THE OXFORD HANDBOOK OF

AMERICAN SPORTS LAW

THE OXFORD HANDBOOK OF

AMERICAN SPORTS LAW

Edited by
MICHAEL A. McCANN

OXFORD
UNIVERSITY PRESS

OXFORD
UNIVERSITY PRESS

Oxford University Press is a department of the University of Oxford. It furthers the University's objective of excellence in research, scholarship, and education by publishing worldwide. Oxford is a registered trade mark of Oxford University Press in the UK and certain other countries.

Published in the United States of America by Oxford University Press
198 Madison Avenue, New York, NY 10016, United States of America.

Library of Congress Cataloging-in-Publication Data
Names: McCann, Michael A., author.
Title: The Oxford handbook of American sports law / Michael A. McCann.
Description: New York: Oxford University Press, 2018.
Identifiers: LCCN 2017030141 | ISBN 9780190465957 (hardcover)
Subjects: LCSH: Sports—Law and legislation—United States.
Classification: LCC KF3989 .M325 2018 | DDC 344.73/099—dc23

About the Editor

Michael A. McCann is the Associate Dean for Academic Affairs at the University of New Hampshire School of Law, where he is also Director of the Sports and Entertainment Law Institute and a Professor of Law. He has published articles in the *Yale Law Journal*, *Boston College Law Review*, and *Harvard Journal of Sports and Entertainment Law*, among other leading law reviews. He is also an investigative writer and legal analyst for *Sports Illustrated*. He has written over 600 articles for *Sports Illustrated* since joining the publication in 2007 and was the first journalist to interview Lance Armstrong after his 2013 interview with Oprah Winfrey. He is also a sports attorney and served as a member of the legal team that represented Ohio State University running back Maurice Clarett in his historic case against the National Football League (NFL) and its eligibility rule. McCann is also collaborating with Ed O'Bannon on *Court Justice*, a book that details O'Bannon's path-breaking case against the National Collegiate Athletic Association (NCAA).

Contents

Acknowledgments

In all facets of life, but especially sports, nothing is accomplished without collaboration and teamwork. This has proven unquestionably true with *The Oxford Handbook of American Sports Law.*

To that end, I would like to acknowledge the sizable contributions of several key individuals.

First, I thank Nicholas Danforth, a student of mine at the University of New Hampshire School of Law. Nicholas was with me on Day 1 and provided terrific editorial assistance throughout.

I also thank the wonderful OUP staff, including Timothy Allen, Haley Anderson, Alyssa Callan, Robyn Curtis, Tithi Jana, Meredith Keller, David Pervin, and Shereen Shafi. I could not have worked with a kinder and more thoughtful group of persons.

I am also incredibly grateful to my wife, Kara McCann, for her love and support—and sublime proof reading skills.

Last, but not least, I am indebted to my parents, Dr. and Mrs. William P. McCann, for their unending encouragement and inspiration.

I hope you enjoy the *Handbook* as much as I do.

Michael A. McCann

Contributors

Thomas A. Baker III is Associate Professor of Sport Law in the Sport Management and Policy Program at the University of Georgia and Editor-in-chief for the *Journal of Legal Aspects of Sport* (JLAS).

Erin E. Buzuvis is Professor of Law and Director of the Center for Gender & Sexuality Studies at Western New England University.

Alexander Chester is a counsel with O'Melveny & Myers LLP.

Todd Clark is Professor of Law at North Carolina Central University School of Law.

Christopher R. Deubert is the Senior Law and Ethics Associate for the Football Players Health Study at Harvard University.

Ed Edmonds is Professor Emeritus of Law in the Notre Dame Law School at the University of Notre Dame.

Gabe Feldman is Paul and Abram B. Barron Associate Professor of Law and Director of the Sports Law Program at Tulane University.

Roger Allan Ford is Associate Professor of Law at the University of New Hampshire School of Law and Faculty Fellow at the Franklin Pierce Center for Intellectual Property.

Jon M. Garon is Professor of Law and Dean of Shepard Broad College of Law at Nova Southeastern University.

Ryan Gauthier is Assistant Professor of Law in the Faculty of Law at Thompson Rivers University.

Jimmy Golen is a sports writer for the Associated Press and former Knight Journalism Fellow at Yale Law School.

Nathaniel Grow is Associate Professor of Business Law and Ethics at Indiana University's Kelley School of Business.

N. Jeremi Duru is Professor of Law in the Washington College of Law at American University.

Richard T. Karcher is Associate Professor in the School of Health Promotion & Human Performance at Eastern Michigan University.

Dionne L. Koller is Professor of Law and Director of the Center for Sport and the Law at the University of Baltimore.

Michael A. McCann is Associate Dean for Academic Affairs, Professor of Law and Director of the Sports and Entertainment Law Institute at the University of New Hampshire.

Alan Milstein is a shareholder in the law firm Sherman Silverstein and Adjunct Professor of Law at Temple University.

Sean F. Nolon is Associate Professor of Law at Vermont Law School.

Nicholas M. Ohanesian is an administrative law judge in the Social Security Administration.

Brian L. Porto is Professor of Law at Vermont Law School.

Irwin P. Raij is a partner and Co-Chair of the Sports Industry Group in Entertainment, Sports & Media at O'Melveny & Myers LLP.

Geoffrey Rapp is Harold A. Anderson Professor of Law and Values and Associate Dean of Academic Affairs at the University of Toledo College of Law.

Alexandra J. Roberts is Assistant Professor of Law at the University of New Hampshire School of Law and Fellow of the Yale Law School Information Society Project.

Stephen F. Ross is Professor of Law and Executive Director of the Center for the Study of Sports in Society at The Pennsylvania State University.

Jimmy Sanderson is Visiting Assistant Professor in the New College of Interdisciplinary Arts and Sciences at Arizona State University.

Jeffrey Standen is Dean and Professor of Law at Northern Kentucky University.

Daniel L. Wallach is a shareholder at the law firm of Becker & Poliakoff, P.A.

Maureen A. Weston is Professor of Law and Director of the Entertainment, Media, & Sports Law Program at the Pepperdine University School of Law.

Glenn M. Wong is Executive Director of the Sports Law & Business Program and Distinguished Professor of Practice–Sports Law in the Sandra Day O'Connor College of Law at Arizona State University.

Warren K. Zola is Executive Director of the Boston College Chief Executives Club in the Carroll School of Management at Boston College.

CHAPTER 1

INTRODUCTION

American Sports Law Through Deflategate

MICHAEL A. MCCANN

1. Why Sports Law Doesn't Fit with Other Categories of Law

Many in the legal community espouse the view that "sports law" doesn't exist. Instead, they argue, sports law is merely a catchall phrase for the wide range of laws that apply to actors in the sports industry. Legal controversies involving athletes, for example, might implicate contract law, criminal law, agency law, antitrust law, labor law, trademark law, tax law, tort law, immigration law, or any other category of law customarily recognized by legal scholars. The gist of this viewpoint is that there is no center to "sports law"—that the phrase means everything and nothing at the same time. Even some of the most famous American sports litigations, such *as Curt Flood v. Bowie Kuhn* and *Maurice Clarett v. National Football League*, are commonly portrayed as controversies that implicate labor law, antitrust law or some other established category of law and that connect with sports only through the happenstance of the parties involved.

The fact that sports are fundamentally about games and leisure doesn't help sports law, either. Other categories of law emanate from decidedly more meaningful concerns, including the constitutional rights of citizens, the duties that accompany ownership in real property, and legal protections for persons who receive health care. No matter how much we care about whether Tom Brady was fairly treated by the National Football League (NFL), whether daily fantasy sports is unlawful gambling or lawful diversion, or whether Ryan Lochte "overexaggerated" his experiences at the Rio 2016 Olympics, those debates are ultimately more provocative than they are impactful. Brady sitting out four games and the "right" to select a fantasy sports lineup are simply not that important in the grand scheme of things. Sports law, therefore, is easy to trivialize. Unlike other categories of law, it normally centers on things that don't sway the essentials of life and well-being.

At least one U.S. Supreme Court Justice has expressed skepticism that sports law is an actual category of law. Back in 2006, I attended a reception at Mississippi College School of Law, where I was a professor, and the late Justice Antonin Scalia was the guest of honor. I spoke with him for a few minutes. Justice Scalia asked me which courses I taught and I told him that I taught sports law. He quizzically responded, "Sports law, what's that?"

It's true that sports law is a field that doesn't exhibit an obvious center of gravity. This is in part a function of the absence of an overarching federal sports law or regulatory body. There's no U.S. Sports Code or a Federal Sports Act. There's no U.S. Department of Sports or Federal Athletics Agency. There is a U.S. Anti-Doping Agency, but it is a private not-for-profit entity that betrays its government-sounding name.

The absence of a unifying sports law or government body also doesn't comport with the tendency of humans to categorize information and to anchor to those categories. As social psychologists have uncovered, the human brain takes myriad shortcuts to manage an incessant and multifaceted array of stimuli. These shortcuts, more technically called heuristics, rely on predictive cues to classify and make sense of sensual perception at any given moment (Chen and Hanson, 2004). To illustrate, social psychologists have observed that we tend to assume reciprocity in how other people view us. As a result, if you believe that the person with whom you are speaking is generous, you tend to assume that this person believes you are generous too (Carlson and Barranti, 2016). The propensity to make this assumption is one of the many subconscious devices that the brain uses to facilitate interaction.

As part of the brain's quest to simplify and act as a "cognitive miser," the brain tends to place information in discrete categories and to repel challenges to those categories. By doing so, we're able to generalize experiences and organize them in what seem like logical boxes.

How we teach the law is a telling illustration. Guided by the Langdellian model, we teach law students primarily through traditional courses—such as contracts law, tort law, and criminal law—and we frame these courses as having established doctrines. We also teach these courses as if they are, basically, unconnected from one another. A first-year torts course typically covers negligence, intentional torts, and products liability and not much else. This structure is logical since the legal community recognizes these doctrines as comprising what we conceive of as torts. If torts were a person, we would say it owns certain doctrines. This allows torts to have something of a script that is uniquely, well, *torts*.

While organized and neat, teaching torts as one island in the archipelago of laws is dissociated from the practice of torts. An attorney who practices torts law normally would not call herself a "torts attorney," since such a moniker would not align with her work. Indeed, a "torts" claim doesn't arise and end within the tidy boundaries of torts. Usually insurance law plays a decisive role in any torts claim. Further, a lawsuit alleging negligence often invokes other categories of law in asserting additional claims, such as breach of contract, breach of warranty, fraud, misrepresentation, infringement, and antitrust violation. If a torts lawsuit is resolved out of court through a settlement, a contract—from the category of law called contracts—is signed. If instead the court decides the lawsuit, a judgment will be entered. If the plaintiff prevails in the judgment, he may seek assistance from a sheriff and other law enforcement actors to collect. State licensing boards might also play a role if the case involves a physician or other licensed professional who acted negligently.

The same exercise could be done for other legal topics as they operate in practice. Torts, contracts law, and other traditional categories of law are organizations of doctrine that frequently blend together in the real world. From that lens, these categories function a little bit like sports law in that they blur the lines that law professors find so helpful when teaching.

2. Why Sports Law Has Become Its Own Unique Category of Law

Even if traditional categories of law are more malleable than they seem while studied in law school, they still claim a doctrinal core—whether it's negligence for torts, the model penal code for criminal law, or the U.S. Constitution for constitutional law. As explained earlier, sports law lacks such a feature.

But that doesn't mean sports law can't constitute a category of law. There are other ways a category of law could be identified and recognized as legitimate.

For instance, I've found that sports law courses have increasingly resembled one another. Since starting as a law professor in 2005, I've periodically reviewed the syllabi of my sports law colleagues as a way of keeping up with the latest practices. Through this admittedly informal method of review, I've noticed that the cases and laws selected as materials have become much more standardized than they were back in 2005.

Every sports law class teaches *Flood v. Kuhn*, in which the U.S. Supreme Court upheld Major League Baseball's long-standing, if dubiously reasoned, exemption from federal antitrust law. Every sports law class has a lengthy section on collective bargaining and the unique applications of the nonstatutory labor exemption to pro athlete employment. Every sports law class extensively covers athlete drug testing and the distinctive goals and controversies of such testing in the context of sports. Every sports law class explores gender equity and the impact of Title IX, ostensibly an education and civil rights law that has become known as a sports law. Every sports law course explores whether college athletes—and their idiosyncratic mix of school and sports—ought to be considered employees.

Sports law is also taught as a context course in the same way other areas of law are taught. While there are courses where legal principles are applied throughout—in torts, students study how to make an injured party whole again; in criminal law, students learn about punishment and blame—certain courses are fundamentally about how the law governs a particular *context*. Patent law is one such course. In it, students learn how the law governs creation and innovation, and how various legal tools equip attorneys who practice in that space. Internet law is yet another. Students in an Internet law course explore legal principles and controversies found within the context of online activities. Health care law courses are designed similarly. Health care law professors lecture on select applications of contract, antitrust, and regulatory laws to the health care industry. There are many other examples of areas of law taught through context courses.

One could plausibly argue that context courses are unnecessary and that their underlying legal concepts can—and should—be taught instead in principles courses, where students learn about the theoretical underpinnings that bind together laws irrespective of their application. Judge Frank Easterbrook of the U.S. Court of Appeals for the Seventh Circuit is perhaps the most prominent advocate of such a viewpoint.

In 1996, Easterbrook rejected the logic of establishing a separate category of law for the nascent, but clearly burgeoning, online industry. Easterbrook used "the law of the horse" to illustrate why, in his view, one is more likely to learn about how the law intersects with a particular context in a principles course than in a context course. Easterbrook observed that various cases center on legal controversies related to horses. These controversies run the gamut of legal issues, from the sale of horses to injuries caused by horses to the licensing of horse races and to many other "horse" situations that implicate seemingly disparate areas of law. "Any effort to collect these strands into a course on The Law of the Horse," Easterbrook wrote, "is doomed to be shallow and to miss unifying principles." Easterbrook explained that studying applications of different areas of law to one industry—whether it's horses, the Internet or sports—runs the risk of ignoring the relevant purposes and theories of those areas of law (Easterbrook, 1996, 207–208).

Easterbrook's concern about context courses is understandable but also anticipatable and correctable. A sports law professor can shape his or her lectures and syllabi to ensure that students understand the relationship between a legal controversy in sports and the broader areas of law implicated by that controversy. For instance, a sports law professor who lectures on discrimination of minority coaching candidates can—and typically does—lecture on related principles of employment discrimination law and their underlying purposes. To be sure, such background information is neither as detailed nor as extensive as would be found in a semester's worth of employment law lectures. Yet it mitigates, if not cures, the learning risks identified by Easterbrook.

Regardless of Easterbrook's critique, context courses exist because they center on important aspects of society that interact with the law. As a market, sports comprise a very lucrative and extensive business. As a cultural phenomenon, sports consist of athletes and teams that people care passionately about. By lecturing on "sports law," a professor can furnish a richer understanding of a topic that society has deemed to be consequential and interesting. Further, sports law students can adapt and hone the tools they learned in first-year courses to legal controversies in sports. They will become better attorneys for it. The same basic points can be said of other context courses. While law schools may not "need" to offer context courses, they likely improve legal education by doing so.

Taken together, there may be an organizing principle or at least gravitational pull of doctrine thought of as "sports law." Sports law may not have the "center" that other courses feature, but a script for teaching sports law has surfaced and it spotlights a context of substantial interest in society. Through that script, sports law has become a stand-alone topic.

The chapters you'll read in the *Handbook of American Sports Law* constitute, in my view, a powerful and engaging version of that script. And it is an ideal time for it to be written. The business and scope of sports have exploded in recent years. An industry that used to be about games and player contracts is now also about 4K broadcasts, streaming media, eSports, wearable technology, genetic testing, and so on. The accompanying legal regimes have evolved as well. New laws and cases have transformed the study of sports law from a narrow specialty into a robust discipline. The canon of sports law expands each year.

The *Handbook of American Sports Law* offers a critical examination of the direction of this bourgeoning category of law. In the United States, the relationship between league commissioners and players is clearly in a transformative era. The same can be said for the relationship between universities and student-athletes, particularly in regard to whether student-athletes should be compensated for their labor or their names, images, and likenesses. The free movement of players and anti-doping measures are also in flux. Further, businesses that participate in the sports industry are consistently presented with new legal challenges in protecting intellectual property and analytics. As found in the *Handbook of American Sports Law*, authoritative perspectives on contemporary sports law debates are valuable to academics, students, and professionals who participate in the community of American sports law.

The *Handbook of American Sports Law* also establishes a foundation for future research on sports law issues. As technology and social media alter the ways fans, athletes, and team officials interact, legal doctrine will be challenged to adapt. The *Handbook of American Sports Law* forecasts these future debates and outlines where the law may be headed.

While the *Handbook of American Sports Law* intentionally focuses on U.S. (American) sports law, the chapters alert readers to points of comparison between U.S. sports law and other countries' conceptions of sports law. This is a crucial component to the book. The industry actors and governing bodies of sports—and the many relevant legal regimes that intersect in sports—are often global and remarkably interconnected. There are thus valuable points to be made about comparative applications of law to sports.

3. Measuring Sports Law Through Deflategate

Earlier in this chapter I compared the legality of Tom Brady's suspension to other topics that interact with the law. My basic point was that Brady's suspension, although of great interest to many, was decidedly less consequential than other noteworthy legal crises of our day. The relationship between federal health care law and the Constitution, for example, or the rights of inmates on death row are—obviously—more important than whether Brady or Jimmy Garoppolo played the first four games of the Patriots' 2016 schedule.

But what made Brady's suspension so compelling to attorneys and sports fans alike is what often makes sports law so compelling: it induces people to think about what the law is and ought to be. Indeed, the NFL suspending Brady for his alleged involvement in a scientifically dubious and seemingly insignificant equipment dispute became *the* transcendent sports law controversy of the nascent twenty-first century. Perhaps only in the category of sports law could Deflategate exist and thrive.

As in any legal controversy, the origin of Deflategate is a debatable point. That said, a description of the most relevant rule is a logical way to begin.

In the NFL, each team controls its own footballs for use in games. This is an unusual approach to sports equipment. Neutral referees and game organizers normally possess and provide the core instruments of play—be they soccer balls, tennis balls, baseballs, basketballs, or pucks. Referees, it is thought, prevent the risk of equipment tampering that might favor one side and interfere with fair play.

But in the NFL, quarterbacks and kickers are extremely sensitive and quite vocal about how their footballs feel. Players in these positions are known to blame the football's surface and weight when throws and kicks go astray. Their preferences about the "feel" of the football—footballs used in NFL games are made of cowhide leather and inflated with air—run the gamut. Some quarterbacks, like Aaron Rodgers, prefer the footballs to be very hard, meaning as inflated as possible. It is easier to throw a tight spiral on a hard football. Other quarterbacks, like Brady, prefer a slightly softer football, meaning one that is not inflated to the max. A softer or lighter football tends to be easier to catch. Still other quarterbacks have been known to manipulate footballs by heating them in cold-weather games. Players who man other positions are also sensitive to the football. Receivers, for example, sometimes apply substances to their gloves to make it easier to catch.

While the NFL permits some variance in the weight and feel of game footballs, the league also instructs its referees to inspect the footballs prior to each game. This inspection is designed to ensure that game footballs comply with a bevy of NFL equipment requirements. One of those requirements is that the footballs weigh between twelve and a half and thirteen and a half pounds per square inch (PSI). Teams that impermissibly tamper with footballs' qualities, including weight, are subject to a minimum punishment of a $25,000 fine (Wells, Karp, and Reisner, 2015). More often, the footballs pass inspection. The referees then return the footballs to an equipment assistant for each team. The two assistants then walk to the field with the footballs in a respective bag and the game begins shortly thereafter.

This sequence took place prior to the New England Patriots playing the Indianapolis Colts in the American Conference Championship Game on January 18, 2015. Referee Walt Anderson inspected and approved each team's twelve game footballs, and then permitted a Patriots locker room assistant named Jim McNally to escort the Patriots footballs to the field. Instead of going directly to the field, McNally took the bag containing the Patriots footballs into a men's bathroom for about one minute and fortyseconds. After McNally exited the bathroom with the bag of balls, he brought them to the field. Brady and other Patriots players would use those balls in the game.

The game wasn't competitive at all. The Patriots trounced the Colts by a score of 45 to 7. Brady excelled, throwing three touchdown passes and completing 66% of his passes. Brady, however, made one notable mistake. In the second quarter, Colts linebacker D'Qwell Jackson intercepted a Brady pass. Colts officials, who days earlier had expressed concerns to the NFL about the inflation level of Patriots footballs, thought the football felt a little bit soft and asked an intern to weigh it. Using a digital pressure gauge, the intern found that the football weighed 11.0 PSI—far less than the 12.5 PSI minimum. An NFL game official then weighed the football three times and found it weighed less than 12.0 PSI on each test.

During halftime of the game, the referees tested the eleven other Patriots footballs and four of the Colts footballs. All but one of the fifteen tested footballs—one of the Colts' balls—weighed less than 12.5 PSI. The actual readings by the referees varied as they used two different types of pressure gauges that yielded different results (Goldberg, 2015). All of the footballs were fully inflated and used in the second half. The Patriots outscored the Colts 28 to 0 in that second half. By beating the Colts, the Patriots earned the right to represent the AFC in Super Bowl XLIX, which would be played two weeks later.

4. A Strange Accusation About Footballs Becomes a National Controversy

As Patriots fans celebrated their team's victory in the AFC Championship, a story would emerge hours after the game that cast a cloud over the Patriots' victory. At 1:55 a.m. on Monday, January 19, Bob Kravitz, a columnist at WTHR Indianapolis, tweeted: "A league source tells me the NFL is investigating the possibility the Patriots deflated footballs Sunday night."

Kravitz's report initially brought bemusement. For one, the footballs thrown by Brady were clearly not "deflated" in any commonsensical understanding of the word. They may have been slightly underinflated but not deflated. Deflated footballs would have been obvious to the human eye and hindered, not helped, Brady. The report also seemed like sour grapes. The Patriots had just embarrassed the Colts on national TV in a critical playoff game. Perhaps the Colts leaked a rumor to a local media member that both undermined the authenticity of the Patriots' victory and distracted attention from the Colts' failings.

But in the days that followed, the controversy—which in the beginning was alternatively dubbed "Deflategate" and "Ballghazi"—swelled. A dispute that was initially perceived to concern deflated footballs morphed into one about slightly underinflated footballs and potential competitive benefits for Brady in throwing such balls. The fact that the controversy involved the NFL's best quarterback and the NFL's best team only amplified interest. Plus, many NFL fans outside New England dislike and distrust the Patriots, who in 2007's "Spygate" controversy were found to have violated an NFL rule about where teams can videotape other teams. The major television networks covered Deflategate as if it was a news story rather than a trifling sports dispute.

Almost immediately, Brady and his coach, Bill Belichick, denied any involvement in a deflation conspiracy, though Brady's less-than-defiant denial—when asked by a journalist, "Can you answer right now, is Tom Brady a cheater?" Brady modestly responded, "I don't believe so"—did little to quell suspicions (Putterman, 2015). Two days after the game, the story would morph into a true crisis. The most prominent sports media outlet, ESPN, reported that eleven of the twelve Patriots footballs measured more than two pounds under 12.5 PSI (Mortensen, 2015). If that had been true, the torts doctrine of *res ipsa loquitur* would have seemed applicable: the thing (substantial deflation) speaks for itself and the Patriots must have been guilty. The scandal quickly became the topic of national news broadcasts. Did the Patriots cheat their way to the Super Bowl?

5. A Not-So-Independent "Independent" Report and Dubious Science

As a response to the allegations and escalating frenzy, NFL commissioner Roger Goodell assembled what he termed an "independent" investigation team. The team would probe what happened to the footballs. NFL general counsel Jeffrey Pash and New York City attorney Ted Wells were tapped to lead the probe. The word "independent" seemed misplaced. The investigation was co-led by the NFL's top attorney, who is obviously not "independent." As another source of conflict, the NFL employed the referees who were assigned to the AFC Championship game. Those referees played a complicating role in the controversy—they admitted that they had failed to record which of the two pressure gauges was used to inspect the footballs. The NFL, however, was under no obligation to outsource the investigation, let alone through a purportedly independent vehicle. The league could have handled the investigation internally, just like the NBA had done a year earlier with the Donald Sterling controversy (for more on Sterling, see "Leagues and Owners: the Donald Sterling Story," this volume).

Over a three-month period, Pash, Wells, and their associates met with various Patriots employees, including Brady, Belichick, McNally, and John Jastremski, a locker room attendant who had communications with Brady. The investigators also sought and obtained electronic correspondence and other communications between relevant

Patriots employees. Further, the investigators retained the engineering firm Exponent—which years earlier had defended the tobacco industry in mass torts litigation—and Princeton University physicist Dr. Daniel Marlow to offer expert opinions on the footballs' apparent deflation.

On May 6, 2015, Wells and his colleagues released a 234-page report titled "Investigative Report Concerning Footballs Used During the AFC Championship Game on January 18, 2015." The document quickly became known as "the Wells Report." It asserted that McNally and Jastremski knowingly tampered with the game footballs' air pressure. These two men did so, the report charged, so that the footballs would be below 12.5 PSI. The report also insisted that it was more probable than not that Brady was "at least generally aware" of McNally and Jastremski's plot.

The accusation against Brady was based on inference as opposed to direct evidence. No video, recording, or electronic message implicated Brady, and not one witness connected Brady to any deflation plot. The deflation plot itself was lacking proof. While Wells postulated a theory of what happened to the footballs, the absence of evidence of tampering was a glaring omission.

Instead of connecting the dots, the Wells Report circled around a conclusion. The report offered five main reasons why it concluded that the Patriots and perhaps Brady were guilty:

1. The report spent considerable energy discussing a single text message sent by McNally to Jastremski in May 2014, eight months before the game in question and during a time of year when no games are played. In the text, McNally referred to himself as "the deflator"—suspicious, to be sure, particularly given that by May 2015, the scandal was popularly called Deflategate. Yet neither the text message in question, nor any text messages prior or after it, linked to Brady or to deflating footballs.
2. The report highlighted that in October 2014, Brady complained to Jastremski that footballs used in a game against the New York Jets felt overinflated. Brady's complaints, however, did not include an instruction that the footballs be deflated below 12.5 PSI.
3. Multiple pages in the Wells report dwell on McNally's trip to the bathroom. The fact that McNally brought the footballs into the men's room prior to the game naturally raised eyebrows, but there was no proof that he deflated footballs while in the bathroom. Further, a logical and seemingly more likely assumption is that McNally simply used those 100 seconds in the bathroom to relieve himself.
4. The report also homed in on how well Brady treated the Patriots locker room staff. Indeed, Brady—whose net worth is reportedly about $180 million and whose wife, super model Gisele Bündchen, is reportedly worth about $380 million—regularly provided gifts to Jastremski and other Patriots locker room staff. The gifts, in the report's view, implied that Brady might have paid for special football treatment. This speculation was countered by the fact that NFL quarterbacks routinely buy

gifts for locker room staff, many of whom earn less than $50,000 a year and are part-time workers.

5. The report also criticized Brady for not sharing his personal cell phone with investigators. Brady, however, was under no legal obligation to share his phone. Further, he may have had reason to distrust the NFL. The ESPN report of eleven of twelve footballs being more than two pounds under 12.5 PSI turned out to be false and was attributed to an anonymous source from the commissioner's office. Moreover, much of the content in Brady's phone was already in the NFL's possession, as the NFL had all of the texts sent by Brady to the locker room staff and also had a listing of all of Brady's phone calls.

Meanwhile, distinguished members of the scientific community began to mount an assault on conclusions reached by the Wells Report. Most notably, Dr. John Leonard, an engineering professor at the Massachusetts Institute of Technology and self-described diehard fan of the Philadelphia Eagles, conducted his own experiments and used data publicly shared by Wells and the NFL. He found that the Patriots football measurements corresponded not with an elaborate human conspiracy but rather with simple weather and atmospheric conditions found on the kind of chilly and rainy evening in which the AFC Championship game was played (Leonard, 2016).

Leonard applied Ideal Gas Law, a basic formula taught in high school physics that measures pressure when temperature, volume, and number of gas moles are known. He determined that the footballs measured exactly as science would predict and that Exponent's methodology in testing the footballs was flawed and seemingly motivated to reach a particular conclusion. For the same reason that tires tend to lose air pressure in the winter, Leonard observed, footballs also lose air pressure in cooler environments. Leonard's findings, which other scientists replicated, debunked the central thesis of Deflategate. In contrast, not one neutral scientist confirmed conclusions reached by Wells and the NFL.

6. Goodell Shocks the Sports World with His Deflategate Punishments While the Patriots and Brady Hatch Their Legal Strategies

While science suggested Deflategate was little more than hot air, Goodell and other NFL officials anchored to the belief that the Patriots had pulled a fast one—even on, it seems, science. Goodell imposed arguably the most severe penalty assigned to a team in league history. He fined the Patriots $1 million—the maximum amount under league rules—and revoked the Patriots' first-round draft selection in 2016 and fourth-round draft selection in 2017.

Goodell also suspended Brady for four games, which amounted to one-quarter of the regular season and which at the time was twice as severe as the penalty assigned to NFL players who committed domestic violence. Goodell reasoned that the Patriots and Brady had badly damaged the integrity of the game by plotting to use slightly underinflated footballs and by failing to fully comply with a league investigation.

Patriots fans were outraged. How could the NFL punish the Patriots and Brady for conduct that science indicated didn't happen? Doesn't evidence matter?

As those fans would learn over the following year and a half, the NFL was contractually authorized by the Patriots and Brady to take whatever steps the league deemed correct—even if the evidence indicated otherwise.

Consider first the Patriots' penalty. The team's fans demanded that the Patriots owner, Robert Kraft, sue the league. They were aware that the late Oakland Raiders owner Al Davis had sued the NFL in the 1980s and 1990s. Invoking antitrust law, Davis argued that the NFL and other teams had conspired against the Raiders in trying to block relocation of his team from Oakland to Los Angeles and then back to Oakland. The litigation was ultimately resolved in a way that enabled Davis to relocate his teams (McCann & Raiola, 2017).

Guided by the Raiders' litigation, some Patriots fans wondered if Deflategate might reflect an anticompetitive conspiracy between the NFL and teams jealous of the Patriots' success. After all, Colts and NFL officials had exchanged emails prior to the game about the Patriots footballs. Plus, there were rumors that other teams' officials, including those employed by the Baltimore Ravens, might have complained to the NFL about the Patriots footballs.

Kraft declined to sue for one very good reason: the law. NFL team owners contractually assent to refrain from suing the league or other teams as a condition of owning an NFL franchise. Further, the league constitution, which governs the relationship between owners and the league, dictates that the commissioner has final authority on disciplinary matters. The Raiders litigation was also not on point. Davis invoked antitrust law to challenge restrictions on movement of a business, a conventional concern of antitrust law. Kraft, in contrast, would have sued in an attempt to defeat the traditional power of a sports league commissioner to issue final discipline of teams. Further, Kraft would have faced the tall task of convincing a court that his situation permitted a circumvention of the express language of the league constitution and other NFL documents. A lawsuit would have proven futile and the seventy-four-year-old billionaire wisely declined (McCann, 2016).

Brady was in a superior legal position to mount a challenge, but the odds of success were stacked against him. Brady's legal rights stemmed from his membership in the National Football League Players' Association (NFLPA), the union for NFL players. In 2011, the NFLPA and NFL negotiated a collective bargaining agreement (CBA) that governs the employment of NFL players through the 2020 season. Article 46 of the CBA details the power of the commissioner to discipline NFL players and the rights of players to appeal any imposition of discipline. Unfortunately for Brady, Article 46 allows the commissioner to hear appeals through the NFL's version of arbitration. As the arbitrator (presiding officer of an appeal hearing) Goodell reviews the decision making of the person who originally punished the player. In other words, Goodell reviews Goodell, meaning an "appeal" is not so much an appeal as we understand that word in law but rather a request for reconsideration.

Despite the fact that Goodell, the arbitrator, would decide if Goodell, the commissioner, was correct in suspending him, Brady invoked his Article 46 right to appeal. Brady met with Goodell in June 2015. While voluntarily testifying under oath, Brady insisted that he knew nothing about a football deflation scheme. Through his attorneys, Jeffrey Kessler and David Greenspan, Brady also highlighted how other NFL players accused of similar types of equipment wrongdoing received either no sanction or modest penalties. For instance, no player caught using the prohibited Stickum substance—which makes footballs easier to catch—has ever been suspended. The same is true of any players found to have heated footballs in cold weather games. Likewise, another NFL quarterback who refused to turn over his phone in a league investigation—Jets quarterback Brett Favre, who was investigated for sexually harassing a female Jets employee—was only fined $50,000 and not suspended. A four-game suspension for an equipment issue and for not being fully cooperative, Brady's attorneys stressed, was wildly disproportionate in light of precedent.

Goodell, as the arbitrator, was unmoved. In July 2015, Goodell issued his arbitration award: he upheld the four-game suspension that Goodell the commissioner had issued two months earlier. In doing so, Goodell portrayed Brady not merely as aware of others' misconduct but as an active participant in a nefarious plot to deflate footballs. He also characterized Brady's replacing—or, as Goodell wrote, "destroying"—his personal phone as an obvious indication of guilt.

7. Deflategate Plays Out in Court

Brady and the NFL then began a nearly yearlong federal litigation over the lawfulness of Goodell upholding a suspension that Goodell had earlier imposed. For two reasons, the NFL was considerably advantaged in this litigation.

First, Article 46 is written in a way that insulates the commissioner's fact-finding and determination of penalty from meaningful scrutiny. Indeed, Article 46 empowers Goodell to determine a form of discipline that he deems appropriate for conduct that the commissioner deems "detrimental to the integrity of, or public confidence in, the game of professional football." Further, Article 46 makes clear that the commissioner's decision "will constitute full, final and complete disposition of the dispute."

Second, the relevant standard of review used by courts to evaluate Goodell's arbitration award heavily favored the NFL. Under the two relevant laws—the Labor

Management Relations Act and the Federal Arbitration Act—as well as applicable case law, arbitrators in union-management disciplinary matters must only offer a plausible rationale for an arbitration award to be considered lawful. Under this toothless standard, Goodell was under no obligation to explore the science of Deflategate. Goodell, in fact, could have incorrectly determined the facts in Deflategate and yet still have lawfully suspended Brady. All Goodell's award needed to exhibit was the mere appearance of reasonableness.

Many Patriots fans and members of the media found the relevant legal regime to be at odds with their understanding of our legal system. How could facts not matter in the pursuit of justice?

As those fans and media would gradually learn, whether Brady "did it" would not dictate the outcome of the litigation. Brady's only pathway to victory would be to demonstrate that Goodell's method of review was so fundamentally flawed that the arbitration award ought to be vacated.

Brady initially succeeded in that goal. U.S. District Judge Richard Berman of the Southern District of New York heard the first round of arguments. He made clear that he found Goodell's conduct as arbitrator to be extremely problematic. In criticizing Goodell as having "dispensed his own brand of industrial justice," Berman would vacate Goodell's arbitration award on three grounds.

First, Brady was never notified that he could be suspended for alleged involvement in an alleged plot to slightly underinflate footballs. Not one other player in the NFL's nearly 100-year history had been suspended for an equipment infraction. Berman regarded a four-game suspension for Brady's supposed offense as arbitrary and capricious, and as inconsistent with any basic understanding of notice. The suspension also, in Berman's view, violated the "law of the shop," a common law principle that compels arbitrators to both provide sufficient notice of possible punishments and issue awards with an appreciation of precedent.

Second, Berman stressed Goodell's disregard for procedural fairness. While Berman cautioned that Goodell was accorded some degree of deference as the arbitrator, that deference, Berman maintained, should be limited in light of the unique circumstances. Goodell "had a personal stake in the outcome of the appeal," Berman remarked in a March 2017 interview. "That is, he had an incurable conflict of interest, evident partiality, and could not possibly be fair" (Kahler, 2017).

In his September 2015 order, Berman concluded that Goodell unlawfully denied Brady's attorneys a chance to cross-examine Pash during the appeal hearing. Pash, as mentioned previously, was co-lead investigator and played a role in the drafting of the Wells Report. Goodell, as the arbitrator, reasoned that Pash's testimony would have been redundant to testimony already provided by Wells. Berman disagreed, reasoning that Pash, who had an equal title to Wells, may have offered information relevant to Brady's appeal. To be sure, Pash's role as general counsel of the NFL suggests he would have testified from a very different perspective from that of Wells, an outside attorney. By denying Brady a chance to cross-examine Pash, Berman concluded, Goodell denied Brady a fair hearing.

Third, Berman objected to Goodell's prohibiting Brady from reviewing the league's investigative notes into Deflategate. Those notes contained the league's scientific findings and data collection methods. Had Brady obtained that information, he likely would have been able to mount a more effective defense in his appeal hearing. Indeed, Brady might have been able to disprove the underlying allegations—particularly since Daniel Nash, an attorney for the NFL, would admit to Berman that there was no direct evidence of Brady playing any role in the controversy. Instead, Brady could only deny the accusations. Further, Berman noted, Goodell had permitted access to investigative notes in other player disciplinary matters. For Goodell to refuse to do so with Brady seemed hypocritical and unfair.

By vacating Goodell's arbitration award and thus nullifying Brady's suspension, Berman enabled Brady to play the entire 2015 season. As expected, however, the league filed an appeal with the U.S. Court of Appeals for the Second Circuit. In March 2016, a three-judge panel on the Second Circuit heard oral arguments. I sat in the front row of the hearing, which pitted attorney Jeffrey Kessler, on behalf of both the NFLPA and Brady, against former U.S. Solicitor General Paul Clement, who argued for the NFL. It was clear that two of the three judges—Judges Barrington Parker, Jr. and Denny Chin—would side with the NFL, while Chief Judge Robert Katzmann appeared more in line with Berman's view.

The hearing did not proceed as expected, however, as the judges were surprisingly fixated on the factual record, incomplete as it was. At one point, in fact, Judge Chin inexplicably remarked that, "the evidence of the ball tampering is compelling, if not overwhelming." Many of us in the courtroom wondered, "*What evidence is he talking about?*" Further, the remark prompted Kessler to ponder aloud why there was so much discussion of facts when the appellate hearing was supposed to concern whether Judge Berman correctly interpreted the law in vacating Goodell's suspension.

The views of Judges Chin and Parker became law a month later when, in a 2-1 vote, the panel reversed Judge Berman. As a consequence, Brady's suspension was reinstated. He would thus be set to miss the first four games of the 2016 regular season.

Writing on behalf of himself and Judge Chin, Judge Parker attempted to simplify and substantially limit what he found to be the relevant legal question: Did Goodell comply with Article 46 in upholding his earlier suspension of Brady?

Noting that Goodell's power under Article 46 was "especially broad" and that federal courts are obligated to provide high deference to arbitrators, Judge Parker reasoned that Goodell met the very minimal requirements of Article 46. After all, the commissioner afforded Brady an arbitration hearing after Brady filed an appeal, and the commissioner allowed Brady to be accompanied by counsel of his choice. Article 46, however, did not obligate Goodell to be consistent or persuasive in his decision, or make a person available as a witness or require the NFL to share investigative notes. The fact that Goodell wore multiple hats—fact-finder, punisher, and arbitrator—also didn't bother Judges Parker and Chin because the NFLPA agreed to such a framework in the CBA. In fact, Judge Parker observed that even if Goodell, as the arbitrator, made "mistakes of fact or law"—that is, even if Goodell completely fumbled Deflategate—Goodell would have complied with the law "so long as he acted within the bounds of his bargained for authority." Given that Article 46 required so little of Goodell, it is difficult to conceive of how Brady could have prevailed under the framework constructed by Judges Parker and Chin.

In his dissent, Judge Katzmann described Goodell as having disregarded any basic notions of fairness. Judge Katzmann articulated that Goodell's award ought to have been vacated based on his "shifting rationale for Brady's discipline." Namely, Goodell never explained why after the appeal (arbitration hearing), Goodell described Brady as an active member of a deflation plot whereas Goodell previously punished Brady on grounds he merely had "general awareness" of Jastremski and McNally allegedly plotting to Deflategate footballs. As Judge Katzmann explained, it seemed as if Goodell changed the rationale for punishing Brady. If such a depiction was correct, then Brady effectively had no right to an appeal: he never had a chance to appeal the new rationale that Goodell imported during the appeal. From that lens, Goodell disregarded the most basic procedural requirements of Article 46.

Brady then petitioned for a rehearing en banc, where all of the active judges on the Second Circuit would have reheard the case. Famed arbitrator Kenneth Feinberg, the AFL-CIO, Dr. Leonard, the Patriots, and other prominent voices filed amicus briefs on Brady's behalf. In sum, they insisted that Brady's suspension constituted an injustice and an affront to both science and federal arbitration laws. But petitions for rehearings en banc in the Second Circuit are granted less than 1% of the time and only in extraordinary situations. Unfortunately for Brady, his petition, while newsworthy, wasn't deemed appropriate for a rehearing and was promptly denied.

Brady then could have petitioned the U.S. Supreme Court, but he would have again faced incredibly low odds. Instead, Brady simply withdrew the case and placed his focus back on his football career. He sat out the first four games of the 2016 regular season. He then returned to play the remaining twelve regular games, leading his team to victories in eleven of them. Brady and the Patriots then entered the playoffs as a favorite to win Super Bowl LI. Defeating the Houston Texans and the Pittsburgh Steelers in Divisional Round and AFC Championship Games, respectively, the Patriots would advance to play the Atlanta Falcons in the Super Bowl. After trailing 28-3, Brady led the Patriots to a dramatic 34-28 victory. Named Most Valuable Player of the Super Bowl, Brady would receive the award from Goodell at a presentation ceremony. The two smiled politely on the stage and declined to say anything about Deflategate. Judge Berman, however, offered a response: "I think Deflategate is finally put to rest by that Super Bowl."

8. Conclusion

If American sports law could be encapsulated in one legal controversy, that controversy would be Deflategate. Some might say Brady's case was fundamentally a dish of arbitration law and labor law—with a side of contract law—dressed up with famous NFL players and celebrity. Others might argue Deflategate was compelling merely because of its stark disconnect between science and law. There would be more than a nugget of truth in those observations.

But there's something else going on, too. Deflategate indeed mixed traditional categories of law and the uneasy relationship between law and science. It also, however, became its own legal creature, with its own name and power to influence. It taught Americans about the law and led them to question the rules and customs of law. Sports law may not fit the traditional categories of law, but it surely influences how people view the law.

Acknowledgments

I thank Roger Ford and John Greabe for their valuable feedback and insights. I also thank Jordan Budd, Margaret McCabe, and the University of New Hampshire School of Law for their generous support.

References

Chen, R., and Hanson, J. (2004). "The Illusion of Law: The Legitimating Schemas of Modern Policy and Corporate Law." Michigan Law Review 103: 62–70.

Carlson, E., and Barranti, M. (2016). "Metaperceptions." *The Social Psychology of Perceiving Others Accurately* 172.

Easterbrook, F. (1996). "Cyberspace and the Law of the Horse." *University of Chicago Legal Forum* 1996: 207–216.

Goldberg, D. (2015, May 14). "The Wells Report in Context." Morgan Lewis. Available at https://wellsreportcontext.com/.

Kahler, K. (2017, Marcb 17). "Richard Berman: 'Deflategate is finally put to rest.'" MMQB.com, Available at http://mmqb.si.com/mmqb/2017/03/17/nfl-judge-richard-berman-deflategate-tom-brady-super-bowl-51-ted-wells-wells-report-roger-goodell.

Leonard, J. (2016, October 4). "Tom Brady Has Done His Time for Deflategate, But the Science Says He's Not Guilty." *SI.com* Available at www.si.com/nfl/2016/10/04/tom-brady-deflategate-ideal-gas-law.

McCann, M. (2016, January 17). "Deflategate, One Year Later: The Anatomy of a Failed Controversy." SI.com. Available at www.si.com/nfl/2016/01/18/deflategate-one-year-later-tom-brady-bill-belichick.

McCann, M., & Raiola, R. (2017, January 17). "Sin City? How Raiders Players and Coaches Would Become Richer in Las Vegas." SI.com. Available at www.si.com/nfl/2017/01/17/raiders-moving-las-vegas-tax-implications.

Mortensen, C. (2015, January 21). "11 of 12 Pats Footballs Underinflated." Available at www.espn.com/boston/nfl/story/_/id/12202450/nfl-says-new-england-patriots-had-inflated-footballs-afc-championship-game.

Putterman, A. (2015, May 7). "Deflategate Quotes, Then and Now." SI.com. Available at https://www.si.com/nfl/2015/05/07/deflategate-quotes-new-england-patriots-tom-brady.
Wells, T. V., Karp, B. S., and Reisner, L. L. (2015, May 6). "Investigative Report Concerning Footballs Used During the AFC Championship Game on January 18, 2015" (New York: Paul, Weiss, Rifkind, Wharton & Garrison LLP). Available at www.documentcloud.org/documents/2073728-ted-wells-report-deflategate.html.

Cases

Flood v. Kuhn, 407 U.S. 258 (1972).
Clarett v. National Football League, 306 F. Supp. 2d 379, 387 (S.D.N.Y. 2004), *rev'd* 369 F.3d 124 (2d Cir. 2004).

CHAPTER 2

THE EVOLUTION OF THE POWER OF THE COMMISSIONER IN PROFESSIONAL SPORTS

JIMMY GOLEN AND WARREN K. ZOLA

1. Introduction

The commissioner of a major sports league, whether college or pro, has not one job but many. He may be operating as the CEO (chief executive officer) of a multi-billion-dollar business, obligated to cultivate old revenue streams and forage for new ones. He—and they are all, in fact, men—must worry about the bottom line, and look for ways to grow the sport nationally and internationally. He must ensure the safety of the athletes under his watch (or, as is often the case, answer for his failure to do so). He, or his office, also negotiates television and other media contracts that are in some sports the largest source of revenue. And, with the emergence of players unions, the commissioner is also the face of, if not the actual force behind, negotiations over collective bargaining agreements (CBAs) that determine the relationship between players and owners and help shape the future of the game.

This executive role also casts the commissioner as the game's top regulator—the office ultimately responsible for deciding how to define a charging foul, how long an extra point should be, or whether to count a no-hitter if the game was shortened by rain. The commissioner's office oversees the umpires, officials, and referees who implement these rules. It is the author of the league schedule, including regular-season games, drafts, all-star games, and playoffs. It is the keeper of official statistics and custodian of the history of the game.

There is a judicial aspect to the job as well, and it is here where we are often introduced to the vague-sounding but near-omnipotent "best interests of the game" powers. As the sport's chief disciplinarian, the commissioner has the power to punish players, owners, officials, and even ancillary employees (including, as we shall see, game-day equipment managers) when he considers it necessary to protect the integrity of the game. He arbitrates disputes between teams, using the league charter or bylaws as his guide. NBA (National Basketball Association) Commissioner Adam Silver forced Los Angeles Clippers owner Donald Sterling to sell his team, but lesser penalties have been handed down against owners for extreme behavior, including baseball owners Marge Schott and George Steinbrenner, or smaller crimes like videotaping opponents' signals. Players have been banned for life for gambling or for drug use. Commissioners have also, with varying success, tried to use their power to limit relocation or force league realignment.

Not to be overlooked, however, is that the commissioner is also a politician—both outwardly, as he makes his sport's case to the public, and internally, where he must maintain the support of the owners who elevated him to power. In his public-facing role, the commissioner lobbies governments for funds for youth leagues or for legislation that will benefit the business. He schmoozes politicians to ease up on safety regulations (or overlook past transgressions), or to cough up money for a new stadium. He monitors the relationships with colleges, minor leagues, and other player training grounds that provide his sport with prospects—either at no cost or at least more cheaply than he could do on his own. He is also the face of a charity designed to engender goodwill in the community, and the head of a media company that increasingly controls the sport's story.

But it is the need for commissioners to politic internally, cultivating support among the owners who hired him, that marks one of the least examined yet most important aspects of their role. Early occupants of the position—Kenesaw Mountain Landis first among them, in 1920—saw themselves as above the fray, a neutral who was independent of both the owners and players and had only the game's best interests at heart. That image persisted until the resignation of baseball commissioner Fay Vincent in 1992, which stripped the veil from this pervasive (though productive) myth. Recent commissioners are no longer seen as an impartial guardian of the game but as a mere appointee, who is paid—quite well, of late—to do the owners' bidding. Now earning more in some cases than the highest-paid player in his game, the commissioner is increasingly beholden to the owners and unwilling to cross them, lest the checks stop coming.

In later chapters we will see examples of commissioners who are so beholden to the check-writing owners that they seem incapable of exerting independent power. We will see commissioners who make questionable legal or business decisions that seem designed to pander to a majority of owners at the expense of one or a few. We will see one commissioner lose his job when he falls out of favor with this important constituency.

This chapter will investigate how the commissioner came to be the figure that fans see handing out the trophy after the championship game, defending his sport's safety record in Congress, or announcing yet another work stoppage. It will examine the evolution of the commissioner's power from its original, autocratic incarnation in the form of Landis to the more one-sided—but still quite powerful—owners' mouthpiece we see today. And, while other chapters will delve more deeply into some of the legal cases that tested and shaped the commissioner's powers, this chapter will provide a road map for the major developments that led us to the more varied and nuanced commissionerships seen in modern sports.

2. The Rise of the Commissioner

Baseball isn't the game that it was when I was a boy, or when I was President of the National League. I know that it is a better game in many ways because it has developed from the good start we gave it. What I like about it is that it has not departed so much from the old way of playing that I cannot enjoy it. (Arcidiacono, 2010)

– Morgan Bulkeley, the first president of the National League

2.1. Early Years

Sports need rules, and then very soon after that, they need someone to enforce them. Baseball achieved the former in the middle of the nineteenth century thanks largely to Alexander Cartwright, a New York bank clerk turned Hawaiian fire chief who was a founder of the Knickerbocker Base Ball Club. Contrary to the romantic but apocryphal myth, it was Cartwright in Hoboken, New Jersey, and not Abner Doubleday in Cooperstown, New York, who shaped the sport into the one we see today. Playing "the New York game," which included such now fundamental regulations as nine players per side and four bases, ninety feet apart, clubs formed into a loosely conglomerated National Association of Base Ball Players and crowned a champion. Thus standardized, baseball became popular among Civil War soldiers and proliferated across the nation after the war when they returned home. By 1869, the interest in top players created a market for their services, leading to a split between the professionals and the amateurs. In 1876, the National League began play as the first true major professional league, stating among its goals "to make baseball playing respectable and honorable" (Spalding Guide, 1876, 59).

In addition to rules governing play and limiting membership—any team willing to pay $10 had been allowed to join the National Association—the original National League Constitution established a five-member board, chosen at random from the club representatives. The board selected a president from among its members, and the position went first to Morgan Gardner Bulkeley, the principal owner of the Hartford Dark Blues. The only member of the Baseball Hall of Fame to have enlisted in the Civil War, Bulkeley traced his ancestry to the Mayflower and served as the head of the Aetna Life Insurance Co., a family business. He lasted only one season atop the National League, with an eye more toward politics than sports; he would go on to serve as the Mayor of Hartford, as Governor of Connecticut, and as a U.S. Senator from the state.

In his place, the board selected coal magnate William Hulbert. The president of the Chicago White Stockings, Hulbert had struggled to convince players to play for him on baseball's western frontier; likewise, East Coast teams would often balk at making the expensive trip West at the end of the season with the pennant no longer at stake. In six years as the league president (he died of a heart attack in 1882), Hulbert consolidated many of the powers we see in a modern commissioner: enforcing rules against gambling, player poaching, and such immoral activities as Sunday baseball. He expelled teams from New York and Philadelphia for failing to complete their schedules. He permanently banned four players from the Louisville Grays for fixing games. He kicked Cincinnati out of the league for playing on Sunday—and serving beer, no less. And most important, he also established the first reserve clause that tied players to their teams in an era when contracts were frequently ignored, often in mid-season.

Meanwhile, competition was coming in a "Junior Circuit" run by a former sports writer named Byron Bancroft "Ban" Johnson. As a sports writer for the *Cincinnati Commercial Gazette*, Johnson railed against the rowdiness in the National League, impressing (or annoying) Red Stockings manager Charles Comiskey enough that he recommended him to the struggling Western League. As president, Johnson empowered umpires to eliminate rough play and suspended players for swearing, all with the goal of making the league more family friendly. As it thrived, he renamed it the American League (A.L.), declared it a major league on par with the National League (N.L.), and poached freely from the more established circuit's rosters.

In order to steal the best talent from the N.L., the A.L. declared the reserve clause illegal and embarked on a bidding war for elite players; more than 100 jumped from the N.L. to the A.L. for the 1901 season. Among the most notable was Philadelphia second baseman Napoleon Lajoie, who was embroiled in contract spat with the Phillies when the crosstown Athletics offered him a deal. The Phillies' attempt to obtain an injunction (based on the reserve clause) failed, and Lajoie played for the A's in 1901, leading the A.L. in batting average, home runs, and RBIs (runs batted in) to win the league's triple crown. After the season, the Phillies won an appeal that barred Lajoie from playing in Pennsylvania for any other team, with the court declaring: "(Lajoie) may not have been the sun in the baseball firmament, but he is certainly a bright particular star" (*Philadelphia Ball Club v. Lajoie*). But rather than return him to the Phillies—and unwilling to have him sit out every home game—the A's traded him to Cleveland; whenever the Blues, as they were then known, would play in Philadelphia, Lajoie would wait for his teammates in Atlantic City and rejoin them after the series.

2.2. National Agreement

It was this untenable dynamic that led the leagues in 1903 to agree to a truce called the National Agreement. (Similar attempts to bring peace between professional leagues, dating as far back as 1884, achieved limited success before collapsing.) The 1903 pact incorporated many of the protocols of past governing documents, including territorial rights and respect for existing contracts. But it also put at the head of the enterprise a National Commission consisting of the American and National League presidents along with a third person chosen by them. For the purposes it was established—settling disputes over player contracts—this body was effective, amicably deciding seventy-three such cases in the 1905 season alone (the bulk of them in favor of the major leagues over the minor leagues) (Zelinsky, 2011).

But faced with other challenges, the weakness of the three-man National Commission was a looming problem. Boston Red Sox owner Harry Frazee was among those who recognized this, and he argued in November 1918 for a single person to assume the role of commissioner—a month before his infamous decision to sell Babe Ruth to the New York Yankees. Along with New York Giants owner Harry Hempstead, Frazee offered former U.S. President William Howard Taft the ability to be the "sole arbiter of the National Commission." Several more owners publicly supported Taft, including William Baker of the Philadelphia Phillies, Charles Ebbets of the Brooklyn Dodgers, and Barney Dreyfuss of the Pittsburgh Pirates. However, others were angry that Frazee and Hempstead failed to consult them, resulting in a stalemate. (But it didn't hurt Taft, who eventually landed on the U.S. Supreme Court.) The weakness of the Commission was finally laid bare in 1919, when it proved incapable of responding to a pair of very different crises.

2.3. *American League Baseball Club of New York v. Johnson*

He was the most brilliant baseball man the game has ever known. He was more responsible for making baseball the national game than anyone in the history of the sport.

– A.L. President and Baseball Hall of Famer Will Harridge

In theory, the three members of the National Commission had equal power; in truth, it was dominated by Ban Johnson. But his authority was challenged in 1919 when Boston Red Sox pitcher Carl Mays—frustrated over a lack of run support, dissatisfied with his contract, eager to play for a contender, and also perhaps preoccupied with a fire that burned down his Missouri farmhouse—walked off the mound in the middle of a game and left the team. (He might also have been woozy, having just been beaned by his catcher's attempt to throw out a base-stealer.) When the Red Sox tried to rid themselves of him and trade him to the New York Yankees, Johnson stepped in and suspended Mays. "Baseball cannot tolerate such a breach of discipline," the league president said. "It was up to the owners of the Boston club to suspend Carl Mays for breaking his contract and when they failed to do so, it is my duty as head of the American League to act" (Wood, 2017). The ensuing legal dispute threatened to tear the league apart, with the three clubs that opposed Johnson contemplating defection to the N.L.

The case went to New York Supreme Court, leaving Judge Robert F. Wagner to determine if Johnson had acted, as the Yankees claimed, as an "unmolested despot" (Lynch, 2008). One issue was whether Johnson was attempting to punish the ballclubs or Mays himself, but Wagner quickly dispensed with the former: "The president is given no authority whatever to discipline the clubs which are members of the league," he wrote, noting that such power was vested in the board of directors (*American League Baseball Club of New York v. Johnson*). Searching for an authority to punish Mays, Wagner turned to Section 20 of the N.L. Constitution:

> *The President in the performance of his duties, shall have the power to impose fines or penalties, in the way of suspension or otherwise, upon any manager or player who, in his opinion, has been guilty of conduct detrimental to the general welfare of the game.*
>
> (N.L. Constitution, 1877)

But Wagner determined that Johnson's decision to suspend Mays was not properly "in the performance of his duties." On the contrary, the president was empowered "to suspend any umpire, manager or player for offering, agreeing, conspiring or attempting to cause any game to result otherwise than on its merits. The constitution is barren of any further grant of power to the president." The playing rules gave the president "the right and duty . . . to regulate the actual playing of the game on the field and to enforce the rules instituted for the governing of the game" (National Agreement, 1903). But this did not apply in Mays's case either, Wagner decided. "Doubtless his powers would extend to the discipline of players for any infringement of these rules upon the field or for an overt act committed by a player on the field in violation of the rules," Wagner wrote. "Beyond that power, however, it does not seem that the president may proceed" (*American League Baseball Club of New York v. Johnson*). Instead, the power to suspend Mays was given to the teams themselves: "Each club belonging to this league shall have the right to regulate its own affairs, to establish its own rules, and to discipline, punish, suspend or expel its manager, players or other employees" (N.L. Constitution, 1877). Mays, who had finished the 1919 season in New York under a temporary injunction, was free to return to the Yankees in 1920.

Wagner's decision, it should be noted, was issued on October 25, 1919, less than two weeks after the conclusion of that year's World Series. Although there was rampant suspicion even then about the effort of the heavily favored Chicago White Sox, who lost the best-of-nine Series to Cincinnati in eight games, it would be almost a year before the failure of the National Commission to contain and respond to the crisis would lead to its demise.

3. Creation of the Office of the Commissioner

Gambling, and the corresponding danger of match-fixing, was an open secret in sports dating back to the ancient Olympics, and a constant worry for baseball's early governors.

3.1. Black Sox Scandal

As far back as 1877, the National League's second season, four Louisville Grays players were banned from baseball for life after the team, coasting to the pennant, lost ten of eleven games; the Grays folded after the season (Bock, 2017). So when whispers began circulating even during the 1919 World Series that the Chicago White Sox had taken bribes to throw the championship, it was not entirely unprecedented. After the Reds beat the White Sox five games to three in the Series, newspapers openly questioned the effort and intentions of the Chicago players.

The National Commission took the Homer Simpson approach: Ignore it, and hope it goes away. White Sox owner Charles Comiskey, whose penurious ways were blamed for the players seeking outside income, offered a $20,000 reward for proof of a fix and then, claiming to have investigated himself, declared the matter closed, saying: "These yarns are made out of the whole cloth and grow out of bitterness due to losing wagers" (Fountain, 2016, 126). The rumors persisted until August 1920, when a Cook County, Illinois, grand jury convened to look into the allegations of fraud.

Two players offered statements described as confessions, including Game 1 starting pitcher Ed Cicotte, who hit the first batter he faced with the second pitch—an apparent signal to the gamblers that the fix was on. Outfielder "Shoeless" Joe Jackson, whom Babe Ruth had called the greatest hitter he'd ever seen, admitted taking $5,000, though he maintained he gave his full effort during the Series—he batted .375, tops among the regular hitters—and his confession seemed more of a complaint that he hadn't been paid the whole $20,000 he was promised. Claude "Lefty" Williams, the starting pitcher in Games 2, 5, and 8, also gave a statement, but perhaps the more damning evidence was that Williams, who went 23-11 with a 2.36 earned run average in the regular season, was 0-3 in his three Series starts. Five more players were charged with conspiracy and fraud: first baseman Arnold "Chick" Gandil, third baseman Buck Weaver, shortstop Charles "Swede" Risberg, utility infielder Fred McMullin, and centerfielder Oscar "Happy" Felsch. (A teammate, Shano Collins, was listed as one of the injured parties, having been cheated out of $1,784 by losing the World Series rather than winning it.) Much like Capt. Louis Renault in "Casablanca" when he was confronted with backroom gambling, Comiskey had no alternative: With just a few games left in the season, he suspended the players and ended the ballclub's chance at another pennant.

3.2. The Lasker Plan

The baseball community, which had tolerated the occasional fix since the game's beginnings, could not stomach such chicanery in the sport's championship. Critics—many of them taking aim at Ban Johnson himself—focused on the National Commission and charged that it had done "nothing while the game was being debauched because of the [internal] petty politics" (Zelinsky, 2011, 29). Some saw the problem in the Commission's structure: With the two league presidents holding control, it would naturally tend to support the owners and not represent the best interests in the game as a whole (Smith, 1970).

To address this issue, Chicago advertising mogul and Cubs co-owner Albert D. Lasker proposed a newly constituted Commission. Under the "Lasker Plan," the sport would be controlled by three powerful businessmen from outside baseball with the hope that they would be "representatives of the public," and not just the game's owners. The Comiskey-friendly Chicago Herald & Examiner declared that:

> *The practical operation of this agreement would be the selection of three men of such unquestionable reputation and standing in fields other than baseball that the mere knowledge of their control of baseball, in itself, would insure that the public interests would first be served, and that, therefore, as a natural sequence, all existing evils would disappear.*
>
> (*Chicago Herald & Examiner*, 1920)

3.3. Kenesaw Mountain Landis

Support for the new Commission of Baseball grew, with the *Chicago Herald & Examiner* calling it "the supreme court of baseball" and editorializing that "there would be no chance of crookedness or complaint" (Smith, 1970, 167). Among those considered to serve on the Commission was Judge Kenesaw Mountain Landis, who had been appointed to the federal bench by President Theodore Roosevelt in 1905 and presided over an early antitrust suit against organized baseball. Landis delayed his decision in the case; while waiting, the sides settled and, ultimately, the upstart league was forced to fold. When approached to serve on the new Commission, though, Landis argued for a singular, and thus more powerful, authority. With owners in no position to bargain—and players with even less power to resist—the new commissioner demanded and was vested with almost unlimited authority and secured an oath from the owners who hired him. Authority the owners would ultimately seek to curb in the future. However, at the time, they declared:

> *We, the undersigned . . . hereby pledge ourselves loyally to support the Commissioner in his important and difficult task; and we assure him that each of us will acquiesce in his decisions even when we believe them mistaken and that we will not discredit the sport by public criticism of him and one another.*
>
> (Abrams, 1998, 95)

Landis was named "the final arbiter of disputes between leagues and clubs and disputes involving players and to impose punishment and pursue legal remedies for any conduct that he determined to be detrimental to the best interest of the game" (Parchman, 1990, 1415). He was also given the explicit power to "determine, after investigation, what preventative, remedial or punitive action is appropriate in the premises, and to take such action either against Major Leagues, Major League Clubs or individuals, as the case may be" (Major League Constitution, from *Landis*, 1931).

The Judge, who retained his spot on the bench, wasted no time making use of this power. Although the eight White Sox players were acquitted in court in August 1921 of the conspiracy, that wasn't good enough for Landis. One day later, Landis banned all of them for life and consigning them to history as the "Black Sox":

> *Regardless of the verdict of juries, no player who throws a ballgame, no player that undertakes or promises to throw a ballgame, no player that sits in conference with a bunch of crooked players and gamblers where the ways and means of throwing a game are discussed and does not promptly tell his club about it, will ever play professional baseball.*
>
> (Ginsburg, 2003, 144)

Note that Landis said "professional baseball," and not merely "in the major leagues." The Commissioner believed—with good reason—that he reigned over the entire sport, and not just the leagues that had hired him. And he also believed deeply in his duty to protect the sport at all levels from evils such as gambling. In his biography, *Judge and Jury: The Life and Times of Judge Kenesaw Mountain Landis*, David Pietrusza wrote:

> *The game was not 'saved' when Landis banished obvious crooks like Gandil and Risberg and Cicotte. Nor did it become simon-pure because the dim-witted Joe Jackson was bounced for taking $10,000 [sic]. Landis' most important action in the Black Sox case was his most controversial: Banning Buck Weaver. Unlike Jackson, Weaver took no cash from gamblers. From all accounts, he took no action to purposely throw the Series. Nor did he give his assent in any manner to the plot.*
>
> *Landis knew all that. When he wrote that 'no player that sits in a conference with a bunch of crooked players and gamblers where the ways and means of throwing games is planned and discussed and does not promptly tell his club about it, will ever play professional baseball' he was referring to the hapless Weaver.*
>
> *. . . What Landis did in banning Weaver was to ex post facto place guilty knowledge of crooked play on the same level as the deed itself. Landis ratcheted baseball's moral code up several notches, making it akin to West Point's Code of Honor.*
>
> (Pietrusza, 2001, 194)

Thus empowered, Landis next set his sights on Ruth, the sport's biggest name. The New York Yankees star planned to conduct a "barnstorming" tour after the 1921 World Series but didn't ask Landis for permission until the day before the tour was to begin. (Once commonplace, such tours were curtailed in 1911.) Landis summoned Ruth to his office, but the Brobdingnagian slugger refused with a dismissive, prompting the following salvos between Landis and Ruth as they battled:

> *'Who does that big monkey think he is? It seems I'll have to show somebody who's running this game.'*
>
> – Kenesaw Mountain Landis on Babe Ruth, October 15, 1921

> *'Aw, tell the old guy to jump in a lake.'*
>
> – Babe Ruth, October 15, 1921 (Price, 2015)

Landis once again invoked his "best interest" authority, suspending Ruth and teammate Bob Meusel for the first five weeks of the 1922 season and fining them \$3,362—the equivalent of their World Series pay. As with the Black Sox, the message was received: The "Dictator of the National Pastime" (*Washington Post*, 1920) had virtually limitless power, and he intended to use it.

3.4. *Milwaukee American Association v. Landis*

Landis's reign remained largely unchallenged until 1931, when he again deployed his "best interests" authority—this time to stop an otherwise legal player transaction. St. Louis Browns owner Phil Ball had been shuttling outfielder Fred Bennett between the major league club and minor league teams that were secretly under Ball's control. When Landis learned of the interclub relationship, he blocked Bennett's transfer to Milwaukee and declared him a free agent. At Ball's behest, Milwaukee sued Landis, arguing that he had no authority to intercede where no rules prohibited the underlying actions. While the ballclub conceded that Landis had the authority to prevent actions that were not in baseball's best interests, it argued that his authority was limited to those expressly stated or exclusively defined as detrimental. Where the Major League Agreement allowed an action, it should not be struck down because of an ancillary effect on the game. Citing his "best interests" authority, Landis argued he had unrestrained authority to take whatever action he deemed appropriate.

The owners had no one to blame but themselves. In the Major League Constitution, originally adopted as the Major League Agreement on January 12, 1921, they unambiguously included among the commissioner's functions the power:

> *"To investigate . . . any act, transaction, or practice charged, alleged or suspected to be* ***not in the best interests*** *of the national game of Baseball"* (emphasis added).
>
> (Article II, Section 2(b), Major League Constitution, 1921)

In its ruling, the U.S. District Court for the Northern District of Illinois agreed with Landis and his interpretation of the scope of his authority. In a ruling that served to formalize his power, the court said that the Major League Agreement was designed to:

> *. . . endow the commissioner with all the attributes of a benevolent but absolute despot and all the disciplinary powers of the proverbial pater familias. . . . the provisions are so unlimited in character that we can conclude only that the parties did not intend to so*

> *limit the meaning of conduct detrimental to baseball, but intended to vest in the commissioner jurisdiction to prevent any conduct destructive of the aims of the code.*
>
> (*Landis*, 1931)

In dismissing Milwaukee's case, the court further determined that Landis was granted the authority:

> *... with the expressed desire to achieve certain ends, that is, to keep the game of baseball clean, to promote clean competition, to prevent collusive or fraudulent contracts, to protect players' rights, to furnish them full opportunity to advance in accord with the abilities and to prevent their deprival of such opportunities by subterfuge, covering or other unfair conduct.*
>
> (*Landis*, 1931)

It was only after Landis died in 1944 that owners moved to limit his successors' power, deleting from the Major League Agreement the section where they waive their right to challenge the commissioner's decisions in court. A section added to the Major League Agreement would also strip A. B. "Happy" Chandler and Ford Frick, who followed Landis, of the power he employed against the Milwaukee club in 1931:

> *No Major League Rule or other joint action of the two Major Leagues, and no action or procedure take in compliance with any such Major League Rule or joint action of the two Major Leagues shall be considered or construed to be detrimental to baseball.*
>
> (Article I, Section 3, Major League Agreement)

Upon Frick's retirement in 1964, the Major League Agreement was changed again, reversing the 1944 amendments and changing the phrase "detrimental to baseball" to "not in the best interests of baseball."

3.5. *Molinas v. NBA*

Meanwhile, other professional sports leagues were investing in their leaders similar powers. Although the NBA did not appoint its first commissioner until 1971, the president effectively filled that role from the league's founding in 1946. Maurice Podoloff was the NBA president in 1953 when Fort Wayne Pistons forward Jack Molinas admitted to gambling on games. Although Molinas claimed—as Pete Rose would later—that he only bet on his team to win and never gave less than a full effort, Podoloff suspended Molinas indefinitely, calling him "a cancer on the league," and rebuffed repeated applications for reinstatement (*Molinas v. NBA*).

While serving his suspension, Molinas, who had played for Columbia University before becoming the fourth overall draft pick, attended and graduated from Brooklyn

Law School and, in spite of his gambling priors, was admitted to the New York State Bar. He also played in the Eastern Basketball League. More to the point, he sued the NBA in New York State Supreme Court, alleging due process violations and also questioning Podoloff's authority to hand down an indefinite suspension. When his state court case was rejected, he pursued an antitrust claim in federal court that challenged the NBA's reserve clause, arguing that Podoloff's indefinite suspension was an unreasonable restraint of trade.

In dismissing the case, the district court took as sacrosanct Podoloff's authority to protect his sport. Alluding to point-shaving scandals at the time that threatened to undermine the integrity of college basketball, the court concluded that "it was absolutely necessary for the sport to exhume gambling from its midst for all times in order to survive" and therefore that "it is certainly reasonable for the league and Mr. Podoloff to conclude that this conduct could not be tolerated and must, therefore, be eliminated" (*Molinas v NBA*). As for the antitrust claims, Judge Irving R. Kaufman affirmed the right of a league to regulate itself:

> *Surely, every disciplinary rule which a league may invoke, although by its nature it may involve some sort of a restraint, does not run afoul of the anti-trust laws. And, a disciplinary rule invoked against gambling seems about as reasonable a rule as could be imagined.*
>
> (*Molinas v NBA*)

4. Players Unions and a New Limit on the Commissioners' Powers

While the influence of league commissioners would ebb through time, one aspect of sports changed little: Team owners and their leagues maintained a consistent upper hand in relations with the players. That would change with the rise of players unions, which were able to collectively bargain for rights that served as a check on commissioners' previously unfettered powers.

4.1. Marvin Miller

When the Major League Baseball Players Association (MLBPA) hired Marvin Miller as its executive director in 1966, the average player's salary was $19,000—with a minimum salary of $6,000. There was no free agency, and few of the privileges that players in all sports now consider their birthright (Goldstein, 2012). By the time he retired in 1982, the average salary was $241,497 and Miller had forged what may be the nation's strongest labor union, earning through collective bargaining agreements a greater share of the sport's prosperity ("Average Baseball Salary," 2008). According to arbitrator Peter Seitz, who in 1975 overturned the reserve clause in the Messersmith and McNally cases, Miller was "the Moses who had led Baseball's Children of Israel out of the land of bondage" (Miller, 1989, 331).

Beyond the tangible benefits he helped obtain for players, Miller also obliterated the perception of the commissioner's office as an impartial protector of the best interest of the sport. The union head complained about this myth in his autobiography, calling out baseball writers who opted:

> *... for a romantic view of the commissioner as some kind of Socrates or Solomon whom baseball people flock to for an objective view of a current crisis. The owners select the commissioner and pay his salary, and they do not pay him to be objective.*
>
> (Miller, 1992, 406)

Miller made it his goal, and the goal of the MLBPA, to ensure that the public knew this, letting no management claim go uncontested (and, in negotiations, brooking little compromise). Writing in the *New York Times*, Miller called claims of commissioner benevolence—or even neutrality—"hokum":

> *Commissioners have most often used their office precisely as the owners always intended: in the interest of the owners. It would be improbable to expect any other result. The commissioner of baseball always was and is an employee of the owners.... It is no surprise, therefore, that commissioners do what they are told by the owners, or they find themselves another line of work.*
>
> (Miller, 1989)

4.2. *NFLPA v. NLRB*

In football, a similar struggle was afoot. In 1971, the NFL Players Association (NFLPA) brought a lawsuit against the National Labor Relations Board (NLRB) in an attempt to answer a simple question: Does the commissioner work for the owners, owing them some fiduciary responsibility, or can he really be viewed as an impartial actor beholden to no one?

In response to a rash of violent, on-field injuries, NFL Commissioner Pete Rozelle urged the league's owners to pass a rule that would result in a $200 fine for any player leaving the bench during a fight (*NFLPA v. NLRB*) Rozelle fined nearly 100 players for violating the rule during the 1971 season, leading NFLPA President Ed Garvey to protest that the rule had not been collectively bargained for, and was thus unenforceable.

Garvey filed an unfair labor practice charge with the NLRB. Rozelle argued that his ability to promulgate rules, and fine players as a result, was vested in him both via the CBA and the NFL Constitution, By-Laws, and Standard Player Contract. He also claimed that it fell within the commissioner's purview to draft such rules and enforce them; he was not merely acting on the owners' instructions. The NLRB disagreed, ruling that the commissioner's actions were management actions, and thus neither impartial nor separate from the collective bargaining process.

4.3. *Finley v. Kuhn*

For most of his tenure, MLBPA President Marvin Miller's foil was Bowie Kuhn, who served as the baseball commissioner from 1969 to 1984. But perhaps the single most pointed conflict between their visions for the sport was actually a dispute between Kuhn and an owner.

Although baseball's owners had attempted to reign in the commissioner's power after Landis, Kuhn attempted to restore the office to its full influence when he took over in 1969. In challenging this power, Miller had an unintentional ally in Oakland Athletics owner Charlie Finley. With free agency looming after the 1976 arbitration case involving Andy Messersmith and Dave McNally, Finley decided to strike preemptively and sell off his biggest stars. In the middle of the season—less than two years after the A's won their third consecutive World Series (a feat that hasn't been repeated since)—Finley agreed to sell Joe Rudi and Rollie Fingers to the Boston Red Sox for $1 million apiece and Vida Blue to the New York Yankees for $1.5 million. (Rudi and Fingers were to be free agents at the end of the year, and Blue had just signed a three-year extension that would be passed along to New York.) Kuhn intervened, annulling the deals as "inconsistent with the best interests of baseball, the integrity of the game, and the maintenance of public confidence in it" (*Finley v. Kuhn*). His reasoning: the transactions would debilitate the Athletics and destroy competitive balance by initiating a system in which the wealthier teams could buy talent from others.

The ever-litigious Finley sued, claiming that "the action of Kuhn was arbitrary, capricious, unreasonable, discriminatory, directly contrary to historical precedent, baseball tradition, and prior rulings and actions of the Commissioner" (*Finley v. Kuhn*). While also raising antitrust claims and accusing Kuhn of acting maliciously because of past dust-ups, Finley argued that it was "procedurally unfair" for Kuhn to negate the deal without prior warning that he would "disapprove large cash assignments of star players even if they complied with the Major League Rules." Upon appeal, Seventh Circuit Judge Robert Sprecher posed the question thusly: "whether the Commissioner of baseball is contractually authorized to disapprove player assignments which he finds to be 'not in the best interests of baseball' where neither moral turpitude nor violation of a Major League Rule is involved" (*Finley v. Kuhn*). Citing fifty years of "numerous exercises of broad authority under the best interests clause," and noting that such powers were inscribed in the Major League Agreement that Finley had signed, the court decided that Kuhn was within his rights: "The broad authority given to the Commissioner by the Major League Agreement placed any party to it on notice that such authority could be used" (*Finley v. Kuhn*).

The price of Kuhn's victory, however, would be steep: The *Finley* case began a slow erosion of his office and contributed to the union's power—something even Miller himself noted:

> *[Kuhn's] moves constantly backfired . . .. His ability to distinguish between reality and his prejudices, his lack of concern for the rights of players, sections of the press, and even of the stray, unpopular owner—all combined to make Kuhn a vital ingredient in the growth and strength of the union. To paraphrase Voltaire on God, if Bowie Kuhn had never existed, we would have had to invent him.*
>
> (Miller, 1992, 91)

During his tenure, Miller was able to significantly alter the public's perception of the commissioner—and, in fact, the reality of his power. Via collective bargaining, Miller earned for players the right to have some salary disputes settled by an impartial arbitrator. Grievance and arbitration procedures are now negotiated rather than established by fiat by owners. Though free agency was established through arbitration that struck down the reserve clause, the precise terms and process players use to shop their services are also dictated by the CBA. It was Miller who defined the terms of the neutral arbitrators who would inherit much of the power that had previously belonged to commissioners: "Arbitrators are hired and paid by both parties to a dispute. They must be impartial, with no connection whatever to either party. No sports commissioner in history qualified for the role" (Miller, 1989, 10). Miller stepped down in 1983 and was briefly replaced by Kenneth Moffett before MPBPA General Counsel Donald Fehr took over later in 1983. He guided the union through its next evolution, often continuing Miller's work by chipping away at the authority of the commissioner's office, until his retirement in 2009.

5. Modern Developments and Incidents

5.1. *Rose v. Giamatti*

> *I'd walk through hell in a gasoline suit just to play baseball.*
>
> – *Pete Rose* (Reston, 1991, 5)

Gambling once again became the target of the commissioner's "best interest" powers when Bart Giamatti, who had been chosen to succeed Peter Ueberroth as commissioner but had not yet taken office, learned of rumors that then-Cincinnati Reds manager Pete Rose had been betting on baseball. A professor of English Renaissance literature at Yale University who had served as president of the National League, commissioner-elect Giamatti hired Washington lawyer John Dowd to look into it. Following a three-month investigation, Dowd concluded that Rose had regularly bet on the Reds (but never against them)—fifty-two times during the 1987 season alone, the 225-page report documented, at a minimum of $10,000 per day.

Giamatti shared the report with Rose's lawyers and set a hearing for June. But in the meantime, the commissioner also wrote a letter on behalf of one of the witnesses interviewed by Dowd, who was awaiting sentencing in federal court in Cincinnati on drug and income tax charges. Giamatti's letter, which vouched that informant Ron Peters was "candid, forthright and truthful," convinced Judge Carl Rubin, a Reds fan, that the commissioner had a "vendetta" against Rose. He alerted Rose's lawyers, who sued in state court to prevent Giamatti from disciplining Rose, accusing the commissioner of "actual displayed bias and outrageous conduct" (*Rose v. Giamatti*).

First came a jurisdictional hearing, with everything at stake: To avoid the possibility of another pennant-waving judge, Giamatti needed to show diversity of citizenship in order to remove the case to federal court. Rose argued that Major League Baseball was the true party to the suit, and it was merely "a trade name utilized by the professional baseball clubs," including Ohio-based Reds. But U.S. District Judge John D. Holschuh found the commissioner's office to be a "juridical entity" in itself. Tracing the development of Major League Baseball from the 1903 National Commission, he concluded that

> *... the Major League Agreement ... creates the office of Commissioner of Baseball and vests extraordinary power in the Commissioner. The Commissioner has unlimited authority to investigate any act, transaction or practice that is even suspected to be "not in the best interests" of baseball.*
>
> (*Rose v. Giamatti*)

In any case, Holschuh also determined that Giamatti was the true defendant, saying: "The complaint is replete with allegations of wrongdoing on the part of Giamatti" (*Rose v Giamatti*).

Deprived of his home-court advantage, Rose settled three weeks later and withdrew his suit. The all-time hit king, who neither admitted nor denied having bet on baseball, was banned from baseball and permanently ineligible to associate with any major league or minor league club, although he could apply for reinstatement in a year. (A rule change at the Baseball Hall of Fame would later make him ineligible for enshrinement.)

Days later, Giamatti died of a heart attack. Deputy Commissioner Francis "Fay" Vincent, Giamatti's friend and former Yale Law School alum, succeeded him and promised to maintain Rose's banishment.

> *Today's courts have an unhealthy itch to supervise and fine-tune virtually every equity judgment in American life. Rose's legal strategy was to find a judge willing to insinuate himself into baseball's disciplinary procedures. If Rose had succeeded, the commissioner's office would have been irreparably damaged. Its core function, which is disciplinary, would permanently have been put into question.*
>
> (Will, 1999, 201)

5.2. *Chicago National League v. Vincent*

A former Columbia Pictures chairman and Coca-Cola vice president, Vincent never escaped the tumult in which his tenure began. Barely a month after he assumed office, an earthquake devastated the Bay Area and forced the World Series between San Francisco and Oakland to be postponed for ten days. The following February, owners locked players out of spring training before Vincent intervened to force a compromise (opening day was pushed back a week). And, during his first season, Vincent suspended New York Yankees owner George Steinbrenner for what turned out to be two years for paying a small-time gambler to "dig up dirt" on outfielder Dave Winfield.

In 1991, Vincent again found himself in the middle of quarreling owners when he determined that American League teams would share the expansion fees paid by new National League teams in Miami and Denver. Historically, each league had kept such fees, but with the A.L. teams forced to participate in the expansion draft, Vincent determined that they should share $42 million, or $3 million apiece (N.L. teams would get the bulk of the $190 million in fees) (MLB.com). This led one A.L. owner to state, "That's it. Fay Vincent is history" (Cozzillio et al., 2007, 97). But it was the ensuing spat over divisional realignment that brought the spat to fruition.

In an attempt to find a home for the Rockies and Marlins, while also maintaining regional rivalries, Vincent decreed that the Chicago Cubs and the St. Louis Cardinals would move from the N.L. East to the N.L. West, with the Atlanta Braves and the Cincinnati Reds to switch from the West to the East. The Cubs, a charter member of the National League and also of the N.L. East, which was created in 1969, balked, arguing that they would lose a traditional rivalry with the New York Mets and also forego revenue as a result of playing many more games on the West Coast. They vetoed the transfer under clause in the National League Constitution that gave any team being move the right to reject realignment. (It also required a three-fourths vote of the other clubs in the league; the vote was 10-2, with the Cubs and the Mets against.)

Despite the Cubs' veto, Vincent argued that the Major League Agreement and the best interests powers superseded the National League Constitution by conferring upon the commissioner the exclusive right to decide. The relevant portion of the Major League Agreement read as follows:

> *. . . all disputes and controversies related in any way to professional baseball between clubs . . . other than those whose resolution is expressly provided for by another means . . . in the constitution of either Major League.*
>
> (Reinsdorf, 1996, 225)

The Cubs asked the court for an injunction, and U.S. District Judge Suzanne B. Conlon granted it, declaring that "the broad authority granted the Commissioner by Article I of the Major League Agreement is not as boundless as he suggests." Conlon distinguished the case from *Finley*, noting, "Unlike the Chicago Cubs, Oakland was not acting pursuant to any contractual right authorized by the American League Constitution." The result of the injunction, which would prevent realignment in time for the 1993 season, didn't just set a new limit on the commissioner's powers. Unable to fire Vincent due to a clause that prevented his powers from being diminished during his term, owners instead voted 18-9 (with one abstention) to ask him to quit. Vincent refused, then thought better of it—ironically, citing the "best interests of baseball" in his resignation statement:

> *I cannot govern as Commissioner without the consent of owners to be governed. I do not believe that consent is now available to me. Simply put, I've concluded that resignation – not litigation – should be my final act as Commissioner "in the best interests" of baseball.*
>
> (Sell, 1992, A1)

5.3. Latrell Sprewell

NBA Commissioner David Stern was also reminded of the limits of his power after Golden State Warriors guard Latrell Sprewell got into an altercation with his head coach, P. J. Carlesimo, on December 1, 1997. After being told to leave practice, Sprewell attacked Carlesimo, grabbing him by the throat, dragging him to the ground, and choking him for ten to fifteen seconds before other players intervened. Banished to the showers, Sprewell returned nearly twenty minutes later to again attack Carlesimo. This time, Sprewell connected on several punches before being dragged away.

Sprewell, who was averaging 21.4 points per game in the first year of a four-year, $32 million contract, apologized to his fans and teammates—but not Carlesimo; the team initially suspended him for ten days without pay. Two days later, the Warriors sent him a letter terminating his contract. Stern then announced that Sprewell would be suspended from the league for one year, declaring "a sports league does not have to accept or condone behavior that would not be tolerated in any other segment of society" (Javier, 2000, 212). The union objected to the voiding of a lucrative and otherwise guaranteed contract. "You're talking about a lot of money [and] a player's career [which] I'm sure he's been banking on and looking forward to," Chicago Bulls forward Scottie Pippen said "... then you snatch it all away."

The NBA's 1995 CBA gave Sprewell the right to a grievance in front of a neutral arbitrator jointly appointed by the NBA and National Basketball Players Association (NBPA). Six times in its history, the league noted, it had fined or suspended a player under the "conduct detrimental" standard. When gambling is involved, the Uniform Player's Contract (UPC) gives the commissioner "the power in his sole discretion to suspend the player indefinitely or to expel him as a player for any member of the Association, and the Commissioner's finding and decision shall be final, binding, conclusive and unappealable." But the NBPA responded that such unfettered power is limited to gambling; the previous longest non-gambling suspension was the twenty-six-game penalty for Los

Angeles Lakers forward Kermit Washington after he punched Houston Rockets forward Rudy Tomjanovich during an on-court melee, fracturing his skull and knocking him unconscious.

For arbitrator John Feerick, the dean of the Fordham University Law School, the key factor was whether Sprewell acted with premeditation when he returned to the court. Feerick decided that the two confrontations were parts of a single punishable act; he reinstated Sprewell's contract and terminated the suspension effective July 1, 1998, clearing him to return at the start of the next season. Stern did not take it well, saying: "You cannot choke your boss and hold your job unless you play in the NBA" (Javier, 2000, 209).

5.4. John Rocker

It does not require violent behavior, like Sprewell's (and Washington's)—or any action at all, really—for a commissioner to invoke his best interest powers, as the case of Atlanta Braves pitcher John Rocker showed. But Bud Selig's response to Rocker's racist comments also showed that the commissioner's powers have limits, even when the sport's reputation and business interests are endangered.

Rocker first drew attention for his controversial opinions in 1999 during a series in New York against the Mets and again in the National League Championship Series, when he called Mets fans "stupid" and accused them of throwing batteries and insulting his mother. But it was in a *Sports Illustrated* interview over the offseason that Rocker, in Selig's view, put baseball's best interests at risk. As reporter Jeff Pearlman watched, Rocker gave fans the finger, called a black teammate a "fat monkey" and complained profanely about immigrants, female Asian drivers, New York City, "some queer with AIDS" and even Sprewell, saying "Do you think if he was Keith Van Horn—if he was white—they'd let him back? No way" (Pearlman, 1999). After the article was published, the Braves issued a statement distancing themselves from the comments. The Atlanta City Council unanimously passed a resolution condemning Rocker's remarks. Selig noted that the comments not only hurt the sport's image but posed a security concern wherever Rocker took the field. The ballplayer apologized, saying in a statement released through his agent: "Even though it might appear otherwise from what I've said, I am not a racist. I should not have said what I did because it is not what I believe in my heart. I was angry and basically firing back at the people of New York" (Thornton, 2010, 29).

Still, Selig suspended Rocker for spring training and the first twenty-eight days of the regular season. He also ordered Rocker to undergo sensitivity training and fined him $20,000. In announcing the punishment, Selig said:

> *Major League Baseball takes seriously its role as an American institution and the important social responsibility that goes with it. We will not dodge our responsibility. Mr. Rocker should understand that his remarks offended practically every element of society and brought dishonor to himself, the Atlanta Braves and Major League Baseball.*

> *The terrible example set by Mr. Rocker is not what our great game is about and, in fact, is a profound breach of the social compact we hold in such high regard.*
>
> (Chass, 2000, A1)

The players appealed, with union head Gene Orza calling the length of the suspension excessive and saying: "It is literally unprecedented to impose a penalty on a player for pure speech, offensive though the speech may be." According to research by the union and commissioner's office, Rocker was the first player to be disciplined for speech since 1938, when Landis suspended New York Yankees outfielder Jake Powell for ten days for disparaging African Americans during a radio interview.

Baseball's neutral arbitrator, Shaym Das, heard testimony from Selig, Rocker, Braves President Stan Kasten, baseball security chief Kevin Hallinan, and Atlanta City Councilman Derrick Boazman, who brought with him a group of protestors and spoke of the effects of Rocker's remarks in the community. In his decision, Das agreed that speech is a punishable form of conduct—not just in baseball, but in other sports, too—and that where leagues have sought to limit the commissioner's powers to punish it they have said so expressly in their governing documents. Nor was there any dispute about the nature of Rocker's conduct, with Das calling it "truly unprecedented in the history of sports in terms of its vileness and the public condemnation that it precipitated." While accepting baseball's claims that Rocker's comments hurt baseball and the Braves; created a security risk; undermined the team's and the sport's minority outreach efforts; and damaged Rocker's ability to work with his coaches and teammates, Das did question whether the damage was so severe as to merit an unprecedented penalty. "This suspension is more than twice as long as any previous nondrug-related suspension," the arbitrator wrote. "The Commissioner simply has not proffered a justifiable basis for this disparity." He cut in half the regular-season suspension, trimmed the spring training ban to time served and accepted the union's contention that the maximum fine for off-field behavior was $500. (*Major League Baseball Arbitration, MLBPA v. Commissioner of MLB*)

5.5. Pistons/Pacers Brawl

> *The events at last night's game were shocking, repulsive, and inexcusable—a humiliation for everyone associated with the NBA.*
>
> – *David Stern, NBA Commissioner* (Commissioner's Statement, 2004)

In a rematch of the 2004 Eastern Conference Finals at the Palace at Auburn Hills outside Detroit, Indiana was leading the Pistons by fifteen points with forty-six seconds left in the game when Pacers forward Ron Artest committed a foul on Ben Wallace, who was driving for a meaningless layup. The Pistons forward took exception to the physical play and responded with a full-chest bump and two-handed shove. While coaches and officials tried to calm the situation, Artest cooled off, lying on his back on the scorer's table until someone threw a drink that hit him. Artest went into the stands and began fighting with the fans, setting off a new—and largely unprecedented melee that came to be known as "The Malice at the Palace."

The game was called; nine spectators were injured in what was a public relations disaster for a league that struggling to control its image. Commissioner David Stern suspended nine players, costing them over $10 million, with Artest receiving the longest penalty in NBA history for on-court violence: eighty-six games, or more than a full season. (Michigan prosecutors also charged five players and seven spectators with assault and battery.) The NBPA challenged the suspensions, arguing that the players' behavior was literally "off-court," thus entitling them to arbitration rights they would not have if the punishment were for on-court behavior.

A federal arbitrator upheld all of the player's suspensions except for that of Indiana's Jermaine O'Neal, who had his twenty-five-game penalty reduced to fifteen games. The NBA appealed to federal court, asking that Stern's entire punishment be upheld. The federal judge issued a temporary injunction allowing O'Neal to play while the case was resolved. However, after playing in two more games, the federal court upheld the arbiter's decision noting that O'Neal's conduct was "off-court" conduct and as a result, Stern's punishment was subject to review.

5.6. David Stern/Chris Paul

With the fourth pick in the 2005 NBA draft, the New Orleans Hornets selected Chris Paul from Wake Forest University. Paul went on to win the 2006 Rookie of the Year before becoming a perennial all-star. But the Hornets struggled financially, and the team's owners put it up for sale. With no buyers stepping forward, the NBA itself purchased the Hornets in late 2010 for approximately $300 million, putting the league's other twenty-nine owners in control of the franchise (NBA.com, 2010).

The team's biggest star at the time, Paul had the option to become an unrestricted free agent at the end of the 2011-2012 season and informed the team that he would not sign an extension. Hornets General Manager Dell Demps sought to trade him and settled upon a three-team deal with the Houston Rockets and Los Angeles Lakers that would have brought four players and a first-round draft choice to New Orleans. Some of the NBA's other owners urged Commissioner David Stern to veto the trade; he did, saying:

> *... All decisions are made on the basis of what is in the best interests of the Hornets.... We decided, free from the influence of other NBA owners, that the team was better served with Chris in a Hornets uniform than by the outcome of the terms of that trade.*
>
> (NBA.com, 2010)

It should be noted that the Paul trade talks coincided with a lockout that delayed the start of the season until Christmas. While the fight was over the usual matters—division of revenues, the length of contracts, an age limit—owners also argued for measures that would help small-market teams retain their stars. It was in this milieu that Stern nixed the deal, announcing the veto shortly before the league was to reopen for business, which left players and even some owners convinced he was attempting to govern through the NBA ownership of the Hornets in ways the league wasn't able to win through collective bargaining. It should also be noted that Stern relied upon his authority as a team executive to veto the deal, and did not argue that it was detrimental to sport's best interests, a move that would have left him open to a challenge as in *Finley v. Kuhn*. Ultimately, Stern authorized a different trade, sending Paul to the Los Angeles Clippers for three players and a first-round draft pick—a deal that appeared to bring back fewer assets to New Orleans than the original, three-team trade.

5.7. Bountygate

In March 2012, the NFL released a report accusing New Orleans Saints players and coaches of maintaining a "bounty" system that would pay cash to defensive players who injured opponents or knocked them out of games. This pay-per-hit scandal that came to be known as "Bountygate" allegedly included twenty-two to twenty-seven Saints players and ran 2009 until 2011 (Pacifici, 2014). NFL Commissioner Roger Goodell also determined that head coach Sean Payton was aware of the program, and that defensive coordinator Gregg Williams engaged with leaders of the defense to oversee it. He also found that team officials instructed players to lie about the program, prolonging and obstructing the investigation, and "deemed . . . the involvement of the coaching staff, and three years of denials and willful disrespect for the rules . . . unacceptable" (Cowherd, 2012). The commissioner suspended Payton for an entire season and banned Williams indefinitely. He also suspended General Manager Mickey Loomis for eight gamesand assistant coach Joe Vin for six and fined the Saints $500,000 while docking it second-round picks in each of the next two drafts.

Citing "conduct detrimental to the integrity of and public confidence in the game of professional football," Goodell in early May suspended four players for their role in Bountygate: linebacker Jonathan Vilma, for the entire 2012 season; defensive lineman Anthony Hargrove, for eight games; defensive lineman Will Smith, four games; and linebacker Scott Fujita, three games (Complaint, *NFLPA v NFLMC* (2012)). The players appealed directly to the commissioner, and they were denied.

As allowed under the CBA, the players and the NFL Players Association filed non-injury grievances, arguing that Goodell had exceeded his authority as commission and deprived them of bargained-for due process. On the eve of the regular season, a three-person appeals panel lifted the suspensions and told Goodell to reconsider the suspensions under both the Article 14 of the CBA, which prohibited undisclosed compensation, and Article 46, Commissioner Discipline. Goodell issued new suspensions, reducing some but leaving those against Vilma and Smith the same. And the players appealed again; in arguments that would be a precursor to Deflategate, the NFLPA said Goodell to recuse himself, claiming he could not be a neutral arbitrator. In what was seen as a "major surprise," Goodell agreed and appointed former NFL Commissioner Paul Tagliabue to review the case (Holder, 2012). (The players would also ask Tagliabue to recuse himself, without success.)

After hearings that were delayed for Hurricane Sandy, with the players to remaining active in the meantime, Tagliabue issued a decision on December 11 that upheld Goodell's findings but nonetheless vacated the player discipline. The former commissioner noted that he was "guided by rules and policies embedded in the CBA," as well as legal precedents defining his role as arbitrator. He did not review the commissioner's findings de novo, saying: "if the parties had intended such a review, they would have written it into the CBA." Nor did he substitute his judgment for Goodell's. Instead, he said he was "reviewing the discipline for consistency of treatment, uniformity of standards for parties similarly situated and patent unfairness or selectivity." Placing the bulk of the blame on the coaches, and citing the pressure on players to please the staff, Tagliabue said the punishments were too harsh and inconsistent with the NFL's willingness to wink at bounty schemes in the past. And, though Tagliabue insisted that his decision should not set a precedent, his endorsement of Goodell's role in the case would help cement the commissioner's authority to act as an arbitrator on appeal from his own decisions. This, combined with Tagliabue's decision to vacate the suspensions, no doubt influenced Goodell's thinking when he declined to recuse himself in the Deflategate case to follow.

6. Conclusion

> *[The commissioner] can and does wield enormous power through two less formal weapons: persuasion and myth.*
>
> – Leonard Koppett

Like the Wizard of Oz, professional sports commissioners for most of the twentieth century ruled from behind a curtain designed to obscure their true role. From the creation of the Lasker Plan until baseball's Fay Vincent was forced from office in 1992, it was possible to imagine a commissioner's work in noble—and neutral—terms as they professed to put the "best interest of the game" above all other considerations.

That useful fiction eroded with the rise of player unions, as the commissioner took an active role in labor negotiations and his job was exposed to be less as a guardian of the game and more of a hireling representing the interest of the owners who hired him. In baseball, the transformation was nakedly public and obvious: Vincent, after employing his "best interest" powers in a way that displeased his bosses, was replaced by Selig—an actual owner. And any remaining claim the office had to neutrality was destroyed. Vincent was dubbed, and in fact titled his autobiography, "The Last Commissioner." But players' union head Marvin Miller would maintain that the owners' move to overthrew him merely lifted the veil from a what had always been true: "Baseball, in the phrase 'best interest of baseball' is a euphemism," Koppett wrote, "code for 'club owners'" (Koppett, 1991, 265).

Still, the "best interest" authority remains—for now—inscribed in league constitutions and CBAs that continue to define the relationship between teams and their players, and teams and their leagues. Recent cases, which we will examine in later chapters, have tested the powers, with differing outcomes: NBA Commissioner Adam Silver's decision to strip Los Angeles Clippers owner Donald Sterling of his team seems to have bridged the management-labor divide in his league, while also consolidating his power among the owners. Conversely, NFL Commissioner Roger Goodell's penalties in Deflategate, while welcomed by some teams, created a rift between Goodell and a longtime ally who was one of the league's most powerful owners. The long-running, dubiously managed, and expensive investigation also left players concerned about the danger of unchecked "best interest" power; they are already girding themselves for negotiations over their next collective bargaining agreement, which is scheduled to expire after the 2020 season, when they will no doubt attempt to curtail the commissioner's power. (Whether they will stand firm on this point, or trade it away for more tangible benefits, also remains to be seen.)

Other players' unions will no doubt watch closely to see whether a century of power consolidation can be reversed.

And followers of sports law will as well.

References

Abrams, Roger. (1998). *Legal Bases: Baseball and the Law* (Philadelphia, PA: Temple University Press).

Arcidiacono, David. (2010). *Major League Baseball in Gilded Age Connecticut; the Rise and Fall of the Middletown, New Haven, and Hartford Clubs* (Jefferson, NC: McFarland Press).

"Average Baseball Salary." (2008, December 4). ESPN.com. Accessed April 6, 2017, www.espn.com/espn/wire/_/section/mlb/id/3744821.

Bock, Hal. (2017). *Banned: Baseball's Blacklist of All-Stars and Also-Rans* (New York: Diversion Publishing).

Chass, Murray. (2000). "Baseball Suspends Rocker 'til May for Comments." *New York Times*, January 31.

Chicago Herald & Examiner. November 5, 1920.

"Commissioner's Statement." (2004, November 20). NBA.com. Accessed March 29, 2017, www.nba.com/news/commissioner_statement_041120.html.

Cowherd, Kevin. (2012). "Discipline of Saints speaks loud and clear." *Baltimore Sun*, March 22.

Cozzillio, M., Levinstein, M., Dimino, M, Sr., and Feldman, G. (2007). *Sports Law: Cases and Materials* (Durham, NC: Carolina Academic Press).

Fountain, Charles. (2016). *The Betrayal: The 1919 World Series and the Birth of Modern Baseball* (Oxford: Oxford University Press).

"Francis T. Vincent." MLB.com. Accessed April 6, 2017, http://mlb.mlb.com/mlb/history/mlb_history_people.jsp?story=com_bio_8.

Ginsburg, Daniel E. (2003). *The Fix Is In: A History of Baseball Gambling and Game Fixing Scandals* (Jefferson, NC: McFarland).

Goldstein, Richard. (2012, November 28). "Marvin Miller, Union Leader Who Changed Baseball, Dies at 95." *New York Times*. Accessed April 2, 2017, www.nytimes.com/2012/11/28/sports/baseball/marvin-miller-union-leader-who-changed-baseball-dies-at-95.html.

Holder, Larry. (2012, October 19). "Roger Goodell Recuses Himself from New Orleans Saints Bounty Appeal Hearings." *The Times-Picayune*. Accessed April 7, 2017, www.nola.com/saints/index.ssf/2012/10/nflpas_demaurice_smith_says_ro.html.

Javier, Roger A. (2000). "'You Cannot Choke Your Boss and Hold Your Job Unless You Play in the NBA': The Latrell Sprewell Incident Undermines Disciplinary Authority in the NBA." *Villanova Sports & Entertainment Law Journal* 7: 209.

Koppett, Leonard. (1967). *A Thinking Man's Guide to Baseball* (New York: Dutton).

Koppett, Leonard. (1991). *The New Thinking Man's Guide to Baseball* (New York: Simon & Schuster).

Lynch, Michael T. (2008). *Harry Frazee, Ban Johnson and the Feud that Nearly Destroyed the American League* (Jefferson, NC: McFarland).

Major League Constitution. Originally adopted as Major League Agreement on January 12, 1921. Accessed April 6 and available for download at www.law.uh.edu/assignments/summer2009/25691-b.pdf.

Miller, Marvin. (1989). "The Power of Baseball's Commissioner Is a Myth." *New York Times*. Accessed April 2, 2017, www.nytimes.com/1989/11/05/sports/views-of-sport-the-power-of-baseball-s-commissioner-is-a-myth.html.

Miller, Marvin. (1992). *A Whole Different Ball Game: The Inside Story of Baseball's New Deal* (New York: Simon & Schuster).

National Agreement for the Government of Professional Base Ball Clubs. (1903). Accessed April 3, 2017, http://roadsidephotos.sabr.org/baseball/1903NatAgree.htm.

National League Constitution and Playing Rules. (1877).

"NBA completes Hornets Purchase." (2010, December). NBA.com Accessed March 29, 2017, http://www.nba.com/2010/news/12/20/hornets-sale.ap/.

Pacifici, Adriano. (2014). "Scope and Authority of Sports League Commissioner Disciplinary Power: Bounty and Beyond." *Berkeley Journal of Entertainment and Sports Law* 3(1): 93–116.

Parchman, Matthew B. (1990). "Limits on Discretionary Powers of Professional Sports Commissioners: A Historical and Legal Analysis of Issues Raised by the Pete Rose Controversy." *Virginia Law Review* 76: 1409.

Pearlman, Jeff. (1999, December 27). "At Full Blast Shooting." SI.com. Accessed April 3, 2017, https://www.si.com/vault/1999/12/27/271860/at-full-blast-shooting-outrageously-from-the-lip-braves-closer-john-rocker-bangs-away-at-his-favorite-targets-the-mets-their-fans-their-city-and-just-about-everyone-in-it.

Pietrusza, David. (2001). *Judge and Jury: The Life and Times of Judge Kenesaw Mountain Landis* (South Bend, IN: Diamond Communications).

Price, S. L. (2015, September 8). "The Shrinking Commish: Are Goodell's Days as Disciplinarian Numbered?" Accessed April 6, 2017, www.si.com/nfl/2015/09/08/roger-goodell-deflategate-nfl-commissioner-discipline-power-tom-brady.

Reinsdorf, Jonathan M. (1996). "The Powers of the Commissioner in Baseball." *Marquette Sports Law Journal* 7: 225.

Reston, James. Jr. (1991). *Collision at Home Plate: The Lives of Pete Rose and Bart Giamatti* (New York: Burlingame Books).

Sell, Dave. (1992). "Baseball's Vincent Resigns." *Washington Post*, September 8.

Smith, Leverett T. Jr. (1970). *The American Dream and the National Game* (Bowling Green, OH: Bowling Green University Popular Press).
Spalding Guide. (1876). Cooperstown, NY: Baseball Hall of Fame and Museum.
Thornton, Patrick. (2002). *Sports Law* (Burlington Mass: Jones & Bartlett Learning).
Vincent, Fay. (2002). *The Last Commissioner: A Baseball Valentine* (Philadelphia: Temple University Press).
Will, George F. (1999). *Bunts* (New York: Simon & Schuster).
Wood, Allan. "Carl Mays." Accessed March 30, 2017, http://sabr.org/bioproj/person/99ca7c89.
Zelinsky, Aaron S. (2011). "The Supreme Court (of Baseball)." *Yale Law Journal Online* 121: 143.

Cases

American League Baseball Club of N.Y. v. Johnson, 109 Misc. 138, 179 N.Y.S. 498 (1919).
Complaint, NFLPA v. NFL Mgmt. Council, 2:12-cv-01744-SSV-SS (E.D. La. July 7, 2012).
Finley v. Kuhn, 569 F.2d 525 (7th Cir. 1978).
Major League Baseball Arbitration, MLBPA v. Commissioner of MLB re: John Rocker. (2002). Accessed April 4, 2017, www.law.uh.edu/assignments/summer2009/25691-c.pdf.
Milwaukee Am. Ass'n v Landis, 49 F.2d 298 (N.D. Ill. 1931).
Molinas v. NBA, 190 F. Supp. 241 (S.D.N.Y. 1961).
NFLPA v. NLRB, 503 F.2d 12 (8th Cir. 1974).
Philadelphia Ball Club v. Lajoie, 51 A. 973 (Pa. 1902).
Rose v. Giamatti, 721 F. Supp. 906 (S.D. Ohio 1989).

CHAPTER 3

LEAGUES AND OWNERS

The Donald Sterling Story

MICHAEL A. MCCANN

1. The Complex Relationship Between Owners, Their League, and Its Commissioner

League commissioners and owners are aligned in many ways. Most crucially, commissioners work for owners. Only owners can hire commissioners, and only they can fire them. On behalf of owners, commissioners negotiate collective bargaining agreements (CBAs) with players' associations and contracts with companies in the television, apparel, and other sports markets. The public perception of commissioners and owners is that they are seated at the same side of the table.

Usually they are.

While typically aligned, the interests of commissioners and owners are not designed for perfect harmony. Commissioners are entrusted with pursuing the best interests of the league—rather than the best interests of owners. This is a distinction with meaning.

Among the "big four" U.S. sports leagues—the National Football League (NFL), the National Basketball Association (NBA), Major League Baseball (MLB), and the National Hockey League (NHL)—the idea of a "league" refers to a joint venture of independently owned, sellable, and competing franchises. Owners, then, can be thought of as present-day custodians of franchises. Different persons or entities will at some point own those franchises.

Owners' interests are not fully aligned with those of other owners or even those of the league itself. Each owner wants his or her team to win games and championships. These are goals that require teams to defeat other teams. Consequently, owners *must* compete in a competitive sports league. An owner also wants the team to succeed as an asset.

Success as an asset is typically measured by the asset's capacity to turn a profit and to increase in value from the time it was purchased to the time it will be sold. A team's value is impacted by a league's business choices as well as by policies the league negotiates with its respective players' association. An owner's optimal financial interests for his or her team might align with those of the league, but not necessarily so.

A league, in contrast, is structured to maximize the interests of *all* of its teams, in both the short and long term. This objective requires the league to empower each of its teams with legitimate opportunities for success. Otherwise, fans and prospective fans would doubt that their favorite team has a viable chance to succeed. Accordingly, their interest in their favorite team might wane and their dollars, time, and energy might be invested elsewhere. Along those lines, a league doesn't prefer that any particular team win. In fact, a league adopts and implements various procedures to make it almost impossible for one team to win all of the time.

Consider, for example, how leagues utilize player entry drafts to restrict how teams hire amateur players. These drafts award the worst teams with exclusive opportunities to hire the most coveted amateur players. Think of this concept as applied to a more conventional industry. Imagine if the worst engineering firm in the United States, by virtue of being the very worst in the engineering industry, gained the exclusive right to hire the valedictorian of MIT or Caltech. Moreover, imagine that the valedictorian would be contractually bound to this engineering firm for perhaps a quarter of his or her engineering career. Surely, this idea sounds preposterous and unfair. Yet leagues adopt such an approach to the acquisition of new talent because it supplies the worst teams with enhanced opportunities for success. Remember, a league looks out for all but not for any one.

With this framework of owners in mind, commissioners are sometimes thought of as chief executive officers (CEOs) in that both positions are the most powerful in their organizations. This analogy makes sense on multiple levels, at least on the surface. Consider a textual level. League constitutions expressly include the employment duty of "serving as chief executive officer" within their descriptions of the commissioner. Article VI of the NHL Constitution, for example, instructs that the NHL commissioner, "shall serve as the Chief Executive Officer" of the NHL and "shall be charged with protecting the integrity of professional hockey and preserving public confidence in the League."

The CEO-commissioner analogy is also persuasive from a functional standpoint. Like CEOs, commissioners are ultimately responsible for the organization's success or failure. They also share an overarching authority to act in the best interests of that organization. Further, lawmakers, journalists, and other constituencies regard CEOs and commissioners as their organization's official voice.

Yet the CEO-commissioner analogy encounters complications when viewing these two positions' respective sources of power. CEOs rely on board members' delegations of power through bylaws, and are thus beholden to boards. While corporate governance commentaries warn that some boards insufficiently supervise CEOs, the more central point is that the CEOs are accountable to boards.

Commissioners, in contrast, derive independent and autonomous power through league constitutions and accompanying documents. Commissioner authority, in other words, exists not through owner decree but through contractual instruments that are designed to outlast owners.

Take, for example, Article 24 of the National Basketball Association's Constitution. It dictates that the commissioner is the NBA's CEO. Within that authority, the commissioner is responsible for the "general supervision and direction of all business and affairs of the League." Notice that it is the commissioner, rather than owners or a group of owners, who is charged with the overarching power of supervision and direction of the NBA as a business entity. The commissioner of the NBA is also entrusted with important dispute-resolution powers.

As outlined in Article 24, the commissioner shall have "exclusive, full, complete, and final jurisdiction of any dispute" involving two or more teams and ownership groups. The constitutions of other leagues, including the NFL, MLB, and the NHL, offer similar constructions of the commissioner.

A commissioner of a professional sports league is thus accorded powers independent from those of the owners. To be sure, owners retain indirect authority over the commissioner by virtue of the fact that only owners hire the commissioner and only owners can fire him or her. In practice, however, commissioners are not deterred by the possibility of losing their job: not one modern commissioner in the NBA, NFL, MLB, or NHL has been fired. Only in one exceptional circumstance has a commissioner been "pushed out." In 1992, a majority of MLB owners, frustrated by commissioner Fay Vincent's approach to labor relations, voted 18-9 in favor of a resolution that expressed "no confidence" in Vincent and that requested his resignation. Vincent promptly resigned. Other than Vincent's unwanted exit, commissioners are normally seen as exiting their employment at a time of their choosing.

The commissioner is therefore emboldened to pursue the best path for the league as he or she assesses. This is true even if the chosen pursuit is adverse to one or more teams or owners.

In recent years, league commissioners have sometimes pursued "best interest" strategies in direct contravention of certain owners' interests. I will focus on one illustrative example: NBA Commissioner Adam Silver's ouster of Donald Sterling as owner of the Los Angeles Clippers. The removal of Sterling implicated multiple powers of the commissioners and highlighted the critical importance of a commissioner's willingness to challenge an owner.

2. The Rise of Donald Sterling as an Uncooperative Owner and the NBA's Acquiescence to Sterling's Misconduct

The experience of Donald Sterling as owner of the Clippers NBA franchise from 1981 to 2014 is instructive on many levels. For our purposes, it highlights the broad range of commissioner authority to discipline owners while illuminating implicit constraints on the use of that authority.

To fully understand the demise of Sterling's ownership in 2014 would require a trip back in time to the spring of 1981. Back then, the Clippers played in San Diego and were owned by Irv Levin. They were also in the midst of another dismal season. The team was in second to last place in the NBA's Pacific Division and playing out the string of the 1980-81 regular season schedule. Not only were the Clippers bad, they were boring: critics maligned them for playing an uninspired style of basketball. Fans noticed. Attendance at Clippers games had dropped about 50% from two years prior and the superstar player expected to turn around the franchise's fortunes—Bill Walton—couldn't play due to myriad foot injuries. Levin, a film executive who previously owned the Boston Celtics, had recently suffered a personal tragedy with the death of his wife in a car accident. He was "desperate" to sell the money-losing Clippers and move on with his life (Branch, 2014).

NBA Commissioner Larry O'Brien shared Levin's concern about the future of the Clippers. More significantly, O'Brien feared this particular team's misfortunes were a harbinger for the rest of the league. At that time, a number of NBA teams were experiencing deep financial problems. Eighteen of the twenty-three NBA franchises reported net losses that year (Hershey and Dupree, 1981). The possibility of teams going out of business or the league contracting—where franchises are eliminated and players are disbursed to remaining franchises—was not farfetched.

The sources of the NBA's financial woes were substantial and varied. Among them were consumer preferences. American consumers were simply more interested in other forms of sports entertainment and other types of television programs. Consider that NBA Finals games were shown on tape delay, rather than live—an idea nearly incomprehensible in the twenty-first century, where even banal post-game interviews from preseason NBA games are broadcast live. The NBA just wasn't that exciting in the early 1980s.

The economics of pro sports only compounded the challenge for the NBA. At the time, revenue for NBA and other sports teams was largely contingent on gate receipts. Indeed, television and radio rights offered comparatively modest returns. Keep in mind, only about a quarter of Americans had cable TV in 1981 and ESPN was in its infancy. Simply put, NBA owners needed fans to buy tickets to watch games or teams would not generate enough money.

Of course, if O'Brien and owners had a crystal ball, they would have known their fortunes would change radically within a decade. Cable television would soon take off in popularity, with approximately 60% of American homes having cable by the end of the 1980s. For its part, ESPN would quickly become the worldwide leader in sports and, by 1983, would begin airing NBA games to a national audience (Stewart, 2002). Broadcasting revenue for games would surge, particularly as Magic Johnson, Larry Bird,and later Michael Jordan captivated an ever-enlarging NBA fan base. NBA teams located in large media markets, such as New York and Los Angeles, would be the greatest beneficiaries of this revenue bonanza. While NBA teams share revenue from games broadcast through national TV contracts, each team negotiates its own local TV deal, the size of which tends to reflect market size. But in the spring of 1981, given what was known at that time, stabilizing the Clippers' ownership in an era of middling revenues was essential for the NBA.

Levin thought he had found a buyer whom the NBA would embrace in Phil Knight, the billionaire co-founder of Nike, but their deal fell apart. Levin then turned to other prospective buyers, one of whom was Los Angeles attorney Donald Sterling. Sterling had made his fortune buying properties and then renting them or selling them for profit. Although Levin found Sterling to be "a little weird," Sterling was willing and able to pay Levin's asking price of $12.5 million (Branch, 2014). Seeking financial stability above all else, the NBA quickly approved the sale.

In a fitting omen, Sterling began his ownership of the Clippers with a promise that he would not keep. He wrote an open letter to Clippers fans assuring them, "I'm in San Diego to stay" (Branch, 2014). Sterling did stay—but for only a few years. And those three years were turbulent, to put it mildly. Between 1981 and 1984, Sterling managed the San Diego Clippers in often peculiar and penny-pinching ways.

For instance, Sterling hired a former model with no apparent background in basketball to a senior position in basketball operations. He also refused to pay players' salaries and hotel bills, and advocated replacing the team's electric typewriters with cheaper manual ones. Sterling's most bizarre idea revealed his utter disinterest in, if not contempt for, fan relations. Sterling proposed to his staff that Clippers home games be played without a live attendance, meaning no one—including Clippers fans—would be able to attend home games. He reasoned that such a step would relieve the team of the obligation to pay for concessions workers, security, and parking attendants, and the team could capture enough revenue through television and radio broadcasts. The idea went nowhere (Dohrmann, 2014).

Some of Sterling's controversial ideas advanced and became unfortunate realities. A few would even run afoul of the NBA Constitution and bylaws, which Sterling, like all owners upon buying a franchise, contractually assented to follow. And, among those few ideas, two would go so far as to endanger Sterling's continued ownership of the San Diego Clippers.

In 1982, Sterling attempted to make Clippers' season tickets more attractive by offering free nights at the Sands Hotel and Casino in Las Vegas. While the idea might have made sense for certain types of businesses, it did not for an NBA team. The NBA, like other professional sports leagues, expressly prohibits any associations with gambling entities. Article 13(f) of the NBA Constitution, in fact, stipulates that ownership can be terminated for directly or indirectly participating in gambling activities. Sterling, an attorney with over twenty years of experience at that time, either knew or should have been aware of this contractual stipulation.

The NBA was also disturbed by Sterling's glib remarks captured on an audio recording in January 1982. On the recording, Sterling implied that the Clippers should lose games so they would finish last. They would then be able to draft first overall in the 1982

NBA Draft. "Maybe I have to lose the battle to win the war," Sterling observed. "We must end last to draw first to get a franchise-maker" (N.Y. Times Sports desk, 1982).

At the time, the NBA awarded draft picks in direct inverse order of regular season record, meaning that the team with the worst record would receive the first pick and an opportunity to draft the best available amateur player. There are legal problems with teams trying to lose games, more colloquially known as "tanking." Article 13(g) of the NBA Constitution instructs that an ownership can be canceled if teams attempt to lose games. The NBA, like other leagues, markets its games to consumers as ones where players, coaches, and management always strive to compete at the highest level. If teams instead pursue strategies that undermine contractual and advertised pledges to play competitive games, those teams might run afoul of consumer protection and antifraud laws.

The NBA warned Sterling of his apparent misconduct and demanded that he change his ways. Commissioner O'Brien, who fined Sterling $10,000 for his tanking comments, also assembled a special committee of six owners to study whether Sterling ought to be removed as owner. In September 1982, the committee recommended that Sterling be ousted (Rainey, Fenno, and Turner, 2014). O'Brien then set a date for owners of all twenty-two teams to discuss whether to end Sterling's ownership, which per Article 14 of the NBA Constitution, would have required a three-quarters vote by other owners.

It seemed as if Sterling's stewardship of the Clippers would be short-lived. He openly disregarded important league rules and advocated positions at odds with basic notions of a competitive sports league.

But Sterling, perhaps sensing that the NBA needed him more than he needed it, announced his intention to sell the Clippers. This announcement led worried NBA executives to postpone the vote indefinitely. The vote would never be held—Sterling called the owners' bluff. After Sterling made cosmetic changes to the Clippers' operations, then-NBA Vice President (and future commissioner) David Stern hailed the San Diego Clippers as a franchise being run in a "first-class" style (Rainey et al., 2014).

A year later Sterling betrayed his promise to the people of San Diego. He moved the Clippers to Los Angeles and did so without the required approval of the NBA's Board of Governors, some of whom were concerned about the potential saturation effect of two NBA franchises—the Clippers and Lakers—coexisting in one city. In response to this so-called first-class franchise's unauthorized move, the NBA sued Sterling in the U.S. District Court for the Southern District of California. The league argued breach of contract, among other claims, and maintained that Sterling had caused at least $25 million in damages. Never to be outdone, Sterling filed a counter lawsuit in Los Angeles Superior Court for $120 million. Sterling insisted that the NBA and its owners had conspired in violation of antitrust law to prevent him from moving the franchise to a more lucrative locale—Los Angeles. In doing so, Sterling asserted, the NBA wasted league resources to which he contributed by paying dues. Sterling thus disregarded his contractual agreement with other owners and instead sued them so that he would not have to adhere to his commitment.

Sterling's ploy effectively worked. The two sides dropped their lawsuits in 1987 and the Clippers would—just as Sterling angled—play in Los Angeles. In exchange, Sterling only had to pay a modest price. Namely, he agreed to forfeit $6 million in league expansion fees that other owners received when the Charlotte Hornets and Miami Heat entered the league. Commentators regarded it as a decisive victory for Sterling and a defeat for the NBA, its new commissioner, David Stern, and the powers of the commissioner.

Sterling's ownership of the Clippers would remain problematic for the next three decades. On the court, the Clippers were one of the league's worst franchises, suffering losing season after losing season. Basketball writers frequently cited Sterling as a major factor in the team's failures. He was viewed as needlessly spendthrift with players. For example, Sterling failed to resign any of the Clippers' nine players selected as a lottery picks from the 1985 to 1998 drafts after their initial contracts (Dorsey, 2017). Sterling was even accused of taking steps to deflate players' statistics. One former NBA scorekeeper insisted that Sterling demanded that scorekeepers record fewer assists so that Clippers players would accumulate less impressive statistics and thus obtain less leverage in salary negotiations (Craggs, 2009).

Sterling also encountered several legal issues during these three decades. None would lead to repercussions from the NBA, which consistently declined to invoke its powers to punish or expel Sterling.

For example, in both 1996 and 2003, former employees sued Sterling for sexual harassment. There is no indication that the NBA formally investigated the veracity or seriousness of these claims, let alone discipline Sterling. Also, in 2006, the Justice Department sued Sterling and his wife, Shelly Sterling, for discriminatory rental practices. The two had allegedly discriminated on the basis of race and national origin and violated the Fair Housing Act. According to the Justice Department's complaint, the Sterlings openly opined that African Americans and Hispanics were undesirable tenants and the Sterlings' property managers should avoid renting to them. A few years later, the Sterlings settled the lawsuit and agreed to pay a record $2.75 million fine as well as undergo fair housing training (Office of Public Affairs, 2009). The NBA took no public action.

Sterling's poor record with race relations would only continue. In 2009, the Clippers' former general manager, Elgin Baylor, sued Sterling for wrongful termination as well as race and age discrimination. Baylor alleged that Sterling "employed a campaign to get" him to quit by "using ageist comments, repeatedly asking [Baylor] his age [and] reminding Baylor that he was old enough to retire." Baylor also asserted that Sterling engendered a racially hostile environment, telling Baylor he wanted a team "composed of 'poor black boys' from the South and a white head coach." Although a jury in 2011 declined to find liability, the NBA's ability to punish Sterling for allegedly racist remarks was not contingent upon a court finding. The league's Non-Discrimination Policy makes clear that the NBA has zero tolerance for any discrimination on the basis of race or ethnicity—which is also unlawful under the 1964 Civil Rights Act. It is unclear if the NBA formally investigated Baylor's allegations, but there is no record of Sterling being punished over them.

3. Commissioner Adam Silver Invokes His Legal Authority to Order Donald Sterling's Removal from the NBA

Sterling's ability to escape consequences for questionable conduct would end dramatically in 2014. In April of that year, TMZ published a recording of Sterling—who had been married to Shelly Sterling for fifty-nine years at that time—and his girlfriend, V. Stiviano, having an argument (TMZ Staff, 2014). During the argument, Sterling made a series of racist comments. Most notably, Sterling asked Stiviano, "*Why are you taking pictures with minorities?*" and what benefit she received by "*walking publicly with black people?*" He also told Stiviano that he was "bothered" by her posting pictures of herself on Instagram with black people, including former Los Angeles Lakers star Magic Johnson, and that he didn't want her bringing black people to Clippers games. Sterling attempted to mitigate his remarks by stressing that he was fine with Stiviano, who describes herself as black and Mexican, spending time with black people in private. It was only her public appearances with black people, Sterling reasoned, that troubled him. For obvious reasons, Sterling's attempt to qualify his racism made it only worse.

The TMZ story triggered a national controversy for the NBA and its new commissioner, Adam Silver. It would be Silver's first test since he took over the position merely two months earlier.

Silver, along with NBA general counsel Rick Buchanan, faced an unenviable task. For starters, the NBA had to ensure the recording's authenticity before Sterling could face discipline. The source of the recording was unknown, and Clippers executives strategically suggested it might have been altered to defame Sterling. As a mere private business, the NBA could not subpoena TMZ to turn over the recording. Further, the NBA knew that Sterling regarded the recording itself as illegal: it is a crime in California to intentionally record a confidential conversation without the consent of all of the persons in the conversation.

Yet Silver also knew that he had to act swiftly and decisively. Sterling's apparent remarks were abhorrent and well publicized. They attracted widespread scorn and beget a national discussion on race relations in America. Most notably, President Barack Obama took time at a news conference in Kuala Lumpur, Malaysia, to address the escalating crisis. Obama movingly linked Sterling's remarks to the "legacy of race and slavery" in the U.S. and the "vestiges of discrimination" (McCann, 2014a, 2014b). For their part, NBA players—74% of whom are black—were outraged. The Golden State Warriors threatened to boycott the team's playoff game with the Clippers unless, as star player Stephen Curry firmly put it, Sterling received "the maximum punishment" (Boren, 2014).

Still, many were skeptical that the NBA would do much more than fine Sterling and issue a carefully scripted, sternly worded statement repudiating Sterling's remarks. After all, the NBA had acquiesced to Sterling's uncooperative and insolent style of ownership for three decades. The league had several opportunities to expel Sterling, including on grounds related to race, and yet demurred each time.

This time it was different. The NBA was no longer a financially strapped sports league with half-filled arenas and games broadcast on tape delay. By 2014, the NBA and its teams annually generated nearly $5 billion a year in revenue. As explained earlier, the dramatic growth in television revenue—particularly for teams located in large media markets—radically changed the value of NBA franchises. Sterling's franchise was most emblematic of this metamorphosis. Despite their general ineptitude, Sterling's Clippers had increased in value from $13 million in 1981 to approximately $2 billion in 2014. This increase in value was jaw dropping even when accounting for inflation: using the value of a dollar in 2014, the Clippers surged from $31 million to $2 billion under Sterling's ownership.

This was also a different time due to the presence of a different leader. By any objective metric, David Stern was a resoundingly successful commissioner. During his tenure, which spanned from 1984 to 2014, the NBA transformed from a financially unstable venture into a billionaires club. Nonetheless, as discussed earlier, Stern adopted a conciliatory approach to Sterling. Sterling moved the Clippers without the league or Stern's approval. Further, over the course of three decades, Sterling repeatedly engaged in disobliging, if not unlawful, practices that no doubt rankled Stern. Yet Stern never took steps to oust or even severely punish Sterling. Stern's acquiescence might have been the right approach for the NBA at the time. The NBA wanted the public to focus on talented players, not on wayward owners. Yet this approach enabled Sterling to act without fear of consequences.

Through his words and conduct, Silver's approach to Sterling was unmistakable: enough is enough. Within seventy-two hours of TMZ's publication of Sterling's remarks, Silver had (1) dispatched former Assistant U.S. Attorney David Anders, among other attorneys, to Los Angeles to interview all relevant witnesses and verify all of the evidence; (2) reviewed the applicability of the NBA Constitution and Bylaws to Sterling's apparent misconduct; (3) determined an appropriate sanction; and (4) issued the sanction and explained it to the public. Silver, an attorney by trade, could not have more adroitly handled the crisis.

Silver's strongest moment came on April 29, 2014, when he publicly revealed Sterling's punishment. Few could have predicted the tenor and substance of Silver's remarks in that media-packed Hilton Hotel conference room in Midtown Manhattan. "I am personally distraught," Silver reflected, "that the views expressed by Mr. Sterling came from within an institution that has historically taken such a leadership role in matters of race relations and caused current and former players, coaches, fans and partners of the NBA to question their very association with the league." In response, Silver announced, "I am banning Mr. Sterling for life from any association with the Clippers organization or the NBA." Silver also fined Sterling $2.5 million (the maximum amount permitted under the NBA Constitution) and pledged to "urge the Board of Governors to exercise its authority" to force Sterling to sell the Clippers (SI.com staff, 2014).

The NBA's legal argument to expel Sterling was textually logical, if unprecedented. Article 13 of the league's constitution enumerates ten distinct grounds that can justify termination of ownership of an NBA team. Two of those grounds were especially applicable to the case against Sterling. Article 13(a) prohibits willful violation of the league constitution, bylaws or other agreements between any owner and the NBA, while 13(d) contemplates a failure to meet contractual obligations to the NBA, other owners, players, or third parties in a way that causes adverse impact to the NBA or other owners. The relevant contractual obligations were covenants concerning owners' unethical conduct and owners' advocacy of "positions that have a materially adverse effect on the league." These covenants were found in contracts that Sterling, like every NBA owner, had signed. The franchise agreement between Sterling and the NBA and the so-called joint venture agreement, which requires owners to assent that the league and its commissioner have binding and final authority over whether owners had satisfying contractual commitments, were two such contracts.

For the NBA, 13(d) served as more effective means to address Sterling. Unlike 13(a), 13(d) does not require intent, which would have been difficult to establish given that Sterling's remarks to Stiviano were secretly and unlawfully recorded. Sterling presumably would have elected a more public venue to enunciate his views if he had intended for them to be heard. Article 13(a) demands no such intent. It merely asks if the owner failed to fulfill a contractual obligation and if such a failure adversely impacted the NBA or owners. Sterling's remarks clearly caused an adverse impact on the NBA. Carmax, Virgin America, and Mercedes-Benz were among major companies that took steps to end their sponsorships with the Clippers. NBA players, including LeBron James, threatened a boycott of NBA games unless Sterling was removed as Clippers' owner.

Yet removing Sterling would have made the NBA vulnerable to claims of hypocrisy. For decades, Sterling's conduct had, in various ways, "adversely" impacted the NBA. At no time was Sterling's ownership ever threatened.

The NBA also faced the risk of a "slippery slope." If Sterling could be ousted for comments made in a private conversation, could other owners be ousted as well? Surely, Sterling was not alone among owners in making comments that, if they became public, would reflect poorly on the NBA and its sponsors.

In addition, other NBA owners had generated controversy through their alleged conduct and beliefs. For instance, the NBA took no action after the U.S. Securities and Exchange Commission sued Dallas Mavericks owner Mark Cuban in 2008 for insider trading (Cuban would win his trial in 2013). The lawsuit generated controversy and raised questions about Cuban's adherence to ethical and legal rules. At no time did the NBA indicate that it contemplated punishing Cuban. But in a post-Sterling world, would such a controversy require punishment?

Alternatively, some owners have contradicted the NBA's positions on important political and policy matters. For instance, Rich DeVos, who is part of the family that owns the Orlando Magic, has spoken out against marriage equality. While DeVos is certainly within his First Amendment rights to opine on that topic, the NBA has advocated and adopted workplace policies that support marriage equality. Further, it's possible the NBA could conclude that DeVos's position on marriage is counter to the business interests and partnerships of the NBA, which is arguably the most progressive of the major sports leagues. If the NBA punished Sterling for making lawful, albeit offensive, comments, should it also punish owners when they lawfully express views that a substantial percentage of Americans find offensive?

Silver and Buchanan were not worried about these potential criticisms. As they stressed, the focus of the relevant legal analysis is not on the underlying act or how the act became public, but rather on the *impact* of that act once it became public. Indeed, Article 13 stresses that the league's capacity to take action against an owner is contingent upon whether the conduct "affects" the NBA and its owners. As a result, even if Sterling's private comments to Stiviano about black people were morally less reprehensible than Sterling discriminating against black people—as he allegedly did as a landlord—the *impact* of Sterling's private comments caused a much more substantial impact on the NBA's reputation.

Further, the league disputed the significance of whether the recording was unlawful. From the NBA's perspective, the lawfulness of the recording under California law was immaterial to relevant contractual question: whether the *impact* of the recording's public broadcast warranted Sterling's expulsion under the NBA's Constitution. The NBA also stressed that its constitution followed both New York law—which, unlike California law, permits recordings of other without their consent—and standard arbitration rules and procedures, which are relatively flexible and often permit the introduction of evidence that a court might deem inadmissible. Stern, as an NBA owner, contractually accepted all of these conditions as part of his membership in the NBA.

Accordingly, the NBA announced that the league's Board of Governors, which includes the controlling owner of each of the thirty NBA teams, would meet to consider Silver's recommendation that Stern be removed as owner. Article 14 of the league constitution outlines the procedures for an expulsion hearing. Such a hearing is structured as something of a mix between a trial, an arbitration hearing, and a c-level executive conversation. Attorneys for the NBA would present Silver's case against Sterling. In response, Sterling's legal team would articulate a defense. Unlike in a trial, formal of rules of evidence and advocacy would be dispensed in favor of conversation and transparency. Glen Taylor, the chairman of the Board of Governors and owner of the Minnesota Timberwolves, was expected to preside over the hearing. Taylor would have been more of a facilitator than an arbitrator since Taylor would not have been tasked with issuing an award. Instead, the twenty-nine controlling owners of every NBA team except the Clippers were charged as de facto jurors. In order for Sterling's ouster to take effect, twenty-two of the twenty-nine owners had to vote in favor of sustaining Silver's charge against Sterling. If Sterling had been ousted, Silver, as commissioner, would have taken over operational control of the Clippers and put it up for sale.

4. NBA's Legal Efforts Aided by Shelly Sterling and Her Interpretation of the Sterling Family Trust

Sterling's expulsion hearing never took place. The NBA postponed it as Sterling's wife, Shelly Sterling, began a legal effort to remove her husband from control of the Sterling Family Trust.

Shelly Sterling undertook this effort as part of a strategy to sell the Clippers against the wishes of her husband. Although Donald Sterling was on the NBA's Board of Governors and functioned as the owner of the Clippers, his family trust technically owned the team, along with various properties and other assets. Donald and Shelly Sterling were the trust's only members and possessed equal shares. Mrs. Sterling, whom had been estranged from her husband while he pursued a relationship with Stiviano, insisted that the eighty-year-old Donald Sterling had become incapacitated and was unable to discharge his duties under the trust.

Just a few weeks after her husband's infamous recording became public, Shelly Sterling sat down for an interview with ABC's Barbara Walters. Mrs. Sterling, who along with her husband were (as explained previously) sued by the Justice Department in 2006 for racial discrimination in housing practices, insisted that she had never before heard Donald make racist remarks. Shelly Sterling further opined to Walters that her husband's advanced age had clearly impaired his reasoning and cognitive skills.

Shelly Sterling's commentary about her husband's mental capacities made for more than mere celebrity gossip. It also contained legal significance: under the terms of the family trust, if either Donald or Shelly Sterling became incapacitated, the other would obtain full decision-making authority. Either Shelly Sterling genuinely believed her husband had become incapacitated or she saw a fortuitous opportunity to obtain control of the family trust. As her husband ineptly fought exile from the NBA, Mrs. Sterling retained a neurologist and psychiatrist to evaluate her husband, without his consent or even his knowledge. In fact, Donald Sterling would later say his wife "tricked" him into meeting with the two doctors under false pretenses. Nonetheless, the doctors agreed with Shelly Sterling: Donald Sterling was unfit to carry out his duties under the trust.

While it appeared that Shelly Sterling had outmaneuvered Donald Sterling in seizing control of the trust, the public was hardly sympathetic for Donald. After all, he had eviscerated any goodwill through racist words and a history of insensitive misdeeds. In fact, E-Poll Market Research classified Sterling as "the most hated man in America." Further, Sterling's bizarre behavior continued even after the public heard his recorded remarks. For example, he called Silver and other NBA officials "despicable monsters" in response to Silver declaring his intent to oust Sterling. Sterling also made a series of bizarre and cantankerous comments to CNN's Anderson Cooper in a much-publicized interview. In that interview, Sterling bragged that African Americans liked to play golf with him.

He also offered various generalizations about Jewish people (Sterling is Jewish) and labeled Stiviano, who was thirty-one years old, a "girl." While those remarks did not prove that Sterling was mentally unfit—if anything, they seemed consistent with the benighted attitudes that he had expressed for decades—they did nothing to endear him to the public, either.

5. Courts Tell Donald Sterling That Losing the Clippers Was His Own Fault

Never a quitter and always a lawyer, Donald Sterling fought back in court. His first move was to file a lawsuit against a wide-range of opponents—the NBA, Adam Silver, David Stern, Shelly Sterling, and the two physicians Shelly Sterling hired to evaluate Donald—for $1 billion. Sterling's main legal theory was grounded in antitrust law. He postulated that this seemingly disparate group had somehow acted as a cartel to exile him from the league. Further, Sterling reasoned, a forced sale of the Clippers would net less than what the franchise would fetch for sale in a "free market, unfettered by the NBA."

Sterling's antitrust law failed to advance for many reasons. For one, Sterling had contractually assented to the possibility of losing his franchise when he assented to follow Article 13. Second, Sterling's removal from the Clippers was seemingly an economic positive, not negative, for the franchise. After all, he had caused the franchise tremendous embarrassment and his decision making as owner was often ridiculed. From that lens, Sterling's ouster would actually *enhance* economic competition: it would improve the Clippers and make them more appealing to fans, consumers, businesses, and potential franchise buyers. Third, Shelly Sterling had secured a sale of the franchise to former Microsoft CEO Steve Ballmer for $2 billion, the highest dollar amount ever to be paid for an NBA franchise. Sterling's contention that the franchise ought to be worth more than what his wife negotiated flew in the face of common sense. Fourth, the idea of a conspiracy involving physicians hired by Shelly Sterling and current and former NBA commissioners seemed unlikely, to put it kindly. While the NBA likely coordinated with Shelly Sterling—who indemnified the NBA from her husband's lawsuit—in facilitating a sale of the franchise to Ballmer, the notion of a nefarious and far-reaching conspiracy to have Donald Sterling declared mentally incapacitated lacked factual support.

While his billion-dollar antitrust suit was destined for failure, Sterling simultaneously pursued another lawsuit that was much less quixotic. Donald and Shelly Sterling sought an order from Los Angeles Superior Court Judge Michael Levanas over whether she lawfully became the sole trustee of the family trust. This determination was crucial given that Shelly Sterling's legal ability to sell the Clippers was contingent upon her having the capacity to execute such a sale. Judge Levanas was thus asked to determine if Shelly Sterling lawfully concluded that her husband lacked the mental competence to fulfill his obligations under the family trust.

A competency hearing took place, and Judge Levanas heard competing perspectives about whether Donald Sterling was at risk of making serious errors of judgment in managing the trust. Shelly Sterling provided CT scans and PET scans of her husband's brain to contend that he suffered from cognitive impairment and was unable to capably discharge his duties and obligations. Donald Sterling countered with his own expert physicians who insisted that he was fine. Donald Sterling also surmised that Shelly was motivated not by her husband's health but by an opportunity to cash out on the Clippers.

Clippers players and NBA fans were very curious onlookers: if Judge Levanas sided with Donald Sterling, the tentative deal reached by Shelly Sterling and Steve Ballmer would have been rendered void. In that scenario, the NBA would have been forced to conduct an expulsion hearing of Sterling in order to remove him.

Much to the relief of Shelly Sterling and the NBA, Judge Levanas found sufficient evidence for the finding that, as required by the trust, two independent physicians credibly declared Donald Sterling mentally incapacitated. Donald Sterling was thus unable to discharge his responsibilities as a trustee, leaving Shelly Sterling as the sole trustee. The order enabled Shelly Sterling, on behalf of the Sterling family trust, to then sell the team to Ballmer—a transaction the NBA not only approved but also gladly welcomed.

Over the next two years, Sterling would appeal his legal defeats, but none of his appeals prevailed. In November 2016, Sterling withdrew his antitrust case as part of a settlement. Although Donald Sterling lost his NBA team, he and Shelly Sterling evenly split the massive proceeds from the Ballmer sale, which, after federal and state capital gain taxes, reportedly netted the Sterlings $1.34 billion (McCann, 2014a). In other words, in exchange for losing a team that many basketball efforts thought he neglected, Donald Sterling was awarded approximately $717 million—or more than fifty-two times what he paid for that team. Sometimes losing does pay.

6. Conclusion

In a perfect league, the downfall of Donald Sterling as owner of the Los Angeles Clippers would have never taken place. Such a league, after all, would never have approved Sterling as an owner in the first place. Even less idealistic scenarios would have yielded different outcomes. A league with more backbone than the NBA would not have tolerated Sterling and his harmful antics for three decades.

But in the world that existed, Donald Sterling repeatedly partook in distasteful behavior that damaged the brands of his team and the NBA. Sterling acted without fear of any meaningful punishment, a dynamic that only emboldened him. The NBA tolerated Sterling mainly because invoking its ouster authority would have risked injury to the NBA's financial health and precipitated controversy.

By 2014, however, the NBA was in its best financial shape ever. Billionaires sought to pay enormous amounts of money to buy one of the coveted thirty teams. When one such billionaire, Steve Ballmer, offered to pay $2 billion for the Clippers, any logic for retaining Donald Sterling was lost.

Sterling's ouster from the NBA illustrates the legal powers of a commissioner under a league constitution. Perhaps as important, it illuminates how circumstances influence the willingness of a commissioner to invoke those powers.

Acknowledgments

I thank my wife, Kara McCann, for her unwavering encouragement and my research assistant, Nicholas Danforth, for his excellent research. I also thank Roger Ford, John Greabe, Leah Plunkett and Alexandra Roberts for their helpful comments on drafts. Last but not least I thank Jordan Budd, Margaret McCabe, and the University of New Hampshire School of Law for their generous support.

References

Boren, C. (2014). "NBA Players Were 'Ready to Boycott' Games If NBA Hadn't Acted Against Donald Sterling." *Washington Post*, April 30, at www.washingtonpost.com/news/early-lead/wp/2014/04/29/nba-players-were-ready-to-boycott-games-if-nba-hadnt-acted-against-donald-sterling.

Branch, J. (2014). "Clippers for Sale." *The New York Times*, May 10, SP1.

Craggs, T. (2009, August 26). "The Confessions of an NBA Scorekeeper," *Deadspin*, at http://deadspin.com/5345287/the-confessions-of-an-nba-scorekeeper.

Dohrmann, G. (2014). "Recently Banned Donald Sterling Has Long History of Clashing with NBA." *Sports Illustrated*, May 30, at www.si.com/nba/2014/05/30/donald-sterling-history.

Dorsey, J. (2017). "Donald Sterling's Cheapest Moments as Los Angeles Clippers Owner." *Bleacher Report*, January 3 at http://bleacherreport.com/articles/1677590-donald-sterlings-cheapest-moments-as-la-clippers-owner.

Hershey, S., and Dupree, D. (1981). "Free Spenders." *The Washington Post*, October 25.

McCann, M. (2014a). "NBA's Checklist Before Approving Sale of the Clippers." *Sports Illustrated*, May 30, at www.si.com/nba/2014/05/30/steve-ballmer-clippers-nba-approval-checklist-sterling.

McCann, M. (2014b). "Power and Process." *Sports Illustrated*, May 12, pp. 16–18.

N.Y. Times Sports Desk. (1982). "NBA Fines Clippers' owner." *The New York Times*, January 9, p. 19.

Office of Public Affairs. (2009, November 3). "Justice Department Obtains Record $2.725 Million Settlement of Housing Discrimination Lawsuit." *U.S. Dept. of Justice*, at www.justice.gov/opa/pr/justice-department-obtains-record-2725-million-settlement-housing-discrimination-lawsuit.

Rainey, J., Fenno, N., and Turner, B. (2014). "Donald Sterling's Past May Speak to a Present Course with NBA." *The Los Angeles Times*, May 1, at www.latimes.com/local/la-me-sterling-legal-20140502-story.html.

SI.com staff. (2014). "Transcript: Adam Silver Announces Lifetime NBA Ban for Donald Sterling." *Sports Illustrated*, April 29, at www.si.com/nba/point-forward/2014/04/29/adam-silver-donald-sterling-transcript.

TMZ Staff. (2014). "L.A. Clippers owner to GF: Don't Bring Black People to My Games . . . Including Magic Johnson," *TMZ*, April 26, at www.tmz.com/2014/04/26/donald-sterling-clippers-owner-black-people-racist-audio-magic-johnson/.

Stewart, L. (2002). "Lakers Get Christmas Date." *The Los Angeles Times*, July 19, p. 5.

CHAPTER 4

THE COMMISSIONER'S POWER TO DISCIPLINE PLAYERS FOR ON- AND OFF-FIELD MISCONDUCT

RICHARD T. KARCHER

1. Introduction

During the last quarter century, the creation of new media platforms and technologies—the Internet, twenty-four-hour cable television sports coverage, social media, and cell phone cameras—has put professional athletes in a fishbowl. Every aspect of their lives, including every indiscretion, can be captured by someone and exposed for the world to see. This can occur an unlimited number of times and for an unlimited duration. Also, during the last quarter century, the compensation of professional athletes has increased exponentially—and new media platforms and technologies bring to society an unprecedented level of awareness about it. The combination of these two developments has had a profound impact on the societal view of professional athletes as "role models." As society's expectations of professional athletes and how they conduct themselves at work and on their own free time has changed through the years, so too have leagues' expectations.

This chapter addresses the power of professional sports league commissioners to discipline and suspend players for misconduct both on and off the field. First, it will provide a historical perspective of league discipline of players over the past century. This chapter then addresses the source of the commissioner's power and authority to discipline players for misconduct as well as the rationale behind it. Finally, the chapter discusses limitations on the commissioner's power and authority, including the collective bargaining agreements (CBAs) and a few highly publicized arbitration and court rulings that involved suspensions of players by league commissioners.

2. Historical Development of Commissioner Discipline of Players

Historically, league commissioners were reluctant to interfere with the club-player employment relationship. In the limited situations where they did, the discipline of players involved misconduct that had some reasonable nexus to their on-field activities (Edelman, 2009).

In *American League Baseball Club of New York v. Johnson*—one of the earliest cases on record involving league suspension of a player—Boston Red Sox pitcher Carl Mays left the field in the middle of a game and did not return the next day. While American League President Byron "Ban" Johnson was waiting for the Red Sox to discipline Mays for his conduct, the Red Sox sold him to the Yankees, who were in the midst of the pennant race. Johnson then decided to suspend Mays for "deserting his club and breaking contract." This prompted the Yankees to file a lawsuit against Johnson, claiming that he lacked the authority to suspend Mays. According to Johnson, the following clause in the league constitution gave him that authority: "The president, in the performance of his duties, shall have the power to impose fines or penalties, in the way of suspension or otherwise, upon any manager or player who, in his opinion, has been guilty of conduct detrimental to the general welfare of the game."

However, Judge Wagner granted a permanent injunction against Johnson's suspension of Mays. Judge Wagner agreed with the Yankees' position that the individual clubs are responsible for these types of player suspensions pursuant to another clause in the league constitution. This clause provided: "Each club . . . shall have the right . . . to discipline, punish, suspend or expel its manager, players or other employees, and these powers shall not be limited to cases of dishonest play or open insubordination, but shall include all questions of carelessness, indifference, or other conduct of the player that may be regarded by the club as prejudicial to its interest." Although Judge Wagner was of the view that the league president had the authority to discipline players for infringing the playing rules of the game or for committing overt acts on the field in violation of the rules, Mays's offense "was not an overt act committed on the field."

The infamous "Black Sox" scandal, where gamblers bribed White Sox players to "fix" the 1919 World Series games, took place the same year *Johnson* was decided. Team owners and fans believed that the source of the problem was the lax disciplinary approach of the National Commission, which was composed of the American League and National League presidents and a chairman selected by the two of them. As a result, club owners replaced the tripartite commission with a single commissioner, Kenesaw Mountain Landis, who agreed to accept this newly created position on the condition that the league constitution be rewritten to give the commissioner broad sweeping powers (Weiler et al., 2011). Landis was granted the authority to do whatever was necessary to protect the "best interests" of the sport.

The trial of the "Black Sox" players began in June 1921, and with no proof that any crime had been committed, the jury returned "not guilty" verdicts after deliberating for less than three hours (Lamb, 2013). One day after the verdict, Commissioner Landis banned all eight White Sox players for purportedly betting against their team. He issued the following statement:

> Regardless of the verdict of juries, no player that throws a ball game; no player that undertakes or promises to throw a ball game; no player that sits in a conference with a bunch of crooked players and gamblers where the ways and means of throwing ball games are planned and discussed and does not promptly tell his club about it, will ever play professional baseball.... Just keep in mind that, regardless of the verdict of juries, baseball is competent to protect itself against crooks, both inside and outside the game.
>
> (Schiff & Jarvis, 2016, 103)

Subsequent suspensions of players in other professional sport leagues for gambling involvement included National Hockey League (NHL) President Clarence Campbell's suspension of two players in 1948 and the National Basketball Association (NBA) President Maurice Podoloff's suspension of Jack Molinas in 1954 (Edelman, 2009, 635).

Beginning in the early 1980s, players were suspended by league commissioners for illegal drug use and/or possession, and in some cases quite aggressively. In 1983, when Kansas City Royals players Vida Blue, Willie Wilson, Jerry Martin, and Willie Aikens were sentenced to three months in prison for cocaine possession, Commissioner Bowie Kuhn imposed a one-year ban on each player. In 1987, pitcher LaMarr Hoyt was suspended for an entire season for bringing painkillers into the United States from Mexico. Five years later, pitcher Steve Howe was suspended for life for cocaine possession. Labor arbitrators later overturned or reduced several of these unilateral suspensions. For example, arbitrators overturned Kuhn's drug-related suspensions of pitchers Ferguson Jenkins and Pascual Perez (Pollack, 1999).

Although illegal drug possession or use would not have satisfied Judge Wagner's requirement of an overt act committed on the field, the arbitrator in the *Willie Wilson* decision of 1984 opined that "this type of employee misconduct is of serious impact on the employer" and further explained:

> Because baseball players are highly skilled, well compensated and constantly visible, they deserve and receive national attention. Neither the players nor the industry escapes the publicity. And drug involvement, because of its threat to athletes' playing abilities, because it is illegal and because of the related connotation of inroads by organized crime, constitutes a serious and immediate threat to the business that is promoted as our national pastime. Because the perception alone of taint is so potentially damaging, baseball has a substantial interest in the implementation and enforcement of drug prohibitions.
>
> (Weiler et al., 2011, 43)

All the leagues now have collectively bargained comprehensive drug policies and programs that specify prohibited drugs and substances, detailed testing procedures, penalties for violations, and the process for appeals.

In the mid- to late 1990s, there were some highly publicized league suspensions for player misconduct on the field and court. In 1994, Larry Walker of the Montreal Expos charged the mound after being struck by a pitch. Walker was fined $500 and suspended four games. This suspension had particular significance given that an arbitrator determined the Expos were required to pay Walker his salary for those missed games. The arbitrator reasoned that there was a long-running practice in which owners had always paid players their salaries for games missed due to league suspensions for on-field, but not off-field, misconduct (Weiler et al., 2011). Two years later, Baltimore Orioles second baseman Roberto Alomar was suspended five days for spitting in the face of the home plate umpire after a heated argument over a called third strike.

On the court, Vernon Maxwell of the Houston Rockets received a ten-game suspension for entering the stands and striking a fan during the 1994–1995 season. Similarly, Dennis Rodman of the Chicago Bulls received an eleven-game suspension for kicking a cameraman at courtside in a game during the 1996–1997 season. One year later, Latrell Sprewell threatened to kill his coach, P. J. Carlesimo, during a practice session and even choked him for seven to ten seconds—the time it took for other players and coaches to restrain Sprewell. After showering and changing, Sprewell returned to the court to again confront Carlesimo and threw an overhand punch that grazed Carlesimo's cheek. NBA Commissioner David Stern suspended Sprewell for a full year but an arbitrator found it excessive and reduced it to the sixty-eight games remaining in the 1997–1998 season. The suspension resulted in Sprewell suffering a loss of $6.4 million in salary (*Sprewell v. Golden State Warriors*).

On the ice, the NHL has had its share of players receive league suspensions for excessive acts of violence. In 2000, NHL Commissioner Gary Bettman handed Marty McSorley of the Boston Bruins a record-setting twenty-three-game suspension (and $72,000 in lost salary) for viciously attacking another player in the final seconds of a game. Four years later, on March 8, 2004, Todd Bertuzzi of the Vancouver Canucks skated up on Steve Moore of the Colorado Avalanche from behind and violently struck Moore in the back of the head with his forearm, dropping Moore to the ice face first. Moore remained unconscious on the ice for a while and ended up with a broken neck and fractured vertebrae. The NHL suspended Bertuzzi for the rest of the season and reinstated him after a seventeen-month suspension, which cost Bertuzzi more than $500,000 in lost salary (Thornton, 2009).

In the early 2000s, the use of performance-enhancing drugs (PEDs) in Major League Baseball (MLB) took center stage, grabbing all the headlines. In 2005, Congress held hearings and summoned various players and baseball executives to appear before it. Then an influential book entitled *Game of Shadows* was published in 2006. The book, which was written by two investigative reporters for the *San Francisco Chronicle*, provides chilling details of an expansive steroid scandal in baseball. Faced with the possibility of congressional regulation of steroid possession and use in professional baseball,

MLB Commissioner Bud Selig employed former U.S. Senator George Mitchell to undertake a massive investigation. Selig charged Mitchell with determining the extent of PED use by major league players after the substances were banned by the 2002–2006 CBA. The "Mitchell Report" is hundreds of pages long and arguably "the most damning and thorough report ever produced in the history of sports" (Thornton, Champion, and Ruddell, 2012, 241). The report, which MLB made public, concluded that the use of anabolic steroids and other PEDs in baseball was "widespread." Of particular controversy, the report named eighty-nine players who were believed to have used banned PEDs. Mitchell nonetheless recommended to Selig that no disciplinary action be taken against these named players. The report's findings, coupled with the threat of congressional action, ultimately led to the implementation of random drug testing as well as stiffer penalties and sanctions under the collectively bargained substance abuse policy.

Roger Goodell's tenure as commissioner of the National Football League (NFL) began in September 2006. This change in authority was a significant turning point for the manner in which the league handled players charged with, or alleged to have been involved in, criminal activity. Goodell's emphatic view that playing football in the NFL is a privilege led to numerous suspensions under his watch for personal conduct that both occurred away from the field and garnered substantial media attention and scrutiny. The suspensions included those for Adam "Pacman" Jones (battery) and Michael Vick (dog fighting) in 2007; Donte Stallworth (DUI manslaughter) in 2009; Ben Roethlisberger (sexual assault) in 2010; Ray Rice (domestic violence) and Adrian Peterson (child abuse) in 2014; and Greg Hardy (domestic violence) in 2015.

3. League Adoption of Personal Conduct Policies

The adoption of personal conduct policies at the league level is based in large part on a changing view in society that professional athletes should hold themselves to higher standards of responsible conduct. A survey from the mid-1990s revealed that 76% of adults and 82% of teens in the United States think it is "bad for society" to allow athletes to continue their sports careers when convicted of a violent crime (Withers, 2010, 146). Further, only 14% of adults and teens think allowing athletes to go unpunished is "good because it shows people deserve a second chance" (Withers, 2010, 147). According to American sports journalist Don Yaeger, it should be no surprise that many NBA players have been arrested; he deemed NBA players adolescents "who are excessively paid and over hyped to play a boy's game while living in a cocoon where they are pampered, protected, and never told no" (Benedict, 2004, 216).

Under the June 2000 NFL Personal Conduct Policy, the NFL clubs vested power in the commissioner to fine, suspend, or banish any player who was convicted of criminal activity or admitted to engaging in wrongdoing (Edelman, 2009, 637). In April

2007, less than one year after Roger Goodell was appointed the new commissioner, the NFL Personal Conduct Policy was strengthened by adding longer suspensions, indefinite suspensions, and the right to suspend players for noncriminal behavior (Edelman, 2009). Goodell had demanded a stricter policy because, at that time, NFL players were perceived as out of control, even though only a small percentage of players were getting into trouble with the law (McCann, 2014).

The advent of twenty-four-hour news distributed via a variety of media platforms certainly makes it seem that player arrests are a growing problem in the NFL. However, there is virtually no evidence to suggest that is the case. One might recall some of the headlines in 2000 involving NFL players Ray Lewis (murder charge), Rae Carruth (charged with murder in the shooting death of his pregnant girlfriend), Mark Chmura (sexual assault charge), and Peter Warrick (charged with grand theft). League officials that year also reported that the number of players arrested for violent crimes actually *dropped* from thirty-eight players in 1997 to twenty-six in 1999. Moreover, as noted by an NFL spokesman, the number of players arrested can be misleading because it includes instances where charges are dropped (Karp, 2008).

The current NFL Personal Conduct Policy, which was revised again by the owners in August 2014, details an extensive list of prohibited conduct:

> If you are convicted of a crime or subject to a disposition of a criminal proceeding (as defined in this Policy), you are subject to discipline. But even if your conduct does not result in a criminal conviction, if the league finds that you have engaged in any of the following conduct, you will be subject to discipline. Prohibited conduct includes but is not limited to the following:

- Actual or threatened physical violence against another person, including dating violence, domestic violence, child abuse, and other forms of family violence;
- Assault and/or battery, including sexual assault or other sex offenses;
- Violent or threatening behavior toward another employee or a third party in any workplace setting;
- Stalking, harassment, or similar forms of intimidation;
- Illegal possession of a gun or other weapon (such as explosives, toxic substances, and the like), or possession of a gun or other weapon in any workplace setting;
- Illegal possession, use, or distribution of alcohol or drugs;
- Possession, use, or distribution of steroids or other performance enhancing substances;
- Crimes involving cruelty to animals as defined by state or federal law;
- Crimes of dishonesty such as blackmail, extortion, fraud, money laundering, or racketeering;
- Theft-related crimes such as burglary, robbery, or larceny;
- Disorderly conduct;
- Crimes against law enforcement, such as obstruction, resisting arrest, or harming a police officer or other law enforcement officer;

- Conduct that poses a genuine danger to the safety and well-being of another person; and
- Conduct that undermines or puts at risk the integrity of the NFL, NFL clubs, or NFL personnel.

(National Football League, 2014)

The policy further provides that a "disciplinary officer"—a member of the league office with a criminal justice background—makes the disciplinary decisions. A first offense that involves assault, battery, domestic violence, dating violence, or child abuse, as well as other forms of family violence or sexual assault involving physical force or committed against someone incapable of giving consent, is subject to a baseline suspension of six games without pay. A player who commits a second offense is subject to a permanent banishment from the league and may petition for reinstatement after one year. The disciplinary officer's initial decision can be appealed to the commissioner, with no right of appeal to a neutral arbitrator or panel of arbitrators.

In baseball, the league and the players association reached agreement on a collectively bargained domestic violence policy in August 2015. The commissioner may place a player accused of domestic violence, sexual assault, or child abuse on paid administrative leave for up to seven days while the allegations are being investigated. The commissioner decides the appropriate discipline, with no minimum or maximum penalty set forth under the policy, and punishment is not dependent on whether the player was convicted of a crime or pled guilty.

Unlike the NFL's policy, the player can appeal before a three-person arbitration panel comprised of representatives of the league and the players association and an "agreed-upon" independent arbitrator. If a suspension arises from the punishment, the player is not paid and does not accrue major league service time. The team is not allowed to issue punishment to the player, unless the commissioner defers to the team. A board comprised of members of the commissioner's office and the Major League Baseball Players Association (MLBPA) evaluate a player's conduct and help to determine treatment options, including counseling, psychological evaluations, and other measures to protect a spouse or children, depending on the incident (Hagen, 2015).

4. The Commissioner's "Best Interests" Power

The commissioner's sweeping authority in regard to player discipline arises from various provisions contained in the league constitutions, whereby the club owners expressly grant the commissioner the authority and power to act in the "best interests" of the sport, to protect the "integrity of the game," and to suspend players for conduct that is "prejudicial or detrimental" to the league. This sweeping authority of league commissioners includes disciplinary powers and the authority to enforce independently a disciplinary process that provides rudimentary due process protections necessary to avoid judicial oversight of the commissioner's decisions (Mitten et al., 2013). While the commissioner's authority in disciplinary matters traditionally has been "plenary" in nature, the commissioner's power may also be limited by the league constitution (Yasser et al., 2015, 423 n. 4).

If legally challenged, courts generally take a "hands-off" approach and defer to the commissioner's decision as long as the commissioner acted in good faith and has followed the basic rudiments of due process of law. In other words, the rules of procedure for conducting investigations adopted by the commissioner must satisfy a minimum requirement of due process pursuant to which a party is entitled to notice of the alleged misconduct and a fair opportunity to be heard (*American League Baseball Club of New York v. Johnson*). Thus, whether the commissioner's decision is right or wrong is beyond the competence and jurisdiction of courts to decide (*Charles O. Finley v. Bowie Kuhn*).

Commissioner discipline raises a threshold question: When is a player's misconduct connected to the best interests of the sport or the integrity of the game such that discipline by the league is warranted? The connection is obvious when the misconduct involves *on-field* activities, such as fighting or intentionally injuring someone, violating the rules of the game, cheating, and inappropriate or obscene language and gestures. However, the connection becomes more tenuous when it involves *off-field* misconduct. A legitimate argument could be made that league discipline of players for off-field misconduct should be limited to misconduct that influences or affects the competition on the field or court. This is the approach taken by the National Collegiate Athletic Association (NCAA), which leaves the responsibility of disciplining players for any off-field misconduct to the team/university unless the misconduct involves gambling or a drug testing violation.

With respect to team-imposed discipline, the team is caught in somewhat of a predicament. On the one hand, the team wants to deter players from engaging in misconduct to the extent it constitutes a distraction to the team or has a detrimental impact on the team. But on the other hand, the team's ability to win games may be impacted if a star player is suspended and unable to play. Provisions contained in the standard player contracts entered between the players and the teams, which the league and the players association collectively bargain, generally permit termination or discipline by a team should a player "fail, refuse or neglect to conform his personal conduct to the standards of good citizenship and good sportsmanship" (MLB standard player contract).

Perhaps the team is the more appropriate entity than the league to discipline players for misconduct. The team is in a superior position to assess whether a particular player's misconduct is a distraction or has a detrimental impact on that team. The team is also better able to assess the appropriate disciplinary action to be taken under the circumstances. In addition, the team, which is the employer, should have the ability to establish team rules and curfews it deems necessary and appropriate. The team, as the employer, has a greater incentive than the league to impose discipline that is fair but also not too lenient to maintain discipline and control. Thus, if a player is alleged to have been involved in on- or off-field misconduct or is charged with a crime, the team should have the discretion whether to discipline the player. As an example, on the day that Sprewell choked and threatened Carlesimo, the Warriors suspended him for a minimum of ten games and then two days later exercised its right to terminate Sprewell's contract (*Sprewell v. Golden State Warriors*). In another example, the NFL's Carolina Panthers suspended its star receiver, Steve Smith, two games in 2008 for punching out a teammate. At the time, ESPN's Ron Jaworski opined:

> It really was a courageous decision. It would have been easy for the coach to fine the player and play him. From a football perspective, I would think that was the thing to do. But he took it a step further. He fined him and played two games without him. Most people thought it was a suicide move. Sit your best, most explosive player?
>
> (Corbett, 2008)

Hums and MacLean (2013) provide four reasons why dealing with off-field misconduct is difficult from the league's perspective: (1) off-field incidents are widely covered in the media; (2) if the league takes punitive action, it may give the appearance of guilt even if the legal system has not yet passed judgment on the accused athlete; (3) if the league controls information about the incident, it is often accused of covering up information; and (4) the issue of how the players association will react to punishing players for incidents that occur away from the field or court.

The public's knee-jerk reaction to off-field misconduct tends to be, "I would be fired if I did that." But this is not necessarily so. Employers typically have no interest in what their employees are doing when they are off-duty. If an employee is involved in a barroom brawl or gets arrested for drunk driving or marijuana possession over the weekend, chances are that the employee is not likely to be fired or even disciplined by the employer. And, indeed, the employer would have every right to do so if the employee is employed at will (which most employees are), meaning that the employee can be terminated for any reason or no reason.

Granted, professional athletes, unlike typical employees, are in the public eye and the public holds them to a higher standard. As such, professional athletes are subjected to greater scrutiny by the media because of their "public figure" status; however, it is quite another thing to suggest that they should be subjected to league suspension because of their "role model" status. It should not be overlooked that league suspensions interfere with the team-player employment relationship and constitute "a form of discipline which may have severe economic consequences for the athlete involved" (Weistart, 1977, 706). Judge Wagner wrote in the *Johnson* decision that "[s]uspension of a player . . . not only interferes with his individual contract, but may also interfere with the reputation and collective ability of the club" (140).

5. Due Process Concerns and Collectively Bargained Limitations on the Commissioner's Authority to Discipline Players

Off-field misconduct is laden with factual issues, which distinguishes it from misconduct on the field where there are multiple camera angles to capture and record the behavior. When the commissioner decides to impose discipline for off-field misconduct, the commissioner performs his own factual investigation and formulates an opinion. However, the commissioner's investigation of the facts is limited because the commissioner has no subpoena power and, thus, he cannot force witnesses to testify. Moreover, the typical safeguards afforded the accused in criminal proceedings are lacking, such as cross-examination of witnesses. Thus, there are due process concerns surrounding disciplinary action prior to a conviction; until a conviction or its equivalent there are merely allegations of wrongdoing. As an example, the NFL suspended James Lofton in 1986 at the end of the season because of a rape charge, and then Lofton was acquitted during the off-season.

Perhaps more important, a player disciplined by the commissioner for allegedly committing a crime prior to a conviction can be prejudiced in any criminal proceeding. Prosecutors may subpoena the results of the internal league investigations and use them against the player at trial. Under the previous violent crime policy created and administered by former NFL commissioner Paul Tagliabue, punishment was triggered only by a conviction or its equivalent, including a plea of no contest or a plea to a lesser charge. Commissioner Goodell changed that in April 2007 and now players can be disciplined even when the conduct itself has not yet resulted in the conviction of a crime.

However, professional athletes in league sports are not at-will employees; they are employed under long-term contracts and unionized. Because the players are members of certified labor unions, a professional sports league must operate within the confines of labor law and the CBA entered between the league and the union. The subject of player discipline falls into the category of mandatory subjects of collective bargaining under the National Labor Relations Act (NLRA) because it impacts players' hours, wages, and other working conditions. As such, the league cannot unilaterally create rules relating to the extent to which players are disciplined and under what circumstances they can be disciplined; the disciplinary rules and procedures must be collectively bargained with the union. For example, a federal court of appeals held it was an unfair labor practice within the NLRA for NFL club owners to unilaterally create a rule providing for an automatic fine to be levied against any player who left the bench area while a fight or altercation was in progress on the football field (*National Football League Players Association v. National Labor Relations Board*).

Thus, the CBA may modify, limit, or otherwise affect the commissioner's power to discipline players as established by the league constitution (Yasser et al., 2015). Collectively bargained limitations on the commissioner's disciplinary authority may take a variety of forms, including (1) defining the types of misconduct (which might distinguish between on-field and off-field behavior) subject to disciplinary action by the commissioner, (2) defining the level and extent of disciplinary action that may be imposed by the commissioner under those circumstances, and (3) providing the right of appeal to a neutral arbitrator or panel of arbitrators. Exactly where these lines should be drawn is for the union and league to decide.

With the exception of the NFL, CBAs contain heavily negotiated provisions regarding procedures for independent and neutral arbitration, including the mutual selection of the arbitrator(s), to resolve player challenges to commissioner disciplinary actions for on- and off-field misconduct. Courts have routinely upheld arbitration procedures arising from provisions contained in CBAs entered between the players association and the league (*Mandich v. North Star Partnership*; *National Hockey League Players Association v. Bettman*). Also, if the CBA lacks a procedural right, a court may be unwilling to create one. In its ruling upholding Goodell's four-game suspension of Tom Brady in the Deflategate controversy, judges for the U.S. Court of Appeals for the Second Circuit stressed how the NFL CBA failed to contractually stipulate the procedural safeguards that Tom Brady and the players association believe ought to exist (McCann, 2016).

The NFL CBA, Article 46, provides that the commissioner has the power to punish a player for (1) conduct occurring on the playing field and (2) conduct that is "detrimental to the integrity of, or public confidence in, the game of professional football." A player who is disciplined for off- and on-field misconduct can only appeal to the commissioner himself (or his designee). However, disputes involving the *interpretation* of the NFL CBA are resolved under different procedures utilizing neutral arbitrators. Also, appeals involving commissioner discipline for unnecessary roughness or unsportsmanlike conduct are resolved by hearing officers who are jointly selected on an annual basis.

In the NBA, Article 35 of the league constitution provides that the commissioner has sweeping authority to suspend players for "conduct that does not conform to standards of morality or fair play, that does not comply at all times with all federal, state, and local laws, or that is prejudicial or detrimental to the NBA." A disciplinary decision involving a player who wagers on the outcome of a game is binding and unappealable. However, Article 35(h) of the league constitution provides that all other actions of the commissioner can be appealed to an arbitrator pursuant to the grievance procedures set forth in the CBA. As an important limitation, the CBA, provides that discipline imposed for "conduct on the playing court" can only be appealed to the commissioner himself.

With respect to off-court misconduct, however, Article VI of the NBA CBA limits the commissioner's authority. The CBA provides that "[w]hen a player is convicted of (including a plea of guilty, no contest, or nolo contendere to) a violent felony, he shall immediately be suspended by the NBA for a minimum of ten (10) games." Thus, merely being charged with a violent crime is not enough; league suspension is only allowed if a player is convicted of, or pleads guilty to, a felony. McCann (2014) argues this is a "remarkably tolerant standard for players who commit domestic violence, one of the most difficult crimes to prosecute, [because] [v]ictims of domestic violence often refuse to testify against their significant others, thus denying prosecutors of their most crucial witness." Moreover, while a ten-game suspension might sound substantial, it only equates to approximately one-eighth of the NBA's eighty-two-game season.

The MLB CBA (referred to as the Basic Agreement), in Article XII regarding discipline, provides that players "may be subjected to disciplinary action for just cause by his Club, the Senior Vice President, Standards and On-Field Operations or the Commissioner. Therefore, in Grievances regarding discipline, the issue to be resolved shall be whether there has been just cause for the penalty imposed." According to Hylton (2001, 184), "[s]ince 1970, for better or for worse, the right to grievance arbitration has been a major source of power for baseball players in their dealings with team owners and the Commissioner's Office."

6. Arbitral Review of the Commissioner's Disciplinary Actions

With the exception of the NFL, players who are disciplined by the league commissioner generally have the right of appeal to an independent and neutral arbitrator or panel of arbitrators. Neutral arbitrators are typically lawyers who tend to be concerned about the due process that is afforded each individual player, as well as the financial impact that league suspensions without pay will have on a player who is accused of misconduct by the league. An arbitrator determines whether the imposition of discipline for a particular offense as well as the degree of the penalty imposed is supported by "just cause." Just cause is evaluated according to the "common law of the workplace" as well as the terms set forth in the CBA and existing league rules and regulations. In accordance with employment and labor law, just cause essentially means that the league must follow progressive discipline in response to player misconduct, imposing gradually increasing penalties for repeated offenses in an effort to rehabilitate the player and deter future misconduct by the player. "[P]enalties must be carefully fashioned with an eye toward responsive, consistent and fair discipline" (*Major League Baseball Players Association and the Commissioner of Major League Baseball (Steven Howe)*).

Just cause review also ensures that the imposed discipline is not arbitrary, unduly harsh, or contrary to established precedent involving similar situations. It would generally be considered arbitrary under a just cause standard to impose an overly aggressive disciplinary action on an individual player with an ulterior motive of sending the message to players that "this behavior will not be tolerated in this league." How then does an arbitrator determine whether there was just cause?

> [N]o clear standards exist to aid an Arbitrator in finding a conclusive answer to such a question and, therefore, perhaps the best he can do is to decide what a reasonable man, mindful of the habits and customs of industrial life and of the standards of justice and fair dealing prevalent in the community, ought to have done under similar circumstances and in that light to decide whether the conduct of the discharged employee was defensible and the disciplinary penalty just.
>
> (*In re Arbitration Between National Basketball Players Association on Behalf of Player Latrell Sprewell and Warriors Basketball Club and National Basketball Association*)

In the NFL, the owners have fought hard to retain the commissioner's exclusive authority to impose discipline and for the commissioner (or his designee) to serve as the arbitrator over his own decisions, thus avoiding any just cause review. The NFL's Personal Conduct Policy gives the commissioner the discretion to define what constitutes misconduct and to determine the appropriate sanction. Because the commissioner's disciplinary action is not subject to a just cause review by an independent and neutral arbitrator, there is no "check on fairness." Indeed, the National Football League Players Association (NFLPA) has publicly commented that the personal conduct suspensions and fines have been excessive, "particularly in cases where a player has been accused of but not found guilty of a violation of law" (Karp, 2008).

Because the NFL CBA lacks a right to independent and neutral review, some players have brought their grievances to court seeking to overturn the commissioner's (or his designee's) disciplinary sanction, which entails a very difficult burden for the player. Courts give "substantial deference" to the decisions of labor arbitrators and will only vacate an arbitration award if it fails to "draw its essence" from the CBA, such that the arbitrator imposed "his own brand of industrial justice," or when the arbitrator "exceed[ed] the authority given to him by the CBA or decide[d] matters parties have not submitted to him" (*National Football League Players Association v. National Football League*, 88 F.3d at 1089). One of the first court rulings involved Clayton Holmes of the Dallas Cowboys who was suspended four games in accordance with the NFL's Policy and Program for Drugs of Abuse and Alcohol after testing positive for marijuana on four occasions. Holmes had unsuccessfully appealed the suspension to the commissioner, who determined that the appeals of his first three positive tests were untimely and that there was no evidence to suggest that the fourth test was suspect. A federal district court rejected Holmes's argument that his involuntary enrollment in the NFL's drug program breached the CBA and that he was denied due process rights, including the opportunity to confront his accusers, present evidence, and cross-examine witnesses (*Holmes v. National Football League*).

In 2015, Adrian Peterson of the Minnesota Vikings successfully challenged an arbitration award of the commissioner's designated hearing officer, Harold Henderson, who affirmed the commissioner's imposition of a suspension without pay for the remainder of the 2014 season after Peterson pled no contest to a reduced misdemeanor charge of reckless assault for child abuse as a result of a May 2014 incident involving his son. In August 2014, the commissioner had issued an enhanced Personal Conduct Policy (New

Policy), increasing the sanctions for domestic violence and sexual assault incidents. However, a federal court vacated the arbitration award because the commissioner retroactively applied the New Policy to Peterson ("It is undisputed that under the previous Policy, first-time domestic violence offenders faced a likely maximum suspension of two games"). According to the court, "it is not seriously contested that the Commissioner understood he was constrained to apply the New Policy prospectively" and, thus, the arbitration award fails to draw its essence from the CBA and the arbitrator exceeded his authority (*NFLPA v. NFL*, 88 F.3d at 1091–1092). In August 2016, however, the U.S. Court of Appeals for the Eighth Circuit reinstated the arbitration award and highlighted the extensive deference accorded to arbitrators (*National Football League Players Association v. National Football League*, 831 F.3d at 935).

In April 2015, shortly after the court issued its ruling vacating the arbitration award in the Arrington matter, Goodell suspended Greg Hardy of the Dallas Cowboys for ten games after the NFL conducted an investigation and determined that in May 2014 (prior to the adoption of the New Policy) he used physical force in at least four instances against a former girlfriend, which "constitutes a significant act of violence in violation of the personal-conduct policy" (Belson, 2015). One month later, the NFLPA filed a motion to hold the NFL and the commissioner in contempt of court on the grounds that they were doing to Hardy (and possibly other players) what the court's ruling in the Arrington case forbids—retroactive application of the New Policy[1] (NFLPA's Memorandum of Law in Support of Motion, May 19, 2015). Hardy appealed the ten-game suspension and Goodell once again appointed Harold Henderson as the hearing officer. This time Henderson reduced the suspension by more than half, to four games. Henderson felt that a ten-game suspension "is simply too much . . . of an increase over prior cases without notice such as was done last year, when the base line for discipline in domestic violence or sexual assault cases was announced as a six-game suspension" (Belson, 2015, D6).

We will finish this chapter with a look at how independent and neutral arbitrators have reviewed some highly publicized commissioner suspensions in the NBA, MLB, and NFL.

7. NBA

In the infamous Latrell Sprewell case discussed earlier in this chapter, the NBA commissioner suspended Sprewell for one year and the club subsequently terminated Sprewell's contract. The players association filed a grievance on behalf of Sprewell in accordance with the terms of the CBA, which provided that the arbitrator's review of disciplinary action resulting in sanctions in excess of $25,000 and for conduct concerning "the preservation of the integrity of, or the maintenance of public confidence in, the game of basketball" was limited to determining if the commissioner's decision was "arbitrary and capricious." Applying this standard, arbitrator John Feerick determined that the commissioner's punishment was too severe and reduced the suspension from eighty-two to sixty-eight games (the remainder of the season). He also found that the club did not have just cause to terminate Sprewell's multiyear contract (under the provision that prohibits "acts of moral turpitude") given that the league's suspension already made it impossible for Sprewell to play and that the conduct in question was born out of anger and passion, not an act of moral turpitude (*In re Arbitration Between National Basketball Players Association on behalf of Player Latrell Sprewell and Warriors Basketball Club and National Basketball Association*).

In another highly publicized incident, a spectator threw a beverage that struck Pacers player Ron Artest during a game against the Pistons in November 2004. Artest and two of his teammates, Stephen Jackson and Anthony Johnson, ran up into the stands and fought with several spectators. Another Pacers player, Jermaine O'Neal, attempted to enter the stands and was restrained by an arena official, but O'Neal pushed the official away and then struck a spectator who had descended from the stands onto the court. The NBA commissioner invoked his "best interests" powers and suspended Artest for the remainder of the season, Jackson for thirty games, O'Neal for twenty-five games, and Johnson for five games.

The NBPA (National Basketball Players Association) appealed to an arbitrator who upheld the suspensions of Artest, Jackson, and Johnson but found that O'Neal's suspension of twenty-five games was not supported by just cause and reduced it to fifteen games. Interestingly, the NBA objected to the grievance procedure and did not attend the arbitration. The NBA argued to a federal judge that the dispute was not appealable to an arbitrator because the discipline pertained to "conduct on the playing court," which the CBA expressly provides is only appealable to the commissioner himself. The players argued that conduct on the playing court only applied to conduct occurring as *part of the game itself* and relied on Article 35(h) of the league constitution, which provided that all appeals of commissioner discipline except for those relating to wagering on games are subject to the grievance procedure in the CBA. The court agreed with the players and found that, because Article 35(d) of the constitution expressly provided for fines or suspensions for conduct during games (suggesting that punishment for in-game behavior would be appealable under 35(h)), the NBA's broad interpretation of "conduct on the playing court" would render Article 35(h) illusory (*National Basketball Association v. National Basketball Players Association*).

8. MLB

Kansas City Royals players Vida Blue and Willie Wilson appealed Commissioner Kuhn's one-year suspension of each of them for the entire 1984 season after being arrested and convicted for cocaine possession in 1983. The arbitrator agreed with the commissioner that recreational drug use was a legitimate threat to the "best interests of baseball," noting that drug use risked physical harm to players and increased the chance that dangerous criminals could gain control over players. However, the arbitrator reduced Wilson's suspension to one month on the grounds that he had already spent nearly all of the 1983 season in prison. Blue's suspension for the entire 1984 season was upheld by the arbitrator because he determined that his use of cocaine was more extensive than Wilson's (in earlier years) and he also served as a conduit between his drug supplier and other players (Weiler et al., 2011).

In 1991, Steve Howe was arrested and charged with attempted cocaine possession. Howe had been previously suspended by baseball for drug use six times between 1982 and 1988. Based on Howe's history of drug use, the commissioner imposed a lifetime suspension. On appeal, the arbitrator, applying a just cause standard and highlighting the importance of "careful scrutiny of the individual circumstances and the particular facts relevant to each case," noted that the "need for scrutiny is at its zenith here simply because of the nature of the penalty at issue." The arbitrator reduced Howe's suspension to time served, which amounted to 119 days. The arbitrator found that, before imposing such a stringent penalty, the commissioner should have more carefully examined Howe's particular circumstances and evaluated his condition and the adequacy of his treatment, including possibly subjecting Howe to more stringent year-round testing (*Major League Baseball Players Association and the Commissioner of Major League Baseball (Steven Howe)*).

The extent to which a league commissioner may discipline a player for pure speech off the field on the basis that it affects the best interests of baseball was tested in the case of Atlanta Braves pitcher John Rocker, whose insensitive and inappropriate racial epithets were made public in a December 27, 1999, article that appeared in *Sports Illustrated* (*SI*). Rocker told the *SI* reporter he would never play for a New York team because he did not want to ride a subway train "next to some queer with AIDS." He also mocked foreigners. Commissioner Bud Selig barred Rocker from spring training, suspended him for the first month of the season (twenty-eight days), and fined him $20,000. On appeal, the arbitrator determined that while the commissioner has the right to discipline for pure speech off the field that affects the business of baseball, the penalty was unduly harsh and did not comport with the basic fairness due all employees. The arbitrator cut the suspension in half to fourteen days and reduced the fine to $500, the maximum fine allowed under the league constitution for off-field behavior deemed not in the best interests of baseball (*Major League Baseball Players Association v. Commissioner of Major League Baseball (Rocker)*).

9. NFL

As previously noted, Article 46 of the NFL CBA provides that a disciplinary decision may be appealed to the commissioner (or his designee) to review his own decision. Because the NFL CBA lacks an arbitration mechanism by which players have the right to appeal the commissioner's decisions to an independent and neutral arbitrator, the commissioner's ability to be a neutral decision maker has been challenged in the courts (as explained earlier in this chapter). However, as a general principle, agreed upon arbitration procedures may only be avoided in the rare instance when they require a party to submit to a decision maker so biased as to be incapable of providing a fair hearing. An independent and neutral arbitrator (not the commissioner's designee) was used to resolve two disciplinary disputes, the "New Orleans Saints Bounty Scandal" and the Ray Rice matter. In both cases the arbitrator vacated the player suspensions.

The New Orleans Saints Bounty Scandal was probably the most highly publicized, scrutinized, and complex commissioner disciplinary authority dispute in all of the American professional sports leagues. In 2010, the NFL investigated whether the New Orleans Saints were financially incentivizing their defensive players to injure opposing players. Commissioner Goodell concluded that the bounty system existed and, in 2012, penalized the Saints by stripping them of two second-round draft picks, imposing a $500,000 fine, and suspending the general manager as well as multiple players and coaches for various lengths of time. The NFLPA filed an appeal with the commissioner as well as a separate proceeding with an Independent System Arbitrator pursuant to Article 15 of the CBA, arguing that the alleged bounty system was an "undisclosed agreement" and thus subject to the jurisdiction of the System Arbitrator (Mitten et al., 2013, 584).

In June 2012, the System Arbitrator concluded that the alleged bounty system would be more appropriately analyzed as "conduct detrimental to the league" and, therefore, subject to the jurisdiction of the commissioner. In accordance with the CBA, the NFLPA appealed the System Arbitrator's decision to an Appeals Panel. Subsequently, the commissioner denied the NFLPA's appeal that was filed to him and the NFLPA sued the NFL on behalf of three of the four suspended players. In the lawsuit, the players argued that the commissioner, when serving as an arbitrator, is not granted the authority under the CBA "to disregard the essence of the parties' agreement, to conduct proceedings that are fundamentally unfair, and to act with evident bias" (*National Football League Players Association v. NFL Management Council*). The other suspended player, Jonathan Vilma, filed his own suit against the NFL. He claimed that Goodell failed to serve as a neutral arbiter and failed to issue a timely decision on the appeal (*Vilma v. NFL*). Vilma would later file a separate lawsuit against Goodell, claiming that the commissioner had defamed him (*Vilma v. Goodell*).

On September 7, 2012, the Appeals Panel remanded the matter to Goodell to determine whether he issued the suspensions under the "conduct detrimental" clause or the "undisclosed agreement" clause. One month later, Goodell, after meeting with the players and their attorneys, determined that the suspensions were issued for "conduct detrimental" to the league (over which Goodell would have jurisdiction) but he reduced the lengths of the suspensions for two of the four players. All four suspended players appealed the reissued decision and requested that Goodell recuse himself from deciding the appeal. Goodell agreed to recuse himself and designated former NFL Commissioner Paul Tagliabue to hear the appeals in his place (Mitten et al., 2013, 585–586).

On December 11, 2012, Tagliabue vacated the suspensions of all four players. While Tagliabue, for the most part, did not dispute Goodell's factual findings surrounding the scandal, he felt the Saints organization was to blame and the players' suspensions were inappropriate:

> Unlike [the] Saints' broad organizational misconduct, player appeals involve sharply focused issues of alleged individual player misconduct in several different aspects. My affirmation of Commissioner Goodell's findings could certainly justify the issuance of fines. However, this entire case has been contaminated by the coaches and others in the Saints' organization.
>
> (NFL.com, 2012)

Two years later, the NFL had another highly publicized and scrutinized commissioner suspension. This time it involved star running back Ray Rice of the Baltimore Ravens. It followed the public release of a video of Rice dragging his unconscious fiancée out of a hotel elevator—an act that would lead to a grand jury subsequently indicting him on assault charges. In June 2014, Rice met with Goodell and other league representatives about the assault and Goodell subsequently suspended Rice for two games. A firestorm of public criticism followed the suspension announcement, prompting Goodell to publicly admit that he "didn't get it right" and he shortly thereafter (in August 2014) increased the presumptive penalty for domestic violence for first-time offenders under the Personal Conduct Policy to a six-game suspension (which Goodell acknowledged could not, and would not, apply to Rice). On September 8, a second video from the camera inside the elevator aired publicly for the first time. It captured Rice punching and knocking his fiancée out just before he dragged her out of the elevator. On that same day, in response to a furor of public outcry over the second video, Goodell suspended Rice indefinitely. The discipline letter to Rice stated that the heightened sanction was based on the fact that Rice presented a "starkly different sequence of events" to Goodell (at their June meeting) than what was captured in the second video (*In re Ray Rice*).

Rice and the NFLPA appealed the suspension on the basis that the NFL and Goodell knew about the elevator incident and the accompanying second video long before it became public and that Rice was punished twice for the same conduct in violation of the CBA. The question to be answered by the arbitrator, retired federal judge Barbara Jones, was whether the commissioner's decision to increase the original suspension was arbitrary or capricious—in essence, whether the imposition of an indefinite suspension was not fair or consistent. Jones found that it was in fact arbitrary primarily because Rice did not mislead the commissioner and because there were no new facts on which the commissioner could base his increased suspension. As such, the indefinite suspension imposed on Rice was vacated (*In re Ray Rice*).

10. Conclusion

Professional athletes are in the public eye and the public holds them to a higher standard. While the societal demand for professional sports leagues to hold athletes accountable for their misdeeds is loud and clear, disciplinary action can only be imposed within the confines of federal labor law and the CBA. The NFL is unique from the other professional sports leagues in that the player's sole right of appeal is a request for the commissioner (or his designee) to review his own ruling; in other words, there is no right of appeal. Until the NFL CBA affords players the right to appeal commissioner discipline to an independent and neutral arbitrator, the commissioner's rulings will continue to be challenged in court over the disciplinary procedures utilized as well as the commissioner's ability to be fair and impartial, which only serves to intensify the media's coverage of the player's misconduct and the league's handling of the issue.

Note

1. "Hardy was suspended for ten games—five times more than the first-time violator maximum under the Previous Policy. The only way the Commissioner could impose a ten-game suspension would be to apply the new six-game minimum under the New Policy, and then increase the period of suspension for alleged exacerbating factors" (NFLPA's Memorandum of Law in Support of Motion, 21)

References

Belson, K. (2015). "Greg Hardy's N.F.L. Suspension Is Reduced to 4 Games from 10." *New York Times*, July 10, www.nytimes.com/2015/07/11/sports/football/greg-hardys-nfl-suspension-is-reduced-to-4-games-from-10.html?_r=0.

Benedict, J. (2004). *Out of Bounds: Inside The NBA's Culture of Rape, Violence, and Crime* (New York, NY.: Harper Collins).

Corbett, J. (2008). "NFL Insider: Gutsiest Call? Panthers Banning Best Player." *USA Today*, September 18, http://usatoday30.usatoday.com/sports/football/nfl/2008-09-16-nfl-insider_N.htm.

Edelman, M. (2009). "Are Commissioner Suspensions Really Any Different from Illegal Group Boycotts? Analyzing Whether the NFL's Personal Conduct Policy Illegally Restrains Trade." *Catholic University Law Review* 58(3): 631–662.

Hagen, P. (2015). "MLB, MLBPA Reveal Domestic Violence Policy." *MLB.com*, August 21, http://m.mlb.com/news/article/144508842/mlb-mlbpa-agree-on-domestic-violence-policy.

Hums, M. A., and MacLean, J. C. (2013). *Governance and Policy in Sport Organizations* (3rd ed.) (Scottsdale, Ariz.: Holcomb Hathaway).

Hylton, J. G. (2001). "The Historical Origins of Professional Baseball Grievance Arbitration." *Marquette Sports Law Review* 11: 175–184.

Karp, H. (2008). Why the NFL Spies on Its Players. *The Wall Street Journal*, November 7, www.wsj.com/articles/SB122601853947707055.

Lamb, W. F. (2013). *Black Sox in the Courtroom: The Grand Jury, Criminal Trial and Civil Litigation*. eBook.

McCann, M. (2014). "Why the NBA Won't Touch Its Domestic Violence Policies Anytime Soon." *Sports Illustrated*, October 1, www.si.com/nba/2014/10/01/nba-domestic-violence-policy-michele-roberts-jeff-taylor.

McCann, M. (2016). "Tom Brady Faces Long Odds After NFL Wins Deflategate Appeal." *Sports Illustrated*, April 25, www.si.com/nfl/2016/04/25/tom-brady-deflategate-suspension-nfl-appeal-roger-goodell.

Mitten, M. J., Davis, T., Smith, R. K., and Duru, N. J. (2013). *Sports Law and Regulation: Cases, Materials, and Problems* (3rd ed.) (New York: Wolters Kluwer Law & Business).

National Football League. (2014). "NFL Owners Endorse New Personal Conduct Policy." December 10, www.nfl.com/news/story/0ap3000000441758/article/nfl-owners-endorse-new-personal-conduct-policy.

NFL.com. (2012). "Paul Tagliabue Vacates Saints Player Bounty Suspensions." December 11, www.nfl.com/news/story/0ap1000000109646/article/paul-tagliabue-vacates-new-orleans-saints-bounty-suspensions.

Pollack, J. M. (1999). "Take My Arbitrator, Please: Commissioner 'Best Interests' Disciplinary Authority in Professional Sports." *Fordham Law Review* 67: 1645–1712.

Schiff, L. H., and Jarvis, R. M. (2016). *Baseball and the Law: Cases and Materials* (Durham, N.C.: Carolina Academic Press).

Thornton, P. (2009). "Rewriting Hockey's Unwritten Rules: *Moore v. Bertuzzi*." *Maine Law Review* 61(1): 205–217.

Thornton, P. K., Champion, W. T., Jr., and Ruddell, L. S. (2012). *Sports Ethics for Sports Management Professionals* (Sudbury, Mass.: Jones & Bartlett Learning, LLC).

Weiler, P. C., Roberts, G. R., Abrams, R. I., and Ross, S. F. (2011). *Sports and the Law: Text, Cases and Problems* (4th ed.) (St. Paul, MN: West).

Weistart, J. C. (1977). "Player Discipline in Professional Sports: The Antitrust Issues." *William & Mary Law Review* 18: 703.

Withers, B. P. (2010). "The integrity of the Game: Professional Athletes and Domestic Violence." *Harvard Journal of Sports and Entertainment Law* 1: 145–179.

Yasser, R., McCurdy, J. R., Goplerud, C. P., and Weston, M. A. (2015). *Sports Law: Cases and Materials* (8th ed.) (New Providence, N.J. and San Francisco, Calif.: Matthew Bender).

Cases

American League Baseball Club of N.Y. v. Johnson, 109 Misc. 138, 179 N.Y.S. 498 (1919).

Arbitration Between Nat'l Basketball Players Ass'n on Behalf of Player Latrell Sprewell and Warriors Basketball Club and Nat'l Basketball Ass'n, In re (Feerick, Arb., March 4, 1998).

Finley v. Kuhn, 569 F.2d 527 (7th Cir. 1978).

Holmes v. National Football League, 939 F. Supp. 517 (N.D. Tex. 1996).

Major League Baseball Players Ass'n and the Comm'r of Major League Baseball (Steven Howe) (Nicolau, Arb., 1992).

Major League Baseball Players Ass'n v. Commissioner of Major League Baseball (Rocker), Panel Decision No. 104 (Arb. 2000).

Mandich v. North Star P'ship, 450 N.W.2d 173 (Minn. Ct. App. 1990).

National Basketball Ass'n v. National Basketball Players Ass'n, 2005 WL 22869 (S.D.N.Y. Jan. 3, 2005).

National Hockey League Players Ass'n v. Bettman, No. 93 Civ. 5769, 1994 WL 738835 (S.D.N.Y. Nov. 9, 1994).

NFLPA's Memorandum of Law in Support of Motion to Hold the NFL in Civil Contempt (May 19, 2015).

National Football League Players Ass'n v. National Football League, Case No. 14-cv-4990 (DSD/JSM, 2015).
National Football League Players Ass'n v. National Football League, 88 F. Supp. 3d 1084 (D. Minn. 2015).
National Football League Players Ass'n v. National Football League, 831 F.3d 935 (8th Cir. 2016).
National Football League Players Association v. National Football League Mgmt. Council, No. 2:12-cv-01744 (E.D. La. 2012).
National Football League Players Association v. National Labor Relations Board, 503 F.2d 12 (8th Cir. 1974).
Ray Rice, In re (Jones, Arb., Nov. 28, 2014).
Sprewell v. Golden State Warriors, 266 F.3d 979 (9th Cir. 2001).
Vilma v. National Football League, No. 2:12-cv-01718 (E.D. La. 2012).

CHAPTER 5

THE REGULATION OF DOPING IN U.S. AND INTERNATIONAL SPORTS

MAUREEN A. WESTON

1. Introduction: Doping in Sports

ELITE athletes competing at the highest levels of sport face tremendous pressure to win. In some cases, athletes, and perhaps the teams, personnel, and even governments that support them, succumb to the temptation to engage in doping in a seeming effort to boost athletic performance and team success. Society's emphasis on winning, together with certain athletes' desire to be champions, has created a veritable global epidemic (Nafziger, 2004). News that high-profile athletes, such as Major League Baseball's Mark McGuire or Alex Rodriguez, cycling's nine-time Tour de France winner Lance Armstrong, or tennis favorite Maria Sharapova, have tested positive for doping roiled the public and sporting world, and cost the athletes involved tens of millions of dollars in prize money, sponsorships, and secondary business pursuits. Each year, numerous athletes become ineligible and are stripped of titles due to violations of increasingly strict anti-doping regulations.[1]

On the eve of the 2016 Summer Olympics, the International Olympic Committee[2] (IOC) deliberated on whether to ban the entire country of Russia for a government-sponsored doping operation created for its Olympic athletes. An investigation commissioned by the World Anti-Doping Agency (WADA), the regulatory authority for enforcing anti-doping rules in international sport, determined that Russia had been involved in State-sponsored doping programs, which involved a systematic scheme to enhance the performance of both its Olympic and Paralympic athletes. Two weeks before the start of the Rio Games, the IOC issued a decision requiring Russian athletes to prove their compliance with anti-doping rules to individual sport federations. Appeals were heard in expedited on-site arbitration by the Court of Arbitration for Sport (CAS), which is the exclusive tribunal charged with adjudication of Olympic-related eligibility disputes. (IOC, Olympic Charter, Rule 61).[3] Although some Russian athletes were cleared to participate in the Rio Olympic Games, the entirety of both Russia's track and field and weightlifting teams faced a total ban. The International Paralympic Committee (IPC) banned the entire Russian delegation from the 2016 Paralympic Games (Paraolympic.Org Staff, 2016). The reports of State-sponsored doping led to retesting of doping tests from the 2014 Winter Olympics in Sochi, Russia, the 2012 Games in London, and the 2008 Olympics in Beijing, with resulting violations found. (Richard McLaren, Independent Commission Investigation into State-Sponsored Doping, 2016)

The barrage of reports of doping in sport is numbing. As noted, "Sports doping is cascading into international sports chaos that affects world-wide events, major nations and every competitor" (Katz, 2016). The use of a banned substance to gain an advantage over a competitor changes the nature of the competition, jeopardizes the health and safety of athletes, threatens the integrity of the game, and is outright cheating. This is a sad phenomenon in which "the doper can literally make millions of dollars" while the real champion is denied the glorious moment and the financial opportunities afforded title recognition while being largely lost to undeserved obscurity (Katz, 2016).

The fight or "war" against doping in sport is truly global. In some situations, however, innocent athletes are penalized while intentional dopers manage to race ahead of the testers. Testing procedures may be faulty or unable to detect prohibited substances used by some athletes able to stay ahead of the technology. Drug testing of athletes also raises concerns about privacy invasion, regulatory overreach, education, research, and testing reliability.

This chapter examines the regulatory governance structures and procedures for addressing doping and drug testing of athletes in U.S. collegiate, professional, Olympic, and international sport.

2. U.S. Sports Anti-Doping Laws and Policies

Doping is generally defined as the presence, use or attempted use, trafficking, possession, or administration of any prohibited substance or method—as well as evading, refusing, or failing to either submit to sample collection or file whereabouts information, or to tampering or attempting to tamper with any part of doping control (World Anti-Doping Code, Art. 2.1 to 2.10). Whether an athlete has committed a doping offense depends on the applicable regulatory scheme.

2.1. U.S. Federal and State Statutes

Athletes are subject to general federal and state legislation, which criminalizes and penalizes certain drug use. In 1990, Congress passed the Anabolic Steroid Control Act[4] in response to reports of the increasing use of anabolic steroids in Olympic and professional sport including a purported "silent epidemic" of steroid use in high schools.[5] Passage of the Act followed the media frenzy involving Canadian sprinter Ben Johnson, who was stripped of a gold medal at the 1988 Seoul Olympics for testing positive for the steroid Stanozolol. The race, identified by some as "the dirtiest race in history," triggered controversies that increased public awareness about doping as a serious threat to sport (Collins, 2006). The Act classifies certain performance-enhancing substances as a crime punishable by various penalties. Although the Act was intended to penalize steroid use in sport, few professional, Olympic, or elite-level players have ever been prosecuted or arrested, much less imprisoned, for steroid use. Many states have their own versions of statutory schemes similar to federal controlled substances laws, with similarly limited enforcement with respect to athlete use (Mitchell, 2007).

2.2. U.S. Sports Regulation

While legislation may address certain uses of steroids and illegal drugs, individual sport leagues and governing bodies have specific and more comprehensive anti-doping policies governing athletes and associated personnel.[6] These policies address substances or methods that may be legal to use as a matter of state or federal law but which are prohibited for use by athletes due to potential performance-enhancing, masking, or adverse health effects. As doping is considered cheating and a threat to the integrity of sport, sport anti-doping policies are governed under the law of private association in that individuals agree to abide by these policies as a matter of contract and condition of participating in the sport.

In the United States, athletes at the collegiate and professional levels are subject to drug testing and anti-doping disciplinary sanctions, which include possible expulsion from sport. The anti-doping policies, testing and disciplinary procedures, and sanctions regulating U.S. athletes vary depending on whether an athlete competes in U.S. professional sport leagues that contain a players' association union, in National Collegiate Athletic Association (NCAA) college sport, or in an international sport wherein athletes are held to the uniform policies and procedures of the WADA World Anti-Doping Code (WADA Code). These policies may be subject to U.S. constitutional privacy and due process restrictions only where administered by a public entity or state actor, such as the drug testing of interscholastic or intercollegiate athletes in public schools. By contrast, professional sport leagues are private associations of member clubs that own and operate teams within the respective sport. Players contract with individual teams but are collectively represented by a players' association union, which acts as the players' exclusive bargaining representative in negotiations with the league. Drug testing policies in major U.S. unionized professional sport are topics that must be negotiated with the players, rather than imposed unilaterally, under the federal labor law, and therefore adopted as set forth in the respective leagues' collective bargaining agreement (National Labor Relations Act, 9 U.S.C. §§ 157, 158(1)). While no similar statutory or labor protections exist for Olympic or international sport athletes, they are generally bound by fundamental contract law based on their acceptance of membership in a sport federation and the application of that federation's rules, which include anti-doping proscriptions, to their individual sport participation.

The following discusses the anti-doping policies in U.S. collegiate and major professional league sport, as well as Olympic sport. However, doping is an issue in sport at all levels and is found in every type of sport. A direct comparison of the policies is difficult due to the varied policies adopted and, mostly, enforced by the respective sport organization (e.g., baseball has rules governed by the collective bargaining agreement between Major League Baseball (MLB) and the MLB Player Association (MLBPA), but the international game is regulated by the IOC-recognized international federation and is subject to the WADA Code). The policies even vary on the definition of doping, the concept of the athlete's strict responsibility for all substances consumed, the focus on treatment (if any), how to address recreational use, testing procedures, and sanctions (Gandert & Ronisky, 2010). For example, the concept of strict liability for all substances consumed is stated in anti-doping policies for Olympic sport but not expressed in the MLB or National Basketball Association (NBA) policies directly. All policies recognize a medical necessity exception for use of banned substances, where athletes comply with a process for receiving a therapeutic use exemption (TUE). The need to address doping as cheating in sport and for education and prevention through anti-doping policies is a driving force motivating all of the anti-doping programs.

At the collegiate level, student-athletes at NCAA member institutions are required to comply with the NCAA Drug Testing Program. The NCAA bans eight classes of drugs, including stimulants, anabolic agents, diuretics and other masking agents, peptide hormones, and steroids, and it posts a nonexhaustive list of the banned substances. The NCAA conducts testing for these substances year-round, as well as for other street/illicit drugs and stimulants at championships and post-season bowl games. Member institutions may also test student-athletes. Sanctions include loss of one year of eligibility for the first offense and complete and permanent ineligibility for a second violation. Appeals of a positive drug test are brought by member institutions upon request of the student-athlete and heard for final determination before the NCAA Committee on Competitive Safeguards and Medical Aspects of Sport in a telephonic conference. The bans on performance-enhancing substances and street drugs are intended to protect athlete health and safety and the integrity of sport competition. The legality of the NCAA's drug testing program has been repeatedly upheld. This in in spite of significant challenges based upon balancing athlete privacy concerns with protecting the health and safety of athletes and maintaining program reputation (*See Hill v. NCAA*).

2.3. Anti-Doping and Drug Testing Policies in U.S. Professional Team Sports

Each of the major U.S. professional sport leagues, such as the National Football League (NFL), NBA, MLB, and National Hockey League (NHL), has adopted anti-doping policies and procedures. However, none of the U.S. leagues has adopted the WADA Code. As players in these leagues are unionized and represented by player associations, drug testing policies are negotiated and regulated through collective bargaining agreements or individual contracts. Thus, the rules for drug testing and sanctions in professional sport are varied and depend upon the negotiated policy for each league. With union involvement in the process, the policies focus also on education and treatment of substance abuse, rather than only on punishment.

2.3.1. *National Football League Drug Policy*

The NFL was the first U.S. professional sport league to develop a policy banning performance-enhancing drugs in 1987, but its substance abuse policy dates to the 1970s (Wolf, 2011). The NFL's Policy and Program on Substances of Abuse addresses the "illegal use of drugs and the abuse of prescription drugs, over-the-counter drugs, and alcohol" (NFL, 2015). A key aspect of the substance abuse policy is also "to offer programs of intervention, rehabilitation, and support to players who have substance abuse problems" (*id.*). The NFL's prohibition on marijuana is highly controversial, particularly as marijuana use has become legal for medical and recreational use in a number of states and as it offers an alternative to, often addictive, opioid pain killers (Hruby, 2014). Heralded NFL players, such as Ricky Williams and Josh Gordon, have incurred career-ending suspensions and millions in lost earnings for marijuana use. Williams is a vocal proponent for allowing NFL players to use marijuana citing the pain relief benefits and problems of opioid addiction.

In 2015, the NFL Management Council and NFL Player Association (NFLPA) agreed upon the NFL Policy on Performance-Enhancing Substances. This policy sets forth the NFL's anti-doping regulations and identifies an extensive list of prohibited substances. Under the NFL Program, all players are tested through urine sampling pre-employment and at least once a year. Ten players per team are randomly tested throughout the season. Specimens collected from athletes are divided into two separate bottles—an A and B sample. Players whose "A" sample tests positive or who are suspected of drug involvement may be subjected to additional testing under the Reasonable Cause Testing Program. Players are also subject to up to six blood tests annually for human growth hormone (HGH). A player testing positive is notified and entitled to request "B" sampling analysis observed by a forensic toxicologist.

The NFL has adopted a strict liability standard, providing that, "Players are responsible for what is in their bodies and a positive test will not be excused because a Player was unaware that he was taking a Prohibited Substance" (NFL, 2015). A player found in violation of the substance abuse policy is subject to discipline "[a]t the discretion of the Commissioner, including suspension up to six games for a first violation or, if appropriate, termination of the individual's affiliation with an NFL Club" (*id.*, Section 5, Discipline for Violations, at 9). The policy sets forth a schedule of suspension length and related discipline, which varies upon whether the positive test resulted from use of a diuretic or masking agent (two games), stimulant or anabolic steroid (four games), or prohibited substance and tampering or attempting to tamper with the test process (six games). Appeals of the disciplinary sanctions are to be heard by an arbitration panel unaffiliated with the NFL, NFLPA, or clubs. However, "[a]n Appeals Settlement Committee consisting of the NFL Commissioner and the NFLPA Executive Director or their respective designees shall have authority to resolve any appeal under this Policy, which resolution shall be final and binding" (*id.*). Appeals of the reasonable cause testing are heard exclusively by the commissioner or his or her designee. The appeals process is a fair way to challenge the NFL's rulings, and it could result in an eliminated or reduced suspension. Recent NFL players who have taken advantage of the appeals process are Pittsburgh Steelers running back Le'Veon Bell, for a missed drug test, during the 2016 season and Seattle Seahawks cornerback Richard Sherman, for a positive performance-enhancing drug (PED) test, during the 2012 season. Bell's appeal forced the league to reconsider suspending him for the full four games, and it resulted in his settling with the league on a three-game suspension (Brady, 2016). Sherman won his appeal by successfully casting doubt on the techniques of the testing team (Weinrich, 2012).

2.3.2. *NBA Anti-Drug Program*

The NBA and Players Association Collective Bargaining Agreement (2011) provides for an anti-drug program (National Basketball Association, Collective Bargaining Agreement, Article XXXIII, Anti-Drug Program, 335–398 (2011)). Under the NBA Substance Abuse Policy, the NBA and Players Association jointly select a medical director and an independent expert experienced in substance abuse detection to administer the program and jointly form a Prohibited Substance Committee. Urine testing is conducted for more than 160 prohibited substances, which include steroids, PEDs and masking agents, marijuana, and other substances the committee deems necessary to ban. Players are encouraged to "voluntarily come forward" under the drugs of abuse or marijuana program and enter treatment programs. Players may be randomly tested six times per year, or additionally at any time for reasonable cause. Notice of a positive test is sent to the Players Association and involved player, who may request testing of the B sample within five days. A player determined to have used, possessed, or distributed a prohibited substance may appeal in grievance arbitration, and if unsuccessful, he may face immediate dismissal or disqualification from the NBA. Players may seek reinstatement after a period of at least one to two years from the disqualification. However, the NBA's recent record in PED testing is not an exemplary one. Only eight players have been suspended for PED use since 2000 raising questions about the program's effectiveness (NBA Suspends Magic's Turkaglu for Positive Steroid Test, 2013).

2.3.3. *MLB's Joint Drug Prevention and Treatment Program*

MLB was last among the major U.S. professional sport leagues to establish an anti-doping policy in 2004, in response to intense pressure by Congress and the public. The reason for this could have been a combination of greed and denial. The fallout from a 1994 strike and lockout led to decreased attendance at ballparks in the ensuing years (Fainaru-Wada and Williams, 2007). The steroid-fueled 1998 home run race, which resulted in Mark McGuire breaking the single-season home run record, brought fans back to the game in droves (Fainaru-Wada and Williams, 2007). Steroids were lining the pockets of owners and players taking away any incentive for MLB to have a doping policy. This changed in 2003 when a law enforcement raid on the offices of the Bay Area Laboratory Cooperative (BALCO), owned and operated by Victor Conte, uncovered evidence of widespread use of performance-enhancing substances and masking agents implicating a number of star baseball players and other elite athletes. This federal criminal investigation, as well as information that indicated rising steroid use among youth, prompted MLB to commission a formal investigation led by former U.S. Senate majority leader George Mitchell. The Mitchell Report indicated that each of the thirty clubs had players who had been involved with performance enhancing drugs at some point, describing this as the "steroids era" in MLB. Players linked to the BALCO scandal or other steroid use included Mark McGuire, Barry Bonds, Jason Giambi, and Marvin Bernard. The Mitchell Report confirmed extensive steroid use among MLB players and that "the players' union, owners, team physicians, trainers, and even the Commissioner himself" knew of the rampant doping and did nothing about it (Wolf, 2011, 1611). Congress also held formal investigative hearings into MLB's drug testing program (*Steroids in Sports: Cheating the System and Gambling Your Health*, 2005).

In the wake of congressional threats to apply a uniform testing policy, such as the WADA Code, to all U.S. professional sport, the MLB and MLBPA addressed drug testing in the 2005 Collective Bargaining Agreement.[7] The 2005 Policy on Joint Drug Prevention and Treatment required random testing only upon "reasonable cause" and only penalized steroid use. Suspensions ranged from ten to thirty to sixty days for the first three violations, respectively, while a yearlong suspension was imposed for the fourth.

In 2015, the MLB and MLBPA agreed to adopt a more stringent policy in the MLB's Joint Drug Prevention and Treatment Program (Joint Drug Program). The reason for this was that the old program did not provide an effective enough deterrent as nearly forty players were suspended for PED use between 2005 and 2015 including at least three multiple offenders (Gehring, 2015. It was worth the risk for players to be suspended for a mere ten days for a first offense by a using a substance that could greatly benefit their careers. The Joint Drug Program is administered by the MLB Health Policy Advisory Committee (HPAC), which includes members selected by both the MLB and MLBPA. The Joint Drug Program tests for 134 prohibited substances, but the list is not exhaustive.

Under the MLB Joint Drug Program, players are tested once during spring training and once during the regular season, which consists of 162 games (MLB Joint Drug Prevention and Treatment Program, 2015). The policy also provides for additional random urine tests (3,200) and blood tests (260) conducted during the season and 350 random urine tests and 140 random blood tests conducted during the off-season, used solely to detect HGH. The samples are tested at a WADA-accredited laboratory in Montreal, Canada. Penalties for violations include a 50-game suspension for the first offense, 100 games for a second, and a lifetime ban for a third—all without pay.

2.3.4. *Other U.S. Professional Sports*

Anti-doping programs are also in effect in other professional team and individual sport. The collective bargaining agreement between the NHL and NHL Players' Association includes a Performance Enhancing Substances Program (Collective Bargaining Agreement Between National Hockey League and National Hockey League Players' Association, 2013). Major League Soccer also has an anti-doping program (Collective Bargaining Agreement Between Major League Soccer and Major League Soccer Players Union, 2015–2020). Individual professional sport have also adopted anti-doping rules and testing. Purportedly the first professional sport to adopt an independently administered anti-doping program, the Ultimate Fighting Championships (UFC) contracted with USADA in 2016 to conduct testing of fighters but did not adopt the strict WADA Code or its procedures (U.S. Anti-Doping Agency, 2016). Even emerging sport, such as competitive video gaming or eSports, are considering doping regulation amidst reports that gamers use pharmaceutical neuroenhancers, such as Adderall and Ritalin. Electronic Sports League (ESL), founded in 1997, now with over six million registered users and over one million teams engaged in competitive video gaming, such as the League of Legends Championships and "Intel Extreme Masters," announced in 2016 that it would adopt the WADA banned substances list, but testing would only occur at ESL's discretion and only during competition (Blicharz, 2015; Loria, 2016).

2.3.5. *A Critique of the U.S. Sports Self-Regulatory Approach to Fight Doping*

Notably, doping regulation and implementation in U.S. professional sport is done by the sport itself. Major professional sport league doping policies result from collective bargaining negotiations between the league and respective player union. Other non-Olympic, professional sport, such as the UFC, establish their own anti-doping regulations. Arguably, this arrangement has a vested interest in athlete performance and protecting the sport image and brand from the scandal of doping revelations. This is viewed skeptically by some because of the apparent conflicts of interest and limited effective regulation for dealing with new doping issues. In this scheme, the players and owners agree on how to define and penalize doping. A crucial element of the fight against doping is missing: independence (Gandert & Ronisky, 2010). Sport leagues, such as MLB in the 1990s, have little incentive to police themselves when large amounts of revenue and popularity are being brought to the sport by drug-infused athletes. By contrast, in the Olympic and international sport realm, anti-doping policies are unilaterally established and regulated by an agency independent of the sport—WADA and national counterparts, such as USADA.

3. The World Anti-Doping Code in Olympic and International Sports

Doping at the Olympic and international sport level is regulated under the auspices of WADA. WADA was established in 1999 in connection with the IOC's World Conference on Doping in Sport in 1999 as a private foundation governed under Swiss law with headquarters in Montreal. WADA is funded equally by the sport governing bodies within the Olympic movement and various governments of the world. WADA promulgates, administers, and enforces the WADA Code. The Code is the core document that provides the framework for harmonized anti-doping policies, rules, and regulations within sport organizations and among public authorities. The WADA Code sets forth specific anti-doping rules, definitions of doping, burdens of proof, prohibited substances and methods, and addresses standards for testing, sample analysis, sanctions, appeals, confidentiality, reporting, and statute of limitations (USADA, 2005). USADA, established by federal charter in 2000, administers this policy for U.S. Olympic, Paralympic, and Pan American athletes.

The Olympic Charter mandates that all members of the Olympic Movement, including the IOC, IPC, international sport federations, National Olympic Committees, and sport governing bodies, adopt and implement the WADA Code.

Acceptance of the Code is mandatory for all athletes in the Olympic Movement by virtue of their membership in sport governing bodies and by their participation in sport events.

The purposes of the WADA Code and the Anti-Doping Program that supports it are "[t]o protect the Athletes' fundamental right to participate in doping-free sport and thus promote health, fairness and equality for athletes' worldwide, and to ensure harmonized, coordinated and effective anti-doping programs at the international and national levels with regard to detection, deterrence, and prevention of doping" (WADA Code, 2015). Doping is considered cheating and antithetical to the spirit of sport. The WADA anti-doping program seeks to protect clean athletes by enforcing strict anti-doping regulations.

3.1. The 2015 WADA Code

The WADA Code first took effect in 2004, was substantially revised in 2009, and amended again with the 2015 WADA Code. The Code contains one of the most comprehensive lists of prohibited substances and methods and also provides for perhaps the most stringent penalties among all sport anti-doping programs.

3.1.1. *Anti-Doping Violations*

The Code defines doping as "[t]he occurrence of one or more anti-doping violations set forth in Article 2.1 through 2.10 of the Code."[8] An anti-doping rule violation (ADRV) is established by any of the following:

- *The Presence of a Prohibited Substance or its Metabolites or Markers in an Athlete's Sample* (Section 2.1), such where the athlete waives analysis of the B sample and the B sample is not analyzed, or where the athlete's B sample is analyzed and the analysis of the athlete's B sample confirms the presence of the prohibited substance or its metabolites;

- *Use or Attempted Use by an Athlete of a Prohibited Substance or a Prohibited Method* (Section 2.2), regardless of intent, fault, negligence, or knowing use;
- *Evading, Refusing or Failing to Submit to Sample Collection* (Section 2.3);
- *Whereabouts Failures* (Section 2.4), such as a combination of three missed tests and/or filing failures within a twelve-month period by an athlete in a registered testing pool;
- *Tampering or Attempted Tampering with any part of Doping Control* (Section 2.5);
- *Possession of a Prohibited Substance or a Prohibited Method* (Section 2.6), unless the athlete establishes that the possession is consistent with a TUE granted in accordance with Article 4.4 or other acceptable justification;
- *Trafficking or Attempted Trafficking in any Prohibited Substance or Prohibited Method* (Section 2.7);
- *Administration or Attempted Administration to any Athlete In-Competition of any Prohibited Substance or Prohibited Method, or Administration or Attempted Administration to any Athlete Out-of-Competition of any Prohibited Substance or any Prohibited Method that is prohibited Out-of-Competition* (Section 2.8);
- *Complicity* (Section 2.9); and
- *Prohibited Association* (Sections 2.1-2.10).

3.1.2. *The Prohibited List and Monitored Substances*

The WADA Code identifies the official list of prohibited substances and methods that constitute doping in the "Prohibited List." The Prohibited List comprises two categories. First, substances that have the potential to enhance performance in future competitions (e.g., anabolic agents) or that feature masking potential, some of which are prohibited at all times (i.e., both in competition and out of competition) and others in competition only. Prohibited methods include blood doping and tampering with the doping control process.[9] The prohibited list also includes a "catch-all" provision referring to "other substances with a similar chemical structure or similar biological effects."[10] Thus, an athlete may test positive for a substance not specifically listed. Standards for granting TUEs provide for authorized medical use of otherwise prohibited substances.

WADA has a monitoring process to follow patterns that may identify new substances. In collaboration with its members, WADA publishes a list of substances that are not on the Prohibited List but still monitored as part of an ongoing effort to detect the new shapes of potential doping or to possibly add to the list in the future. Strict anonymity rules apply with regard to such tests, and positive samples of these substances would not constitute a violation of anti-doping rules.[11] Meldonium is an example of a monitored substance that became prohibited in January 2016 and resulted in a wave of positive tests (nearly 300 cases), primarily of Eastern European athletes where the drug was initially produced and widely distributed. Meldonium, originally used for increasing blood flow in coronary diseases, was monitored by WADA during 2015 and, with evidence of athletes using it for performance enhancement, added to the list of prohibited substances as of January 1, 2016.

Top-level professional tennis player Maria Sharapova was among the athletes who had used Meldonium based on samples collected during the 2016 Australian Open. The International Tennis Federation (ITF) banned Sharapova two years. However, Sharapova's suspension was reduced to fifteen months after an appeal to CAS, and most of the other 300 cases were dismissed after reports revealed that WADA could not verify exactly how long Meldonium remained in an athlete's system.

3.1.3. *Strict Liability and Random Testing*

The WADA Code holds athletes strictly liable for knowing the anti-doping rules, for knowing the prohibited substances and methods, and for any prohibited substance found in their samples.[12] Accordingly, a rule violation may be established without proof of intent, fault, negligence, or knowing use on the athlete's part. One primary change from the 2009 to the 2015 Code was to distinguish between inadvertent and intentional doping and to authorize flexibility in the sanctions based on such circumstances.[13] "Intentional" is defined as a knowing violation or manifest disregard for the risk of a violation and is intended to identify those athletes who cheat. However, the burden is on the athlete to prove no fault or negligence, or no significant fault or negligence, to reduce the otherwise mandatory four-year sanction.

The Code authorizes WADA or the appropriate national anti-doping organization (ADO) to test, both inside and outside competition, athletes who are nationals, residents, license holders, or members of the sport organizations of that country. Athletes may be required to provide a sample at any time and at any place by any ADO with jurisdictional testing authority. Athletes in the "Registered Testing Pool" are required to file a *Whereabouts* report identifying a specific sixty-minute time slot every day between 5 a.m. and 11 p.m. This report anchors the athlete to a specific location where the athlete must be available for testing. Whereabouts are filed quarterly and submitted on a date specified by the anti-doping organization (WADA International Standard for Testing and Investigations, 1.3.1). Any combination of three missed tests and/or filing failures constitutes an ADRV (WADA Code, Art. 2.4).

3.1.4. *Testing Procedures*

The WADA Code testing procedure is set forth in the International Standard for Testing and Investigations, the latest version effective January 1, 2017. WADA has two different processes for urine samples and blood samples. The "Athletic Biological Passport" program, which monitors an athlete's biological attributes over a period of time, features longitude profiling of an athlete. Under this program, WADA can test anytime, anywhere, with no advanced notice. The testing can even occur in locations not listed on whereabouts filings. Athletes are to provide photo identification for the sample collection process and have the right to have a representative present. Athletes may be asked to provide urine, blood, or both samples. Before opening the container, the athlete is advised to check the collection vessel, inspect it carefully, and rinse his or her hands.

Thereafter, the athlete should keep control of the container until it is sealed and secured. A doping control officer directly observes the sampling. An athlete who refuses to provide a sample without compelling justification, deliberately avoids a doping control official to evade notification or testing, or engages in acts that undermine the doping control process, such as intimidating a potential witness, offensive behaviors toward a doping officer, or breaking the B bottle, violate the WADA Code (Art. 2.5).

3.1.5. *Proof of Doping*

WADA, or the jurisdictional ADO, must establish an ADRV to the "comfortable satisfaction" of the hearing panel. An ADRV may be established by any reliable means, even without a B sample confirmation, including athlete admission, witness statements, documentary evidence, conclusions drawn from longitudinal profiling or analytical data collected as part of the athlete biological passport, or other information.[14] A positive test conducted by a WADA-accredited laboratory is presumptively valid. The burden is on the athlete to prove the test resulted from a departure from International Standards of Laboratory (ISL) practice and that such departure caused the adverse finding.[15]

3.1.6. *Sanctions on Individuals*

Article 10 of the WADA Code sets forth the schedule of sanctions on individuals guilty of an ADRV. Generally, an ADRV results in disqualification of the athlete's individual results obtained in the event in which the ADRV occurred, forfeiture of any medals, and a period of ineligibility. A four-year suspension is the sanction for a finding of the presence, use or attempted use or method, or possession of a prohibited substance or prohibited method; or for evading, refusing or failing to provide a sample, or tampering or attempting to tamper with any part of the doping control, unless the athlete can establish that the ADRV was not intentional. The four-year suspension is intended to punish cheaters and intentional rule violators. A minimum penalty of a four-year suspension and a maximum penalty of a lifetime ban, depending upon the seriousness of the violation, is imposed for trafficking or attempted trafficking or administration of prohibited substances or methods (WADA Code, Art. 2.7). Assisting, encouraging, aiding, abetting, conspiring, covering up, or any other type of intentional complicity, depending on the seriousness of violation, is sanctioned with two to four years of ineligibility For other ADRVs, such as professionally associating with or serving as an intermediary for someone who has already been suspended, the period of ineligibility is two years (WADA Code, Art. 10.3). The degree of fault plays a role when the violation is a whereabouts failure, where the suspension is a minimum period of one year and a maximum of two years.

The ineligibility period may be eliminated if the athlete proves exceptional circumstances of no fault or negligence for the ADRV, such as sabotage by a competitor despite due care (WADA Code, Art. 10.5, "Sabotage by those within the athlete's circle or contaminated supplements do not constitute no fault, as athletes are responsible for everything they ingest. Such circumstances, however, could qualify as no significant fault or negligence"). Where an athlete can prove no significant fault or negligence for the ADRV, the sanction may be reduced, ranging from a reprimand to two years of ineligibility. The period of ineligibility sanction may also be eliminated, reduced, or suspended should the athlete provide "[s]ubstantial Assistance in Discovering or Establishing Anti-Doping Rule Violations" (WADA Code, Art. 10.6). Additional mitigating grounds include an admission of an ADRV in absence of other evidence, or prompt admission upon notice of a violation (WADA Code, Art. 10.6. Providing substantial assistance to an anti-doping organization, criminal authority, or professional disciplinary body may also in some circumstances result in elimination, reduction, or suspension of a period of ineligibility).

Failure by anti-doping organizations to follow their rules and regulations can also be a basis to overturn the sanctions. In *Vadim Devyatovskiy & Ivan Tsikhan v. IOC*, the CAS panel upheld the appeal by the athletes and restored their medals and diplomas, finding violations in laboratory standards regarding "documentation and reporting requirements." The same analyst tested both A and B samples of two athletes in the 2008 Beijing Olympics violating mandatory procedural safeguards and justifying the annulment of test results.

Athletes who commit a second or multiple ADRV become ineligible for "[t]he greater part of: (a) six months; (b) one-half of the period of Ineligibility imposed for the first anti-doping rule violation . . .; or (c) twice the period of Ineligibility otherwise applicable to the second anti-doping rule violation treated as if it were a first violation."[16] A third anti-doping rule violation generally incurs a lifetime ban. If during an event more than two members of a team in a team sport violated the anti-doping rules, the governing body of the event shall impose suitable sanctions that can range from point deductions to disqualifications.

3.1.7. *Appeals to Court of Arbitration for Sport*

Athletes and other persons subject to the WADA Code are entitled to a "Fair Hearing and Notice" of a decision. Appeals of an ADRV determination are made exclusively to the CAS, whose decision is final and binding (WADA Code, Art. 8.5, 13). Since 1995, the Olympic Charter has provided that "any dispute arising on the occasion of or in connection with the Olympic Games shall be submitted exclusively to the Court of Arbitration for Sport (CAS) in accordance of the Code of Sports-Related Arbitration."[17] The athlete, the ADO with results management responsibility, WADA, and any other ADO that would have had a right to appeal a first-instance hearing decision to the CAS, has authority to appeal sanctions and acquittals directly to the CAS with no requirement for a prior hearing.

3.2. Anti-Doping as International Law: The International Convention Against Doping in Sport

While the WADA Code operates as a contractual obligation upon sport organization members and athletes, it has the force of international law through the International

Convention Against Doping in Sport (ICADIS). The hybrid nature of WADA as a quasi-private international organization with close cooperation between non-governmental organizations and governments, and their shared power in the decision-making process, created a legal vacuum where many states were not bound by WADA rules despite their adoption by most sporting organizations. Motivated in part by the use of doping by athletes in sport and the consequences thereof for their health, the United Nations Educational Scientific and Cultural Organization (UNESCO) led the efforts for the international community to develop an international treaty with binding powers on government that extends its legal authority to the WADA Code. Other concerns that drove UNESCO to act include an appreciation for both the principle of fair play and the critical objective of the elimination of cheating in sport and an observance of the important role of governments in the fight against doping.

In effect since 2007, ICADIS provides a legal framework that organizes all governmental and non- governmental efforts in a joint process to fight doping. Over 162 signatory governments enforce anti-doping rules against those not covered under WADA, such as individuals engaged in the trafficking of prohibited substances. As such, ICADIS helps to formalize anti-doping rules, policies, and guidelines on a global level. The purpose of ICADIS is to promote the prevention of, and the fight against, doping in sport. The ultimate ambition of ICADIS is to eliminate doping in sport.

The United States ratified ICADIS in 2008 and since then has been obliged by its provisions. As a result, governments, sport federations, and civil societies—as well as the Olympic movement—are provided with a binding legal instrument.

3.3. Summary of WADA Code ADRV Sanctions

WADA Code Anti-Doping Violation		Period of Ineligibility Sanction, WADA Code 2015
2.1	Presence of a Prohibited Substance or its Metabolites or Markers in an Athlete's Sample	2-4 years (Art. 10.2.1)
2.2	Use or Attempted Use by an Athlete of a Prohibited Substance or a Prohibited Method	2-4 years (Art. 10.2.1)
2.3	Evading, Refusing or Failing to Submit to Sample Collection	2-4 years (Art. 10.3.1)
2.4	Whereabouts Failures	1-2 years (Art. 10.3.2)
2.5	Tampering or Attempted Tampering with any part of Doping Control	4 years (Art. 10.3.1)
2.6	Possession of a Prohibited Substance or a Prohibited Method	4 years (Art. 10.2.1)
2.7	Trafficking or Attempted Trafficking in any Prohibited Substance or Prohibited Method	4 years to lifetime ban (Art. 10.3.3)

WADA Code Anti-Doping Violation		Period of Ineligibility Sanction, WADA Code 2015
2.8	Administration or Attempted Administration	4 years to lifetime ban (Art. 10.3.3)
2.9	Complicity	2–4 years (Art. 10.3.4)
2.10	Prohibited Association	1 Year (Art. 10.3.5)

4. Comparison: Doping Policies in U.S. & International Sport

	Testing	1st Violation	2nd Violation	3rd Violation
NFL	Year-round random. Minimum once a year.	4 game suspension without pay	8 game suspension without pay	1 year without pay
NBA	4 in-season 2 off-season	Veteran – 2 year First year – 1 year	10 games/ Counseling	25 games * treatment 4th: min. 2 year
MLB	Urine/Blood (HGH & Steroids)- Spring training Min. once in season Various random	10-day suspension without pay	30 games, without pay	60 games, without pay; thereafter, 1 year and per Commissioner
NHL	Once during training, min. once in season	20 game suspension without pay and treatment referral	60 game suspension and referral	Permanent suspension
Olympic/ International	Urine/blood Year-round 365 days/year 24 hours/day Top 5 finishers Whereabouts Biological Passports	Reprimand to Four Year Ineligibility	Lifetime Ban	

5. High-Profile Doping Case Examples

The following discussion highlights three well-known doping controversies. Each is instructive of the key legal principles at play.

5.1. *U.S. Anti-Doping Agency v. Lance Armstrong*

Professional U.S. cyclist Lance Armstrong was one of the most prominent athletes in the world before his career was ruined with a notorious doping scandal.

Armstrong won the Tour De France seven times between 1999 and 2005. He regularly faced doping allegations until official federal investigations between 2010 and2012 uncovered clues about Armstrong doping. Criminal proceedings were closed without any charges against him, but the USADA accused Armstrong of doping after the trial ended. Based on blood samples from 2009 and 2010 and testimonies, including from teammates, Armstrong was subsequently banned from competitions by the International Cycling Union. Armstrong did not appeal this decision to CAS. His scandal also led to the revelation of other U.S. cyclist doping violations, mostly his teammates.

5.2. *Major League Baseball v. Alex Rodriguez*

MLB's case against Alex Rodriguez was a very unusual case because of the way MLB was able to establish Rodriguez's second violation of the Joint Drug Program. Rodriguez never actually tested positive for steroids. Instead, MLB authorities connected his PED use to Biogenesis, an anti-aging clinic in Florida, through the use of witnesses and eventually a paper trail. The fallout from the case was dramatic. Rodriguez along with twelve other players were handed suspensions by the league (Lengel & Bushfield, 2013). However, Rodriguez was the only player suspended for more than fifty games because he tried to interfere in the investigation. He was suspended for 211 games, but he appealed the decision accusing MLB of intimidating witnesses and other unsavory tactics to get information against him (Elfrink and Garcia-Roberts, 2014). Ultimately, Rodriguez's suspension was reduced to 162 games by arbitrator Frederic Horowitz (Elfrink and Garcia-Roberts, 2014). It was still the longest suspension ever handed down by MLB over PED use (Hagen, 2014). It was the last major scandal in MLB's ugly PED history.

5.3. Russian State-Sponsored Doping Scandal

The revelation of State-sponsored doping in Russia shook the sport community around the world. It was the first known incident after the Nazi's systematic use of steroids and then Eastern Germany's doping programs after the Cold War (Longman, 2013).

Based on the investigations conducted by WADA, the Russian sport ministry, through various techniques, was deeply involved in the manipulation of Russian athletes' doping results (McLaren, 2016). According to the report, the "corruption" of doping control officers, cooperation of medical personnel with coaches to make them aware of washing periods, failing to comply with WADA rules regarding the rapid enforcement of athletes' biological passport, controlling WADA accredited laboratory to cover up the doping cases, sample swapping, bottle cap removing, and after all other efforts failed, disappearing positive results as the last resort were all conducted and administered by Russian officials (McLaren, 2016). The report states that "beyond a reasonable doubt... [t]he surprise result of the Sochi investigation was the revelation of the extent of State oversight and directed control of the Moscow Laboratory in processing, and covering up dirty urine samples of Russian athletes from virtually all sport before and after the Sochi Games" (WADA, 2016). The scandal led the IOC to impose a ban on Russian athletes on the eve of the 2016 Rio Olympic Games, although athletes who met certain standards were cleared to participate. While the mere reality of doping by individual athletes is a huge challenge in the sport world, the idea of governmental involvement in such activities exacerbates a situation that has a huge impact on international sport events and their huge audience throughout the world.

New aspects of this scandal surfaced in a second report published in December 2016 extending the scope of governmental programs to other big international events implicating more than 1,000 Russian athletes in State-sponsored doping. Revelations showed that London 2012 was corrupted on an unprecedented scale. Through its systematic cheating, Russia hijacked London competitions and has been might be described as "deceiving" sport fans for years. (McLaren, 2016).

The second report addressed the 2012 London Games, 2013 Universidad Games, 2013 Moscow IAAF World Championships, and 2014 Sochi Winter Olympics. It also identified fifteen Russian medalists in the London 2012 Olympics on the Washout List. Finally, the report added sample swapping as another method for manipulating the samples, which occurred when investigations revealed male DNA in two female hockey players' urine samples. Investigations also showed that a new combination of drugs known as "Duchess" was built with a very short detection window to help the doped athletes evade the doping control process.

It remains to be seen how a significant sporting power like Russia will be permitted to return to unfettered competition in international sport. Investigations of systematic doping in other countries and legal action against WADA by Russia may follow in the future if the country feels that its athletes are unfairly targeted by WADA.

6. Criminalizing Sports Doping and the Future of the Fight

Years fighting doping by spending millions of dollars, banning violators, toppling medal podiums, "turning medals into metals," imposing harsh testing standards, forcing athletes to ignore their privacy, dealing with the stress of whereabouts failures, and other punitive efforts have failed to stop some athletes from cheating. This failure has recently increased calls for criminalizing doping in some jurisdictions.

Despite all efforts, the doping problem persists. Adding to the pressure is the stance adopted by governmental and judicial figures in different countries arguing that sport authorities alone had proven not to be a strong enough deterrent in the fight against doping. The unstoppable flow of PEDs into the veins of athletes resulted in some jurisdictions adopting a criminal approach to solve the problem.

This is despite the fact that the event that caused the creation of WADA was criminal charges against Tour De France athletes in 1998, during which "the French police found doping substances in the possession of certain teams and proceeded to arrest not only officials, but also athletes. The sight of athletes being led away by the police, to face possible criminal charges, was most dramatic" (Siekmann, 2012, 315).

The challenge appears to be a conflict of administrative regulations between organizations fighting doping (WADA) and criminal policies of sovereign States. These States, despite being members of WADA and ratifying the 2005 UNESCO convention against doping, are increasingly moving to criminalize doping offenses.

6.1. National Legislation: Sports Doping as a Crime

Due to the intractability of the doping crisis, various countries have sought to address the problem through the criminalization of doping (Hoberman, 2011). In both Europe and North America, policymakers have used legislative powers to address doping, primarily by imposing criminal sanctions. In 1065, France first outlawed the use of certain substances in connection with sport competitions (Lindholm, 2013). Before the 2008 Tour de France, France moved to sanction athletes caught possessing or trafficking doping products with criminal sanctions. Austria has also responded to doping through criminal law in the Austrian Anti-Doping Act. Italy's Sports Activities and the Fight Against Doping Activities Act provides for criminal doping offenses. According to this legislation, both athletes and support personnel procuring, administering, or consuming (or even encouraging the use of) WADA Code prohibited substances or methods with the aim of improving an athlete's competitive performance or to modify the results of an anti-doping test are imprisoned from three months to three years and fined anywhere from $2,700 to $53,980. After *Operacion Puerto* scandal in 2005, which involved a network of doping including athletes, cycling managers, and doctors, Spain similarly enacted legislation classifying doping as a criminal conduct.

After news of the 2016 State-sponsored doping scandal, Russia proposed to criminalize doping whereby coaches and specialists in sport medicine and training who induce athletes to use PEDs face punishment, including monetary fines, bans in sport, and imprisonment.

In 2015, Germany enacted its Anti-Doping Act which extends criminal sanctions, punishable up to ten years in jail, against the production, trade, and possession of doping use or possession. "Elite athletes of organized sport" or those who generate directly or indirectly substantial income out of sporting events, who use or attempt use of doping substances or methods with the aim to obtain an undue advantage in a competition are subject to sanction. The Act is considered to apply to all athletes irrespective of their nationality, and thus also applies when athletes of foreign nationality participate in competitions in Germany (Klein & Keidel, 2015).

6.2. National Legislation: Non-Criminalization of Sports Doping

In Bulgaria, the "attempted use," "attempted trafficking," and "attempted administration" of a prohibited substance and/or method are not considered anti-doping rule violations given that the Penal Code of the Republic of Bulgaria defines the "attempt" at committing a violation as a criminal offense while anti-doping rule violations are considered administrative violations. In Poland, the implementation process of the WADA Code has for many different reasons been abandoned, mainly because of collision with the general rules of the Criminal Code (Flemish Minister Report, 2010).

6.3. Doping as Sporting Fraud

Intentional doping is cheating, and athletes and support personnel engaged in doping may also face criminal or civil liability for fraud (McKenzie, 2007). For example, an athlete who wins a major sport event, prize money, and endorsements but who has doped, is stripped of the title and winnings. The clean athlete in second place may later move up but has been denied the glory of the winning moment. "Is the second placed athlete a victim of fraud?" (Blickenstaff, 2015). It would also be difficult to define a victim in these cases: is it just the second place competitor, or is it every competitor who participated? Most of foregoing legislation believes that doping is obtaining money, property, services, benefits, or advantages dishonestly or by deceit, and thus is trying to establish a separate type of crime known as sporting fraud. This way the crime falls under the public and criminal policies of legal jurisdictions, and therefore more financial and human resources are available to fight it.

6.4. Summary: National Sports Anti-Doping Legislation

Generally, by 2010, the trade and distribution of doping products was a criminal offense prohibited and sanctioned by criminal code in eight European Union (EU) countries (Cyprus, the Czech Republic, Finland, Hungary, Lithuania, the Netherlands, Slovenia, and Italy), by drug laws in ten EU countries (Austria, Belgium, Denmark, Germany,

Ireland, the Netherlands, Portugal, Romania, Sweden, and the United Kingdom), and by sport acts in four EU countries (France, Greece, Luxembourg, and Spain).

Japan, slated to host the 2020 Olympics, is also considering new legislation considering "whether breaches of a law would result in criminal charges and how it would tackle those who supply athletes with prohibited substances." Qatar, with its ambitious acts during the past decade in the sport industry, also proposed to criminalize the import and use of PEDs.

In the United States, the first governmental action was the 1990 passing of the Anabolic Steroid Control Act, which in fact added steroids to provisions of the Controlled Substances Act. After the BALCO scandal and presidential response against doping in baseball, the Anabolic Steroid Control Act of 2004 was passed to expand the scope of prohibited substances. Under the circumstances surrounding the situation, Congress passed the three bills discussed earlier.

6.5. INTERPOL-WADA Partnership

Although the WADA Code as adopted by sporting organizations and covered athletes as a matter of private associational contract law, the anti-doping rules are taking on as rules of law through ICADIS and increasingly, criminal law, with international law enforcement joining the fight against doping in sport. The line between treating sport doping as cheating and a rule violation versus a crime is sometimes elusive. Yet, INTERPOL (International Police), the world's largest police organization with a network of police forces from over 190 countries worldwide, has joined forces with WADA in "Project Energia" to target the manufacturing and trafficking of drugs to athletes (Associated Press, 2016). INTERPOL views the trafficking of doping into sports as a form of organized crime. According to this organization, the "reality is that when an athlete takes illegal performance-enhancing drugs, this is just one piece in a larger network of crime" that might be connected to crimes such as corruption, match-fixing, illegal gambling, bribery, and money laundering. The task force, funded by WADA, uses criminal analysis in tandem with both organizations to cooperate in the fight against doping, including finding the link between organized crime and drug trafficking of prohibited substances. (INTERPOL, 2015,).

Although the current framework for fighting doping has focused on the professional and elite level, INTERPOL officials reveal the horrifying reality of doping in amateur and semiprofessional sport. Clément de Maillard, a criminal intelligence officer at Interpol, believes that "[i]t's not necessarily in the area of professional sport, but the sport for amateurs and semi-professional sport, we know that there is more performance-enhancing drug consumption" (Blickenstaff, 2016). He adds, "[w]e note some criminal behavior among athletes regarding the financial stakes of sport, and the way they cheat? I consider the way they cheat as a type of fraud" (Rumsby, 2014). WADA Chief David Howman believes that organized crime controls 25% of world sport.

INTERPOL played a role in investigating the case of professional cyclist Lance Armstrong. INTERPOL also contributes to international operations to dismantle criminal organizations related to the trafficking of PEDs. In May 2015, a global alert was issued by INTERPOL for 2.4-dinitrophenol (DNP), an illicit and potentially lethal drug used as a dieting and bodybuilding aid.

INTERPOL initiated a program in October 2016 that through its expertise in cybercrime and forensic analysis, especially in chemical and physical profiling methods, aims to help member countries understand and combat the trafficking of performance-enhancing drugs through targeted criminal analysis.

While INTERPOL involvement in doping issues might be interpreted as a sign of its criminal nature, another sign is the exclusion of doping cases from the mediation procedures of CAS. Although that power imbalance in doping cases may be a reason to exclude it from mediation, looking more deeply in their nature shows that governing bodies in these cases need to impose their authority to maintain the integrity of the game. That pushes these violations close to criminal conduct in nature.

6.6. Controversy on Criminalizing Sport Doping

The approach to combat doping in competitive athletics has been twofold: the imposition of administrative penalties by the sports agencies for those who test positive for the drugs and the imposition of sanctions to criminalize those who manufacture, traffic, or possess them unlawfully, regardless of sports involvement. The focus in both instances is on the drugs or substances themselves. Recently action and national legislation to criminalize sport doping and athlete use is not without controversy. WADA issued a statement regarding various countries which have enacted legislation criminalizing sport doping. WADA acknowledged that criminalizing prohibited substance trafficking can be effective in catching athlete support personnel who possess or traffic PEDs. However, WADA believes that the Code's current stringent sanction process for athletes, which includes a four-year period of ineligibility and the right to a hearing before the CAS, has been globally accepted by sport and governments. As such, "the Agency does not believe that doping should be made a criminal offence for athletes" (WADA, 2015).

6.7. Burdens of Proving Criminalized Doping versus WADA Sanctions

Despite the laws governing doping, an athlete has rarely been prosecuted criminally for doping. The few filed cases related to athlete doping involved activities around an athlete, such as false testimony, lying, or possession of prohibited substances. For example, the U.S. government's case against Barry Bonds was not about whether he actually took HGH. It was about whether he perjured himself when he did not take HGH (Dolan, 2015).

Proof of intention is a crucial aspect of defining a crime. Sport cases show that a majority of doping violations are unintentional, such that the athlete unknowingly used or was misinformed regarding a prohibited substances (e.g., Meldoniom). These cases are adjudicated by arbitrators under sport-arbitration procedural rules. Sport arbitrators must have demonstrated competence in the fields of both sport law and international arbitration.

Sport doping adjudicated by criminal courts must establish intention beyond a reasonable doubt. Inadvertent use of prohibited substances if proven can be a strong mitigating factor that sets aside prison terms and criminal punishments before the case is ready to be submitted to administrative procedures of sport organizations.

The cost of the war on doping is certainly high. Sporting government bodies don't have the financial resources to test deep into the amateur ranks, and even if they did, the testing laboratories don't have the capacity to process all those tests. Law enforcement faces similar resource limitations. There is no denying that each government and sport body has an instrumental role in aiding the anti-doping fight. The pressures of the subpoena and the threat of jail time (no matter how minimal) may not particularly deter future doping, but it most certainly triggered dopers to turn on one another and provide evidence (Sigman, 2008).

Drug testing continues to be a game of cat-and-mouse as new performance-enhancing compounds and masking techniques emerge; catching up to the cheaters can take decades (Collins, 2006). Delayed discovery is currently impacting athletes. Usain Bolt was just stripped of his 4 x 100 meters relay gold medal from 2008 because it was discovered that one of his teammates was doping (Lewis, 2017). It is even possible that if a sample C is taken from the athletes and is analyzed at least two decades later then everybody would be shocked by the results.

Neither targeting trafficking, administrative procedures, nor criminalizing doping is free of problems. But a combination of these procedures are part of the coordinated effort to combat doping in sport.

7. Conclusion

Few events provide a more unifying and inspiring experience than watching our favorite athletes and teams compete at the highest levels in sport: winning the Tour de France, securing the Pennant, and going for the Gold. These athletes captivate our hearts, serve as role models to our youth, and become our collective heroes. As Nelson Mandela has said, "Sport has the power to change the world, the power to inspire, the power to unite people in a way that little else can . . .. Sport [can] spread hope to the world."

Our reality about what is elite and humanly possible is altered when we learn that some of these revered athletes resorted to using prohibited substances. In short, cheating in sports is like fraud. It gives spectators an inflated view of what their favorite athletes can actually accomplish.

Doping is not a mere moral consideration anymore, when in the lucrative sport industry each achievement, goal, title, and medal has the potential to change the whole life of an athlete. Doping "can be viewed as a form of cheating that taints the entire product" (Sigman, 2008, 180). The fight against doping in sport still rages today and continues to evolve as both drug user and drug enforcement continue to become more technological. It will persist as long as there is the temptation of sports glory waiting on the other side of victory.

The specter of doping casts suspicion and skepticism over many athletic events and professional sport leagues, calling into question the integrity of all athletes—and that's not fair. Most athletes are abiding by the rules, but the high-profile cases suggest a culture of sport far from the Olympic ideals of excellence, achievement, and fair play. This public health issue requires a multifaceted response, starting with educating the world's youth about the dangers of the drugs and the moral depravity of cheating. The glory and riches gained may be enticing, but the infamy gained from cheating will outlast it. One only needs to ask Lance Armstrong, Mark McGuire, or Alex Rodriguez for proof of that statement.

Notes

1. World Anti-Doping Agency (2015) (reporting 850 anti-doping rule violations in 2015, with more than thirty athletes sanctioned through the Athlete Biological).
2. *Olympic Charter* (as in force August 1, 2016). Available at https://stillmed.olympic.org/media/Document%20Library/OlympicOrg/General/EN-Olympic-Charter.pdf#_ga=1.204155664.1229088166.1485210766.
3. Olympic Charter (www.Olympic.org/Documents/olympic_charter_en.pdf).
4. Anabolic Steroid Control Act, 21 U.S.C. §§ 802 *et seq.* (classifying steroids as controlled substances and limiting their lawful use to treating disease or other recognized medical illness; unlawful use or distribution is classified as a felony punishable by imprisonment). The Act classifies five schedules of controlled substances *Id.*, § 802.
5. Wolf (2011) (reporting on rampant use of steroids in professional football and baseball and noting steroid use since the 1950s in U.S. weightlifting and by at least three professional football teams by the 1960s, with many more following course in the 1970s and 1980s).
6. Milot (2014) (analyzing the "[g]ap between how legal and sporting authorities, on the one hand, and elite athletes, on the other, approach, understand, and react to the risk of harm from the use of performance-enhancing substances.").
7. Mitten (2006) (noting that commissioners from the four major sport leagues appeared before Congress, which proposed drug testing legislation, prompting the leagues to develop more stringent policies to avoid federal regulation); Linderman (2011).
8. WADA Code, Art. 1.
9. WADA Code, Art. 4.2.1.
10. *Id.*
11. WADA Code, Art. 4.5.

12. WADA Code, Art. 2.1.
13. WADA Code, Art. 10.5.
14. WADA Code, Commentary, § 2.2.
15. WADA Code, Art. 3.2.
16. WADA Code, Art. 10.7 (an anti-doping rule violation for which an athlete or other person has established no fault or negligence is not deemed a prior violation).
17. Olympic Charter, Art. 46.

References

Associated Press. (2016, October 4). "WADA and INTERPOL Join Forces to Target Trafficking." *USA Today*. Available at http://www.usatoday.com/story/sports/olympics/2016/10/04/wada-and-interpol-join-forces-to-target-trafficking/91522476/.

Bishop, Greg. "*Ricky Williams Takes the High Road.*" *Sports Illustrated*, http://www.si.com/longform/2016/ricky-williams-weed/.

Blicharz, Michal. (2015, March 22). *Intel Extreme Masters Katowice 2016 becomes ESL's largest ever sports event*. Available at www.eslgaming.com/.

Blickenstaff, Brian. (2015, April 23). "Criminalized Doping and Sending Cheaters to Jail." *Vice Sports*. Available at https://sports.vice.com/ca/article/criminalized-doping-and-sending-cheaters-to-jail.

Blickenstaff, Brian. (2016, April 15). "The New Doping Issue Is Not a Sports Issue, It's a Health a Public Health Issue." *Vice Sports*. Available at https://sports.vice.com/en_us/article/the-new-doping-crisis-is-not-a-sports-issue-its-a-public-health-issue.

Brady, Nation. (2016, August 19). "Le'Veon Bell Suspension Reduced from 4 Games to 3." *SB Nation*, /www.sbnation.com/2016/8/19/12319364/leveon-bell-suspension-appeal-steelers-reduced.

Collective Bargaining Agreement Between Major League Soccer and Major League Soccer Players Union. (2015, February 1–2020, January 31). Art. 12, Drug Testing, www.mlsplayers.org/images/Collective%20Bargaining%20Agreement%20-%20February%201,%202015.pdf.

Collective Bargaining Agreement Between National Hockey League and National Hockey League Players' Association. (2013, February 15). Art. 47, Performance Enhancing Substances Program, www.nhl.com/nhl/en/v3/ext/CBA2012/NHL_NHLPA_2013_CBA.pdf.

Collins, Rick. (2006). "Changing the Game: The Congressional Response to Sports Doping via the Anabolic Steroid Control Act." *New England Law Review* 40: 753.

Dolan, Maura. (2015, April 22). "Barry Bonds' Obstruction of Justice Conviction Overturned." *Los Angeles Times*, www.latimes.com/local/lanow/la-me-ln-barry-bonds-conviction-overturned-20150422-story.html.

Elfrink, Tim, and Garcia-Roberts, Gus. (2014). *Blood Sport* (New York: Penguin).

Fainaru-Wada, Mark, and Williams, Lance. (2006). *Game of Shadows* (New York: Penguin).

"France Stiffens Anti-Doping Laws." (2009, April). *Cycling News*, www.cyclingnews.com/news/france-stiffens-anti-doping-laws/.

Gandert, Daniel, and Ronisky, Fabian. (2010). "American Professional Sports Is a Doper's Paradise: It's Time We Make a Change." *North Dakota Law Review* 86: 816.

Gehring, Chris. (2015, March 17). "10 Years Later, A Look at Every MLB Player Suspended for PEDs." *Sportingnews*, www.sportingnews.com/mlb/news/baseball-players-suspended-steroids-peds-list-all-time-policy/dki1hp6z3olo1rab6qnapzt3z.

Hagen, Paul. (2014, January 11). "Arbitrator: A-Rod Suspended for 2014 Season." MLB.com, http://m.mlb.com/news/article/66433260/arbitrator-rules-alex-rodriguez-to-be-suspended-for-2014-season/.

Hruby, Patrick. (2014, September 17). "The NFL's Hazy Logic." *The Atlantic*, available at www.theatlantic.com/entertainment/archive/2014/09/the-nfl-embraces-marijuana-finally/380246/.

Hoberman, John. (2011). "Athletes in Handcuffs? The Criminalization of Doping." In *Doping and Anti-Doping Policy in Sport*, edited by Mike McNamee and Verner Moller (Morgantown, W. Va.: Fitness Information Technology).

International Convention Against Doping in Sport. (2007). Available at www.unesco.org/new/en/social-and-human-sciences/themes/anti-doping/international-convention-against-doping-in-sport/.

INTERPOL. *Organized Crime and Professional Sports* www.interpol.int/Crime-areas/Crimes-in-sport/Doping; www.interpol.int/News-and-media/News/2015/N2015-050.

Japan Times. (2016, January 12). "Japan considers new law to curb doping ahead of 2020 Olympics," available at www.japantimes.co.jp/sports/2016/01/12/olympics/japan-considers-new-law-curb-doping-ahead-2020-olympics/.

Katz, Ron. (2016, May 20). "Sports Doping Should Be Criminalized." *Forbes*, available at www.forbes.com/sites/rkatz/2016/05/20/sports-doping-should-be-criminalized/?elqTrackId=f772154b83a146b0937c792852ca752c&elq=8e52165dea2e46498d8d08cf6123f2de&elqaid=4103&elqat=1&elqCampaignId=2626#78e3bc913b75.

Klein, Christian & Keidel, Nicolas. (2016, February 10). *Should Doping in Sport Be Criminalised? A Review of Germany's New Anti-Doping Act*, www.lawinsport.com/articles/item/should-sports-be-criminalising-doping-a-review-of-germany-s-new-anti-doping-act#references; www.dw.com/en/germanys-anti-doping-law-comes-into-force/a-18928499.

LA Times Staff. (2015, September 28). "A Look at NHL Drug Policy, Other Major Sports." *LA Times*, available at www.latimes.com/sports/kings/la-sp-with-nhl-drug-policy-20150929-story.html.

Lewis, Amy. (2017, January 25). "Usain Bolt: Sprinter Loses One Olympic Gold over Teammate's Failed Dope Test." CNN, http://edition.cnn.com/2017/01/25/sport/usain-bolt-triple-triple-nesta-carter-doping-gold-medal-beijing-2008-relay-4x100m/.

Lengel, David, and Busfield, Steve. (2013, August 5). "Alex Rodriguez and 12 Other Players Suspended in Biogenesis PEDs Scandal." *The Guardian*, www.theguardian.com/sport/2013/aug/05/alex-rodriguez-suspended-mlb-peds-drugs.

Linderman, Lee A. (2011). "A Congressional Carve Out: The Necessity for Uniform Application of Professional Sports Leagues Performance-Enhancing Drug Policies." *Southern California Law Review* 84: 751,771–772.

Lindholm, Johan. (2013). "Does Legislating Against Doping in Sports Make Sense?: Comparing Sweden and the United States Suggest Not." Va. Sports & Entertainment Law Journal 13: 21, 37.

Longman, Jere. (2013, August 8). "Study Says West Germany Engaged in Sports Doping." New York Times, http://www.nytimes.com/2013/08/09/sports/west-germany-engaged-in-sports-doping-in-1970s-study-says.html.

Loria, Kevin. (2016, January 15). *Some Competitive Video Gamers Are Abusing Drugs to Get an Edge.* Available at www.businessinsider.com/esports-doping-scandal-investigated-by-espns-otl-2016-1.

Major League Baseball's Joint Drug Prevention and Treatment Program. (2015). Available at http://mlb.mlb.com/pa/pdf/jda.pdf.

McKenzie, Christopher. (2007). "The Use of Criminal Justice Mechanisms to Combat Doping in Sport." *Sports Law ejournal*, 9 (2007), at http://epublications.bond.edu.au/slej/4.

McLaren, Richard. (2016). *Independent Commission Investigation into State-Sponsored Doping.*

Milot, Lisa. (2014). "Ignorance, Harm, and the Regulation of Performance-Enhancing Substances." *Harvard Journal of Sports & Entertainment Law* 5: 91.

Mitchell, George J. (2007, December). *Report to the Commissioner of Baseball of an Independent Investigation into the Illegal Use of Steroids and Other Performance Enhancing Substances by Players in Major League Baseball.*

Mitten, Matthew J. (2006). "Drug Testing of Athletes—An Internal, Not External Matter." *New England Law Review* 40: 797.

Nafziger, J. A. R. (2004). *International Sports Law*. (Ardsley, N.Y.: Transnational).

"NBA Suspends Magic's Turkoglu for Positive Steroid Test." (2013, February 13). NBA.com, www.nba.com/2013/news/02/13/magic-turkoglu-suspended/.

National Collegiate Athletic Association. (2016–2017). Drug Testing Program, 7, www.ncaa.org/sites/default/files/2016SSI_DrugTestingProgramBooklet_20160728.pdf.

NCAA Drug Testing Policy, http://www.ncaa.org/health-and-safety/policy.

National Football League. (2015). *Policy on Performance-Enhancing Substances*, https://nfl-paweb.blob.core.windows.net/media/Default/PDFs/Player%20Development/2015%20Policy%20and%20Program%20on%20Substances%20of%20Abuse.pdf.

Note. (2015). "An American in Paris: The Legal Framework of International Sport and the Implications of the World Anti-Doping Code on Accused Athletes." *Virginia Sports & Entertainment Law Journal* 7: 149 (2015).

Paraolympic.Org Staff. (2016, August 7). "The IPC Suspends the Russian Paraolympic Committee with Immediate Effect." Paraolympic.Org. Available at www.paralympic.org/news/ipc-suspends-russian-paralympic-committee-immediate-effect.

Reuters. (2015, November). "New Law in Doping Criminalize Inducement to Doping: RIA Novosti." Bloomberg News, www.reuters.com/article/us-sport-doping-russia-idUSKBN12Y1GV.

Rumsby, Ben. (2014, October 670). "Organized Crime Controls 25 Percent of World Sport: Warns WADA Chief David Howman." *Telegraph*, at www.telegraph.co.uk/sport/othersports/11144807/Organised-crime-controls-25-per-cent-of-world-sport-warns-Wada-chief-David-Howman.html.

Showalter, Brent D. (2007). "Steroid Testing Policies in Professional Sports: Regulated by Congress or the Responsibility of the Leagues?" *Marquette Sports Law Review* 17: 663.

Siekmann, Robert C. R. (2012). *Introduction to International and European Sports Law* (New York: Springer).

Sigman, Shayna M. (2008). "Symposium: Doping in Sports: Legal and Ethical Issues: Are We All Dopes? A Behavioral Law and Economics Approach to Legal Regulation of Doping in Sports." *Marquette Sports Law Review* 19: 125, 181.

Steroids in Sports: Cheating the System and Gambling Your Health: Hearings Before the Subcomm. on Commerce, Trade & Consumer Prot. and the Subcomm. on Health of the Comm. on Energy and Commerce, 109th Cong. 4 (2005).

USADA. (2005). "Harmonization Through the World Anti-Doping Program." *Play True* 3.

WADA. (2016, July 18). "WADA Statement: Independent Investigation confirms Russian State manipulation of the doping control process." Available at https://www.wada-ama.org/en/media/news/2016-07/wada-statement-independent-investigation-confirms-russian-state-manipulation-of.

Wagner-McGoun, Sean. (2016, February 2). "Ricky Williams Explains His Belief That Cannabis Can Help NFL Players." CBS, www.cbssports.com/nfl/news/ricky-williams-explains-his-belief-that-cannabis-can-help-nfl-players/.

Walker, Lesley. (2015, April 14). "Draft law in Qatar aims to criminalize performance-enhancing drugs." *Doha Times*, https://dohanews.co/draft-law-in-qatar-aims-to-criminalize-performance-enhancing-drugs/.

Weinrich, Marc. (2012, December 27). "Richard Sherman Wins Drug Test Appeal, Will Not Be Suspended." *Sports Illustrated*, www.si.com/si-wire/2012/12/27/richard-sherman-suspension-drug-test-sue-seahawks-nfl.

Weston, Maureen A. (2009). "Doping Control, Mandatory Arbitration, and Process Dangers for Accused Athletes in International Sports." 10 *Pepperdine Disputes and Resolutions Law Journal* 10: 5.

Wolf, Roberta F. (2011). "Conflicting Anti-Doping Laws in Professional Sports: Collective Bargaining Agreements v. State Law." *Seattle University Law Review* 34: 1605, 1609.

World Anti-Doping Agency. (2015). Annual Report, at https://wada-main-prod.s3.amazonaws.com/resources/files/wad-020_annual_report_2015_vf_high_1006_final.pdf.

World Anti-Doping Agency. *WADA History*. Available at www.wada-ama.org/en/who-we-are; https://www.wada-ama.org/en/funding.

WADA. (2015, October 15). *Statement on Criminalization of Doping in Sport*, available at www.wada-ama.org/en/media/news/2015-10/wada-statement-on-the-criminalization-of-doping-in-sport.

Cases

Hill v. NCAA, 865 P.2d 633 (Cal. 1994) (upholding a drug testing program for student athletes as reasonably related to a legitimate interest in fair intercollegiate athletics),

Vadim Devyatovskiy v. International Olympic Comm., CAS 2009/A/1752 and CAS 2009/A/1753 Ivan Tsikhan v. IOC, award of 10 June 2010, http://jurisprudence.tas-cas.org/Shared%20Documents/1752,%201753.pdf.

CHAPTER 6

DRUGS IN PROFESSIONAL SPORTS

TODD CLARK

1. Introduction

THE issue of drugs, both recreational and performance enhancing, has substantially impacted the sports world and has become a hot topic for sports writers, academics, and legislators. The impact of drugs in professional sports has affected political concerns, legal validity, player safety, and competitive spirit. While drugs are prevalent in all sports, professional and amateur, this chapter pays primary attention to how drug issues affect players and teams in the National Football League (NFL), the National Basketball Association (NBA), and Major League Baseball (MLB or Baseball). Although other professional sports leagues are affected by drug use and drug policies, this chapter only focuses on three most prominent and highest-revenue-generating sports leagues in America. As a preliminary mechanism for illustrating how drugs have affected professional sports, consider the following examples:

- NFL player, Josh Gordon, wide receiver for the Cleveland Browns, was suspended for an entire season without pay for violating the NFL's Policy and Program for Substance of Abuse. Gordon's suspension resulted after he tested positive for alcohol—a direct violation of the terms and conditions of the substance abuse program he was required to follow after getting charged with driving while under the influence (DUI).
- In December 2015, the NBA suspended Charlotte Hornets center Al Jefferson for five games after he violated the NBA's anti-drug policy. While neither party articulated the basis for Jefferson's suspension, it was likely attributable to a positive marijuana test since the anti-drug policy contained in the NBA's collective bargaining agreement provides for a five-game suspension the third time a player tests positive

for marijuana. More recently, on July 1, 2016, the NBA suspended O. J. Mayo for two years after a drug test revealed a "drug of abuse" in his system.

- One of the most famous cases of drug abuse in professional sports occurred in the context of Baseball after Jose Canseco released his tell-all book entitled *Juiced: Wild Times, Rampant 'Roids, Smash Hits and How Baseball Got Big* in 2005. In his book, Canseco claimed that approximately 85% of MLB players used performance-enhancing drugs (PEDs). Canseco also allege that he personally injected several players, including Mark McGuire, with PEDs. Canseco's allegations against McGuire were extremely scathing considering that in 1998, McGuire had broken one of the most highly regarded records in all of baseball—Roger Maris's sixty-one home runs in one season record—after McGuire hit seventy home runs (a few years later, Barry Bonds would break McGuire's record by hitting seventy-three home runs in one season). Initially, McGuire denied Canseco's accusations but he ultimately confirmed Canseco's claims in a public statement in 2010. Although Canseco and McGuire admitted to using PEDs, neither player was ever suspended. While MLB prohibited the use of steroids as early as 1991, league-wide testing did not occur until 2003, after both Canseco and McGuire had retired.

This chapter focuses on drug policies and how issues of abuse and enforcement affect the legal environment within the realm of professional sports. To facilitate this discussion, section 2 will provide background of the collective bargaining process and how it applies to the regulation of drugs in professional sports. Section 3 will highlight the drug policies that are in effect in the three major sports leagues in America. Finally, sections 4, 5, and 6 will explore the relevant legal issues affecting both drugs of abuse as well as PEDs in the context of professional sports.

2. The Collective Bargaining Process in Professional Sports

The National Labor Relations Act (NLRA) is the primary piece of legislation that regulates the relationship between owners of professional sports teams and professional athletes. The NLRA provides private-sector employees with the express right to form unions for the purpose of protecting employee rights. To accomplish this task, employees aggregate their efforts by unionizing to increase their power during the bargaining process with management. Through this process, the hope is that employees and management can "collectively" bargain for fair and reasonable terms and conditions. In the professional sports context, athletes do not individually bargain. Instead, the players are members of a players' association that represents the rights of the athletes in negotiations with the owners.

Pursuant to Section 8(d) of the NLRA, owners and athletes are required to negotiate in good faith with respect to "wages, hours, and other terms and conditions of employment...." Based on this provision, owners cannot unilaterally mandate any requirement that affects any of the previously listed items. If, however, an issue is not deemed "mandatory" and is instead considered "permissive" or "non-mandatory" owners may unilaterally take action without approval from the players' association. An issue is permissive when it is "fundamental to the basic direction of a corporate enterprise . . .," or when it only impinges "indirectly upon employment security" (*Fibreboard Paper Products Corp. v. NLRB*). In 1989, the National Labor Relations Board in two separate cases, *Johnson Bateman Co.* and *Minneapolis Star Tribune*, specifically determined that drug testing is a condition of employment and is therefore subject to mandatory arbitration. Therefore, professional sports leagues must collectively bargain before any requirement, modification, enactment or amendment to collective bargaining agreement (CBA) may take effect.

3. Drug Testing Policies in Professional Sports

This section provides a brief overview of the rules, regulations, enforcement mechanisms, and penalties associated with drug policies of the NFL, NBA, and MLB.

3.1. National Football League

As detailed below, policies and procedures for drug testing of NFL players are designed to balance player health, competitiveness and privacy.

3.1.1. *When Was the Policy Enacted?*

The NFL's first drug-related policy was issued in 1971 and prohibited "the use of drugs not prescribed or approved by a team physician." This policy was merely an educational policy and primarily focused on educating players about the dangers of substance abuse. It was not until 1973 that the policy was amended to provide disciplinary provisions. Today, the NFL has two separate polices, one policy for "substances of abuse" and a second for "steroids."

3.1.2. *What Substances Are Testable Pursuant to the Policy?*

According to the NFL's policy, the following "Substances of Abuse" are testable:

- Cocaine (benzoylecognine), no more than or equal to 150 ng/ml
- Marijuana (Delta 9-THC-carboxylic acid), no more than or equal to 35 ng/ml

- Amphetamine (or any analogous substance), no more or equal to 300 ng/ml
- Opiates (total morphine and codeine), no more than or equal to 300 ng/ml
- PCP (phencyclidine), no more than or equal to 25 ng/ml
- MDMA (methylenedioxymethamphetamine, or any analogous substance)
- Alcohol, no more than or equal to .06g/dl (grams per deciliter)
- Alcohol is only prohibited if a specific player's treatment plan explicitly prohibits alcohol.

For their part, steroids are also subject to NFL testing. Indeed, the NFL's PED policy prohibits anabolic agents, masking agents, and stimulants.

3.1.3. *When Can an Athlete Be Tested?*

The timing and frequency of testing is also a matter of negotiation between the NFL and NFLPA. The following outlines the key policies on when an NFL player can be tested.

3.1.3.1. *Substances of Abuse*

There are four separate types of testing pursuant to the NFL's the drug testing policy: pre-employment, preseason, intervention program testing, and testing by agreement.

Pre-employment testing can be administered to rookies or to veteran players who wish to sign a contract with an NFL team and who were not under contract to a previous team at the time of the team's last game of the immediately preceding season. Results from these tests are made available to interested teams.

Pre-season testing can be administered once to all players under contract between April 20 and August 9. Testing can be administered to an entire team or to specific positional groups, but not on an individual-by-individual basis unless the player is excused by the medical advisor. If so, the excused player may be tested individually as long as it occurs before the first regular season game unless there is a showing of "extenuating circumstances." Finally, any player signed or acquired after the pre-season testing date may be tested individually if the player has not already been administered.

Under the intervention program, players who have failed a drug test are required to provide a specimen whenever instructed by the medical advisor. "For players in Stage One, the Medical Director will determine the frequency of testing for the player. For players in Stages Two and Three, the Medical Advisor will determine the frequency of testing" (NFL Policy and Program on Substance Abuse, 2015).

Testing by agreement occurs when an NFL team and a player agree to unannounced testing during the player's contract, as long as the club has a reasonable basis for requesting testing. A positive result places the player into Stage One of the intervention program.

3.1.3.2. *Steroid Policy*

There are six different circumstances that can compel an NFL player or prospective NFL player to be tested for steroids: pre-employment, annual, preseason/regular season, postseason, off-season, and reasonable cause testing for players with prior positive tests or under other circumstances. Under each type of test, a player's urine or serum (the liquid part of blood) may be tested. The nature of the test influences the terms, conditions, and extent of the testing.

First, pre-employment urine and serum testing can be administered to free agents, veterans, or rookies. Urine testing can also be administered at the NFL's scouting combine, which is a forum for prospective NFL players to showcase their talents to NFL teams. Pre-employment serum testing at the scouting combine, however, is limited to thirty randomly selected players.

Second, annual urine testing will be administered to all players at least once per year. This testing will occur at training camp or whenever a player reports to camp. Annual serum testing will be administered to 20% of a team's randomly selected players.

Third, preseason/regular season urine testing will be administered to ten randomly selected players, from each team, from the preseason through the regular season. Preseason/regular season serum testing will be administered to five randomly selected players, who are picked from eight randomly selected teams. Such testing may occur from the preseason through the regular season.

Fourth, postseason urine testing will be administered to ten randomly selected players on each playoff team, each week, as long as the team remains in the playoffs. Postseason serum testing will be administered to five of the ten players who were randomly selected for urine testing.

Fifth, offseason urine testing will be administered to players under contract and who are not subject to reasonable cause testing; however, no player will be subject to more than six offseason tests. The rules for selecting players for offseason testing are the same as those for regular season testing. Offseason serum testing will be randomly administered to 10% of a team's players. Players who have notified the NFL in writing that they have retired are not subject to offseason testing. However, if a player later signs a contract to continue his career, the player will be placed back in the pool.

Sixth and finally, so-called reasonable cause testing—testing where there are sufficient indicia of steroid use—will be administered to three categories of players: (1) players who have previously tested positive, (2) players for whom there is "credible" evidence of steroid use within two seasons of their college football draft or before their scouting combine, and (3) players for whom there is credible evidence of a policy violation or a medical condition that warrants testing. Any player who is placed in the reasonable cause testing program based on a failed test must remain in the program for the lessor of two years or two full seasons. A player placed in reasonable cause testing may be tested via urine or serum testing at the discretion of an independent administrator.

3.1.4. *What Are the Penalties for Violating the Policy?*

3.1.4.1. *Substance Abuse Policy: Suspensions and Discipline (Intervention Stages)*

All players are eligible for entrance into the intervention program. Entrance into the program can occur in one of three ways: (1) a positive test result, (2) behavior that, in the opinion of the medical director, reflects signs of substance abuse, or (3) the player voluntarily refers himself to the program.

Pursuant to the NFL's Substance Abuse Policy, there are three stages of the intervention program. The nature of the player's discipline is determined by the relevant stage.

Stage One: Within Stage One, the medical director determines whether a player should be disciplined and when the player will be tested. No player may remain in stage one for more than ninety days unless the medical director decides to extend the treatment plan. Such an extension can only last up to ninety days. Therefore, the maximum time that any player will be in Stage One is 180 days. If a player is found to have violated the terms and conditions of his Stage One placement, the player will be subject to a fine equal to three-seventeenths of the amount in his NFL contract. A positive test advances player to Stage Two. Self-referred players cannot be fined and will remain in Stage One unless one of three circumstances is triggered: the player is mandatorily entered into Stage One by testing positive for a substance outside the player's normal treatment plan; the medical director learns from an outside source the that player has engaged in a new abuse; or the player does something new that would indicate to the medical director that the player is abusing drugs (e.g., the player is arrested on drug charges).

Stage Two: Within Stage Two, a player's discipline is determined by the number of violations. A player will remain in Stage Two for twenty-four months or for two seasons, whichever is shorter, unless he is released earlier.

For a player's **first** violation in Stage Two, a player who completed Stage One is assessed a fine of four-seventeenths of the player's NFL Player Contract One. If, however, the player failed to complete Stage One, he would be subject to a suspension without pay for four games (including regular/postseason and Pro Bowl).

For a player's **second** violation in Stage Two, the player will be assigned to Stage Three. If he was previously fined, he will be suspended without pay for four games (including regular/postseason and Pro Bowl). Alternatively, if he was previously suspended for Stage Two noncompliance, he will be suspended without pay for six regular and/or postseason games. Furthermore, a positive test will advance player to Stage Three.

As Americans' attitudes about marijuana have become more permissive—if not supportive—the NFL and National Football League Players Association (NFLPA) have relaxed their sanctions for players who test positive for marijuana. To wit, if a player's first positive test result under Stage Two is for marijuana, he is subject only to a fine of two-seventeenths of the player's NFL player contract.

Stage Three: Within Stage Three, a player can be tested at any time but cannot be tested more than ten times in one month. A player will remain in Stage Three for the remaining part of the player's career unless, after twenty-four months, it is determined that the player should be discharged from treatment. If a player fails to comply with the terms and conditions of his treatment in Stage Three, the player will be banished from the NFL for at least one year.

As in Stage Two, if a player's first positive test in Stage Three is for marijuana a moderated punishment is applied: the player will receive a ten-game suspension. If the player tests positive for marijuana yet again, the player will then be banished for a minimum of one year.

3.1.4.2. *Steroids Policy: Suspensions and Discipline*

Any player or person governed by the NFL's steroid policy who is convicted, admits to conduct that amounts to a violation of the policy, or for whom there is credible evidence that the player or person has violated the policy is subject to discipline from the commissioner. The commissioner may suspend the offender for up to six games. If, however, the circumstances warrant, the commissioner may terminate the offender's contract.

Suspensions and discipline (intervention stages) are determined pursuant to a three-step process.

Step One applies to a player's first violation.

- A positive test for a diuretic or masking agent results in a regular and/or postseason two-game suspension.
- A positive test for a stimulant or anabolic agent results in a regular and/or postseason four-game suspension.
- A positive test for a prohibited substance plus a diuretic or masking agent, attempt to alter a specimen, or attempt to manipulate a test result will result in a regular and/or postseason six-game suspension.

Step Two applies to a player's second violation and will result in a regular and/or postseason ten-game suspension.

Step Three applies to a player's third violation and will result in banishment from the league for at least two seasons; however, the player's banishment is subject to appeal.

3.2. National Basketball Association

3.2.1. *When Was the Policy Enacted?*

In 1983, the NBA and the National Basketball Players Association (NBPA) agreed to include drug testing as part of the NBA's collective bargaining agreement. This policy was largely focused on recreational drugs, also known as drugs of abuse. Heroin, cocaine, and LSD all fall within the category of recreational drugs or drugs of abuse. While the NBA's initial drug testing policy did not prohibit PEDs, in 1999 the NBA and the NBA Players Association agreed to prohibit them as well.

3.2.2. *What Substances Are Testable Pursuant to the Policy?*

- Drugs of abuse (cocaine, heroin, LSD, etc.)
- Marijuana
- Steroids, PEDs, and masking
- Diuretics

3.2.3. *When Can an Athlete Be Tested?*

Once the NBA or the NBPA has been presented with evidence that a player has used, possessed, or distributed a drug of abuse, marijuana, or a PED, an independent expert will be appointed to determine whether reasonable cause exists. If the independent expert finds reasonable cause, he or she will issue an "authorization for testing." Once the authorization for testing is issued, the player may be tested at any time, without notice. Players may be randomly selected for testing up to four times, at any time, during the season. Additionally, players may be randomly selected and tested, no more than two times, at any time during the offseason.

3.2.4. *What Are the Penalties for Violating the Policy?*

The penalties are determined by the nature of the drug testing violation. To illustrate, if the player tests positive for a drug of abuse or if the player refuses to submit to a drug test without a reasonable explanation, he will be immediately dismissed and disqualified from playing in the NBA for at least two years. As an accompanying sanction, the player's contract will be voided.

Marijuana is treated much more permissively by the NBA and NBPA's collectively bargained rules. If a player tests positive for marijuana, he is not disqualified for at least two years, as he would with other drugs of abuse. In fact, he is not disqualified for any length of time. He is merely required to enter the NBA's marijuana program. As a second offense, he must pay a $25,000 fine but still does not receive a suspension. Only on a third offense for marijuana will a player be suspended, and then it is for five games.

As to testing positive for a steroid or performance-enhancing drug (SPED), a first-time violation calls for a twenty-game suspension and admission to the NBA's SPED program. A second violation carries a forty-five-game suspension. Finally, a third violation disqualifies the player for at least two years and voids his contract.

3.3. Major League Baseball

3.3.1. *When Was the Policy Enacted?*

MLB's first drug policy was enacted in 1971 and specifically provided that all MLB personnel must "comply with federal and state drug laws." However, it was not until 1991 that MLB's policy contained language banning steroids and it did not begin testing players for PEDs until 2003.

3.3.2. *What Substances Are Testable Pursuant to the Policy?*

A. Drugs of Abuse
- Cocaine
- LSD
- Marijuana

- Opiates
- MDMA
- GHB
- PCP (phencyclidine)
- Ephedera

B. Steroids

3.3.3. *When Can an Athlete Be Tested?*

3.3.3.1. *Drugs of Abuse*

MLB does not test for drugs of abuse unless the player is part of a treatment program. A player suspected of using a drug of abuse will go before the treatment board. If the board establishes that the player used, possessed, or sold a drug of abuse, the player is then placed in a treatment program. A player in a treatment program is subject to testing but is not subject to suspension and will only be liable for a series of fines unless (1) the player flagrantly disregards his treatment program and (2) the commissioner determines that the player's drug use poses a threat to the safety of the other players.

3.3.3.2. *Steroids*

3.3.3.2.1. ***Urine Testing*** A player is subject to unannounced urine testing upon reporting to Spring Training. Once the season begins, 3,200 random urine samples are collected at unannounced times. In addition, during the offseason, 350 random urine samples are collected. There is no limit on how many times a player may be subjected to random urine testing.

3.3.3.2.2. ***Blood Collection*** A player is subject to unannounced blood collection during Spring Training. Once the season begins, 260 random blood specimens are collected at unannounced times, post-game, from the player's nondominant arm unless the player request otherwise. During the offseason, 140 blood specimens will be collected at unannounced times during each offseason. There is no limit on how many times a player can be randomly selected for blood testing.

3.3.3.3. *Reasonable Cause Testing*

A player is subject to Reasonable Cause Testing if a party presents sufficient evidence that a player has used, possessed or sold PEDs, stimulants, dehydroepaindrosterone (DHEA), or drugs of abuse in the previous twelve months. If the basis of the inquiry is for anything other than drugs of abuse, the player is subject to urine or blood testing within forty-eight hours. If the inquiry is for drugs of abuse, the player is subject to testing as determined by the board. If a player disputes that there is reasonable cause, the player can commence a proceeding within forty-eight hours of receiving the reasonable cause notification.

3.3.4. *What Are the Penalties for Violating the Policy?*

3.3.4.1. *Performance-Enhancing Substance Violations*

A player's first violation will result in an eighty-game suspension. The second violation will result in a 162-game/183-days-of-pay suspension. The third violation will result in a permanent suspension from MLB and Minor League Baseball. However, the player can apply for reinstatement after a minimum of two years.

3.3.4.2. *Stimulant and DHEA Violations*

A player's first violation will result in follow-up testing. The second violation will result in a twenty-five-game suspension. The third violation will result in an eighty-game suspension. A fourth violation could end the player's career: he faces possible permanent suspension.

3.3.4.3. *Failure to Comply with Evaluation or Treatment Program*

A player who refuses to submit to an evaluation or who refuses to participate in mandatory sessions is subject to discipline. The first violation will result in a suspension of at least fifteen games but not more than twenty-five. The second violation will result in a suspension of at least twenty-five games but not more than fifty games. The third violation will result in a suspension of at least fifty games but not more than seventy-five games. The fourth violation will result in a suspension of at least one year. Any further violation will result in a penalty to be determined by the commissioner.

4. Legal Issues Involving Drugs in Professional Sports

Today, concerns relating to drugs of abuse and PEDs have created a host of complex legal issues. The following sections will provide a comprehensive commentary regarding drugs in professional sports and the accompanying legal issues engendered by their use.

4.1. Drugs of Abuse in Professional Sports

The concept of "drugs of abuse" includes a host of illegal substances, including: cocaine, heroin, opium, LSD (lysergic acid diethylamide), crack cocaine, Ecstasy, and psychedelics. However, the drug that has garnered the most attention in the context of professional sports is marijuana. Twenty-five states and the District of Columbia have legalized marijuana in some capacity. Four of these states—Alaska, Oregon, Washington, and Colorado—have legalized marijuana for recreational purposes. As a result of increased efforts to legalize marijuana, professional sports leagues are approaching an ethical and legal crossroads about whether to acquiesce to rising pressures to allow athletes to use it.

The primary argument advanced by those in favor of legalization of marijuana is that it has proven to be a valid mechanism for combating pain and other medical conditions. There are countless stories of athletes using marijuana for the purpose of pain relief. Former NBA player Jay Williams estimated that approximately 80% of the players in the NBA use marijuana to treat pain and other ailments. While leagues allow players to use prescription opioids, such as Vicodin or Percocet, to treat pain, no league authorizes players to use marijuana. Surprisingly, opioids are perceived as a safer, less risky, less addictive, and less dangerous alternative to marijuana. Yet, history has proven that opioids can be extremely harmful and often have highly addictive properties. In fact, Williams was addicted to oxycontin for more than five years. Williams's opioid addiction is not an isolated story. His narrative is consistent among players across all sports leagues. For example, numerous NFL players have alleged that NFL coaches, physicians, and trainers routinely pass out pain killers like candy to ensure that players are able to play when called on without any regard to the side effects, dosage limitations, or consequences. These stories became so rampant in the NFL that in May 2015, over 1,500 players filed a class action law suit against the NFL alleging that NFL teams and their staffs "intentionally" misled players about the health risk of pain killers and often distributed them without any prescription. As of this writing, the lawsuit remains in litigation.

According to the Centers for Disease Control and Prevention (CDC), while almost 26,000 people died from opioid abuse in 2015, there are no reported cases to date of death from a marijuana overdose. In fact, the likelihood of a person overdosing from marijuana is extremely unlikely. According to Drug Enforcement Administration (DEA) administrative law judge Francis L. Young, to overdose and die from marijuana consumption, "a marijuana smoker would have to consume 20,000 to 40,000 times as much marijuana as is contained in one marijuana cigarette" (*In re Marijuana Rescheduling Petition*). Stated another way by Administrative Law Judge Francis Young in *In re Marijuana Rescheduling Petition*, a marijuana user would have to consume "nearly 1,500 pounds of marijuana within about 15 minutes to induce a lethal response." This information bolsters the arguments of marijuana proponents to authorize its use because marijuana is substantially less likely to result in overdose or death than opioids.

In addition to possibly serving as a safer and more efficient option to treat pain, some research suggests that marijuana may also be effective at treating brain trauma. This possibility is extremely promising to athletes, especially athletes in the NFL where there are extensive issues, both legal and health related, based on head trauma and concussions. According to researchers from the Department of Veterans Affairs and Boston University, 96% (eighty-seven of ninety-one) of the NFL brains they tested from deceased NFL players tested positive for chronic traumatic encephalopathy (CTE). According to the Brain Injury Research Institute, CTE

> is a progressive degenerative disease which afflicts the brain of people who have suffered repeated concussions and traumatic brain injuries, such as athletes . . .. The brain of an individual who suffers from chronic traumatic encephalopathy gradually deteriorates and will over time end up losing mass. Certain areas of the brain are

> particularly liable to atrophy, though other areas are prone to becoming enlarged. Another aspect of CTE is that some areas of the brain experience an accumulation of tau protein, a substance which serves to stabilize cellular structure in the neurons but which may become defective and subsequently may cause major interference with the function of the neurons.
>
> (Brain Research Institute, 2017)

Given the apparent prevalence of CTE among athletes, specifically among athletes in the NFL, some advocates argue that marijuana may be a viable and safe alternative for treating CTE.

> Cannabinoids may play a role in neuroprotection in disorders such as stroke, Parkinson's disease, traumatic brain injury and epilepsy. These disorders may be caused by the generation of free radicals, reactive oxygen species, and pro-inflammatory cytokines. Emerging data suggest that natural- and synthetic-cannabinoids show a potent anti-oxidant activity and anti-inflammatory reaction . . .. In the last 10 years, it has been possible to demonstrate that [cannabidiol, a.k.a. CBD] has the following unique therapeutic profile: 1) a cannabinoid receptor-independent mechanism, 2) long-lasting cerebro-protective effect after ischemic stroke, and lack of development of tolerance. Moreover, CBD has almost no side effects, including psychotropic activity. Preliminary studies highlight the fact that the multifunctional actions of CBD may lead to benefits in more complex systems within the brain after ischemic stroke.
>
> (Hayakawa, Mishima, and Fujiwara, 2010)

Moreover, according to a study published in the *Journal of Bone and Mineral Research*, CBD has also been shown to make bones stronger and more resistant to fracture. It has also proved to as a viable mechanism for shortening the healing time of bone fractures.

4.2. Marijuana Regulation

If marijuana is truly the wonder drug that some suggest, why has no major professional sports league in the United States approved it for use? The first and most compelling reason is that marijuana is illegal under federal law. Pursuant to the Federal Control Substances Act, marijuana is a "Schedule 1" drug. A Schedule 1 drug is one that has a high potential for abuse, no currently accepted medical use in treatment in the United States, and for which there is a lack of accepted safety for use of the drug or other substance under medical supervision. Marijuana's classification as a Schedule 1 drug is of significant importance. Since Schedule 1 drugs "have no medical purpose" they cannot be prescribed. As a result, Marijuana and other Schedule 1 drugs are not studied as extensively as other drugs for potential medicinal benefits. However, there is some push to reclassify marijuana from a Schedule 1 to a Schedule 2 drug. If this reclassification occurs, it would allow researchers to conduct more robust analysis on its properties to determine whether it can legitimately be used as a viable medical treatment option.

The second reason that marijuana has yet to be authorized by any sports league is that marijuana usage carries a negative stigma. It is commonly thought that marijuana gained its negative stigma from its status as a "gateway drug," or from its addictive and psychedelic properties. However, Isaac Campos (2012), postulates that marijuana acquired a stigma in North America because of its link to negatively perceived groups such as prisoners and indigenous persons in Mexico. When marijuana was first introduced in Mexico in the early 1500s it was perceived as a fiber plant that was used to make various products including, clothing, boat sails, and rope. Over the next 400 years, marijuana in Mexico gained a closer connection with unfavorable tribes, poor persons, and criminals. As a result, marijuana's link to its undesirable citizenry earned it a reclassification from a "fiber" plant capable of creating important goods to a demonic by-product. As a result, in 1920 marijuana was banned in Mexico, approximately seventeen years before the same result occurred in the United States. According to Campos, Mexico's treatment of marijuana influenced American ideology, law, and policy. Consequently, Campos advances that marijuana's illegality and, more important, its stigma, is rooted in the ethos of discrimination by Mexico's power structure against Mexico's undesirables.

In light of the aforementioned reasons for marijuana's illegality, there is growing sentiment for its legalization. Until that time, there are a host of legal possibilities and outcomes. The first of which is exemplified by the Colorado Supreme Court's holding in *Coats v. Dish Network*. In *Coats*, Colorado's Supreme Court was asked to determine whether an employer could terminate an employee who lawfully used marijuana under Colorado State law. Specifically, the employer terminated a paraplegic employee after he failed a drug test. The employee, however, had lawfully obtained a state-issued license to use marijuana for medical purposes. The employee used marijuana at home, after work, as authorized by his license and further, by Colorado State law. Nonetheless, he was terminated for violating the employer's drug policy after testing positive for marijuana.

The employee argued that his termination was unlawful because it violated a Colorado State statute that provided that "[i]t shall be a discriminatory or unfair employment practice for an employer to terminate the employment of any employee due to that employee's engaging in any lawful activity off the premises of the employer during nonworking hours" unless certain exceptions apply" (Colo. Rev. Stat. Ann. § 24-34-402.5(1)). The employee's primary argument was that his use of marijuana was "lawful" under Colorado State law and therefore his employer discriminated against him pursuant to the aforementioned statute by terminating him for participating in "lawful" conduct away from his employer's premises. The court disagreed and reasoned that while the conduct may have been lawful under state law, marijuana is illegal pursuant to federal law and therefore, the employee did not engage in "lawful" conduct. The court interpreted the term "lawful" to apply to conduct that is legal under both federal and state law. Moreover, the court reasoned that there was no language in the statute that suggested that the term "lawful" was limited to state law. Instead the court opined that the legislature used the term "lawful" "in its general, unrestricted sense, indicating that a 'lawful' activity is that which complies with applicable 'law,' including state and federal law."

While *Coats* is merely a decision of the Supreme Court of Colorado, it provides the most probable outcome of a case involving a professional athlete who seeks to argue that his use of marijuana is lawful in a jurisdiction where marijuana has been legalized. More specifically, it is highly likely that a court would enforce a professional league's punishment for a player's use of marijuana regardless of whether such use is lawful at the state level. This will be true as long marijuana remains illegal under federal law.

Interestingly, the NFL's existing policies might permit the use of medical marijuana. Indeed, some scholars and commentators highlight that while the NFL's drug policy identifies marijuana as a prohibited substance, the NFL's collective bargaining agreement prohibits only the "illegal use" of marijuana. A reasonable argument therefore exists that a player in a state where marijuana is lawful would be permitted to use it without penalty. While the technical variation in language between the two policies may offer hope to marijuana proponents, the likelihood of prevailing on such argument is low. The more plausible outcome is one that is consistent with the *Coats* court, which held that "lawful" use is use that is legal under both state and federal law. Based on this interpretation, the NFL's policy prohibiting marijuana would be upheld. The NFL and other professional sports leagues would be incentivized to advocate for this outcome, as otherwise players in certain states could use marijuana while players in other states would be forbidden. Such an inconsistent framework might endanger competitive balance within leagues.

As explained previously, although marijuana usage is currently illegal under federal law, there is growing sentiment for its legalization. There is also speculation—as alluded above—that the DEA might reclassify marijuana from a Schedule 1 drug to a Schedule 2 drug in the near future. Schedule 2 drugs are drugs that "have a high potential for abuse, that have a currently accepted medical use in treatment in the United States or a currently accepted medical use with severe restrictions, and that may lead to severe psychological or physical dependence." Reclassifying marijuana would substantially impact marijuana access, its legality, and its impact on professional sports. First, reclassifying marijuana as a Schedule 2 drug would allow for greater research on the drug to validate or invalidate its alleged benefits. Second, a marijuana reclassification would legalize marijuana for medical purposes. Such a distinction would allow marijuana to be issued for a "legitimate medical purpose" by a registered practitioner.

Should marijuana be reclassified as a Schedule 2 drug, it is unlikely that any of the professional sports leagues would continue to subject players to tangible consequences for marijuana usage. This is because of the Americans with Disabilities Act (ADA), which substantially restricts the types of information an employer can seek from an employee or prospective employee. One type of information deemed off-limits for questioning is the prescription medications an employee is currently using. The ADA prohibits "covered employers," which is generally defined as employers with fifteen or more employees, from discriminating against employees on account of an actual or perceived disability.

A professional sports team is a covered employer pursuant to this definition since they all have more than fifteen employees. The ADA also prohibits employers from asking employees "what prescription medications they are taking," unless it can be established that such inquiry is "job related and consistent with business necessity." Generally, this inquiry is lawful when the employee is engaged in employment that affects public safety or if the employer can demonstrate that an "employee's inability or impaired ability to perform essential functions will result in a direct threat." In evaluating the concept of a "direct threat," an employer is given more latitude when the threat is to the public or to third parties. As the EEOC highlights in its ADA enforcement guidelines,

> a police department could require armed officers to report when they are taking medications that may affect their ability to use a firearm or to perform other essential functions of their job. Similarly, an airline could require its pilots to report when they are taking any medications that may impair their ability to fly. A fire department, however, could not require fire department employees who perform only administrative duties to report their use of medications because it is unlikely that it could show that these employees would pose a direct threat as a result of their inability or impaired ability to perform their essential job functions.
>
> (Enforcement Guidance, 2005)

Given these examples, it seems unlikely that a team could establish a legitimate argument for proving that an inquiry into a player's use of medical marijuana is job related and consistent with business necessity. For example, in basketball, if a player is impaired as a result of marijuana usage, it is likely that the player may miss more shots or turn the ball over more frequently. Such conduct, however, is unlikely to pose physical harm to other players, coaches, or spectators. MLB teams would have similar problems because of the lack of physical contact between players. Teams in the NFL would have the highest probability of establishing that an impaired player posed a legitimate safety risk since contact in the NFL is rather violent. Consider what would happen to an unsuspecting quarterback if he were blindsided by a fast-approaching defensive lineman because one of his offensive linemen was "high" and failed to block the defensive lineman. This type of hit could cause permanent damage to the quarterback's person. As illustrated by this example, determining the probable legal outcome in certain sports situations is difficult—particularly because the Equal Opportunity Employment Commission's (EEOC's) guidelines and the case law dealing with this issue are relatively sparse. Generally, however, an inquiry into an employee's use of lawful medications is prohibited.

In light of the current climate, relevant legal discourse, and existing medical research, it appears that the use of marijuana in professional sports may occur in some capacity in the not too distant future. As evidence of this possibility, the commissioners for both the NFL and NBA have acknowledged the possibility of authorizing the use of marijuana through collective bargaining. NFL Commissioner Roger Goodell recently stated that the NFL "will obviously follow signs. We will follow medicine and if they determine this could be a proper usage in any context, we will consider that. Our medical experts are not saying that right now" (Strauss, 2014). Similarly, NBA Commissioner Adam Silver has expressed that the NBA is "much more concerned about human growth hormone (HGH) testing and designer performance-enhancing drugs. This is a policy matter, and it's our strong preference that our players do not consume marijuana. We believe it will affect their performance on the court. That said, marijuana testing is something that's collectively bargained with the players' association, and we adjust to the times" (Mandell, 2014). While neither commissioner's statement was an outright proclamation that marijuana authorization is imminent, their statements suggest that both leagues are cognizant of the developing arguments for marijuana authorization.

5. PEDs in Professional Sports

One the most compelling and "fair" discussions about steroids occurred in the well regarded and highly controversial 2008 documentary "Bigger, Faster, Stronger . . ." Directed by Christopher Bell, this documentary film attempted to evaluate the accuracy of news stories that depict steroid abuse as rampant and harmful. While the film capably balanced fact versus the reality of steroid use, its single most memorable part occurred when Bell highlighted relevant statistics from the CDC. Those statistics revealed that only three people died in 2007 from steroid abuse, while two legal substances—alcohol and tobacco—were responsible for approximately 75,000 and 475,000 deaths, respectively. Assuming this information is correct, why are PEDs perceived in such a negative light?

Unlike marijuana, there is no major national initiative to legalize or authorize PEDs in professional sports. More accurately, there is a widespread campaign to eliminate the use of PEDs because of the perception that these types of drugs harm athletes' health, undermine the integrity of the sport, and negatively influence young persons who look up to athletes. Indeed, PEDs are riddled with side effects that can have both immediate and long-term effects on an athlete. These side effects can manifest themselves physiologically as well as psychologically. Physiologically, an athlete can experience acne, tumor growths, hair loss, stunted growth, liver damage, reduced sperm count, testicular shrinkage, impotence, cardiovascular disease, nausea, seizures, and high blood pressure. Psychologically, an athlete may experience "roid rage" or increased aggression, drastic mood swings, insomnia, loss of memory, anxiety, and depression resulting from steroid withdrawal. In addition, there is a compelling argument that steroids hurt the competitive spirit of sports. Athletes who "cheat" by using steroids to gain a competitive advantage over other athletes destroy the competitive spirit of the game and tarnish the integrity of sport. PED use by one athlete also encourages use by other athletes. This dynamic creates a game-theory-based prisoner's dilemma for athletes.

> Suppose we have two athletes (A, B), playing against each other in a competitive sport, with two choices (Stay Clean, Dope). If they both stay clean, the situation is as normal: what will separate their performances is a combination of natural ability, hard work, training and luck. If one of them dopes and the other doesn't, the doper will gain a significant competitive advantage, while the clean athlete may well have to look for another line of work. In the parlance of the Prisoner's Dilemma, this represents a "Sucker's Payoff" for the clean athlete. Conversely, if they both choose to dope, the competitive advantage is cut away and once again a combination of natural ability, hard work and training will decide the day. Although the net result of both athletes doping is no different from the situation in which both stay clean, game theoretic axioms assume that the both doping scenario is more likely. This is because doping strictly dominates staying clean: the athlete that dopes does better, no matter what his opponent does.
>
> (Danaher, 2012)

When such a phenomenon occurs, it increases health risks for all players. Bigger, faster, players cause bigger, faster collisions, hits, punches, and other types of contact that result in greater injury.

It is also important to recognize that players are role models even if some of them reject the premise. As such, their conduct encourages similar conduct, especially from children. Therefore, increased steroid use by athletes encourages and would likely increase steroid usage by children.

5.1. Types of PEDs in Sports

Generally speaking, there are six types of PEDs: anabolic steroids, blood doping, HGH, stimulants, masking agents, and diuretics.

Anabolic steroids trick an athlete's body into developing muscle mass and endurance. Once steroids are introduced to the body, they are broken down into smaller components called molecules. These molecules penetrate cells in the body and attach themselves to androgen receptors. Androgen receptors dictate what function a cell will perform. Once steroid molecules attach themselves to androgen receptors, a signal is sent to the cell to produce more protein. In turn, more protein builds more cells and muscle.

Lyle Alzado's experience with anabolic steroids is arguably one of the most famous and important cases of steroid abuse in sports history. After a stellar career in the NFL as a defensive end, Alzado died at the age of 43 from a brain tumor. While it has never been confirmed that steroids caused his death, it is uncontroverted that he was an avid user of steroids and that steroids could have caused or worsened the tumor's deadly growth. Alzado's death played a substantial role in bringing the perils of steroid abuse to the forefront of the American consciousness.

Blood doping refers to a process used by athletes to increase the number of oxygen-carrying red blood cells in the body. By increasing the number of red blood cells, the amount of oxygen that can be carried to an athlete's muscles also increases. As a result, the athlete experiences less fatigue and higher endurance levels. One of the most commonly utilized methods of blood doping involves the injection a hormone called erythropoietin (EPO), which regulates the body's oxygen delivery system. The most famous case of blood doping involved bicyclist Lance Armstrong, winner of the Tour de France a record seven times. Armstrong admitted to using EPO after the U.S. Anti-Doping Agency released a 1,000-page report chronicling his abuse.

HGH is a naturally occurring protein hormone in the body that is produced by the pituitary gland. Once HGH is secreted into the body, the liver converts it into growth factors, the most important of which is insulin-like growth factor 1 (IGF-1). Once this occurs, the body uses IGF-1 for a host of processes including muscle repair, muscle development, hair growth, sex drive, and reducing the effects of degenerative diseases. HGH supplementation has gained substantial press and infiltration into professional sports because an athlete's levels of HGH decrease with age. This is partially why older athletes tend to heal slower and often struggle to develop and maintain muscle mass.

Diuretics are primarily used by athletes to assist in weight loss. Diuretics operate by inducing the kidneys to release more salt and water into the body's urine. When high levels of salt are present in the body, it causes fluid buildup in the blood vessels. Such buildup, in turn, causes blood pressure to increase. Although diuretics were intended as a mechanism to lower blood pressure, athletes use them to cut weight as well as to mask the presence of other substances. Diuretics operate to assist in the weight loss process by reducing the amount of water in the body. Professional athletes in combat sports like mixed martial arts (MMA), wrestling, and boxing often use diuretics as a weight-control method to qualify for their relevant weight class.

At the same time, diuretics can function as masking agents because they flush the body of fluids. This lowers the concentration of performance-enhancing agents and makes it more difficult to test for unauthorized substances via urine testing. Masking agents can thus "cover up" an individual's consumption of a banned substance. The most common type of masking agent is a diuretic. Other types of masking agents include probenecid, which specifically reduces the concentration of anabolic steroids in urine, and plasma expanders, which conceal evidence of blood doping.

Athletes use stimulants to increase attentiveness, increase alertness, and reduce tiredness. Stimulants operate by increasing the level of dopamine in the brain. Dopamine is a neurotransmitter that controls brain functions including pleasure, movement, and attention. Caffeine is largely regarded as the most prevalent stimulant. While stimulants are not as detrimental to the body as their other performance-enhancing counterparts, there is a growing interest in regulating them because they can lead to dehydration, muscle cramps, dizziness, or possibly death.

5.2. History of Laws Regulating PEDs in Professional Sports

In the 1970s it was well known that professional athletes were using steroids to gain competitive advantages. As a response in 1981, Congress amended the Food, Drug, and

Cosmetic Act to require a physician's prescription for steroid use. The amendment also assigned oversight of steroids to the Food and Drug Administration (FDA). Congress believed its amendment would limit access to steroids to those persons who possessed a proper prescription. It did not fully appreciate that a significant black market existed for the sale and purchase of steroids or that steroid users would use them for nonmedical purposes. When Congress finally recognized the severity and complexity of steroid usage, and that steroids posed a risk to children, it passed Anti-Drug Abuse Act of 1988. This act criminalized the unlawful distribution or possession of steroids. Although steroids were illegal after 1988, they were not defined as "controlled substances" under the Controlled Substance Act (CSA). As a result, the mechanism for enforcement was limited. Defining a substance as a "controlled substance" subjects it to enforcement by the DEA, which enhances enforcement capacity. Classification as a controlled substance also encourages individual states to create statutes that criminalize the same conduct, thereby adding additional enforcement mechanisms at the state level. To remedy the problem of limited enforcement, Congress began to explore the possibility of reclassifying steroids as "controlled substances. . . ." The critical issue that Congress had to overcome was evidence, or lack thereof: to this day, there is no peer-reviewed evidence proving the existence of physical or psychological dependence with steroids, and thus steroids do not meet the necessary criteria for classification as "controlled substances." For this reason, the FDA, the DEA, the National Institute on Drug Abuse, and the American Medical Association (AMA) strongly opposed Congress's desire to classify steroids as controlled substances. In light of the discontent of these agencies, and the definitional limitations of the CSA, Congress recognized that it had to act. As a result, Congress passed the Anabolic Steroid Control Act (1990), which defined anabolic steroids as Schedule III drugs—that is, substances that have a medically acceptable use and pose only a moderate risk of addiction or abuse—under the CSA. Finally, in 2004 Congress amended and expanded the scope of the CSA to redefine the definition of anabolic steroids by eliminating the requirement that a substance improve muscle growth. In addition, the 2004 amendments brought certain "precursors," which are substances that turn into full active hormones at a later point in the body, within the definition of an anabolic steroid.

5.3. Legal Issues Involving PEDs in Professional Sports

This is where the law and the intersection of PEDs get interesting. Consider the following hypothetical: you are watching Monday Night football and the game is in the middle of the fourth quarter. The home team is down ten points and the ball is on the forty-yard line. It is third and ten and both teams realize that this is a critical point in the game. The home team must convert a first a down or score a touchdown if it has any hope of pulling out the victory. As the home team breaks the huddle and lines up, the quarterback notices the middle linebacker hedging toward the line of scrimmage. This movement indicates that a blitz is forthcoming, as it suggests that the middle of the field will be open. To take advantage of this opportunity, the quarterback calls an audible signaling his top receiver to run a slant route across the middle of the field. Thereafter, the quarterback yells "hike" to initiate the play and exactly as the quarterback suspected, the linebacker blitzes and the middle of the field is wide open. The receiver's route takes him to precisely where the quarterback audibled him to go and immediately the quarterback releases a beautifully placed ball that hits the receiver in full stride.

However, the quarterback fails to notice the strong safety sitting in short zone coverage. After the receiver catches the ball, the safety launches himself, helmet first, and slams his helmet into the unsuspecting receiver's helmet. The receiver fumbles the ball and he is knocked out cold. Another defender from the visiting team picks up the ball and runs it in for a touchdown, sealing the victory for the visiting team.

In the midst of the visiting team's celebration, the receiver continues to lay motionless on the ground. After the receiver is carted off the field by the medical staff, it is learned that the safety's hit paralyzed the receiver and that the receiver's career has ended—he will never play the game he loves again nor will he ever walk. The instant replay clearly reflects that a targeting penalty should have been called because of the safety's helmet-to-helmet contact. It is also learned that the safety tested positive for PEDs and has been using them for the past two seasons. Prior to using the drugs he weighed 180 pounds and was a third string safety that rarely played. But after approximately two years of PED usage, he transformed himself into a 220-pound monster who is substantially bigger, faster and stronger. Given these facts, what is the likelihood that the receiver could successfully sue over his injuries given that the PEDs likely contributed to those injuries? Could the receiver sue his team or the safety's team?

This scenario presents several interesting legal issues. While some may be inclined to argue that the receiver assumed the risk of injury by playing a violent sport, other readers may perceive that the PEDs created a risk that was not naturally within the scope of the game. After all, the play should have resulted in a penalty and PEDs are both illegal and prohibited by the NFL's policies. However, before this question can thoroughly be answered, consider the relevant case law and scholarly commentary on this issue.

To establish a viable tort claim for sport injuries in professional sports, there are three independent theories that plaintiffs have relied upon: negligence, recklessness, and intentional conduct.

The Restatement (Second) of Torts thoroughly explains how reckless misconduct differs from both negligent and intentional misconduct. In regard to the distinction between reckless and negligent misconduct, it provides that reckless misconduct:

> differs from that form of negligence which consists in mere inadvertence, incompetence, unskillfulness, or a failure to take precautions to enable the actor adequately to cope with a possible or probable future emergency, in that reckless misconduct requires a conscious choice of a course of action, either with knowledge of the serious danger to others involved in it or with knowledge of facts which would disclose this danger to any reasonable man. It differs not only from the above-mentioned form of negligence, but also from that negligence which consists in intentionally doing an act with knowledge that it contains a risk of harm to others, in that the actor

> to be reckless must recognize that his conduct involves a risk substantially greater in amount than that which is necessary to make his conduct negligent. The difference between reckless misconduct and conduct involving only such a quantum of risk as is necessary to make it negligent is a difference in the degree of the risk, but this difference of degree is so marked as to amount substantially to a difference in kind.
>
> (Restatement (Second) of Torts, 1965)

Furthermore, reckless misconduct also differs from intentional misconduct.

> While an act to be reckless must be intended by the actor, the actor does not intend to cause the harm which results from it. It is enough that he realizes or, from facts which he knows, should realize that there is a strong probability that harm may result, even though he hopes or even expects that his conduct will prove harmless. However, a strong probability is a different thing from the substantial certainty without which he cannot be said to intend the harm in which his act results.
>
> (Restatement (Second) of Torts, 1965)

More clearly, reckless conduct exists where the actor intends to do harm but does not fully appreciate the magnitude of the resulting harm. In contrast, intentional conduct requires that the actor have the specific intent to cause harm or, more generally, that the actor acted with substantially certainty that harm would occur. In some regard, recklessness, because of its reduced focus on the resulting harm, may be perceived as a lesser included act of intent.

Generally, courts have been unwilling to allow plaintiffs to prevail in professional sport torts cases based on the negligence standard. This is mainly because of the doctrine of assumption of the risk, which generally refers to acceptance of inherent risks in an activity. While assumption of risk operates as a valid defense in cases involving negligence, it does not apply in cases of reckless or intentional conduct. The primary reason that assumption of the risk is a valid defense in professional sports negligence cases is that these activities pose an elevated degree of difficulty, competition and, more importantly, danger. As a result, it is—and should be—more difficult to prove the necessary breach of duty to establish negligence.

To illustrate, in *Turcotte v. Fell*, the court accepted the defendant's assumption of the risk defense because the defendant was negligent—at best—and because there was no evidence of reckless or intentional misconduct. In *Turcotte*, the plaintiff, a professional jockey, was injured after the defendant, also a jockey, violated a track rule by riding into the plaintiff's lane of travel. This caused the plaintiff to fall from his horse and resulted in injuries that left him paraplegic. Later, the plaintiff sued the defendant as well as the track owner who the plaintiff alleged failed to properly maintain the track. The court dismissed both claims, holding that that the defense of assumption of the risk was available to the defendants since there was no evidence of intentional or reckless conduct. While the court agreed that the defendant jockey violated a track rule by "riding foul," the court held that such conduct was within the realm of the sport. The court highlighted that horse racing, by its nature, is an inherently dangerous sport considering the massive size of the horses. The court also cited the small stature of the jockey, the history of injury the jockey's experience, and the difficulty of controlling the horses. Given these reasons, the court reasoned that the plaintiff had assumed the risk. In regard to the track owner, the court also dismissed that claim because the plaintiff testified that he was aware of the conditions and had never ridden on a track that did not have the condition for which he complained. In addition, the jockey admitted that he had observed the track condition before the race that caused his injury.

While courts rarely apply the negligence standard, evidence of intentional conduct—though often difficult to prove—is a legitimate basis to establish a professional sports tort. To gain an appreciation for the extent of conduct that is necessary to establish intentional conduct, consider the 2003 case of *Marcus Williams v. Bill Romanowski*. This case is largely regarded as one of the first cases to allow a professional athlete to recover in tort for intentional conduct (assault and battery). In this case, two NFL players got into an altercation after a play ended during a training camp team scrimmage. Williams, a tight end, had blocked Romanowski, a linebacker, during the course of a play. After the play, the Romanowski ripped off Williams's helmet and punched him in the face. The punch caused Williams substantial injuries including a concussion, shattered eye socket, chipped tooth, and depression. According to Williams, this incident led to the end of his NFL playing career. Williams filed suit against Romanowski, requesting in excess of $3 million. He alleged that Romanowski's conduct was outside the scope of the game.

Several players testified in *Williams v. Romanowski* that fighting during training camp was a common occurrence and that scuffles happened rather frequently. In opposition, Williams introduced testimony from a team representative that indicated that while fights occurred, the nature of the defendant's attack was unlike anything he had ever observed. Williams also sought to introduce evidence of Romanowski's alleged steroid abuse to establish that his conduct was a function of "roid rage" but the court denied it. Ultimately, the jury found for the plaintiff and awarded him $340,000, of which $300,000 constituted lost wages and remainder reflected medical bills. However, the jury rejected the plaintiff's claim for emotional and punitive damages. Williams considered appealing or seeking a new trial but ultimately settled the case in exchange for another $75,000. In total, Williams received $415,000.

In determining liability in the context of sports related torts, the majority of courts apply the recklessness standard. In fact, the recklessness standard can be perceived as a middle ground between negligence and intentional conduct. In defining the contours of the negligence standard, *Nabozny v. Barnhill* and *Hackbart v. Cincinnati Bengals, Inc.* are the two most frequently discussed cases on this issue. *Nabozny* involved a soccer game. In it, the defendant kicked the plaintiff in the head, severely injuring him, while the plaintiff was in a "penalty area" that restricted any contact to the plaintiff's person. The witnesses testified that the incident could have been avoided because it was clear that the plaintiff was in the penalty area and that the defendant had ample time to stop his motion. The plaintiff brought suit and the trial court directed verdict in the defendant's favor. The court of appeals, however, reversed and remanded, holding that the proper standard was that of recklessness. The court reasoned that athletes in competition owe each other a duty to refrain from conduct prohibited by the applicable safety rules of the game. In determining whether such duty has been breached a player may be found liable when he or she engaged in conduct that revealed deliberate or reckless disregard for the safety of the other player and caused injury to that other player. Although *Nabozny* involved amateur athletes, its legal analysis is consistently applied in the context of professional sports torts.

Along with *Nabozny, Hackbart* is probably the most widely cited case applying the recklessness standard. In *Hackbart*, the plaintiff, a defensive player, was struck in the back of the head by the defendant, an offensive player, after one of the plaintiff's teammates intercepted a pass from the defendant's quarterback. At trial it was established that the defendant was acting out of anger and frustration, and that he intended to hit the plaintiff but without a specific intent to injure. According to the defendant, he delivered the blow because he knew that the interception meant that his team would lose the game. Although the defendant's actions should have resulted in a penalty, one was not called because the referees did not see the incident. After the game ended, the plaintiff experienced neck pain but continued to play for the next two weeks until he finally learned that he had a serious neck fracture. Thereafter, he brought suit against the defendant. The district court judge ruled in favor of the defendant based on the premise that football is a physical sport and noted that injuries—even intentional ones—are a part of the game, and by playing the sport the plaintiff assumed the risk and/or contributed to the harm. Moreover, the trial court judge reasoned that it is unlikely that social values against violence would be furthered by holding the defendant liable since football itself is inherently dangerous. It was also the trial judge's opinion that the proper remedy for the defendant's conduct was not through use of the court system but through NFL penalties and suspensions. The circuit court disagreed with the trial court's ruling, holding that recklessness was the proper standard and that the facts of the case should be judged against that standard. The court opined that the defendant:

> admittedly acted impulsively and in the heat of anger, and even though it could be said from the admitted facts that he intended the act, it could also be said that he did not intend to inflict serious injury which resulted from the blow which he struck. In ruling that recklessness is the appropriate standard and that assault and battery is not the exclusive one, we are saying that these two liability concepts are not necessarily opposed one to the other. Rather, recklessness . . . might be regarded, for the purpose of analysis at least, a lesser included act. Assault and battery then call for an intent, as does recklessness. But in recklessness the intent is to do the act, but without an intent to cause the particular harm. It is enough if the actor knows that there is a strong probability that harm will result. Thus, the definition fits perfectly the fact situation here. Surely, then, no reason exists to compel appellant to employ the assault and battery standard which does not comfortably apply fully in preference to the standard which meets this fact situation.
>
> (*Hackbart*, 601 F.2d at 524–525).

The circuit court did not reject the possibility that the defendant could be liable for assault and battery. Instead, it reasoned that the facts of the case may give rise to a showing of recklessness and, pursuant to that standard, proof of an intent to cause harm is not material to a finding of liability.

A player may also choose to sue a professional sports team. Lawsuits against teams must overcome additional hurdles. Specifically, these suits are limited by three constraints: (1) workers' compensation laws, (2) collective bargaining agreements (CBAs), and (3) vicarious liability limitations.

First, pursuant to the "no fault system," workers' compensation laws generally prohibit employees from suing their employer unless there is evidence of intentional misconduct or fraud. As noted earlier, professional athletes are employees of the teams for which they play. As part of that arrangement, employers pay to provide workers' compensation insurance as an exclusive means of redress for most types of work-related injuries. In exchange, employers are exempt from work injury lawsuits. In order for a professional athlete to bypass this limitation, he or she would have the difficult task of establishing intentional or fraudulent conduct.

Second, CBAs tend to contain language that bars player lawsuits against teams. Since CBA are contracts and are normally negotiated by competent and sophisticated parties, courts are usually willing to enforce the terms and conditions of the CBAs rather than allow the parties to use state tort law. All three of the CBAs discussed in this chapter have provisions that require that disputes between players and teams be settled via binding arbitration. Therefore, any limitation on the extent of recovery or the remedies available to a player will be governed by the terms and conditions of the CBA and not the courts.

Finally, if a player seeks to hold another team liable for the tortious conduct of one of its players, the limitations associated with *respondeat superior* will apply. Pursuant to this doctrine, a master (employer) is not liable for the tortious conduct of its servants (employees) unless the servant's conduct is considered to be within the scope of employment. Generally, intentional torts are not considered to be within the scope. Given these limitations, this type of liability seldom applies.

Then again, *Tomjanovich v. California Sports, Inc.* is one of the few cases where a player of one team was able to hold another team liable for the acts of its players. In *Tomjanovich*, the plaintiff, NBA player Rudy Tomjanovich, was punched by Kermit Washington, a player on the defendant team (Lakers), after Tomjanovich tried to break up a fight between one of his teammates and a Lakers player. As a result of the punch, Tomjanovich suffered fractures to his nose, jaw, and skull as well as facial lacerations, a concussion, loss of blood, and a detached retina. Tomjanovich brought suit against the Lakers, alleging that the team was liable for his injuries based on the doctrines of vicarious liability and negligence. To establish these claims, Tomjanovich introduced evidence that established that the Lakers encouraged violent behavior. Evidence also showed that the Lakers paid fines for players who engaged in violent conduct, encouraged the perpetrator's conduct by labeling him an enforcer, and failed to discipline Washington for his actions against Tomjanovich. In response, the Lakers argued that the plaintiff assumed the risk because Tomjanovich was aware that physical altercations were a part of the game and because Tomjanovich interjected himself into the physical altercation. The court rejected the Lakers' defense and ruled that Tomjanovich's evidence was sufficient to establish that Washington's conduct was within the scope of his employment. In addition, the court reasoned that the Lakers were independently negligent because they promoted, encouraged, and ratified Washington's conduct. In essence, the court applied the negligence theory but rejected the Lakers' assumption of the risk or contributory negligence defense.

At this point we can now analyze the hypothetical posed at the beginning of this section. In summary, it would be difficult to hold the safety or his team liable for the receiver's injuries. First, it is unlikely that the receiver can prevail under a negligence standard because most courts do not apply it in the context of sports torts. Further, and more important, it is highly likely that the receiver assumed the risk by engaging in the sport—a sport that is consistently identified as an extremely dangerous activity. There is a compelling argument that the facts of the hypothetical fit squarely into the facts of *Turcotte* which would necessitate a similar outcome that prohibits the receiver's suit. Both cases involved a clear violation of the rules of the sport. Nonetheless, it is unlikely that this fact alone would be sufficient to establish liability since the violation occurred within the scope of the game. There was no evidence that the hypothetical football safety or that the defendant in *Turcotte* intentionally or maliciously disregarded the rules of the game. In fact, the evidence suggests that the defendants in both cases were merely acting to secure a competitive advantage without a desire to injure or violate the rules of either sport. The only extenuating factor that is present in the hypothetical and not in *Turcotte* is the PED issue. While PED usage might militate in favor of holding the safety liable, it is unlikely to work based on the assumption of the risk defense. By all accounts, PEDs are widely used in the major sports leagues, including the NFL. As such, even though such use is specifically prohibited, the receiver was probably aware or should have been aware of the rampant use of steroids by NFL players. Thus his continued participation could be perceived as his assumption of the risk of injury or as his own contributory fault.

Second, while the recklessness and intentional standards are not limited by the assumption of the risk defense, these standards are substantially more difficult to establish. Given the level of proof courts require to establish the intentional standard, as evidenced by *Romanowski*, it is unlikely that the receiver could establish an intentional tort. The hit that the safety executed in the hypothetical was not specifically executed to injure the receiver. Moreover there is no evidence that the safety acted with a substantial certainty that serious injury would occur on the play. An even more tenuous argument would be that steroid use itself was the intentional act that caused the receiver's harm. As noted previously, the intentional act in *Romanowski* was a punch, an act that is substantially more connected to the victimized player's injuries than using PEDs. It is clear that a punch is specifically designed to cause harm whereas PEDs are used to gain a competitive advantage. Athletes use PEDs to make them run faster, jump higher, act quicker, and heal more efficiently, not necessarily to physically injure fellow competitors. Given this critical distinction, it is unlikely that the receiver could establish an intentional tort.

A better argument for the hypothetical receiver would be one that focuses on the concept of recklessness. The holdings from *Nabozny* and *Hackbart* would offer the receiver the greatest chance of recovery. In both of these cases, as well as in the hypothetical, the plaintiffs' injuries occurred within the context of the game after an illegal act by the defendant. In both *Nabozny* and *Hackbart*, the defendants could have avoided their respective rule violations. Also, it was obvious to both defendants that a harm outside the scope of the game would result. In *Nabozny*, the act was a kick to the plaintiff's head while the plaintiff was in an area where the defendant knew contact was prohibited. In *Hackbart*, the act was an elbow to the back of the plaintiff's head while the plaintiff was on both knees, with his back turned, in a defenseless position. Similarly, in the hypothetical, the act was an illegal helmet-to-helmet hit against a defenseless receiver. However, this is where the similarities end. There is no evidence in the hypothetical that the safety had any appreciation for the risk that he was creating with tackle. Therefore, again, the plaintiff's claim might fail.

The hypothetical receiver's best argument is that the safety's use of steroids should be a factor in evaluating whether the safety's conduct was reckless. Although the U.S. Court of Appeals for the Tenth Circuit overturned the district court's decision in *Hackbart*, there is language from the district court judge's opinion that sheds insight into the perception of football at the time the case was adjudicated. Specifically, the district court judge reasoned that, "in the case of football it was questionable whether social values would be improved by limiting the violence." While professional football continues to be a violent sport, there seems to be some retrenchment on the notion of violence. For example, since *Hackbart* was decided, the NFL has enacted rules prohibiting helmet-to-helmet contact, requiring sideline concussion protocols, and stopping game play when a runner's helmet comes off. When *Hackbart* was decided almost forty years ago, no one could have anticipated that the NFL would enact these types of safety regulations. At the time, violence was a welcomed, desired, and expected part of the professional football experience. However, the traumatic and debilitating experiences that numerous retired NFL players have faced in recent years has forced the NFL to recognize the need to make the game safer. In fact, modern social values require it. Given this evolution, the court system might be willing to consider PEDs as a factor in player injury litigation—thereby increasing the possibility of liability in the context of sports torts. Interestingly, the plaintiff in *Hackbart* tried to introduce evidence of the defendant's steroid usage to establish the defendant's violent nature. The court denied the evidence on grounds it would be prejudicial. As such, the rules of evidence could also operate as an obstacle to introducing evidence of PEDs as a factor in whether recklessness has been established.

6. Conclusion

As this chapter highlights, drugs in professional sports create issues that affect a host of legal concerns. In addressing these concerns, the modern lawyer must possess a comprehensive understanding of the social perspective on drug usage, a knowledge of the medical and scientific manner that drugs affect the body, a gauge for the political climate regarding current and future regulation, and an appreciation for the financial and safety dynamics at play.

References

Bigger, Faster, Stronger. (2008). Christopher Bell, director. Magnolia. DVD.

Brain Research Institute. (2017). "What Is CTE?" Available at www.protectthebrain.org/Brain-Injury-Research/What-is-CTE-.aspx. Last visited January 30, 2017.

Campos, I. (2012). *Home Grown: Marijuana and the Origin of Mexico's War on Drugs* (Chapel Hill: University of North Carolina Press).

Danaher, J. (2012). "Doping and Competitive Advantage: Chwang's Argument (Part One)." Available at http://philosophicaldisquisitions.blogspot.com/2012/10/doping-and-competitive-advantage.html.

Enforcement Guidance. (2005). "Disability-Related Inquiries and Medical Examinations of Employees Under the Americans With Disabilities Act." Available at www.eeoc.gov/policy/docs/guidance-inquiries.html.

Hayakawa, K., Mishima, Kenichi, and Fujiwara, Michihiro. (2010). "Therapeutic Potential of Non-Psychotropic Cannabidiol in Ischemic Stroke." *Pharmaceuticals* 3: 2197–2212.

Mandell, N. (2014, November 24). "Adam Silver on Marijuana Use in the NBA." *USA Today*. Available at http://ftw.usatoday.com/2014/11/adam-silver-marijuana.

Restatement (Second) of Torts § 500 cmt. f (Am. Law Inst. 1965).

Restatement (Second) of Torts § 500 cmt. g (Am. Law Inst. 1965).

Strauss, C. (2014, January 23). "Goodell: NFL Would Consider Allowing Medical Marijuana." *USA Today*. Available at www.usatoday.com/story/sports/nfl/2014/01/23/commissioner-roger-goodell-marijuana/4797267/.

Cases

Coats v. Dish Network, 350 P.3d 849 (Colo. 2015)

Fibreboard Paper Prods. Corp. v. NLRB, 379 U.S. 203 (1964).

Hackbart v. Cincinnati Bengals, Inc., 601 F.2d 516 (10th Cir.1979), *cert. denied*, 444 U.S. 931 (1979).

Johnson Bateman Co., 295 N.L.R.B. 180 (1989).

Marijuana Rescheduling Petition, Docket No. 86-22. In re (1988).

Minneapolis Star Tribune, 295 N.L.R.B. 543 (1989).

Nabozny v. Barnhill, 334 N.E.2d 258 (Ill. App. 1975).

Williams v. Romanowski

Tomjanovich v. California Sports, Inc., No. H-78 243, 1979 WL 210977 (S.D. Tex. Oct. 10, 1979).

Turcotte v. Fell, 502 N.E.2d 964, 970 (N.Y. 1986).

CHAPTER 7

BLOOD SPORTS IN AN AGE OF LIABILITY

JEFFREY STANDEN

1. Introduction

Blood sports involve combat. The aim of the contest is to injure one's opponent, to beat him into submission, or even at times to kill. Blood sports can be usefully separated into three categories: human versus human contests, human versus animal sports, and animal versus animal fighting. For over a century, blood sports have been under both social and legal attack, to the point where most of the historic forms of combat have been prohibited by law worldwide, or significantly modified to improve safety. Many traditional human-against-human contests, such as bare-knuckle boxing, cudgels, swords, and wrestling, have been banned or sharply regulated. One contemporaneous newspaper account, recorded in Gorn's book, provides a startling description of what is said to be the first death in America from the blood sport, resulting from a bare-knuckle contest between fighters Lilly and McCoy. The account is also suggestive of why prohibitions arose.

> Round 70th—McCoy was now indeed a most unseemly object: both eyes were black—the left one near closed, and indeed that whole cheek presented a shocking appearance. His very forehead was black and blue; his lips were swollen to an incredible size, and the blood streamed profusely down his chest. My heart sickened at the sorry sight. When he came up he appeared very weak, and almost gasping for breath, and endeavored, while squaring away, to eject the clotting fluid from his throat.
>
> (Gorn, 2010, p. 75)

According to Gorn, McCoy's seconds, all with large wagers on their man, refused to concede the fight, as did McCoy. Over the course of the contest, McCoy was knocked down eighty times. At the end of the last round, McCoy collapsed and died, having drowned in his own blood. The fight lasted for two hours and forty-one minutes. This fatality, reportedly the first in America from the new sport, drew public outrage, even as the contemporary public, remarkably, demanded more fights. As a result of public outcry, bare-knuckle fighting has evolved into modern gloved boxing, featuring more sensible, safer rules of combat.

For blood sports where humans square off against animals, such as bull fighting and fox hunting, social opprobrium has combined with legal restrictions to diminish the frequency and impact of the spectacle. Although certain human-animal blood sports remain prevalent, such as hunting and fishing, in nearly all circumstances the blood sport is today closely regulated to manage wildlife populations, protect endangered species, preclude unnecessary wounding or animal discomfort, and promote safety. Animal-versus-animal combat sports bear near-universal condemnation and legal prohibition. Today, for example, cock fighting is illegal in every U.S. state, with Louisiana being the last to have enacted a ban in 2007. Thirty-three states have made this crime a felony, and in forty states it is illegal even to spectate at a cockfight. Dog fighting is illegal in all U.S. states. Yet animal-versus-animal combat reportedly continues both in the United States and worldwide, in most places underground. Bear baiting and other gruesome animal contests seem to have disappeared entirely. With a few exceptions, the disturbing images of animals or humans fighting to a brutal conclusion, including death, have been relegated to the past or to the margins of society.

Nonetheless, a popular taste for violent sports seems to persist. Today, along with the remnants of the historic blood sports, some cousins or descendants of blood sports remain prominent. Mixed martial arts (MMA), a modern variant of human fighting where combatants fight until voluntary submission or incapacity, has emerged and appears vibrant. Although at times bloody, the rules of the contest limit the blows and strikes combatants may employ, precluding hair pulling, eye gouging, strikes to the spine or back of the head, kneeing a downed opponent, and so forth. A referee is present in the ring to stop fights when necessary. Modern boxing is similarly subject to rules that restrict fighter strikes, equipment, preparation, and eligibility, and it is governed by regional or national boxing commissions or other boards of control. Hunting or fishing for sport, as mentioned, is restricted by regional authorities that stipulate seasons, define prey, prohibit certain equipment, limit catch-totals, and at times even prohibit harvesting certain animals altogether.

Speaking generally, blood sports have devolved in status from popular to prohibited due to a combination of forces. Social disfavor loomed large, stemming from a growing awareness of the value of human life, an enlightened appreciation of animal suffering, and an increased consciousness of the coarsening effect of blood sports on community sentiment. Legislative and regulatory responses were paramount, as well. One additional, and sometimes overlooked, agent in this sweeping development has been judicial action. Civil liability assessments and criminal convictions have been crucial in inducing changes in legality. Chronologically, legislative prohibitions typically followed liability assessments. Thus it was the courts, and not usually the legislative lawmakers, that were the leading players in the eventual regulation or prohibition of blood sports.

2. Violent Sports Today

Although the historical blood sports have been nearly eliminated, the sporting public's taste for violence apparently persists. Combat sports have been mostly supplanted by contact sports. Today, the most popular violent sports are contact sports such as American football, ice hockey, MMA, boxing, and wrestling. With respect to football, although it is not a combat sport, and thus not a blood sport, it presents the most visible modern expression of a blood sport, with its "gladiatorial" heritage, regular physical violence, and recurrent bodily injuries, which sometimes included death during football's formative years. Football has in recent decades been the most popular of American sports, filling stadia and broadcast schedules with both amateur (collegiate) and professional games.

In one salient fact, modern contact sports mirror the historical blood sports. Like their violent predecessors, contact sports involve physical blows to the body, and often result in injuries that are different or beyond what people confront in normal life. Few ordinary pursuits in life, for example, involve the risk of concussive head injury that is common in organized football. Because of the comparative violence and the injuries participants sustain, certain contact sports are becoming increasingly controversial. They generate controversy for reasons similar to blood sports. In a further parallel, a small yet noticeable emergence of civil liability claims portends that today's contact sports, which exist at the violent end of the spectrum of popular sports, might suffer the same fate as the blood sports, with civil damages leading eventually to legislative prohibition or regulation.

Lawsuits brought during the blood sport era often involved claims by combatants against fellow combatants. These suits formed the basis for the eventual demise of the combat sport on the generalized grounds of "public policy." For example, in *Bell v. Hansley*, the court stated, "[o]ne may recover in an action for assault and battery, although he agreed to fight with his adversary; for such agreement to break the peace [is] void . . . ." Other courts were more explicit. The court in *Logan v. Austin* stated that, "[p]ublic policy will not authorize one man to beat another, although he consent to it, as it is against morality, and might lead to a violation of the public peace . . . ." Criminal prosecutions for bare-knuckle fighting were also common. In *Regina v. Lewis*, the opinion stated that "no one is justified in striking another, except it be in self-defence; and it ought to be known, that, whenever two persons go out to strike each other, and do so, each is guilty of an assault" (875). Some courts, such as the Supreme Court of Ohio in *Champer v. State*, were more lenient. "[A]n indictment against A, for an assault and battery upon B., is not sustained by evidence that A. assaulted and beat B. in a fight at fisticuffs, by agreement between them" (437).

Today's lawsuits that stem from injuries suffered in contact sports are nearly always brought by former players seeking redress. These suits typically target league owners or event organizers. This is not a new phenomenon. Event organizers or game owners have long been defendants in suits brought by players, as have other players. Even modern players have also been defendants in the rare criminal case. Nonetheless, the modern suits are distinguishable in nature from the historic suits arising out of bare-knuckle fighting. The bare-knuckle fighters brought lawsuits for injuries that were a direct and anticipated consequence of their sport: in other words, a fighter suing for injuries to his head was in effect suing for damages he would fairly anticipate occurring, and thus stemmed directly from his decision to engage in the sport. In contrast, modern suits, at least until recently, alleged injuries that resulted not from the ordinary course of play but rather from activity that was either directly prohibited by the rules of the sport or from injuries suffered from violence that occurred during stoppages in play. In other words, these modern suits did not seek compensation for injuries from the sport itself but for extra-legal or extraneous conduct. As such, these suits did not pose an existential threat to the sport.

3. Criminal Prosecutions

In *Regina v. Green* and *Regina v. Maki*, two criminal prosecutions that arose from a single exchange of prohibited stick slashes to the head during an exhibition hockey game, both players involved in the altercation were prosecuted. The stick slashes were specifically prohibited by the rules of the sport; the prosecutions arose from conduct that transgressed what the rules permit, and thus arguably beyond the contact to which an athlete could be deemed to have consented. Most criminal prosecutions and private lawsuits that arise from contact sports similarly involved conduct or contact specifically prohibited by the rules of the game.

It is interesting that the judges in the *Green* and *Maki* cases shared different perspectives on the same incident. Said the judge in the *Green* case:

> There is no doubt that the players who enter the hockey arena consent to a great number of assaults on their person, because the game of hockey as it is played in the National Hockey League, which is the league I am dealing with, could not possibly be played at the speed at which it is played and with the force and vigour with which it is played, and with the competition that enters into it, unless there were a great number of what would in normal circumstances be called assaults, but which are not heard of. No hockey player enters on to the ice of the National Hockey League without consenting and without knowledge of the possibility that he is going to be hit in one of many ways once he is on that ice (594).

The judge in the *Maki* decision had a different view: "[T]here is a question of degree involved, and no athlete should be presumed to accept malicious, unprovoked or overly violent attack" (782).

Similarly, in a criminal prosecution arising out football, the court in the 1976 opinion in *People v. Freer* held that an athletic participant could not legally consent to an "overly violent" activity, stating that "there is a limit to the magnitude and dangerousness of a blow to which another is deemed to consent" (978). The conviction stemmed from a football game in which the victim, a defensive player, punched the ball carrier while tackling him. This initial punch, the court ruled, was properly consented to, since using a punching motion while tackling in the game of football is part of the game. After the rough tackle, as the play drew to a close, the ball carrier punched the tackler back. This second punch gave rise to the criminal prosecution, where the court denied the defendant the opportunity to present evidence of consent as a defense. Instead, the court ruled, as a matter of law, that the participants could not consent to an "overly violent" attack of this kind.

> Initially it may be assumed that the very first punch thrown by the complainant in the course of the tackle was consented to by defendant. The act of tackling an opponent in the course of a football game may often involve "contact" that could easily be interpreted to be a "punch." Defendant's response after the pileup to complainant's initial act of "aggression" cannot be mistaken. Clearly, defendant intended to punch complainant. This was not a consented to act (978).

The court reasoned that "any attack which the defendant may have believed was being made upon him was terminated by the pileup which ensued after the initial contact between the [victim] and the defendant at the time of the tackle" (979). Thus the judge drew a careful distinction between contact that occurred as part of the game's play and conduct that was permitted by rule or, here, at least appeared to be legal, and that which occurred subsequent to the referee's whistle or the normal conclusion of play. Thus, the *Freer* decision suggests that there is a limit to the type of blow to which a party will be deemed to have consented, even in a violent sports contest in which the consent to participate is otherwise valid or legal.

The contention that the injuring contact involved a transgression of the known rules of the sport, or its customs, or occurred after the play had ceased, is common. In *State v. Shelley*, the court stated that athletes are deemed to have consented to both the injury and the conduct that led to it that are the "reasonably foreseeable hazards of joint participation in an athletic contest" (490). The fact that the injurious contact may constitute a penalty or foul under the rules of the game does not necessarily render the conduct beyond justification under the consent defense. The trial court reasoned, "consent is to contact that is contemplated within the rules of the game and that is incidental to the furtherance of the goals of that particular game" (491). On appeal, the court declined to limit consent to what is contemplated by the rules or goals of the game, instead holding that "[c]ertain excesses and inconveniences are to be expected beyond the formal rules of the game," and that consent is formed by the players' reasonably foreseeable hazards of joint participation in a lawful athletic contest. . . ." (492). Nonetheless, the appellate court upheld the ruling that the defendant's conduct, involving a punch to the opponent's face, exceeded the scope of consent.

4. Civil Suits

Modern civil suits arising from contact sports similarly involved injuries stemming from play or contact that violated the rules of the sport, either before or subsequent to stoppages in play. With respect to suits against co-combatants, the tort defense of assumption of risk was often stricken, on the grounds that people could not consent to conduct that involved a breach of the peace. The reasoning of the North Carolina court in the 1821 civil suit *Stout v. Wren*, which arose from a bare-knuckle boxing match, is as instructive as any other. "A man shall not recover a recompense for an injury received by his own consent, provided the act from which the injury is received be lawful; but where two fight by consent, and one is beaten, he may recover damages for the injury, because fighting is an unlawful act" (420). A more recent suit pitting participants against each other is illustrated by the *Ordway* litigation, from 1988 in California. There, veteran horse jockey Judy Casella was thrown from her horse during a race and badly injured when her mount rolled over her. Casella's horse had stumbled after becoming entangled with another horse whose jockey violated a race rule by "crossing over without sufficient clearance, causing interference," for which violation the jockey was later suspended. The court dismissed Casella's suit on the grounds that she had assumed the risk of her fall, even though it resulted from the breach of a rule by a competitor. "Routine rule violations," the court reasoned, are common occurrences and thus within "the parameters of the athletes' expectations" (544). Only where a competitor's misconduct was obviously outside the normal expectations of participants in the sport is liability appropriate. Civil liability between competitors does not ordinarily attach for mere negligence on the part of a player but instead requires recklessness or intentional conduct (*Kabella v. Bouschelle*; *Ross v. Clouser*).

Despite the reluctance of courts to hold co-competitors liable in civil suits founded on negligence, numerous judicial decisions assess liability against other actors pertinent to the sports contest on a mere allegation of negligence. Civil liability for negligence has been assessed in lawsuits alleging that the game equipment or playing conditions were unsafe. *Ashcroft v. Calder Race Course, Inc.* held that a horse jockey did not assume the risk of a negligently located exit gap on the racetrack. Suits have been brought raising allegations of negligence or product liability concerning football helmets, baseball bats, hockey helmets, trampoline springs, and many other pieces of playing equipment. Nonetheless, suits alleging negligence in field preparation or conditions often fail on a theory of assumption of risk. For example, an outfielder injured while playing baseball on a wet field was denied recovery on the ground that he was aware of the obvious risk and consented to play in the game (*Maddox v. City of New York*). A baseball player was denied recovery by his assuming the risk of playing the game on a baseball field with visible ruts and depressions (*Zachardy v. Geneva College*). Similarly, a tennis professional assumed the risk of playing on a court with imperfections in the surface (*Heldman v. Uniroyal, Inc.*).

Negligence suits and product liability actions arising from sports also pose difficult problems of establishing causation. For instance, in *Testerman v. Riddell*, a football player alleged that the manufacturer's representative fitted him with undersized shoulder pads, leading to a serious injury. The suit was dismissed for failure to establish causation. The injury, stated the court, could have resulted from an opponent's blow or from contact with the ground, and in any event the area injured might not have been covered with a shoulder pad at the moment of impact even if properly fitted, and might have happened even if the plaintiff had been wearing larger pads.

5. The "Concussion Suits"

The more recent law suits, which I will loosely term the "concussion suits," pose a fundamentally different and arguably greater challenge to the contact sports. For the most part, criminal and civil suits from the annals of sports stemmed from extra-legal conduct, specifically injurious behavior that happened during stoppages in play, or from game conduct that constituted an egregious violation of the rules or norms of the contest. Suits arose from conduct that was not an essential part of the game, and indeed, was likely an unwelcome and unforeseen by-product of a closely contested athletic contest. Unlike the suits from blood sports' past, these modern suits did not threaten to alter fundamentally or even banish altogether the sports from which they came.

Today's concussion suits differ in kind. They are aimed at addressing the consequences of the game when played as it was designed to be played, and not for conduct prohibited by the rules of the contest or by public law. In other words, these concussion suits arise from injuries suffered while players were playing the game according to its prescribed rules and within the reasonable expectations of its contestants. In the past, where suits arose from extra-legal contact, the remedy to avoid liability was to more closely enforce the rules of the game, and to more sharply circumscribe egregious conduct. Similarly, where suits arose from the negligence in the design or manufacture of game implements or playing surfaces, the remedy if imposed was to acquire better equipment or improve playing surfaces. With the modern concussion suits, the only remedy to preclude future harm is to change the rules of the game in a very fundamental way, or to stop playing the game entirely.

American football provides the salient example. With its constant blocking and tackling, football is a sport that inevitably inflicts a significant amount of physical damage on its participants, even when the sport is played within the rules. In one characterization, the sport is patently designed to result in injury, an inevitable by-product of the high-speed collisions of two determined players. Tackling a ball carrier means forcibly pushing or dragging him to the ground, an inherently unsafe and potentially injurious act.

Thus, because the novel "concussion suits" against organized football stem from permitted game play, the incentive to avoid subsequent law suits suggests that the rules of the sport themselves must be changed. In the case of football, where blocking and tackling are the very essence of the sport, liability concerns obviously pose an existential threat to the game. Of course, football players and fans have long been aware of the physical risks of the sport, with its images of veteran or retired players struggling to live with diminished mobility. What is new is the discovery of latent, chronic brain injuries, leading to a markedly diminished lifestyle and even early dementia.

Popular attention to the problem of latent, chronic brain injuries from football began when medical researchers examined the brain matter of diseased former players. A widely watched news documentary on public broadcasting (Breslow, 2015) reported the startling claim that eighty-seven of ninety-one former NFL players tested positive for the brain disease, according to the nation's largest brain bank focused on the study of traumatic head injury. Researchers with the Department of Veterans Affairs and Boston University identified the degenerative disease as chronic traumatic encephalopathy (CTE), in 96% of NFL players they examined and in 79% of all football players. CTE can lead to conditions such as memory loss, depression, and dementia. In a study of former available data, one commentator (Culhane, 2012), discussing the problem as a matter of public health, reported that an article in the journal *Neurology* found that veterans of the NFL were between three and four times more likely than the general population to die from various brain injuries. The *Neurology* study found that "speed players" (essentially all but the linemen) were at much greater risk for head injury than their more stationary teammates.

CTE has four stages. In stage one, CTE causes a protein known as "tau" to form around the brain's blood vessels, interrupting normal functioning and killing nerve cells. Stage two is characterized by rage, impulsivity, and depression, as the defective tau protein affects more nerve cells in the brain's frontal lobes. In the third stage, characterized by confusion and memory loss, tau deposits expand from the frontal section to the temporal (side) section, affecting the amygdala and hippocampus, which impairs emotion and memory. Finally, in stage four, advanced dementia results from tau deposits overwhelming the brain, killing many nerve cells and shrinking the brain, leaving it deformed and brittle, with a resultant severe limitation in cognitive function. CTE is a progressive degenerative disease which afflicts the brain of people who have suffered repeated concussions, like athletes. The brain of an individual who suffers from CTE gradually deteriorates and loses mass.

Bennet I. Omalu, M.D., and Julian Bailes, M.D., were the first to diagnose CTE in a professional football player in 2002 (Brain Injury Research Institute, 2015). The condition has so far only been diagnosable through the postmortem examination of the brain of an individual suspected of suffering from CTE, and has been found in several notable cases which received widespread media attention, including the suicide deaths of NFL player Junior Seau and professional wrestler Chris Benoit, who committed suicide after murdering his wife and son. Professor Geoffrey Rapp (2012) argues in favor of a link between concussions and suicide. He states that "[d]ata supports the following linkage, which is entirely logical: brain injury increases the likelihood of depression, depression leads to higher 'suicidal ideation,' and higher suicidal ideation rates increase the likelihood of suicide attempts and suicides" (43). After years of denial, the NFL's top health officer acknowledged a link between football-related head trauma and CTE during a roundtable discussion on concussions convened by the U.S. House of Representatives' Committee on Energy and Commerce.

Most of the popular reporting on CTE, including particularly the NFL response, has been to attribute the CTE outbreak to incidences of concussions. The disease, however, is widely believed to stem from repetitive trauma to the head, suggesting that the relatively minor, yet highly repeated, blows to the brain from blocking and tackling both in games and in practices are at fault in causing the disease. In theory, if it is only concussions that lead to the disease, then they can be minimized or treated with greater care. If CTE results from repetitive stresses, however, then no remedy short of quitting the game seems plausible.

Suits involving brain injuries from contact sports have been brought for many years (Scheuerman, 2012). Recently, however, the volume and size of the complaints have increased, led by the *Turner* class action litigation brought in federal court in Pennsylvania. In *Turner*, former NFL players retired prior to 2014 brought suit for alleged brain injuries, with the parties agreeing to a settlement requiring NFL make payouts, over sixty-five years, expected to exceed $1 billion. The settlement agreement included $5 million for diagnosis of ALS; $4 million for posthumous diagnosis of CTE; up to $3.5 million for Parkinson's and Alzheimer's victims; $3 million for neurocognitive impairment (moderate dementia); $1.5 million for early dementia; and up to $75 million for a program of baseline examinations of players for potential brain impairment, counseling, and treatment. The *Turner* settlement applies to 25,000 former NFL players, if retired by July 2014, and 9,000 relatives of deceased players.

Although the *Turner* settlement came from the NFL, potential liability for other defendants for head trauma remains. Helmet manufacturers have also been subject to concussion suits. Riddell, a helmet manufacturer, is being sued by over 1,000 former NFL players who claim the company knew about the risks of concussions and kept it a secret. The former NFL players who accepted the *Turner* settlement are free to sue Riddell, leading to this second suit being termed the players' "other suit" In re Riddell Concussion Reduction Litigation). A recent newspaper article states that new evidence has been produced that suggests that the defendant manufacturer and the NFL knew more about concussion risks than has been previously disclosed (Kosman, 2016). Riddell was also sued over allegations that it defectively designed a helmet that caused a high school player to suffer brain damage. Riddell was found not liable, with the court reasoning that helmets were created to prevent some injuries but not to prevent concussions.

Another physical contact sport, ice hockey, is also involved in concussion-related litigation. In a case pending in Minnesota, former National Hockey League (NHL) players allege that defendant NHL is responsible for "the pathological and debilitating effects of brain injuries caused by concussive and sub-concussive impacts sustained during their professional careers" (In re NHL, 2015). The complaint defined a mild traumatic brain injury (MTBI) as consisting of "trauma to the head and a resulting transient loss of normal brain function." According to plaintiffs, repeated MTBI can trigger progressive degeneration of brain tissue and can lead to Alzheimer's disease, dementia, and CTE. Another suit against the NHL, *Leeman et al. v. NHL*, alleges that the league is responsible for "the pathological and debilitating effects of brain injuries caused by concussive and sub-concussive impacts sustained . . . during their professional careers" (2). The plaintiffs' primary request is medical monitoring for the roughly 4,800 living former players, plus additional unspecified relief.

Amateur sports participants have also brought claims for damages. In a class action suit filed over high school concussions, the plaintiffs, former players, sought court supervision over how high schools manage football head injuries and called for the defendant high school association to pay medical testing to former high school players extending back to 2002 (*Pierscioinek v. Illinois High School Association*). The class action status was denied. College athletes have also sued over head injuries, as current and former players have claimed that the National Collegiate Athletic Association (NCAA) breached certain contractual obligations and common law duties in the way it handled student-athlete concussions and concussion-related risks. The plaintiff class and the NCAA settled the dispute for approximately $75 million. The NCAA also agreed to make changes to its concussion-management and return-to-play policies. The settlement reserved to the plaintiffs the right to bring tort claims against NCAA for future brain injuries.

Injured athletes have sued leagues and associations for injuries other than to the brain, but where the injury resulted from permissible game play. In a suit against a youth football association, parents of a quadriplegic youth football player sued Pop Warner league claiming coaches trained their son to tackle with his helmet, increasing the likelihood of injury (*Dixon v. Pop Warner Little Scholars*). In another matter, the parents of a youth athlete sued for their son's suicide, claiming it was the result of repeated concussions and the league's failure to warn of the dangers of youth football (Pyka v. Pop Warner Little Scholars).

Injuries from sports have not all arisen from physical injuries to the brain or other body parts. Some of the more suspect behaviors generally associated with some modern contact sports include the unauthorized use of pain medications, reportedly common in the professional ranks. One case, arising in California, was a class action alleging improper administration of pain medications to professional football players in the NFL (*Dent v. NFL*). The court ruled that because the relationship between players and leagues is governed by a collective bargaining agreement, the agreement preempted resorting to private tort litigation. In another complaint, a class action of more than 1,300 players, the plaintiffs alleged that the NFL supplied them with illegally obtained drugs and painkillers throughout their careers, without advising them of the risks. As a result, the players claimed they were kept on the field although injured and are now suffering debilitating medical complications including drug dependency. Once again the judge found that the collective bargaining agreement preempted the private suit. Another suit reprised some of the same allegations as a previous claim but added a claim of intentional activity, not negligence, on the part of the defendant league. The suit contended that NFL teams and their medical staffs withheld information from players about the nature and seriousness of their injuries, supplying them painkillers to mask the pain and minimize lost playing time. Another painkiller suit contends NFL teams and their medical staffs withheld information from players about the nature and seriousness of their injuries. A similar suit by a former hockey player was dismissed (*Boogaard v. NKL*).

The advent of suits by athletes injured in contact sports has predictably generated significant academic attention. Professor Culhane argues that consent is the central legal issue in sports injury cases. Boxers cannot sue each other for the injuries inflicted in a sanctioned match because what would otherwise be acts of battery are not actionable when the parties consent to such contact. Scholars have also explored the workers' compensation system and its limitations on compensation for professional athletes' disabilities. Some states statutorily exclude athletes, while other states are statutorily silent on the matter. Only Kansas statutorily includes professional athletes. California implicitly includes pro athletes by placing restrictions on out-of-state athletes' filing claims within the state.

The particular problem of head injuries appears especially worrisome. The causative element remains unclear. Concussion prevention and postconcussion protocols can mitigate some the effects of head injury, but it remains uncertain whether chronic brain injuries result from concussions or more from the repeated, lower-grade head impacts that occur regularly, in every football down, from youth league to professional. If the very action of the sport incurs liability, then the sport cannot survive.

Two solutions seem possible. First, the defense of "assumption of risk" could preclude widespread liability. Indeed, in effect the NFL appears to be relying on this defense. After settling the litigation mentioned earlier, the NFL publicly acknowledged, for the first time, a causative link between playing football and suffering CTE. This admission has the legal effect of placing players who choose to play professional football on notice that the game's play creates this significant risk. After the NFL's admission, people who knowingly choose to assume such a risk cannot later be heard to complain about it through legal redress. The NFL could remain liable, however, despite assumption of risk, if it becomes aware of additional risks, or more significant known ones, and fails to disclose that new information publicly.

Second, the owners of the leagues that promote contact sports could seek legislative intervention. Intervention would most likely follow the pattern set by boxing, where government-sanctioned commissions and other regulatory bodies were empowered to set the important terms of engagement. State-sanctioned football, for example, would absolve the defendant leagues or other sports organizations from liability. It would also, however, take from the owners the ability to stage contests at their discretion. Each possible solution will be examined.

6. Assumption of Risk

In the sports arena, assumption of risk raises two issues. The courts that preside over these cases first need to define "the game" at issue. Specifically, if a court is asked to determine whether or not an athlete consented or assumed the risk to play a game, the normal course of which led to his injury, the court must first resolve the contours or scope of what conduct comprises that game or sport. To what exactly did a player consent when he consented to play football, for instance? The second issue stems from the first. It asks how sports associations or leagues may modify the rules of their respective games to create a different set of expectations that players are presumed to assume.

7. Defining the Game

In baseball, four pitched balls produce a walk; three strikes and the batter is out. Rules such as these enable the game to be played, and organized baseball leagues could vary them at will. Other rules in baseball create prohibitions, such as the rule against a pitcher purposely throwing at a batter. Although a batter can expect pitches in the form of both balls and strikes, it is more problematic to conclude that the batter should also expect a pitch purposely thrown at him, in violation of the rules. The doctrine of assumption of risk is founded on consent. Can a player be said to consent to conduct that the rules of the game expressly prohibit?

The *Avila* case brings the matter into sharp relief (Davis, 2006). There, a college baseball pitcher, upset at the fact that his teammate had been hit by a pitch the previous inning, apparently decided to hit the next batter from the opposing team. The pitcher threw a fastball at the opponent's head, hitting it, splintering his protective helmet and causing severe and permanent injury to his brain. In the subsequent suit brought by the injured batter against the county, which had hosted the game and operated the college, the defendant presented the defense of assumption of the risk, arguing that the batter, by agreeing to participate in the game of baseball, took the risk of being hit by an inside pitch, even though the rules of the game expressly prohibit purposeful "beanballs." The Supreme Court of California on appeal ruled, as a matter of law, that a batter being hit by a beanball is an "inherent" risk of baseball. In other words, the risk of the beanball inheres in the sport, no matter what rules are arrayed against it. The batter, by choosing to play in a baseball game, assumed the risk of being thrown at by an opposing pitcher, even if the pitch were aimed at his head in anger and intentionally, and even where the rules of the sport explicitly preclude the conduct at issue.

California divides the doctrine of assumption of risk into two: primary and secondary. Under the latter, the pitcher in this case would owe the batter a duty of care, a duty not to negligently or intentionally injure the batter, and the question would be whether or not the batter knowingly exposed himself to the risk of the pitcher's failure to meet that duty. However, under the former, "primary" assumption of risk doctrine, the pitcher owes the batter no duty of care at all. Being thrown at is just part of the game, and no matter what the pitcher intended or of what the batter had knowledge, no liability attaches. The California Supreme Court applied the doctrine of primary assumption of risk to hold that, as a matter of law, a pitcher intentionally throwing at a batter is part of the game, and thus one of the risks the batter assumes when he steps into the box.

The determination that batters reasonably expect beanball pitches seems a factual, empirical question, involving the frequency of the event. Yet the court's resolution was derived from anecdote: the court's opinion recites various instances of beanballs and statements concerning beanballs and concludes that beanballs are within the common expectation of batters. This form of offhand empiricism is a poor substitute for the real thing. Yet grand empirical pronouncements based on anecdote, if based on anything at all, permeate legal decisions, especially in the context of sports. With this decision, whether based on an accurate factual finding or not, as a matter of law in California the intentional beanball is within the field of risks that batters assume.

Although the court posed what appeared to be an empirical question, in fact it may have not been interested in a "correct" empirical answer. Instead, as is the case repeatedly in the application of the assumption-of-risk defense, the more plausible observation is that the California court chose, for unstated reasons, to define "the sport of baseball" to include within its normal activity the illicit beanball. This choice suggests a larger role for the assumption-of-risk defense, one that is infused with policy considerations. The California courts, in particular, have made this objective, judicially controlled aspect of the choice clear. In *Knight v. Jewett*, where the defendant broke the plaintiff's finger in a touch football game, the court stated that "the question of the existence and scope of a defendant's duty of care is a legal question which depends on the nature of the sport or activity in question and on the parties' general relationship to the activity, and is an issue to be decided by the court, rather than the jury" (706). Similarly, in Shin v. Ahn, the court held that "a court need not ask what risks a particular plaintiff subjectively knew of and chose to encounter, but instead must evaluate the fundamental nature of the sport and the defendant's role in or relationship to that sport in order to determine whether the defendant owes a duty to protect a plaintiff from the particular risk of harm" (584).

One policy that appears important to courts in tort suits arising from sports contests are concerns about the introduction or intrusion of tort liability to sporting activities. For example, in the aforementioned *Knight v. Jewett* case, the California court noted that, "even when a participant's conduct violates a rule of the game and may subject the violator to internal sanctions prescribed by the sport itself, imposition of legal liability for such conduct might well alter fundamentally the nature of the sport by deterring participants from vigorously engaging in activity that falls close to, but on the permissible side of, a prescribed rule" (710). Similarly, the court in *Avila* stated that, "it is one thing for an umpire to punish a pitcher who hits a batter by ejecting him from the game, or for a league to suspend the pitcher; it is quite another for tort law to chill any pitcher from throwing inside" (394). Tort liability for wrongful pitches would involve judges and juries assessing the unstated intentions of pitchers. It would also involve asking if the club or coach followed the proper standard of care in training the pitcher and did not negligently employ a pitcher without adequate control. The introduction of tort law would put a premium on control pitchers over hard-throwing but comparatively wild pitchers, and perhaps would introduce a measure of self-dealing into game decisions, as coaches might put less effective but better-control pitchers on the mound, even if the team interests were otherwise, in order to avoid personal liability.

Second, courts liberally applying the assumption-of-risk defense might conclude that opposing teams can minimize the frequency and danger of brushback pitches better than judicial tribunals. By concluding that the batter "assumed the risk" as a matter of law, the California court was effectively deciding that the intentional harm done by the pitcher would result in no legal remedy. Under these circumstances, the batter's remedy is retaliation: the payback pitch where his teammate throws at an opposing batter. The denial of a legal remedy makes sense if the teams can together minimize the joint costs of batting by working together, under the implicit threat of retaliation, to take care not to unnecessarily throw at opposing batters.

8. Resetting Expectations

What is problematic about this methodology, in which patently empirical questions are resolved by anecdote and resort to amorphous public policy, apart from the fact that it may well produce incorrect answers, is that the judicial fact, once announced, sets the standard for future cases. Once a court determines, on the basis of testimony and similar cases, that a baseball batter "expects" to be subject to an intentional beanball from the pitcher, for example, then a batter in a subsequent game who is subject to an identical harm may not claim he did not expect it. The prediction is self-fulfilling; the judge's determination of expectations defines the sport itself.

For example, in *Bourque v. Duplechin*, the defendant, running from first to second base during a softball game, veered a few feet out of the base path in an effort to prevent the second baseman, the plaintiff, from completing a double play. The court ruled that the plaintiff assumed the risks from a batted ball or from a runner if the plaintiff had remained on the base path, both "common occurrences." The plaintiff did not, however, "assume the risk of [the defendant] going out of his way to run into him at full speed when [the plaintiff] was five feet away from the base" (43). This conduct, the court ruled, was "unexpected and unsportsmanlike." In a similar case, also arising out of a softball game, *Picou v. The Hartford Insurance Co.*, the court ruled that the risk of collision at second base inheres in the game. Decisions on these grounds are intensely factual and resist easy generalization. It is speculative to assess which fact of the defendant's conduct comprised the unexpected and thus unconsented to aspect that gave rise to the defendant's liability: the fact that the collision came at full speed or was outside the baseline or was five feet outside that line, and not four or three. Yet the court in *Bourque* ruled as a legal matter that the plaintiff did not assume of the risk of defendant's conduct, thus precluding the defendant's main defense. Despite the elusiveness of capturing the scope of plaintiff's consent as to base runners, the decision is illustrative of the unmistakable import from this and other decisions: through tort decisions, the courts have come to define the expectations of participants in sporting contests.

Participants in an athletic contest are deemed to have consented to assaults and batteries when both the injury and the conduct that caused it are "reasonably foreseeable hazards of joint participation in an athletic contest." Thus, the fact that certain conduct may constitute a "foul" or "penalty" under the particular rules of the sport does not necessarily render the conduct beyond justification under the consent defense. In *State v. Shelley*, the defendant was playing a basketball game when he was the victim of a hard foul that resulted in a scratch to his face. The defendant subsequently returned to the game and hit the victim (the perpetrator of the initial hard foul) in the face, breaking the victim's jaw in three places. The defendant argued that the blow to the face was not intentional but rather happened in the course of play as a reactive, unthinking response. The defendant argued that because of the previous hard foul by the victim, the defendant expected another, and thus reacted to a perceived imminent hard foul. The defendant also raised the defense of consent, arguing that the victim was injured in the course of normal, if violent, basketball play.

The trial court stated that as a matter of law, the defense of consent was not available because the defendant's conduct in striking another player with a blow to the face exceeded what is considered to be permissible within the rules of the sport of basketball. "Consent is to contact that is contemplated within the rules of the game and that is incidental to the furtherance of the goals of that particular game" (491). The appellate court disagreed. It reasoned that the consent defense is necessary to an assault action arising out of a sports contest. If a consent defense was not available to a sports-related assault, then most athletic contests would need to be banned because many sports involve invasions of physical integrity. The court reasoned that "society has chosen to foster sports competitions," and therefore players must, by necessity, be able to consent to physical contact with each other when playing the game. The appellate court rejected a reliance on the rules of the game by themselves to limit the athlete's scope of consent. The commentaries to the Model Penal Code provide:

> There are, however, situations in which consent to bodily injury should be recognized as a defense to crime. . . . There is . . . the obvious case of participation in an athletic contest or competitive sport where the nature of the enterprise often involves risk of serious injury. Here, the social judgment that permits the contest to flourish necessarily involves the companion judgment that reasonably foreseeable hazards can be consented to by virtue of participation.

The court determined that a reliance on the rules of the game to form the limit of consent would be too constricting to athletic play, as "[c]ertain excesses and inconveniences are to be expected beyond the formal rules of the game. It may be ordinary and expected conduct for minor assaults to occur" (492). Instead, the court held that the limits of consent are formed by the reasonably foreseeable hazards of joint participation in a lawful athletic contest or other competitive sport not forbidden by law. Despite these conclusions of law, in the final analysis, the appellate court held that the magnitude and dangerousness of the defendant's conduct were beyond the limits of permissible consent.

The appellate court found that there was no question that the defendant intended to hit the victim and explained that "[t]here is nothing in the game of basketball, or even rugby or hockey, that would permit consent as a defense" to the defendant's lashing out at the victim with sufficient force to land a substantial blow to the jaw (493).

The court's reasoning raises two substantive issues. First, if a court, following the Model Penal Code, holds that the limits of consent are not formed by the rules of the respective sport or game but rather by the "reasonably foreseeable hazards" of joint athletic participation, then the ruling bodies of sports would theoretically be unable to utilize their control over the rules of a sport to modify the conduct of players. For example, assume the NHL wished to make illegal stick checks no longer "part of the game." To further this desire, assume the NHL passed a stringent rule against all illegal contact with hockey sticks and added severe penalties for infractions. At this point, illegal stick checks would clearly be prohibited by the rules of the game. Yet under the Model Penal Code approach, criminal prosecutions for assault of players who committed an illegal stick check and severely injured an opponent would be subject to an absolute defense of consent; despite their strict prohibition under hockey's rules, stick checks are presently and would remain a reasonably foreseeable hazard of joint participation in a NHL hockey game. If the rule makers and governing authorities of a sport are unable to alter the nature of their game, at least as far as criminal liability is concerned, then it is unclear how exactly a sport could go about altering the nature of its contest. This result is problematic, for sports are simply games, lacking any inherent qualities or necessary attributes. Thus, if an organizer of a game wants to create a contest involving ice skating, sticks, and pucks, but without stick checks or body checks, and call the sport *X*, no tribunal or legislature should have cause to gainsay that creation. But a legal standard, such as that reflected in the *Shelley* decision, that divorces the scope of participant consent from the rules of the contest, fails to recognize and respond to the only written representation as to what risks the participant, had he or she read the rules, actually agreed to undertake. The U.S. Supreme Court suggested as much in *PGA Tour, Inc. v. Martin*. In *Martin*, a golfer who was unable to walk the golf course due to a disability sued to be permitted to use a golf cart. The rules of the PGA expressly required all competitors to walk the course. In holding for Martin, the court ruled that the game of golf involves only striking a ball into a hole, and that walking was not part of the game, despite the PGA rule stating that it is. Thus, *Martin* implies that the sport of golf has an existence and nature apart from its rules.

The second problem with the court's reasoning in *Shelley*, which declines to use the rules of a sport to define the scope of conduct to which a player consents, is that the "reasonably foreseeable hazard" standard creates a difficult matter of factual interpretation, both for the player in playing the game and for the tribunal in assessing the player's conduct after the fact. For instance, the defendant in *Shelley* argued that his blow to the victim's face was unplanned and an immediate reaction to what he perceived to be a threatened hard foul. Moreover, the defendant's blow came during the play of the sport and from the "weak side," or the side away from the ball, and happened while the two players were looking at the ball. It is not at all obvious to the player that such a blow to the face of an opponent would subject him to criminal liability. Ignoring this possibility, the appellate court declared that "there is no question" but that the defendant intended to hit the victim, a strong conclusion that seems unsupportable in light of the court's recitation of the facts of the case. Indeed, the only pertinent fact available in the trial record cited by the appellate court was the defendant's insistence that the blow was not intentional. The decision also raises an issue under the rule of lenity traditionally applied in criminal cases. The court's mention of the sport of hockey, albeit in dicta, suggests the ambiguity of the court's standard. In hockey, blows to the head and other parts of the opponent's body with a gloved hand are not uncommon yet can result in severe injuries, thus suggesting the need for flexibility in the application of criminal law. As the court held in *People v. Schacker*, "If cross checking, tripping and punching were criminal acts, the game of hockey could not continue in its present form" (309).

9. Legislative Intervention

Assuming that the defense of assumption of risk is not applied vigorously to defeat future tort claims, then the best hope for contact sports to survive the wave of liability for latent, chronic injuries to the brain of players is through the intervention of state or federal legislatures. Legislative intervention could obviate private tort liability as a means to define a sport and regulate the risks endemic to it. Such intervention, however, would come at a cost.

The evolution of modern boxing from its bare-knuckle ancestor is instructive. Initially, the occasionally brutal spectacle of bare-knuckle prize fighting was checked by a form of self-regulation. Rules for these contests were first devised by the famous bare-knuckle fighter Jack Broughton, who established seven rules at Tottenham Court Road in 1743. The most important of Broughton's Rules, in a notable change from the past, permitted the fighter to lose by submission or a refusal to continue. The rules also provided for a "knockout," albeit on a thirty-second count, a "referee," although present merely to keep the peace, and prohibited hitting an opponent who was down. Another great bare-knuckle fighter, John L. Sullivan, joined with U.S. President Theodore Roosevelt to engineer the gradual replacement of the rugged Broughton Rules with the more modern Queensbury rules. The Queensbury rules featured timed rounds and gloved hands, and prohibited the clinches and wrestling-like moves that enabled superior bare-knuckle fighters to deliver dangerous blows. Despite these innovations designed to promote fighter safety, there was a public perception that the self-interest of fight promoters and the desperation of boxers generated bouts that were unevenly matched due to differences in weight, experience, skill level, or health. Boxers too were thought to not earn a proper share of the proceeds of the contests. As a result, in most states in the nation, and in many countries, boxing is today regulated by state or national commissions, unions, or boards. In a few countries it is banned. Where permitted, the primary function of boxing boards is to sanction fights. They also modify the rules of the contest to promote safety, specifying weight and skill parameters, match length, glove weight and equipment, and other dimensions of the contest. Although their approaches vary widely, these sanctioning boards also typically require promoter registration, the provision of various health and safety equipment, the presence of medical personnel, and so forth. In many U.S. states, MMA bouts have been brought under the supervision of the boxing commission.

Governmental or state-sanctioned licensing commissions add a significant cost to the production of a boxing contest. They inhibit the ability of promoters and fighters to maximize their earnings through staging contests. Although the ability of participants in boxing to pursue profits is somewhat reduced, the exchange might nonetheless be a profitable one. The creation of enlightened and relatively uniform boxing rules and conditions has allowed for the growth of a robust market for private insurance, both for fighters and promoters. As long as the fight is properly sanctioned by the appropriate governing body, the promoter will not be liable for staging the fight, although of course he could be liable for other practices that are deemed illegal, such as a conspiracy to violate antitrust laws. The respective commission, as an agency performing a government function in issuing a permit for the fight, is immune from private suit.

Consequently, the arrival of state regulation brings a strong measure of relief from liability for damages. It also introduces a new actor to the staging of sports contests, both for better and for worse. Historically, the owners of sports leagues or contest organizers, in boxing or other sports, were free to stage contests and tournaments with the goal of maximizing the return from the ownership. Players were similarly free to sell their labor, choosing to accept the obvious risk of injury in exchange for outsized professional salaries. Regulatory oversight would most likely inhibit the free exchange of labor, even to the extent of modifying rules of the contest in order to promote the well-being of players. The recent advent of concussion litigation could lead to the prohibition of certain contact sports. More likely, however, our newfound knowledge about the inherent risks of contact sports will lead to a growing intervention of public authorities into sports, with the eventual effect of making the sport less recognizable to the contemporary fan, and perhaps relegating a popular activity to the sidelines.

References

Abrams, Roger I. (2014, July 24). "Painkiller Lawsuit Against the NFL Will Cause the League a Serious Headache." *The Huffington Post*. Accessed February 24, 2016, www.huffingtonpost.com/roger-i-abrams/painkiller-lawsuit-agains_b_5385699.html.

Associated Press. (2014a, May 20). "Ex-NFL Players Allege League Illegally Supplied Them with Drugs." *CBSNews*. Accessed February, 24 2016, www.cbsnews.com/news/ex-nfl-players-allege-in-lawsuit-league-illegally-used-drugs/.

Associated Press. (2014b, July 7). "Federal Judge Approves NFL Concussion Settlement." *nfl.com*. Available at www.nfl.com/news/story/0ap2000000363672/article/federal-judge-approves-nfl-concussion-settlement.

Associated Press. (2014c, December 17). "Former NFL Players May Appeal after Painkillers Lawsuit Dismissed." *CBSNews*. Accessed February 24, 2016, www.cbsnews.com/news/former-nfl-players-may-appeal-after-painkillers-lawsuit-dismissed/.

Brain Injury Research Institute. (2015). "What Is CTE? Chronic Traumatic Encephalopathy Explained." n.p. Accessed February 11, 2016, www.protectthebrain.org/Brain-Injury-Research/What-is-CTE-.aspx.

Breslow, Jason M. (2015, September 18). "87 Deceased NFL Players Test Positive for Brain Disease." *Frontline*. Available at www.pbs.org/wgbh/frontline/article/new-87-deceased-nfl-players-test-positive-for-brain-disease/.

Campbell, Dave. (n.d.). "105 Former NHL Players Are Plaintiffs in Class-Action Concussion Lawsuit Against League." *Boston.com. The New York Times*.Accessed April 6, 2016.

Culhane, John G. (2012, Fall). "Not Just the NFL: Compensation, Litigation, and Public Health in Concussion Cases." Florida International University Law Review 8: 5.

Davis, Timothy. (2006). "*Avila v. Citrus Community College District:* Shaping the Contours of Immunity and Primary Assumption of the Risk." Marquette Sports Law Review 17: 259.

ESPN Internet Ventures. (2015, January 27). "Ex-players Appeal Dismissal of Suit." *ESPN*. Accessed March 2, 2016, http://espn.go.com/nfl/story/_/id/12238510/former-nfl-players-appeal-dismissal-lawsuit-painkillers.

Fainaru, Steve. (2016, March 15). "NFL Acknowledges, for First Time, Link Between Football, Brain Disease." *ESPN*. Accessed March 20, 2016, http://espn.go.com/espn/otl/story/_/id/14972296/top-nfl-official-acknowledges-link-football-related-head-trauma-cte-first.

Friede, Matthew. (2015). "Professional Athletes Are 'Seeing Stars': How Athletes Are 'Knocked-Out' of States' Workers' Compensation Systems." *Hamline Law Review* 38(3): 519–555.

Gannett. (2015, May 21). "Former Players: NFL Teams 'Conspired' to Push Painkillers." *USA Today*. Accessed March 2, 2016, www.usatoday.com/story/sports/nfl/2015/05/21/former-players-nfl-teams-conspired-to-push-painkillers/27722609/.

Gorn, Elliott J. (2010). *The Manly Art: Bare-Knuckle Prize Fighting in America*, Updated Edition (Ithaca, N.Y.: Cornell University Press).

Hanna, Cheryl. (2001). "*Sex Is Not a Sport: Consent and Violence in Criminal Law.*" *British Columbia Law Review* 42: 239 (2001)

"Judge Nixes First Class-Action Lawsuit over High School Concussions." (2015, October 28). *CBS News*. n.p. Accessed February 29, 2016, www.cbsnews.com/news/concussions-lawsuit-against-illinois-high-school-association-dismissed-by-illinois-judge/.

Karon, Daniel R. (1991). "Winning Isn't Everything, It's the Only Thing: Violence in Professional Sports: The Need for Federal Regulation and Criminal Sanctions." *Indiana Law Review* 25: 147.

Knoll, Corina. (2014, March 20). "Helmet Maker Not to Blame in Football Player's Injury, Jury Finds." *Los Angeles Times*. Accessed March 20, 2014.

Kosman, Josh. (2016, February 15). "Ex-NFL Players: We Have Proof Helmet Maker Hid Concussion Risks." *New York Post*. n.p. Accessed February 29, 2016, http://nypost.com/2016/02/15/nfl-helmet-maker-takes-another-hit-in-concussion-lawsuit/.

Lehman, Everett J., Hein, Misty J., Baron, Sherry L., and Gersic, Christine M. (2012, September 5). "Neurodegenerative Causes of Death Among Retired National Football League Players." *Neurology*. Available at http://nflconcussionlitigation.com/wp-content/uploads/2012/09/EMBARGOED-NFL-Players-and-Death-From-ADALS-Lehman-titled-copy.pdf.

Maese, Rick. (2014, December 17). "Federal Judge Dismisses NFL Painkiller Case." *Washington Post*. Accessed February 24, 2016, www.washingtonpost.com/sports/

redskins/federal-judge-dismisses-nfl-painkiller-case/2014/12/17/3af89414-8630-11e4-abcf-5a3d7b3b20b8_story.html.
Martinez, Michael. (2016, March 9). "Pop Warner Settles Concussion Suit Filed by Ex-Player." *CNN*. Cable News Network. Accessed April 6, 2016.
Orentlicher, David, and David, William S. (2012, Fall). "Concussion and Football: Failures to Respond by the NFL and the Medical Profession." *Florida International University Law Review* 8: 23 (Fall, 2012)
Rapp, Geoffrey Christopher. (2012, Fall). "Suicide, Concussions, and the NFL." *Florida International University Law Review* 8: 5.
Scheuerman, Sheila B. (2012, Fall). "The NFL Litigation: A Critical Assessment of Class Certification." *Florida International University Law Review* 8: 5.
Standen, Jeffrey. (2009). "The Manly Sports: The Problematic Use of Criminal Law to Regulate Sports Violence." *Journal of Criminal Law & Criminology* 99: 619.
Wexler, Evan. (2013, October 8). "How CTE Affects the Brain." *Frontline*. Accessed February 11, 2016, www.pbs.org/wgbh/frontline/article/the-four-stages-of-cte/.

Cases

Acuna v. Riddell Sports, Inc., No. LC090924 (Cal. Super Ct.).
Ashcroft v. Calder Race Course, Inc., 492 So. 2d 1309 (Fla. 1986).
Avila v. Citrus Cmty. Coll. Dist., 131 P.3d 383 (Cal. 2006).
Bell v. Hansley, 48 N.C. 131 (1855).
Boogaard v. NKL, 2015 WL 9259519 (N.D. Ill. 2015).
Champer v. State, 14 Ohio St. 437 (1863)
Dent v. NFL, 2014 WL 2058098 (ND Cal 2014).
Dixon v. Pop Warner Little Scholars, 2014 Cal. Super. LEXIS 259 (Nov. 14, 2014).
Freer, People v., 381 N.Y.S.2d 976 (N.Y. 1976).
Heldman v. Uniroyal, Inc., 371 N.E.2d 557 (Ohio 1977).
Kabella v. Bouschelle, 672 P.2d 290 (N.M. 1983).
Knight v. Jewett, 834 P.2d 696 (Cal. 1992),
Leeman et al. v. NHL, Civil Case No. 13-CV-1856 (D.D.C. 2013).
Logan v. Austin, 1 Stew. 476 (Ala. 1828).
Maddox v. City of New York, 487 NYS2d 354 (1985).
NCAA Student-Athlete Concussion Injury Litig., In re, No. MDL No. 2492, 2014 U.S. Dist. LEXIS 174334, at *6 (N.D. Ill. Dec. 17, 2014).
NHL, In re (2015).
NHL Players' Concussion Injury Litig., In re, No. 14-2551 (SRN), 2015 U.S. Dist. LEXIS 38755, at *2 (D. Minn. Mar. 25, 2015).
Ordway v. Superior Ct. of Orange County (re: Judy Casella), 243 Cal. Rptr. 536 (1988).
Picou v. The Hartford Ins. Co., 558 So. 2d 787 (La. Ct. App. 1990).
Pierscioinek v. Illinois High Sch. Ass'n, 2015 Ill. Cir. LEXIS 24.
Pyka v. Pop Warner Little Scholars, Inc., No. 15-cv-00057 (W.D. Wis.).
Regina v. Green, 1 OR 591 (Can. 1971).

Regina v. Lewis, 174 Eng. Rep. 874 (Q.B. 1844).
Regina v. Maki, 3 OR 780 (Can. 1970).
Riddell Concussion Reduction Litig., In re, CA No. 13-7585 (2015 U.S. Dist. Ct. LEXIS 101415 (D.N.J. Aug. 3, 2015).
Ross v. Clouser, 637 SW2d 11 (Mo. 1982).
Schacker, People v., 670 NYS2d 308 (1998),
Shelley, State v., 929 P.2d 489 (Wash. Ct. App. 1997).
Shin v. Ahn, 42 Cal. 4th 482 (2007).
Stout v. Wren, 8 N.C. 420 (1 Hawks) (1821).
Testerman v. Riddell, 161 Fed. Appx. 286 WL 41193 (4th Cir. 2006).
Turner v. NFL, LexisNexis. U.S. Dist. Ct. (E.D. Pa. July-Aug. 2014).
Zachardy v. Geneva Coll., 733 A2d 648 (Pa. 1999).

CHAPTER 8

SPORTS AND AMERICAN TORT LAW

GEOFFREY RAPP

1. INTRODUCTION

AMERICAN sports are violent and dangerous. Even the seemingly idyllic "pastime" of baseball is punctuated by moments featuring the application of tremendous physical force to objects, and to people—a collision at home plate or an outfielder running at full speed into a stadium wall are just two examples. Sports commonly thought of as more violent, such as football and hockey, might be best characterized as sports for which violence is an essential constituent component. With violence—whether deliberate or accidental—comes injury. As a result, it is not surprising that, certainly for well over a century and perhaps long before that, injuries have occurred in connection with sports at all levels in this country.

Tort law, which serves to provide a civil recourse for injured persons in pursuit, primarily, of damages, has thus long had an intersection with professional and amateur sports. Over the course of time, in encounters with injuries arising from or connected in some way to sports, American courts have developed nuanced and peculiar—and not always internally consistent—rules to govern the right to recover for injuries, accidental or otherwise, connected to sports.

A tort, in short, is an act or an omission which the law considers wrongful, such that a person suffering an injury (actual physical harm in many cases and in some only an injury in terms of a right invaded) may bring a claim that does not require the existence of a contract. Broadly speaking, American tort claims are divided into two categories. *Accidental tort* claims involve injuries arising by accident—meaning, the person legally responsible for the injury did not act (or fail to act) intentionally. *Intentional tort* claims, in which the law is generally less hospitable to defendants, involve wrongdoers who acted (or failed to act) purposefully. This chapter discusses tort rules and cases involving sports using this broad division, before taking up separate considerations relating to economic torts, privacy torts, and sports torts relating to product defects and latent injuries.

One important point about tort law is that in America it is largely "common law," meaning that tort rules are the sum of published judicial decisions resolving individual cases. This can be distinguished from areas of law in which federal (or even state) statutes provide at least seemingly clear answers. As a result, one speaking about tort rules must often avoid generalization without sufficient caveat. Rules differ from one state to another, and represent the sum total of decided cases but may not always be neat and clean. In some jurisdictions, particular issues in tort law may never have been litigated, and therefore the jurisdiction's approach may not be possible to delineate.

2. Accidental Torts

When a person is injured as the result of an accident, the primary claim the injured person asserts in a tort lawsuit is known as negligence. Negligence, the workhorse of accident law, has four elements—that is, four components a plaintiff must convince a judge and/or jury, by a preponderance of the evidence, apply. Like the required elements of a molecule in your high school science class, any missing element in a tort case defeats the plaintiff's effort to recover. The four required elements of a negligence claim are (1) *duty*, (2) *breach*; (3) *causation*; and (4) *damages*.

The plaintiff must first establish that she was owed a duty by the defendant. This means that the defendant had a legal obligation to conduct him- or herself in a certain way, and owed that obligation to the plaintiff and others in the same category as the plaintiff. Typically and traditionally, a defendant's duty is to conduct him- or herself in a reasonable manner, and that duty is owed to any individual who could be foreseeably injured by the failure, on the part of the defendant, to meet that duty. More recently, prominent academics and legal thinkers, acting through the American Law Institute, have taken the position that anyone who is injured as the result of unreasonable conduct on the part of a defendant should be said to have been owed a duty unless there are policy reasons for saying that "no duty" applies. As I discuss in sections 2.1 and 2.2, sports cases involving participants and spectators are one of the areas in which courts have found policy considerations favor not applying the ordinary rules of duty.

Once the plaintiff establishes that the defendant owed her an obligation to conduct him- or herself reasonably, the next step is "breach." The plaintiff must show that the defendant failed to meet that applicable standard of care. Showing breach usually means demonstrating a lack of reasonable care—that level of care that a person of ordinary prudence would have used under those circumstances. Examples would be acting carelessly, thoughtlessly, and heedless of risk, and failing to take appropriate steps to reduce the riskiness of one's actions. Mistakes—if of a sort that a reasonable person would not make—can be the basis for a claim of negligence.

The plaintiff must then establish causation—that the defendant's wrongful conduct *caused* the plaintiff's injuries—and damages. Though these elements are complex in the law of torts, most of the special considerations in sports cases center on the issues of duty and breach, and therefore, in the interests of economy, this chapter largely omits a discussion of causation and damages.

While negligence claims are certainly brought in sports injury cases, one of the more distinctive features of sports torts law has to do with the limitations courts have placed on plaintiffs seeking to recover for mere negligence. Both for participants—especially in "contact" sports—and for spectators, courts have tended to limit recovery to cases in which the defendant's conduct deviated from appropriate standards to a greater degree, such that it might be said to be not just "negligent" but "reckless."

2.1. Participants

For participants in sporting events (i.e., the players), courts have frequently held that negligence alone is insufficient to state a cause of action. That is, a defendant should not be held liable for an injury caused to another participant because the defendant failed to exercise *care* for the plaintiff's safety. Instead, to recover for an injury caused by a fellow sporting participant, courts have often held that plaintiffs must demonstrate a higher level of deviation from the appropriate level of care—usually that associated with recklessness.

The origins of this important distinction between sports torts law and tort law applicable in other areas of activity are found in the defense known as *primary assumption of risk*. The word "assumption" here is used to describe situations in which the plaintiff assumed, that is, took upon her own shoulders, the financial responsibility associated with injuries she might suffer in a particular circumstance. Primary assumption of risk is one of three uses of the term "assumption of risk" in tort law.

Express assumption of risk involves the use of words to limit the risks as to which the defendant will be legally responsible to the plaintiff. Examples would include contractual waivers and limitations on liability, such as releases signed before participation.

Secondary implied assumption of risk involves attributing to the plaintiff responsibility for her own injury because the plaintiff knew of the danger presented by an activity for which the defendant was responsible, plaintiff appreciated its extent, and plaintiff willingly exposed herself to that danger. The tort law equivalent of "buyer beware" was described by Justice Cardozo using the Latin phrase *volenti non fit injuria* (roughly, to a willing person, no injury is done). A plaintiff who sees water in a pool and goes into the pool would have no legal right to complain about getting wet. In modern approaches, where a plaintiff was actually aware of danger, a jury will assign a share of fault (meaning, legal responsibility) to the plaintiff to account for that awareness. The result would typically be to reduce the plaintiff's ability to recover; even if a defendant was careless, the plaintiff can only force the defendant to pay for a portion of her injuries. Where the plaintiff bears a particularly large share of the blame—either due to awareness of risk or due to her own carelessness—she may be unable to recover at all.

Primary assumption of risk, the rule most distinctively applied to sports (and other forms of recreational) injuries, does not involve either the use of words or proof by a defendant that the plaintiff actually understood the dangers involved. Instead, this form of assumption of risk is "primary" in that it negates the element of duty and simply requires a showing that the plaintiff participated in an activity and was injured as a result of something that would be described as an inherent or essential aspect of the activity. Even if the defendant failed to act with sufficient carefulness, a plaintiff cannot recover if his or her injury resulted from an ordinary, expected aspect of the activity. This is true even if the plaintiff him- or herself did not appreciate the dangers involved. The difference, in part, between primary assumption of risk and secondary implied assumption of risk is that the latter requires actual awareness of danger by the victim, while the former simply requires a judicial determination that the danger is obvious, expected, or an essential aspect of that activity.

In sports participation cases, what this means is that courts will say that plaintiffs assume risks that are inherent in participation in that particular sport. Plaintiffs are denied the chance to argue that a defendant's conduct was careless if the thing the defendant did or for which the defendant is responsible amounts to a customary and well-understood part of that particular sport. In downhill skiing, this might mean that defendant ski resorts aren't responsible for the fact that ice or snow is slippery. In football, it precludes a plaintiff from asserting that a tackle was "unreasonably careless."

When one participant injures another, the injured person can't complain about matters that involved understood dangers of sports participation. In various cases, courts have found the following to be risks covered by this doctrine:

- Hitting a fellow hockey player with the butt-end of a hockey stick, according to a Massachusetts court in *Gauvin v. Clark*;
- Falling and hitting a hard object while running and kicking a soccer ball, according to a New York court in *Cohen v. Massapequa Union Free School District*;
- Being hit by a carelessly thrown softball while warming up to play a game, according to a California court in *Mann v. Nutrilite*;
- Being struck in the head while competing for possession of the ball with another player during a college soccer game, according to a Connecticut court in *Trujillo v. Yeager*; and
- A tackle during a prison inmate football game, according to an Ohio court in *Schnetz v. Ohio Department of Rehabilitation and Correction.*

Courts apply this rule in many other circumstances, and they defend it on a couple of grounds. First, courts assert that injuries in sports are commonplace, and that allowing lawsuits over obvious and expected risks would unleash a "flood of litigation," requiring wasteful expenditure of judicial resources resolving such cases. Relatedly, particularly when discussing athletic injury cases arising in scholastic sports (whether at the secondary or postsecondary level), courts will often express concern about the costs of potential liability reducing the availability of sporting activities.

Second, courts assert that for sports to serve their functions—whether that be promoting physical fitness or providing diversion from life's stresses in the case of recreational sports, or entertainment in the case of professional sports—participants must be free to participate vigorously without concern over the risk of being sued. If a football player has to worry about "careless tackling" being the basis for a lawsuit, he will tackle with less force, and to the court, that might undermine the core objecive of the sport of football: to stop the advancement of the ball. In *Knight v. Jewett*, a case involving an injury in a flag football game, the California Supreme Court opined that "imposition of legal liability . . . might well alter fundamentally the nature of the sport by deterring participants from vigorously engaging in activity." (834 P.2d 696, 710).

Primary assumption of risk does not mean, in many jurisdictions, that plaintiffs can never recover. First, although plaintiffs cannot recover for simple negligence on a defendant's part, many courts have said that the rule applicable to sports is not a "no duty" rule but rather a "limited duty" rule. It is not that co-participants are free from any responsibility for each other's safety, just that they are free from responsibility for carelessness and mistake. They retain a limited duty to avoid recklessness. Recklessness, sometimes equated in the law to gross negligence or wanton and willful misconduct, is, I have argued elsewhere, a somewhat poorly defined middle ground of misconduct between negligence (the least extreme form of misconduct) and intentional tort (covering the most extreme forms of misconduct). A person is reckless if he or she ignores risks that are particularly substantial, especially where the risks create the possibility of grievous injury to a helpless victim. Driving while distracted as one fumbles with a CD might be careless, but driving while texting might be reckless. Conduct between co-participants in an athletic setting would be actionable in tort if it rises to the level of recklessness.

As courts have sought to apply these legal principles to sports injury cases, they have teased out issues along a number of dimensions.

First, they have discussed whether all sports are subject to these rules limiting co-participant liability, or whether this protection from liability should only apply to "contact" sports. The idea that participants need to be protected from liability so that they engage in vigorous athletic participation might apply with more force to sports involving expected contacts; whether such legal protection is needed to foster appropriately enthusiastic participation in sports thought of as less dangerous is another matter. Some courts have therefore restricted the application of the "limited duty" rule to contact sports but allowed negligence claims to be brought for non-contact sports. This has led some courts and legal writers to refer to primary assumption of risk or limited duty doctrine, as applied to sports cases, as the "contact rule exception." The critical difference in outcome created by the contact-vs.-non-contact distinction embraced in some jurisdictions, of course, begs the question of whether a particular sports is, or isn't, a contact sport. This prompted one Ohio court in *LaMalfa v. Aquila*, to pose what is doubtless one of the most pressing legal questions ever asked: is potato sack racing a contact sport? (The court ruled that it was not.) While some courts have loosened the definition of "contact sport" to include dangerous but not combative sports like cheerleading, others have decided to apply the limited duty to non-contact sports as well.

Second, courts have discussed how, if at all, the rules of a game should relate to legal liability. The rule of primary assumption of risk or limited duty prevents recovery for simple negligence in cases involving the ordinary, expected, and well-understood aspects of participating in a particular sport. The question this raises is whether a participant assumes the risks of only those contacts permitted in the rules, allowing them to recover whenever a co-participant violates the rules, or whether there is some range of "illegal" conduct under the rules of a sport that is nonetheless considered to be so commonplace or acceptable that it is also subject to the protective force of primary assumption of risk. For instance, it may be against the rules of football to "rough" a passer. Does that mean that a quarterback injured by a play that would violate that rule can sue, but one injured while still in possession of the ball cannot? Logically, there should be some range of rule-breaking conduct that is nonetheless customary and expected and would be subject to the same limited duty approach. The Supreme Court of New Jersey concluded this was the case in *Crawn v. Campo*, finding that a claim could not be brought against a softball player in a "no slide" pickup game in spite of the rule:

> The relationship among sports participants is derived from a consensual arrangement that involves both articulated and unarticulated rules, obvious and obscure conventions, and clear and not-so-clear expectations. Some rules are broken, yet their transgression is tolerated. Certain practices are customary yet others are followed inconsistently. Some conventions are well understood, others are not always known or appreciated by all participants (643 A 2d, 606).

Some courts have distinguished between rules that, if violated, should trigger tort liability and rules that would not, by focusing on the purpose or aspiration of the rule. In *Nabozny v. Barnhill*, an Illinois court emphasized that violation of "safety rules"—such as the rule at issue in that case prohibiting contact with a soccer goalie then in possession of the ball—should be given special consideration in deciding whether to impose legal liability. Rules that exist for reasons other than player safety would, if violated, be less likely to lead to a finding that the rule violator acted recklessly.

In addition to the rules of a sport, its customs also may influence a court in deciding whether particular conduct should trigger tort liability for a participant. In golf, for instance, there may be no rule but a custom involving yelling "fore" when striking a ball in the direction of another player on the course. Does that mean that the failure to yell "fore" is reckless?

Third, courts have discussed whether the level of play should matter. In general, the more advanced the level of play, the greater the obvious or known danger is said to be. Contacts that might be ordinary (and thus assumed risks) of professional football might be unacceptable in Pop Warner football. Courts can be expected to be more protective of the safety of players at more junior levels, which allowing more liberal recovery in injury claims might serve. A Connecticut court wrote in *Babych v. McRae*, that a professional athlete is "[m]anifestly . . . more aware of the dangers of the activity, and presumably more willing to accept them . . . ."

2.2. Spectators

A second area in which sports cases have embraced distinctive approaches to tort law involves injuries to spectators. Originally in cases involving baseball games (and therefore often known as the "baseball rule" even after extension to other sports), courts limited the ability of spectators to recover from sports facility operators for injuries caused by flying objects; namely, baseballs hit into the stands or other areas in which fans might be.

The rule has been justified by the same sort of ideas applied in co-participant cases, though the policy reasons are somewhat divergent. Flying baseballs enter the stands so regularly, and the risks created by them are so well understood, that arenas have only limited duties to screen the most dangerous areas of the baseball park, or provide protected seating to those who request it. It matters not if a particular plaintiff is aware of how common baseballs flying into the stands are (or are not); since this is a form of primary rather than secondary implied assumption of risk, the subjective knowledge of the plaintiff (or lack thereof) is irrelevant.

Sometimes wistfully, courts have opined that balls flying into the stands are not just common and expected dangers but actually one of the reasons why fans come to games. In *Rudnick v. Golden West Broadcasters*, a California court wrote, "the chance to apprehend a misdirected baseball is as much a part of the game as the seventh inning stretch or peanuts and Cracker Jack" (156 Cal. App. 3d, 802). Imposing liability on teams might lead them to screen off more seats, which would obstruct views and reduce the intimacy of watching a baseball game live.

As baseball was joined by other spectator sports during the twentieth century, courts confronted the question of whether this same protection should apply in other settings. The issue arises less frequently in football and soccer, where balls are softer and travel more slowly, and are thus far less likely to cause fractures or eye injuries sufficient to motivate litigation. But hockey pucks can be as dangerous as baseballs. In early cases, courts often declined to apply the baseball rule to limit recovery by hockey fans; hockey, a somehow "foreign" Canadian sport, was less well understood than the national pastime, baseball. In 1939, for instance, a California court wrote that it was "not common knowledge that pucks used in ice hockey games are liable to be batted into the section occupied by the spectators" (*Thurman v. Ice Palace*, 36 Cal. App. 2d, 368). ut as hockey became more widespread, popular, and well understood, courts increasingly applied the same approach to limit recovery by injured fans as had been applied in baseball. The risk became known. Interestingly, however, the National Hockey League (NHL) and an arena paid a $1.2 million settlement to the family of a 13-year-old girl killed at a Columbus Blue Jackets hockey game. The NHL likely had a strong argument to offer in defense of that case but chose to settle the matter to avoid bad publicity.

Another issue presented by the "baseball rule" is whether injuries should not be subject to tort claims only if caused by a flying ball, or also if those injuries are caused by other projectiles flying into the stands, such as broken bats. Courts have reached mixed results. *Benajem v. Detroit Tigers*, involved a ten-year-old girl whose fingers were grievously damaged after a broken bat left the field of play, curved around protective netting, and struck her. The plaintiff initially won a $1 million jury verdict after the trial court declined to apply the baseball rule to a fragment of a broken bat. On appeal, however, a court reversed that decision and tossed out the verdict, finding that the limited duty rule also protected the Tigers from liability for a flying shard of a broken bat.

Courts have also held that while the risk of batted balls may be assumed by fans, teams and arenas can be liable if they increase the dangers associated with being a spectator beyond their "natural" levels. For instance, in *Jones v. Three Rivers Management Corp.*, a fan was injured while standing in the concourse outside the Pittsburgh baseball stadium. The court defined the problem not as an inherent risk of baseball but as one arising from the architectural features of the stadium, which allowed balls to reach the concourse but limited the view of anyone standing in the concourse in ways that prevented them from seeing the field. The stadium owner could be liable there, since the architectural design had increased the danger of attending a game.

Courts have also allowed recovery where a fan was distracted by a mascot. In *Lowe v. California League of Professional Baseball*, a fan turned away from the game after being touched by a seven-foot-tall dinosaur mascot and was then struck by a flying ball. Because the mascot's presence was not necessary to the game, and increased the danger to the fan, the fan's lawsuit was permitted to proceed. Other times, however, courts have not allowed distraction by a mascot to serve as a method for avoiding primary assumption of risk. In *Harting v. Dayton Dragons Professional Baseball Club*, the Ohio Supreme Court found that "team mascots and their antics are a common phenomena, and the mascots are normally present during the entire course of the game" (870 N.E.2d, 770). In what is perhaps a sad statement on a number of levels, the court opined, "In many cases, the team mascots are more popular than the team itself" (*Id.*). In conclusion, "The fact that the Chicken appeared while the game was being played does not absolve [plaintiff] from the duty to protect herself from the ordinary risks inherent in the sport" (*Id.*).

Courts appear likely to deviate from the baseball rule and characterize conduct as increasing the danger beyond the "natural" level where victims are particularly sympathetic. The baseball rule, however, has arguably forced plaintiffs to twist the way in which they argue cases. To the extent plaintiffs must cabin their argument into the territory of architectural features and off-field distractions, this may distort the litigation process. Instead of focusing on the core question of whether an arena operator has done enough to protect fans from danger, we focus on whether an exception to the baseball rule should apply in a particular case.

At times, courts have resisted the idea that arena owners should have a limited duty and allowed fans to recover on negligence principles. Most recently, an appellate court in New Mexico, in *Edward C. v. City of Albuquerque*, questioned whether there was a "compelling reason" to provide immunity to stadium operators not provided to other landowners which invite members of the public to their properties. The court would have allowed the plaintiff to recover under a negligence theory. On appeal, the state supreme court reversed the lower court, adhering to the baseball rule but emphasizing that the victim was not in the stands but rather in an inadequately protected "multi-use area."

More threatening to the seeming immunity enjoyed by baseball arena operators are efforts not to overcome the limited duty rule but to redefine the extent of the duty by broadening its limits. In the fall of 2015 a class action lawsuit was filed against Major League Baseball, its teams, and the arenas in which games are played, asserting that the baseball should be held liable for failing to extend netting further down the sidelines.

Courts have also had to consider cases involving injuries to fans resulting not from the activity on the court or field but from activity in the stands. These claims often focus on inadequate security and/or the excessive sale of alcohol to intoxicated persons. Because these claims have little to do with sport itself (and could as easily be filed against arenas hosting concerts and other public gatherings), this chapter does not discuss them further.

3. Intentional Torts to Persons

As is the case with accidental injuries, courts have also developed discrete rules relating to injuries to participants in athletic activities that resulted from intentional conduct.

The most common intentional tort claim involving harmful physical contact is the tort of battery. Winning a battery claim requires showing that a defendant acted with intent, meaning with a desire or purpose or knowledge that a result is substantially certain to occur. The defendant must have intentionally caused a harmful or offensive *contact*. Punching, kicking, and perhaps spitting would all be legally cognizable batteries.

As in negligence cases, plaintiffs are limited by an important principle. Where a plaintiff has *consented* to a contact, she cannot bring a battery claim. Courts have held that participants consent to all risks that are commonplace, expected, and inherent aspects of a particular sport. Where one has reason to expect that intentional (and perhaps harmful) contact may occur during a sport, battery claims cannot be brought successfully.

In claims involving participants against other participants, an additional consideration may involve whether a person legally responsible for another's actions can be held vicariously liable. This is most likely to surface in pro sports, where an athlete whose conduct causes injury is employed by a team. Can the injured player sue the person causing injury? The law of agency governs the responsibility of employers for their employees' misconduct. Often, courts hold that employers are *not* liable for intentional misconduct by their employees but *are* liable for the negligent acts. Such conduct is considered outside the "scope of employment."

For employees whose job involves an understanding that the employee may need to engage in violence, however, such violence can be found to fall within the ambit of the employer's legal responsibility. Classic examples would be security personnel or bar bouncers. In sports cases, courts have confronted questions of whether violence—even outside the course of play—may be an expected or understood part of an athlete's role. In *Nathans v. Offerman*, a Connecticut court heard a case involving injuries caused by former major league player Jose Offerman who, at 38 years old and in the "twilight of his career," played for the minor league Long Island Ducks. The pitcher for the rival Bridgeport Bluefish struck Offerman on the leg, prompting Offerman to charge the pitcher's mound with his bat in hand. The plaintiff, the catcher for the Bluefish, ran toward the mound and in the fight that followed was struck in the head by Offerman's bat. Offerman's employer sought dismissal, but the court found it sufficiently unclear as to whether he had deviated from the scope of employment when he rushed the mound and allowed the case to go to trial. It was possible, to the court, that a jury might find Offerman was attempting to further his employer's business interests by engaging in physical violence.

4. Economic and Dignitary Harms

Tort law regulates more than just physical security. It also protects intangible interests like privacy and reputation. Sports stars have valuable images and reputations, and tort law has recognized claims that they may have to protect such intangible interests.

One of the tort claims—with origins in the common law and often embodied in statute—that exists to protect one's image and likeness is the "right of publicity." A person owns his or her name, image, and likeness, and can bring a tort claim against a party that uses such indicators of identity without permission in a manner that provides a commercial advantage. Often, the issue in sports cases involves whether a stylized rendering of an athlete's image is sufficient to constitute use of the name, image, and likeness of the athlete.

In *Newcombe v. Adolf Coors*, Don Newcombe, a major league pitcher, sued the beverage manufacturer after an image Newcombe claimed was his was utilized in an advertisement for Killian's Irish Red Beer. Newcombe, a recovering alcoholic, was particularly incensed that his image was used to promote beer sales. Though the ad itself utilized a painted graphic, Newcombe argued that the pitcher depicted was clearly him, based on his distinctive windup, his skin color, and the player's number ("39," a slightly modified take on Newcombe's "36"). Siding with Newcombe, the U.S. Court of Appeals for the Ninth Circuit found that the image was readily identifiable as Mr. Newcombe.

More easily resolved are cases in which the player's actual picture is used without permission. After Yahoo! used Tom Brady's image, without permission, in ads promoting its fantasy sports services (both in *Sports Illustrated*, and, according to Brady, in banner ads which appear on web browsers), Brady's marketing firm, "TEB Capital Management LLC," sued the Internet company.

At some point, however, an athlete's publicity rights give way to the First Amendment's guarantee of freedom of expression. Defendants in name-image-likeness lawsuits will argue that their use of an athlete's likeness represented a transformative use, making the use itself expression subject to First Amendment protection. Sometimes, courts find these arguments unpersuasive. For instance, hockey player Tony Twist, known as an aggressive "enforcer" on the ice, was lampooned in the form of a *Spawn* comic book gangster named "Antonio Twistelli" (and a considerably altered physical appearance). Twist won his case—receiving a $15 million jury award before eventually settling after successfully defending against appeals. The appellate courts found that if the predominant use of the athlete's name and likeness was artistic in nature, it would be protected by the First Amendment, but that if its predominant use was to achieve a commercial advantage the athlete could prevail.

Similarly, in *Keller v. EA Sports*, former Arizona State and Nebraska quarterback Sam Keller challenged the NCAA Football video game's use of his likeness as a character. Unlike in the Twist case, Keller's name was not included in the video game, but he argued successfully that the digitized avatar was his. It had the same height, weight, skin tone, hair color, and style and utilized the same playing style Keller had demonstrated during his athletic career. The court found that Keller's likeness was used without sufficient transformation, and thus that his claim prevailed.

In other cases, however, First Amendment claims have been successful. There are not always clear points of distinction, leaving open the question of when the First Amendment trumps a tort right-of-publicity claim. In *ETW Licensing v. Jireh*, the licensing entity of golfer Tiger Woods sued a company which sold a print of a painting, *The Masters of Augusta*, celebrating the Master's golf tournament that prominently featured a graphic of Woods striking a golf ball. The court sided with the "public interest in freedom of expression," emphasizing the elements of the painting that were not Woods's likeness in finding the use sufficiently transformative as to enjoy the full protection of the First Amendment.

Another tort claim that serves to protect reputational interests is defamation, which can involve statements harmful to another person's reputation in written (libel) or oral (slander) form. Athletes accused of misconduct by others will often threaten, and sometimes file, defamation claims. Lance Armstrong, for instance, filed lawsuits against media outlets accusing him of doping—engaging in what the *ABA Journal* called "lawsuit bullying" prior to his admission that he had, in fact, engaged in the use of prohibited performance-enhancing substances.

Again, the freedom of expression serves to temper the rights of a plaintiff bringing a defamation claim. Statements of opinion are not actionable in the law of defamation, even if the opinion is quite negative or harmful to reputation. Moreover, rhetorical hyperbole is protected expression.

For instance, former NBA (National Basketball Association) player Danny Fortson filed a lawsuit against Phoenix Suns owner Jerry Colangelo, who referred to the player as a "thug" after Fortson ended the season of a talented Suns rookie. Fortson also sued *New York Post* columnist Peter Vecsey, and the paper, after the columnist referred to

Fortson as "thugged out" and a "wanksta." The court opined that "[t]o foreclose the use of hyperbole, under the threat of civil liability, 'would condemn [sports commentary] to an arid, desiccated recital of bare facts.' "

5. Product-Related Torts

In addition to accidents and intentionally harmful conduct, the law of torts also provides claims to those injured as a result of defective products. Product defects fall into three categories. First, manufacturing defects involve flaws in a product resulting from problems during the production process—a single unit of a product is more dangerous than it should be. Second, design defects—the lion's share of product liability claims—involve products that were designed in ways that pose risks outweighing the benefits of the chosen design. Where a technologically feasible and safer alternative design is available, a product is deemed to have a design defect. Third, products may be defective even without a manufacturing flaw or design problem if they fail to contain an adequate warning. Sports products liability claims have been filed in all three areas.

Importantly, products liability claims do not require a showing of breach (as in the case of negligence) or intent on the part of the defendant (as in the case of battery). Instead, these are "strict liability" torts, which means that once a plaintiff proves a defect, and that his injury arose because of that defect and not because he misused the product or altered it in a significant way, the plaintiff will win his claim.

Often, a plaintiff will bring all three kinds of products liability claims. For instance, in a case eventually decided by the Montana Supreme Court, *Patch v. H & B*, the family of an American Legion youth baseball player killed after being struck by a batted ball sued the manufacturer of the aluminum bat that had been used in the game, claiming that the bat increased the velocity speed of a struck ball and thus made it harder for infielders to protect themselves from grievous, and in this case fatal, injuries. The plaintiffs asserted manufacturing and design defects; the trial judge dismissed the manufacturing defect claim, and the jury found that the bat was not defectively designed, but that it was defective due to a failure to warn of the enhanced risks associated with aluminum bats. To avoid being deemed defective under a failure-to-warn claim, a warning must be reasonable—both in terms of its placement and appearance (it must be visible to a user) and in terms of its substantive content (it must include sufficient clarity on the risks, their severity, and any necessary steps to avoid those risks).

6. Latent Injuries

Among the interesting recent developments in potential tort law issues relating to sports concerns latent injury claims, most notably those associate with traumatic brain injuries in football and hockey. Latent injury cases—involving injuries that manifest themselves years after a victim participated in an activity—are complicated throughout the law of torts. Workplace claims involving asbestosis and silicosis (sometimes fatal lung conditions experienced by workers exposed to harmful substances) were a dominant feature of courts' tort dockets in the 1970s and 1980s.

In football, recent scientific advances, covered extensively in the media, have suggested that concussions and subconcussive injuries can, over time, lead to the onset of a condition known as chronic traumatic encephalopathy (CTE). While the science is still in development, it suggests that CTE victims' brains' resemble those of a patient with Alzheimer's or dementia, and various conditions including depression have been linked to CTE.

Typically, workers are restricted from suing their employers for injuries which occurred on the job. Instead, such workers, under state statute, must file claims for workers' compensation. However, where an employer engaged in fraud or intentional tort, workers might be able to get around that statutory exclusion and file a lawsuit.

The length of time between the contacts causing a latent injury and the actual physical manifestations of that injury present complicated legal problems of proof. In asbestos-related claims, that may involve difficulty distinguishing the relative contribution of breathing asbestos fibers and smoking cigarettes for a victim who, years later, develops lung disease. In football- and hockey-related brain injury cases, other factors, such as lifestyle choices and genetic predisposition, may complicate the relationship between playing a sport and developing CTE or other long-term brain disease.

Nonetheless, plaintiffs have been successful in extracting settlements in at least the professional football context, based on the assertion that the NFL (National Football League) engaged in fraud with respect its knowledge of mounting evidence that concussions and other head trauma could cause lasting health problems for retired NFL players.

7. Conclusion

The landscape of torts cases relating to sports is quite broad—it would be impossible to cover the subject in all of its detail except in a freestanding book. This chapter has attempted to highlight some of the key legal principles and tort claims that arise in connection with sports. Notably, tort law has been adapted to address special policy considerations arising from an injury's connection to a sporting event.

References

American Law Institute. (1998). *Restatement of the Law Third—Torts: Products Liability* (Philadelphia, Pennsylvania: American Law Institute).

American Law Institute. (2009). *Restatement of the Law Third—Torts: Liability for Physical and Emotional Harm* (Washington, D.C.: American Law Institute).
American Law Institute. (2012). *Restatement of the Law Third—Torts: Liability for Physical and Emotional Harm* (Philadelphia, Pennsylvania: American Law Institute).
Edelman, Marc, and Geoffrey Rapp. (2015). *Careers in Sports Law* (Chicago: American Bar Association).

Cases

Babych v. McRae, 41 Conn. Super. 280 (1989).
Benajem v. Detroit Tigers, 635 N.W.2d 219 (Mich. Ct. App. 2001).
Cohen v. Massapequa Union Free School Dist., 285 A.D.2d 577 (N.Y. 2d Dep't 2001).
Crawn v. Campo, 643 A. 2d 600 (N.J. 1994).
Edward C. v. City of Albuquerque, 241 P.3d 1086 (N.M. 2010).
ETW Licensing v. Jireh, 332 F.3d 915 (6th Cir. 2003).
Gauvin v. Clark, 404 Mass. 450 (1989).
Harting v. Dayton Dragons Professional Baseball Club, 870 N.E.2d 766 (Ohio Ct. App. 2007).
Jones v. Three Rivers Management Corp., 394 A.2d 546 (Pa. 1978).
Keller v. EA Sports, 724 F.3d 1268 (9th Cir. July 31, 2013).
Knight v. Jewett, 834 P.2d 696 (Cal. 1992).
LaMalfa v. Aquila, 114 Ohio St. 3d 1481 (2007).
Lowe v. California League of Professional Baseball, 56 Cal. App. 4th 112 (1997).
Mann v. Nutrilite, 136 Cal. App. 2d 729 (1955).
Nabozny v. Barnhill, 31 Ill. App. 3d 212 (1975).
Nathans v. Offerman, 922 F. Supp. 2d 271 (D. Conn. 2013).
Newcombe v. Adolf Coors, 157 F.3d 686 (9th Cir. 1998).
Patch v. Hillerich & Bradsby Co., 361 Mont. 241 (2011).
Rudnick v. Golden West Broadcasters, 156 Cal. App. 3d 793 (1984).
Schnetz v. Ohio Dep't of Rehabilitation and Correction, No. 2006-07406, 2009 Ohio 1573 (2009).
Thurman v. Ice Palace, 36 Cal. App. 2d 364 (1939).
Trujillo v. Yeager, 642 F. Supp. 2d 86 (D. Conn. 2009).

CHAPTER 9

THE INCREASING ROLE OF DISABILITY ISSUES IN U.S. SPORTS LAW

DIONNE L. KOLLER

1. Introduction

U.S. sport traditionally has enjoyed considerable freedom from government intervention. All levels of sport are regulated by leagues or governing bodies that establish athlete eligibility requirements and other rules that must be satisfied in order for an athlete to participate (Mitten and Davis, 2008). Sports governing bodies have substantial authority to set the terms for participation in their respective sport, and courts generally give deference to how sports regulators choose to enforce them. Federal and state law is rarely used to regulate directly the games or how they are played (Koller, 2016).

In recent years, however, there has been growing interest in using law to effect change in sports. For instance, all fifty states and the District of Columbia have enacted legislation mandating that youth athletes who are suspected of suffering a concussion be removed from play and may not return until cleared by an appropriate medical professional (Harvey, Koller, and Lowrey, 2015). The combination of sports concussion litigation and legislation has caused a rethinking of sports, how they are played, and how the games, as currently constructed, might be changed. Perhaps not coincidentally, there has also been increased interest in using law and policy to include more individuals with disabilities in the world of sports.

The Centers for Disease Control and Prevention report that one out of every five adults has a disability and the U.S. Department of Education reports that 12.9% of all public school students have some type of disability (Centers for Disease Control, 2016). Research demonstrates that athletic participation provides all individuals with numerous benefits, including increased self-esteem and better overall health and wellbeing. Children who participate in sports tend to develop important life skills and exhibit better academic outcomes (Looby, 2012). For adults and children with disabilities, sports participation provides the added benefits of helping to mitigate the effects of chronic disease and the emotional and social impact of their condition (Dearden Ferrin, and Dulaney, 2012). Individuals with disabilities, however, are often not able to enjoy the benefits of athletic participation either because of a lack of appropriate sports opportunities or because of a lack of accommodation within existing sports programs.

Although there is no constitutional right to participate in sports, two federal statutes aimed at ensuring that individuals with disabilities are able to access public accommodations, services, and educational opportunities have relevance in the athletics context: the Rehabilitation Act of 1973 (Rehabilitation Act) and the Americans with Disabilities Act of 1990 (ADA). These statutes prohibit discrimination and have been interpreted to provide individuals with disabilities an equal opportunity to participate in sports. A third statute, the Ted Stevens Olympic and Amateur Sports Act (Amateur Sports Act), seeks to provide separate programming for disabled athletes through the Paralympic Movement.

While all three statutes have been in force for decades, there is increasing momentum behind putting their provisions to work and expanding participation opportunities for athletes with disabilities. This momentum is occurring against the backdrop of a childhood obesity epidemic, and children with physical and developmental disabilities are among the population of youth with the greatest need for sports programming. Obesity rates for children with disabilities are 38% higher than for children without disabilities, and children with autism are even more at risk. As a result, greater use of law to provide opportunities for children with disabilities is an important issue. This chapter focuses on the increasing role the Rehabilitation Act and the ADA play across all sports contexts, from interscholastic and intercollegiate to professional and Olympic, and ways that law and policy can effect even greater change in the future.

2. Statutory Overview

U.S. law provides protections and opportunities for athletes with disabilities primarily through the Rehabilitation Act, the ADA, and the Amateur Sports Act. Both the Rehabilitation Act and the ADA prohibit discrimination against individuals with disabilities. The Amateur Sports Act provides athletic opportunities for individuals with disabilities through the Paralympic Movement. An important goal of the Rehabilitation Act and the ADA, which apply to most sports teams and regulators, is to break down barriers to allow individuals with disabilities to enjoy equality of opportunity and fully participate in American society (Weston, 2005).

Most entities that sponsor sports programs are covered by either the Rehabilitation Act or the ADA, and in some cases both. The Rehabilitation Act provides that "no otherwise qualified individual with a disability," be excluded from, or subject to, discrimination in "any program or activity receiving Federal financial assistance." (Rehabilitation

Act, 29 U.S.C. § 794(a).) The Supreme Court has held that an "otherwise qualified individual" is "one who has met all of a program's requirements in spite of his handicap" (*Southeastern Community College v. Davis*, 442 U.S. at 406). To state a claim under the Rehabilitation Act, a plaintiff must show that (a) the program or entity receives federal financial assistance; (b) the plaintiff has a disability within the meaning of the statute; (c) the plaintiff is "otherwise qualified" to participate in the athletics program, with or without reasonable accommodations; and (d) the plaintiff was excluded from participating in the program because of his or her disability.

The primary difference between the Rehabilitation Act and the ADA is that the coverage of the ADA is much broader, extending to most private entities and employers. Courts have held that the same standards and case law should be used for determining violations of the Rehabilitation Act and the ADA. As a result, the requirements for a claim under the ADA are essentially the same as those for a claim under the Rehabilitation Act, except that a plaintiff bringing a claim under the ADA need not show that the defendant is a recipient of federal financial assistance. The ADA states that "no qualified individual with a disability shall, by reason of such disability, be excluded" from participation in programs or activities of a covered entity. (Americans with Disabilities Act, 42 U.S.C. § 12132.)

To state a claim under the ADA, a plaintiff must show that the defendant is a "public entity" or a place of "public accommodation" operated by a private entity and therefore covered by Title II or Title III of the ADA. Most state high school athletic associations and professional sports teams are covered by the ADA. The plaintiff must also show that (a) he or she is an individual with a "disability" as defined by the statute; (b) that he or she is "otherwise qualified" to participate, with or without reasonable accommodations; and that, (c) because of his or her disability, he or she has been excluded from participation in the athletic program.

An individual is disabled within the meaning of the Rehabilitation Act and the ADA if he or she has "a physical or mental impairment that substantially limits one or more major life activities." (Americans with Disabilities Act, 42 U.S.C. § 12102(1).) As with the Rehabilitation Act, an individual is "qualified" for purposes of the ADA if he or she can meet the "essential eligibility requirements," with or without reasonable modification. (Americans with Disabilities Act, 42 U.S.C. § 12131(2).) It is not necessary for the plaintiff to show that the defendant engaged in intentional discrimination. Instead, a plaintiff may establish discrimination by showing that the defendant could have made a reasonable accommodation that would allow the plaintiff to participate but refused to do so.

To determine whether a reasonable accommodation should be made, the Supreme Court has made clear that athletic associations and sponsors of sports programs must make an "individualized inquiry" and not rely on stereotypes or generalizations (*PGA Tour, Inc. v. Martin*). It is permissible to exclude an individual with a disability from an athletic program by refusing to make a requested modification if the athlete's requested modification would "fundamentally alter" the nature of the program or impose an undue administrative or financial burden on the program. (Americans with Disabilities Act, 42 U.S.C. § 12182(b)(2).) A fundamental alteration in this context would include altering an "essential" aspect of the game itself, altering the nature of the competition by providing a competitive advantage, or posing a safety issue for other competitors.

In the area of sports, the ADA and the Rehabilitation Act (when applicable) have most frequently been used to challenge sports stadium designs, competition rules, and athlete eligibility requirements (Cottingham et al., 2016). The ADA has had perhaps its greatest impact on sports facilities, and not on the games themselves. Researchers have concluded that ADA compliance is "well ingrained" in the sports venue culture—due to the use of best practices, professional training, and technical assistance—so that accommodating patrons with disabilities is "seamlessly" integrated into facility operations. In contrast, while progress has been made, there has not been the same dramatic change in the design and operation of sports programs that is evident in sports stadiums (Grady and Moorman, 2016). Instead, progress in the area of sports rules and programming has primarily come through the case-by-case process of litigation, with courts applying the ADA and Rehabilitation Act in various athletic contexts, as explained in later sections.

3. Interscholastic Sports

The most expansive legal and policy response to the issue of individuals with disabilities participating in sports is happening at the interscholastic level. In this context there is perhaps the greatest potential for the transformation of sport for persons with disabilities. This is because of the substantial number of sports opportunities provided for children through schools and the legal obligations to provide equal participation opportunities for students with disabilities.

The National Federation of State High School Associations states that more than 7.8 million children participate in high school sports. Nevertheless, it is well documented that in the United States, rates of physical inactivity and childhood obesity are high (U.S. Department of Education, 2011). Because of numerous barriers to participation, researchers have found that children with disabilities are 4.5 times less active than their peers (Aspen Institute, 2016). In general, youth with disabilities participate in "very little" physical activity at school (U.S. Department of Education, 2011). Research also demonstrates that students with cognitive or intellectual disabilities participate on sports teams at greater rates than students with certain types of physical disabilities, at least in part because there are fewer athletic programs that are designed to meet the needs of those with physical disabilities (McPeters, 2015).

A range of issues involving individuals with disabilities who seek to participate in sports occur at the interscholastic level. The most common issue subject to legal action is to what extent, if any, eligibility and other participation rules must be modified to allow an athlete with a disability to participate in an existing sports program. While litigation has effected significant change in some respects, it has not brought about sweeping reform. A report by the U.S. Government Accountability Office (GAO) found that despite legal requirements to provide equal opportunity and access for students with disabilities, participation opportunities were limited (U.S. Government Accountability Office, 2010). As a result, an increasingly important policy issue is the movement to eliminate barriers to participation by adding new sport opportunities and teams to existing programs. Some states, such as Maryland, have made access to sport a priority by requiring local school boards to develop policies to provide students with disabilities with reasonable accommodations to enable them to participate on existing sports teams and, where necessary, provide students with disabilities access to alternative sports programs.

Because eligibility rules are often established by state high school athletic associations that do not generally receive federal funding, legal challenges at this level are often brought under the ADA. Common legal challenges in the interscholastic context are to facially neutral rules that, without modification, prevent students with disabilities from participating in sports. These include challenges to rules that prohibit participation by athletes on the basis of age (declaring a student ineligible when he or she reaches the age of nineteen) and on the basis of duration of participation (declaring a student ineligible when he or she has attended school for eight semesters). Most high school athletic associations have "age nineteen" and "eight semester" rules, and these rules can have a substantial impact on students with disabilities, who may be older or enrolled in high school longer than typical students.

Students with disabilities challenging "age nineteen" and "eight semester" rules generally argue that they are "qualified" to participate in athletics if the rule in question is waived. These individuals argue that a waiver is a reasonable modification of the program that is necessary for them to participate. However, athletic associations are not legally obligated to waive eligibility rules if doing so would fundamentally alter the nature of the athletic program or where a procedure for granting a waiver would pose an "undue burden" on the association. Athletic associations often argue that eligibility rules were promulgated for important policy reasons—such as protecting the safety of other students who might be younger and smaller and promoting fairness by allowing all students an opportunity to participate—so that waiving the rules would "fundamentally alter" the nature of the sports program. To determine whether a reasonable modification through waiver of an eligibility rule is required, courts hold that athletic administrators must undertake an "individualized inquiry."

Because these cases rely on individualized assessments and fact-specific analysis, results differ widely. Thus, students with the same disability may not be entitled to the same protections under the ADA, given the sport involved and the athlete's particular size and skill. Courts have stated that relevant factors to consider include the student's age, athletic experience, and the potential risk of harm to other athletes due to the individual's strength, size, and speed, and the sport. For instance, in *Baisden v. West Virginia Secondary Schools Activities Commission*, the court stated that an individualized inquiry was required for a student with learning disabilities who sought a waiver of the athletic association's "age nineteen" rule to allow him to play football. Due to his disability, Baisden had to repeat two years of his education, resulting in his turning nineteen before his senior year. The court held that the association's "age nineteen" rule was not essential and may be waived in an appropriate case. However, the court found that Baisden's size (six feet four and 280 pounds) and his athletic ability (he ran a forty-yard-dash in 5.3 seconds) meant that the safety of younger, smaller students would be compromised and he would have a competitive advantage. As a result, the court found that waiving the "age nineteen" rule would "fundamentally alter" the nature of the athletic program. The athletic association was therefore not required to waive the rule to allow Baisden to participate (*Baisden*, 568 S.E.2d at 44).

In contrast, in *Cruz v. Pennsylvania Interscholastic Athletic Association*, the court held that an athletic association was required to modify its eligibility criteria by waiving the "age nineteen" rule to permit a student with learning disabilities to participate in football and track and field. The court noted that the student was not a "star" player and was relatively small in size, so he was not a safety risk and had no competitive advantage over other students. Moreover, because the track and football teams did not make "cuts," the student would not displace others. The court also held that a process whereby students could request a waiver of the "age nineteen" rule would not place an "unreasonable burden" on the association (*Cruz*, 157 F. Supp. 2d at 499).

Although the ADA provides student-athletes with a right to an individualized assessment of whether a reasonable modification of a challenged eligibility rule is possible, it does not provide additional opportunities that are not available to other students. Thus, in *Starego v. New Jersey State Interscholastic Athletic Association*, an autistic student sought a waiver of an "eight semester" rule which limited high school students to eight consecutive semesters of athletic eligibility, and an "age nineteen" rule. The court held that granting a waiver of these rules would not pose an "undue burden" and that granting a waiver would be a reasonable accommodation. However, the court emphasized that Starego could not show that he was excluded from the athletic program because of his disability. The court found that because he had played four years of football, granting Starego a waiver to play a fifth year would "provide a benefit to which other students are not entitled," and that while the ADA puts the student "on an equal footing with" others, it does not provide additional opportunities (*Starego*, 970 F. Supp. at 314–315).

Courts have also considered challenges to the way high school athletic associations treat adaptive sports in comparison to traditional sports. In *Badgett v. Alabama High School Athletic Association*, an elite wheelchair athlete brought suit against the high school athletic governing body alleging that it discriminated against her when it refused to allow her to compete against able-bodied track and field athletes and refused to allow points she earned in competition to be included in her high school's track and field point total. The court held that the modifications made by the association, including establishing a separate wheelchair division for track and field (in which schools could win a state championship), allowing wheelchair athletes to earn individual points, establish state records, and earn individual honors, were sufficient. The court emphasized that the ADA and the Rehabilitation Act did not entitle an athlete to the "best," or "requested" modification, only a "reasonable" one.

The court found that Badgett's requested modification to race with able-bodied athletes and have her individual points count toward her school's total were not reasonable because they would fundamentally alter the nature of the state's track and field program. The court credited the association's evidence that the norm in track and field was to have a separate wheelchair division. Further, the court did not find it reasonable to require the association to make separate evaluations of whether a particular wheelchair athlete could safely participate with able-bodied runners. The court also explained that because points were awarded to teams based on the essential skills of "running and jumping," it would fundamentally alter the program to award team points for wheelchair racing, which is a distinctly different activity (*Badgett*, 2007 WL 2461928).

More recently, there has been a growing movement to provide separate programming for students with disabilities who are unable to participate in traditional sport offerings. The effort to accommodate students with disabilities who seek to participate in a school sports program gained momentum with the publication in 2013 of a "Dear Colleague" letter from the Department of Education's Office of Civil Rights (OCR) which provided guidance to elementary and secondary schools regarding their obligations under Section 504 of the Rehabilitation Act. The OCR stated that school-based sports of all levels are "an important component" of an education program, and that a GAO report found that students with disabilities were not being provided with an equal opportunity to participate in school-based sports. (U.S. Department of Education, Office for Civil Rights, 2013.)

The OCR explained that a school must operate its sports program in a way that provides "qualified students with disabilities" an "equal opportunity" to participate. According to the OCR, schools are therefore required to provide qualified students with disabilities with an equal opportunity to participate in an "integrated manner," to the greatest extent possible, including making reasonable modifications, unless doing so would fundamentally alter the sports program. To evaluate whether a proposed modification is required, the school must make an "individualized inquiry" and not rely on generalizations or stereotypes. The OCR was clear, however, that an "individualized inquiry" does not mean that every student with a disability is guaranteed a place on an athletic team if other students must try out. Thus, schools may require a level of athletic skill in order to participate.

The greatest impact of the OCR's "Dear Colleague" letter is with respect to schools offering separate or different athletic opportunities for students with disabilities. The OCR emphasized that providing "unnecessarily" separate or different athletic programs is discriminatory. However, the OCR stressed that for students with disabilities who are not able to participate in a school's existing program (even with reasonable modifications), schools should create additional opportunities and support these programs as it does with its traditional athletic activities. The OCR stated that disability-specific teams such as wheelchair basketball can be fielded on a district-wide basis, and it also urged schools to consider mixing male and female students and offering teams where students with and without disabilities can participate together.

In this regard, the OCR's guidance resembled the approach it has taken with Title IX to achieve equal opportunity for women and girls to participate in school-based sports. For example, in the "Dear Colleague" letter, the OCR spoke of "fully and effectively" accommodating the "interests and abilities" of students with disabilities, and creating separate programs where appropriate to take into account the "unmet interests" of students with disabilities. This language is similar to that used in the gender equity context, and the success in that area can provide a blueprint for effecting change in the way schools allocate athletic opportunities for students with disabilities (Milani, 1998).

In addition, legal requirements to provide "equal opportunity" for students with disabilities can drive important innovation in sport. The GAO's report highlighted the fact that we have relatively little information about providing opportunities for physical activity and sports programming to individuals with disabilities. Lack of attention to the issue has perpetuated the barriers to participation, and recent government action, through the GAO report and the OCR's "Dear Colleague" letter, are providing an effective stimulus for schools to do more. Thus, while current law focuses mainly on incorporating students with disabilities into existing sports programs, going forward, a mix of approaches—both inclusion and the development of new sport experiences—has the potential to stimulate the greatest change in sports. Through a hybrid approach, American schools can be a laboratory for developing new opportunities and changing norms around the issue of who is an "athlete" and what is a "sport" as those terms are commonly understood.

For instance, new sports such as "cup stacking" enable a range of students with different abilities to participate in sports. Groups such as the American Association of Adaptive Sports Programs are providing guidance and programming to school systems so that they can implement adaptive programs in sports such as wheelchair basketball and sitting volleyball (Seminara, 2016). Additionally, schools are increasingly integrating athletes with disabilities into existing programs in sports such as track and field and swimming, so that students with disabilities may participate alongside students without. With continued expansion of these efforts at the interscholastic level, there will likely be change at more advanced levels of sport—especially in the intercollegiate athletic context.

4. Intercollegiate Sports

To be eligible for participation in college athletics, students must meet minimum academic requirements set by the National Collegiate Athletic Association (NCAA) and the physical and skill-based requirements set by the institution for which the athlete seeks to compete. The number of students entering colleges and universities with a disability is on the rise, particularly in the area of cognitive and mental health impairments. The NCAA lists numerous "education-impacting" disabilities, including learning disabilities, attention deficit hyperactivity disorder, and autism spectrum disorder. These are in addition to physical disabilities such as medical conditions or hearing impairments. With the rising number of students entering postsecondary education with a diagnosis of a learning disability or other mental health impairment, there have been—and likely will continue to be—legal challenges to NCAA eligibility criteria.

The NCAA requires entering student-athletes to have graduated from high school and completed the requisite number of "core" high school courses. Prospective student-athletes must also achieve a minimum score on a standardized college entrance examination (the SAT or ACT) that is indexed to a student's high school grade point average. Once enrolled, students must meet continuing eligibility standards set by their institution as well as the NCAA's progress-toward-degree rules.

Students with learning disabilities have challenged these rules. Although the NCAA is only subject to the Rehabilitation Act if it receives federal financial assistance, courts have held that the NCAA is subject to the ADA. In 1998, the NCAA entered into a consent decree with the U.S. Department of Justice (DOJ) to resolve the DOJ's determination that the NCAA's initial eligibility requirements discriminated against students with learning disabilities in violation of Title III of the ADA. Although the NCAA did not admit liability, it did agree to change several aspects of its bylaws relating to initial eligibility and a student athletes' high school course work. Specifically, the NCAA agreed under certain conditions to accept courses designed for students with learning disabilities as meeting the requirements for "core" high school course work. The NCAA also agreed to grant students with learning disabilities who did not meet the initial eligibility requirements an additional year of athletic eligibility (*United States v. National Collegiate Athletic Association*).

Courts have indicated that initial eligibility criteria are "essential" and therefore the NCAA is not required to waive them completely to accommodate a student-athlete with a disability. In *Cole v. NCAA*, an athlete with a learning disability failed to meet the NCAA's initial eligibility requirements. The athlete filed an application for a waiver under NCAA rules, and the NCAA, after an individualized assessment of the athlete's academic record, denied the request. The athlete challenged the NCAA's refusal to waive the eligibility rules under the ADA (*Cole*, 120 F.Supp. 2d 1060).

The court ultimately held that the claim was moot, as the athlete had achieved "partial-qualifier" status and was able to practice with his college team. Nevertheless, the court stated that the eligibility requirements serve the important interest of ensuring that entering student-athletes are prepared to succeed academically. As a result, if, after the NCAA gives the prospective student-athlete individualized consideration of a waiver request, it is determined that he or she does not meet the requirements, the NCAA is not obligated to waive the eligibility rules to allow the athlete to participate. The court stated that the NCAA was entitled to deference in its assessment of whether a student-athlete was entitled to a waiver of the eligibility requirements (*Cole*, 120 F. Supp. 2d 1060). Because the NCAA has established a process for considering, on an individual basis, requests to waive initial-eligibility requirements, it is likely that courts will follow the reasoning in *Cole* and defer to the NCAA's determination.

In contrast, there is some indication that enrolled students may have greater success when seeking modification of academic eligibility rules. For instance, in *Matthews v. NCAA*, the court held that a student-athlete with learning disabilities was protected by the ADA, and that accommodating the student by waiving the NCAA's rule requiring a certain percentage of an athlete's course work be completed by his or her second year of enrollment, and during the academic year, would not "fundamentally alter" the NCAA's regulatory purpose (*Matthews*, 179 F. Supp. 2d at 1209).

Outside the context of NCAA eligibility requirements, courts will also defer to institutions to determine whether an athlete is physically qualified, and therefore eligible to participate. The leading case, *Knapp v. Northwestern University*, demonstrates the extent to which courts will defer to institutions to make reasonable determinations about an athlete's ability to participate. In *Knapp*, a basketball player suffered from a heart condition that increased his risk of sudden cardiac death. Although Northwestern honored his scholarship, the university would not clear him to play on its basketball team.

Knapp brought suit under the Rehabilitation Act seeking, among other things, an injunction that would require Northwestern to allow him to play. Northwestern agreed that it was covered by the Rehabilitation Act and that Knapp was excluded from the team solely because of his condition. However, the school argued that Knapp was not an "otherwise qualified individual with a disability" under the meaning of the Act. To demonstrate that he had a "disability" within the meaning of the statute, Knapp was required to establish that he had a physical impairment "which substantially limits one or more of his major life activities." Although a cardiovascular condition was a physical impairment within the meaning of the statute, the court found that Knapp could not show that this impairment substantially limited a major life activity.

The court explained that under the Rehabilitation Act, "major life activities" were basic functions such as walking, seeing, or hearing. Knapp claimed that his cardiovascular condition—an increased risk of harm that otherwise did not affect his daily life—affected the major life activity of learning, because with the condition he was not eligible to play intercollegiate basketball. The court held that the "major life activity" of learning could not be defined to include playing intercollegiate sports. As a result, the court held that Knapp was not "disabled" under the meaning of the Rehabilitation Act.

The court also rejected Knapp's claim because he could not establish that he was "otherwise qualified" to play basketball at Northwestern. The court noted that an "otherwise qualified" individual is one who is able to meet a program's requirements in spite of his handicap. Importantly, the court explained that physical qualifications may be essential to participating in certain programs, and that a "significant risk" of personal injury may disqualify an individual in cases where the risk of harm cannot be eliminated. Although Knapp produced medical opinions that his risk of cardiac death was within an acceptable range, and he and his parents agreed to execute liability waivers, the court deferred to Northwestern.

Significantly, the court held that decisions over whether an athlete was medically eligible to participate are "best left to team doctors and universities" as long as those decisions are reasonably made and based on an individualized inquiry. The court explained that such decisions must be based on sufficient medical evidence and with reference to any reasonable accommodations. Thus, the court emphasized that schools have the authority to decide whether an athlete with a disability is otherwise medically qualified to participate, and the court's role will be limited to ensuring that any decision to disqualify an athlete with a disability is made after an individualized, reasonable inquiry based on competent medical evidence.

Finally, students struggling with mental health issues may have difficulty establishing that they are "disabled" within the meaning of the Rehabilitation Act and ADA. In *Costello v. University of North Carolina*, the court held that an athlete who suffered from obsessive-compulsive disorder (OCD) could not show that he was "disabled," and therefore entitled to legal protection, because his OCD was not a "substantial impairment." Specifically, the court explained that a "mere medical diagnosis of an impairment" was not enough. In this case, the student-athlete could not show that his OCD was so severe as to substantially limit a major life activity, especially since his treatment mitigated the effects (*Costello*, 2006 WL 3694579).

In general, while the NCAA and individual colleges and universities are subject to the ADA and the Rehabilitation Act, courts will give deference to their determinations of whether an athlete is academically and physically qualified to participate in sports. Consistent with interpretations of the ADA and Rehabilitation Act, courts will ensure that the NCAA and educational institutions give individualized consideration of an athlete's particular circumstances. However, the NCAA and individual institutions are generally not required to waive completely eligibility requirements to allow an athlete with a disability to participate.

This approach makes for good policy. Given the temptation to "win at all costs" that is well documented in college sports, the NCAA is appropriately concerned with ensuring that individuals who participate in intercollegiate athletics are qualified to be students as well as athletes. The requirement that the NCAA and institutions make individualized determinations, and courts giving deference to this process, strikes the right balance between the policies underlying federal disability law and the educational goals that the NCAA and its member institutions seek to serve.

However, while the NCAA has made important strides in accommodating athletes with learning and other disabilities into existing sports programs, more should be done to achieve equality of opportunity by creating adaptive varsity intercollegiate sports programming. The NCAA generally supports such efforts (and at least one athletic conference has adopted an "inclusive sport strategy" that features varsity adaptive sports offerings) (ECAC Sports, 2015). Beyond this, the OCR should work to ensure that, like Title IX, the ADA and the Rehabilitation Act are robustly enforced to provide the full measure of equality to intercollegiate student-athletes with disabilities.

5. Professional Sports

The ADA also provides athletes with protection against discrimination in the context of professional sports. The leading case in this area is *PGA Tour, Inc. v. Martin*. In this case, professional golfer Casey Martin brought a claim against the PGA Tour seeking the right to use a cart during the third stage of a PGA Tour qualifying event. Although the PGA Tour had permitted Martin to use a cart during the first two stages, it stated that all athletes must walk the course during the third stage. It was agreed that Martin was an individual with a disability under the meaning of the statute due to a degenerative condition that affected his ability to walk, and that his disability prevented him from walking the course during a golf tournament.

The Court first held that the PGA Tour was a "public accommodation" and therefore covered by Title III of the ADA. The Court then explained that the ADA defines discrimination as failing to make the necessary modifications to afford access to individuals with disabilities, unless it can be shown that making such a modification would "fundamentally alter" the nature of the program or service that the covered entity provides. The PGA Tour argued that it need not modify its walking requirement to accommodate Martin because doing so would "fundamentally alter" the nature of the game.

The Court recognized that a sport could be fundamentally altered in two ways. First, the Court stated that a modification could alter an "essential" element of the game so that "it would be unacceptable even if it affected all competitors equally." The Court gave as an example a request to modify the game of golf by "changing the diameter of the hole from three to six inches." The Court held that using a cart was not "an essential attribute" of the game.

The Court stated that a second type of fundamental alteration would be one that gave the individual with a disability an advantage over other players, thereby altering the "character of the competition." The PGA Tour argued that any waiver of a competition rule at the "highest level" would fundamentally alter the game because all players must compete under the same rules. The Court rejected this by stating that it amounted to a claim that the PGA Tour was exempt from the ADA's "reasonable modification" requirement, and that Congress had not exempted elite athletics from the ADA's coverage.

Finally, the Court held that the PGA Tour violated the ADA by refusing to consider Martin's particular condition and circumstances in determining whether a modification of the no-cart rule would fundamentally alter the game by giving Martin an advantage over other players. In fact, the Court found, Martin endured greater physical fatigue and stress even with a cart than able-bodied players did with walking. The Court held that "an individualized inquiry" must be undertaken to determine whether a requested modification to accommodate a person's disability would be reasonable.

Justice Scalia, writing in dissent, emphasized that the Court's analysis of rules that were "essential" (and therefore not subject to waiver or modification) and those that, as the majority found with respect to the golf cart rule, were peripheral, was an "impossible . . . Alice in Wonderland" determination, given that rules of sport are "arbitrary" and "made up." Moreover, Scalia argued that the requirement of an "individualized determination" would increase the number of future cases. Indeed, Scalia even predicted a scenario where the parents of a Little League player with attention deficit disorder would try to convince a court that the child needed four, instead of the usual three, strikes when batting.

Since *Martin*, there has been little evidence of excessive litigation seeking to overturn rules of competition or that Little League has been compelled to provide four strikes. The rules of sport and games as traditionally played remain intact. However, there are two effects of the Court's opinion that have been wide-reaching. First is the holding that professional sports are covered by the ADA, and there is no exception for elite athletics. Congress has not amended the ADA in response to this result. The second effect is that sports regulators must make an individualized inquiry to determine whether reasonable accommodations can be made to allow an athlete with a disability to participate. As noted previously, this is now the standard at all levels of sport.

Given the Court's holding in *Martin* that the ADA can be applied in the context of professional sports, interesting legal issues are presented when an athlete with disabilities is a member of a team, and not an individual performer, and where the disability is mental and not physical. Such an issue was presented by basketball player Royce White, who suffers from generalized anxiety disorder and OCD. In connection with these issues, White experienced severe fear of flying and he was not able to adapt to the substantially increased number of flights required of a player in the National Basketball Association (NBA). White ultimately was released by his team and did not resume an NBA career.

Were he to have resumed playing, however, White, or an athlete who similarly suffered from anxiety, would have had several options. First, he could have sought accommodations from a team that employed him. If the team did not agree to accommodate his anxiety, he could also seek redress through the players' union using the process outlined in the NBA's collective bargaining agreement. If an agreement with the team could not be negotiated, a player like White could seek a legal remedy by resorting to the process for those who are employed by ADA-covered entities by filing a charge of discrimination through the Equal Employment Opportunity Commission (EEOC). If the EEOC could not mediate a resolution, then the player could file a claim against the team and the NBA under the ADA.

Importantly, the collective bargaining relationship between the players' union and the league does not displace the protections of the ADA. That is, while the collective bargaining process largely insulates professional sports leagues from antitrust challenges (so as not to undermine the labor law goals achieved through collective bargaining), no such exemption exists in the case of the ADA. However, a player like White suffering from anxiety over flying would have a difficult case. Like the student-athlete with OCD in *Costello*, a professional athlete with a fear of flying might have difficulty demonstrating that he is "disabled" under the ADA. In addition, a player like White would have to show that the team failed to provide a "reasonable accommodation." The nature of professional sports would make this very difficult. While allowing a player to travel to some away games by ground transportation would be possible, it likely would not be a reasonable accommodation to allow the player to miss road games and the resulting team meetings and other activities that take place when a professional team travels by air to games (McCann, 2014). As a result, the unique and demanding nature of professional sports means that while athlete-employees may attempt to claim coverage under the ADA, they likely will have a difficult time prevailing.

The Supreme Court's opinion in *Martin* was an important reminder that a sports organization's rules and practices—including those related to athlete eligibility and the "rules of the game"—are subject to the ADA. Despite the fact that the dissent in *Martin* predicted that the decision could detrimentally affect sport, the unique facts presented by Martin's level of skill and his physical disability have meant that the case, at least at the professional level, has not had significant effects.

The *Martin* decision's greatest impact, however, is that courts now mandate an individualized inquiry into whether a request for a reasonable accommodation by an athlete with a disability would "fundamentally alter" the athletics program. This mandate has had the greatest application at the level of interscholastic and intercollegiate sports, likely due to the greater number of participants and lower level of skill required to participate. At least one scholar also noted that *Martin's* effects have been muted at the professional level due to the "ethos of competition," such that a competitor would not want to be perceived as having an advantage (Greely, 2004). Going forward, the culture that deters individuals with disabilities from coming forward and seeking greater opportunities to participate in sports likely will be changed by the numbers of athletes with disabilities competing at lower levels of sport and by the visibility and success of Paralympic athletes.

6. Olympic Movement Sports

The Paralympic Movement has been at the forefront of providing athletic opportunities for individuals with disabilities through traditional sports such as archery, fencing, and swimming, and through adaptive sports such as sled hockey and wheelchair basketball. The first Paralympic Games of Olympic-style competition was held in Rome in 1960. Since then, the Paralympics have been held every four years, in coordination with the Olympic Games. Paralympic sports have rules and eligibility standards that correspond to the types of physical disabilities that are accommodated, such as limb loss, spinal cord injury, visual impairments, and brain injury. An important motivation for the Paralympic Movement is to provide the benefits of athletic participation to injured military personnel.

In the United States, the Paralympic Movement is administered by the U.S. Olympic Committee (USOC) subject to the requirements of the Amateur Sports Act. Through the Act, the USOC is charged with exercising "exclusive jurisdiction" over all matters relating to U.S. participation in the Paralympic Games and organization of the Paralympic Games if they are held in the United States. The USOC is also charged with, among other things, assembling the best possible athletes to represent the United States in the Paralympic Games, and encouraging and expanding opportunities for athletes with disabilities. The USOC advances these goals by developing participation opportunities for athletes with disabilities to participate in programs and competitions with able-bodied athletes. The most significant issues in this context are the allocation of resources for separate adaptive sports competition through the Paralympic Movement and integrating disabled athletes into competition with able-bodied athletes.

In *Hollonbeck v. U.S. Olympic Committee*, several elite Paralympic athletes claimed that the USOC discriminated against them in violation of the Rehabilitation Act and the ADA by providing less funding and fewer privileges and benefits than those available for able-bodied athletes in the Olympic program (*Hollonbeck*, 464 F. Supp. 2d at 1072). The court held that the Amateur Sports Act did not impose a duty on the USOC to provide the same level of support and benefits to the Paralympic program as it does with the Olympic program, and that the Rehabilitation Act and ADA do not impose such an obligation. The court concluded that the plaintiffs were challenging the quality of their experience in the Paralympic program, which is separate from the Olympic program. As a result, the court found that the Rehabilitation Act and the ADA did not apply, and that the harms alleged by the athletes were policy issues for the legislative or executive branches, and not the courts.

Although the case was unsuccessful in forcing the USOC to provide the same benefits to Paralympic athletes that it provides to Olympic athletes, scholars have credited the suit with spurring members of the Olympic and Paralympic movements to develop new policies and practices to further develop Paralympic sports and athletes (Grady and Moorman, 2016). While more work needs to be done, athletes today credit the Paralympic movement with changing the perceptions of athletes with disabilities and legitimizing adaptive sports, which ultimately contributes to more resources and better training opportunities. In addition to providing elite athletes with disabilities the opportunity to compete and reap the rewards, the Paralympic Movement can also be credited with creating greater legitimacy for such athletes. This undoubtedly has an important psychological effect at all levels of sport and can serve to encourage children with disabilities to get involved in sport and advocate for opportunities to participate.

Another important issue involving athletes with disabilities in the Olympic Movement is the extent to which such athletes can be integrated into competition with able-bodied athletes. The leading case involved sprinter Oscar Pistorius. Pistorius was a double amputee who raced with the use of so-called Cheetah prosthetic legs. The international federation for track and field, the IAAF (International Association of Athletics Federation), banned Pistorius from competition based on a rule it adopted which prevented an athlete from using "any technical device . . . that provides the user with an advantage." (CAS 2008/A/1480). Pistorius appealed the IAAF's decision to the Court of Arbitration for Sport (CAS), the entity which has exclusive authority to decide cases involving disputes between the IAAF and international-level athletes.

The CAS arbitration panel determined that the IAAF improperly applied its rule to Pistorius, in that the IAAF did not properly determine that the "Cheetah" prosthetics provided Pistorius with an "overall net advantage" over other athletes. Specifically, the panel found that the IAAF's determination was the result of a flawed process, because the IAAF adopted the rule with Pistorius in mind and employed an unfair procedure for enforcing it. The panel also found that the IAAF made its decision based on a flawed scientific report, the contents of which were heavily influenced by the IAAF. The panel concluded that the IAAF did not meet its burden of demonstrating that Pistorius had an advantage over other, able-bodied competitors, and it declared that Pistorius was eligible to compete.

Notably, like the U.S. Supreme Court in *Martin*, the CAS panel stated that in determining eligibility, the IAAF must make an individual determination, and that it must consider whether an individual athlete with a disability has an "overall net advantage," and not simply generalize that a prosthesis or other such device provides one. As with *Martin*, the effects of the *Pistorius* decision have been limited in that there has not been another athlete with disabilities who has successfully challenged an eligibility rule and secured a right to compete in Olympic Movement sport with able-bodied athletes.

However, both cases illustrate that at least some sports governing bodies struggle to integrate qualified athletes with disabilities into their programs in a way that balances the rights of athletes with disabilities with the desire to maintain what are thought to be the essential rules and character of the sport. Indeed, in both *Pistorius* and *Martin*, the relevant governing body implemented the challenged rule in response to the athletes' success in competing with able-bodied athletes. This suggests an unwillingness to consider that an athlete can be anyone other than those able-bodied individuals who typically have achieved in sports, and the requirement of an "individualized inquiry" will help prevent such ossified thinking.

7. Conclusion

For athletes with disabilities, the law's primary focus is providing equal opportunity to participate by prohibiting discrimination in existing programs. The effect is to provide greater opportunity for athletes with disabilities to participate by being integrated into existing sports programs. In this regard, the legal development of most consequence for athletes with disabilities is the requirement, articulated by the Supreme Court in *Martin*, that sports regulators conduct an individualized inquiry into whether reasonable modifications may be made to eligibility requirements or competition rules that would allow the athlete to participate. Courts have applied this "individualized inquiry" requirement across sports contexts, with the greatest effect on interscholastic and intercollegiate sports.

Aside from the law's impact on participation opportunities, however, is the potential for the law to erode other barriers faced by athletes with disabilities. For example, since the ADA, athletes with disabilities report that they enjoy greater legitimacy and perceive fewer social barriers to their participation. In this respect, the law has served a function outside the litigation context by signaling that individuals with disabilities can be athletes and are valued for their achievements (Cottingham et al., 2016). In this way, the effort to provide meaningful sports participation opportunities for individuals with disabilities is not unlike the decades-long struggle to provide opportunities for women and girls to participate through the use of Title IX. Using law to create participation opportunities can, as it did with gender equity under Title IX, serve as a catalyst to develop interest in sports participation within the community of persons with physical and mental disabilities who might not otherwise consider participation in sports.

Unlike Title IX, however, change through legal action ultimately may not be as sweeping as would be hoped. This is because the Rehabilitation Act and the ADA have not been interpreted to fully reach the most important issue facing individuals with disabilities who would participate in sports. Because the law is primarily aimed at ensuring equality of opportunity for those who are "qualified" to participate in existing programs, many individuals with disabilities may never be able to contemplate sports participation. As a result, many individuals will never develop the fundamental motor skills and desire necessary to become an "athlete" as that term is currently constructed in American society and reflected in American sports law (Aspen Institute, 2016).

Thus, to effect meaningful change, we must focus on the lack of widespread sports programming for persons with disabilities. Recent legal developments through the OCR's "Dear Colleague" letter, emphasizing the obligation of schools to provide athletic opportunities for students with disabilities when traditional sports programming is not sufficient, is an important step to expand the number of individuals with disabilities who participate in sports. However, while it is clear that an important feature of securing participation opportunities for individuals with disabilities is the antidiscrimination paradigm of the ADA and the Rehabilitation Act, we must go beyond simply including "qualified" athletes with disabilities into existing sports programs. Instead, we must balance the antidiscrimination approach with a structural equality approach, by creating and providing opportunities for individuals with physical and developmental disabilities who might not otherwise be able to participate in traditional programs. In doing so, we must consider our definition of what is a "sport," and continue seeking to create new games, or modify existing ones, so that our notion of an "athlete" is expanded to fully include persons with disabilities.

References

Aspen Institute. (2016). "Project Play: Physical Literacy in the United States: A Model Strategic Plan, and Call to Action," at 5, available at assets.aspeninstitute.org/content/uploads/files/content/docs/pubs/PhysicalLiteracy_AspenInstitute.pdf.

Centers for Disease Control and Prevention. (2016). "53 Million Adults in the US Live with a Disability," at www.cdc.gov.

Cottingham, M., Carroll, M., Lee, D., Shapiro, D., and Pitts, B. (2016). "The Historical Realization of the Americans with Disabilities Act on Athletes with Disabilities." *Journal of the Legal Aspects of Sport* 26: 5–7, 15–18.

Dearden, A., Ferrin, S., and Dulaney, S. (2012). "Promoting Greater Inclusion of Disabled Student-Athletes in Interscholastic Sports Programs." *Education Law Report* 278: 1–2.

ECAC Sports. (2015). "ECAC Board of Directors Cast Historic Vote to Add Varsity Sports Opportunities for Student-Athletes with Disabilities in ECAC Leagues and Championships," at www.ecacsports.com.

Grady, J., and Moorman, A. (2016). "The Americans with Disabilities Act 25th Anniversary: Assessing Progress, Opportunities, and Challenges." *Journal of the Legal Aspects of Sport* 26: 1–3.

Greely, H. (2004). "Disabilities, Enhancements, and the Meanings of Sports." 15 *Stanford Law and Policy Review* 15: 99–111.

Harvey, H., Koller, D., & Lowrey, K. (2015). "The Four Stages of Youth Sports TBI Policymaking: Engagement, Enactment, Research, and Reform." *Journal of Law, Medicine & Ethics* 43: 87.

Koller, D. (2016). "Putting Public Law into 'Private' Sport." *Pepperdine Law Review* 43: 681, 685.

Looby, J. (2012). "Reasonable Accommodations for High School Athletes with Disabilities: Preserving Sports While Providing Access for All." 19 *Sports Law Journal* 19: 227, 229.

McCann, M. (2014). "Do You Believe He Can Fly? Royce White and Reasonable Accommodations Under the Americans With Disabilities Act for NBA Players With Anxiety Disorders and Fear of Flying." *Pepperdine Law Review* 41: 428–429.

McPeters, T. (2015). "The Rehabilitation Act of 1973: Why the OCR's Small Reminder Will Likely Spark Big Changes for High School Athletics in 2014 and Beyond." *Marquette Sports Law Review* 25: 413–417.

Milani, A. (1998). "Can I Play?: The Dilemma of the Disabled Athlete in Interscholastic Sports." 49 *Alabama Law Review* 49: 817–820.

Mitten, M., and Davis, T. (2008). "Athlete Eligibility Requirements and Legal Protections of Sports Participation Opportunities." *Virginia Sports & Entertainment Law Journal* 8: 71–72, 132–133.

Seminara, Dave. (2016). "Cup Stacking: A Sport Whose Growth Runneth Over." *The New York Times*, March 31, B9.

U.S. Department of Department of Education, Office for Civil Rights. (2013). "Dear Colleague Letter," at www2.ed.gov.

U.S. Department of Education, Office of Special Education & Rehabilitative Services, Office of Special Education Programs. (2011). "Creating Equal Opportunities for Children and Youth with Disabilities to Participate in Physical Education and Extra Curricular Athletics," at www2.ed.gov.

U.S. Government Accountability Office. (2010). "Students with Disabilities: More Information Guidance Could Improve Opportunities in Physical Education and Athletics," GAO-10-519, at www.gao.gov.

Weston, M. (2005). "Health Law Symposium: The Intersection of Sports and Disability: Analyzing Reasonable Accommodations for Athletes with Disabilities." *St. Louis Law Journal* 50: 137–138.

Cases

Badgett v. Alabama High Sch. Athletic Ass'n, 2007 WL 2461928 (N.D. Ala. 2007).

Baisden v. West Va. Secondary Sch. Activities Comm'n, 568 S.E.2d 32 (2002).

Cole v. NCAA, 120 F. Supp. 2d 1060 (N.D. Ga. 2000).

Costello v. University of N.C., 2006 WL 3694579 (M.D.N.C. 2006).

Cruz v. Pennsylvania Interscholastic Athletic Ass'n, 157 F. Supp. 2d 485 (E.D. Pa. 2001).

Hollonbeck v. U.S. Olympic Comm., 464 F. Supp. 2d 1072 (N.D. Colo. 2006), aff'd, 513 F.3d 1191 (10th Cir. 2008).

Knapp v. Northwestern Univ., 942 F. Supp. 1191, 1198-99 (N.D. Ill. 1996), rev'd, 101 F.3d 473 (1996).
Matthews v. NCAA, 179 F. Supp. 2d 1209 (E.D. Wash. 2001).
PGA Tour, Inc. v. Martin, 532 U.S. 661 (2001).
Southeastern Cmty. Coll. v. Davis, 442 U.S. 397, 406 (1979).
Starego v. New Jersey State Interscholastic Athletic Ass'n, 970 F. Supp. 2d 303 (D.NJ. 2013).
United States v. National Collegiate Athletic Ass'n, Consent Decree (D.D.C. May 26, 1998).

CHAPTER 10

COLLECTIVE BARGAINING AND WORKFORCE PROTECTIONS IN SPORTS

NICHOLAS M. OHANESIAN

1. Collective Bargaining

The importance of collecting bargaining in U.S. sports cannot be overstated. Perhaps more than any other factor, it shapes the legal relationship between athletes, teams and leagues in the major pro leagues. This section examines the foundations of collective bargaining and their application to professional sports in the United States.

1.1. The Relationship Between Antitrust Law and American Professional Sports

In order to properly understand collective bargaining as it relates to professional sports in the United States, it is necessary to understand antitrust law. Collective bargaining involves restraining an employer, employees, or both parties by limiting how the parties deal with one another. If a group of employees refuses to work unless they are paid a certain wage, this constitutes a restraint on the employer. In contrast, if a group of employers refuse to pay employees more than a certain wage per hour, a restraint on employees occurs.

Passed in 1890 as a reaction to the rise of large trusts cornering the market in certain industries, the Sherman Antitrust Act banned agreements that unreasonably restrained interstate commerce. Despite its clear populist roots, subsequent court decisions interpreting the Sherman Antitrust Act would apply the law to employees who attempt to deal with their employer collectively through a labor union. Congress would pass the

Clayton Act in 1917 and the Norris-LaGuardia Act in 1932 as legal instruments to restrict antitrust law from being applied in this manner. These acts led to varied success until a change of the federal courts occurred under President Franklin Roosevelt.

Unlike many industries where the workforce pool is large and thus employees seek to work through labor unions to improve their position, the workforce pool for professional sports has traditionally been much smaller. Instead of employees coming together to protect each other, professional sports teams of the past came together to protect their interests from what they saw as unreasonable demands from their workforce. In contrast to the situation discussed previously—where employers in industrial sectors sought to use the Sherman Antitrust Act against employees working together through labor unions—professional athletes found themselves set upon by restraints on trade exercised by professional sports associations, such as Major League Baseball (MLB), the National Football League (NFL) and the National Basketball Association (NBA). It is against this backdrop that we examine the four cases that explore the contours of antitrust law and professional sports in the United States.

a. *Loewe v. Lawlor*

In 1901 the D.E. Loewe & Company declared it would operate its hat making business located in Danbury, Connecticut, without its employees being represented by the United Hatters Union of North America (UHU). At the time the UHU represented seventy of the eighty-two hat manufacturing companies in the United States. In response to Loewe's position, the UHU instituted a consumer boycott and encouraged the retailers, the wholesalers, and the public not to purchase products from Loewe. Loewe sued 240 members of the UHU for violating the Sherman Antitrust Act. The U.S. District Court for Connecticut held the Sherman Antitrust Act did not apply to the conduct of the UTU. The U.S. Court of Appeals for the Second Circuit would affirm this finding. The U.S. Supreme Court, however, reversed and remanded the case, concluding that the Act indeed applied to the UTU's conduct. The Court reasoned that the Act applied to all restraints on trade regardless of the method and source. The Court further found the de minimis involvement in interstate commerce to be immaterial.

In *Loewe v. Lawlor*, the U.S. Supreme Court reached out broadly to conclude that the efforts of organized labor were within the scope of the Sherman Antitrust Act. In the next case, decided fourteen years later, the Court was called upon to resolve whether MLB was engaging in interstate commerce and thus reachable under the Sherman Antitrust Act. In the interim, Congress passed the Clayton Act, which among other purposes sought to exempt organized labor from the reach of the Sherman Antitrust Act. Ask yourself whether these decisions are consistent with how interstate commerce is viewed.

b. *Federal Baseball Club v. National League*

In 1915 the Federal Baseball Clubs (Federal) ceased operations. Federal was a rival baseball league of Major League Baseball. Federal filed suit alleging that the MLB had conspired to monopolize baseball in the United States. After prevailing at trial and on appeal the case reached the U.S. Supreme Court. The Court's decision was both unanimous and short in length. The Court declared that MLB was not engaged in interstate commerce. It found the games themselves to be local affairs not involved in interstate commerce. Further, the fact that teams needed to travel to reach the games was deemed merely incidental. Justice Oliver Wendell Holmes reasoned that, ". . . the Chautauqua lecture bureau sending out lecturers, does not engage in such commerce because the lawyer or lecturer goes to another state" (209).

It is certainly a debatable point whether the *Loewe* Court and the *Federal Baseball Club* Court were correct in their application of the interstate commerce clause and in their respective applications of the Sherman Antitrust Act. What is undoubtedly striking, however, is when the two decisions are viewed side by side. In *Loewe,* the Court construed interstate commerce broadly to capture the efforts of organized labor within the law's ambit. Yet in *Federal Baseball Club* the Court cut a narrow path. It focused solely on baseball games—"exhibitions" in the Court's vernacular—to the exclusion of the effects on interstate commerce that the Loewe court had seized upon. Further, despite the Court's analysis in *Loewe* of the intentions of Congress, Congress acted to correct this interpretation of law. It first did so with the passage of the Clayton Act and later with passage of the Norris LaGuardia Act. Congress took no such action with respect to *Federal Baseball Club.*

c. *Wickard v. Filburn*

In 1938, as part of the New Deal, President Franklin D. Roosevelt signed the Agriculture Adjustment Act (AAA) into law. The purpose of the law was to help stabilize the boom-or-bust cycle of agricultural commodity prices. One of this law's key tools was the use of quotas in regard to the amounts of products that could be grown by farmers. These quotas thus regulated supply and demand. In 1941 Roscoe Filburn grew winter wheat in excess of his quota established under the AAA for the purpose of private consumption on his own farm. When the AAA levied a penalty against Filburn, he filed suit for relief in federal court where he initially succeeded. The United States then appealed directly to the U.S. Supreme Court. Filburn's core complaint was that the wheat he grew was never placed into interstate commerce—the wheat was purely for consumption on his farm. The Court took perhaps its broadest view of interstate commerce yet, finding that although Filburn did not sell his excess his wheat, he also did not need to buy wheat for his farm. In this finding the Court reasoned that Filburn's action posed a substantial impact on interstate commerce.

While the *Wickard* decision is unrelated to antitrust law and has even less to do with sports, the decision nonetheless serves as a trail marker for interstate commerce jurisprudence. An invigorated interstate commerce clause would go on to serve as the constitutional backbone for much of the twentieth century's most important legislation. With this new understanding of interstate commerce, how would the Courts treat professional sports? The answer to this question would be decidedly mixed.

d. *Haywood v. NBA*

Spencer Haywood played on the 1968 Olympic Basketball Team for the United States at the age of 18. After attending college for a few years he turned pro, signing a contract with the American Basketball Association. Thereafter, at age 21, he signed a contract with the Seattle Supersonics of the NBA. Haywood's contract with the Supersonics was problematic because the NBA had an eligibility rule that prevented athletes from being signed until four years after graduating from high school. Haywood did not meet this requirement and the NBA threatened to levy sanctions against both Haywood and the Supersonics.

Haywood sought relief in federal court, alleging that the NBA was engaged in a group boycott. After an injunction was entered *pendente lite* by a federal district court, the U.S. Court of Appeals for the Ninth Circuit vacated the injunction. Haywood ultimately appealed to Supreme Court Justice William O. Douglas in his capacity as the Ninth Circuit's Circuit Justice. Justice Douglas had no problem limiting *Federal Baseball* to MLB. Justice Douglas then found Haywood's career would suffer irreparable harm by being denied the opportunity to play professional basketball.

Following the decision of Justice Douglas, the NBA reached a settlement with Haywood allowing him to play in the NBA. Haywood went on to play with the Seattle Supersonics, New York Knicks, New Orleans Jazz, Los Angeles Lakers, and Washington Bullets. He made four All-Star teams and was recently elected to the Basketball Hall of Fame.

e. *Radovich v. NFL*

In 1938 the Detroit Lions signed Bill Radovich. Following service in World War II, Radovich requested a trade to the Los Angeles Rams to be closer to his ailing father. The Lions' owner denied the request and further warned Radovich that if he played anywhere else, he would be blacklisted. After Radovich's contract with the Lions had expired, he signed with the Los Angeles Dons of the All-America Football Conference, a rival of the NFL. In 1948 Radovich was offered a contract as a player/coach with the San Francisco Clippers, a minor league football team affiliated with the NFL. At some point after finding out about the blacklist, the Clippers withdrew their offer to Radovich.

Radovich then filed suit against the NFL, alleging violations of the Sherman Antitrust Act. Radovich lost at the district and circuit court levels under the theory that football was indistinguishable from baseball, which enjoyed an exemption since *Federal Baseball Clubs*. The Supreme Court reversed and found that the exemption to antitrust laws enjoyed by baseball was limited to baseball. Although the Court felt bound by *stare decisis* with respect to baseball, it identified no compelling policy in favor of extending the exemption to football. With changes in how courts defined viewed interstate commerce and with a majority in *Radovich* willing to differentiate professional football from baseball, how long would baseball's antitrust exemption stand? The next major challenge to this exemption would be a game-changer.

f. *Flood v. Kuhn*

At age 18, Curtis "Curt" Flood signed his first major league contract in 1956. He did so with the Cincinnati Reds. A couple of years later, the Reds traded Flood to the St. Louis Cardinals, for whom Flood would play for over a decade. During this time Flood became a star. He played in three World Series, batted over .300 in six seasons and netted seven Gold Gloves.

In October 1969, Flood learned from a reporter that the Cardinals had traded him to the Philadelphia Phillies. Flood was irate, particularly given that he had been subjected to racial taunts by Phillies fans when the Reds played there. Flood wrote to Bowie Kuhn, the commissioner of MLB, and asked to be declared a free agent. Flood had no right to free agency because of the so-called reserve clause, a standard term in baseball and other sports contracts in that era. The reserve clause dictates that a team holds the exclusive rights to negotiate with a player for one year following the expiration of the player's contract with his team. Kuhn said no.

Flood then brought suit against MLB alleging that the reserve clause violated the Sherman Antitrust Act. Flood insisted that competing teams joining hands to prevent themselves from competing with one another for players on an open market was inherently anticompetitive. Flood, however, lost at the district and circuit court levels on the strength of *Federal Baseball*. The reasoning was simple: baseball was exempt from antitrust scrutiny.

Flood then petitioned the Supreme Court and former Supreme Court Justice Arthur Goldberg would argue on his behalf. This effort also failed. Like the lower courts, the Court invoked *stare decisis* and ruled that MLB was not subject to the Sherman Antitrust Act. In so doing the Court recognized that MLB was undoubtedly engaged in interstate commerce. However, the Court chose to adhere to the precedent of *Federal Baseball Clubs*.

Flood v. Kuhn continued baseball's exemption from antitrust laws and failed to produce free agency, the goal of Flood in his lawsuit. Although the majority flatly acknowledged that the commerce argument originally made in *Federal Baseball Club* was no longer tenable, the majority rested its affirmation of the antitrust exemption on *stare decisis* grounds alone. As noted by Justice Douglas in the *Haywood* decision and the *Flood* court, other major team sports leagues received no such exemption from antitrust laws. When juxtaposed with *Wickard v. Filburn*, the argument that baseball is not engaged in commerce falls even more flat.

Despite the Supreme Court's refusal to permit the Sherman Antitrust Act to be applied to MLB, it was baseball that made the first move toward free agency among the major sports. In 1974, pitchers Andy Messersmith and Dave McNally decided to challenge the reserve clause through the grievance arbitration system created under the first collective bargaining agreement (CBA) signed by MLB and the Major League Baseball Players Association (MLBPA) (this CBA, which was reached in 1968, will be discussed in the next section). Arbitrator Peter Seitz ruled in 1975 that the reserve clause only permitted baseball clubs to renew baseball player contracts for one year following the expiration of their contract and not in perpetuity as the baseball clubs had long maintained. With this decision in hand, the MLBPA was able to negotiate free agency for players after six years of service to their club. The NFL followed suit in 1992, followed by the NHL in 1995 and the NBA in 1996.

1.2. Collective Action in Sports

In American labor law there are two ways that a union can become the collective bargaining representative for a group of employees. The first is through the National Labor Relations Board's (NLRB) election process. The second method involves a union securing voluntary recognition from the employer.

1.2.1. *NLRB Process*

a. NLRB procedures
b. *American League Baseball Clubs*

Under Section nine of the National Labor Relations Act (NLRA), a labor union can file a petition to hold an election. If the union presents evidence that a sufficient percentage of employees wish to have an election held, the NLRB will order an election. In most instances, the parties agree on elections. If, however, an agreement cannot be reached, the NLRB will conduct a hearing to resolve any disputed terms. The elections are conducted either at the employer's facilities or through mail ballot. If, in the aftermath of the election, there are disputes concerning the conduct of the election, the NLRB will hold a hearing to resolve the issues. The decisions reached at hearing are appealable to the five members of the NLRB, who are appointed by the President of the United States. The decisions of the NLRB, in turn, are ultimately appealable to the appropriate U.S. Courts of Appeals and the Supreme Court. Although most elections are resolved within sixty days of filing, the possibility exists for an NLRB elections process to drag out over a period of years.

While many issues are subject to litigation before the NLRB, the first and most fundamental question in all cases is whether the employer involved is an "employer" within the meaning of the NLRA. If the employer does not meet the definition, then the NLRB will not hold an election. The following decision of the NLRB addresses this issue: *American League of Professional Baseball Clubs & Association of National Baseball League Umpires.*

In 1968 the Association of National League Baseball Umpires filed a petition for an election with the NLRB seeking an election to represent umpires employed by the American League of MLB. The American League conceded that it was engaged in interstate commerce, much as MLB would do in *Flood v. Kuhn*. The American League also argued, as MLB would later in *Flood*, that the NLRB should honor *stare decisis* under *Federal Baseball.* Consequently, the American League reasoned, the NLRB should not assert jurisdiction under the NLRA. Unfortunately for the American League, the NLRB saw the concession of interstate commerce by the American League as dispositive. Further, the NLRB concluded, a request to an administrative agency (as opposed to a court) to decline jurisdiction was a policy matter and did not implicate stare decisis. On the basis of this distinction, the NLRB asserted jurisdiction of the American League and all of MLB.

1.2.2. *Voluntary Recognition*

a. MLBPA
b. NBAPA
c. NFLPA
d. NHLPA

We learn from the *American League of Professional Baseball Clubs* decision that MLB was prepared to wage a battle in order to prevent their umpires from unionizing. This may have been a surprise to the umpires given that baseball had granted "voluntary recognition" to the baseball players in 1968. As a general matter, the term "voluntary recognition" refers to when an employer chooses to recognize that a majority of its employees have signed union authorization cards. Consequently, the union comes into existence and the employer can bargain with it. All the major professional sports unions were granted voluntary recognition. None, therefore, needed to resort to the NLRB elections process utilized by the baseball umpires. The National Basketball Players Association (NBPA) gained recognition, and signed its first collective bargaining agreement, in 1964. The National Football League Players Association (NFLPA) gained its first contract and voluntary recognition in 1970 from the NFL. Finally, the National Hockey League Players Association (NHLPA) gained voluntary recognition from the NHL in 1967. A reasonable question to ask is why the four major sports leagues decided to grant voluntary recognition to their respective players' unions, while declining to do so elsewhere, as shown by the baseball umpires saga discussed earlier.

The explanation is quite simple: through the nonstatutory labor exemption, a CBA provides a legal shield to antitrust liability for player drafts, free agency, and any number of other limits on competition that would otherwise run afoul of the Sherman Antitrust Act. In contrast, when collective bargaining with the referees, concessionary workers, and ticket sellers, sports league are less concerned with how negotiated rules interact with antitrust laws. Indeed, when hiring referees, concessionary workers, and ticket sellers, professional sports typically do not negotiate rules that would otherwise run afoul of antitrust law. Accordingly, MLB chose to challenge the umpires over unionization while voluntarily recognizing the MLBPA with respect to the players.

1.2.3. *Economic Warfare in Professional Sports*

a. Strikes
b. Lockouts
c. Impasse and implementation

If collective bargaining is the diplomatic method of achieving a CBA, strikes and lockouts are the economic warfare method of reaching the same result. Striking is the act of workers withholding their services in an attempt to extract concessions from their employer. Conversely, a lockout is the act of an employer refusing to employ workers until such time as the labor union makes concessions to the employer. Professional sports unions and professional sports leagues have used both tools.

The NLRB has imposed important limitations on strikes and lockouts. If a union strikes solely for economic reasons, the employer has the right to hire temporary or permanent replacement workers during the duration of the strike, retain the permanent replacements following the end of the strike and further displace striking workers until vacancies occur. In contrast, if a union goes on strike in part, or solely, to protest unfair labor practices committed by an employer, the employer can only hire temporary workers for the duration of the strike and must reinstate the strikers following the end of the strike. In a lockout, an employer can only hire temporary employees.

A reasonable question might be why are strikes ever necessary? Unions strike and employers lockout employees because of an inability to reach an agreement at the bargaining table. If the parties reach an impasse over terms of the agreement, an employer has the right to declare impasse and propose its best and final offer at the table.

1.3. Filling in the Blanks Through Collective Bargaining

So what do the parties want to negotiate over anyway? To this point, much of this chapter has been concerned with getting the union and the employer to the negotiating table. Once they are there, what are they going to seek at the table? And what happens if the negotiations fail—where do the parties go from there? This chapter now turns to those considerations.

1.3.1. *The Relationship Between CBAs and Antitrust Law*

a. Reserve clause (arbitrator decision for free agency)
b. Salary caps
c. Grievance arbitration (deflate gate)

The most fundamental issue at the bargaining table—and what sets sports unions and the big four sports apart from traditional collective bargaining relationships—is a reserve system. A reserve system normally limits a player to negotiating with only one team. The other teams are prevented from competing with one another for the services of the player. This reduction in competition reduces overall wages for players, who are normally paid through employment contracts with teams. All of the major sports in the United States also feature some form of a player entry draft whereby each team selects players and thereby acquires the rights to exclusively negotiate with drafted players for a set period of time (usually lasting at least one year).

The reserve system in each of the major sports leagues predates CBAs and the involvement of sports unions generally. As discussed earlier in the chapter, reserve systems were challenged due to their antitrust implications. The major reason for unionization among professional athletes was to foment opposition to the reserve system and to advance a desire for free agency. Each of the major sports leagues now permits players to enter free agency after a certain number of years in a respective league. Free agency is just what it sounds like: the ability to negotiate with any team desiring the services of the player. Free agency introduced competition for players' services. Not surprisingly, free agency led to a steady climb in player wages that continues to this day.

The rise in player salaries as a result of free agency led to leagues seeking limits on how much each team could spend on player salaries. Salary caps are an anathema to unions because they artificially keep player wages low. Teams typically frame a salary cap as a method of insuring "competitive balance," which refers generally to the idea that each team should have a legitimate opportunity to win. Without a cap on salaries, less wealthy franchises tend to be outbid for the services of the best players by more profitable teams. The NFL, NBA, and NHL all employ some form of a salary cap on player salaries. These three leagues also utilize some form of revenue sharing among the teams to ensure an element of competitive balance. To this point, however, MLB has not been able to negotiate a salary cap with the MLPBA. Instead, MLB has negotiated a luxury tax whereby teams that spend over a certain threshold pay a penalty to the league. This penalty is meant to encourage more wealthy franchises to moderate their spending. Not surprisingly, baseball player salaries average higher than players in the other sports that are subject to a salary cap.

1.3.2. *The Decertification and Antitrust Law*

a. Brady v. NFL

Given how substantially management tends to value antitrust protections and given the limitations of management to implement a reserve system without a CBA, a fair question to ask is whether players would be better off without a labor union altogether. Of the major players' associations in the United States, only the NFLPA has used the threat of decertifying during collective bargaining negotiations. Under the NLRA, a union may disclaim interest in continuing to represent a group of employees at any time. While many employers would welcome a union deciding to no longer represent employees, professional sports organizations would view such a decision differently. Such an act would make a league vulnerable to antitrust litigation. This has put professional sports in an unusual position in labor law: fighting to prevent a labor union from disclaiming interest in representing their employees. As can be seen the following case, the NFL has gone to court to accomplish this feat.

On March 11, 2011, the CBA between the NFL and the NFLPA expired. The NFL had informed the NFLPA that the league intended to lock out the players if an agreement on a new CBA was not reached by the time the existing CBA expired. Rather than run the risk of a prolonged lockout, the NFLPA disclaimed interest in representing the NFL players. Additionally, the NFLPA amended their bylaws to prohibit representing the players.

The now unrepresented players immediately filed suit against the NFL. On behalf of other players, nine named plaintiffs—including stars Tom Brady and Drew Brees—alleged that the lockout of unrepresented players violated the Sherman Antitrust Act. U.S. District Judge Susan Nelson agreed with the players, noting that the NFLPA's disclaimer was valid and effective. As part of her order, Judge Nelson issued an injunction enjoining the lockout.

On appeal the U.S.. Court of Appeals for the Eighth Circuit sided with the NFL. The Eighth Circuit identified a problem with the issuance of the injunction under the Norris-LaGuardia Act (NLA). The NLA was enacted in 1932 to restrict federal courts from enjoining labor disputes without complying with certain procedural safeguards. From a historical standpoint, the NLA was designed to constrain the use of injunctions by the Courts as a means of protecting employers during labor disputes. The NFLPA argued, first, that there was not a labor dispute because the NFLPA had disclaimed interest in representing the players. Second, the NFLPA insisted, even assuming there was a labor dispute within the meaning of the NLA, Judge Nelson had complied with the requirements for the issuance of the injunction. These arguments failed. A majority of the three-judge appellate panel found that the labor dispute continued despite the NFLPA's disclaimer of interest. The panel further determined the NLA applied to injunctions to enjoin a lockout. This decision forced the parties back to the bargaining table and, for the time being, removed them from antitrust litigation. The parties eventually reached a new collective bargaining agreement.

2. Workforce Protections

Athletes and other workers are impacted by policies that regulate their workplace conditions and that shape the scope of their job responsibilities. This chapter now turns to those issues.

2.1. Just Who Do You Work for Anyway?

1. Employees
2. Independent contractors

Central to any employer and employee relationship is whether the participants are employees or independent contractors. This distinction is crucial. If a professional athlete is an employee of his or her team, the protections under the NLRA apply. In addition, most, if not all, workforce protection laws only apply to employees and not to independent contractors. Courts and administrative agencies such as the U.S. Department of Labor and the Internal Revenue Service typically apply some version of the "right of control" test to determine whether a person is functioning as an independent contractor or as an employee. The right of control means that in order to establish the employer/employee relationship, the employer must exercise control over the manner and means that the work is performed. Under this test, the professional athletes in team sports tend to be regarded as employees. Such a classification makes sense. The franchises—through coaches and managers—direct how and when athletes perform. Further, the teams set practice times, arrange games, and direct players on how to perform their duties during the games. By contrast, the professional athletes in individual sports tend to be independent contractors. Consider boxers, for example; they negotiate the rates of pay with promoters and pay trainers themselves. During the boxing matches, while there are rules that apply, boxers are free to employ whatever strategies they deem most effective within the confines of the rules. The same considerations apply to tennis players and golfers.

2.2. FLSA

The Fair Labor Standards Act (FLSA) was originally passed in 1938 and is enforced by the U.S. Department of Labor and through private litigation. The law sets a minimum wage for hourly employees, requires overtime pay for hours worked over forty per week, and requires payment for work performed. The law further provides a federal cause of action to collect unpaid wages due to employees.

While a casual observer may find little convergence between professional sports and the FLSA, NFL cheerleaders have proven to be the exception. In 2014, NFL cheerleaders began filing lawsuits against the NFL and its teams over failure to pay minimum wages and for failing to pay them for hours worked. Although many of these cases have settled, the threshold issue is whether the cheerleaders are independent contractors or employees. Given the settlements, this issue has not been resolved.

2.3. OSHA

The Occupational Safety and Health Administration (OSHA) is a federal agency that regulates workplace safety. OSHA sets standards governing workplace safety and illnesses. It also investigates workplace injuries and illnesses. Given the number of injuries in professional sports—especially among the contact sports—one would assume that OSHA has taken an active role in the NFL and the NHL. The reality is that it has not. However, there have been notable exceptions. In 2001 a Minnesota Vikings offensive tackle died due to heat stroke following summer practice. OSHA investigated the matter and found that the team provided adequate hydration to players. The team also placed medical staff nearby in the event a health problem surfaced. A more consequential sports-related question for the OSHA to answer is whether and how the agency should address cumulative injuries and illnesses sustained by NFL players over their careers. These injuries range from traumatic arthritis to chronic traumatic encephalopathy (CTE).

2.4. Title 7 and the Equal Pay Act

Title 7 of the Civil Rights Act of 1964 prohibits discrimination in employment on the basis of sex, race, color, national origin, and religion. Similarly, the Equal Pay Act of 1963 requires employers to pay employees the same for performing the same work, regardless of gender. This issue has arisen in sports played by both men and women. Recently, members of the U.S. Women's Soccer Team have filed suit against the U.S. Soccer Federation alleging that the women are paid less than the men. What is exceptionally striking about this circumstance is the on-field success of the women compared to the men and the higher pay rates for members of the men's team compared to the women's team.

2.5. Concussion Litigation

Research has been emerging for a number of years concerning the long-term impact of repeated concussions sustained by athletes in contact sports, primarily football. A number of prominent former football players have committed suicide during their retirement years, allegedly due to the impact of these conditions. A number of athletes have willed their brains to science in order to study the impact of CTE. Of the ninety-four brains donated to this point, ninety have tested positive for CTE. A major class action lawsuit filed by former NFL players against the NFL recently settled for approximately $1 billion, a figure that will be paid out over sixty-five years.

2.6. Criminal Charges for On-the-Field Conduct

It is generally known that among the contact sports (hockey and football) a certain amount of violence is not only accepted but expected. However, at some point, athletes may go too far and can commit crimes. Identifying that point is extremely challenging. One key problem in viewing contact sports as grounds for criminal charges is the legal defense of consent. By agreeing to participate in a contact sport, an athlete is expected to hit and be hit by other players. In rare instances, criminal charges have been imposed and most of the examples have involved hockey players. The amount of force applied, the resulting injuries sustained, and the proximity to the game itself are all crucial factors in the imposition of these charges. Indeed, of the half a dozen incidents where charges have been filed for on-the-ice conduct, there were fractures, concussions, and even vertebrae broken. Likewise, most of the incidents took place on the ice but not near the action of the game. Neither player, furthermore, was defending the puck nor attempting to score at the time the assault occurred.

3. Conclusion

Professional athletes have two options when seeking to protect or improve their terms and conditions of employment. The first method is through collective action via unionization. Due to accompanying antitrust protections, professional sports teams have unique incentives to cooperate with this process. The second option is through protective legislation at the federal and state levels. As discussed in this chapter, workforce protections do not always neatly apply to professional athletes. Finally, it must be acknowledged that professional athletes in non-team sports face special hurdles as much of the traditional protections available to professional athletes in team sports do not exist

References

Alford, Sean W. L. (2009). "Comment: Dusting off the AK-47: An Examination of the NFL Players Most Powerful Weapon in an Antitrust Lawsuit Against the NFL." *North Carolina Law Review* 88: 212.

Banner, Stuart. (2013). *The Baseball Trust: A History of Baseball's Antitrust Exemption* (New York: Oxford University Press).

Hobel, Michael S. (1982). "Note: Application of the Labor Exemption after the Expiration of Collective-bargaining Agreements in Professional Sports." *New York University Law Review* 57: 164.

Osborne, Amy Beckham. (2005). "Baseball and the Law: A Selected Annotated Bibliography, 1990-2004." *Law Library Journal* 97: 335.

Shields, Marjorie A. (2003). "Award of Worker's Compensation Benefits to Professional Athletes." *American Law Reports* 5th 112: 365.

Snyder, Brad. (2007). *A Well Paid Slave: Curt Flood's Fight for Free Agency in Professional Sports* (New York: Penguin Press).

Cases

American League of Professional Baseball Clubs & Association of National League Umpires, 180 N.L.R.B. 190 (1970).

Brady v. NFL, 664 F.3d 661 (8th Cir. 2011).

Federal Baseball Club v. National League, 259 U.S. 200 (1922).
Flood v. Kuhn, 407 U.S. 258 (1972).
Haywood v. NBA, 401 U.S. 1024 (1971) (Douglas, C.J.).
Loewe v. Lawlor, 208 U.S. 274 (1908).
Radovich v. NFL, 352 U.S. 445 (1957).
Wickard v. Filburn, 317 U.S. 111 (1942).

CHAPTER 11

COLLECTIVE BARGAINING IN PROFESSIONAL SPORTS

The Duel Between Players and Owners and Labor Law and Antitrust Law

GABE FELDMAN

1. Introduction

The history of collective bargaining negotiations in professional sports is dotted with long periods of labor strife. In many ways, collective bargaining in professional sports is a mirror image of collective bargaining in traditional, non-sports industries—management and labor exercise their economic weapons, including strikes and lockouts, to gain leverage at the bargaining table. Professional sports leagues and players associations, however, have unique attributes that present complex challenges and legal issues in the collective bargaining context. Like virtually every aspect of sports in our modern culture, labor struggles and potential work stoppages in professional sports leagues play out in the heat of the public spotlight. The true uniqueness and complexity in sports labor negotiations, however, emanates from the clash of labor law and antitrust law that is at the heart of many of the collective bargaining struggles between players and owners. Most recently, this clash played out in the National Football League (NFL) labor negotiations that led to *Brady v. National Football League* and the National Basketball Association (NBA) negotiations that led to *Anthony v. NBA*. Most of the questions raised in those cases about the conflict between labor and antitrust law remain unanswered. It is largely inevitable, however, that this conflict will arise again, and the resolution of these issues could help shape the future of collective bargaining in professional sports. This chapter will provide a brief background of the basic principles of labor law and the unique aspects of professional sports leagues and their athletes, present a summary of the history of collective bargaining in the "Big Four" U.S. sports leagues (the National

Football League, National Basketball Association, National Hockey League, and Major League Baseball), and analyze the recent labor battles and the evolution of the law in this area. The chapter concludes with a look forward to the potential future of labor negotiations between players and owners in professional sports leagues.

2. Federal Labor Law Background

The fundamental policy underlying collective bargaining is to encourage management and labor to enter voluntarily into collective bargaining agreements without government interference. Federal law seeks to promote two primary goals as part of this overall policy: good faith bargaining between labor and management and the opportunity for both labor and management to gain concessions from each other at the bargaining table. Federal labor law thus provides unions and employers with roughly equal bargaining power and creates a process that facilitates the ability of the parties to create the terms of their own agreements. Labor law attempts to create a balance of bargaining power by providing employees with the right to strike and employers the right to lock out their employees. A strike is the right of the employee to withhold his or her services, while the lockout is the employer's countervailing right to exclude the employee from employment.

Courts have recognized that these economic weapons help induce voluntary agreements between management and unions (LeRoy, 2012). The role of the government is thus to serve only as the "referee" in the economic struggle between the parties (LeRoy, 1996). As Professor Weistart has explained, "[f]ederal labor policy accepts that the prevailing principle should be freedom of contract: the parties can agree to whatever terms they wish, and courts will not inquire into the wisdom or reasonableness of the bargain struck" (Weistart, 1981, 131).

In the late nineteenth and early twentieth centuries, however, a power imbalance existed between labor and management, with employers maintaining significant control and leverage over their employees. This imbalance was amplified by the fact that courts consistently held strikes to be illegal under antitrust law and enjoined strikes to force the employees to return to work. Amidst the backdrop of this management-tilted power imbalance, Congress enacted a series of laws designed, in part, to level the playing field between labor and management. The Norris-LaGuardia Act, passed in 1932, limited the jurisdiction of district courts to issue an injunction "in a case involving or growing out of a labor dispute," thus preventing courts from enjoining striking employees (29 U.S.C. § 101 (2006)).

The National Labor Relations Act (NLRA) (also known as The Wagner Act, 29 U.S.C. § 151) and the Labor Management Relations Act (LMRA) (also known as the Taft-Hartley Act, 29 U.S.C. § 141) were then passed to establish collective bargaining as the process and regime to govern the relationship between employers and unionized employees. The NLRA and LMRA require employers and employees to negotiate in good faith with respect to wages, hours, and other terms and conditions of employment. Both the NLRA and the LMRA reflect Congress's intent to allow the parties, free from governmental or judicial interference, to reach the terms of their own agreements through the carefully regulated collective bargaining process. A key development of this process has been the rise of the employer lockout, which we explore in the next section.

3. Brief Overview of the Lockout as Management's Economic Weapon

To get a clear picture of modern labor negotiations in sports and non-sports industries, it is important to understand the evolution of the lockout from a defensive maneuver to an offensive tactic designed to give the employer leverage at the bargaining table. The employer's right to lock out was recognized under common law, prior to the passage of the NLRA. Although the term "lockout" has never been explicitly defined by the federal labor statutes, the generally accepted definition of a lockout is the "cessation of the furnishing of work to employees in an effort to get for the employer more desirable terms" (Feldman, 2012, 837–38 (quoting *Iron Molders' Union No. 125 of Milwaukee, Wisconsin v. Allis-Chalmers Co.*, 166 F. at 52)). Conversely, a strike is generally defined as the "cessation of work by employees in an effort to get for the employees more desirable terms" (Feldman, 2012, 838. (quoting *Iron Molders' Union No. 125 of Milwaukee, Wisconsin v. Allis-Chalmers Co.*, 166 F. at 52)). These weapons "set up a game of labor/management chicken—a contest to see which side can hold out the longest before economic pressure forces one of them to concede at the bargaining table" (Feldman, 2012, 838).

Historically, however, an asymmetry existed between strikes and lockouts. The lockouts receive no explicit statutory protection under labor law, while strikes are expressly protected by the NLRA. This reflected the NLRB's early view that strikes and lockouts were *not* equal counterparts. Instead, the NLRB viewed the strike as a mechanism for reducing the economic disparity between union and management, while the lockout was seen as an aggressive (rather than corrective) tactic (Johannesen, 1964; Feldman, 2012). Early commentators highlighted that employers had other economic weapons to use during negotiations. For example, employers were permitted to hire replacement workers during a strike, a tactic used by the NFL owners in 1987 to pressure the NFL players to end their strike.

Early on, the NLRB held that lockouts were only permitted when motivated by legitimate business considerations and where the lockout did "not impinge upon the employees' rights to organize and to engage in other concerted activity protected by the Act" (Feldman, 2012 839 (quoting *Great Falls Employers' Council, Inc.*, 123 N.L.R.B. at 978)). Lockouts designed to interfere with or harm unions were viewed as destructive to the collective bargaining process and held illegal.

The NLRB eventually concluded that this restricted view of the lockout created an imbalance of bargaining power that tipped the scales too far in favor of employees. The

Supreme Court expanded the permitted uses of the lockout in *NLRB v. Truck Drivers Local Union No. 44*, allowing employers to lock out striking employees to pressure them to return to work. The Supreme Court's approval of this "defensive lockout" signaled the end of the presumption of illegality of lockouts and replaced it with a more symmetrical view of labor law that sought to balance management and labor interests. This view ultimately paved the way for employers to use lockouts in a variety of different defensive ways.

The approval of the use of the "offensive lockout" marked the next, and most significant, step in the evolution and expansion of the lockout. In *American Ship Building Co. v. NLRB*, the Supreme Court held that employers can lock out employees as a tactic for gaining leverage at the bargaining table. The Court held that "there is nothing in the Act which gives employees the right to insist on their contract demands, free from the sort of economic disadvantage which frequently attends bargaining disputes" (313). The Court noted that permitting offensive strikes but not defensive lockouts created an unfair and unnecessary asymmetry in labor negotiations and concluded that "the employer's use of a lockout solely in support of a legitimate bargaining position is [not] in any way inconsistent with the right to bargain collectively or with the right to strike" (310).

The NLRB further expanded the use of lockouts with two key rulings. First, in *Darling & Co.*, the Board announced that management could lock out employees prior to impasse. Second, in *Harter Equipment, Inc. v. Local 825*, the Board held that the use of temporary replacement works was permitted during offensive lockouts. Allowing employers to lock out their employees prior to impasse helped transform the lockout from a weapon of "last resort" to an offensive weapon, while use of temporary replacement workers provided additional strength to this weapon. Both rulings legitimized the lockout as an offensive economic weapon that could be used by employers to gain leverage during a negotiation and marked a "critical stage in the evolution of the lockout from a purely defensive tactic to a weapon that served as a corollary to the strike and led to the modern era in labor-management relations" (Feldman, 2012, 842). In the sports industry (and labor management relations in general), the offensive lockout has thus evolved into the weapon of choice by employers. The next section highlights the rise of the lockout in professional sports and provides a brief overview of the labor struggles between players and owners.

4. Brief History of Collective Bargaining in Professional Sports

Collective bargaining agreements in professional sports govern a wide range of terms and conditions of employment, including the player entry draft, free agency restrictions, minimum and maximum salaries, salary caps and luxury taxes, revenue sharing, roster sizes, player discipline, drug testing, practice times, season length, travel expenses, health benefits, and myriad other issues impacting the players and owners. All these terms are the product of the collective bargaining struggle between players and owners, and the trajectory of collective bargaining across the "Big Four" professional sports leagues has followed a similar arc. In the early days of each of the players associations, players fought for basic economic rights, including pensions, health benefits, minimum salaries, and greater ease of movement between teams. As the players gained more rights and more leverage, the battleground shifted to percentage of league-generated revenues and salary caps and other limits on player salaries.

Major League Baseball (MLB) experienced a tumultuous stretch of labor management relations from the inception of the Major League Baseball Players Association (MLBPA) through the late 1990s. The key issues at stake in the MLB collective bargaining negotiations included pension payments, minimum salaries, free agency, salary caps, and revenue sharing. The players engaged in strikes in 1972, 1980, 1981, 1985, and 1994–1995, while the owners locked out the players in 1973, 1976, and 1990 (Levinstein et al., 2007). Several of work stoppages led to missed games, including the 1994–1995 strike, which resulted in the cancellation of 920 games as well as the entire postseason and World Series. Following the 1994–1995 strike, however, MLB and the MLBPA have experienced over twenty years of relative labor peace without a single work stoppage.

The NFL, NBA, and National Hockey League (NHL) have all experienced similar patterns of labor strife. From 1968–1994, the NFL, NBA, and NHL experienced seven work stoppages—all seven of them were player strikes. As in baseball, the key issues were pensions, minimum salaries, and free agency (Feldman, 2012). Since, 1994, the NFL, NBA, and NHL have experienced seven additional work stoppages—all seven of these have been lockouts. Although the specific issues varied from league to league, owners across all three leagues often claimed "poverty" and locked out the players to gain reductions in player salaries and benefits (Feldman, 2012). These lockouts have led to significant numbers of missed games, including the 2004 NHL lockout, which resulted in the cancelation of the entire season and postseason, including the Stanley Cup finals.

This shift in the dynamics of the labor struggle—from player strikes to employer lockouts—is a microcosm of the transformation of labor relations in traditional, non-sports contexts, keyed by the evolution of the lockout from a defensive shield to a sanctioned offensive weapon for employers. Despite the similar arc of labor relations in sports and non-sports industries, there are unique aspects of collective bargaining in professional sports that could alter the balance of power between players and owners. The next section discusses the unique aspects of labor relations in professional sports.

5. Unique Aspects of Collective Bargaining in Professional Sports

On its surface, the labor strife between players and owners is not dissimilar to the periods of strikes and lockouts suffered in other industries. Beneath the surface, however, the conflict between antitrust and labor law presents a unique battleground for labor negotiations in professional sports. Although there are many distinctions between the collective bargaining relationship in professional sports leagues and other non-sports industries, this section focuses on two key distinctions.

First, professional athlete unions are unique compared to traditional industrial unions. In traditional, non-sports industries, employees possess relatively homogeneous skills and are relatively easy to replace. Most professional athletes, in contrast, have highly specialized skills that are difficult to replace. Additionally, professional athletes—and NFL players in particular—have relatively short careers. In addition to short careers and nontransferable skills, most top-flight professional sports leagues in the United States have significant market share, which leaves athletes with a limited employment market. For example, the NFL has a virtual monopoly in the production of elite professional football and a virtual monopsony in the labor market for elite professional football players. Thus, buyers (e.g., consumers) have no substitutes when buying the professional sports product, and sellers (e.g., the players) have no alternatives when selling their services to professional teams. The lack of employment options for players outside their respective leagues deprives them of the leverage they would have if they could "jump," or threaten to jump, to a rival employer. These factors also virtually eliminate the strike as a viable option for most professional athletes. As Professor Lock has noted:

> Strikes . . . jeopardize a disproportionate percentage of career earning potential for players with short careers and, in many cases, few alternative career opportunities. The [absence of other employment options] of the players further limits their ability to withstand a strike and, consequently, the union's leverage at the bargaining table. With no competing league, most players have no legitimate alternative job opportunity and thus, are unlikely to outlast management in a labor dispute.
>
> (Lock, 1989, 346)

Similarly, the relatively short careers and lack of options for professional athletes magnify the impact of a lockout because a work stoppage (either via a lockout or strike) jeopardizes a disproportionately large percentage of their playing careers and earning potential (Feldman, 2012).

Second, professional sports leagues engage in "multiemployer bargaining," whereby the separately owned teams join together to negotiate with the players as one unit. Multiemployer bargaining is not limited to sports leagues and is actually fairly common across different industries. The reason for engaging in multiemployer bargaining is, however, unique to sports leagues. In non-sports industries, firms engage in multiemployer bargaining because it allows them to offer programs jointly that they could not offer on their own and reduces the transaction costs of multiple negotiations. Although professional sports teams also benefit from the efficiencies of a single multiemployer bargaining unit, professional sports teams bargain as one unit (the league) because of the highly interdependent nature of the teams and the need for uniform rules across the league. For example, leagues must have uniform schedules, rules of the game, mechanisms for signing and trading players, and other terms and conditions of employment. Allowing the teams to negotiate as a single unit ensures that these rules will be consistent and uniform across the league and allows the game itself to exist. After all, teams cannot play a game unless they agree to play the game at a certain time in a certain place under certain rules. Multiemployer bargaining is thus necessitated (or at least consistent with) the interdependence of the teams and inherent need for cooperation across team owners.

While multiemployer bargaining is an efficient mechanism for professional teams, it does raise potential antitrust issues, because the multiemployer unit is essentially an agreement among owners. Collective bargaining agreements in professional sports leagues thus represent not only an agreement between the players and the league but also an agreement among the teams within the league. For example, free agency restrictions in the NFL are the product of an agreement between the players and the owners and between the owners themselves (as part of the multiemployer bargaining unit). Labor tactics of the multiemployer unit—including lockouts—also represent an agreement among owners. These agreements, in turn, are subject to scrutiny under Section 1 of the Sherman Act.

Section 1 of the Sherman Act condemns "[e]very contract . . . or conspiracy, in restraint of trade or commerce among the several States." A threshold issue in Section 1 cases is whether the challenged conduct constitutes a "contract, combination . . . or conspiracy" (15 U.S.C. § 12). For purposes of Section 1, a "contract" requires an "agreement," and an agreement requires more than one entity. For years, professional sports leagues argued that they were single entities incapable of reaching an agreement under Section 1. Although, as discussed earlier, courts have recognized that sports teams are uniquely interdependent, they routinely rejected the leagues' single-entity argument and held that a professional sports league is a combination of teams that is capable of reaching an agreement in violation of Section 1. In 2010, the Supreme Court definitively held that NFL teams—despite their often-overlapping interests—are not single entities and therefore their agreements are subject to scrutiny under Section 1 (*American Needle, Inc. v. National Football League*). MLB was historically protected from antitrust attack under the anomalous baseball antitrust exemption, thus eliminating the conflict between labor law and antitrust law for baseball owners and players. Congress repealed this exemption in the Curt Flood Act of 1998, giving baseball players the same access to antitrust law as other professional athletes going forward (15 U.S.C. § 26b (2006)).

The collective bargaining agreements between players and owners—which encompass agreements among the owners themselves—thus present a unique conflict between federal antitrust and labor law. The next section of this chapter fleshes out and highlights these conflicts.

6. Antitrust Law vs. Labor Law

There is an inherent conflict between federal antitrust and labor law. On the one hand, antitrust law promotes competition and prohibits cooperation among competitors. On the other hand, federal labor law encourages cooperation among competitors. In fact, a foundational principle of federal labor law is that employees may form unions to gain leverage at the bargaining table *by eliminating competition* among themselves. Courts and Congress have struggled with this conflict. For more than twenty years after the passage of the Sherman Act, courts routinely held that unions were illegal restraints of trade in violation of antitrust law.

Congress minimized this conflict by creating the "statutory labor exemption" in the Norris LaGuardia Act (29 U.S.C. § 101 (2006)) and Sections 6 and 20 of the Clayton Act (15 U.S.C. § 12). This exemption protects unilateral union conduct—including strikes and the formation of unions—from antitrust challenge. Section 6 of the Clayton Act states that the "labor of a human being is not a commodity or article of commerce" and the Norris-LaGuardia Act prevents courts from enjoining labor activities (Feldman, 2012). As the Supreme Court explained in *United States v. Hutcheson*, the statutory labor exemption establishes that "labor unions are not combinations or conspiracies in restraint of trade, and exempt[s] specific union activities . . . from the operation of the antitrust laws" (622).

The statutory exemption did not, however, eliminate the entire conflict between antitrust and labor law, because it did not reach agreements between unions and nonlabor parties (*Connell Construction Co. v. Plumbers & Steamfitters Local Union No.* 100,). In other words, the statutory exemption did not immunize the collective bargaining process or the terms of the collective bargaining agreement from antitrust attack. The Supreme Court filled this gap through the creation of the "non-statutory labor exemption" (421 U.S. at 621–622).

As the Supreme Court explained in *Brown v. Pro Football, Inc.*:

> As a matter of logic, it would be difficult, if not impossible, to require groups of employers and employees to bargain together, but at the same time to forbid them to make among themselves or with each other any of the competition-restricting agreements potentially necessary to make the process work or its results mutually acceptable. . . . [and] some restraints on competition imposed through the bargaining process must be shielded from antitrust sanctions . . . to give effect to federal labor laws and policies and to allow meaningful collective bargaining to take place. (518 U.S. at 237)

The non-statutory labor exemption recognizes that antitrust law must give way to labor law when necessary to allow the collective bargaining process to work. This implied repeal of antitrust law in favor of labor policy reflects a preference for resolving labor disputes through voluntary agreement (and labor policy) rather than through judicial interference (and antitrust law). The Supreme Court first established the nonstatutory labor exemption in *Local Union No. 189, Amalgamated Meat Cutters & Butcher Workmen of North America v. Jewel Tea Co.*. In *Jewel Tea*, employers argued that a term in the collective bargaining agreement prohibiting meat markets from operating during certain hours was an antitrust violation. Justice White, in a plurality opinion, held that the agreement was immune from antitrust attack because it was "of immediate and direct" concern to the employees and only tangentially or indirectly harmful to competition in the product market (691). Justice Goldberg, authoring a separate plurality opinion, determined that nonstatutory labor exemption protects all "collective bargaining activity concerning mandatory subjects of bargaining under the Labor Act" (710). The Court later clarified the scope and rationale of the exemption in *Connell Construction Co.*, explaining that "a proper accommodation between the congressional policy favoring collective bargaining under the NLRA and the congressional policy favoring free competition in business markets requires that some union-employer agreements be accorded a limited non-statutory exemption from antitrust sanctions" (421 U.S. at 625–626). But, the Court made clear that the exemption does not apply where the agreement has substantial anticompetitive effects that "would not follow naturally from the elimination of competition over wages and working conditions" (421 U.S. at 625–626).

Although these early cases established the general framework for the nonstatutory labor exemption, it remained a relatively shapeless and amorphous doctrine. It has more fully developed over the last few decades through a series of cases involving the NFL and NBA. The next section highlights these cases and the further development of the nonstatutory labor exemption. It is important to note that the evolution of the exemption is not a theoretical matter—it has a significant impact on the leverage each side has during the labor negotiations.

7. Harmonizing Labor Law and Antitrust Law: The Evolution of the Nonstatutory Labor Exemption in Professional Sports League Cases

The landmark professional sports league case in the evolution of the nonstatutory labor exemption was *Mackey v. NFL*, where the Eighth Circuit held that the exemption immunizes the terms of a collective bargaining agreement from antitrust attack. In *Mackey*, NFL players challenged a rule in the collective bargaining agreement (known as the "Rozelle Rule") that severely restricted free agency. The Eighth Circuit recognized that employers (e.g., team owners) would have limited incentive to negotiate a collective bargaining agreement if the agreement itself could expose them to treble damages under antitrust law. The Eighth Circuit therefore held that the Rozelle Rule was immune from antitrust attack. A three-factor analysis, known as the "*Mackey* test," emerged from that case to help courts determine if the nonstatutory exemption should apply. According to the *Mackey* test, the terms of a collective bargaining agreement are exempt from antitrust as long as three factors are met: (1) the terms of the agreement primarily impacted only the parties to the collective bargaining relationship; (2) the terms were mandatory subjects of bargaining; and (3) the agreement was the result of good-faith, arm's-length negotiations. In such cases, antitrust policy must give way to federal labor policy and the collective bargaining agreement is exempt from antitrust scrutiny.

The scope of the exemption then expanded to protect the owners' unilateral implementation of terms and conditions of employment after a collective bargaining agreement has expired (*Powell v. NFL*). In *Powell,* after the expiration of the collective bargaining agreement, the NFL owners unilaterally implemented the "right of first refusal" free agency restriction that was contained in the previous agreement. The players challenged the restriction under the Sherman Act, arguing that the nonstatutory labor exemption ended with the expiration of the collective bargaining agreement. The Eighth Circuit disagreed, holding that antitrust law must still give way to labor law after the expiration of the collective bargaining agreement because post-expiration union and employer conduct is still governed by a "comprehensive array of labor law principles" (1301). These principles strictly define the obligations and rights of the parties. For example, prior to impasse, each side has a continuing duty to bargain, and the employers are obligated to maintain the status quo with respect to wages and other terms of employment (Feldman, 2012). After impasse, an employer is permitted to, among other things, maintain the status quo or implement its "last, best offer," which includes any *new* terms of employment that were "reasonably contemplated" within their pre-impasse proposals. Employees, in turn, are provided with their own rights under labor law, including the ability to file a number of unfair labor practice charges.

In other words, the collective bargaining process continues even after the expiration of a collective bargaining agreement (both pre- and post-impasse). As the Eighth Circuit explained in *Powell,* permitting the NFL players to challenge the owners' decision to maintain the status quo would "improperly upset the careful balance established by Congress through the labor law" and would "treat[] a lawful stage of the collective bargaining process as misconduct by [the owners], and in this way conflicts with federal labor laws" (*Powell,* 930 F.2d at 1302).

The Supreme Court further expanded the scope of the nonstatutory labor exemption to cover *new* terms unilaterally implemented by the owners (post-impasse) as part of their "last, best offer" after the expiration of the collective bargaining agreement (*Brown,* 518 U.S. at 241–242). In *Brown,* the NFL unilaterally implemented—as contemplated by their last, best offer—a fixed salary for players on teams' developmental squads. The NFL players challenged the terms under the Sherman Act, but the Supreme Court held that the exemption covers old and new terms lawfully (as defined under labor law) implemented after the expiration of the collective bargaining agreement.

To an extent, *Brown* is the natural extension of the reasoning in *Powell.* Implementation of the last, best offer—like maintenance of the status quo—is part of the heavily regulated collective bargaining process. Allowing the players to bring an antitrust suit challenging the implement of the last, best offer would interfere with the carefully calibrated balance between labor and management that is central to federal labor policy (Feldman, 2012). It would also place the owners in a no-win situation. If the owners exercised their right to implement their last, best offer, they would be exposed to antitrust liability. If the owners changed their offer, they would be exposed to labor law liability. The nonstatutory exemption does, however, have limits. As the Supreme Court explained in *Brown*, the exemption lasts only until the "collapse of the collective bargaining relationship," which could occur through the dissolution of the union. (250).

Faced with the Eighth Circuit's decision in *Powell* (and while *Brown* was still working its way through the courts), the NFL players took an extreme step to gain access to antitrust law. The NFLPA dissolved its union by disclaiming interest in serving as the players' representatives. The NFL players then filed an antitrust suit in Minnesota challenging the league's free agency restrictions. The district court judge in Minnesota held that the dissolution of the players' union terminated the collective bargaining relationship between the players and owners, which terminated the non-statutory labor exemption, which allowed the players' antitrust suit to proceed (*McNeil v. NFL*, 1992 WL 315292). A jury then found that the NFL's free agency restrictions violated antitrust law and awarded the players over $30 million in damages.

8. The Current and Future Labor Battleground in Professional Sports: The Lockout vs. Antitrust Law

The conflict between antitrust and labor law in sports labor negotiations continued to evolve during the NFL and NBA lockouts in 2011, as both players and owners continued to jockey for leverage at the bargaining table. In both the NFL and NBA, progress stalled during collective bargaining negotiations, the owners locked out the players, and the players dissolved their unions and challenged the lockouts under antitrust law. The issues raised by the NBA and NFL conflicts were similar, but this section focuses on the NFL negotiations because the NBA-NBPA battle settled before any judicial decisions were issued, while the NFL-NFLPA struggle spawned multiple judicial opinions and a lengthy discussion of the relevant issues (*Anthony v. NBA*; *Brady v. National Football League*).

In the NFL-NFLPA negotiations, the NFL had made it clear that it planned to lock out the players if they did not reach a new collective bargaining agreement before the March 11, 2011, expiration of the previous deal. Shortly before the expiration of the collective bargaining agreement, the NFLPA informed the owners that it had dissolved its union (through a disclaimer of interest) and restructured itself as a professional trade association instead of a union. A group of nine NFL players (led, alphabetically, by Tom Brady) and one prospective NFL player (Von Miller) then filed a class action lawsuit arguing, among other things, that the lockout was a per se illegal group boycott and a price fixing violation designed to coerce the players "to agree to a new anticompetitive system of player restraints" that will economically harm them (*Brady*, 779 F. Supp. at 1042). The complaint also noted that "the players in the NFL have determined that it is not in their interest to remain unionized if the existence of such a union would serve to allow the NFL to impose anticompetitive restrictions with impunity" (21). The players also moved for a preliminary injunction to prevent the owners from locking them out. The owners locked out the players on March 12, 2011.

The NFL owners raised three primary arguments in response to the players' request to enjoin the lockout. First, the owners argued that the Norris-LaGuardia Act strips federal courts of the power to enjoin lockouts. Second, they argued that the lockout was immune from antitrust attack under the nonstatutory labor exemption. Among other things, the owners contended that the NFLPA's disclaimer of interest was a "sham" and that the collective bargaining relationship still existed. Third, they argued under the primary jurisdiction doctrine that the court should defer to the NLRB's ruling on the validity of the NFLPA's disclaimer of interest before proceeding with the case.

The district court rejected all of the league's arguments and enjoined the lockout. Judge Nelson summed up the rationale for her decision as follows:

> The nation's labor laws have always applied only where an action involves or grows out of a labor dispute. Such a labor relationship exists only where a union exists to bargain on behalf of its members. Where those employees effectively renounce the union as their collective bargaining agent—and accept the consequences of doing so—and elect to proceed in negotiating contracts individually, any disputes between the employees and their employers are no longer governed by federal labor law (1042).

Judge Nelson held that the Norris LaGuardia Act's restriction on injunctions only applied during "labor disputes," and that this situation was no longer a labor dispute because the players had dissolved their union. Judge Nelson emphasized that the players had "sacrificed their union representation and the protection of labor laws" and added that it would be "ironic if a statute that had been enacted to protect the rights of individual employees from improper actions by employers and the courts were turned against those employees and used to justify the continued application of a system found illegal under the Sherman Act" (1026).

Judge Nelson also held that the nonstatutory labor exemption no longer applied because "the parties have left the collective bargaining framework entirely," and "once the union disclaims its role as the bargaining agent for its members . . . the protection provided employers by the non-statutory labor exemption is lifted" (1040). Consistent with *McNeil*, Judge Nelson concluded that the dissolution of the union ended the collective bargaining relationship and thus ended the nonstatutory labor exemption. Once the union ceased to exist, the employees gave up their rights and protections under labor law and gained access to antitrust law and its protections against restraints of trade.

Relying on *Mackey*, Judge Nelson also noted that "federal labor policy trumps the contrary policies of the antitrust laws only where, among other requirements, the agreement sought to be exempted concerns mandatory subjects of collective bargaining" (1041). Because a lockout is not a subject of collective bargaining but rather a procedural tool of bargaining, Judge Nelson held that the application of the nonstatutory labor exemption was inappropriate. Judge Nelson further held that lost playing time was sufficient to constitute irreparable harm and noted that the harm "is underscored by the undisputed brevity and precariousness of the players' careers in professional sports, particularly in the NFL" (1035) (internal quotation omitted).

The Eighth Circuit, in a divided panel, reversed the district court's decision and dissolved the injunction, noting that a "labor dispute" does not require the existence of a union (*Brady*). The court did not address the existence of the nonstatutory labor exemption but held that the disclaimer of interest (regardless of its impact on the exemption) "did not suddenly [cause the labor dispute to] disappear just because the Players elected to pursue the dispute through antitrust litigation rather than collective bargaining" (673). Although the prevailing view had been that the anti-injunction protections in the Norris-LaGuardia Act were designed solely to protect unions and employees, the Eighth Circuit took an expansive view of the Act, holding that its protections were bilateral and protected both labor and employer conduct. The court thus held that the Norris-LaGuardia "deprives a federal court of power to issue an injunction prohibiting a party to a labor dispute from implementing a lockout of its employees" (680-81). The parties eventually settled the case, the players re-formed the NFLPA as a union, and both sides reached a new collective bargaining agreement.

The NBA-NBPA labor struggle in 2011 proceeded along a similar track, with the NBA owners locking out the players and the players dissolving their union and challenging the owners' lockout under antitrust law (*Anthony v. NBA*, No. 11-5525 (N.D. Cal. Nov. 15, 2011)). The NBA owners and players, however, settled the litigation and reached a new collective bargaining agreement before any of the key legal issues were decided.

9. The Future of Collective Bargaining in Sports

The NFL-NFLPA labor struggle in *Brady* (and the comparatively brief NBA-NBPA struggle in *Anthony v. NBA*) clearly framed the key question in the latest stage of the evolution of the conflict between players and owners and between labor and antitrust law—does the nonstatutory labor exemption immunize a lockout from antitrust attack after the dissolution of a union? The resolution of this and related issues may help shape the collective bargaining relationship between players and owners for decades to come and tip the scales to either the players or the owners. If the nonstatutory labor exemption ends upon dissolution of the union, the owners' lockout will lose some of its power as the players may choose to forego (or threaten to forego) their labor rights to gain access to antitrust law. If the exemption extends past dissolution, the lockout will maintain its strength and the aggressive bargaining of professional sports owners is likely to continue.

From the leagues' perspective, immunizing post-dissolution lockouts (and other activity that would otherwise be legal under labor law) from antitrust attack is the logical extension of the nonstatutory labor exemption and provides the proper balance between labor and antitrust policy (Feldman, 2012). The leagues argue that the dissolution of the union in this context is a "sham," designed solely to provide the players with leverage at the bargaining table, and that the union will immediately reform (and re-engage in collective bargaining) when they have gained that leverage. The leagues argue that the dissolve-and-sue strategy thrusts a "powerful new [labor] weapon" into the negotiations that would upset the carefully calibrated balance created by the labor process and would ultimately destroy the collective bargaining process (*Brown*, 518 U.S. at 237). And, ending the nonstatutory labor exemption at the point of union dissolution would leave the owners in a Catch-22: either accede to the demands of the players at the bargaining table or unilaterally agree on terms and conditions of employment (or labor tactics) that can be attacked under antitrust law (237).

The players, in contrast, argue that they have a statutorily protected right to choose *not* to be in a union and can make that choice at any time. They also contend that the dissolution of the union, regardless of when it happens or how long it lasts, is not a sham because it deprives them of their rights under labor law. At that point, the owners are free to implement any terms of employment they wish, subject only to potential scrutiny under antitrust law. Immunizing employer conduct from antitrust attack post-dissolution of a union would thus deprive the players both of their antitrust rights and their labor rights and frustrate both federal labor and antitrust policy (Feldman, 2012).

10. Conclusion

There are no simple answers to the questions raised by the conflict between antitrust and labor law that arise during labor negotiations in professional sports. The NBA and NFL lockouts in 2011 provided a preview of the issues, but most of the key questions remain largely unanswered. It is likely only a matter of time before the conflict arises again and the players respond to a lockout by dissolving their union and bringing an antitrust lawsuit. The resolution of that labor battle will not only impact the leverage in that particular negotiation but will also help dictate the strength of each side's bargaining position for years to come.

References

Feldman, G. (2009). "The Puzzling Persistence of the Single-Entity Argument for Sports Leagues: *American Needle* and the Supreme Court's Opportunity to Reject a Flawed Defense." *Wisconsin Law Review* 2009: 835–916.

Feldman, G. (2012). "Antitrust Versus Labor Law in Professional Sports: Balancing the Scales After *Brady v. NFL and Anthony v. NBA*." *University of California Davis Law Review* 45: 1221–1300.

Johannesen, D. B. (1964). "Lockouts: Past, Present, and Future." *Duke Law Journal*, 1964: 257–281.

LeRoy, M. (1996). "Lockouts Involving Replacement Workers: An Empirical Public Policy Analysis and Proposal to Balance Economic Weapons Under the NLRA." *Washington University Law Quarterly* 74: 981–1058.

LeRoy, M. (2012). "The Narcotic Effect of Antitrust Law in Professional Sports: How the Sherman Act Subverts Collective Bargaining." *Tulane Law Review* 86: 859–899.

Levinstein, M., Cozzillio, M., Dimino, M. & Feldman, G. (2007). *Sports Law: Cases and Materials*, 2nd ed. (Durham, N.C.: Carolina Academic Press).

Lock, E. (1989). "The Scope of the Labor Exemption in Professional Sports." *Duke Law Journal* 38: 339–419.

Weistart, J. (1981). "Judicial Review of Labor Agreements: Lessons from the Sports Industry." *Journal of Law & Contemporary Problems* 44: 109–146.

Cases

American Needle, Inc. v. National Football League, 560 U.S. 183 (2010).

American Ship Bldg. Co. v. NLRB, 380 U.S. 300 (1965).

Anthony v. NBA, No. 11-5525 (N.D. Cal. Nov. 15, 2011).

Brady v. National Football League, 644 F.3d 661 (8th Cir. 2011).

Brady v. National Football League, 779 F. Supp. 2d 992, 1042 (D. Minn.), *vacated*, 644 F.3d 661 (8th Cir. 2011).

Brown v. Pro Football, Inc., 518 U.S. 231 (1996).

Connell Constr. Co. v. Plumbers & Steamfitters Local Union No. 100, 421 U.S. 616 (1975).

Darling & Co., 171 N.L.R.B. 801 (1968).

Great Falls Employers' Council, Inc., 123 N.L.R.B. 974 (1959).

Harter Equip., Inc. v. Local 825, 260 N.L.R.B. 597 (1986).

Iron Molders' Union No. 125 of Milwaukee, Wis. v. Allis-Chalmers Co., 166 F. 45 (7th Cir. 1908).

NLRB v. Truck Drivers Local Union No. 44 (Buffalo Linen), 353 U.S. 87 (1957),

Local Union No. 189, Amalgamated Meat Cutters & Butcher Workmen of N. Am. v. Jewel Tea Co., 381 U.S. 676 (1965).

Mackey v. NFL, 543 F.2d 606 (8th Cir. 1976).

McNeil v. NFL, 1992 WL 315292 (D. Minn. Sept. 10, 1992) (No. 4-90-976).

Powell v. NFL, 930 F.2d 1293 (8th Cir. 1989).

United States v. Hutcheson, 312 U.S. 219 (1941).

CHAPTER 12

THE SINGLE-ENTITY DOCTRINE OF ANTITRUST AS APPLIED TO SPORTS LEAGUES

STEPHEN F. ROSS

1. Introduction

LIKE most competition law regimes around the world, the Sherman Act differentiates between collaborative action among multiple parties and unilateral action by a single firm. Collaborative action by those who do not face vigorous rivals can harm consumers by restricting output, raising price, or inhibiting output responsive to consumer preference. Indeed, in some cases output can be limited even below the level set by an efficient monopolist, when collaborators adopt rules that further parochial interests of individual parties. Whether the collaboration serves useful economic purposes or is anticompetitive is generally ascertained by applying the antitrust law's Rule of Reason.

Since sports other than baseball became serious economic enterprises in the 1950s, a debate has persisted as to whether sports leagues should have to justify their rules under the Rule of Reason. Although there are principled policy arguments in favor of exempting sports from antitrust challenge, ultimately the Supreme Court concluded that sports leagues that do not face serious competition in the marketplace should not be able to harm consumers or others without any justification, or to adopt overly restrictive rules in pursuit of legitimate objectives. Judicial scrutiny is particularly important because of the serious risk that club-run sports leagues will adopt rules that not only exploit consumers but may not even be in the best collective interest of the league, protecting instead parochial interests.

Those favoring an immunity from justification first tried, but failed, to persuade Congress to expand a judicially created exemption for baseball. Next, they sought to shield sports leagues from meaningful antitrust scrutiny by characterizing league policies as products of a "single entity." *American Needle, Inc. v. National Football League* reaffirmed the Sherman Act's potency in protecting against anticompetitive, inefficient decisions potentially motivated by the parochial interest of club owners. More recently, league advocates have seized on dicta in a recent non-sports decision to shield so-called core activities from the Rule of Reason. Such a shield is unwarranted. It is inconsistent with well-settled non-sports precedents, and sports leagues that genuinely fear undue antitrust scrutiny can easily avoid Rule of Reason scrutiny by delegating all competition-related policies to a single competition organizer with the economic and legal incentives to pursue policies solely in the best interest of the entire sport.

2. The Sherman Act's Differentiation Between Collaborative and Unilateral Conduct

The Supreme Court clearly established in *Copperweld Corp. v. Independence Tube Corp.*, and reaffirmed in *American Needle, Inc. v. National Football League*, the different ways in which antitrust courts analyze challenges to conspiracies to restraint of trade under Section 1 and monopolization under Section 2 of the Sherman Act. This is consistent with textual structure of the act, but also with sound competition policy. The long-standing American view is that unilateral action threatens competition only when it excludes competitors by means that harm consumers: conduct that puts rivals out of business due to a firm's superior product benefits consumers, and even higher prices may reflect an appropriate reward for innovation that—absent exclusionary tactics—will attract new rivals to serve consumers if exploitive (Hovenkamp, 2011). In contrast, *Copperweld* observes that concerted activity is "is fraught with anticompetitive risk" insofar as it "deprives the marketplace of independent centers of decisionmaking that competition assumes and demands" (467 U.S. at 768–769).

The specific issue in *Copperweld* was an "agreement" between a parent corporation and its wholly owned but legally distinct subsidiary. Rejecting the application of Section 1 to this agreement, the Court noted that "general corporate actions are guided or determined not by two separate corporate consciousness, but one. They are not unlike a multiple team of horses drawing a vehicle under the control of a single driver" (467 U.S. at 771).

Because sports league governing typically involves complex structures, the characterization of a challenged rule as the product of a single firm (the League) or an agreement among club owners often has outcome-determinative significance for antitrust liability. Absent practices targeting potential rivals, a single firm virtually escapes scrutiny, while a policy attributed to multiple competition participants is subject to extensive scrutiny under the Rule of Reason.

To be sure, collaboration often reaps economic benefits but can also harm consumers in two discrete ways. Consumer welfare, which in a general sense refers to preserving the difference between the amount consumers are willing to spend and the amount they actually spend while buying in an efficient marketplace, may be significantly reduced by eliminating competition between the parties in the relevant market. In such a case, the appropriate antitrust result is to bar collaboration and restore rivalry between the joint venture principals. Consumer welfare may be enhanced by some form of collaboration among the parties, but policies or agreements that flow from the self-interest of the individual parties may reduce consumer welfare. A parochially structured joint venture with market power is likely to produce a result akin to a problem economists have identified as one of "double monopoly," where consumers are harmed by monopoly profits and further harmed if a second monopolist handles distribution. (Gilbert, 2004). Indeed, a test distinguishing collaborative and unilateral conduct based on whether the actual decision makers' legal and economic incentives are to act for the putative entity as a whole is consistent with the presumption in economics that a "firm" constitutes an independent profit maximizing entity (Hovenkamp, 1995). Thus, the Second Circuit rejected a single-entity characterization for sports leagues, reasoning that owners might adopt policies where the benefits to the league as a whole were outweighed by anticompetitive effects, or distinctly where "the restraint might be one adopted more for the protection of individual league members from competition than to help the league." Thus, the court concluded that the "sound and more just procedure is to judge the legality of such restraints according to well-recognized standards of our antitrust laws rather than permit their exemption on the ground that since they in some measure strengthen the league competitively as a 'single economic entity,' the combination's anticompetitive effects must be disregarded" (*North American Soccer League v. NFL*, 670 F.2d at 1257).

As detailed, in *American Needle*, the Supreme Court applied *Copperweld* in the sports context, holding that policies adopted by National Football League (NFL) owners were subject to Rule of Reason inquiry. Ascertaining whether courts should accept the Court's reasoning or instead seek creative new ways to shield sports leagues from justifying their rules requires an understanding of what the Rule of Reason is, and whether competition policy warrants an exception for sports.

3. The Rule of Reason

At its essence, antitrust analysis of agreements challenged under Section 1 as unreasonable restraints of trade requires defendants whose business practices will not be quickly checked by vigorous interbrand rivalry to justify their rules as procompetitive. Courts often cite the original articulation of the Rule of Reason in *Board of Trade of Chicago v. United States*, calling for unspecified consideration of almost any relevant factor in reaching a conclusion as to whether the challenged restraint "merely regulates and thereby promotes competition or whether it is such as may suppress or even destroy competition" (246 U.S. at 238). However, in practice, courts use a three-step approach.

First, courts employ a "market power screen" to eliminate the need for continued judicial analysis where the defendants' products face "reasonable substitutes" in the marketplace so that there is no likely consumer harm. (Lower courts have increasingly imposed far more demanding standards than those contemplated by *Continental T.V., Inc. v. GTE Sylvania Inc.* (noting that consumers can't be exploited when "vigorous interbrand competition" exists (433 U.S. at 52 n.19)) and *Valley Liquors, Inc. v. Renfield Importers, Ltd.* (justifying screen because if a firm without power sought to exploit consumers, "market retribution will be swift" (678 F.2d at 745), but that issue is beyond the scope of this chapter).

Second, defendants who can potentially exploit consumers must establish that their practice meaningfully serves a legitimate procompetitive goal. It would appear that the scope of legitimate justification is encompassed by goals that tend to lower price or raise a product's consumer appeal, based on the Supreme Court's observation that the "hallmark" of an antitrust violation is an agreement that raises price or renders output unresponsive to consumer preference (*National Collegiate Athletic Association v. Board of Regents*, 468 U.S. at 107).

Finally, the plaintiff can still prevail by showing that the challenged rule is overly restrictive; that is, that the consumer benefits that the defendants use to justify the rule can be achieved by less restrictive means. This is consistent with a long tradition emanating from the common law of restraint of trade, which upheld noncompete clauses in buyer-seller and employer-employee agreements, but only if appropriately tailored to protect legitimate interests (Heydon, 1999), as well as William Howard Taft's landmark decision in *United States v. Addyston Pipe & Steel Co.* (upholding agreements where "reasonably necessary" (85 Fed. at 283) to achieve broader legitimate purposes).

In short, the key to Rule of Reason scrutiny is its requirement that those not likely to be disciplined by the marketplace have to justify restraints that harm consumers.

4. Should Sports Leagues Have to Justify Their Rules?

During the *Lochner* era, the Supreme Court strictly limited the scope of "interstate commerce" as that termed was defined in Article I, Section 8 of the Constitution and in Section 1 of the Sherman Act. To illustrate, in *United States v. E.C. Knight Co.*, the Court held that the Sherman Act did not apply to the acquisition of virtually all the sugar refineries in Philadelphia, because "manufacturing" was not "commerce." Likewise, the Court held in *Federal Baseball Club v. National League* that the "business of giving exhibitions of base ball" was a purely state matter and the fact that a national competition required "free persons to cross state lines" was "not enough to change the character of the business" (259 U.S. at 208–209). Although *E.C. Knight* was overruled when the New Deal Court expanded the scope of "interstate commerce," the Court affirmed *Federal Baseball* on grounds of *stare decisis* in *Toolson v. New York Yankees, Inc.* However, shortly thereafter the Court refused to extend *Federal Baseball* to boxing (*United States v. International Boxing Club*), and football in *Radovich v. NFL*. In the latter case, the Court, without expressly answering the question whether sports leagues should have to justify their rules, hinted that new sports-specific legislation, following congressional hearings involving all stakeholders, would "more likely to protect the industry and the public alike" (*Radovich*, 352 U.S. at 452).

During the 1950s, advocates for various stakeholders turned to Congress seeking standards that would alternatively hold baseball owners accountable or shield all sports leagues from the risk of antitrust liability (Ross, 2011a). As *Toolson* was on appeal, a House Judiciary Subcommittee held extensive hearings and produced a 232-page report on why a broad antitrust exemption should not be approved (H.R. Rep. No. 82-2002, at 1 (1952)). It concluded that the Rule of Reason was adequate for the purpose. After *Radovich*, the subcommittee again considered legislation, this time favorably reporting a bill that would have subjected baseball, football, basketball, and hockey to the antitrust laws, but expressly exempted agreements that were "reasonably necessary" to (1) the equalization of competitive playing teams, (2) the right to operate in exclusive geographic territories, (3) the preservation of public confidence in the integrity of sports contests, and (4) the regulation of broadcasting rights (H.R. Rep. No. 85-1720, 85th Cong., 2d Sess. (1958)) (Sobel, 1977). Baseball won a floor fight, however, persuading the full House of Representatives to amend the committee bill by eliminating the words "reasonably necessary," and thus completely shielding any rules relating to competitive balance, territorial exclusivity, integrity, and broadcasting. The amendment's chief advocate argued: "Can anyone say with conviction that there is reason for foisting upon the already overburdened courts of this land an ill-suited role as arbiters of disputes within the sports family?" Responding to committee chair Emmanuel Celler's objection that the amendment would shield multiple-club ownership in hockey, wholesale broadcast shifts to pay-per-view, and the Yankees' power to block a new baseball team in New York, Rep. Kenneth Keating acknowledged that sports policies were not perfect but "that their record has been generally good; that they can be relied upon to continue to improve if they are let alone" (104 Cong. Rec. 12085 (1958)). That bill died in the Senate, and when a similar bill passed the Senate in 1965, Chairman Celler killed it in the House Judiciary Committee (Ross, 2011a, 50).

The concern about applying the Rule of Reason to sport clearly affected the Supreme Court as well. In continuing the baseball exemption, the Court's opinion in *Flood v. Kuhn* repeatedly demonstrated the majority's discomfort in applying the justificatory provisions of the Rule of Reason to sports leagues (Ross, 2011a).

Although sports leagues do have special characteristics, these are fully capable of consideration by courts under the Rule of Reason; there are no persuasive public policy reasons why sports leagues whose anti-consumer policies will not face swift market retribution should be able to harm consumers or others without any justification, or should be permitted to freely adopt overly restrictive rules. In many cases, courts have indeed upheld league policies under the antitrust laws, including the right to consider and impose fees for franchise relocations (*Los Angeles Memorial Coliseum Commission v. NFL* and *NBA v. San Diego Clippers Basketball Club*), compete in a broader marketplace for memorabilia (*Major League Baseball Props., Inc. v. Salvino, Inc.*), collectively negotiate with players who had reasonable options to play in other leagues (*Fraser v. Major League Soccer*), reject expansion (*Mid-South Grizzlies v. NFL*), reject a particular owner (*Levin v. NBA*), and protect the live gate of struggling teams (*United States v. NFL*). Where complex labor issues are best resolved by collective bargaining, the Supreme Court has held that antitrust courts must avoid the fray as long as a union is representing the players (*Brown v. Pro Football, Inc.*).

In most cases where courts have found league policies to be unreasonable restraints of trade under Section 1, the courts have acknowledged the leagues' legitimate concerns but found that the challenged rule went far beyond what was necessary to achieve league goals. *Mackey v. NFL* recognized that the NFL "has a strong and unique interest in maintaining competitive balance among its teams" but observed that the challenged "Rozelle Rule" seriously inhibited *any* movement among *any* players. *Chicago Professional Sports Ltd. v. NBA*, affirming an injunction against a rule barring out-of-market telecasts, acknowledged that leagues can prevent free riding by individual clubs on cooperative efforts, but noted that this could not justify an output ban because of the alternative of charging a fee. Indeed, the district court decision affirmed in that case had found little actual damage to other clubs to justify the rule. (Ross, 2011b, discusses the bidding dynamics.)

Judicial scrutiny under the Rule of Reason remains important particularly because the structure of major sports leagues allows owners to adopt policies that not only may exploit consumers but may constitute inefficient rules simply designed to protect parochial interests—even those interests contrary to league as a whole. Notable examples include the unwillingness of English Premier League clubs to telecast more than sixty of their games because of an inability to divide profits, the over-six-year process to move a failing Montreal Expos baseball team to Washington, D.C., because of opposition from the Baltimore Orioles, and industrial disruption and suboptimal labor market rules to prevent owner competition that would enhance league appeal. In contrast, innovations implemented by NASCAR executives who do not require the approval of racing teams likely would have been forestalled by a parochial governance structure (Ross & Szymanski, 2008). Indeed, when sports leagues do act in a unified manner, it is widely attributed to an enormously successful league commissioner who has been able to overcome the obstacles of owner self-interest to achieve an efficient result (Harris, 1986; Zimbalist, 2006). This seems to support Judge Cudahy's conclusion that the club owners' parochial interests might "distort the way the joint product is managed" (*Chicago Professional Sports Ltd. Partnership v. WGN*, 95 F.3d at 603 (hereafter *Bulls II*), 95 F.3d at 603 (concurring op.)).

5. The Supreme Court's Decision in *American Needle*

This lawsuit arose from a decision by NFL owners, who had previously agreed to grant an exclusive license to all club logos and other merchandise-related intellectual property to an entity called NFL Properties, which they controlled, to relicense a merchandise apparel license exclusively to Reebok. The lower courts dismissed the challenge on the ground that these decisions were those of a single firm. The Supreme Court reversed and remanded, holding that NFL policies providing for the collective sale of intellectual property licenses for merchandise had to be considered by the district court under the Rule of Reason. The Court concluded that the NFL was collaborative rather than unilateral, reasoning that the policies were adopted by owners with a conflict of interest between the best interests of their own club and the best interests of the league as a whole (*American Needle*, 560 U.S. at 198). A decision to market intellectual property through a collective entity (NFL Properties) plausibly promoted efficiency, but also could have been adopted by a majority of owners for their own interest: NFL Properties was an "instrumentality of the teams" (*American Needle*, 560 U.S. at 201 (quoting *United States v. Sealy, Inc.*)). This seems correct, because NFL Properties had the power to adopt policies to prevent more efficient rivals from doing a superior job of promoting its club's logos and trademarks, and to avoid the need for less innovative owners to compete on this aspect of their rivalry.[1]

In reversing the Seventh Circuit, the Court implicitly rejected the reasoning in an earlier case from that court, *Bulls II,* where Judge Easterbrook's majority opinion suggested that sports leagues were single entities because an analogy between club owners and a corporate board of directors was "apt" (95 F.3d at 597), and that too strong a reliance on *Copperweld*'s language requiring a "complete unity of interest" (467 U.S. at 771) was "silly" because corporate divisions often have competing interests (*Bulls II*, 95 F.3d at 598). Conflicts are "endemic" in firms like General Motors or IBM, Judge Easterbook observed, "but they do not imply that these large firms must justify all of their acts under the Rule of Reason" (*Bulls II*, 95 F.3d at 598).

In *American Needle,* Justice Stevens exposed flaw in *Bulls II*'s reasoning. Internal divisions among executives at General Motors or IBM are eventually resolved by a CEO or board of directors whose sole economic incentive and fiduciary duty is to the corporation as a whole. In contrast, the marketing decisions of NFL Properties were made collectively by club owners, and "each team's decision reflects not only an interest in NFLP's profits but also an interest in the team's individual profits" (*American Needle,* 560 U.S. at 201). The Court cited with approval its prior decision in *United States v. Sealy, Inc.* finding that a formally vertical territorial licensing scheme adopted by a corporation was in fact an agreement among rival mattress manufacturers who controlled the principal. *American Needle* quoted *Sealy* (388 U.S. at 353): "we are moved by the identity of the persons who act, rather than the label of their hats" (560 U.S. at 192). Unlike GM (or a true sports single entity, like NASCAR), the unanimous Court correctly concluded that when decisions about licensing NFL intellectual property are made by club owners, they are not "pursuing the 'common interests of the whole' league but [are] instead pursuing interests of each 'corporation itself'" (*American Needle*, 560 U.S. at 197 (quoting *Copperweld*, 467 U.S. at 770)). When a league is governed by its member clubs, "they are still separate, profit-maximizing entities, and their interests in licensing team trademarks are not necessarily aligned" (*American Needle*, 560 U.S. at 198). As *Copperweld* phrased it, much as Commissioners Adam Silver or Rob Manfred might wish, sports leagues are not under the control of a "single driver."

Earlier work (Ross, 2011b) illustrates this point by distinguishing between NFL Properties, which the Supreme Court concluded was an agreement among the thirty-two NFL club owners, and Major League Baseball Advanced Media (MLBAM). Unlike NFL Properties, which is governed by all NFL club owners, MLBAM was established in 2000 as a business entity governed by a board of directors including the MLB president (an executive working under the commissioner) and some but not all owners. Assuming that MLBAM's confidential governing documents do not contain bizarre terms that would allow this subset of owners to put their own club's interests over those of the other owners who are shareholders in the venture, decisions by MLBAM of how to license properties assigned to it would presumptively be considered the decision of a single entity. Because MLBAM is governed by a board of directors whose members have a legal obligation to act only in the best interests of MLBAM as a whole, a plaintiff seeking to challenge a specific MLBAM decision would have to show that the directors' economic interests were sufficiently parochial as to trump their fiduciary duties. Absent such a showing, decisions should be considered to be those of a single economic actor. Thus, the only legitimate antitrust challenge to an MLBAM decision would be to attack the initial assignment of club assets for the purpose of collective licensing.

6. The Latest Guerilla Tactic: Precluding Rule of Reason Scrutiny of "Core" Activities

In *Texaco, Inc. v. Dagher*), the Supreme Court reversed a Ninth Circuit decision condemning as illegal per se price fixing a term in a joint venture agreement providing for identical pricing of two different brands of gasoline sold by the joint venture. At one point in his opinion, Justice Thomas, in reasoning wholly unnecessary to the decision, explained that the ancillary restraints doctrine, a version of the Rule of Reason that analyzes restrictions imposed by a legitimate business collaboration on non-venture activities (547 U.S. at 7), had "no application here, where the business practice being challenged involves the core activity of the joint venture itself—namely, the pricing of the very goods produced and sold by" the venture (547 U.S. at 7–8).

Having failed to persuade Congress to exempt sports from antitrust scrutiny, and failed to persuade the Supreme Court to declare sports "single entities" by adopting a broader test, league advocates have now seized upon this imprecise dicta from *Dagher* in yet another effort to preclude Rule of Reason scrutiny for sports league decisions. Noted sports litigator James Keyte started his analysis with the insight that intellectual property that is owned by the league, such as the NFL's famous shield, "can in no sense be viewed as a competitive asset 'owned' by any individual team." He then jumps to the conclusion that all "core activities" of sports leagues can be upheld without justification (Keyte, 2010, 53). In *Dagher,* the Court made it clear that the very arrangement attacked in the case could have been challenged under the Rule of Reason if plaintiffs had been willing to do so (they didn't) and had the plaintiffs produced evidence that the venture had an actual competitive impact (547 U.S. at 7) ("If Equilon's price unification policy is anticompetitive, then respondents should have challenged it pursuant to the Rule of Reason.") Read in terms of sound competition policy, *American Needle* is better read as holding that licensing of the NFL shield is a product of a "single entity" when the decision maker (under the current regime, NFL Properties, an entity controlled by all thirty-two owners) has no conflicts of interest, but the product of an agreement when parochial interests could affect the decision. Thus, a decision to license the NFL shield as part of a youth development program with USA Football would be the decision of a single entity; the decision to license the NFL shield to Budweiser as the exclusive and official beer of the NFL, to the exclusion of any club beer licensing programs, might not be, especially where some club might prefer to have beer sponsorships arranged on a decentralized basis.[2]

A key aspect of the joint venture challenged in *Dagher* was that the principals agreed to share *all* profits from the venture. Sports leagues could indeed protect themselves under *American Needle* "where the members contribute the ownership and control of all of their respective 'competitive' assets to the venture" (Keyte, 2010, at 50). However, sports league apologists' designs go much further. Thus, Keyte argues that if clubs assigned all intellectual property rights to a league entity, then all decisions made by that entity (an entity controlled by the owners, who owe no fiduciary duty to maximize the entity's profits) would be immune from Section 1 scrutiny. This is inconsistent with *American Needle*'s insistence on a single "driver" of multiple horses. Suppose all NBA clubs assigned intellectual property to NBA Properties, and then as governors of that entity, the thirty owners voted 29-1 to reject a proposal to license Brooklyn Nets' logos to their Russian owner for marketing in Russia, because they feared that his profits will result in a competitive advantage. Keyte's doctrine would immunize this decision. In contrast, this is precisely the conflict that Justice Stevens correctly concluded required an assessment under the Rule of Reason.

One recent lower court decision supports this view. In *Laumann v. NHL*, the court rejected the defendants' motion to dismiss a complaint challenging the NHL and MLB policies allocating exclusive geographic territories to each team for licensing local broadcast rights. The defendants argued that the production and distribution of live broadcasts was "core activity" (907 F. Supp. 2d at 488) immune from antitrust scrutiny. The court held that the Rule of Reason applied.

That *Dagher*'s single reference to "core" activity does not support a new way for sports leagues to avoid antitrust scrutiny is illustrated by a non-sports landmark precedent cited approvingly by Justice Thomas in that opinion. In *Broadcast Music, Inc. v. Columbia Broadcasting System, Inc.* (hereafter *BMI*), the Court held that the category of agreements warranting per se condemnation under Section 1 of the Sherman Act did not apply to all cases of "literal" price fixing but rather only those agreements that we "plainly anticompetitive" without "redeeming virtue" (441 U.S. at 8, 9). However, although a collaboration to sell a blanket copyright license was a new product that could not be offered by any individual defendant and that collective fixing of price was an "obvious necessity" (441 U.S. at 20), *BMI* did not uphold the challenged agreements as lawful "core activities of the venture itself." Rather, the Court remanded the case (which was on appeal from per se condemnation by the Second Circuit) for further consideration under the Rule of Reason. On remand, the lower courts exonerated the defendants' practices, but only because buyers dissatisfied with the collaborative products offered could obtain licenses from individual copyright holders directly.[3] The clear implication from the post-*BMI* reasoning is that if licensees did *not* have an alternative means to obtain the desired product, the Rule of Reason might well have invalidated the scheme.

To apply *Dagher* to preclude antitrust scrutiny of sports leagues effectively overrules *BMI*, a conclusion wholly unsupported by the rest of the reasoning in *Dagher* or any other case. Indeed, this *dicta*, if read as league advocates desire, is inconsistent with *Dagher's* positive citation of *National Collegiate Athletic Ass'n v. Board of Regents*—which applied the Rule of Reason to a sports league television restraint. Moreover, it has been described as a "peculiar and unprecedented" limitation on the ancillary restraints doctrine (Areeda & Hovenkamp, 2009, 328). The "guerilla warfare" aspect of this effort to use *Dagher* to revive a shield against Rule of Reason scrutiny can be foreshadowed by the Justice Department's *amicus* brief on the certiorari petition in *American Needle* (*Dagher*, 547 U.S. at 19 n.7): "the NFL respondents consider virtually all aspects of league operations to be 'core venture functions' subject to single-entity treatment."

7. Conclusion

Sports leagues were initially formed as collaborative ventures because, with a nascent league, there is no one other than the participants willing to fund and organize the competition. (For a historical description of the creation of the National League in 1876, see Szymanski and Zimbalist, 2005.) When leagues become dominant enough to wield market power, and thus have their restrictions seriously considered under the Rule of Reason, the club owners that control the leagues have the option of delegating rulemaking authority to an independent competition organizer who would be a single entity.

This is precisely what race car drivers did prior to the formation of NASCAR in the 1940s. As one observer noted, to achieve success required "a central racing organization whose authority outranked all drivers, car owners, and track owners" (Hagstrom, 2001, 28).

Consider why, today, club owners object to delegating such authority. It is precisely so that they can retain policy control, in order to protect their own club's parochial interests. This is precisely why a Rule of Reason is needed and why sports league owners should have to justify decisions that demonstrably restrain trade.

Notes

1. *See also Chicago Prof'l Sports Ltd. P'ship v. WGN* (hereafter *Bulls II*) (Cudahy, J., concurring) (fact that owners of league are owners of participating teams creates "potential for inefficient decisionmaking regarding the joint product of 'league basketball' ").
2. *See, e.g, New York Yankees P'ship & Adidas Am., Inc. v. Major League Baseball Enter., Inc., et al.* (lawsuit, eventually settled without judicial resolution, challenging MLB refusal to allow Yankees to enter into shoe sponsorship).
3. *See, e.g., Buffalo Broad. Co. v. American Soc'y of Composers, Authors & Publishers.*

References

Areeda, P., & Hovenkamp, H. (2009 suppl.). *Antitrust Law* (3rd ed.). (New York: Aspen Publishers).

Gilbert, R. J. (2004). "Antitrust for Patent Pools: A Century of Policy Evolution." *Stanford Technology Law Review* 3, 7.

Hagstrom, R. G. (2001). *The NASCAR Way: The Business That Drives the Sport* (New York: John Wiley & Sons).

Harris, D. (1986). *The League: The Rise and Decline of the NFL* (New York: Bantam Books).

Heydon, J. D. (1999). *The Restraint of Trade Doctrine* (2d ed.). (Sydney: Butterworths).

Hovenkamp, H. (1995). "Exclusive Joint Ventures and Antitrust Policy." *Columbia Business Law Review* 1, 7.

Hovenkamp, H. (2011). *Federal Antitrust Policy: The Law of Competition and Its Practice* (4th ed.). St. Paul, Minn.: West Academic.

Keyte, J. A. (2010). "*American Needle*: A New Quick Look for Joint Ventures." *Antitrust* 25: 48.

Ross, S. F. (2011a). "The Story of *Flood v. Kuhn* (1972): Dynamic Statutory Interpretation, at the Time." In *Statutory Interpretation Stories*, edited by W. N. Eskridge, Jr., P. P. Frickey, and E. Garrett, eds. (New York: Foundation Press), xx.

Ross, S. F. (2011b). "The Supreme Court's Renewed Focus in Inefficiently Structured Joint Ventures." *University of Pennsylvania Journal of Business Law* 14: 261.

Ross, S. F., and Szymanski, S. (2008). *Fans of the World, Unite! A (Capitalist) Manifesto for Sports Consumers* (Stanford, CA: Stanford University Press).

Sobel, L. S. (1977). *Professional Sports and the Law* (New York: Law-Arts Publishers).

Szymanski, S., & Zimbalist, A. (2005). *National Pastime: How Americans Play Baseball and the Rest of the World Plays Soccer* (Washington, D.C.: Brookings Institution).

Zimbalist, A. (2006). *In the Best Interests of Baseball? The Revolutionary Reign of Bud Selig*, (Hoboken, N.J.: John Wiley & Sons).

Cases

American Needle, Inc. v. National Football League, 560 U.S. 183 (2010).
Board of Trade of Chicago v. United States, 246 U.S. 231, 238 (1918).
Broadcast Music, Inc. v. Columbia Broad. Sys., Inc., 441 U.S. 1 (1979).
Brown v. Pro Football, Inc., 518 U.S. 231 (1996).
Buffalo Broad. Co. v. American Soc'y of Composers, Authors & Publishers, 744 F.2d 917 (2d Cir. 1984), *cert. denied*, 469 U.S. 1211 (1985).
Chicago Prof'l Sports Ltd. v. NBA, 961 F.2d 667 (7th Cir. 1992).
Chicago Prof'l Sports Ltd. P'ship v. WGN, 95 F.3d 593, 603 (7th Circ. 1996) (Cudahy, J., concurring).
Continental T.V., Inc. v. GTE Sylvania Inc., 433 U.S. 36 (1977).
Copperweld Corp. v. Independence Tube Corp., 467 U.S. 752 (1984).
Federal Baseball Club v. National League, 259 U.S. 200 (1922).
Flood v. Kuhn, 407 U.S. 258 (1972).
Fraser v. Major League Soccer, 284 F.2d 47 (1st Cir. 2001).
Laumann v. NHL, 907 F. Supp. 2d 465 (S.D.N.Y. 2012).
Levin v. NBA, 385 F. Supp. 149 (S.D.N.Y. 1974).
Los Angeles Mem'l Coliseum Comm'n v. NFL, 719 F.2d 1356 (9th Cir. 1986).
Mackey v. NFL, 543 F.2d 606 (8th Cir. 1976).
Major League Baseball Props., Inc. v. Salvino, Inc., 542 F.3d 290 (2d Cir. 2008).
Mid-South Grizzlies v. NFL, 720 F.2d 772 (3d Cir. 1983).
NBA v. San Diego Clippers Basketball Club, 815 F.2d 562 (9th Cir. 1987).
National Collegiate Athletic Ass'n v. Board of Regents, 468 U.S. 85 (1984).
New York Yankees P'ship & Adidas Am., Inc. v. Major League Baseball Enter., Inc., et al., Case No. 98-civ-0129 (S.D.N.Y.)
North Am. Soccer League v. NFL, 670 F.2d 1249 (2d Cir.1982).
Radovich v. NFL, 352 U.S. 445 (1957).
Texaco, Inc. v. Dagher, 547 U.S. 1 (2006).
Toolson v. New York Yankees, Inc., 346 U.S. 356 (1953).
United States v. Addyston Pipe & Steel Co., 85 Fed. 271, 283 (6th Cir. 1898)
United States v. E.C. Knight Co., 156 U.S. 1 (1895).
United States v. International Boxing Club, 348 U.S. 236 (1955).
United States v. NFL, 116 F. Supp. 319 (E.D. Pa. 1953).
United States v. Sealy, Inc., 388 U.S. 350 (1967).
Valley Liquors, Inc. v. Renfield Importers, Ltd., 678 F.2d 742 (7th Cir. 1982) (Posner, J.).

CHAPTER 13

ELIGIBILITY RULES IN PROFESSIONAL SPORTS

GLENN M. WONG AND
CHRISTOPHER R. DEUBERT

Authors' Note:
Some of the content of this chapter is the result of research done as part of the Football Players Health Study at Harvard University. The authors thank Harvard University for granting permissions.

1. Introduction

This chapter examines the rules governing when individuals are eligible to play in professional sports leagues and organizations. Specifically, we analyze the rules of the National Football League (NFL), Major League Baseball (MLB), National Basketball Association (NBA), National Hockey League (NHL), Major League Soccer (MLS), and the Women's National Basketball Association (WNBA). We also include a brief discussion of eligibility rules for the PGA Tour in men's golf; the Ladies PGA (LPGA) Tour in women's golf; the Association of Tennis Professionals (ATP) for men's tennis; and the Women's Tennis Association (WTA) for women's tennis. The NFL, MLB, NBA, NHL, MLS, and WNBA are team sports, whereas the PGA Tour, LPGA Tour, ATP, and WTA are individual sports. The different nature of the sports leads to differences in the eligibility rules.

Ultimately, because of the unique nature and needs of the organizations and their athletes, a comparative analysis of the eligibility rules might not be particularly useful. The comparative analysis is particularly complicated by the general lack of public data that would support any of the eligibility rules. Nonetheless, this chapter can serve as a useful reference for anyone wishing to understand the leagues' and organizations' eligibility rules and perhaps serve as an impetus for rules that are more grounded in reliable data.

Before explaining each of the organization's eligibility rules, provided are: (A) information on the eligibility rules' legal standing; (B) general information about the leagues' drafts (where applicable) that correspond to their eligibility rules; (C) an explanation of the NCAA and its relevance to the eligibility rules; and (D) insurance options that might be available to players before joining one of the organizations.

1.1. Legal Status of the Eligibility Rules

The legal standing of an eligibility rule is different for each sports organization depending on the league's structure.

The NFL, MLB, NBA, and NHL consist of member clubs that are individually owned and operated, with the league serving as a centralized, governing body. The clubs compete both on and off the field, court, or ice. Off the field, most notably, clubs compete in the labor market for players' services, bidding against one another on the terms of a contract in hopes of persuading a player to sign with their club. Eligibility rules put a limitation on this market by prohibiting certain potential players from participating in the market. The clubs—through the eligibility rules—have collectively agreed not to bid and contract for the services of particular individuals.

The clubs' eligibility rules have the potential to violate antitrust laws. Section 1 of the Sherman Antitrust Act prohibits contracts, combinations, or conspiracies that unreasonably restrain trade (15 U.S.C. § 1). The eligibility rules restrain trade by prohibiting potential players from contracting with clubs. Whether this restraint is "unreasonable" requires a complicated antitrust analysis of a variety of legal and factual factors (*American Needle, Inc. v. National Football League*, 560 U.S. at 186).

Nevertheless, the leagues' eligibility rules have been generally treated as not subject to antitrust scrutiny. Certain collective actions by the clubs are exempt from antitrust laws under what is known as the "non-statutory labor exemption." The nonstatutory labor exemption exempts restrictions imposed by a multiemployer unit (such as sports clubs) where the restrictions were negotiated with a labor organization (i.e., a union, as part of the collective bargaining process) (*Brown v. Pro Football, Inc.*). For each of the NFL, MLB, NBA, NHL, MLS, and WNBA, there is a corresponding union that represents the players and negotiates a collective bargaining agreement (CBA) with the league. Consequently, based on at least the Second Circuit's decision in *Clarett v. National Football League*, it appears that as long as the eligibility rules are negotiated with the union, they will be exempt from the antitrust laws.[1]

The eligibility rules in the NFL, NBA, NHL, and WNBA are all collectively bargained with those leagues' respective players associations and are thus exempt from antitrust law.[2] Next, we discuss each of these leagues' eligibility rules as well as the unique circumstances of eligibility rules in MLB and MLS.

The eligibility rules of the golf and tennis organizations have a different legal status. While there are no member clubs in these sports, the PGA Tour, LPGA Tour, ATP, and WTA all govern a series of tournaments which have agreed to abide by the organization's rules, including the eligibility rules. Thus, while one might argue that clubs in the other sports have violated antitrust laws by agreeing to exclude players who are not yet considered eligible in the individual sports, one might argue that the PGA Tour, LPGA Tour, ATP, and WTA have violated antitrust laws by coordinating the exclusion of a player from the different tournaments.

Importantly, there are also no labor organizations representing the golfers on the PGA Tour or LPGA Tour, or the players on the ATP Tour or WTA Tour. Consequently, these organizations do not enter into CBAs with the athletes concerning eligibility rules or any other matter. As a result, the eligibility rules of the PGA Tour, LPGA Tour, ATP, and WTA do not enjoy the benefit of the nonstatutory labor exemption and are thus subject to antitrust scrutiny.

Nevertheless, the absence of the nonstatutory labor exemption does not mean that the organizations' eligibility rules violate antitrust law. To establish a violation of antitrust law, an athlete would likely have to prove that the rule is "unreasonable" (i.e., if the rule's anticompetitive effects outweigh its procompetitive effects). This is a challenging and complicated legal and economic analysis. Thus, it is perhaps not surprising that no athlete has brought a legal challenge against these organizations' rules in American courts.

However, the WTA's eligibility rule (which will be explained further later) did face a legal challenge in Australia. In 1998, Mirjana Lucic, a fifteen-year-old Croatian who was barred from playing a tournament in Sydney, Australia, sued the WTA alleging that the rule violated Australian antitrust law. Australian antitrust law bans restraints of trade where there was a "manifest failure by a person who created or joined in creating the restraint to attempt to make the restraint reasonable." Based on an extensive analysis conducted by the WTA prior to enacting the eligibility rule, the Australian court held that it could not find that there had been a manifest failure by the WTA in creating the rule.

1.2. Leagues' Drafts

In team sports, the leagues' eligibility rules are designed, in part, to require players to enter the leagues through their respective drafts. The drafts are intended in large part to provide the poorer performing clubs the opportunity to draft (i.e., acquire) the best draft-eligible players first, and thus level the competitive playing field in the league. As discussed later, the size of these drafts can have important impacts on player decisions concerning their eligibility. Table 13.1 provides information about the drafts.

As they are not team sports, there are no drafts in the PGA Tour, LPGA Tour, ATP, or WTA.

1.3. The NCAA

The National Collegiate Athletic Association (NCAA) is a nonprofit, unincorporated association headquartered in Indianapolis through which the nation's colleges and universities govern their athletic programs. The NCAA is made up of over 1,200 member institutions, all of which participate in the creation of NCAA rules and voluntarily

Table 13.1 Leagues' Drafts

	NFL	MLB	NBA	NHL	MLS	WNBA
Month	April/May	June	June	June	January	April
Length	7 Rounds	40 Rounds	2 Rounds	7 Rounds	4 Rounds	3 Rounds
Approximate Number of Players	255	1,215	60	210	84	36

submit to its authority. To oversee its affairs, the NCAA's member institutions hire a president, currently Mark Emmert, formerly the president of the University of Washington.

As we demonstrated later, the majority of players in team sports leagues played college sports at NCAA member institutions and thus adhered to the NCAA's rules before joining their respective leagues. The NCAA's rules have a substantial impact on players and their decisions about when to join one of the professional leagues.

NCAA Bylaw 12.01.1 declares that "[o]nly an amateur student-athlete is eligible for intercollegiate athletics participation[.]" Moreover, NCAA Bylaw 12.01.2 states there must be "a clear line of demarcation between college athletics and professional sports." Consequently, student-athletes are generally barred from receiving any compensation of any kind for their athletic ability other than a scholarship (NCAA Bylaws 12.02.9, 12.02.10, 12.1.2.1, 12.2, 12.4, 12.5, 12.01.4).

The NCAA Bylaws also limit a student-athlete's options concerning joining one of the leagues. The effect of certain NCAA Bylaws are discussed in the course of this chapter, but here we highlight two specific bylaws that affect player eligibility.

First, NCAA Bylaws generally prohibit players from hiring agents (NCAA Bylaw 12.1.2), or retaining a lawyer to represent them in contract negotiations (NCAA Bylaw 12.3.2). Were they permitted in NCAA sports, agents and attorneys would have the ability to communicate with professional clubs about a player's future prospects. Moreover, if the player has been drafted but has collegiate eligibility remaining (as will be explained later), the agents and attorneys would be able to negotiate with the club so the player can make an informed decision relative to the financial end—namely, about whether to return to college or turn professional. While some student-athletes may have the sophistication or support to do this by themselves or with guidance from family members, it stands to reason that they could benefit from the advice of experienced counsel. Nevertheless, NCAA Bylaws prohibit players from having lawyers who have any direct contact with professional clubs (NCAA Bylaw 12.3.2.1).

There is, however, an important caveat to this discussion. In 2014, the NCAA approved allowing the five most competitive and highest revenue-producing conferences (ACC, Big 12, Big Ten, Pac-12, and SEC) to write their own rules on certain matters. As a result, in 2016, these conferences agreed to allow high school baseball players who are drafted to have an agent negotiate a potential contract with a MLB club. The player must pay the agent a market rate and if the player chooses to enroll in college rather than sign with the MLB club, he must terminate the relationship with the agent. This rule, which can be adopted by other conferences, provides baseball players with a meaningful opportunity to consider whether to turn professional instead of enrolling in college.

Second, NCAA Bylaws prohibit basketball and football student-athletes from returning to intercollegiate athletics if they are eligible for the draft but are not drafted.[3] College basketball student-athletes are, however, permitted to declare for the NBA Draft and attend pre-draft workouts and return to school provided they withdraw their name from the NBA Draft. Nevertheless, the players still are unable to actually weigh the results of having been drafted against the possibility of returning to school. Thus, players in both basketball and football must weigh whether they are physically, emotionally, and intellectually ready for the professional ranks or whether to return to college and not be paid for playing while risking an injury that might jeopardize their ability to ever play professionally.

The NCAA and some of these bylaws are currently the subject of lawsuits throughout the country.[4] The lawsuits principally contend that the NCAA's prohibition against student-athletes earning pay while playing violates various legal doctrines and laws, notably the Sherman Antitrust Act's prohibition against agreements that unreasonably restrain trade. Nevertheless, the NCAA Bylaws are still in existence as of this publication and thus play an important role in analyzing leagues' eligibility rules and their effect on player health.

To address the concerns of student-athletes who are weighing whether to turn professional, in 1990 the NCAA created the Exceptional Student-Athlete Disability Insurance (ESDI) program (Wong and Deubert, 2010). We discuss the ESDI and other insurance options next.

1.4. Players' Insurance Options

In light of the NCAA's rules prohibiting players from being compensated while playing college sports (as many are effectively required to do for reasons explained later), some athletes might want insurance policies to protect against an injury preventing or reducing their future professional earnings. Such athletes generally have two options: (1) the NCAA's ESDI program and (2) loss of value insurance policies through private insurers.

1.4.1. *The NCAA's Exceptional Student-Athlete Disability Insurance Program*

Student-athletes who demonstrate that they have the potential to be selected in the first three rounds of the NHL Draft, first two rounds of the NFL Draft, or the first round of the NBA, MLB, or WNBA Draft are eligible for the program. If a player suffers a permanent total disability, the program pays student-athletes a lump-sum payment twelve months later.

The amount of insurance coverage is determined by the insurer "based upon [the student-athlete's] prospective status in the upcoming draft." The premiums cost approximately $3,000 and $6,000 annually for each $1 million of coverage (depending on the sport and the player's position), which is considered a few thousand dollars less expensive than a private policy. Beginning in 2014, the NCAA has permitted colleges to pay the premiums on behalf of the player. Alternatively, student-athletes may take out loans to pay for the insurance without losing their amateur status for the NCAA. Approximately forty to fifty athletes participate in the ESDI program each year, and the majority of those athletes are college football players.

1.4.2. *Loss of Value Insurance*

In addition to the ESDI program, players might also consider obtaining a loss of value (LOV) insurance policy through a private insurance company. LOV policies provide benefits to players whose draft stock, and thus the expected value of their contract, decreases due to injury. For example, if a highly touted college player suffered an injury that prevented him from being the first overall pick in the draft, a LOV policy would have paid him the difference between the contract of the first overall pick and the player's actual, lesser contract.

In 2014, the NCAA approved permitting players to obtain loans based on the player's future earnings to pay for the premiums of LOV policies. And because LOV policies are provided by private insurers rather than the NCAA, any player is able to obtain one if an insurance company is willing to provide coverage.

While LOV policies have reportedly become more common in recent years, research has not revealed any publicly available data on how many players are obtaining the policies or whether any have had difficult repaying the loans used to pay the premiums.

By way of example, in 2015, former Oregon and current NFL cornerback Ifo Ekpre-Olomu collected on a LOV policy. Ekpre-Olomu was projected as a first round pick in the 2015 NFL Draft before tearing his ACL (anterior cruciate ligament) toward the end of the 2014 college season. As a result of his injury, Ekpre-Olomu dropped to the seventh round of the NFL Draft. Ekpre-Olomu's policy provided him with a $3 million payment as a result.

With this background information covered, we are now ready to examine the NFL's player eligibility rules before comparing them to the other leagues.

2. Player Eligibility Rules in the NFL

The 2011 NFL CBA provides: "No player shall be . . . eligible for the [NFL] Draft, until three NFL regular seasons have begun and ended following either his graduation from high school or graduation of the class with which he entered high school, whichever is earlier." Because there are no football leagues in the world comparable to the NFL in terms of skill and pay, the NFL's eligibility rule effectively requires almost all players to attend college for at least three seasons before they can enter the NFL Draft.[5]

The NFL's eligibility rule has faced legal challenges. In 2004, former Ohio State running back Maurice Clarett initiated an unsuccessful legal challenge to the NFL's eligibility rule (*Clarett v. National Football League*, 306 F. Supp. 2d at 387). After a stellar freshman season in the fall of 2002 in which he led Ohio State to the national championship, Clarett was suspended by the NCAA for the entire 2003 season due to a variety of NCAA rules infractions. Rather than not play the 2003 season and then seek an uncertain reinstatement from the NCAA for the 2004 season, Clarett wished to enter the NFL Draft. However, because he was not yet three years removed from his high school graduation, Clarett was ineligible for the draft.

Clarett sued the NFL, arguing that the NFL's eligibility rule violated antitrust laws. After initially winning in the U.S. District Court for the Southern District of New York, the U.S. Court of Appeals for the Second Circuit, in an opinion written by then-Judge Sonia Sotomayor, reversed. The Second Circuit held that the NFL's eligibility rule, even though it was not contained within the CBA, had been collectively bargained with the NFL Players Association (NFLPA) and was thus immune from antitrust law pursuant to the nonstatutory exemption. In 2006, to help avoid future challenges, the NFL and NFLPA added the eligibility rule to the CBA.

The NFL's eligibility rule creates pressures on two groups of potential players. First, the NFL's eligibility rule affects those college players who have already proven themselves as NFL prospects but are not yet eligible for the draft. These players might be concerned about remaining healthy until they are eligible for the draft (e.g., freshmen and sophomores). For example, in 2012, sophomore South Carolina defensive lineman Jadeveon Clowney established himself as the most dominant player in college football. Many in the media argued that Clowney would have been the first overall pick in the 2013 draft if not for the NFL's eligibility rule. However, because of the eligibility rule, Clowney was forced to return to South Carolina for the 2013 season. Clowney had a less impressive 2013 season, including missing several games due to injuries. Clowney's diminished performance and missed game time caused some, including South Carolina's head coach Steve Spurrier, to speculate that Clowney was more concerned with protecting his NFL Draft status than playing college football. Clowney was ultimately selected with the first overall pick in the 2014 NFL Draft.

While Clowney's story still ended with him being highly drafted, there have been many players who suffered injuries in college and, as a result, saw their NFL Draft stock drop significantly. For example, Adewale Ogunleye, from the University of Indiana, was one of the country's best defensive players between 1996 and 1999 and considered leaving college early after his junior season in 1998. However, Ogunleye returned to college and suffered a knee injury during the 1999 season that caused him to go undrafted and left him unable to play in 2000. Ogunleye ultimately went on to have a successful ten-year career in the NFL.

Clowney's former teammate at South Carolina, Marcus Lattimore, provides another interesting example. Lattimore, a running back who was First-Team All-SEC in his freshman year, tore multiple ligaments in his knee in both his sophomore and junior seasons. Lattimore was drafted by the San Francisco 49ers in the fourth round of the 2013 NFL Draft but never played in an NFL game before retiring in 2014 due to ongoing knee problems. Fortunately, Lattimore reportedly was eligible for a $1.7 million payment from a disability insurance policy.

The Clowney, Ogunleye, and Lattimore stories all demonstrate the perils of being prevented from entering the NFL. A football player might suffer health problems at any time, but at least if the player is in the NFL, he will have earned (or be entitled to) some money before facing such problems.

The second group of potential players affected by the NFL's eligibility rule is comprised of those players who are eligible for the draft and who also have college eligibility remaining (e.g., juniors) but are considering entering the NFL Draft. These players often face a difficult choice between entering the draft or playing another year of college football—during which time they may improve their skill and improve their draft prospects, play for a championship at the collegiate level with their current teammates, finish (or come closer to finishing) their education, but also risk injury.

The NFL's eligibility rule, coupled with the short average duration of NFL careers, rookie contract structures, and free agency rules collectively place at least some pressure on players to leave college early for the NFL Draft. The average NFL career of a drafted player is about five years ("Average NFL Career Length," 2014). NFL rookie contracts are limited to four years plus a club option for a fifth year for first-round picks and four years for all other draft picks (2011 NFL CBA, Art. 7, § 3). In addition, the form of rookie contracts is restrictive, limiting the amount of money players can potentially earn to amounts far below what unrestricted free agents might earn on the open market (Deubert, Wong, and Howe, 2012). Finally, players cannot even become unrestricted free agents until they have played at least four seasons. Consequently, the typical player might only have one year left in his career when he is finally able to reach free agency and offer his services to the highest-bidding club.

These dynamics cause some players to believe they need to be in the NFL as soon as possible to capitalize on the limited timespan for which they can expect to be a healthy and productive NFL player. In particular, it is common to hear coaches or the media discuss the limited "lifespan" or "tread on the tires" for running backs. If not for the NFL's eligibility rule, it is likely that some players would choose to enter the NFL Draft after their freshman or sophomore year of college, or maybe even high school, in order to maximize the perceived potential length of their NFL careers.

To assist these players, in 1994, the NFL created an Advisory Committee to help student-athletes determine their potential draft round in the NFL Draft and assist them in making the decision whether or not to leave school early. The Advisory Committee is comprised of NFL club general managers, personnel directors, and scouts, and performs evaluations of student-athletes upon request from the student-athlete or his athletic department. The Advisory Committee provides the student-athlete with projection in one of five categories: "As high as the first round; as high as the second round; as high as the third round; no potential to go in the first three rounds; and no potential to be drafted." The Advisory Committee's assessments are confidential and therefore it is impossible to judge their accuracy unless a player discloses them.

Despite the Advisory Committee's work, recent data suggests that many players declare for the NFL Draft before they are ready. In 2014, 45 of the 107 players (42%) who left college early were not drafted; in 2015, 24 of the 84 early entrants (29%) went undrafted; and, in 2016, 30 of the 107 early entrants went undrafted (28%).[6] Although those players had the opportunity to sign as undrafted free agents with any club, they were not guaranteed any compensation if they did so and their careers are likely to be shorter than those of drafted players ("Average NFL Career Length," 2014).

A player also cannot go through the draft process and then, if not drafted, return to college football. Pursuant to NCAA Bylaw 12.2.4.2.3, a player who declares for the NFL Draft has only seventy-two hours to rescind his declaration or he cannot return to play college football. The NFL requires student-athletes to declare for the NFL Draft (which takes place in April or May) by January 15. Thus, if a player has gone through the draft in April or May, he is long past the January 18 (January 15 plus seventy-two hours) deadline to return to college football.

Even if the deadline for a player to rescind his declaration for the draft were extended until after the draft, NCAA Bylaws create an additional hurdle to players considering entering the draft. A college football season ends in December or January but the NFL Draft is not until April or May. In that interim period, almost all prospective NFL players undergo extensive training to improve their conditioning and skills to enable them to perform well at the NFL Combine and in other workouts. The costs of that training and the player's living expenses during this time period—which are typically at least $30,000—are almost always paid for by agents. Consequently, to enter the NFL Draft, a player generally needs an agent—something forbidden by NCAA rules. Thus, a player who enters the NFL Draft and undertakes the requisite training to be drafted essentially gives up his NCAA eligibility, which prevents him from playing college football in the future.

Despite the pressures the NFL's eligibility rule creates, the NFL's stated purposes for the rule are largely to protect players. In the *Clarett* case, the NFL offered four reasons for its eligibility rule:

> [1] Protecting younger and/or less experienced players – that is, players who are less mature physically and psychologically – from heightened risks of injury in NFL games; [2] protecting the NFL's entertainment product from the adverse consequences associated with such injuries; [3] protecting the NFL clubs from the costs and potential liability entailed by such injuries; and [4] protecting from injury and self-abuse other adolescents who would over-train – and use steroids – in the misguided hope of developing prematurely the strength and speed required to play in the NFL.
>
> (*Clarett*, 306 F. Supp. 2d at 408)

The NFL's eligibility rule imposes a strict delay on when players can enter the league. Given the injury concerns about playing football, players are often anxious to get to the NFL as soon as possible to maximize their potential earnings. Nevertheless, players must weigh their desire to enter the league with an understanding of whether or not they are physically prepared for the NFL.

3. Player Eligibility Rules in MLB

Players' eligibility to play in MLB is based on the player's residency. The eligibility rules differentiate players who are residents from the United States (including territories) or Canada from those who are not, although the rules do not define the term "resident."

American and Canadian players who have never previously contracted with a major or minor league baseball club are subject to MLB's First-Year Player Draft, known as the "Rule 4 Draft," because the Draft is set out in Rule 4 of MLB's Major League Rules (MLR) (but not the CBA).[7] Additionally, when players are eligible for the Rule 4 Draft depends on their education status.

The principal result of the Rule 4 Draft is that, generally, once a player enters college, he cannot enter the draft again until after his junior year of college (unless he is twenty-one years old). If the player plays beyond his junior year, he cannot enter the draft until his collegiate eligibility has expired, which is typically after his senior year. Next, we provide a more detailed description of the Rule 4 Draft's nuances.

High school players are not eligible for the draft while "the student is eligible for participation in high school athletics" (MLR 3(a)(2)(A)). High school athletic eligibility typically terminates at the earlier of eight semesters of enrollment or graduation. A high school player may become eligible for the draft prior to graduation if he has become ineligible for high school competition due to his age, because he has completed the maximum number of allowable semesters of attendance without graduation, or if "the maximum number of seasons in which the player was eligible to participate in any major sport has passed." Though in no case may a high school player be obligated "to report for service prior to the normal graduation of the class with which [he] originally entered high school" (MLR 3(a)(2)(A)(i)–(iii)). Additionally, a high school player who drops out of high school prior to the expiration of his athletic eligibility must remain out of school for "365 days including the date of withdrawal" before he is eligible for the Rule 4 Draft (MLR 3(a)(2)(A)).

Of the 1,216 players drafted in 2016's Rule 4 Draft, only 300 (24.7%) were drafted directly out of high school. The remaining players all played at least some college or junior college baseball. However, once a player decides to enter college, his eligibility for the Rule 4 Draft becomes restricted.

Subject to a number of exceptions discussed later, a college player is ineligible for the Rule 4 Draft from the "date [he] attends the first class in [his] freshman year" until "the graduation of the class with which [he] originally entered college," or the graduation of a subsequent undergraduate class "if [he] retains eligibility to play baseball at [his] college in [that] year" (MLR 3(a)(3)(B)).

The general rule that a college player is not eligible until the graduation of the class with which he entered college does not apply to a college player:

(i) who is at least twenty-one years old and is currently between school years;
(ii) who has completed [his] junior year and is currently between school years;
(iii) who has completed the full period of [his] eligibility for intercollegiate baseball;
(iv) whose association with [his] college has been terminated by reason of scholastic deficiency; or
(v) who withdraws from college and remains out [of college] for at least 120 days (including the date of withdrawal).

(MLR 3(a)(E)(i)-(v)).

Some high school players may also enter junior colleges. Junior college players are eligible for the draft after either their first or second year at the school.

MLB's different rules result in the possibility that a player can be drafted multiple times. A player drafted after high school may choose to enter college instead of signing with the club that drafted him. Players might believe they will have more opportunity to play and develop in college than in the minor leagues. Then, if the player enters a four-year college, he cannot be drafted again until he is twenty-one years of age or after his junior year. If he again does not sign, he can return for his senior season. In each case, the player does not choose to enter the draft—he is automatically subject to the draft. Therefore, a player could be drafted after high school, his junior year of college, and then a third time after his senior year of college.[8]

While MLB's Draft rules provide considerable flexibility, there have been occasions where players thought they were sufficiently prepared for MLB before they could be drafted. After completing his sophomore year of high school in 2009, during which he batted .626, Bryce Harper earned his General Educational Development (GED) and enrolled in a junior college to face better competition. After one year in junior college, Harper was selected as the first overall pick in the 2010 Rule 4 Draft at the age of seventeen. Nevertheless, Harper's situation (and talent) is considered anomalous.

We now discuss the eligibility rules for foreign (i.e., non-U.S./non-Canadian) players, assuming they have not entered an American or Canadian college or otherwise become a resident of the United States. These foreign players are not subject to the Rule 4 Draft. Instead, an international player is eligible to sign a professional contract if he is "17 years old at the time of signing, or . . . will attain age 17 prior to either the end of the effective season for which the player has signed or September 1 of such effective season, whichever is later" (MLR 3(a)(1)(B)(i)–(ii)).

In lieu of a draft, MLB clubs engage in a competitive scouting and bidding process for international talent, particularly as the rate of foreign-born players has increased. In 2016, 27.5% of players on clubs' opening day rosters were foreign-born. Moreover, 22.3% of all MLB players were from South or Central American countries.

Unfortunately, the scouting and bidding process has been fraught with problems. In the Latin American countries, young baseball players, some not even in their teens, are often found and then controlled by "buscones," or street agents (Kalthoff, 2014). The buscones control MLB clubs' access to the players and can effectively sell the players to the clubs, taking a portion of the players' signing bonus for themselves. MLB club personnel have also been caught defrauding their clubs by taking a portion of the signing bonus allocated for the player and often splitting it with the buscone (Kalthoff, 2014). In addition, there are widespread problems with identity fraud. Players desperate to reach MLB purport to be younger than they are or might even pretend to be someone else entirely. While MLB and MLB clubs have taken steps to prevent identity fraud and to eliminate the influence of buscones (by having their own academies), many have also argued that the best way to resolve the issues is through an international draft (Lopez, 2009; Williamson, 2013).

The 2011 CBA created an International Talent Committee charged with "discuss[ing] the development and acquisition of international players, including the potential inclusion of international amateur players in a draft, and to examine the rules and procedures pursuant to which international professional players sign contracts with Clubs." As part of its mandate, the International Talent Committee is to provide the MLBPA and MLB with advice on "[t]he appropriate age at which international amateur players should be signed to professional contracts." Other than its first meeting in 2012, our research has not revealed any output from the International Talent Committee.

During the 2016 CBA negotiations, it was reported that MLB and the MLBPA seriously discussed the possibility of a draft for international players. However, the sides were not able to reach an agreement. Instead, the parties agreed that clubs would be subject to a "Signing Bonus Pool" that limited the amount of compensation clubs could provide to international players. The Signing Bonus Pool is a maximum of $5.75 million, growing annually with league revenues.

Importantly, regardless of how a player ends up with a MLB club—whether through the draft or as an international signee—almost all players will play several seasons with the minor league clubs affiliated with the MLB club that drafted them before signing a MLB contract or playing in a MLB game, if they ever do. Indeed, only about 17% of drafted players ever reach the major leagues. Players signed to minor league contracts are not members of the MLBPA and are not entitled to the same rights and benefits as major league players. Whereas the minimum salary for a major league player is $500,000, minor league players often earn between $10,000 and $20,000 per season.

MLB's eligibility rules generally do not affect a player's decision about how to proceed with their professional eligibility, for either domestic or international players.

International players generally want to get into international camps or onto minor league clubs affiliated with MLB clubs as soon as possible (i.e., as soon as they are eligible). MLB's eligibility rule permits international players to sign at age seventeen (or slightly earlier) and thus is a minimal (if any) barrier to entry for international players. These camps and clubs generally provide international players with the best resources—including coaching, housing, and health care—that they have ever experienced, while also increasing their chances of one day making the major leagues. In so doing, these players forfeit the right to ever play college baseball—an unlikely career trajectory for international players anyway. Thus, international players generally gain little by not entering into a professional contract as soon as they are able.

MLB's eligibility rules also do not cause concern for American and Canadian players. MLB's eligibility rules do not prevent American and Canadian players, apart from very rare circumstances (e.g., Bryce Harper), from entering MLB as soon they believe it is in their best interests. They have the opportunity to become a major leaguer at various times and as early as age seventeen. By the time a player reached the skill level necessary to be drafted by a MLB club, he almost certainly would have reached the age of seventeen. Thus, MLB's eligibility rule generally does not force players to make difficult decisions.

NCAA eligibility rules, however, can affect an American or Canadian player's choices. American or Canadian players who have been drafted by MLB clubs often have to consider whether to forego a signing bonus worth tens or hundreds of thousands of dollars from a MLB club to play or continue playing in college. Choosing to remain in college subjects the player to the risk of career-ending or threatening injury without compensation. As discussed previously, the NCAA's ESDI program attempts to alleviate some of these concerns.

4. Player Eligibility Rules in the NBA

The NBA's eligibility rules differentiate between American players and international (including Canadian) players.

American players must meet three criteria to be eligible for the NBA Draft, summarized as follows:

1. The player must be at least 19 years old during the calendar year in which the Draft is held;
2. At least one NBA season must have elapsed since the player's graduation from high school (or the graduation of the class with which the player would have graduated high school); and
3. The player must meet one of the following seven conditions:

    a. The player has graduated from a four-year college or university in the United States (or is to graduate in the calendar year in which the Draft is held) and has no remaining intercollegiate basketball eligibility; or
    b. The player is attending or previously attended a four-year college or university in the United States, his original class in such college or university has graduated (or is to graduate in the calendar year in which the Draft is held) and he has no remaining intercollegiate basketball eligibility; or
    c. The player has graduated from high school in the United States, did not enroll in a four-year college or university in the United States, and four (4) calendar years have elapsed since such player's high school graduation; or

d. The player did not graduate from high school in the United States, and four (4) calendar years have elapsed since the graduation of the class with which the player would have graduated had he graduated from high school; or
e. The player has signed a player contract with a "professional basketball team not in the NBA" . . . and has rendered services under such contract prior to the January 1 immediately preceding such Draft; or
f. The player has expressed his desire to be selected in the Draft in a writing received by the NBA at least sixty (60) days prior to such Draft (an "Early Entry" player)[.] (2011 NBA CBA Art. X, § 1)

International players must meet two criteria to be eligible for NBA Draft:

1. The player must be at least 19 years old during the calendar year in which the Draft is held; and,
2. The player must meet one of the following three conditions:

   a. The player is or will be twenty-two (22) years of age during the calendar year of the Draft; or
   b. The player has signed a player contract with a "professional basketball team not in the NBA" . . . that is located in the United States, and has rendered services under such contract prior to the Draft; or
   c. The player has expressed his desire to be selected in the Draft in a writing received by the NBA at least sixty (60) days prior to such Draft (an "Early Entry" player). (NBA CBA Art. X, § 1)

The NBA's eligibility rules and their evolution have been controversial. Prior to 1971, the NBA required players to be four years removed from high school graduation in order to be eligible for the draft. In 1970, Spencer Haywood, a former Olympic basketball player who chose to play in the professional American Basketball Association (ABA) rather than finish college, sued the NBA, alleging that the NBA's eligibility rule violated antitrust laws (*Denver Rockets v. All-Pro Management, Inc.*). The U.S. District Court for the District of California agreed and enjoined the NBA from enforcing its eligibility rule. Two weeks after the district court's decision, the U.S. Court of Appeals for the Ninth Circuit stayed the injunction pending the NBA's appeal (*Denver Rockets v. All-Pro Management, Inc.*). However, two weeks later, the Supreme Court of the United States reinstated the injunction (*Haywood v. National Basketball Association*). Haywood and the NBA then settled the case, with the NBA agreeing to allow players who were less than four years removed from high school graduation to enter the NBA if they could demonstrate "financial hardship." In 1976, the financial hardship rule was eliminated, allowing any player to declare for the draft.

Despite the NBA's removal of the eligibility rule, almost all players continued to enroll in college for at least some time before entering the NBA. Between 1976 and 1995, no players entered the NBA without first attending college. In 1995, Chicago high school star Kevin Garnett was chosen with the fifth overall pick in the draft, beginning a wave of high school players trying to make the leap straight to the NBA. Between 1995 and 2005, thirty-five high school student-athletes were selected in the NBA Draft.

However, some high school student-athletes went undrafted or otherwise had unsuccessful NBA careers, causing many to believe that they tried to enter the NBA too soon. As a result, the NBA sought and obtained the current eligibility rule as part of the 2005 CBA. Nevertheless, many have also criticized the current eligibility rule for the creation of so-called one-and-done players—that is, players who play one season of college basketball (as required by the eligibility rule) before entering the NBA Draft. These players are able to enroll in college, take the minimum number of classes in their first semester, go to some of their classes as the college basketball season winds down in their second semester, declare for the draft, and drop out of school having completed only four or five general education classes (Wong, Zola, and Deubert, 2011). Since the initiation of the current eligibility rule, eighty-one players have left college after only one season and were drafted by an NBA club, with mixed success in the NBA.

There are also college players who are eligible for the draft but debate whether to return to college (assuming they have collegiate eligibility remaining). For these players, the NBA's eligibility rule is not a concern. Instead, these players are likely concerned with their readiness for the NBA and the potential for injury at the collegiate level. The NCAA's ESDI program, discussed earlier, is an attempt to alleviate some of the concerns about possible injury. In addition, beginning in 2016, the NCAA amended its rules to permit underclassmen players to participate in the NBA's pre-Draft Combine to allow players to better gauge their potential. Following the Combine, a player now has ten days to withdraw from the draft and return to college (provided he never signed with an agent).

Instead of playing NCAA basketball, some American players have chosen to play professionally in foreign countries before entering the NBA Draft, with mixed success. In 2008, Brandon Jennings, a highly acclaimed high school basketball player from California, decided to play professional basketball in Italy instead of playing college basketball. After one season in Italy, Jennings was selected tenth overall in the 2009 NBA Draft and has had a successful NBA career. Jeremy Tyler, another California basketball player who, in 2009, opted to play professionally overseas rather than college basketball in the United States, had less success.[9]

In addition to playing NCAA basketball or overseas, players have one other option before they are eligible for the NBA. Players can play in the NBA Development League (D-League). Created in 2001, the D-League is the NBA's official minor league, consisting of twenty-two clubs with players hoping to reach the NBA. Indeed, more than 30% of current NBA players have played in the D-League at some point. Of most relevance, the minimum age to play in the D-League is eighteen years old, one year less than the NBA's requirement that a player be nineteen years old. However, no high school player has ever foregone the NCAA for the D-League[10] and most D-League players are undrafted former college players or NBA veterans trying to make a comeback. The low salaries (reportedly between $19,500 and $26,000) likely deter players from considering the D-League as their best option.

The NBA's eligibility rule is generally considered the most controversial in sports. To its critics, the rule prevents young men capable of playing in the NBA from pursuing their dreams (or at least choosing to try to play in the NBA) and instead forces them to enroll in college for a brief period of time even if they have no interest in academics. Others believe requiring players to mature more before entering the NBA is essential for their development as both players and people. Additionally, some have suggested that by having rookies play at least one year of college basketball, they will be more familiar to fans and thus be more interesting and marketable in the NBA (Kerr, 2012; Harper, 2014). Consequently, leading up to the 2017 CBA negotiations, the NBA suggested requiring players to be at least two years removed from high school before entering the NBA Draft. Nevertheless, the NBPA has resisted those suggestions and no changes were made to the eligibility rule in the 2017 CBA.

5. Player Eligibility Rules in the NHL

To be eligible to play in the NHL, a player must be at least eighteen years old and have sufficient vision in both eyes (a requirement discussed further later) (2013 NHL CBA, Art. 8, § 8.4(a)). To reach the NHL, players are subject to the NHL Draft unless the player is at least twenty-two years old or is at least twenty-one years old and played hockey for at least one season in North America when he was eighteen, nineteen, or twenty (2013 NHL CBA, Art. 8, § 8.4(a)).

The NHL's draft and eligibility rules are complicated by the international nature of the NHL. In the 2015–2016 season, 48.6% of the players were Canadian, 23.5% were American, and the remaining 27.9% of players were from sixteen different European nations. All players are subject to the draft, regardless of their nationality.

The four principal sources of NHL Draft picks are as follows: (1) the Canadian Hockey League, an organization of three hockey leagues (Quebec Major Junior Hockey League, Ontario Hockey League, and the Western Hockey League) (Canadian Juniors); (2) the United States Hockey League (USHL), an American junior hockey league; (3) American colleges; (4) European professional leagues; and (5) American high schools. The Canadian Juniors are for players between the ages of sixteen and twenty and operate like a semiprofessional league: the players generally continue to be in school of some kind and receive hundreds of dollars a month as a stipend. The NCAA considers Canadian Juniors to be professional leagues due to the compensation and benefits the players receive (NCAA Bylaw 12.2.3.2.4). Consequently, many young players face a difficult choice between playing hockey for American colleges or playing in Canadian Juniors. About 50% of NHL players played in Canadian Juniors, while about 30% of NHL players went to an American college. While the USHL is also for players between the ages of sixteen and twenty, it does not provide players a stipend and players thus retain their NCAA eligibility.

The NHL's and NCAA's eligibility rules provide flexibility for players. High school and college players can be drafted and choose to instead play college hockey, provided the player did not request to be placed on the list of draft-eligible players (NCAA Bylaw 12.2.4.2). The drafting NHL club generally holds the player's rights until he graduates college (meaning no other club can draft or sign the player) (2013 NHL CBA, Art. 8, § 8.6(c)). In the case of non-North American players, the drafting NHL club holds the player's rights for four years if the player is eighteen or nineteen, or two years if the player is twenty (2013 NHL CBA, Art. 8, § 8.6(d)). After each collegiate season, the player can decide whether to return to college or to begin his NHL career with the club that drafted him.

The purpose of the NHL's age requirement is unclear. However, in deciding to return to college as opposed to enter the NHL, several players have cited the need to continue to grow physically and to gain weight to be prepared for the NHL. Thus, assuming age is a proxy for physical size, the NHL's eligibility rule prevents players that might not be physically ready for the NHL from entering prematurely.

Concerning the vision requirement mentioned at the beginning of this section, the NHL Bylaws declare ineligible "[a] player with only one eye, or one of whose eyes has a vision of only three-sixtieths (3/60ths) or under," (NHL Bylaw § 12.7). In the 1970s, NHL draftee Greg Neeld, who had lost his left eye in a Juniors game, sued the NHL, alleging that the rule violated antitrust laws (*Neeld v. National Hockey League*). The NHL's rule was ultimately determined to be reasonable and not in violation of antitrust laws (*Neeld*, 594 F.2d at 1300). The U.S. Court of Appeals for the Ninth Circuit determined that "the primary purpose and direct effect of the League's by-law was not anticompetitive but rather safety," as there was "bound to be danger to players who happen[ed] to be on Neeld's blind side."

The NHL's eligibility rules are generally flexible and do not force players to either abstain or enter the NHL. Players have a variety of options and generally enter the NHL when their skills and size have sufficiently developed to play in the NHL.

6. Eligibility Rules in MLS

In contrast to all of the other leagues, MLS does not have an eligibility rule. Players need not be of a certain age or have reached a certain level of education to play in MLS. Indeed, in the 2015 season, there were nineteen teenagers on MLS rosters, with the youngest player being seventeen. Notably, Freddy Adu began playing with MLS's D.C. United Club in 2004 at the age of fourteen.

Although there is no eligibility rule, players arrive at MLS via a wide variety of paths. The path by which a player arrives at MLS determines the process by which the player reaches his club.

- *Allocation Process:* U.S. Men's National Team players, elite youth U.S. National Team players, and former MLS players returning to MLS after playing with a non-MLS Club for a transfer fee of greater than $500,000 are allocated to slubs pursuant to MLS's Allocation Ranking List (which is in the reverse order of the prior season's standings).

- *SuperDraft:* Clubs can nominate players to be in the MLS SuperDraft and only nominated players are eligible to be drafted.[11] College players, non-collegiate international players, and players from Generation Adidas (an elite program between MLS and Adidas) are eligible for the SuperDraft.
- *Discovery Process:* Clubs can scout and sign players who are not under contract and who are not subject to the Allocation Process or SuperDraft. The Discovery Process is typically used to sign foreign players who were not nominated for the SuperDraft.
- *Homegrown Players:* Clubs may sign players to their first professional contract without subjecting them to the SuperDraft if the player has been a member of the club's youth academy for at least one year.

Normally, MLS's different drafting and signing processes do not place pressure on players. There are a wide variety of soccer leagues around the world and generally, if a player is good enough, he will have opportunities. MLS rules are generally designed to assist MLS in competing against more talented and better-paying European leagues for players' services. For example, players signed from Generation Adidas are given incentive-laden contracts that provide the opportunity for greater compensation than if the player had completed his college degree while also placing money in escrow for them to complete their college education.

7. Eligibility Rules in the WNBA

Like the NBA, the WNBA eligibility rule differentiates between American players and international players.

American players are eligible for the WNBA Draft if they meet one of five criteria:

1. The player will be at least 22 years old during the calendar year of the Draft;
2. The player has graduated from a four-year college or university prior to the Draft;
3. The player is on track to graduate from a four-year college or university within three months after the Draft;
4. The player's original class from a four-year college or university has graduated; or
5. The player's original class from a four-year college or university is scheduled to graduate within three months after the Draft. (WNBA CBA, Art. XIII)

In each case, the player must also have either exhausted her intercollegiate eligibility or renounced her remaining intercollegiate eligibility by written notice to the WNBA at least ten days prior to the draft.

The WNBA's eligibility generally steers players toward graduating from college before joining the WNBA by requiring players to be twenty-two and generally on track to graduate. Whether or not players are actually able to graduate before joining the WNBA is complicated by the fact that the WNBA Draft occurs in April and the WNBA regular season begins in May, months during which the player might have otherwise been completing her college education.

Nevertheless, some players have left college before the completion of their senior season for the WNBA. Candace Parker of the University of Tennessee was the first to do it in 2008, after having led Tennessee to back-to-back national championships. Parker was selected with the first overall pick in the 2008 WNBA Draft. In 2015, Notre Dame's Jewell Lloyd left college after her junior year and Amanda Zahui B. of Minnesota left after her sophomore year. In all three cases, the players turned twenty-two the year of the draft and were thus eligible.

In the event an American player is not yet eligible for the WNBA Draft but wants to capitalize on her playing ability, playing in international leagues is an option. In 2009, after her junior season at Rutgers, Epiphanny Prince chose to leave school and play professionally in Europe until she was eligible for the WNBA Draft in 2010. Prince played in Russia and Turkey before being selected with the fourth overall pick in the 2010 WNBA Draft.

The rules for international players are simpler. An international player is eligible for the WNBA Draft if she will be at least twenty years old during the calendar year of the draft (2014 WNBA CBA, Art. XIII). An international player means "any person born and residing outside of the United States who participates in the game of basketball as an amateur or professional." However, if the international player plays college basketball in the United States, she is subject to the same rules as an American player.

While the WNBA's eligibility rules appear restrictive for players, they likely have minimal effect on college players' decision-making process. Salaries for WNBA rookies are approximately $40,000–$50,000. Thus, the sums the players are foregoing by remaining in college for another year or two are significantly less than the amounts in the NBA and many other professional sports leagues. Moreover, if a player desires to turn professional, she can play in Europe, where many of the leagues pay salaries far higher than those in the WNBA.

From the WNBA's perspective, there are several benefits to the current eligibility rule: (1) by reducing the number of draft-eligible players, it makes scouting players for the draft easier, which is important considering there is generally only about a week or two between the end of the college basketball season and the WNBA Draft; (2) players who have played all four years of college are more likely to have maximized their skill set and public awareness, improving their play in, and value to, the WNBA; (3) having players who have graduated from college fits with the WNBA's theme of providing powerful role models to young female fans; and (4) players with a college degree will be better prepared for life after basketball, particularly in light of the relatively low WNBA salaries (Duru, 2015).

8. Eligibility Rules in Individual Sports

Sports organizations governing individual sports also have rules restricting the eligibility of their participants. While not a comprehensive review, we provide some basic information about the eligibility rules for the PGA Tour, LPGA Tour, ATP, and WTA.

8.1. PGA Tour Eligibility Rules

To be eligible for membership on the PGA Tour, a golfer must be at least eighteen years of age (PGA Tour, 2015–2016). Nevertheless, even if a golfer is age-eligible, he still must qualify to play in PGA Tour tournaments, which golfers typically do either through tournaments as part of Qualifying (Q) School or the Web.com Tour, a smaller and less lucrative tour for aspiring PGA Tour members.

Moreover, even if a golfer is not yet eligible for PGA Tour membership (i.e., he is under eighteen), he can still play in some PGA Tour events, either through specific qualifying tournaments (e.g., U.S. Open qualifiers) or via sponsor exemptions. Sponsor exemptions are a limited number of spots that the sponsor of a golf tournament can offer to any golfer it would like (e.g., Sony as part of the Sony Open). It is not uncommon in men's or women's golf for the sponsors to select young, well-performing amateur golfers who are not yet eligible for their respective tour. PGA Tour membership provides a golfer with more playing opportunities and at more prestigious tournaments, depending on the golfer's success.

8.2. LPGA Tour Eligibility Rules

The LPGA's Constitution provides that any golfer eighteen years of age or older is eligible to be a member of the LPGA Tour. However, golfers from the ages of fifteen through seventeen can apply for membership "by satisfactorily demonstrating to the [LPGA] Commissioner their capacity to assume the professional and financial responsibilities" of playing on the LPGA Tour. Thus, no golfer under the age of 15 can be a member of the LPGA Tour. The LPGA Tour's eligibility rule was adopted in the 1970s (Marikova Leeds and Leeds, 2015). To date, four players have successfully petitioned the LPGA Tour for early membership status: Aree Song at age seventeen in 2004; Morgan Pressel at age seventeen in 2006; Lexi Thompson at age sixteen in 2011; and, Brooke Henderson at age seventeen in 2015.

As with the PGA Tour, the fact that golfers cannot be members of the LPGA Tour does not mean that they cannot play in LPGA Tour events. Golfers who are not members of the LPGA Tour can play in LPGA Tour events through sponsor exemptions, up to a maximum of six events.

8.2.1. *ATP Eligibility Rules*

The ATP has a graduated eligibility rule depending on the player's age as of the first day of the tournament (Association of Tennis Professionals, 2016). Table 13.2 summarizes the rule.

Table 13.2 Maximum Number of ATP Tournaments Based on Age

Age	Maximum Number of Tournaments
13 or younger	None
14	8
15	12
16	Unlimited

2016 ATP Official Rulebook, § 7.02.

8.2.2. *WTA Eligibility Rules*

The WTA, like the ATP, has a graduated eligibility rule depending on the player's age as on the first day of the tournament. Table 13.3 summarizes the rule.

Table 13.3 Maximum Number of WTA Tournaments Based on Age

Age	Maximum Number of Tournaments
13 or younger	None
14	8
15	10
16	12
17	16
18	Unlimited

Source: WTA 2016 Official Rulebook, § XV. Players can also earn increases in the number of tournaments they are allowed to play, up to four, based on their playing record.

WTA's eligibility rule, probably more than that of any other sports organization, is the result of considerable analysis and study. In the early 1990s, there was concern about the well-being and career longevity of teenage players competing on the WTA Tour (McGuire, 2007). At the time, fourteen- and fifteen-year-olds were permitted extensive play on the WTA Tour. In 1994, the WTA Tour formed an Age Eligibility Commission to study the tour's eligibility rule. The Age Eligibility Commission, consisting of sports medicine and sports science professionals, gathered extensive anecdotal, statistical, medical, and scientific evidence that led to the recommendation of a revised eligibility rule. That rule, which the WTA adopted in 1995, is substantially similar to the current rule. Among the data gathered was evidence that an early start to a player's career correlated to an earlier departure from the tour.

9. Analysis

The organizations' eligibility policies vary. MLS has the most liberal eligibility policy (no age requirement) while the NFL and WNBA have the most restrictive (requiring several years of college).

All of the eligibility rules seemingly are at least partially concerned with when a player is "ready" to enter a professional league. Readiness is an important concept here but difficult to define and is likely defined differently by the various stakeholders. In our view, a player is ready when he is able to enter the league safely, in terms of protecting his health, and maximize his success across various domains, including physically, mentally, and emotionally. Each of the leagues (often through negotiations with their respective unions) has made a judgment as to when it thinks the typical player is ready, or at least ready enough. In so doing, the leagues have helped protect clubs from drafting and investing in players who are not ready, and also potentially helped to protect players who need more time to prepare for a successful and healthy career. However, without empirical analysis, one cannot say for certain when players (individually or collectively) are ready and thus whether the eligibility rule is fair or successful. No such data currently exists and would be challenging to gather.

The NBA is the one league that potentially has the data to inform its eligibility rule. Between 1995 and 2005, thirty-five high school student-athletes were selected in the NBA Draft. Concerned that many of these players were not ready for the NBA, the NBA instituted its current eligibility rule in the 2005 CBA. Since the initiation of the current eligibility rule, eighty-one players have left college after only one season and were drafted by an NBA club. One could, in theory, compare the career and health outcomes of the high school student-athletes who entered the NBA with those of the one-and-done players (as well as upperclassmen) to potentially elucidate whether the NBA's eligibility rule has been effective at preventing players from entering the NBA before they are ready. Such a comparison would be helpful in understanding the value of delaying eligibility, but such data would likely not be generalizable to the other leagues due to the different demands of each sport.

The eligibility rules that require players to play in college (NFL and WNBA) might ensure that only sufficiently physically and emotionally mature players enter those leagues, but they also require players to risk their physical health longer without getting paid. While the NCAA's Bylaws do not dictate these eligibility considerations—its ESDI program tries to alleviate some of these concerns—players have legitimate concerns that they will suffer a career-altering or ending injury before they are even able to reach the professional level and earn any money from their athletic skills. This is at least in part a problem resulting from the NCAA's prohibition on student-athletes being compensated. Whether the NCAA's rules are fair is beyond the scope of this chapter, but it is clear that the rules create a problem for players who have the potential to reach the professional ranks but are required (or might prefer) to continue playing in college.

While more data on the issue of readiness would be helpful, it certainly would not definitively determine who is or is not ready for the draft. There will always be players who are widely considered ready for the professional ranks who do not end up performing well while, alternatively, there will be players who were relatively unknown before playing professionally who end up becoming stars. Thus, we cannot say that any of the organizations' current eligibility rules are unreasonable. Some of the rules seemingly prevent players from joining the professional organizations before they are ready, which both protects those players from injury and the clubs (where applicable) from investing in players who are not yet ready. While there are likely players who are ready to join the professional organizations earlier, there are going to be outliers to any rule and, without data suggesting otherwise, we cannot say the eligibility rules are not reasonable.

In light of the uncertainty about when players are ready for the professional ranks, there is a clear need to accommodate and assist those athletes who either go undrafted or who are unable to put together a successful professional career. Most of the assistance along these lines would likely come from the NCAA and its member institutions. The types of steps that could be taken include, but are not limited to, providing better information and resources for student-athletes considering turning professional, permitting student-athletes to retain agents or attorneys, letting undrafted players regain their college eligibility, and providing players who have left school the opportunity to return and finish their college education at no cost. These and other considerations for helping student-athletes are frequently discussed and merit serious consideration.

From the professional side, better pay in the minor leagues could help ease the transition for players from amateur play to professional ranks. In football, the existence of any minor league would potentially allow players to develop their skills while earning a salary.

Nevertheless, the implementation of any of these reforms faces considerable challenges. Student-athletes and minor league players cannot unionize and thus lack the collective authority to change policies. Instead, these athletes often try to force change through litigation, which has had varied success. Moreover, the NCAA and professional leagues have little incentive to make changes that increase their costs and decrease their level of control over athletes, unless they can be convinced it is in their best interests. Additionally, while the NCAA might prefer changes to certain eligibility rules, it is not a part of the collective bargaining relationship between the league and union that determines the eligibility rules.

In sum, the leagues' eligibility rules, while at times controversial and seemingly supported by minimal data, are challenging to change. Nevertheless, in an era of increased attention on the health and welfare of student-athletes and professional athletes, we hope that all of the parties involved will seriously consider better methodologies for determining their eligibility rules and for assisting the athletes affected by them.

Notes

1. Some scholars have debated whether other circuit courts would find that eligibility rules are protected by the nonstatutory labor exemption (Edelman and Wacker, 2010; McCann, 2010).
2. Unions are empowered to negotiate terms and conditions that might affect future employees, even if those employees are not yet a part of the union's bargaining unit. *See Clarett*, 369 F.3d at 139 (discussing union's rights to "preserve jobs for current players to the detriment of new employees and the exclusion of outsiders"); *Wood v. National Basketball Ass'n*, 809 F.2d 954 (2d Cir. 1987) (denying prospective NBA player's antitrust challenge to CBA provisions negotiated between NBA and NBPA).
3. The NCAA's bylaws suggest that these players can return, but in reality they cannot. NCAA Bylaw 12.2.4.2.1.1 declares that a basketball student-athlete can return to college if he declares his intention to do so "before the first day of the spring National Letter of Intent signing period for the applicable year." However, the first day of the National Letter of Intent signing period for basketball is in April and the NBA Draft is in June. Thus, the player cannot go through the Draft in June and still meet the April deadline to declare his intention to return to college. Similarly, NCAA Bylaw 12.2.4.2.3 declares that a football student-athlete can return to college if he declares his intention to do so "within 72 hours following the National Football League draft declaration date." However, the NFL requires student-athletes to declare for the NFL Draft by January 15 and the NFL Draft is in April or May. Thus, the player cannot go through the Draft in April or May and still meet the January deadline to declare his intention to return to college.
4. *See*, e.g., Jenkins v. NCAA, 14-md-2541, 2016 WL 4154855 (N.D. Cal. Aug. 5, 2016) (denying NCAA's motion for judgment on the pleadings in antitrust lawsuit brought by former NCAA student-athletes).
5. A notable exception was former University of Pittsburgh wide receiver Larry Fitzgerald. Fitzgerald had attended five years of high school and was thus eligible for the 2004 Draft after only two years of college football. Fitzgerald was chosen with the third pick of the 2004 Draft and has had a stellar career with the Arizona Cardinals.
6. It is important to know that while many (if not most) of the players who left college early did so because they thought they had the skill necessary to play in the NFL, at least some were likely forced to leave college for academic, personal, or institutional reasons.
7. The Major League Rules are not a part of the CBA and are not necessarily collectively bargained with the MLBPA. While the CBA mentions multiple Major League Rules, MLB's eligibility rules are not an explicit part of the CBA and thus might be slightly more prone to an antitrust attack as compared to the eligibility rules of the NFL, NBA, NHL, and WNBA for the reasons discussed in "1. Introduction."

8. It is even possible to be drafted four times. Some players go from high school to junior college, where you can be drafted after your second year. Hypothetically, a player could be drafted after high school, enter a junior college and be drafted after junior college, then enroll in a four-year college, be drafted after his junior year, and be drafted a fourth time after graduating from, or completing his eligibility at, the four-year college.
9. Tyler, decided to leave high school after his junior year and play professional basketball in Israel and Japan until he was NBA eligible. While Tyler eventually made it to the NBA as a second-round NBA Draft pick in 2011, he was not a successful NBA player, and currently plays in China. As another example, in 2014, Emmanuel Mudiay from Texas went to play in China rather than for an American college. Mudiay, who escaped from war in the Congo as a child, chose playing overseas due to potential problems concerning the NCAA's academic eligibility and amateurism requirements. In the 2015 NBA Draft, Mudiay was selected as the seventh overall pick by the Denver Nuggets.
10. In 2009, Latavious Williams did go directly from high school to the D-League. However, Williams had little choice—after committing to play at the University of Memphis, Williams could not meet NCAA academic requirements to play.
11. Although it is called the "SuperDraft," the SuperDraft is simply MLS's draft.

References

Association of Tennis Professionals. (2016). *The 2016 ATP Official Rulebook*.

"Average NFL Career Length." (2014, April 30). *Sharp Football Analysis*. Available at www.sharpfootballanalysis.com/blog/?p=2133. Archived at http://perma.cc/4EZY-E7ML.

Camporesi, S. (2016). "Ethics of Regulating Competition for Women with Hyperandrogenism." *Clinics in Sports Medicine* 35: 293.

Deubert, C., Wong, G., and Howe, J. (2012). "All Four Quarters: A Retrospective and Analysis of the 2011 Collective Bargaining Process and Agreement in the National Football League." *UCLA Entertainment Law Review* 19(1): 52–61.

Duru, N. J. (2015). "Hoop Dreams Deferred: The WNBA, The NBA, and the Long-Standing Gender Inequity at the Game's Highest Level." *Utah Law Review* 3: 559.

Edelman, M., and Wacker, J. (2010). "Collectively Bargained Age/Education Requirements: A Source of Antitrust Risk for Sports Club-Owners or Labor Risk for Players Unions?" *Penn State Law Review* 115: 341.

Harper, Z. (2014, November 24). "Commissioner Adam Silver Still Wants Age Limit of 20 for Draft Eligibility." *CBS Sports*. Available at www.cbssports.com/nba/eye-on-basketball/24838071/commissioner-adam-silver-still-wants-age-limit-of-20-for-draft-eligibility, *archived at* https://perma.cc/TX6U-QH6M.

Kalthoff, M. (2014). "Out of Sight, Out of Mind: Confronting the Legal, Economic and Social Issues Raised by Major League Baseball's Peculiar Treatment of Foreign Talent," *Connecticut Journal of International Law* 29: 353, 360–365.

Kerr, S. (2012, May 8). "The Case for the 20-Year-Old Age Limit in the NBA." *Grantland*. Available at http://grantland.com/features/steve-kerr-problems-age-limit-nba/, *archived at* https://perma.cc/BU6U-8T8R.

Lopez, R. (2009). "Signing Bonus Skimming and a Premature Call for a Global Draft in Major League Baseball." *Arizona State Law Journal* 41: 349.

Major League Baseball-Major League Baseball Players Association Collective Bargaining Agreement. (2012).

Major League Baseball. (2008). *Major League Rules.*

Marikova Leeds, E., and Leeds, M. (2015). *Handbook on the Economics of Women in Sports* (Cheltenham, UK: Edward Elgar).

McCann, M. (2010). "Justice Sonia Sotomayor and the Relationship Between Leagues and Players: Insights and Implications." *Connecticut Law Review* 42: 901.

McGuire, B. (2007). "Age Restrictions in Women's Professional Tennis: A Case Study of Procompetitive Restraints of Trade." *Journal of International Media & Entertainment Law* 1: 199 (2007).

NCAA Division I Manual. (2015–16).

PGA Tour. (2015–2016). *Player Handbook & Tournament Regulations.*

Rodenberg, R. (2010). "Gender Policies and Impact of Litigation: *Lawless v. LPGA*." *World Sports Law Report* 8(12): 6–7.

Rodenberg, R., and Stone, D. (2010). "The Short and Long-Run Labor Market Effects of Age Eligibility Rules: Evidence from Women's Professional Tennis." *Journal of Labor Research* 32: 181.

Rodenberg, R., Gregg, E., and Fielding, L. (2009). "Age Eligibility Rules in Women's Professional Golf: A Legal Eagle or an Antitrust Bogey?" *Journal of Legal Aspects Sport* 19: 103 (2009).

Williamson, D. (2013). "Part of the Team: Building Closer Relationships Between MLB Teams and Independent Agents in the Dominican Republic Through an MLB Code of Conduct." *NYU Journal of Intellectual Property & Entertainment Law* 2: 369.

Wong, G., and Deubert, C.. (2010). "The Legal and Business Aspects of Disability Insurance Policies in Professional and College Sports." *Villanova Sports & Entertainment Law Journal* 17: 473, 506.

Wong, G., Zola, W., and Deubert, C. (2011). "Going Pro in Sports: Providing Guidance to Student-Athletes in a Complicated Legal & Regulatory Environment." (*Cardozo Arts & Entertainment Law Journal* 28: 553, 577 (2011).

Cases

American Needle, Inc. v. National Football League, 560 U.S. 183 (2010).

Brown v. Pro Football, Inc., 518 U.S. 231 (1996).

Clarett v. National Football League, 306 F. Supp. 2d 379, 387 (S.D.N.Y. 2004), rev'd 369 F.3d 124 (2d Cir. 2004).

Denver Rockets v. All-Pro Mgmt., Inc., 325 F. Supp. 1049, 1055 (C.D. Cal. 1971).

Denver Rockets v. All-Pro Mgmt., Inc., 71-cv-1089, 1971 WL 3015 (9th Cir. Feb. 16, 1971).

Haywood v. National Basketball Ass'n, 401 U.S. 1204 (1971)).

Neeld v. National Hockey League, 594 F.2d 1297 (9th Cir. 1979).

Wood v. National Basketball Ass'n, 809 F.2d 954 (2d Cir. 1987).

CHAPTER 14

ATHLETE REPRESENTATION

ED EDMONDS

1. Introduction

In the contemporary professional sports setting, the athlete's agent is a critical participant. Although best known for negotiating his client's contract, the agent can perform a vast array of services that advance the player's interest. Although the roots of sports agency in the United States began in the 1920s, their rise in prominence and importance is largely confined to the final three decades of the twentieth century. Unfortunately, not all stories are ones of success or even of legally proper behavior. The rise of agent representation created conflicts with academic institutions promoting the concept of amateurism embodied in the rules of the National Collegiate Athletic Association (NCAA). Unethical behavior and shoddy investment strategies defrauded professional athletes of assets. The actions of agents against each other vying for the rights to represent certain athletes was at times ruthless and unseemly. These and other problematic activities fostered state legislation including one of the most successful endeavors of the National Conference of Commissioners of Uniform State Laws (NCCUSL)—the Uniform Athlete Agents Act of 2000. This effort was bolstered by the federal government with the 2004 passage of the Sports Agent Responsibility Trust Act.

The foundation of the relationship between an athlete and an agent is embodied in Paragraph 1.01 of the *Restatement of Agency 3d*: "Agency is the fiduciary relationship that arises when one person (a 'principal') manifests assent to another person (an 'agent') that the agent shall act on the principal's behalf and subject to the principal's control, and the agent manifests or otherwise consents so to act." The initial component of the relationship is expanded ever so slightly in the initial section of Chapter eight, "Duties of Agent and Principal to Each Other" explaining that "an agent has a fiduciary duty to act loyally for the principal's benefit in all matters connected with the agency relationship." The original *Restatement of the Law of Agency* was promulgated in 1933, one decade after the establishment of the American Law Institute. Thus, the legal contours of the principal-agent engagement are long-standing.

The functions of an agent can be basic player-management contract negotiations or the procurement of endorsements. However, it often far exceeds these activities to include investment advice and income management, legal and tax counseling, career and estate planning, incorporation of the client and related businesses, sports medicine and physical health consultations, public relations support, and insurance matters.

For an agent to be effective, he or she must be intimately familiar with the collective bargaining agreement for unionized sports coupled with agent and financial advisor regulations and applicable drug policies or, in a non-unionized sport like golf or tennis, the nature of the business norms and revenue streams. The sheer length of the agreements underscores the complexity involved in attaining a thorough knowledge. The current agreement between the National Football League (NFL) and the National Football League Players Association (NFLPA) is 301 pages; the 2012—2016 Basic Agreement between Major League Baseball (MLB) and the Major League Baseball Players Association (MLBPA) runs 298 pages; and the collective bargaining agreement between the National Hockey League (NHL) and the National Hockey League Players Association (NHLPA), covering September 16, 2012—September 15, 2022, checks in at 517 pages. The salary cap in the National Basketball Association (NBA) is complex and a thorough understanding of it is critical to successful representation. Recent changes creating a slotting system for salaries for rookies entering a sport like football or baseball through the draft starts with a basic understanding of the system coupled with differentials based upon positions or philosophies. In baseball, high school players may have an alternate collegiate sport opportunity such as football or baseball. This is in contrast to the different degree of leverage a collegiate junior holds over his senior counterpart who cannot return for another season. Understanding these differences could be crucial in negotiating the best deal for the client.

In football and baseball, even those agents with a substantial number of clients typically do not negotiate as many contracts annually as the general manager on the opposite side of the deal. It is incumbent for that agent to try to match the general managers' knowledge of the team roster, including familiarity with each and every position that might impact the client's interests, the nature of the contractual obligations to every team member, the available replacements from a multitude of sources, and the total overall revenue pattern for the league and the team's owners. Furthermore, the agent must have a comprehensive knowledge of the salaries of comparable players. In the four major team sports, the players association maintains databases to assist certified agents. Also, an agent must understand the types of bonuses that are available and the advantages of different strategies as they relate to the athlete the agent represents. Plus, an agent needs to gather as much information as possible about each team's metrics and evaluation methods to select a proper salary range prior to entering negotiations. With this knowledge, the agent can sit down with the client and discuss the team's needs and how their client's skills fit those needs. Before a successful strategy is finalized, an agent must understand the tax consequences presented by the location of the team, including the impact of the jock tax, state income tax consequences, and property taxes. Next, the medical needs of the client must be considered. Are those needs well covered by the collective bargaining agreement or must additional protection be negotiated or procured separately? With the relatively short careers of nearly all athletes, an effective agent must prepare the client for a career after his playing days are complete. Establishing a solid post-career plan usually requires appropriate preparation through aligning the client's interests with the necessary educational attainment or training. To maintain the proper fiduciary relationship, the client should be advised to seek the assistance of an independent review of all financial transactions. One of the key traits of a good agent is the capacity to effectively handle not only the financially challenging aspects of a player's career but other matters beyond the game to allow the player to focus on training and competition.

In certain ways, a good agent is more critical to a player without the attributes of a highly desirable player. By the time the NFL draft gets into the seventh round, an agent and his client are staring at either a selection by one team that will force negotiations with only that potential employer versus an effort to find the best possible fit as an undrafted free agent. After all, making an NFL roster is a predicate to any type of playing career in the NFL. In basketball, the low number of NBA roster slots often means weighing overseas options against a possible spot in the NBA Development League. For a high school player drafted into MLB, the client and his family need to carefully consider a signing offer against a collegiate offer that will foreclose another draft selection for three years or the possibility of heading to a junior college and postponing both the draft or a four-year college offer. The NCAA changed its rules recently to allow high school baseball players to retain the use of an agent in negotiating a deal as long as they sever ties with the agent if they choose to attend college. However, college players are only allowed to use the advisor system authorized by the NCAA. A similar problem exists with respect to hockey players where elite collegiate teams are often a combination of players already drafted by an NHL team and those without a team relationship. Collegiate hockey players face numerous points in their career where professional offerings must be considered carefully.

2. History of Athlete Representation

The decade following the end of World War I, often referred to as the Roaring Twenties, is one of the most significant in American history. The rise of radio brought mass culture to a country that, for the first time, became more urban than rural. The decade was also dubbed the Golden Age of Sports with legendary figures pushing baseball, boxing, college football, golf, horse racing, and tennis to new heights of public attention. This rise in sports popularity also created the first sports agents.

On February 20, 1921, Christy Walsh, stymied on numerous attempts to meet Babe Ruth to discuss a business proposition, laid in wait at a local delicatessen near Ruth's suite at the Ansonia Hotel in New York City. Walsh, a lawyer and former sports cartoonist had worked with World War I flying ace Eddie Rickenbacker as a ghostwriter. Walsh was convinced that Ruth would be an even more attractive business partner. Walsh's big break came when the Babe called the local delicatessen for a case of bootleg beer. Walsh volunteered to deliver the brew to Ruth's suite, where, once inside, he seized the opportunity that would forge one of the greatest promotional relationships of the decade. Walsh convinced Ruth that his syndicate ghost-writing plan would be lucrative. The next day, Walsh hustled to Penn Station to garner Ruth's signature on a short one-page contract before Ruth headed for Hot Springs, Arkansas, to begin needed training for the upcoming season. As a result, Walsh became baseball's first player agent. Walsh expanded his writing activities to become Ruth's business manager and booking agent while also parlaying the Babe's enormous appeal into an advertising pitchman for a broad range of products. Walsh soon expanded his group of clients to include Ty Cobb, Jack Dempsey, Lou Gehrig, John McGraw, and Knute Rockne.

A few years later, Charles C. Pyle, a Champaign-Urbana theater owner convinced University of Illinois football star Red Grange to hire him as Grange's business manager and agent. When Grange signed with the NFL's Chicago Bears for $3,000-per-game and a percentage of gate receipts that ultimately netted him $100,000, "Cash and Carry" Pyle (Reisler, 2009) joined Walsh as successful agents for their clients. In 1926, Pyle joined with tennis star Suzanne Lenglen to create the first professional tennis tour. Pyle and Walsh worked together with their clients as Hollywood emerged as the driving force in the movie industry producing numerous films for Ruth and Grange, in particular.

In the 1950s, Frank Scott, a former traveling secretary for the NFL's Brooklyn Dodgers and MLB's New York Yankees turned a meeting with Yogi and Carmen Berra into an endorsement bonanza. Scott added Mickey Mantle and Roger Maris as clients before expanding his athlete group to a larger group of local athletes. Eventually, Scott would push beyond New York to attain a national group of sports stars. Scott, like Walsh and Pyle before him, did not negotiate contracts in the era before free agency but, instead, concentrated on personal appearances, television show appearances, and endorsements.

In 1960, Mark McCormack, a former collegiate golfer at William & Mary and an attorney at Cleveland's Arter & Hadden, created International Management Group (IMG) with golfing legend Arnold Palmer as his initial client. McCormack soon added Jack Nicklaus and Gary Player to his client list. McCormack used these clients to expand his empire beyond athlete representation to IMG-sponsored tournaments with corporate sponsors advised by IMG and a television production company. Thirty years later, E.M. Swift wrote a *Sports Illustrated* article entitled "The Most Powerful Man in Sports," detailing McCormack's career.

A decade after McCormack started IMG, Donald Dell, a three-time All-American tennis player at Yale University and a United States Davis Cup player in 1961 and 1963 with two championship team captaincies, followed a path similar to McCormack's. Building upon his work for Washington, D.C., law firm Hogan & Hartson and for Peace Corps founder Sargent Shriver, Dell joined with Frank Craighill and Lee Fentress in 1970 to create ProServ with Dell's Davis Cup teammates Arthur Ashe and Stan Smith as their primary clients. Craighill and Fentress would ultimately split with Dell in 1983 and create Advantage International. David Falk would move ProServ forward by shifting from individual sports clients to represent team athletes Patrick Ewing and Michael Jordan.

Although these agents were enormously successful in creating significant financial rewards for themselves and their clients with endorsement and personal appearance opportunities, agents were still not involved in the negotiations of salaries for team-sport athletes. General managers and owners maintained their superior bargaining position by using various reserve systems and player or draft-choice compensation regimens to thwart efforts by players to either become free agents or use free agency to improve their salaries or relocate to a different team. Anyone attempting to seek the aid of an agent was treated with disdain or worse.

The most oft-repeated example of this negative reaction to the presence of an agent involves legendary Green Bay Packers coach and general manager Vince Lombardi and future Hall-of-Fame center Jim Ringo. By 1963, Ringo was an eleven-year veteran who had contributed mightily to Green Bay's success as an outstanding blocker in the Packers vaunted power sweep. However, Ringo was now thirty-two years old and seeking a healthy salary increase. Ringo also appeared interested in playing closer to his Philadelphia home. Ray Kennedy and Nancy Williamson offered a version of the story in *Sports Illustrated*. This version appeared in an article entitled "For the Athlete, How Much Is Too Much?," which was part of the magazine's series on "Money and Sports." According to Kennedy and Williamson

> In the early 1960s a man entered the Packers' office, identified himself to Vince Lombardi as an agent and announced that he had come to negotiate Jim Ringo's contract with the Green Bay Packers. Lombardi excused himself, walked into his personal office and closed the door. Returning a few minutes later, he told the agent, "You are negotiating with the wrong team. Mr. Ringo has just been traded to Philadelphia." (1978, 47, col. 3)

According to Lombardi biographer David Maraniss in *When Pride Still Mattered: A Life of Vince Lombardi*, the author revealed that Ringo's negotiations were actually taking place with personnel director Pat Peppler. As Peppler told Maraniss:

> The apocryphal story of Ringo's quick exit was perpetuated largely because Lombardi wanted it to be believed. Rather than correct the tale, he spread it himself, Peppler said, in the hope that it might discourage players from hiring agents or making difficult contract demands. His bark, for the most part, was worse than his bite, and like all general managers, Lombardi out of necessity found himself dealing with agents and lawyers during the latter half of the sixties. (1999, 354–355)

Furthermore, in a 2003 article by Rob Reischel in the *Milwaukee Journal-Sentinel*, Ringo remarked, "I really don't know how that story got going."

After a successful 1965 season concluded with a seven-game World Series win over the Minnesota Twins, Don Drysdale and Sandy Koufax, who contributed forty-nine wins to the Los Angeles Dodgers championship season, felt that they should be rewarded for their efforts with a salary increase. Koufax received $85,000 for his efforts in 1965, and Drysdale had an $80,000 deal. No pitchers had yet broken through the $100,000 salary ceiling reserved for only a handful of everyday position players. Furthermore, Dodger general manager Buzzie Bavasi used a time-honored tactic of salary misinformation by telling each player what another player was supposedly seeking by altering the actual facts. When the two players compared information they each grew agitated by Bavasi's deceptive practices and decided to holdout collectively for a three-year, $1 million deal shared equally. The pair had consulted noted Hollywood entertainment attorney J. William "Bill" Hayes about their concerns. Years later, Bavasi reacted angrily to a claim in Koufax's autobiography with Ed Linn (1966) that Hayes acted as an intermediary—"if I did that, I opened the door to more trouble than baseball ever dreamed in its worst nightmares. If I gave in and began negotiating baseball contracts through an agent, then I set a precedent that's going to bring awful pain to general managers for years to come." Despite the substantial leverage provided the Dodgers by baseball's reserve system, Hayes was quite familiar with California's De Havilland Law, an important film industry statute that prevented the specific performance of a personal services contract that exceeded seven years. The legislation acquired its nickname from actress Olivia de Havilland who successfully sued the Warner Brothers in the 1940s over the studio's use of suspensions to attempt to push her contract beyond seven calendar years. Don Drysdale hinted at the importance of Hayes's knowledge in his autobiography with Bob Verdi (1990):

> And I think Mr. O'Malley must have realized we were on to something, because it wasn't a week after Bill Hayes made his discovery that our holdout ended. I'm convinced that was the major reason why the Dodgers moved, because we knew they had found out about Bill Hayes's little discovery. I can't prove it, but my guess is that the Dodgers realized they were playing with fire and that if we went to court, they might lose us both and get nothing in return (130).

The two pitchers had also signed a movie deal with Paramount Studios to accept minor acting roles in the movie "Warning Shot." The duo demonstrated enough collective action to force Bavasi and owner Walter O'Malley to give the two hurlers a substantial raise. Koufax signed for $125,000 for what proved to be his final season while Drysdale inked a $110,000 deal.

The resulting concern among owners about collective negotiations provided MLBPA executive director Marvin Miller the power to exact a reciprocal commitment during negotiations. In exchange for language prohibiting collusion by players, the owners agreed to be bound by a similar prohibition. This was particularly important when arbitrators determined that owners colluded to not sign free agents during the 1985, 1986, and 1987 offseasons. Ultimately, the owners were forced into a $280 million settlement with players adversely impacted by their behavior.

The era of the modern sports agents negotiating contracts as well as endorsements and personal appearances is largely the product of Bob Woolf's encounter with Boston Red Sox hurler Earl Wilson in his law office when the player sought help involving a traffic incident. Although Woolf was primarily a general practitioner specializing in criminal matters, Wilson and Woolf quickly became friends, with the lawyer serving as the hurler's confidant and advisor while helping with endorsements and personal appearances. Soon Carl Yastrzemski, Jim Rice, and Luis Tiant sought Woolf's assistance and the client list skyrocketed. After Wilson was traded to the Detroit Tigers in June 1966 and won thirteen of his nineteen decisions, Wilson requested Woolf's assistance in negotiating his 1967 contract with Detroit general manager Jim Campbell. Bowing to the culture in place, Woolf did not accompany Wilson during his negotiations with Campbell. Instead, when contentious points arose between the pair, Wilson would excuse himself from the room and call Woolf who was waiting back in Wilson's apartment to provide advice and emotional support. Wilson successfully obtained a healthy raise including a deferred-compensation agreement, and Woolf was on his way to a successful new career.

The year 1968 was pivotal in the rise of players associations as effective labor organizations working on behalf of their members. The changing balance of powers between management and players would also spur the use of agents to represent players. After a group of MLB players hired Marvin Miller to serve as the executive director of the MLBPA in 1965, the MLBPA negotiated its first collective bargaining agreement in 1968. The union, now moving away from its previous years as a management-controlled organization, negotiated increases in the minimum salary and established a system of arbitration for grievances and salaries. A feature of the union's relationship with its players was an increased use of agents to negotiate salaries beyond the collectively bargained minimum amount.

The NFLPA was officially recognized in 1968 after a strike vote provoked an owner's lockout, and both sides negotiated their first collective bargaining agreement. The unionization efforts in professional basketball made significant strides in 1957 when the Board of Governors of the NBA recognized the NBPA and made modest concessions to the Bob Cousy-led organization. The formation of the American Basketball Association (ABA) in 1967 soon provoked the established league to consider a consolidation that would remove the rival league as an alternative and return normalcy to salaries. In 1970, NBPA president Oscar Robertson filed an antitrust lawsuit on behalf of the organization that stalled consolidation talks. The NBPA, under new president Paul Silas, used the leverage of the *Robertson* suit to negotiate concessions from the NBA. Those concessions included an increase in the minimum salary.

A major change in individual sports also occurred in 1968 when tennis moved to the Open Era allowing professional players their first opportunity to compete in tournaments previously reserved for amateur players. The 1968 British Hard Court

Championships, won by Ken Rosewell, at The West Hants Club was the first open event followed the next month by the first open Grand Slam tournament, the 1968 French Open. Roswell defeated Rod Laver at Roland Garros in the finals. The inclusion of professional tennis players in the sport's elite tournament would help Donald Dell create ProServ two years later. The Olympics would change its rules during the 1980s to allow openly professional athletes to participate. This served as another move that propelled agent representation forward.

By 1975, the MLBPA used the collectively bargained arbitration system to deliver a stunning blow to the reserve system. Their support of a grievance filed by Dave McNally and Andy Messersmith resulted in Peter Seitz's ruling for a three-person arbitration panel that McNally and Messersmith were free agents after playing an entire season under the team's renewal of their contract without signing a new contract containing a similar clause. The long-mandated requirement that players could not report to spring training without signing a new contract had essentially worked to make the reserve system perpetual. In the late 1960s numerous players began the season without signing a new deal, but, eventually at some point during the season, the player and team management would successfully negotiate a new deal. Messersmith, pitching for the Los Angeles Dodgers after an impressive 1974 season when he turned in a 20-6 win/loss performance, refused to accept a new deal. Dave McNally, who had agreed to pursue a grievance as a backup in case Messersmith was persuaded to sign late in the year, retired after starting thirteen games for Montreal Expos. When MLB and the MLBPA agreed that players with six years of credited service could become free agents, the need for agents to negotiate contracts increased dramatically.

Marvin Miller had also successfully negotiated a new system of salary arbitration to begin in 1974. The requirements that compensation disputes for players with more than two years of credited service be resolved by comparing data involving salaries of other players with similar career lengths, positions, and statistics allowed Miller to successfully force MLB to disclose salary information critical to the effective functioning of the system. The released information educated players who had little knowledge of the salaries of other players, even those on their own team. Agent Jerry Kapstein took advantage of this newly acquired information to support his presentation on behalf of numerous Oakland Athletic players in hearings against flamboyant owner Charles Finley. Finley relied on his bombastic style of demeaning his players and their value to his team in front of the arbitrator while Kapstein came prepared with substantial comparative information. When Kapstein's presentations won far more decisions than his rival, the agent was rewarded with enduring loyalty from his Oakland clients who experienced increased paychecks while propelling his agency business forward. Kapstein would ultimately switch to the management side of baseball, while also preferring the name Jeremy, to become president and CEO (chief executive officer) of the San Diego Padres. He would later serve fourteen years as a special advisor for the Boston Red Sox, during which time the Sox won three World Series.

As agents began to assert an influence on the negotiations of contracts, the major professional team sports were undergoing competition from new leagues. The departure of the Dodgers and Giants to Los Angeles and San Francisco, respectively, left the New York metropolitan area with only the Yankees. When attorney William Shea, chair of a committee appointed by New York mayor Robert Wagner to return the National League to New York, was thwarted in his attempts to lure an existing team to relocate, he persuaded retired executive Branch Rickey to join him in the creation of the Continental League as a third major league. Only expansion by the American and National League, including the awarding of a franchise to a Shea-led ownership group for New York, prevented the new league from moving forward. At the same time new owners were attempting to break into the NFL. When they were unsuccessful, they launched the American Football League (AFL). The new league quickly garnered a television contract, and scheduled two more games per season than the NFL, forcing the older league to expand its schedule. The new league spawned a bidding war for top collegiate talent including the New York Jets signing Joe Namath to the highest deal ever for a collegiate star on January 2, 1965. The league obviously pushed agent representation forward. By the end of the decade, the two leagues agreed to merge and institute a common draft, thus removing the leverage agents and players enjoyed in a competitive marketplace. The American Basketball Association began play in 1967. Within a decade the league consolidated with the NBA, providing a home for the surviving four franchises. The World Hockey Association started in 1972 and before the end of the decade four of its successful franchises found a home in the established NHL.

An era of competition was a boon for both players and agents, creating additional jobs and pushing salaries upward. However, it fostered a highly competitive atmosphere that often led to unsavory behavior by those representing athletes. Legislatures, players associations, the NCAA, and agents—particularly lawyers—striving for controls over the unregulated group led to a push for solutions.

3. The Rise of Regulation

It was oft-stated during the 1960s and 1970s that the only qualification required to be an agent was a client. By the mid-1980s the number of agents certified by the NFLPA nearly matched the number of available roster spots. Although athlete representation attracted many attorneys into its ranks, many nonlawyers also joined the field. Attorney-agents, however, initiated the first two efforts to promote professionalism within the industry. In 1975 Jack Mills, Tony Pace, Lloyd Shefsky, Rick Wagenheim, and John Wendel launched the Sports Lawyers Association (SLA). With Shefsky serving as president, the group attempted to defuse the tension between management and players at a time when general managers still maintained substantial control over negotiations and begrudgingly accepted the changes afoot. Three years later the Association of Representatives of Professional Athletes (ARPA) was founded with a goal of advancing "competent and honest representation of professional athletes" among a membership that included attorneys and nonattorneys. ARPA created a Code of Ethics with five canons covering integrity, competence, dignity, management responsibilities, and confidentiality, all based on principles similar to those in effect for practicing attorneys. However, both organizations were seriously limited in their efforts to attract members or to control the activities of those who were beyond their reach.

The first state legislature to step forward was California. In 1981 the body enacted the California Athlete Agents Act, the initial legislative attempt to address athlete representation in an act modeled after the state's regulation of entertainment agents and managers. The Act required registration with the Labor Commissioner, but it also exempted "any member of the State Bar of California when acting as legal counsel for any purpose." Each athlete agency was required to submit a $10,000 surety bond, submit all contract forms to the Labor Commissioner for approval, and file a schedule of fees. One of the true reasons for the statute was quickly revealed with the requirement that all contracts contain a statement in ten-point type that "the athlete may jeopardize his or her standing as an amateur athlete by entering into the contract." The California Act was revised four years later to strengthen a number of the provisions, including an increase of the surety bond to $25,000. The lack of impact of the legislation was underscored by the fact that six years after the implementation of the requirement that agents apply for a license, an inquiring author was told that only fourteen agents had registered.

Other states soon followed through with their own regulatory schemes. The Oklahoma Athlete Agent Act became effective in July 1985. Again, the main focus was on agents who were contacting players at NCAA-member institutions within the state. Texas enacted legislation two years later with a broader coverage than California and Oklahoma. Within the legislation's definition of "agents" not only were contract negotiators included but so too were financial service providers. Again, the main goal was to control agents trying to recruit collegiate athletes. Thus, the statute did virtually nothing to reach potential problems impacting athletes already on professional rosters. Numerous other jurisdictions joined the growing list of states attempting to regulate agent behavior. By the time the NCCUSL decided to seek a uniform solution, over twenty-five additional states had passed a statute.

4. Uniform Athlete Agents Act

The NCCUSL, founded in 1892 to promote the passage of state acts where uniformity "is desirable and practicable," launched their effort to draft a model uniform legislation when they approved the creation of a Study Committee on Athlete Agents on July 16, 1996, an initiative resulting from action taken at their 1996 mid-year meeting. Professor of Law Robert N. Davis of the University of Mississippi School of Law was appointed National Reporter on October 29, 1996. With a need to fund the drafting process, the NCAA stepped forward a few months later with an allocation of $50,000 to support the effort. Thus, from the beginning a clear goal of protecting the interests of NCAA-member institutions was established. The drafting committee produced multiple drafts that were circulated and refined before presenting it for an initial reading by the full NCCUSL body in July 1999. A number of concerns were raised at the Denver, Colorado, meeting and the NCAA and the MLBPA also submitted comments. The Uniform Athlete Agents Act (UAAA) was approved the following year and subsequently presented to state legislatures for consideration.

The narrow focus of the UAAA, targeting specific beneficiaries, is apparent in the definition of "Athlete agent" as "an individual who enters into an agency contract with a student-athlete or, directly or indirectly, recruits or solicits a student-athlete to enter into an agency contract." In turn, a " 'Student-athlete' means an individual who engages in, is eligible to engage in, or may be eligible in the future to engage in, any intercollegiate sport. If an individual is permanently ineligible to participate in a particular intercollegiate sport, the individual is not a student-athlete for purposes of that sport."

Section 4 requires an agent to register with the appropriate state agency, or in the case of representation initiation by the student-athlete, the agent must file an application within seven days after taking the first steps of acting as an agent. The primary enforcement mechanism is that the contract may be voided. Section 6 sets out grounds that permit the state administrative agency to refuse to issue a certificate of registration. Those grounds primarily focus on a conviction of a crime of moral turpitude, dishonesty on the application, or activities that would constitute "conduct that would disqualify the applicant from serving in a fiduciary capacity." Section 10 required any contract to contain a provision that is at the heart of subsequent enforceability of a contract signing that would produce a revocation of any remaining eligibility:

WARNING TO STUDENT-ATHLETE

IF YOU SIGN THIS CONTRACT:

(1) YOU MAY LOSE YOUR ELIGIBILITY TO COMPETE AS A STUDENT-ATHLETE IN YOUR SPORT;
(2) IF YOU HAVE AN ATHLETIC DIRECTOR, WITHIN 72 HOURS AFTER ENTERING INTO THIS CONTRACT, BOTH YOU AND YOUR ATHLETE AGENT MUST NOTIFY YOUR ATHLETIC DIRECTOR; AND
(3) YOU MAY CANCEL THIS CONTRACT WITHIN 14 DAYS AFTER SIGNING IT. CANCELLATION OF THIS CONTRACT MAY NOT REINSTATE YOUR ELIGIBILITY.

Section 15 sets out criminal penalties with wide discretion provided to the states to make violations either misdemeanors or felonies, and Section 16 allows "an educational institution . . . a right of action against an athlete agent or a former student-athlete for damages caused by a violation" of the act.

Ultimately the UAAA was approved by the American Bar Association and supported by the NCAA. Forty-one states passed the UAAA plus the District of Columbia and the Virgin Islands. Montana eventually repealed their Act, and ten states that did not enact the law included California, Massachusetts, Michigan, New Jersey, and Ohio. California revised its statute in 1996 when the legislature enacted the Miller-Ayala Athlete Agents Act.

Although the statute would seem to provide a substantial disincentive to an agent trying to contract with a collegiate athlete and an opportunity to use the legislation against one or both parties for violating the act, there have been relatively few uses of the statute to prosecute violators.

5. Revised Uniform Athlete Agents Act

Despite the wide adoption of the Uniform Athlete Agents Act, by 2013 the need for a revision of the original act surfaced because many states had made amendments that undermined the uniform nature of the various acts. Additionally, many major NCAA-member athletic department officials signed a memorandum pushing for changes including an expansion of the definition of an athlete agent, a provision to provide for reciprocity among states regarding registration, additional requirements to the contract language, and expansion of the notification requirements. The Revised Uniform Athlete Agents Act (RUAAA) was passed by NCCUSL in 2015, and Alabama, Idaho, and Washington became the first three states to enact the new version.

6. Sports Agent Responsibility Trust Act

Despite the success of the UAAA, House Representatives Bart Gordon of Tennessee and Tom Osborne of Nebraska, the former head football coach and athletic director at the University of Nebraska, introduced H.R. 361, the Sports Agent Responsibility and Trust Act (SPARTA), in the 108th Congress in January 2003. The primary purpose of SPARTA, modeled after the uniform act, was to cover the jurisdictions that had not passed the NCCUSL-sponsored legislation. Although the bill that became SPARTA was introduced in 2003, a hearing on a previous bill with the same name was held on June 5, 2002, in the 107th Congress before the Subcommittee on Commerce, Trade, and Consumer Protection of the House Committee on Energy and Commerce. Four individuals testified—Howard Beales, the director of the Federal Trade Commission's Bureau of Consumer Protection, Middle Tennessee State University Athletic Director Boots Donnelly, Representative Osborne, and Bill Saum, the director of the NCAA's Agent, Gambling and Amateurism Activities. An additional hearing was held on May 15, 2003, by the House Judiciary Committee's Subcommittee on Commercial and Administrative Law. Representative Osborne was joined this time by co-sponsor Bart Gordon as well as noted agent Scott Boras. The hearing lasted less than an hour. Floor debate was also brief, and the bill passed the House of Representative on June 4, 2003, and the Senate on September 9, 2004. Public Law 108-304 was approved on September 24, 2004.

The definition of "athlete agent" again focused on student-athlete interactions. Section 3 focused on unfair and deceptive acts and practices by providing enforcement responsibility in the Federal Trade Commission prohibiting such behavior plus prohibiting an agent from "providing anything of value to a student athlete or anyone associated with the student athlete before the student athlete enters into an agency contract." A warning similar to the one in the UAAA is required creating an opportunity to go after agents and student-athletes who violate the act because they are unlikely to follow the directive of notifying the athletic director of the existence of the signed contract. Section 5 allows the state attorney general to commence a civil action if he or she feels an agent has engaged in an unfair or deceptive act to "(A) enjoin that practice; (B) enforce compliance with this Act; or (C) obtain damage, restitution, or other compensation on behalf of the State." Section 6 provides a right of action for an educational institution that was not informed within seventy-two hours of the execution of an agency contract.

7. National Collegiate Athletic Association

The NCAA entered the field of agent regulation in the mid-1970s by prohibiting student-athletes from accepting gifts from an agent or contractually agreeing to representation. In 1984, the NCAA adopted a voluntary "Player Agent Registration Plan." The voluntary nature of this plan seriously undermined its effectiveness. In keeping with its standards promoting amateurism, the NCAA has maintained its efforts to draw a hard line between agents and intercollegiate athletes. However, the Infractions Committee recently sanctioned institutions like the University of Alabama, the University of Miami, and the University of Southern California when inappropriate agent behavior was uncovered.

8. Players Associations

With legislative and NCAA efforts focused on the relationship between agents and intercollegiate athletes, activities to address the problems associated with professional athletes was left to players associations. In 1981, the NFLPA became the first union to establish rules to regulate sports agents when it enacted rules involving "Contract Advisors." Certification was conditioned upon the applicant responding to a series of questions aimed at insuring that the agent had not acted inappropriately by committing criminal or fraudulent acts. Agents were required to use a "standard representation agreement" and submit to certain controls over fees. Three years later, the NBPA adopted a similar set of agent regulations.

In 1988, the MLBPA initiated the regulation of agents. As with the other two players associations, certification by the union was required for an agent to represent a baseball player. The MLBPA regulations were incrementally amended before a major overhaul in 2010. One major change was an increase in coverage beyond direct contract negotiations by establishing "general certification" for the primary individual involved in contract negotiation and "limited certification" for player recruiters generally known as "runners" and those providing "Client Maintenance Services." The MLBPA also changed its attitude toward restrictive covenants directed against agents who left their former agency by allowing enforcement under certain circumstances. Perhaps more important, the new regulations increased the types of disputes between players and their agents that must be submitted to binding arbitration. The regulations also addressed agent switching by requiring players to "consult" with the MLBPA if the player intended to change agents during the offseason.

Although players associations require examinations aimed at ensuring competent knowledge of the applicable collective bargaining agreement, the reach of these efforts has been questioned. Because substantial knowledge of the collective bargaining agreement is critical to effective representation, the players associations are in the best position to protect their members by enforcing a significant commitment to knowledgeable agents.

9. Conflicts of Interest

Conflicts of interest are a common problem in agent representation. Many agents represent multiple players and some also represent coaches, managers, and executives. Certain conflicts of interest are exacerbated by the salary cap aspects in basketball, football, and hockey. Trades of players add to the difficulties that agents have in controlling conflicts because agents lack control over which general manager they might be negotiating with. Players associations have done little to restrict or monitor this area because they generally want to allow the client to choose the individual who represents them.

10. Conclusion

The rise of agent representation of professional athletes coincided with the increased power of players associations during the final third of the twentieth century. As collective bargaining agreements became more complex and salaries rose substantially, effective agents became a critical factor in maximizing the financial potential of an athlete during a typically short career. However, the possibility of unscrupulous behavior or unknowledgeable advice continues to be a real possibility, and regulatory schemes continue to be controlled by players' associations.

The UAAA, the RUAAA, and SPARTA are all focused on protecting NCAA member institutions by prohibiting agents from compromising amateur status and eligibility by contracting with a player prematurely. Despite the existing regulatory schemes, unsavory conduct continues to surface in the intercollegiate games—particularly in the sports of football and men's basketball. Unfortunately, these legislative schemes fail to ensure competent or ethical behavior supporting professional athletes.

References

Creamer, R. (1974). *Babe: The Legend Comes to Life* (New York: Simon and Schuster).

Davis, R. (2001). "Exploring the Contours of Agent Regulation: The Uniform Athlete Agents Act." *Villanova Sports & Entertainment Law Journal* 8:1.

Day, F. (2002). *Clubhouse Lawyer: Law in the World of Sports* (Lincoln, Neb.: iUniverse Star).

Drysdale, D. with B. Verdi. (1990). *Once a Bum, Always a Dodger* (New York: St. Martin's Press).

Dunn, D. (1988). "Regulation of Sports Agents: Since at First It Hasn't Succeeded, Try Federal Legislation." *Hastings Law Journal* 39: 1031.

Edmonds, E. (2009). "The Great Dodgers Pitching Tandem Strikes a Blow for Salaries: The 1966 Drysdale-Koufax Holdout and Its Impact on the Game." In *The Cooperstown Symposium of Baseball and American Culture, 2007-2008*, edited by W. Simons (Jefferson, N.C.: McFarland & Co.), 248.

Edmonds, E., Manz, W., and T. Kettleson (2008). *Congress and Sports Agents: A Legislative History of the Sports Agent Responsibility and Trust Act (SPARTA)* (Buffalo, N.Y.: William S. Hein & Co.).

Feinberg, S. (2015, September 23). "How Yogi Berra Helped to Create the First Sports Agent." *Hollywood Reporter*.

Fluhr, P. (1999). "The Regulation of Sports Agents and the Quest for Uniformity." *Sports Lawyers Journal* 6:1.

Halbertam, D. (1989). *Summer of '49* (New York: William Morrow & Co.).

Heitner, D., Wolf, J., and E. Seidmon (2011). "In Baseball's Best Interest—A Discussion of the October 2010 MLBPA Regulations Governing Player Agents." *Virginia Sports and Entertainment Law Journal* 10: 249.

Helyar, J. (1997, September 5). "ProServ Fell From Top Seed and No Love Is Lost for Dell." *Wall Street Journal*.

Kennedy, R., and Williamson, N. (1978, July 24). "For the Athlete, How Much Is Too Much?", *Sports Illustrated* 34–49.

Koufax, S., with E. Linn (1966). *Koufax* (New York: Viking).

Litsky, F. (1998, June 30). "Frank Scott, 80, Baseball's First Player Agent." *New York Times*.

Maraniss, D. (1999). *When Pride Still Mattered: A Life of Vince Lombardi* (New York: Simon and Schuster).

Montville, L. (2006). *The Big Bam: The Life and Times of Babe Ruth* (New York: Doubleday, 2006).

Reischel, R. (2003, January 31). "Ringo Brings Ring of Truth to Old Lombardi Tale; All-pro Center Says He Never Had an Agent." *Milwaukee Journal-Sentinel*.

Reisler, J. (2009). *Cash and Carry: The Spectacular Rise and Hard Fall of C.C. Pyle, America's First Sports Agent* (Jefferson, N.C.: McFarland).
Ruxin, R. (2010). *An Athlete's Guide to Agents* (Sudbury, Mass.: Jones and Bartlett).
Shropshire, K., and Davis, T. (2008). *The Business of Sports Agents* (Philadelphia: University of Pennsylvania Press).
Sobel, L. (1977). *Professional Sports & The Law* (New York: Law-Arts Publishers).
Staudohar, P. (2009). "The Role of Agents in Baseball." In *The Cooperstown Symposium of Baseball and American Culture, 2007-2008*, edited by W. Simons (Jefferson, N.C.: McFarland & Co.), 217.
Swift, E. (1990, May 21) "The Most Powerful Man in Sports." *Sports Illustrated* 98.
Thomas, R. Jr. (1993, December 1). "Bob Woolf, Lawyer, Dies at 65; A Pioneer Negotiator for Athletes." *New York Times.*
Wagenheim, K. (1974). *Babe Ruth: His Life and Legend* (New York: Praeger).
Walsh, C. (1937). *Adios to Ghosts!* (New York: Author).
Woolf, B. (1976). *Behind Closed Doors* (New York: Atheneum).
Woolf, B. (1990). *Friendly Persuasion: My Life as a Negotiator* (New York: G. P. Putnam's Sons).
Robertson v. National Basketball Association, 556 F.2d 682 (2d Cir. 1977)

CHAPTER 15

IDENTITY AND SPEECH IN SPORTS IN THE SOCIAL MEDIA ERA

JIMMY SANDERSON

1. Introduction

Social media platforms "architected by design to readily support participation, peer-to-peer conversation, collaboration and community" (Meraz, 2009: 682) have rapidly proliferated the sporting world in the past decade (Kassing and Sanderson, 2015; Sanderson, 2011a). On platforms such as Facebook, Twitter, Instagram, Snapchat, Vine, and Periscope, sports organizations, athletes, coaches, reporters, and broadcasters post a sizable amount of information daily that fans consume with an almost insatiable appetite. As people and organizations have turned to social media to communicate, a variety of implications have emerged. Specifically, given the public nature of most social media content, questions have been asked about identity expression and free speech. Indeed, it does not take one long online to find numerous stories documenting employers who have dismissed employees for content posted on social media. Whereas social media are popular tools for personal communication between people, these technologies have also changed boundaries and relationships between individuals and employers (McDonald and Thompson, 2016). In addition, some of the features offered within these social media platforms create grounds for legal issues, such as Facebook's facial recognition, which can identify people in pictures posted by users (Shaw, 2016).

The effects social media has introduced into society also manifest in the sports world. For example, multiple collegiate coaches have publicly acknowledged that they have stopped recruiting a potential student-athlete due to content posted on the recruit's social media account (Trahan, 2014). Discipline resulting from social media content has affected professional athletes such as former National Football League (NFL) player Larry Johnson, who was fined $213,000 for a homophobic slur he posted on Twitter in response to a heckling fan (Ostrow, 2009), owners such as the Dallas Mavericks' Mark Cuban, who has made a habit of criticizing officiating on Twitter (Zillgitt, 2013), and athletes being kicked off of Olympic teams such as Swiss soccer player Michael Morganella (Peck, 2012). Moreover, athletes and sports personalities are not immune from having their actions publicized through social and digital media. For instance, in 2014, recorded phone conversations between Los Angeles Clippers owner Donald Sterling and his then girlfriend, V. Stiviano, wherein Sterling used a variety of derogatory terms in talking about minorities, were released to the public (Wagner, 2014). National Basketball Association (NBA) Commissioner Adam Silver ultimately banned Sterling banned for life, resulting in Sterling's being forced to sell the team (Hirschhorn, 2014).

As social media enables athletes to express more of their identity and personality (Sanderson, 2013, 2014), such communiqués open up a variety of implications for the athletes and sport organization personnel. The social media era has ushered in flattened communication hierarchies (Hutchins and Rowe, 2009) that make regulation of athlete speech on social media more onerous than that of traditional media. Nevertheless, the power that social media offers individuals, such as the ability to post content, at anytime, and to connect with people across the globe, makes it difficult to imagine that this technology will go away in the near future. True, the platforms may come and go, but the overriding technological capabilities are powerful and attractive to users, which accounts for Facebook having 1.8 billion daily active users as of the fall of 2016. Consequently, sports organization personnel must be both cognizant of and proactive in the trends in athlete usage of social media platforms. As they attempt to manage these multifaceted communication structures they must also keep up on related legal protections and safeguards, as well as fan sentiment.

2. Getting More of the Picture: Social Media and Athlete Identity Expression

Athletes have, over time, found ways to express aspects of their identity through traditional media. For example, Muhammad Ali was very vocal about his opposition to U.S. involvement in Vietnam. Yet, as sport grew more commercialized, athletes became more selective about expressing aspects of their identity (Cunningham and Regan Jr., 2012). This trend was perhaps best encapsulated by Michael Jordan's infamous line, "Republicans buy sneakers too" (Granderson, 2012). Nevertheless, through the advent of social media, athletes have begun to share more of their personality and identity on these platforms (Sanderson, 2013, 2014). On one hand, this can provide an effective means for fans to connect with athletes. For instance, Sanderson (2013) investigated identity expression by rookie athletes in Major League Baseball (MLB), the NBA, NFL, and the National Hockey League (NHL) in their rookie seasons. He discovered that athletes shared information such as their popular culture preferences (e.g., favorite music), humor, and family experiences, in addition to seeking information from the audience (e.g., asking for restaurant recommendations in a particular city). Sanderson argued that this personalized content helped fans to identify more with athletes as they self-presented likable and shared experiences that were common to lay audiences.

However, when athletes share these personality traits, they sometimes encounter issues with organization personnel. As one example, Sanderson (2014) examined how MLB player Logan Morrison, then with the Miami Marlins, used Twitter to express identity. Morrison was quite sarcastic on Twitter, and some of his tweets became major news stories. For example, in 2012, Morrison tweeted a photo of a woman breastfeeding her child at Nordstrom's with the comment, "Hey @Nordstrom nothing makes me want to spend $$ like seeing women breastfeeding in your store" (Logan Morrison Sparks Twitter War, 2012). A year later, after being traded to the Seattle Mariners, Morrison had a back and forth with a fan wherein he made a homophobic inference to the fan (Oz, 2013). Further, while he was an employee of the Marlins, Morrison was warned about his Twitter content. Morrison (and others) believed that such a warning along with general concerns about his Twitter activity played a decisive role in the Marlins demoting him to the minor leagues. Morrison would file a grievance over the demotion, contending that he was being unfairly punished for his Twitter activity rather than for his performance (Nelson, 2011). Expressing humor on social media can be a tricky proposition. After all, what an athlete finds funny or humorous others, including mass media, might view quite differently. In Morrison's case, he appeared to be disciplined because of his Twitter activity, and that may have played a role in his team trading him to the Mariners. It might also help to explain his recent trade to the Tampa Bay Rays after the 2015 season (Axisa, 2015). In a similar vein, in 2011 NASCAR driver Kasey Kahne tweeted that seeing a women breastfeeding in public caused him to lose his appetite and stop shopping. Not surprisingly, the tweet received a great deal of criticism. He subsequently apologized on his Facebook page (Llorens, 2011).

While Morrison's and Kahne's content was public, athletes also must be aware that what they find humorous in private social media conversations can bring with it unwelcomed consequences. For instance, in 2012, high school football recruit Yuri Wright was expelled from Don Bosco Prep in New Jersey and had his scholarship offer pulled by the University of Michigan after tweets that were posted from a private account became public and turned into a major news story (Hinton, 2012). Wright's tweets were sexually graphic in nature which may reflect normalized conversation between young men in high school. However, once these tweets were publicized, Wright became a major news story and experienced severe consequences.

As athletes share more of their identity on social media, it provides a unique opportunity for fans to connect with them and see a side of them that is infrequently shown in mainstream media broadcasts. Indeed, via social media, athletes have the ability to selectively choose the aspects of their identity they wish to share. Such a dynamic supplies athletes with more autonomy and a greater capacity to move beyond the scripted, public relations nature that often accompanies mainstream media segments. Certainly, such freedom can at times cause discomfort for sports organization personnel who, arguably, are only one post or tweet away from a major public relations incident. Nevertheless, while humor can often be overlooked, many athletes and other sports figures are taking to social media to express their identity as a dissatisfied worker, voicing dissent (Kassing, 2002) about various aspects of working conditions.

2.1. Dissent as Identity Expression

Dissent occurs when an employee expresses incongruence with his or her expectations of organizational membership, which leads to the development of contradictory opinions (Kassing, 1997). Through social media platforms, athletes and other sports figures have a platform to express these feelings, and perhaps more important, to convey these sentiments in front of a large audience, which can exponentially increase the visibility and awareness of the issue. For example, former Pittsburgh Steelers player James Harrison used Twitter on several occasions to express dissent to NFL Commissioner Roger Goodell (Sikes, 2014). In particular, after Goodell was publicly criticized for the manner in which he handled a domestic violence incident involving Baltimore Ravens player Ray Rice, Harrison tweeted at Goodell, "@nflcommish remains adamant he won't resign, source says: 'Never.' Yea that's what Nixon but then again the CBA gave you more power than him!" (Sikes, 2014). In a similar vein, Dallas Mavericks owner Mark Cuban has been quite active in voicing dissent about NBA officiating and other league issues via his blog and social media accounts. Sanderson (2009) examined how Cuban used his blog as a dissent mechanism and found that Cuban's dissent was primarily focused on promoting change in the NBA. Perhaps one of the more notable outcomes—which occurred on social media—was that blog readers overwhelmingly supported Cuban's dissent. Thus, in addition to getting the message out about issues, social media provides an opportunity to induce support and mobilize fans and other audiences to support the dissent.

Beyond dissent about leadership, social media also offers a vehicle to raise awareness about other issues that may be unlikely to receive much traction outside the athlete raising awareness. This may also include athletes' spouses and family members using social media to sound the alarm. To illustrate, consider when the public learned in 2013 that Tampa Bay Buccaneers kicker Lawrence Tynes was receiving treatment for MRSA, which he apparently contracted at the team's training facility. To assuage concerns, head coach Greg Schiano released a statement stating that Tynes was responding well to treatment. However, Tynes's wife, Amanda, posted a picture of Tynes with an IV in his arm, with the comment, "I hear my husband is responding 'well' to treatment. LOL! He's NOT responding at all yet. This is our #bucslife" (Petchesky, 2013). Along those lines, while it has a different variety of working conditions, social media also has become a place for college athletes to express dissent about the amateur system of intercollegiate athletics. Perhaps the most notable tweet in this respect came from Ohio State quarterback Cardale Jones in 2012, who tweeted, "Why should we have to go to class if we came here to play FOOTBALL, we ain't come to play SCHOOL classes are pointless" (Cardale

Jones, 2012). Jones was suspended for one game as a result of his tweet, though there were those who felt that Jones was conveying an accurate critique of the amateurism system (albeit in perhaps not the most persuasive of ways). Other former student-athletes have used social media to advocate for the overhaul of the intercollegiate athletic system (Davis 2016; Newport, 2014).

That many of these social media posts criticizing the NCAA and the system of amateurism come from former, as opposed to current, college athletes suggests that there may be some reticence to express this form of dissent. Many educational institutions implement social media policies for the athletes in their sports programs (Sanderson, 2011b; Sanderson et al., 2015) and many of these policies are quite restrictive, which may prevent much dissent from manifesting. Although we discuss the efficacy of these policies in Section 2.3 of this chapter, athletes do find the opportunity to express dissent about coaching and playing time, at both the collegiate and the professional level. One of the more infamous cases of such dissent involved Elon University football player Jamal Shuman, who posted a series of tweets expressing his displeasure with his playing time (Burke, 2011). As Shuman's rants continued to grow, several audience members cautioned him to be careful as he might face disciplinary action, to which Shuman responded, "I no everybody that's following me bro, nd not one of them is from the athletic department sir;" and later, "I no I will get in trouble cuz I no one of the ppl who retweet me r gunna tell my coach #smh this is the world we live in today tho" (Burke, 2011). Shuman was ultimately removed from the team.

Social media has created a viable avenue for athletes and sports figures to express support. Those who take advantage of this opportunity generate support from fans and other audience members. Additionally, given that many sports media members diligently cover the social media content posted by athletes and other sports personalities, the ability to raise awareness and generate traction for these issues is immense. These sentiments may or may not be known by organization personnel until the content is posted on social media. Thus, sport organization personnel, at times, find themselves in a reactive position when responding to social media critiques. Whereas criticisms about playing time, coaching, and working conditions can be constructive opportunities for dialogue—and perhaps, in some cases, to facilitate change—one aspect of identity expression where athletes seem to be growing more confident about sharing is the expression of their feelings on political and social issues.

2.2. Social Media and Social Commentary

Through social media, athletes have a mechanism that provides them with the ability to comment instantaneously, outside the control of the team or public relations personnel (Schmittel and Sanderson, 2015). With these capabilities, athletes appear to be growing more comfortable with posting commentary on social and political issues in society. For instance, Schmittel and Sanderson (2015) analyzed tweets sent by NFL players in response to the verdict in the Trayvon Martin case after George Zimmerman, the man who shot Martin, was found not guilty. They discovered that many of the NFL players used Twitter to offer critiques on the American criminal justice system, as well as to share their views on racism in the United States. Their sample was highly proportionate to African-American players, which nevertheless mirrors the composition of NFL rosters. However, the few white players in the sample offered contrasting opinions, suggesting that the criminal justice system was the best model available and that too much sensationalism was being made of the verdict. In particular, there were two noteworthy tweets from NFL players in response to the Zimmerman verdict. Atlanta Falcons wide receiver Roddy White tweeted an insinuation that the jurors in the case should kill themselves (Alper, 2013) and New York Giants wide receiver Victor Cruz tweeted, "Zimmerman doesn't last a year before the hood catches up to him" (Strauss, 2013). At the time of his death, Martin was wearing a hooded sweatshirt. In support of Martin, NBA player Dwyane Wade posted a picture of himself wearing a hoodie on his Twitter and Facebook page while LeBron James posted a picture of the entire Miami Heat team wearing hoodies with the hashtag #WeWantJustice (Heat don hoodies, 2012).

Both White and Cruz subsequently apologized for their comments, yet athletes, particularly minority athletes, have continued to express identity in relation to social issues. For example, after Michael Brown, an African-American male in Ferguson, Missouri, was killed by white police officer Darren Wilson, Kobe Bryant tweeted, "The system enables young black men to be killed behind the mask of the law #Ferguson #tippingpoint #change" (Mandell, 2014). Shortly thereafter, another African-American male named Eric Garner passed away after he was put in a chokehold by an arresting police officer. Garner's last words were "I can't breathe." In response to this incident, athletes such as LeBron James and Derrick Rose began wearing "I can't breathe" t-shirts in pre-game warm-ups (Adande, 2014). The NBA announced shortly thereafter that it would not fine players for wearing the t-shirts, although Commissioner Adam Silver was somewhat cryptic in his public comments, saying "I respect Derrick Rose and all of our players for voicing their personal views on important issues but my preference would be for players to abide by our on-court attire rules" (Report: NBA won't fine players, 2014). In another display, prior to their game on November 30, 2014, five African-American players on the St. Louis Rams—Stedman Bailey, Tavon Austin, Jared Cook, Chris Givens, and Kenny Britt—walked out in pre-game warm-ups with their hands up in the air, representing the "hands up, don't shoot" sign. Protestors used such a sign to challenge police brutality and violence in response to the Brown shooting.

This particular reaction generated a lot of attention from news outlets and triggered a polarized response. For example, the St. Louis Police Officers Association criticized the players' actions and advocated that the NFL take disciplinary action (Fantz, 2014). Moreover, social media became a platform for fan dissent to circulate and mobilize in response to the players' expression. Sanderson, Frederick, and Stocz (2016) chronicled the "Boycott the St. Louis Rams" Facebook page that appeared on the same day as the protest. They discovered that some people renounced their fandom of the Rams, presented their own version of what had transpired in the Brown case, offered their commentary on race relations, and actively encouraged the players to be punished. One of the more notable ways this punishment commentary emerged was through people posting the Twitter accounts and phone numbers of Ram sponsors, encouraging that readers call these sponsors to urge them to cancel their advertising agreements with the Rams. Neither the Rams nor the NFL took any action against the players.

While sports organizations may not take action against players for expressing their political leanings and views on social issues, sponsors represent another important stakeholder. Given their financial contributions, sponsors can exert considerable influence on sports organizations. Additionally, many athletes have sponsorship agreements and their identity expression can certainly impact those relationships. Perhaps one of the more notable examples in this regard involved Pittsburgh Steelers player Rashard Mendenhall. In 2011, shortly after the death of Osama bin Laden was publicly announced, Mendenhall tweeted out statements that expressed concern over the joyful public reaction to this news. Specifically he tweeted, "What kind of person celebrates death? It's amazing how people can HATE a man they have never even heard speak. We've only heard one side . . ." Later, in reference to the September 11, 2001, terrorist attacks on the United States, he tweeted "We'll never know what really happened. I just have a hard time believing a plane could take skyscraper down demolition style" (Rashard Mendenhall doesn't hold back, 2011). In addition to Mendenhall's tweets drawing the ire of Steelers fans and team officials, Champion apparel terminated a contract with Mendenhall that was scheduled to run through 2015 (Bennett, 2011). Champion expressed that the termination was "allowed by and consistent with the language contained in the contract" (McCarthy, 2011). Mendenhall would later sue Champion over the company's invocation of the morals clause, contending that his comments merely reflected his freedom of speech and were not immoral. The lawsuit was ultimately settled out of court.

As the aforementioned cases illustrate, reaction to athletes expressing identity run the spectrum. In some cases, organizations are tolerant or at least acquiesce (such as the Rams not disciplining their players for the hands-up gesture). Other times, players may be allowed to express identity although disapproval may be implied (as with the NBA players and the "I can't breathe" t-shirts). Still, in other instances, discipline may occur either overtly (such as high school recruits losing their scholarships) or covertly (such as Logan Morrison apparently being demoted to the minor leagues because of his Twitter content). Beyond any organizational discipline or sanctions, athletes also can experience endorsers and sponsors cutting ties, making identity expression a costly action.

2.3. Identity Expression and Legal Implications

Certainly, sports organization personnel are likely to have their own risk and tolerance for athletes' identity expression. An athlete being sarcastic on Twitter may be less of an issue than an athlete criticizing a coach, or making a strong comment about a political case or social justice issue. In assessing the tolerance level, organization personnel are likely to balance the resistance and reaction from sponsors and fans versus the cost of disciplining an athlete for what might fall under First Amendment protection rights. Such determinations are likely to depend on how the legal system evolves with technology. For example, the Stored Communications Act of 1986 has been cited as a protection for users from discipline administered for social media content (Shilling, 2013). Yet others have noted that courts tend to struggle in applying technology-related laws passed decades ago to the technology of today (Borchert, Pinguelo, and Thaw, 2015). For example, courts have found that the Stored Communications Act covers Facebook posts. However, when a user's friend, or someone who has been given access shares the post with another party, such as an employer, there is no protection (Wright, 2013). The expectation of privacy that a user has on social media must also be considered Courts have found that there is no expectation of privacy regardless of privacy settings (No reasonable expectation, 2010), including with Facebook photos (Smith, 2015).

Another factor to consider that applies more at the amateur level is whether the organization is a public institution. For instance, many educational institutions implement social media policies (Sanderson, 2011b; Sanderson et al., 2015) and some invoke restrictions on social media for college athletes. To illustrate, both Clemson University and Florida State University restrict football players from using Twitter during the season (Kimes, 2015). Further, in 2015, Old Dominion head football coach Bobby Wilder announced that he was removing a restriction on football players from using Twitter the entire time they were on scholarship (Samuels, 2015). Such a policy was regarded as among "the most restrictive in the United States" (Minium, 2012). Some have argued that such bans are violations of students' First Amendment rights, particularly those at state-funded institutions, such as Clemson and Florida State University (Gay, 2012; Lisk, 2015). Such a legal question, however, has yet to be definitively answered. Additionally, institutions have some recourse through time, place, and manner restrictions, although it has been argued that coaches and athletic directors would incur less exposure to liability if they placed reasonable limitations on social media, provided education, and addressed restrictions on a case-by-case basis (Bentley, 2012). Such a sentiment has been echoed in academic research with student-athletes and their experiences with social media education (Sanderson and Browning, 2013).

In addition to the aforementioned elements, another area that educational institutions must consider is the efficacy of a social media policy. Early research on this topic in Division I (Sanderson, 2011b) found that only seven of the policies in the sample expressed anything positive about social media, and that the policies overwhelmingly framed social media as a fearful enterprise. There are certainly inherent risks in social media, yet Sanderson (2011b) argued that representing social media as solely negative was likely to cause more conflict with college athletes than cooperation. Subsequent work that examined social media policies in Divisions I, II, and III in intercollegiate athletics (Sanderson et al., 2015) found a continued framing of social media as negative, and that many of the policies failed to adapt to the contemporary landscape of social media, still mentioning platforms such as Friendster and Xanga, with minimal mention of more contemporary channels such as Instagram and Snapchat. Sanderson et al. (2015) argued that social media policies continue to lack balance. He also contends that these policies risk alienating the college athlete audience as the policies covered early 2000 platforms that most college athletes nowadays no longer use.

Another issue that must be considered when discussing social media policies is language that requires college athletes to mandatorily submit their social media passwords. Laws in twelve states make the request of social media passwords illegal in educational institutions (Snyder et al., 2015, 50). Thus, athletic department personnel should ensure that their policies comply with relevant state laws and be mindful of language that requires college athletes to mandatorily friend a coach or athletic department representative. To do otherwise would unnecessarily increase exposure to liability or raise legal red flags. As noted by Bentley (2012), education may be a more viable course for athletic departments to pursue and research indicates that college athletes desire training and education on social media (Sanderson, Browning, and Schmittel, 2015).

While sports organizations may not agree with or prefer that players voice opinions, when such opinions are publicized, organization personnel must determine the appropriate course of action. They do so knowing that their response may influence the degree to which players express identity in the future. The legal principles cited previously can be seen in the consequences that were incurred by athletes as a result of identity expression. For an athlete like Yuri Wright—who, even though his comments were posted on a private Twitter account, gave access to someone who shared that content—it provided grounds for his expulsion and loss of a scholarship. In a case like that of Logan Morrison, while the rationale for his demotion is still ambiguous, social media content does not seem to have consistent legal protection, particularly when public, and cannot safeguard against consequences such as fines and demotion. In unionized professional sports leagues, sport administrators may have to proceed more cautiously because, as in Morrison's case, a grievance can be filed. With educational institutions, particularly those in the public domain, while there has not been a definitive challenge to social media restrictions, an approach as advocated by Bentley (2012) involving education, reasonable limitations, and case-by-case discipline may be an advisable path.

Public relations consequences represent another factor to consider when considering responses to identity expression by athletes and other sports figures. There may be times where social media content is problematic (e.g., homophobic, misogynistic) and disciplinary action is warranted). In other cases, even though the stance or commentary expressed by the athlete may run counter to the preferences of team administrators and/or the fan base, it may be more prudent to pass on any disciplinary action. Indeed, any disciplinary action taken against an athlete for his or her political views or advocacy for a social justice issue may bring more negative attention to the organization than just ignoring the comment, an approach the Rams took in their handling of the "hands-up" gesture by their players. While organizational responses will vary, the public relations effect must be considered. Athletes and sports figures can generate considerable support for their position from fans (Sanderson, 2009), which creates counternarratives that position the athlete favorably and the organization negatively (Sanderson, 2011a). Finally, one related point of importance is that social media has a secure hold on society. Children are using social media at younger ages, meaning that athletes will enter high school and college with established social media habits that may or may not have been formed responsibly. Thus, sports administrators should be proactive in their approaches to handling athletes' identity expression.

Whereas identity expression is a vital area that significantly influences the sport and social media landscape, other issues can manifest and affect athletes and sports organizations. These include private content being publicized, organizational responses to athletes receiving death threats via social media, and instances in which team employees use social media in ways that negatively impact athlete protection and sports organizations. Each of these is discussed in the next section.

3. Digital Media Technology and Issues with Protection

Through digital media technologies and the capabilities provided by smart phones, the public can often consume sports figures' communications that the sports figures believe are private. Perhaps one of the most vivid examples here was mentioned earlier, involving former Los Angeles Clippers owner Donald Sterling. Reports indicate that Sterling knew he was being recorded, and in California two-party consent is required for taping phone conversations. Sports figures should be mindful that someone may be recording their conversations and in some states there may be little legal recourse to prevent the contents of those conversations from becoming public. In addition to conversations, sports figures must be vigilant with their behavior, as their conduct can easily become public. Consider former Rutgers University head men's basketball coach Mike Rice, who was fired after a video was released showing him engaging in hostile and arguably physical and verbal abuse toward men's basketball players. Athletic Director Tim Pernetti had addressed these issues with Rice several months prior. However, once the footage became public, the pressure was significant, eventually leading to Pernetti's dismissal as well (Prunty, 2013). Similarly, Rick Vanderhook, the head men's baseball coach at California State University Fullerton, was suspended in 2014 after an audio recording was released that documented Vanderhook speaking to his team with much profanity (Ley, 2014). These cases are not limited to coaches and personnel at high-profile institutions and organizations. In 2012, Matt Mahanic, the men's golf coach at Huntingdon College, a Division III institution, was fired after a recording surfaced of Mahanic using hostile and inflammatory language toward the team, underpinned by significant profanity (Petchesky, 2012). These incidents illustrate the need for athletes and sport organization personnel to be vigilant with both their communication and their actions. When misdeeds become public, it can make it difficult to defend the related behavior. In cases such as Sterling and Rice's, organizations may have little recourse but to enact strict discipline. As will now be discussed, athletes' communication when initiated over social media platforms—particularly with respect to groupies—can also lead to problematic issues.

3.1. Social Media and Private Communication with Groupies

Certainly, athletes and groupies are a relational pair with a long history. However, with the advent of social media, a more public element has been introduced in regard to interactions between these groups. For instance, in 2010, Kansas City Chiefs wide receiver Dwayne Bowe made headlines when he discussed the concept of "importing" while being interviewed for an *ESPN the Magazine* story:

> My rookie year, we were playing in San Diego. You hear stories about groupies hanging out in hotel lobbies, but some of my teammates had it set up so there was a girl in every room. The older guys get on MySpace and Facebook a week before we go to a city; when a pretty one writes back, they arrange to fly her in three or four days in advance. They call it importing.
>
> (Leahy, 2010)

The coordination of groupies may not be altogether problematic, but in this subsequent comment from Bowe, one notable issue manifests: "I told her I had a girlfriend, but she didn't care. She was wearing my jersey, sitting in my lap, making it look like we knew each other. Then she took a picture and put it on Facebook. That almost got me in trouble." The ability to document these encounters could potentially place athletes in a precarious position, particularly if the liaison results in allegations of sexual assault or rape being made. Additionally, people can publicize private messages from athletes that may insinuate the desire for a sexual encounter. Such was the case with Buffalo Bills player Duke Williams, who was sending private direct messages via Twitter to porn star Mia Khalifa, apparently wanting to arrange a liaison with her. Khalifa then posted Williams's messages with the following statement: "Warning: Trespassers in my DM's will be shot and hung out to dry in public" (Kabas, 2015). NBA player J.R. Smith also experienced an issue when he sent a Twitter direct message to a woman, asking her if she was "trying to get the pipe." The direct message was screenshotted, resulting in t-shirts being made. Although many considered the outcome humorous, it nevertheless ends up as a vivid reminder of how easily content that what athletes believe to be private can become public (Heck, 2016).

While it may be difficult to expect athletes to abstain from this behavior entirely, it is still important that they be mindful that their private communications on social media platforms can easily become public and put the athlete and their respective organizations in precarious positions. For example, in April 2016, model Rachel Bush released an Instagram direct message purporting to be from LeBron James (Feldman, 2016). While the content of James's message was trivial—asking "what's up"—it nevertheless became a major news story and put the media spotlight on an area where it need not be. Finally, with a platform like Snapchat, which is predicated on content that quickly disappears, many have a mistaken assumption that content posted on Snapchat will never become public. Through screenshots and mobile applications, it is possible to save Snapchat content and these messages can lead to very problematic outcomes. For instance, a high school wrestler in Montana, Cole Snyder, was arrested in response to allegations that he was requesting that a fifteen-year-old girl send him nude pictures on Snapchat (Devlin, 2015). Certainly, athletes can expose themselves to liability through their social media private messages. Yet athletes can also be harmed by the actions of others on social media, particularly through the expression of death threats, a type of behavior that sports organizations cannot ignore.

3.2. Hateful Messages to Athletes via Social Media

Social media channels have facilitated more interaction opportunities for fans (Kassing and Sanderson, 2015; Sanderson, 2011a). Although these exchanges can be positive, athletes can also be subjected to very hostile and inflammatory behavior, especially those fans with publicly available social media accounts. Whereas some of this behavior may not be problematic, and may merely reflect complaints about the way that the athlete performed, other messages can become hateful, which may lead to negative psychological outcomes for athletes (Olson, 2013). For example, Sanderson and Truax (2014) investigated tweets sent to University of Alabama placekicker Cade Foster after he missed three field goals in a rivalry game against Auburn University. They discovered that while some of the tweets were sarcastic, several contained death threats. In an other instance, NFL player Brandon Jacobs received a death threat from a fan regarding his performance for fantasy football purposes: "On life Brandon, if you don't rush for 50 yards and 2 touchdowns tonight it's over for you and yo family nigga" (Mandell, 2013), and NFL player Mark Sanchez received a tweet in 2012 that stated, "DON'T COME TO PRACTICE WEDNESDAY I PROMISE YOU BULLETTS EVERYWHERE," and "SANCHEZ BETTER HAVE ARMED SECURITY WEDNESDAY AT PRACTICE!! YOU THINK IMMA SIT HERE AND WATCH THIS" (Garafolo, 2012).

In some instances, the threats are not made directly to athletes but to their family members. For example, after Los Angeles Lakers guard Steve Blake missed a shot that would have given the team the lead in the closing seconds of a playoff game against the Oklahoma City Thunder in 2012, Kristen Blake, his wife, received a tweet that read, "I hope your family gets murdered" (Devine, 2012). In the cases of Blake and Sanchez, league security became involved as did law enforcement. The tone of these tweets underscores that threats must be taken seriously. Additionally, when athletes are subjected to a barrage of hateful tweets, even if threats are not involved, organization personnel should reach out to these athletes and ascertain if there are signs of distress that could be ameliorated through mental health resources. Being proactive in these situations could help reduce the chances of an athlete experiencing psychological trauma. Although social media audiences can engage in actions that harm athletes, the actions of organization personnel may harm athletes as well as expose the organization to liability.

3.3. Organization Personnel and Social Media

Organization personnel need to be cautious in their use of social media, particularly when it comes to commentary on athletes. For instance, during a 2015 game against Murray State, the University of Texas El-Paso (UTEP) men's basketball Twitter account began posting critical commentary of player Vince Hunter. Apparently, Senior Associate Athletic Director Jeff Darby believed he was posting the criticism from his personal account (Kaplowitz, 2015). In another case, in May 2016, Texas A&M wide receivers coach Aaron Morehead made news when, after recruit Tate Martell rescinded his commitment to Texas A&M, Moorhead went to Twitter to post comments about loyalty. The tweets did not directly mention Martell yet were perceived as directed at Martell (Khan Jr., 2016). Moorhead later tweeted that he was referring to someone else, but the tweet led recruit Mannie Netherly to pull his commitment (Khan Jr., 2016).

These cases suggest several implications with respect to how sports organization employees' behavior on social media can harm athletes. First, athletes may potentially have grounds for slander or libel against the organization if they are able to show that they experienced harm from the comments. In the UTEP example, such exposure to liability seems particularly plausible since the criticism emerged from the official team account. Second, openly criticizing players, whether via direct mention or by inference, can result in negative press attention and public relations for the organization. Third, consequently, organization personnel should be trained and educated on the nuances of social media platforms and guidance should be provided about usage.

4. Conclusion

Social media technologies have created a number of implications for athletes and sports organizations. Athletes appear to be more confident in expressing aspects of their identity, which includes being critical of organizational decisions as well as offering commentary on political and social issues. Whereas this content may be incongruent with the beliefs and preferences of organizational personnel, discipline for these expressions should be administered cautiously to avoid any infringement on free speech. Although restricting social media may seem like a plausible solution, this strategy has potential legal implications as well, particularly for public institutions. Additionally, with the advent of the Internet and social media, the actions and behaviors of athletes and sports figures can easily become public, which can potentially place these individuals as well as the organization in precarious positions. Thus, it may be advisable for athletes and other organization employees to act as though they are being recorded. Beyond their own content, organization personnel must also be vigilant in protecting athletes from abusive behavior and threats made via social media, including those made to family members. The shifts introduced by social media technologies have influenced athletes' identity expression and its attendant repercussions. As these technologies continue to evolve and influence society, they will most certainly do so in sport. Such a transformation requires that organization personnel be attentive in monitoring user trends as well as legal ramifications. These practices would ensure that athletes' free speech and identity are being protected while concurrently managing organizational risk.

References

Adande, J. A. (2014, December 10). Purpose of "I can't breathe" T-shirts. Retrieved from http://espn.go.com/nba/story/_/id/12010612/nba-stars-making-statement-wearing-breathe-shirts.

Alper, J. (2013, July 14). Roddy White apologizes for post-Zimmerman verdict tweet. Retrieved from http://profootballtalk.nbcsports.com/2013/07/14/roddy-white-apologizes-for-post-zimmerman-verdict-tweet/.

Axisa, M. (2015, November 6). Rays acquire Logan Morrison, Brad Miller in 6-player deal with Mariners. Retrieved from www.cbssports.com/mlb/news/rays-acquire-logan-morrison-brad-miller-in-6-player-deal-with-mariners/.

Bennett, D. (2011, May 6). Rashard Mendenhall's controversial Osama bin Laden tweets cost him a sponsorship. Retrieved from www.businessinsider.com/rashard-mendenhall-champion-sponsorship-2011-5.

Bentley, E. D. (2012). "He Tweeted What? A First Amendment Analysis of the Use of Social Media by College Athletes and Recommended Best Practices for Athletic Departments." *Journal of College and University Law* 38: 452–475.

Borchert, C. J., Pinguelo, F. M., and Thaw, D. (2015). "Reasonable Expectations of Privacy Settings: Social Media and the Stored Communications Act." *Duke Law TechnologyReview* 13: 36–65.

Burke, T. (2011, October 31). The sad saga of a college football player who didn't understand how Twitter works. Retrieved from http://deadspin.com/5854783/the-sad-saga-of-a-college-football-player-who-didnt-understand-how-twitter-works/.

Cardale Jones: Classes pointless. (2012, October 5). Retrieved from http://espn.go.com/college-football/story/_/id/8466428/ohio-state-buckeyes-cardale-jones-tweets-classes-pointless.

Castillo, M. (2014, May 2). Was it legal to record and release Sterling's racist rant? Retrieved from www.cnn.com/2014/04/30/us/nba-sterling-legality/.

Cunningham, G. B., and Regan, M. R. Jr. (2012). "Political Activism, Racial Identity and the Commercial Endorsement of Athletes." *International Review for the Sociology of Sport* 47: 657–669.

Davis, S. (2016, March 17). Warriors player blasts NCAA after self-congratulatory tweet about giving student-athletes free wifi. Retrieved from www.businessinsider.com/festus-ezeli-blasts-ncaa-2016-3.

Devine, D. (2012, May 18). Steve Blake, wife receive death threats via Twitter after Lakers' Game 2 loss. Retrieved from http://sports.yahoo.com/blogs/nba-ball-dont-lie/steve-blake-wife-receive-death-threats-via-twitter-150145008.html.

Devlin, V. (2015, March 31). Documents detail drug, sex charges against Ronan wrestler. Retrieved from http://missoulian.com/news/local/documents-detail-drug-sex-charges-against-ronan-wrestler/article_9854b98d-f8b1-530a-8a90-2e3df6004fdb.html.

Fantz, A. (2014, December 1). Police angry at "hands up" gesture by St. Louis Rams players. Retrieved from www.cnn.com/2014/12/01/us/ferguson-nfl-st-louis-rams/.

Feldman, K. (2016, April 12). LeBron James causes another social media stir after allegedly sending direct message to Instagram to model Rachel Bush. Retrieved from www.nydailynews.com/sports/basketball/lebron-james-allegedly-dms-instagram-model-article-1.2597551.

Garafolo, M. (2012, December 18). Jets QB Mark Sanchez receives Twitter death threats. Retrieved fromwww.usatoday.com/story/sports/nfl/2012/12/18/new-york-jets-quarterback-mark-sanchez-gets-death-threats-on-twitter/1778555/.

Gay, J. W. (2012). "Hands Off Twitter: Are NCAA Student-Athlete Social Media Bans Unconstitutional?" *Florida State University Law Review* 39: 781–805.

Granderson, L. Z. (2012, August 14). The political Michael Jordan. Retrieved from http://espn.go.com/nba/story/_/id/8264956/michael-jordan-obama-fundraiser-22-years-harvey-gantt.

Heat don hoodies after teen's death. (2012, March 24). Retrieved from http://espn.go.com/nba/truehoop/miamiheat/story/_/id/7728618/miami-heat-don-hoodies-response-death-teen-trayvon-martin.

Heck, J. (2016, April 26). J. R. Smith opens up about his infamous, "get the pipe" message. Retrieved from www.sportingnews.com/nba/news/jr-smith-you-trying-to-get-the-pipe-twitter-direct-message-picture/nxecoltvi2rl1w882xqtlkgf6.

Hinton, M. (2012, January 20). Recruits say the dumbest things: Yuri Wright's prospects derailed by vulgar tweets. Retrieved from http://sports.yahoo.com/blogs/ncaaf-dr-saturday/recruits-dumbest-things-blue-chip-cornerback-prospects-derailed-145734774.html.

Hirschhorn, D. (2014. April 29). NBA bans Donald Sterling "for life" after racist rant. Retrieved from http://time.com/81170/donald-sterling-los-angeles-clippers-nba-adam-silver/.

Hutchins, B., and Rowe, D. (2009). "From Broadcast Scarcity to Digital Plentitude: The Changing Dynamics of the Media Sport Content Economy." *Television & New Media* 10: 354–370.

Kabas, M. (2015, July 13). Porn star Mia Khalifa exposes NFL star Duke Williams' shady DMs. Retrieved from www.dailydot.com/irl/mia-khalifa-duke-williams-twitter-dm/.

Kaplowitz, S. (2015, March 17). UTEP Twitter account blasts star player, Hunter, quickly deletes tweet. Retrieved from http://krod.com/utep-twitter-account-blasts-star-player-hunter-quickly-deletes-tweet/.

Kassing, J. W. (1997). "Articulating, Antagonizing, and Displacing: A Model of Employee Dissent." *Communication Studies* 48: 311–332.

Kassing, J. W. (2002). "Speaking Up: Identifying Employees' Upward Dissent Strategies." *Management Communication Quarterly* 16: 187–209.

Kassing, J. W., and Sanderson, J. (2015). "Playing in the New Media Game or Riding the Virtual Bench: Confirming and Disconfirming Membership in the Community of Sport." *Journal of Sport & Social Issues* 39: 3–18.

Khan, S. Jr. (2016, May 5). A&M assistant's tweets add fuel to fire of No. 3 QB's decommitment. Retrieved from football/recruiting/story/_/id/15465600/texas-aggies-lose-second-recruit-night-coach-tweets.

Kimes. M. (2015, June 11). Social media bans may violate college athletes' First Amendment rights. Retrieved from http://espn.go.com/college-sports/story/_/id/13519145/florida-state-clemson-enact-possibly-unconstitutional-social-media-bans.

Leahy, S. (2010, May 20). Dwayne Bowe says Chiefs veterans were "importing" women to hotel rooms on road trips. Retrieved from http://content.usatoday.com/communities/thehuddle//post/2010/05/dwayne-bowe-says-chiefs-veterans-were-importing-women-to-hotel-rooms-on-road-trips/1#.V351kY7Od-t.

Ley, T. (2014, June 25). The secretly recorded videos that got a raging baseball coach suspended. Retrieved from http://deadspin.com/the-secretly-recorded-videos-that-got-a-raging-baseball-1595887560.

Lisk, J. (2015, September 2). College sports social media bans could violate First Amendment. Retrieved from http://thebiglead.com/2015/09/02/college-sports-social-media-bans-could-violate-first-amendment/.

Llorens, I. (2011, December 28). Kasey Kahne, NASCAR driver, tweets against breastfeeding in public, ignites controversy among fans. Retrieved from www.huffingtonpost.com/2011/12/28/kasey-kahne-nascar-breastfeeding_n_1172760.html.

Logan Morrison Sparks Twitter War With Photo of Breastfeeding Mom at Nordstrom. (2012, July 27). Retrieved from www.huffingtonpost.com/2012/07/27/logan-morrison-tweets-breastfeeding_n_1709848.html.

Mandell, N. (2013, October 22). Brandon Jacobs received a death threat from a fantasy football owner. Retrieved from http://ftw.usatoday.com/2013/10/brandon-jacobs-received-a-death-threat-from-a-fantasy-football-owner.

Mandell, N. (2014, November 25). Kobe Bryant on Ferguson: Until the legal system changes "it's going to keep on happening." Retrieved from http://ftw.usatoday.com/2014/11/kobe-bryant-ferguson.

McCarthy, M. (2011, May 6). Champion won't pay Rashard Mendenhall's contract. Retrieved from http://content.usatoday.com/communities/gameon/post/2011/05/champion-wont-pay-out-rashard-mendenhalls-contract-over-0911-tweets-pittsburgh-steelers-osama-bin-laden-nfl/1#.V32JWI7Od-s.

McDonald, P., & Thompson, P. (2016). "Social Media(tion) and the Reshaping of Public Boundaries in Employment Relations." *International Journal of Management Reviews* 18: 69–84.

Meraz, S. (2009). "Is There an Elite Hold? Traditional Media to Social Media Agenda Setting Influence in Blogs Networks." *Journal of Computer-Mediated Communication* 14: 682–707.

Minium, H. (2012, September 15). ODU football ban among most restrictive in U.S. Retrieved from http://pilotonline.com/sports/college/old-dominion/odu-football-twitter-ban-among-most-restrictive-in-u-s/article_a0fcc378-fef6-56cd-8128-3936d1f85b5e.html.

Nelson, A. K. (2011, September 15). Marlins' Logan Morrison files grievance. Retrieved from http://espn.go.com/mlb/story/_/id/6973624/florida-marlins-logan-morrison-files-grievance-demotion.

Newport, K. (2014, March 19). Arian Foster takes shot at NCAA with tweet about March Madness. Retrieved from http://bleacherreport.com/articles/1999163-arian-foster-takes-shot-at-ncaa-with-tweet-about-march-madness,

Newsroom (n.d.). Retrieved from http://newsroom.fb.com/company-info/.

No reasonable expectation of privacy in content posted to social networking websites, regardless of individual privacy settings. (2010, October 13). Retrieved from www.nixonpeabody.com/118536.

Olson, E. (2013, October 29). Players can struggle when heckling turns to hate. Retrieved from http://collegefootball.ap.org/article/players-can-struggle-when-heckling-turns-hate.

Ostrow, A. (2009, October 28). The cost of Larry Johnson's gay slur on Twitter: $213,000. Retrieved from http://mashable.com/2009/10/28/larry-johnson-gay-slur twitter/ #loGTkuag7EqK.

Oz, M. (2013, December 12). Logan Morrison probably isn't making new fans within Seattle's gay community. Retrieved from http://sports.yahoo.com/blogs/mlb-big-league-stew/ logan-morrison-probably-isn-t-making-fans-within-003235550--mlb.html.

Peck, B. (2012, July 30). Swiss soccer player kicked off Olympic team for discriminatory tweet. Retrieved from http://sports.yahoo.com/blogs/fourth-place-medal/swiss-soccer-player-kicked-off-olympic-team-racist-165059693--oly.html.

Petchesky, B. (2013, August 29). Lawrence Tynes's wife blasts the Bucs over MRSA treatment. Retrieved from http://deadspin.com/lawrence-tyness-wife-blasts-the-bucs-over-mrsa-treatme-1221009725.

Petchesky, B. (2012, November 8). Profane rant by D-III Christian College golf coach is a thing to behold. Retrieved from deadspin.com/5959088/fucking-hunky-dory-d-iii-golf-coachs-profane-rant-is-a-thing-to-behold.

Prunty, B. (2013, April 3). Mike Rice fired at Rutgers after abusive behavior on practice tapes comes to light. Retrieved from Retrieved from www.nj.com/rutgers/basketball/index.ssf/ 2013/04/mike_rice_fired_at_rutgers_aft.html.

Rashard Mendenhall doesn't hold back. (2011, May 4). Retrieved from http://espn.go.com/nfl/ news/story?id=6471433W.

Report: NBA won't fine players for wearing 'I can't breathe' t-shirts. Retrieved from www. si.com/nba/2014/12/09/nba-i-cant-breathe-tshirts.

Samuels, D. (2015, July 14). After a four year ban, Old Dominion HC Bobby Wilder is lifting the social media restriction. Retrieved from http://footballscoop.com/news/after-a-four-year-twitter-ban-old-dominion-hc-bobby-wilder-is-lifting-the-social-media-restriction/.

Sanderson, J. (2009). "'Thanks for Fighting the Good Fight': Cultivating Dissent on Blogmaverick.com." *Southern Communication Journal* 74: 390–405.

Sanderson, J. (2011a). *It's a Whole New Ball Game: How Social Media Is Changing Sports* (New York: Hampton Press).

Sanderson, J. (2011b). "To Tweet or Not to Tweet...: Exploring Division I Athletic Departments Social Media Policies." *International Journal of Sport Communication* 4: 492–513.

Sanderson, J. (2013). "Stepping into the (Social Media) Game: Building Athlete Identity via Twitter." In *Handbook of Research on Technoself: Identity in a Technological Society*, edited by R. Luppicini (New York: IGI Global), 419–438.

Sanderson, J. (2014). "Just Warming Up: Logan Morrison, Twitter, Athlete Identity, and Building the Brand." In *Sport and identity: New Agendas in Communication*, edited by B. Brummett & A. W. Ishak (New York: Routledge), 208–223.

Sanderson, J., and Browning, B. (2013). "Training Versus Monitoring: A Qualitative Examination of Athletic Department Practices Regarding Student-Athletes and Twitter." *Qualitative Research Reports in Communication* 14: 105–111.

Sanderson, J., Browning, B., & Schmittel, A. (2015). "Education on the Digital Terrain: A Case Study Exploring College Athletes' Perceptions of Social Media Education." *International Journal of Sport Communication* 8: 103–124.

Sanderson, J., Frederick, E., and Stocz, M. (2016). "When Athlete Activism Clashes with Group Values: The 'Boycott the St. Louis Rams' Facebook Page and Social Identity Threat Management." *Mass Communication and Society* 19: 301–322.

Sanderson, J., Snyder, E., Hull, D., and Gramlich, K. (2015). "Social Media Policies Within NCAA Member Institutions: Evolving Technology and Its Impact on Policy." *Journal of Issues in Intercollegiate Athletics* 8: 50–73.

Sanderson, J., and Truax, C. (2014). "'I Hate You Man!': Exploring Maladaptive Parasocial Interaction Expressions to College Athletes via Twitter." *Journal of Issues in Intercollegiate Athletics* 7: 333–351.

Schmittel, A., and Sanderson, J. (2015). "Talking About Trayvon in 140 Characters: Exploring NFL Players' Tweets About the George Zimmerman Verdict." *Journal of Sport & Social Issues* 39: 332–345.

Shaw, J. (2016, May 7). Facebook is being sued over facial recognition and tagging because . . . paranoia. Retrieved from http://hotair.com/archives/2016/05/07/facebook-is-being-sued-over-facial-recognition-and-tagging-because-paranoia/.

Shilling, C. G. (2013, September 26). United States: Employers liable under Stored Communications Act. Retrieved from www.mondaq.com/unitedstates/x/265214/employee+rights+labour+relations/Employers+Liable+Under+Stored+Communication+Act.

Sikes, C. (2014, September 11). James Harrison confronts Roger Goodell on Twitter. Retrieved from www.sportingnews.com/nfl/news/james-harrison-confronts-roger-goodell-steelers-domestic-violence-suspension/1dkqo28q8khql1uowat8ey28v4.

Smith, E. (2015, January 26). Florida court finds no expectation of privacy on Facebook. Retrieved from www.thenationaltriallawyers.org/2015/01/florida-facebook/.

Snyder, E. M., Hutchens, N. H., Jones W., and Sun, J. (2015). "Social Media Policies in Intercollegiate Athletics: The Speech and Privacy Rights of Student-Athletes." *Journal for the Study of Sports and Athletes in Education* 1: 50–74

Strauss, C. (2013, July 15). Victor Cruz apologizes for controversial Zimmerman tweet. Retrieved from www.usatoday.com/story/sports/nfl/giants/2013/07/15/cruz-explains-zimmerman-tweets/2517965/.

Trahan, K. (2014, August 5). Do college football coaches really drop recruits because of tweets? Retrieved from www.sbnation.com/college-football/2014/8/5/5970569/college-football-recruiting-twitter-coaches.

Wagner, K. (2014, April 27). Exclusive: The extended Donald Sterling tape. Retrieved from http://deadspin.com/exclusive-the-extended-donald-sterling-tape-1568291249.

Wright, P. (2013, August 23). Court finds non-public Facebook posts are covered by the Stored Communications Act—but not posts produced by a user's frenemy. Retrieved from www.employerlawreport.com/2013/08/articles/social-media-2/court-finds-non-public-facebook-posts-are-covered-by-the-stored-communications-act-but-not-posts-produced-by-a-users-frenemy/.

Zillgitt, J. (2013, January 8). NBA fines Mark Cuban $500,000 for Twitter comments. Retrieved from www.usatoday.com/story/sports/nba/mavericks/2013/01/08/dallas-mavericks-owner-mark-cuban-fined/1819001/athletes.

CHAPTER 16

THE "SHIFTING LINE" OF SPORTS BETTING LEGALIZATION

DANIEL L. WALLACH

1. Introduction

WAGERING on sporting events is deeply engrained in our national consciousness. Betting terms, such as the "point spread" and "covering the spread," have long been part of the public lexicon. Even casual sports fans participate in fantasy sports leagues and National Collegiate Athletic Association (NCAA) tournament bracket pools. As one federal appeals court aptly put it, "wagering on sporting events is an activity almost as inscribed in our society as participating in or watching the sports themselves" (*National Collegiate Athletic Association v. Christie*, 730 F.3d at 215). And it is big business too. An estimated $4.2 billion was wagered on Super Bowl 50, and more than $9 billion was bet on the 2016 NCAA Men's Division I Basketball Tournament (Peltz, 2016). The lure of sports betting is so strong that tourists will flock to watch (and bet on) a major sporting event taking place thousands of miles away: the Las Vegas Convention and Visitors Authority reported that the 2015 Super Bowl weekend produced $124.4 million in non-gaming economic impact and attracted nearly 300,000 visitors (Katsilometes, 2016).

However, despite its pervasiveness, sports wagering is illegal in most U.S. jurisdictions. This is largely because of two federal laws—the Interstate Wire Act of 1961 (the Wire Act),[1] which prohibits the transmission of wire communications related to sports betting, and the now-controversial Professional and Amateur Sports Protection Act of 1992 (PASPA),[2] which forbids state governments from authorizing or licensing sports betting, except in those states where it was already legal before PASPA went into effect. As a result of PASPA, Nevada is the only state where traditional single-game sports wagering remains legal. But Nevada's sports books only account for less than 3% of the total amount wagered on sporting events each year in the United States. The remainder is wagered in the "black market," where it is unregulated, untaxed, and illegal. Estimates of the scope of illegal sports betting in the United States range anywhere from between $80 billion and $400 billion (Ruddock, 2016).

Given the rapid proliferation of illegal sports gambling in this country, many have questioned the wisdom—and effectiveness—of PASPA. Enacted under the guise of curbing the spread of sports gambling, PASPA has succeeded only in channeling that activity into illegal markets. Thus, instead of taking place in a regulated environment backed by consumer protections, the vast majority of sports gambling in the United States takes place underground, where it cannot be monitored for suspicious wagering activity. This makes it easier for criminal elements to "fix" games, since the vast amount of wagering would go undetected by law enforcement authorities and the sports leagues. The irony of all this is that PASPA—while originally enacted to protect the integrity of sporting events—has actually served to undermine it by precluding the type of effective monitoring that would occur in a legal and heavily regulated environment. The advent and increasing popularity of the Internet has only served to exacerbate this problem. When PASPA was enacted in 1992, Internet usage and availability was sporadic at best. Online gambling had not yet become as ubiquitous as it is today—the first online gambling site would not even surface until 1995. Fast forward nearly a quarter of a century later, and, today, the Internet has become a dominant form of commerce, blurring state—and even international—boundaries. Due to the rapid growth of the Internet, a law that was designed to curb the spread of sports betting has become powerless to stop it.

Moreover, attitudes about sports betting (and gambling in general) have changed dramatically since PASPA was enacted. In the early 1990s there was growing public dismay about the harms associated with sports gambling. The betting scandal involving legendary baseball player, Pete Rose, was still fresh in the public's mind. But times have changed, and so too have perceptions. Recent polls indicate that more Americans support the expanded legalization of sports betting than oppose it (Fairleigh Dickinson University, 2016). The public's shifting attitude on sports gambling can be attributed to several factors, including (1) recognition that the activity is occurring anyway, so why not just legalize and regulate it, and allow states to benefit economically; (2) the rapid expansion of casino gambling throughout the United States[3]; and, perhaps most prominently, (3) the meteoric rise of fantasy sports—which many consider to be a form of sports gambling—as a staple of American life. The emergence of daily fantasy sports, in particular, may ultimately prove to be the catalyst for change in the U.S. sports betting laws. As more and more states begin passing laws legalizing daily fantasy sports—without opposition from the sports leagues—many have begun to question why some forms of sports gambling are allowed but not others.

Against this backdrop, there has been increasing discussion in recent years about repealing or amending PASPA. In November 2014, NBA Commissioner Adam Silver penned a *New York Times op-ed* urging Congress to "adopt a federal framework that allows states to authorize betting on professional sports, subject to strict regulatory requirements and technological safeguards" (Silver, 2014, A27). While Commissioner

Silver advocates a federal legislative solution, states like New Jersey are pursuing a more aggressive path. In a series of recent court cases, New Jersey has challenged the constitutionality of PASPA, arguing that it impermissibly interferes with state autonomy and allows certain states (like Nevada) to offer sports betting while prohibiting other states from doing so. While New Jersey has been unsuccessful to date, its efforts have exposed significant cracks in PASPA's armor that have left the federal law vulnerable to a successful legal challenge by another state. The "legislative" versus "litigation" path is at the core of the current debate surrounding the legalization of sports betting, which most agree is inevitable. The question is the "when" and the "how." Those questions will likely be answered in the next three to five years, as lobbying and litigation efforts proceed on parallel tracks.

This chapter examines the growing and transformative body of law governing sports betting, with a special emphasis on the Wire Act and PASPA. The provisions of PASPA, in particular, will serve as a launch point to a discussion of the true driver behind current efforts to legalize sports betting in the United States: the recent litigation pitting the State of New Jersey against the four major U.S. professional sports leagues and the NCAA. The pressure and vulnerability created by the New Jersey sports betting litigation—which spawned five court decisions, several stinging dissenting opinions, and the rarely invoked en banc rehearing process—have served to catalyze the current debate on expanded sports betting legalization. This chapter examines the New Jersey sports betting litigation in great depth, and explains how the court rulings—while siding with the sports leagues—have opened up a variety of pathways for states to legalize sports gambling and, at a minimum, have compressed the time frame for federal action to repeal or amend PASPA.

2. The Wire Act

The Interstate Wire Act of 1961 is the primary federal law that prohibits sports betting. The Wire Act was enacted in 1961 as part of then-U.S. Attorney General Robert Kennedy's "war on organized crime." The Wire Act was intended "to assist the states in the enforcement of their laws on gambling, bookmaking, and like offenses, and to aid in the suppression of organized gambling activities by prohibiting the use of wire communication facilities which are or will be used for the transmission of bets or wagers and gambling information in interstate and foreign commerce." In short, the purpose of the Wire Act was twofold: (1) to assist the various states in the enforcement of their gambling laws and (2) to suppress organized criminal gambling activities (*United States v. McDonough*, 835 F.2d at 1104).

The Wire Act makes it illegal for persons engaged in the business of sports betting (e.g., bookies) to offer or take bets over the phone lines or through other wired devices from gamblers located in a state other than where the sports book operator is physically located. The relevant portion of the Wire Act, § 1084(a), provides as follows:

> Whoever being engaged in the business of betting or wagering knowingly uses a wire communication facility for the transmission in interstate or foreign commerce of bets or wagers or information assisting in the placing of bets or wagers on any sporting event or contest, or for the transmission of a wire communication which entitles the recipient to receive money or credit as a result of bets or wagers, or for information assisting in the placing of bets or wagers, shall be fined under this title or imprisoned not more than two years, or both. (18 U.S.C. § 1084(a))

This provision contains two broad clauses. The first bars anyone engaged in the "business of betting or wagering" from knowingly using a wire communication facility "for the transmission in interstate or foreign commerce of bets or wagers or information assisting in the placing of bets or wagers on any sporting event or contest" (U.S. Department of Justice, 2011, p. 4). The second bars any such person from knowingly using a wire communication facility to transmit communications that entitle the recipient to "receive money or credit" either "as a result of bets or wagers" or "for information assisting in the placing of bets or wagers" (U.S. Department of Justice, 2011, p. 4).

To fall within the scope of the Wire Act, a person must be engaged "in the business of betting or wagering" (18 U.S.C. 1084(a)). This requires that a party not only be engaged in the "sale of a product or service for fee" (*United States v. Baborian*, 528 F. Supp. at 329), but that the party also be engaged in a "continuing course of conduct" (*United States v. Scavo*, 593 F. 2d at 842). To satisfy the business-of-betting-or-wagering element of the offense, the Government "'need not establish that making bets or wagers was the defendant's exclusive or even primary source of income," and need not prove any particular "number of bets or dollar volume of bets" (*United States v. Rozenfeld*, 2014 WL at *3). Instead, "[i]t is sufficient . . . if the government establishes that the defendant participated in a regular course of conduct or series of transactions which involved time, attention and labor devoted to betting or wagering for profit" (*United States v. Rozenfeld*, 2014 WL at *3). Consequently, where a gambling operator charges customers for its services, either through accepting or brokering wagers, the continuing activities of that operator will likely constitute being "engaged in the business of betting or wagering" for purposes of the Wire Act (Cabot and Faiss, 2002, p. 19).

In addition to being "engaged in the business of betting or wagering," the Wire Act explicitly requires that a "wire communication facility" be used to take bets on "any sporting event or contest" (18 U.S.C. 1084(a)). The Wire Act defines the term "wire communication facility" broadly to mean "any and all instrumentalities, personnel, and services (among other things, the receipt, forwarding, or delivery of communications) used or useful in the transmission of writing, signs, pictures, and sounds of all kinds by aid of wire, cable, or other like connection between the points of origin and reception of such transmission" (18 U.S.C. § 1081). Several courts have held that the statutory term "wire communication facility" encompasses transactions over the Internet.[4] The Wire Act, however, applies only to sporting events, and does not bar other forms of online gambling, such as lotteries and poker (U.S. Department of Justice, 2011).

The Wire Act also contains a safe-harbor provision (18 U.S.C. § 1084(b)), which exempts from liability certain communications assisting in the transmission of bets or wagers between places where betting on sports is legal. That provision provides:

> Nothing in this section shall be construed to prevent the transmission in interstate or foreign commerce of information . . . assisting in the placing of bets or wagers on a sporting event or contest from a State or foreign country where betting on that sporting event or contest is legal into a State or foreign country in which such betting is legal. (18 U.S.C. § 1084(b))

By its plain terms, the safe-harbor provision in Section 1084(b) requires that the betting be "legal" (i.e., permitted by law) in ***both*** jurisdictions (*United States v. Cohen*, 260 F.3d at 73). Thus, the safe-harbor provision only applies when gambling on the events in question is legal in both the "sending" jurisdiction (i.e., the state from which the information was sent) and the "receiving" jurisdiction (i.e., the state from which it was received) (*United States v. Lyons*, 740 F.3d at713). "Thus, for example, if New York allows betting on horses at race tracks in New York, and if Nevada allows betting in Nevada on the results of New York horse races, then information may be wired from New York to Nevada without violating the statute." (*United States v. Lyons*, 740 F.3d at713). However, because Nevada is the only state that has legalized traditional single-game sports wagering, this exemption has little practical effect with regard to Wire Act prosecutions for illegal sports betting in the United States. This is because there would be no second state where the activity is presently legal, unless, of course, the second place happens to be a foreign country.

A second limitation on the safe-harbor provision is that it only applies to the transmission of "information" assisting in the placing of bets, but not the transmission of the actual bets themselves (*United States v. Lyons*, 2012 WL at *4; *United States v. McDonough*, 835 F.2d at 1104–1105). The Wire Act, however, provides very little guidance in differentiating between an actionable "bet" under § 1084(a) and "information" potentially exempt under § 1084(b). According to one federal district court opinion, "information" would include "knowledge that may influence whether, with whom, and on what terms to make a bet" (*United States v. Ross*, 1999 WL at *5). Thus, "transmissions reporting the results of sporting events, the odds placed on particular contests by oddsmakers, or the identities of persons seeking to place bets would be examples of 'information'" (*United States v. Ross*, 1999 WL at *5). Additional examples of "information" could include the providing of line information, stadium/arena weather conditions, player injury reports, and even statistical data or advanced analytics that would assist a potential bettor in making a bet.

Finally, the Wire Act does not apply to individual bettors or gamblers. According to its language, the Wire Act only applies those "engaged in the *business* of betting or wagering" (18 U.S.C. 1084(a)) (italics added). The courts have steadfastly refused to apply this language to individual gamblers, regardless of the size or frequency of their bets (*see United States v. Anderson*, 542 F.2dat 436; *United States v. Baborian*, 528 F. Supp.

at 329). As one court explained, "Congress intended the business of gambling to mean 'bookmaking, i.e., the taking and laying off of bets, and not mere betting" (*United States v. Baborian*, 528 F. Supp. at 328).

3. Professional and Amateur Sports Protection Act

While the Wire Act provides sweeping criminal penalties for illegal bookmaking, it is not the reason why legal sports betting in the United States is constrained largely to Nevada. That honor belongs to the Professional and Amateur Sports Protection Act (28 U.S.C. §§ 3701 et seq.), commonly referred to by its acronym "PASPA," a 1992 federal law which (1) prohibits most states (and federally recognized Indian tribes) from authorizing or licensing sports betting within their borders and (2) permits professional and amateur sports organizations, in addition to the United States Attorney General, to file civil actions to enjoin violations of its prohibitions.

3.1. Legislative History

PASPA was enacted in 1992 "to stop the spread of State-sponsored sports gambling and to maintain the integrity" of professional and amateur sports (Senate Report 102-248, at 3555). The Report of the Senate Judiciary Committee, the primary source of PASPA's legislative history, identified a number of "harms" caused by sports gambling. The committee believed that "[s]ports gambling threatens the integrity of, and public confidence in, amateur and professional sports," and reasoned that "[w]idespread legalization would inevitably promote suspicion about controversial plays and lead fans to think 'the fix was in' whenever their team failed to beat the point spread" (Senate Report 102-248, 1991, at 3556). Additionally, the Committee was "especially concerned" about "the potential effect of legalized sports gambling on America's youth," noting that technological advances have made gambling more accessible to minors, who at the time comprised some one million of the nation's approximately eight million compulsive gamblers (Senate Report 102-248, 1991, at 3556). The committee thus declared that "[g]overnments should not be in the business of encouraging people, *especially young people*, to gamble" (Senate Report 102-248, 1991, at 3556) (italics added).

Congress made clear, however, that it was concerned primarily with "state-sponsored" sports gambling, and was not trying to eradicate *all* sports gambling. The Report of the Senate Judiciary Committee declares that PASPA's purpose is to "prohibit sports gambling conducted by, or authorized under the law of, any *State or governmental entity*" and to "stop the spread of *State-sponsored* sports gambling" (Senate Report 102-248, 1991, at 3553 & 3555) (italics added). The Senate Report characterized sports gambling as "a national problem," asserting that "[t]he harms it inflicts are felt beyond the borders of those States that sanction it" and adding that "[t]he moral erosion it produces cannot be limited geographically" (Senate Report 102-248, 1991, at 3556). The Senate Report warned of the "domino effect" that could occur absent federal intervention: i.e., that "[o]nce a State legalizes sports gambling, it will be extremely difficult for other States to resist the lure" (Senate Report 102-248, 1991, at 3556). The committee was concerned that "[w]ithout Federal legislation, sports gambling [would] likely . . . spread on a piecemeal basis and ultimately develop an *irreversible momentum*" (Senate Report 102-248, 1991, at 3556) (italics added). These "interstate ramifications," the Committee concluded, were "a compelling reason for federal legislation" (Senate Report 102-248, 1991, at 3556).

3.2. Statutory Language and Scope

PASPA's key provision (§ 3702) provides, in relevant part:

> It shall be unlawful for—
> (1) a governmental entity to *sponsor, operate, advertise, promote, license,* or *authorize by law or compact,* or
> (2) a person to sponsor, operate, advertise, or promote, pursuant to the law or compact of a governmental entity,
> a lottery, sweepstakes, or other betting, gambling, or wagering scheme based, directly or indirectly (through the use of geographical references or otherwise), *on one or more competitive games in which amateur or professional athletes participate,* or are intended to participate, *or on one or more performances of such athletes in such games.* (28 U.S.C. § 3702 (emphasis added))

By its terms, PASPA forbids a "governmental entity" (defined to include a state and its subdivisions, as well as any Indian tribe recognized by the U.S. Secretary of the Interior) from doing any of six things: such entities may not "*sponsor*," "*operate*," "*advertise*," "*promote*," "*license*" or "*authorize by law or compact*" a "lottery, sweepstakes, or other betting, gambling, or wagering scheme" based on the outcome of, or on one or performances within, any professional or amateur sporting event. These six words—especially when construed together (such as under the interpretative tool known as *noscitur a sociis*, more commonly referred to as the "associated words canon") connote an "affirmative" state sanctioning of the activity, i.e., by placing the state's "imprimatur" on sports betting.

PASPA's restrictions on state-sponsored sports wagering apply both to the states and private actors (*see* 28 U.S.C. §§ 3702(1)–3702(2)). However, the prohibition directed to private actors is entirely derivative of a state's violation of PASPA.[5] Thus, in order for a private actor (such as a casino or racetrack) to be subject to the strictures of PASPA, there must be a state legislative act or compact in effect expressly legalizing the sports gambling at issue.

3.3. Standing to Enforce PASPA

There are two mechanisms in place for enforcing PASPA's prohibitions. First, Congress has empowered the Attorney General of the United States (through one of the appropriate regional U.S. Attorney's Offices) to seek an injunction against any violation of PASPA in a federal district court (28 U.S.C. § 3703). Second, Congress granted "professional sports organizations" and "amateur sports organizations" a cause of action for an injunction against a violation of PASPA whenever the organization's *own* "competitive game[s] [are] alleged to be the basis of such violation" (28 U.S.C. § 3703) (italics added). The italicized language makes clear that a sports organization would only have standing under PASPA to protect its *own* games, but not those associated with another sports organization. Thus, for example, while the National Basketball Association could seek a court injunction against any state or federally recognized Indian Tribe that has legalized sports betting on NBA games (since it meets PASPA's definition of a "professional sports organization" with respect to its own games), it would lack standing under PASPA to seek injunctive relief to block the wagering on the competitive games of other sports organizations, such as those sponsored by Major League Soccer or the PGA Tour. This also comports with the constitutional standing principle that a person generally has standing to assert his own legal rights but not those belonging to others. Nonetheless, one federal court recently appeared to gloss over this limitation by entering a blanket injunction prohibiting the State of New Jersey from implementing a law that would have allowed casinos and racetracks to accept wagers on *any* professional or amateur sporting event, even though the only plaintiffs which had filed suit under PASPA were the four major professional sports leagues and the NCAA (*National Collegiate Athletic Association v. Christie*, 61 F. Supp. 2d at 488). The effect of the court's ruling was to permit the major sports leagues to broadly invoke PASPA to prevent states from legalizing betting on a whole host of sporting events that are not even offered by such organizations.

Despite this outlier ruling, the § 3703 standing language—if interpreted literally—could still provide states with an avenue for legalizing sports betting on soccer, golf, tennis, boxing, mixed martial arts, and NASCAR (as well as a number of other "non-major" U.S. sports) since the governing organizations of those sports might not object to such wagering, and, indeed, might tacitly (or even explicitly) support it to increase interest in their sport. Of course, this strategy would only succeed if the U.S. Attorney General (who is empowered to seek injunctive relief against *any* violation of PASPA, irrespective of the sport) opted not to pursue litigation against states that have authorized this limited form of sports gambling. But as we have seen with the recent spate of state legislation approving fantasy sports wagering (which arguably falls within PASPA's broad scope), the U.S. Attorney General has not exactly been a vanguard of PASPA enforcement. In the nearly twenty-five-year history of PASPA, the Attorney General has never initiated a lawsuit against a state for violating PASPA, opting instead for the more subservient role of an intervenor or *amicus curiae* in the two PASPA lawsuits brought by the major sports leagues against the State of New Jersey (as discussed later in this chapter). Although a number of states have explicitly legalized fantasy sports contests through legislative enactments, the U.S. Attorney General has not invoked PASPA to block any of those new laws, and probably never will. Additionally, the 2016 election of a new U.S. President (who, in turn, would appoint a new Attorney General) may bring a more receptive atmosphere for the expansion of legal sports betting. A new presidential administration could decide, for example, that blocking state-authorized sports betting is not a high enough priority (especially when it is supported by the affected sports organizations) and thus direct the new Attorney General not to pursue any legal challenges when the sports betting at issue is legal under state law and is undertaken with the approval or acquiescence of the affected sports organizations. This is one potentially intriguing approach for expanding legal sports betting without repealing or amending PASPA.

3.4. "Grandfathering" Provisions

PASPA also contains a number of exemptions from its application, the most important of which are two "grandfathering" provisions (28 U.S.C. §§ 3704(a)(1)– 3704(a)(2)) which preserve preexisting sports wagering schemes in Nevada, Delaware, Oregon, Montana, and "possibly a few other states" (Senate Report 102-248, 1991 at 3562). § 3704(a)(1) provides that the prohibition does not apply to "a lottery, sweepstakes, or other betting, gambling, or wagering scheme in operation in a State or other governmental entity to the extent that such scheme was actually conducted by that State or other governmental entity during the period beginning January 1, 1976, and ending August 31, 1990" (28 U.S.C. § 3704(a)(1)). This "grandfathering" clause was intended to permit states like Delaware, Oregon, and Montana to continue the limited "sports lotteries" that they had previously conducted (*National Collegiate Athletic Association, Inc. v. Christie*, 730 F.3d at 216).

The § 3704(a)(1) exemption, however, is limited to those sports wagering schemes that were in existence between January 1, 1976, and August 31, 1990, but only "to the extent" that they were actually conducted during that time frame. This is the principal reason that Delaware, Oregon, and Montana—while recognized as being "grandfathered" under PASPA—are nonetheless prohibited from authorizing single-game sports betting. Delaware and Oregon operated only "sports lotteries" (involving multi-game parlay bets) prior to August 31, 1990, whereas Montana operated a sports betting pool (known as "Montana Sports Action") where the winner was determined by the performance of individual football players in games or professional stock car drivers in races. The exemption under § 3704(a)(1) preserved these sports lotteries and sports pools, but did not allow for any expansion beyond that (Senate Report 102-248, 1991, at 3560 ("paragraph (1)[a] does not intend to allow for the expansion of sports lotteries into head-to-head betting.")).

The State of Delaware tested the limits of this exemption in 2009 when it attempted to expand its sports lottery (which had been limited to multi-game parlay bets on NFL teams) to include point-spread bets and "over/under" bets on major professional and college sporting events. In *Office of the Commissioner of Baseball v. Markell*, the Third Circuit held that Delaware's proposed lottery expansion violated PASPA, as the exemption provided under § 3704(a)(1) for preexisting sports wagering schemes only applied "to the extent" that such schemes were actually conducted between January 1, 1976, and August 31, 1990 (*Markell*, 579 F.3d at 304). The court explained that "whatever the breadth of the lottery authorized by Delaware state law in 1976, PASPA requires us to determine 'the extent'—or degree—to which such lottery *was conducted*" (*Markell*, 579 F.3d at 309) (italics in original)). The court found that the only form of sports wagering "conducted" by Delaware between 1976 and 1990 involved multi-game parlay bets on NFL teams. Accordingly, the court held that Delaware was barred from offering single-game sports betting since it had not conducted such wagering during the relevant statutory time frame. As a result of the *Markell* decision, Delaware's version of legal sports betting remains limited to multi-game parlays involving only NFL teams.

The second relevant "grandfathering" exemption—§ 3704(a)(2)—provides that the prohibition does not apply to a lottery, sweepstakes, or other betting, gambling, or wagering scheme in operation in a state or other governmental entity where both (A) such scheme was authorized by a statute in effect as of October 2, 1991, and (B) such scheme actually was conducted in that state or other governmental entity during the period beginning September 1, 1989, and ending October 2, 1991, pursuant to the law of that state or other governmental entity. This "grandfathering" provision was intended to release Nevada from PASPA's clutches (*Christie*, 730 F.3d at 216). Under subparagraph (2), single-game wagering on sporting events was permitted to continue in Nevada because it was actually conducted in Nevada between September 1, 1989, and August 31, 1990 pursuant to Nevada state law (Senate Report 102-248, 1991, at 10). PASPA's legislative history reveals that the reason for the unique treatment of Nevada was to protect Nevada's economy, although political considerations were also a factor.[6] The Senate Judiciary Committee explained that it had no "desire to threaten the economy of Nevada, which over many decades has come to depend on legalized private gambling, including sports gambling, as an essential industry, or to prohibit lawful sports gambling schemes in other States that were in operation when the legislation was introduced." (Senate Report 102-248, 1991, at 3559).

A key distinction between the two "grandfathering" provisions is that § 3704(a)(2) does not "freeze in time" the sports betting schemes that qualify for that exemption. This is in marked contrast to the 3704(a)(1) exemption, which, by virtue of the "*to the extent*" limiting language, prevents qualifying states from expanding their sports betting offerings beyond those actually conducted between 1976 and 1990. This is underscored by the Senate Report's express acknowledgement that Nevada will be able to expand its sports betting options under the 3704(a)(2) exemption. The Senate Report clarifies that "[p]aragraph (2) is not intended to prevent Nevada from expanding its sports betting schemes into other sports so long as it was authorized by state law prior to the enactment of [PASPA]" (Senate Report 102-248, 1991, at 3561). It also makes clear that "sports gambling covered by paragraph (2) can be conducted in any part of the state in any facility in that state, whether such facility is currently in existence" (Senate Report 102-248, 1991, at 3561). This explains why Nevada has been able to more than double the number of licensed sports books in the state since the 1992 enactment of PASPA.

A third exemption—§ 3704(a)(3)—provided states that had previously legalized casino gambling (such as New Jersey) with a "one-year window" to authorize sports betting conducted exclusively in casinos. That exemption was only available, however, if casino gambling had been in operation in a State for the ten-year period preceding PASPA's enactment "pursuant to a comprehensive system of State regulation authorized by that State's constitution" and been confined to a single municipality (28 U.S.C. § 3704(a)(3)). New Jersey was the only state that could satisfy these conditions by virtue of its "Atlantic City-only" casinos. However, New Jersey failed to pass sports betting legislation by the January 1, 1994, deadline. As a result, New Jersey remains subject to PASPA's prohibition against state-sponsored sports betting.

PASPA's fourth and final exception excludes parimutuel animal racing (e.g., horse racing and dog racing) and jai-alai games from its prohibitions (28 U.S.C. § 3704(a)(4)).

4. Legal Challenges to PASPA

Until the recent litigation arising out of New Jersey's efforts to legalize sports wagering, there had been very little PASPA case law on the books (aside from the *Markell* decision, which addressed only the scope of the § 3704(a)(1) exemption). But the seeds of PASPA's discontent may have been sewn some twenty years earlier during the public hearings preceding the enactment of PASPA. Two vocal opponents emerged during the lawmaking process: (1) the U.S. Department of Justice (the DOJ), the current defender of PASPA; and (2) Senator Chuck Grassley (R-Ia.). In a September 24, 1991, letter to the Chairman of the Senate Judiciary Committee, the DOJ expressed its concern that PASPA raised "federalism issues," noting that "determinations of how to raise revenues have typically been left to the states" (Rodenberg & Holden, 2017, at p. 4 n. 18). The DOJ also found it "particularly troubling" that PASPA "would permit enforcement of its provisions by sports leagues" (Rodenberg & Holden, 2017, at p. 4 n. 18). For these reasons, the DOJ opposed the enactment of PASPA.

By far, the most outspoken opponent of PASPA was Senator Grassley, who characterized the bill as a "substantial intrusion into States' rights [that] would restrict the fundamental right of states to raise revenue to fund critical State programs" (Senate Report 102-248, 1991, at 3562). Calling the proposed legislation a "dangerous precedent," Senator Grassley cautioned that it would empower the federal government to interfere with state sovereignty "under the guise of 'interstate commerce,' at the behest of any special interest" (Senate Report 102-248, 1991, at 3562). He vehemently disagreed with the Senate majority's conclusion that PASPA was "consistent with" existing federal law, observing that: (1) "[t]he Federal Government has never sought to regulate purely intrastate activities," (2) PASPA would only prohibit "purely intrastate activities," and (3) "[t]he

Federal Government also has never authorized private parties to enforce such restrictions against the States" (Senate Report 102-248, 1991, at 3563). Indeed, PASPA appears to be the only federal law that gives private parties (e.g., the sports leagues) the right to obtain an injunction against state governments, a unique feature that may leave it vulnerable to a constitutional challenge (Rodenberg, 2016). Senator Grassley also opposed PASPA on the basis that it would "blatantly discriminate between the States" by granting Nevada, Oregon, and Montana "a Federal monopoly on lawful sports wagering to the exclusion of the other 47 states" (Senate Report 102-248, 1991, at 3562). He criticized the statute's grandfathering exemptions as lacking a "rational basis," asserting that "[i]f the professional sports leagues were truly concerned about the risk of 'fixed' games [and] the integrity of professional sports, . . . they would be seeking to prohibit [the] $1.8 billion head-to-head sports wagering industry in Nevada" (Senate Report 102-248, 1991, at 3564).

Although PASPA ultimately sailed through Congress and was signed into law by President George H.W. Bush on October 28, 1992, with an effective date of January 1, 1993, the "federalism" concerns raised by the Department of Justice and Senator Grassley foreshadowed the future legal battles which lay head for PASPA.

4.1. The New Jersey Sports Betting Litigation (Round 1)

The widespread economic downturn stemming from the 2008 financial crisis spurred state lawmakers to consider creative solutions for reducing budgetary shortfalls. As a result, states began to seriously consider the legalization of sports wagering as a way to generate new revenues. New Jersey has been at the forefront of such efforts. In 2010, the New Jersey Legislature held public hearings during which it heard testimony that regulated sports wagering would (1) create new jobs in New Jersey and generate over $600 million in additional gaming revenues for New Jersey's struggling casinos and racetracks, (2) attract millions of dollars of additional revenue from increased tourism, and (3) produce over $60 million annually in direct tax revenues for the state. (Public Hearing Before Senate Economic Growth Committee on Senate Concurrent Resolution 49, 2010 Leg. at 6 (N.J. Apr. 5, 2010)). During these hearings, New Jersey legislators also expressed a desire "to stanch the sports-wagering black market flourishing within [the State's] borders" (*Christie I*, 730 F.3d at 217).

In 2011, New Jersey voters approved, by a nearly 2-to-1 margin, an amendment to the state's constitution to permit the New Jersey Legislature to authorize sports wagering. Following that lead, the New Jersey Legislature enacted the "Sports Wagering Law" (N.J. Stat. Ann. § 5:12A-1), which permitted New Jersey regulators to license sports wagering in casinos and racetracks. On January 17, 2012, New Jersey Governor Chris Christie signed the legislation into law, and, shortly thereafter, the New Jersey Division of Gaming Enforcement promulgated regulations setting forth the procedures by which the State's licensed casinos and racetracks could obtain licenses to conduct sports wagering.

In August 2012, before New Jersey issued any licenses for sports wagering, the four major U.S. professional sports leagues and the NCAA commenced a lawsuit against New Jersey in the U.S. District Court for the District of New Jersey, seeking to prevent the state from implementing its new sports wagering law and regulations. (This case and its ensuing appeal are commonly referred to as "*Christie I*"). The sports leagues contended that, as a matter of law, New Jersey's efforts to authorize and license sports gambling schemes violated PASPA' s express prohibitions. In response, New Jersey challenged the constitutionality of PASPA, arguing that it violates principles of federalism, and, in particular, the "anti-commandeering" doctrine, which forbids the federal government from commanding the states to implement federal laws or policies that would interfere with state sovereignty. In this vein, New Jersey argued that PASPA unconstitutionally commandeers the states in two ways: (1) through its "negative command" prohibiting a state from enacting any law authorizing or licensing sports betting, and (2) through its implicit "affirmative command" requiring a state to maintain existing (but unwanted) sports betting prohibitions under state law. In response, the sports leagues argued that PASPA does not violate the anti-commandeering doctrine because it does not compel the states to do *anything* at all, but rather simply prohibits them from licensing or authorizing sports wagering.

On February 28, 2013, the district court upheld PASPA's constitutionality, granted summary judgment to the sports leagues and enjoined New Jersey from moving forward with its sports wagering regime (*Christie I*, 926 F. Supp. 551). The district court rejected New Jersey's commandeering challenge because, in its view, PASPA "neither *compels* nor *commandeers* New Jersey to take any action" (*Christie I*, 926 F. Supp. at 561 (italics in original)). According to the district court, the anti-commandeering doctrine applies only when the federal government "force[s] States to engage in *affirmative* activity" (*Christie I*, 926 F. Supp. at 570 (italics in original)). By contrast, the district court explained, Congress' "power to *restrict*, rather than *compel*, the actions of States in preempted spheres was, and remains, a settled issue" (*Christie I*, 926 F. Supp. 571 (italics in original)). "The difference between an affirmative command and a prohibition," the district court wrote, "is not merely academic or insubstantial" (*Christie I*, 926 F. Supp. 562). Rather, the court continued, "it is a long held understanding" that "an otherwise permissible congressional action" does not violate the Tenth Amendment when "it excludes a State from enacting legislation in an area in which Congress has made its will clear" (*Christie I*, 926 F. Supp. at 562). In analyzing PASPA through this lens, the district court observed that Congress sought only "to limit the geographic localities in which sports betting is lawful. It does no more or less" (*Christie I*, 926 F. Supp. at 562). Because "[n] o action on the part of the States is *required* in order for PASPA to achieve its ends," the district court concluded that PASPA does not violate the anti-commandeering doctrine (*Christie I*, 926 F. Supp. at 572).

On September 17, 2013, a divided panel of the U.S. Court of Appeals for the Third Circuit affirmed the ruling of the district court (*Christie I*, 730 F.3d 208). The majority observed that "it is hard to see how a Congress can 'commandeer' a state, or how it can be found to regulate how a state regulates, if it does not require it to do *anything at all*" (*Christie I*, 730 F.3d at 231 (emphasis added)). The majority observed that the Supreme

Court has invalidated federal laws on anti-commandeering grounds on only two occasions: in *New York v. United States*, the Supreme Court struck down a "take-title" provision whereby states were required to take title to radioactive waste by a specific date, at the waste generator's request, if they did not adopt a federal program. As the *Christie I* majority noted, this provision "compel[led] the states to either enact a regulatory program, or expend resources in taking title to the waste" (*New York v. United States*, 505 U.S. at 176). Similarly, in *Printz v. United States*, the Supreme Court struck down a federal law requiring state law enforcement officials to conduct background checks of prospective handgun purchasers and perform related tasks. The *Printz* Court explained that Congress "may neither issue directives requiring the States to address particular problems, nor command the States' officers . . . to administer or enforce a federal regulatory program" (*Printz*, 521 U.S. at 935). By contrast, the *Christie I* majority observed, "statutes prohibiting the states from taking certain actions have never been struck down even if they require the expenditure of some time and effort or the modification or invalidation of contrary state laws" (*Christie I*, 730 F.3d at 231).

Acknowledging this "affirmative/negative command distinction," New Jersey made a critical adjustment to its anti-commandeering argument on appeal: instead of arguing that the constitutional violation stemmed from PASPA's "negative command" forbidding a State from licensing or authorizing sports betting, New Jersey asserted that PASPA violates anti-commandeering principles by requiring states to "affirmatively keep" a prohibition against sports wagering on their books, lest they be found to have "authorized" sports gambling by law by "repealing" the prohibition (*Christie I*, 730 F.3d at 232) (emphasis added). The majority agreed that "the affirmative act requirement, if not properly applied, may permit Congress to 'accomplish exactly what the commandeering doctrine prohibits' by stopping states from 'repealing an existing law' " (*Christie I*, 730 F.3d at 232 (quoting *Conant v. Walters*, 309 F.3d 629, 646 (9th Cir. 2002) (Kozinski, J., concurring)). The majority, however, discounted these concerns because it "d[id] not read PASPA to prohibit New Jersey from repealing its own ban on sports wagering" (*Christie I*, 730 F.3d at 232). According to the majority, PASPA was constitutional because "[n]othing in [PASPA's] words *requires* that the states leave any law in place. All that is prohibited is the issuance of gambling 'license[s]' or the affirmative 'authoriz[ation] *by law*' of gambling schemes" (*Christie I*, 730 F.3d at 232).

The majority rejected New Jersey's argument that "repealing" a statute barring sports betting would be equivalent to "authorizing" the activity (which would be barred by PASPA). The majority found that argument "problematic in numerous respects" (*Christie I*, 730 F.3d at 232). "Most basically," the majority wrote, "it ignores that PASPA speaks only of 'authorizing by *law*' a sports gambling scheme," adding that "[w]e do not see how having *no law* in place governing sports wagering is the same as authorizing it by law" (*Christie I*, 730 F.3d at 232 (emphasis in original)). "Second," the majority reasoned, such an argument "ignores that, in reality, the lack of an affirmative prohibition of an activity does not mean that it is *affirmatively* authorized by law" (*Christie I*, 730 F.3d at 232 (emphasis in original)). The majority explained that it would be a "false equivalence" to consider a "repeal" to be the same as an "authoriz[ation] by law" because, following a repeal of prohibitions, "[t]he right to do that which is not prohibited derives not from the authority of the state but from the inherent rights of the people" (*Christie I*, 730 F.3d at 232–233). "In short," the majority concluded, New Jersey's attempt to read into PASPA a requirement that the states must "affirmatively keep a ban on sports gambling on their books" rests on a "false equivalence" between "repeal" and "authorized" and reads the term "by law" out of the federal statute, "ignoring the fundamental canon that, as between two statutory constructions, we ought to prefer one that does not raise a series of constitutional problems" (*Christie I*, 730 F.3d at 233).

But to save PASPA from any constitutional infirmity, the majority gave PASPA a "savings interpretation" that would afford states considerable leeway in crafting their own policies on sports betting, including by "repealing" any existing laws. The majority explained that PASPA's "straightforward prohibition" on state-sponsored sports betting can be recast as providing states with "two choices" that "leave much room for states to make their own policy" (*Christie I*, 730 F.3d at 233). "On the one hand," the majority declared, "a state may repeal its sports wagering ban, a move that will result in the expenditure of no resources or effort by any state official" (*Christie I*, 730 F.3d at 233). "On the other hand," the majority continued, "a state may choose to keep a complete ban on sports wagering, but it is up to each state to decide how much of a law enforcement priority it wants to make of sports gambling, or what the *exact contours* of the prohibition will be" (*Christie I*, 730 F.3d at 233 (emphasis added)). The majority acknowledged that "these are not easy choices," noting that Congress "may have suspected that most states would choose to keep an actual prohibition on sports gambling on the books, rather than rather than permit the activity to go unregulated" (*Christie I*, 730 F.3d at 233). "But the fact that Congress gave the states a hard or tempting choice does not mean that they were given no choice at all, or that the choices are otherwise unconstitutional," the majority reasoned (*Christie I*, 730 F.3d at 233).

The New Jersey parties then appealed to the U.S. Supreme Court. In the federal government's response to New Jersey's petition for writ of certiorari (which was ultimately denied), the U.S. Solicitor General represented that "PASPA does not even obligate New Jersey to leave in place state-law prohibitions against sports gambling that it had chosen to adopt prior to PASPA's enactment. To the contrary, New Jersey is free to repeal those prohibitions *in whole or in part*" (Brief of the United States in Opposition to Petition for Writ of Certiorari, at p. 11 (italics added)). This language echoed earlier statements made by the U.S. Attorney at the Third Circuit oral argument, when he argued that PASPA does not commandeer New Jersey's sovereign functions because, under PASPA, "[i]t is up to the State of New Jersey to determine for itself *the extent* to which it will or will not enforce" its sports betting laws. (Brennan, 2017a) (emphasis in original).

4.2. The New Jersey Sports Betting Litigation (Round 2)

Relying upon the Third Circuit's majority opinion—which left it to a State to "decide how much of a law enforcement priority it wants to make of sports gambling, or what the *exact contours* of the prohibition will be"—and taking the Solicitor General at his word that a State may repeal its sports wagering ban "in part," New Jersey enacted a partial repeal law on October 17, 2014 (the "2014 Law"). The 2014 Law partially repealed all state laws and regulations prohibiting sports wagering, but only in certain circumstances. Specifically, the 2014 Law repealed provisions of New Jersey law governing criminal penalties for gambling, civil penalties for gambling, and other provisions governing wagering at casinos and racetracks, as well as "any rules and regulations that may require or authorize any State agency to license, authorize, permit, or otherwise take action to allow any person" to engage in sports wagering. The 2014 Law, however, only repealed these laws "to the extent they apply or may be construed to apply" to sports wagering at consenting casinos, racetracks, and former racetracks sites (e.g., any racetracks where parimutuel wagering had taken place within the preceding fifteen years). In other words, the partial repeal only affected three classes: casinos, racetracks, and former racetracks. In all other respects, New Jersey's ban on sports wagering remained intact throughout the state.

But the sports leagues viewed this as a circumvention of PASPA and the Third Circuit's prior decision in *Christie I*. On October 20, 2014, the leagues sued New Jersey once again, arguing that the 2014 Law contravenes PASPA because it is tantamount to an "authorization" of sports betting, which is prohibited by PASPA. (This case and its ensuing appeal are commonly referred to as "*Christie II*"). On November 21, 2014, the district court granted summary judgment in favor of the sports leagues and issued a permanent injunction barring New Jersey from "giving operation or effect" to the 2014 Law (*Christie II*). The district court interpreted *Christie I* as holding that PASPA provides states with a binary choice: "a state may either maintain its prohibition on sports betting or may completely repeal its prohibition" (*Christie II*, 61 F. Supp. at 501). "[A]nything outside of these 'two choices,'" the district court added, "would leave states *too much room* to circumvent the ultimate intent of Congress" (*Christie II*, 61 F. Supp. at 504 (emphasis added)). Viewed through this lens, the district court concluded that the 2014 Law was an "authorization" of sports betting in violation of PASPA because it was a *partial* repeal (not a complete repeal), and, further, sought to achieve the same end as the law invalidated in *Christie I*—allowing sports betting in New Jersey's casinos and racetracks (*Christie II*, 61 F. Supp. at 505). The "primary effect" of the 2014 Law, the district court reasoned, "necessarily results in sports wagering with the state's imprimatur, which goes against the very goal of PASPA—to ban sports wagering pursuant to a state scheme" (*Christie II*, 61 F. Supp. at 505) The district court also expressed concern that limiting the repeal to state-licensed casinos and racetracks (the intended beneficiaries of New Jersey's prior unsuccessful attempt to legalize sports betting) would allow New Jersey to accomplish *indirectly* what it cannot do *directly* and lead to other states emulating New Jersey's "roadmap around PASPA," thereby undermining the federal law (*Christie II*, 61 F. Supp. at 492, 504–507).

New Jersey appealed the district court's decision to the Third Circuit, which affirmed the district court's decision by a 2-1 vote. The Third Circuit's opinion, however, was vacated after New Jersey successfully petitioned for a rehearing *en banc* before the full court. The grant of rehearing *en banc*, a rarely invoked process (on average, only one or two cases per year out of hundreds are reheard *en banc* by the Third Circuit) raised New Jersey's hopes for an appellate victory. On rehearing, the Third Circuit considered two issues: (1) whether New Jersey's partial repeal constituted an "authorization" of sports betting in violation of PASPA; and (2) whether PASPA was unconstitutional. Although the *Christie I* panel had already determined that PASPA was constitutionally valid, an *en banc* panel (consisting of all of the court's active judges plus the two senior judges who sat on the original *Christie I* panel) was free to revisit that issue. Indeed, as several of the judges remarked at the *en banc* oral argument, the issue of PASPA's constitutionality was "back in play."

But the result was the same, with the Third Circuit *en banc* panel affirming the district court's decision by a 9-3 vote (*Christie II*). Describing the 2014 Law as an attempt to "skirt" PASPA, the majority concluded that the 2014 Law "authorizes" sports gambling in violation of the federal law. The majority gave three separate reasons for its holding. First, it observed that *without* the 2014 Law, New Jersey's myriad prohibitions against sports betting would apply to casinos and racetracks; thus, the 2014 Law "provides the authorization for conduct that is otherwise clearly and completely legally prohibited" (*Christie II*, 832 F.3d at 396). Second, the majority reasoned that the 2014 Law "authorizes" sports gambling by "selectively dictating" *where* sports gambling may occur (e.g., at casinos and racetracks), *who* may place bets in such gambling (e.g., persons twenty-one and over), and *which* athletic contests are permissible subjects for such gambling (e.g., all professional and collegiate sporting events other than games involving New Jersey college teams or collegiate competitions occurring in New Jersey) (*Christie II*, 832 F.3d at 396). According to the majority, that "selectiveness" constitutes "specific permission and empowerment." (*Christie II*, 832 F.3d at 396, 401 ("To be clear, a state's decision to selectively remove a prohibition on sports wagering in a manner that permissively channels wagering activity to particular locations or operators is, in essence, 'authorization' under PASPA")). Third, the majority pointed to New Jersey's failure to take advantage of the "one-year" opt-out in §3704(a)(3) of PASPA, which was specifically tailored to New Jersey (the only state that met the criteria for the exception). The majority reasoned that the existence of this statutory exception evinced Congress' belief that sports gambling at New Jersey's casinos and racetracks would violate PASPA, otherwise "it would not have needed to insert the New Jersey exception" (*Christie II*, 832 F.3d at 397). In other words, the majority explained, "if sports gambling in New Jersey's casinos does not violate PASPA, then PASPA's one-year exception for New Jersey would have been superfluous . . . [and] [w]e will not read statutory provisions to be surplusage" (*Christie II*, 832 F.3d at 397).

The majority rejected New Jersey's argument—based on the "false equivalence" language in the *Christie I* opinion—that a "repeal" removing sports betting prohibitions is not an "affirmative authorization." Recall that in *Christie I*, the majority explained that states had two choices under PASPA: maintaining sports betting prohibitions or *repealing* them. The *Christie II* majority receded from that earlier statement, declaring that "[t]o the extent that in *Christie I* we took the position that a repeal cannot constitute an authorization, we now reject that reasoning" (*Christie II*, 832 F.3dat 396–397). The majority characterized its discussion in *Christie I* of states having "two choices" as mere "dicta" (meaning not essential to the court's decision). Furthermore, the majority added, any discussion of the "partial versus total repeal" issue in *Christie I* is "similarly unnecessary to determining the 2014 Law's legality because the question presented here is straightforward—i.e., what does the law *do*—and does not turn on the way in which the state has enacted its directive" (*Christie II*, 832 F.3d at 397). As the majority explained, "the presence of the word 'repeal' does not prevent us from examining what the provision actually does, and the Legislature's use of the term does not change that the 2014 Law selectively grants permission to certain entities to engage in sports gambling" (*Christie II*, 832 F.3d at 397). The majority observed that "[w]hile artfully couched in terms of a repealer, the 2014 Law essentially provides that, notwithstanding any other prohibition by law, casinos and racetracks shall hereafter be permitted to have sports gambling" (*Christie II*, 832 F.3d at 397). "That," the majority concluded, "is an authorization" (*Christie II*, 832 F.3d at 397).

Turning next to the constitutional issue, the majority reiterated that PASPA does not violate anti-commandeering principles. However, it refined its commandeering analysis from *Christie I* to address New Jersey's contention that PASPA (as interpreted by the district court) leaves the states "without options" beyond either a *complete repeal* or a *complete ban* on sports wagering, and, thus, unconstitutionally commandeers the authority of the states. Declaring that such an argument "sweeps too broadly," the majority clarified that "PASPA does not command states to take affirmative actions, and it does not present a coercive binary choice" (*Christie II*, 832 F.3dat 401). To interpret PASPA as confining states to an "all-or-nothing" choice (e.g., a complete repeal or no repeal at all) "is to read something into the statute that simply is not there" (*Christie II*, 832 F.3d at 402). But the majority emphasized that its determination that New Jersey's "selective" repeal (limited to casinos and racetracks) amounted to an "authorization" under PASPA "does not mean that states are not afforded sufficient room under PASPA to craft their own policies" (*Christie II*, 832 F.3d at 401). Indeed, the majority allowed that other options "may pass muster" under PASPA, citing as one example a partial repeal of a sports wagering ban to allow *de minimis* wagers between friends and family (*Christie II*, 832 F.3d at 401). However, it refused to pinpoint the line at which a partial repeal becomes an "authorization" (and thereby prohibited by PASPA), noting that "the issue of the extent to which a given repeal would constitute an authorization, in a vacuum, is not before us," and wondering whether such a line could even be drawn (*Christie II*, 832 F.3d at 401). Instead, the majority stated, "[it] is sufficient to conclude that the 2014 Law overstepped it" (*Christie II*, 832 F.3d at 402).

There were two dissenting opinions in *Christie II*. The first dissent was written by Judge Julio Fuentes (the author of the majority opinion in *Christie I*), who was joined by the Third Circuit's newest member, R. Thomas Restrepo. Judge Fuentes disagreed with the majority's view that a partial repeal of prohibitions is tantamount to an "authorization." He maintained that Congress's insertion of the words "by law" after "authorize"—a qualifier conspicuously absent from PASPA's five other prohibited acts (e.g., "sponsor," "operate," "advertise," "promote," and "license")—infused that restriction with "special meaning" such that a state's "authorization by law" of sports betting "cannot merely be inferred" from a repeal of sports betting prohibitions, "but rather requires a *specific legislative enactment* that *affirmatively allows* the people of the state to bet on sports" (*Christie II*, 832 F.3d at 403 (emphasis added)). He reasoned that "[a]ny other interpretation would be reading the phrase 'by law' out of the statute" (*Christie II*, 832 F.3d at 403). Judge Fuentes insisted that this was "exactly" the underpinning of *Christie I*—"that all PASPA prohibits is "the affirmative 'authoriz[ation] by law' of gambling schemes" (*Christie II*, 832 F.3d at 403). Quoting from his majority opinion in *Christie I*, Judge Fuentes reasoned that "nothing prevented New Jersey from repealing its sports betting prohibitions, since, 'in reality, the lack of an affirmative prohibition of an activity does not mean it is *affirmatively* authorized by law" (*Christie II*, 832 F.3d at 403 (italics in original)).

To illustrate what he believed was the flaw in the majority's approach, Judge Fuentes posed a hypothetical in which the state completely repealed its sports betting prohibitions and then added back—over time—"later enacted limited restrictions regarding age requirements and places where wagering could occur" (*Christie II*, 832 F.3d at 405). "Surely," he reasoned, "no conceivable reading of PASPA would preclude a state from *restricting* sports wagering in this scenario. Yet the 2014 Repeal comes to the same result" and is deemed unlawful (*Christie II*, 832 F.3d at 405 (emphasis in original)). Judge Fuentes also rejected the majority's rationale for equating a partial repeal with an "authorization by law," pointedly stating that the majority "fails to illustrate how the 2014 Repeal results in sports wagering *pursuant to state law* when there is effectively no law in place as to several locations, no scheme created, and no state involvement" (*Christie II*, 832 F.3d at 405 (emphasis in original)). In the end, Judge Fuentes concluded that he "do[es] not see how a partial repeal of prohibitions is tantamount to authorizing by law a sports wagering scheme in violation of PASPA" (*Christie II*, 832 F.3d at 406).

In a separate dissent, Judge Thomas Vanaskie criticized as "untenable" the majority's "shifting line approach" to a state's exercise of its sovereign authority (*Christie II*, 832 F.3d at 407). Judge Vanaskie observed that after *Christie I*, a state like New Jersey "*at least* [had] the choice" of either: (1) "repealing, in whole or *in part*, existing bans on gambling on sporting events," or (2) "keep[ing] a complete ban on sports gambling" (*Christie II*, 832 F.3d at 408, 411). Such a choice, he explained, was essential to upholding PASPA's constitutionality in *Christie I* (*Christie II*, 832 F.3d at 408). By contrast, he wrote, the majority's decision in *Christie II* "does not leave a state 'much room' at all" (*Christie II*, 832 F.3d at 408). Following *Christie II*, states "must maintain an anti-sports wagering scheme" by "leav[ing] gambling prohibitions on the books to regulate their citizens" (*Christie II*, 832 F.3d at 408, 411). Judge Vanaskie opined that this essentially "leaves the States with no choice," adding that "[t]he anti-commandeering doctrine, essential to protect State sovereignty, prohibits Congress from compelling States to prohibit such private activity" (*Christie II*, 832 F.3d at 411). Judge Vanaskie was unpersuaded by the majority's assertion that some partial repeal options "may pass muster" (such as the example involving small wagers between friends and family), noting that the majority "does not explain why all partial repeals are not created equal or explain what distinguishes the 2014 Law from those partial repeals that pass muster" (*Christie II*, 832 F.3d at 407). As Judge Vanaskie explained, "[t]he bedrock principle of federalism that Congress may not compel the States to require or prohibit certain activities cannot be evaded by the false assertion that PASPA affords the States some undefined options when it comes to sports wagering" (*Christie II*, 832 F.3d at 407). Contending that the majority opinion "excised" the distinction between a "repeal" and an "authorization," Judge Vanaskie declared that it is "clear" that no repeal of any kind will evade PASPA's command that no State "shall . . . authorize by law sports gambling" (*Christie II*, 832 F.3d at 409). Such commands, Judge Vanaskie concluded, "are fundamentally incompatible with our constitutional system of dual sovereignty" (*Christie II*, 832 F.3d at 409).

5. Supreme Court Review of PASPA May Alter Landscape

In October 2016, the New Jersey parties petitioned the United States Supreme Court to review the Third Circuit's decision in *Christie II*. In their petitions, the New Jersey parties emphasized the Tenth Amendment anti-commandeering principle, framing the question presented as follows: "Does a federal statute that prohibits adjustment or repeal of state-law prohibitions on private conduct impermissibly commandeer the regulatory power of States in contravention of *New York v. United States*, 505 U.S. 144 (1992), and *Printz v. United States*, 521 U.S. 898 (1997)"? As highlighted by the New Jersey petitions (and buttressed by the various *amicus curiae* briefs), the Third Circuit's new interpretation of PASPA presents a much greater threat to state sovereignty than the *Christie I* decision because it can be seen as preventing a state from *repealing* its own laws (with myriad examples highlighted in the State's petitions), and, further, leaves the state without any meaningful (or identifiable) choices. Remember that to "save" PASPA from a commandeering defect, the *Christie I* majority emphasized that states were afforded a "choice" under PASPA: to maintain their state law prohibitions against sports betting or to *repeal* them. The *Christie II* decision all but eviscerates this choice.

Despite the important federalism issues presented in *Christie II*, New Jersey faced an uphill battle in persuading the Supreme Court to accept the case. For one thing, the Supreme Court generally grants less than 2% of all petitions seeking certiorari review. New Jersey's chances for Supreme Court review were also hampered by the absence of any "circuit split" on the issue of PASPA's constitutionality. Most cases accepted for review by the Supreme Court involve conflicting decisions among the lower federal courts on a particular legal issue. Since the *Christie* cases are the only federal court decisions addressing the constitutionality of PASPA, the all-important "circuit split" is lacking here. Additionally, the United States Solicitor General filed an *amicus curiae* brief in May 2017 recommending that the Supreme Court not grant certiorari review in the

Christie II case. The Solicitor General's recommendation carries significant weight with the Supreme Court, and, historically, is followed around 80 percent of the time. (Thompson and Wachtell, 2009, p. 276). The Solicitor General's adverse recommendation thus made it far less likely—at least statistically—that that the Supreme Court would review the *Christie II* case on the merits.

Despite these long odds, the Supreme Court granted certiorari review on June 27, 2017, listing *Christie II* as one of only 26 cases that would be reviewed by the Court during its 2017 Term. While this development surprised many observers, I have consistently maintained that *Christie II* was more "cert-worthy" than *Christie I*. (Wallach, 2017). In the *Christie I* case, New Jersey's anti-commandeering argument was directed to PASPA's "negative command" forbidding states from licensing or authorizing sports wagering. That was always an uphill battle given the Supreme Court precedent limiting the application of the anti-commandeering doctrine to cases where the federal government requires states to engage in some type of "affirmative activity," such as taking title to radioactive waste (as in the *New York* case) or performing background checks on prospective handgun purchasers (as in the *Printz* case). In *Christie II*, however, New Jersey's commandeering argument addresses the flip-side of PASPA: its "affirmative requirement" compelling states to prohibit sports wagering (which would prevent them from "repealing" their sports betting laws—the effect of *Christie II*). This view of PASPA fits more neatly into the Supreme Court's commandeering jurisprudence, and, as such, New Jersey's prospects for Supreme Court review were arguably enhanced.

But it is the "equal sovereignty" argument, addressed in the first lawsuit between New Jersey and the professional sports leagues (the "Christie I" case) and also raised in the *Christie II* petitions, which ultimately may prove to be the perfect vehicle for the Supreme Court. New Jersey's equal sovereignty argument is grounded upon the notion that PASPA does not treat all states equally; instead, it affords uniquely favorable treatment to Nevada and three other states (Delaware, Montana and Oregon) by allowing those four "grandfathered" states to offer sports betting to varying degrees, while banning the other 46 states (including New Jersey) from offering any form of sports gambling.

In *Christie I*, the Third Circuit held that the principle of equal sovereignty does not apply to legislation (such as PASPA) enacted pursuant to the Commerce Clause of the U.S. Constitution. The Third Circuit distinguished *Shelby County v. Holder*, 133 U.S. 2612 (2013), a voting rights act case that was decided on the basis of equal sovereignty, on the ground that PASPA involves the regulation of commerce, as opposed to elections. But nothing in *Shelby County* or any of the Supreme Court's prior decisions appears to suggest that the principle of equal sovereignty is limited to voting rights cases.

While the Supreme Court declined to review *Christie I*, despite the apparent inconsistency with *Shelby County*, it may wish to address the equal sovereignty principle this time around. If that were to occur, PASPA might not survive scrutiny under the *Shelby County* test, which looks to whether the statute's disparate geographic coverage is "sufficiently related to the problem that it targets." This is where PASPA is especially vulnerable, as the reason for the disparate treatment of Nevada, Oregon, Montana and Delaware (the four "grandfathered" states) was to protect the "strong reliance interests" of those states that had legalized sports gaming prior to the enactment of PASPA. But such carve-outs do not appear to be "sufficiently related" to the targeted goals of PASPA, which are to stop the spread of legal sports betting and to protect the integrity of professional and amateur sports.

With the *Christie II* case transitioning from the 'cert-stage' to the 'merits-stage," New Jersey's sports betting prospects have improved dramatically. During the 2016 Term, the Supreme Court reversed federal court of appeals decisions at a stunning 83% rate. (Brennan, 2017b). While this may be a relatively small sample size, the Supreme Court's reversal rate over the past five Terms still exceeds 70%, suggesting that New Jersey should be viewed as a prohibitive favorite to prevail before the High Court. (Brennan, 2017b). This belief is also bolstered by the fact that the Supreme Court granted certiorari review in a case where there was no "circuit split" and departed from the adverse recommendation of the United States Solicitor General. These factors strongly suggest that the Supreme Court may be inclined to reverse *Christie II* and allow New Jersey (and, quite possibly, other states) to offer sports betting as soon as 2018.

6. Beyond *Christie II*: Several Options Remain on the Table

But even if the Supreme Court affirms the Third Circuit's decision in *Christie II*, that would not necessarily be the end of the line for legal sports betting in the Garden State—or elsewhere. There are several legislative avenues that States could still pursue, subject, of course, to any limitations or restrictions imposed by the Supreme Court's eventual decision in *Christie II*. One potential option for New Jersey would be to enact another partial repeal law, though perhaps one not nearly as targeted or selective as the 2014 Law (which decriminalized sports gambling only for casinos, racetracks, and former racetrack sites). While the *Christie II* decision did not provide specific examples of a partial repeal law that would "pass muster"—other than the commercially meaningless "friends and family" exception—it did allow that states had "sufficient room" under PASPA to "craft their own policies." The precise contours of this policymaking room for state lawmakers were not spelled out in *Christie II*, but, clearly, New Jersey would be permitted to partially repeal its state law prohibitions on sports gambling as long as it did not cross the line into an "authorization" of that activity (which would be prohibited by PASPA). So, what kind of partial repeal would "pass muster" with the Third Circuit? Perhaps a partial repeal based on geographic boundaries, such as a law repealing sports gambling prohibitions at any commercial establishment within Atlantic County (where all of New Jersey's casinos are located) and Monmouth County (the home to Monmouth Park Racetrack). While such a law could likewise be viewed as benefitting casinos and racetracks, it would not be nearly as selective or targeted as the 2014 Law: it would decriminalize sports betting within the *entirety* of both counties (and not just at state-licensed casinos and racetracks). A repealer like this would stand a far better chance of passing legal muster, though it would likely lead to more litigation with the sports leagues, which would invariably point to language in the *Christie II* opinion stating that a state law which "channels wagering activity to particular *locations* . . . is in essence, an 'authorization' under PASPA." (832 F.3d at 401). Ironically, this could the tee up the next round of litigation—anyone ready for a "*Christie III*"?—over the meaning, breadth and scope of the word "locations"—that is, whether it refers only to specific venues or encompasses any "geographic-based" repealer (such as a law decriminalizing the activity throughout an entire county or municipality).

A second option—and one completely within New Jersey's control to pull off—is the so-called nuclear option (e.g., a *complete* decriminalization of sports betting statewide). Under a complete repeal, any and all state law prohibitions against sports betting would be removed so that anybody (literally *anybody*) could offer, accept, or place sports wagers without criminal or civil repercussions (or any form of regulation). While this option may seem less than ideal for both political and practical reasons, it does offer one immediate advantage for New Jersey: it would likely withstand a legal challenge from the sports leagues. This is because the Third Circuit's opinion in *Christie II* makes clear that a complete repeal by New Jersey of its ban on sports betting would not violate PASPA. With necessity being the mother of invention, New Jersey may be left with little choice but to pursue this option if it wants to bring sports betting to the Garden State within the next three years, since any congressional repeal or amendment of PASPA seems unlikely before then. The "nuclear option" already seems to be gaining traction in New Jersey. In June 2017, New Jersey state senator Raymond J. Lesniak proposed a bill that would totally remove and repeal the State's prohibitions, permits, licenses, and authorizations concerning sports wagering (New Jersey Senate Bill No. 3375). While such a bill might face long odds in the New Jersey Senate and New Jersey Assembly due to its controversial premise (e.g., having *no* laws on the books prohibiting sports betting), the apparent motivation behind it is to push the sports leagues and Congress to address the issue of expanded sports betting sooner rather than later. The leagues' worst fears—widespread *unregulated* and *unmonitored* sports gambling (with no oversight)—would be realized if New Jersey were to enact such a law, especially with so many professional sports venues being within short driving distance of New Jersey. Thus, the thinking here is that a complete repeal, if enacted, could dramatically shorten the timeline for expanded legal sports betting by forcing the sports leagues and Congress to act more expeditiously in legalizing sports betting nationally. While this "nuclear" option may not be taken seriously by some observers—who see it as nothing more than a "bluff" or a publicity stunt—it is the *only* one of the three remaining options that would guarantee sports betting in New Jersey on day one.

Alternatively, New Jersey may wish to consider a variation of the so-called "nuclear option": completely repealing its state law prohibitions on sports betting and then, over time, adding restrictions to arrive at essentially the same place as the 2014 Law: legal sports betting only at casinos and racetracks. Judge Fuentes alluded to this very possibility in his *Christie II* dissent when he reasoned that "no conceivable reading of PASPA" would preclude a state from "repeal[ing] completely its sports betting prohibitions" and then adding "later enacted limited restrictions regarding age requirements and places where wagering could occur" (832 F.3d at 405). Such a two-tiered legislative approach—which could be spread out over a period of several years—could conceivably allow New Jersey to accomplish over time what it could not achieve in a single legislative act—that is, legal sports betting confined to specific locations of the state's choosing. Of course, such a maneuver would surely be challenged by the sports leagues, which would argue that New Jersey was trying to accomplish indirectly what it was prohibited by *Christie II* from doing directly. But this creative solution offers certain advantages: at the outset, it would guarantee legal sports betting in New Jersey, while potentially providing the state with an opportunity to make appropriate down-the-road adjustments to the law free from the clutches of PASPA. This could represent the pragmatic solution for those state lawmakers hesitant to completely decriminalize sports gambling.

Looking beyond New Jersey, other states may loom as potential courtroom challengers to PASPA, especially if the Supreme Court avoids the constitutional question in *Christie II*. (It is possible that the Court could simply decide the case on the narrow basis that New Jersey's partial repeal law does not constitute an impermissible "authorization" under PASPA). One influential New York lawmaker, J. Gary Pretlow, has already declared that New York will be "looking at challenging the feds" on PASPA and not to be "surprised if you see a state like New York putting through legislation on this very shortly" (Wallach, 2016). And others will surely follow. In recent years, lawmakers in California, Indiana, Michigan, Minnesota, Mississippi, South Carolina, and Texas have proposed legislation that would legalize sports betting. (Stutz, 2015). While such efforts were eventually abandoned, the possibility of other states challenging PASPA in the near future is not so farfetched. New Jersey's litigation efforts (even in a losing cause) have provided other states with a ready-made blueprint to follow in challenging PASPA on constitutional grounds. The arguments for challenging PASPA have already been extensively laid out by New Jersey in numerous court documents, and the dissents in the two Third Circuit court rulings provide further ammunition to a state considering a PASPA challenge in another federal judicial circuit. The same legal issues would be in play, just in a different court. And, perhaps, with a different result next time.

Ironically, the recent state measures to legalize daily fantasy sports may provide state challengers with a creative new argument for toppling PASPA. While PASPA is commonly understood to prohibit "state-authorized" betting or wagering schemes on the *outcomes* of professional and amateur sporting events, it also prohibits state-authorized betting or wagering schemes that are based "on one or more *performances* of athletes in such games." This language arguably encompasses state legislation authorizing daily fantasy sports contests, which are tied to the "performances" of athletes. A plausible argument can be made that the sports leagues are "selectively enforcing" PASPA by opposing state efforts to legalize traditional sports betting, as in the case of New Jersey, but taking no action against those states which have authorized fantasy sports contests (which presumably also violates PASPA). Such an argument could serve to undermine the leagues' assertion in future cases that they would be "irreparably harmed" by expanded legal sports betting when they have neither suffered nor asserted any such harm from other supposed violations of PASPA. Since the leagues would need to demonstrate irreparable harm in order to obtain a preliminary injunction (as that is one of the essential elements that must be proven), the ability of future state challengers to rebut that element through evidence of the leagues' selective enforcement of PASPA could be the key to avoiding a preliminary injunction in the early stages of a case. This would be a significant development, as it could enable a state challenger to offer sports betting throughout the pendency of a case, including any and all appeals, without having to wait for the final resolution of the lawsuit on the merits. While such an argument is not guaranteed to succeed, it provides another possible tool in a state's legal arsenal to topple PAPSA.

7. Is a Federal Legislation Solution Imminent?

New Jersey's efforts to legalize sports betting—while unsuccessful to date—have nonetheless served to catalyze the broader discussion nationally. As a result of the New Jersey litigation, an increasing number of prominent voices have called for Congress to amend or repeal PASPA. In September 2014, NBA Commissioner Adam Silver publicly acknowledged that legalized sports betting is "inevitable" (Levinson and Soshnick, 2014). He reasoned that cash-strapped states would look to pursue sports betting for economic reasons and that the NBA would be open to "participating" in a regulated environment (Levinson and Soshnick, 2014). Silver followed up this eye-opening statement with an even more stunning declaration two months later. In November 2014, Silver penned a *New York Times Op-ed* piece urging Congress to "adopt a federal framework that allows states to authorize betting on professional sports, subject to strict regulatory requirements and technological safeguards" (Silver, 2014, A27). Such requirements and safeguards, as envisioned by Silver, would include "mandatory monitoring and reporting of unusual betting-line movements; a licensing protocol to ensure betting operators are legitimate; minimum-age verification measures; geo-blocking technology to ensure betting is available only where it is legal; mechanisms to identify and exclude people with gambling problems; and education about responsible gaming."

In calling for a "comprehensive federal solution," Silver stressed that "[a]ny new approach must ensure the integrity of the game." Towards that end, Silver has advocated a European-style "integrity monitoring" system that would track the wagering on sporting events in order to detect unusual or suspicious betting patterns that would help identify fixed matches. In a 2015 interview, Silver noted that this type of tracking system is successfully employed in European betting markets. "Because they have all that data, they're able to monitor it," Silver said. "And if there's any irregular activity whatsoever, it's like tracking insider trading on the New York Stock Exchange. If there's a blip, if there's unusual activity, they know to investigate. So first the issue for us is if all this betting is going to go on anyway, *we* should be able to monitor it." Note Silver's use of the pronoun "we, inferring that the leagues would want to have "real-time" access to all of the wagering activity.

The other major U.S. sports leagues, however, remain divided on the subject. Rob Manfred, the Commissioner of Major League Baseball, appears to be the most outwardly supportive of Silver's proposal. In response to a question at the 2015 MIT Sports Analytics Conference, Manfred said that the federal regulation of sports betting "seemed like a pretty good idea" to him (Rodenberg, 2015). Manfred's more recent comments go even further. In early 2017, Manfred declared that Major League Baseball "is ready to join in what I think is going to be a dialogue about how sports gambling regulation *should be changed*." (Gouker, 2017) (emphasis added). His hockey counterpart, NHL Commissioner Gary Bettman, has been somewhat more circumspect about the league's position, insisting that hockey "doesn't lend itself to gambling in the same way that football and basketball do" (Wyshinski, 2016). However, the National Football League—the sport garnering the largest amount of illegal wagering activity in the U.S.—remains vehemently opposed to changing the federal law. At an NFL owners meeting in October 2016, Commissioner Roger Goodell reiterated that the league "remains very much opposed to legalized gambling on sports" (Purdum, 2016b). The NFL's continued opposition poses a significant hurdle to any future federal legislative efforts.

While the leagues may be cautious in their public statements, their recent actions point to a readiness to accept expanded legal sports betting. Within the last two years, all four major U.S. professional sports leagues have entered into groundbreaking deals with European-based technology companies to monitor the worldwide wagering activity on the leagues' games (Maese, 2016; Soshnick, 2016a,b). These companies—the two most prominent of which are Sportradar and Genius Sports—utilize sophisticated algorithms to detect unusual betting patterns in an attempt to identify suspicious betting activity that might lead to fixed matches. Such "integrity monitoring" and fraud-detection technology, which are commonplace throughout Europe, will be the cornerstone of any future regulated sports gambling environment in the United States. The existence of these deals suggests that the U.S. sports leagues are taking the necessary preparatory steps in anticipation of a regulated sports betting environment. Additionally, several of the major U.S. sports leagues have entered into licensing arrangements to distribute their real-time game data and statistics to sports betting operators located overseas (Soshnick, 2016a,b). Another telltale sign of the U.S. sports leagues' inexorable march toward a regulated sports gambling environment is their recent embrace of daily fantasy sports, a variant of traditional sports betting. The NBA is an investor in FanDuel, one of the largest daily fantasy sports operators, and two other major sports leagues—Major League Baseball and the National Hockey League—have taken minority stakes in DraftKings, the major competitor to FanDuel. Along those same lines, many U.S. sports franchises have entered into lucrative advertising sponsorships with either FanDuel or DraftKings. But perhaps the most revealing indicator of the U.S. sports leagues' warming to the idea of expanded legal sports gambling is the NHL's recent decision to place an expansion hockey team in Las Vegas, to be followed potentially by the relocation of the NFL's Oakland Raiders.

Against this backdrop, there is some movement afoot within Congress to enact a federal framework for legalizing sports betting nationally. In October 2016, New Jersey Congressman Fránk J. Pallone—the ranking Democrat on the influential U.S. House of Representatives Commerce, Manufacturing and Trade Committee (which has jurisdiction over "sports-related matters")—revealed in an interview with ESPN that his committee plans on introducing comprehensive federal legislation that will address sports betting, daily fantasy sports and other forms of online gambling (Purdum, 2016c). While Congressman Pallone did not provide a timetable for the new legislation, he stressed that the current federal gambling laws are "obsolete" and "in desperate need of updating." Such an "update" would likely involve amendments to three separate federal anti-gambling laws—PASPA, the Wire Act, and the Unlawful Internet Gambling Enforcement Act of 2006 (UIGEA)—to afford states the option of legalizing sports betting while also insulating private parties acting pursuant to state law from the threat of criminal prosecution.

In May 2017, Congressman Pallone introduced a "discussion draft" of his proposed bill, called the Gaming Accountability and Modernization Enhancement Act (the "GAME Act"). (Purdum, 2017). The GAME Act would repeal PASPA and allow states to legalize sports betting in accordance with the Act's requirements, which include provisions relating to licensing, taxation, underage gambling, safeguards against financial crime, and, critically, "integrity safeguards" aimed at ensuring the integrity of the sporting events. While the specifics of these proposed "consumer safeguards" are rather sparse—requiring states only to implement "appropriate safeguards" in these crucial areas—the GAME Act is still the most detailed federal proposal on the subject of sports betting since the enactment of PASPA some 25 years earlier. Far from a final work-product (it is just a "discussion draft" at this point), the GAME Act is intended to advance a dialogue on legal sports betting with all of the key stakeholders, including the major U.S. sports leagues, with the goal of eventual legalization by 2018 or 2019.

While a new federal regime will likely include many of the elements that Adam Silver envisioned—centered around technology companies monitoring the wagering activity to detect unusual betting patterns, and, perhaps, even the establishment of a national integrity platform—there is a difference of opinion among the key stakeholders as to the optimal approach. One possibility—floated by former NBA Commissioner David Stern—would be for Congress to "amend" PASPA to provide a uniform scheme of federal regulation that would allow states and sports leagues to either "opt-in" or "opt-out." (Purdum, 2016a). However, other groups, such as the American Gaming Association (the lobbying arm of the U.S. casino industry), believe that that the question of whether to legalize sports betting is one that should be left entirely up to the states, and therefore advocate an outright repeal of PASPA. (Gouker, 2016). Additionally, it is expected that any legal framework would compensate the sports leagues for their intellectual property (e.g., their games and data). Along those lines, two New Jersey lawmakers have proposed paying the sports leagues a percentage (0.25%) of every bet wagered on their contests (Friedman, 2014). Such a revenue stream—along with licensing deals and sponsorships—could easily generate hundreds of millions of dollars in new revenues for the leagues annually, making legal sports betting the greatest economic stimulus package for the sports industry since the advent of cable television.

8. Conclusion

Regardless of the approach taken, most seasoned observers believe that a congressional repeal or amendment of PASPA to allow state-sponsored sports betting is at least three to five years away. (Youmans, 2016). Some are even more pessimistic and believe the timeline is considerably longer than five years. (Youmans, 2016). It is this author's opinion that the timeline could be shortened considerably through litigation pressure—either through one state succeeding in court or by a group of states mounting legal challenges to PASPA. New Jersey's litigation efforts underscore the benefits of this approach. This is all about pressure and leverage. The first state that succeeds in overturning PASPA—and all it takes is one—will open the proverbial floodgates to expanded legal sports betting nationwide. This will have an immediate channeling effect that could benefit other states too: the sports leagues would likely respond to one state's courtroom success by immediately lobbying Congress to enact a uniform federal framework (which would allow *all* states to legalize sports betting) to avoid the inevitable patchwork of state laws that would likely emerge following even one successful legal challenge. All it will take is just *one* successful court challenge by a state to create this domino effect. The timing of the legalization of sports betting may depend on it.

Notes

1. Interstate Wire Act of 1961, 18 U.S.C. §§1081 et seq. Available at www.law.cornell.edu/uscode/text/18/1084.
2. Professional and Amateur Sports Protection Act, 28 U.S.C. §§3701 et seq. Available at www.gpo.gov/fdsys/pkg/STATUTE-106/pdf/STATUTE-106-Pg4227.pdf.
3. Eighteen states now have commercial casinos, as contrasted with only three—Nevada, New Jersey, and Mississippi—when PASPA was enacted in 1992 (Montero, 2016).
4. *United States v. Lyons*, 740 F.3d at 716 (noting "[t]he Wire Act's evident applicability to the internet."; *United States v. Cohen*, 260 F.3d at 76 (concluding that "transmitting bets and betting information" over the Internet "violate[s] the statute").
5. *See Christie I*, 730 F.3d at 216 ("The prohibition on private persons is limited to any such activity conducted " 'pursuant to the law or compact of a governmental entity.' ") (citing 28 U.S.C. §3702(2)).
6. 138 Cong. Rec. S7274 & 7278 (daily ed. June 2, 1992) (statement of Sen. Hatch) (Congress had "no choice" but to grandfather in the four states in order to "resolve the problems surrounding getting an important bill like this through . . .. Compromise is frequently necessary around here, of course, in order to enact legislation.").

References

Bonesteel, M. (2016a, August 10). "New Jersey's Attempt at Legalized Sports Betting Suffers Another Big Setback in Court." *The Washington Post*. Available at www.washingtonpost.com/news/early-lead/wp/2016/08/09/new-jerseys-attempt-at-legalized-sports-betting-suffers-another-big-setback-in-court/.

Bonesteel, M. (2016b, October 21). "U.S. Congress to Take First Concrete Step Toward Legalizing Sports Betting." *The Washington Post*. Available at www.washingtonpost.com/news/early-lead/wp/2016/10/21/u-s-congress-to-take-first-concrete-step-toward-legalizing-sports-gambling/.

Brennan, J., and Perez, A. J. (2016, August 9). "Federal Court Rejects New Jersey Bid to Legalize Sports Gambling." *USA Today* Available at www.usatoday.com/story/sports/2016/08/09/new-jersey-sports-gambling-rejected-federal-court/88446564/.

Brennan, J. (2017a, March 13). "U.S. Attorney Who Had Role in NJ Sports Betting Case Resigns" *NorthJersey.com*. Available at http://www.northjersey.com/story/news/business/meadowlands-matters/2017/03/13/us-attorney-who-had-role-nj-sports-betting-case-resigns/99120856/.

Brennan, J. (2017b, June 28). "U.S. Supreme Court track record suggests New Jersey is favored to win sports betting case" *NorthJersey.com*. Available at http://www.northjersey.com/story/news/new-jersey/2017/06/28/supreme-court-history-suggests-nj-favored-win-sports-betting-case/436401001/?platform=hootsuite.

Cabot, A. N. (2010). "The Absence of a Comprehensive Federal Policy Toward Internet and Sports Wagering and a Proposal for Change." *Villanova Sports and Entertainment Law Journal* 17: 271.

Cabot, A. N., and Faiss, R. D. (2002). "Sports Gambling in the Cyberspace Era." *Chapman Law Review* 5: 1, 19.

Carey, D. W. (2013). "Two Lessons of Anticommandeering: The Preemptive Significance of the Professional and Amateur Sports Protection Act." *Willamette Sports Law Journal* 11: 1.

Drape, J. (2015a, August 25). "New Jersey's Effort to Legalize Sports Betting Is Denied on Appeal." *The New York Times*, at B9.

Drape, J. (2015b, October 14). "Appeals Court to Rehear New Jersey Sports Betting Case." *The New York Times*, at B17.

Drape, J. (2016, August 9). "Federal Court Blocks New Jersey Plan to Legalize Sports Betting." *The New York Times*, at B16.

xFairleigh Dickinson University (2016). "More Americans Bet on Legalizing Sports Betting Than Oppose It.," Public Mind Poll, 2 Nov., available at http://view2.fdu.edu/publicmind/2016/161102/.

Friedman, M. (2014, September 17). "N.J. Lawmakers Propose Small Sports Betting Fee to Go to Sports Leagues." NJ.com. Available at www.nj.com/politics/index.ssf/2014/09/atlantic_county_lawmakers_propose_sports_betting_fee_to_go_to_sports_leagues.html.

Goodall, J. C. W. (2015). "Bringing Down The House: An Examination of the Law and Policy Underpinning the Professional and Amateur Sports Protection Act of 1992." *Rutgers University Law Review* 67: 1097.

Gouker, D. (2016, October 7). "Why You Won't Be Seeing A Federal Framework For US Sports Betting Soon" *Legal Sports Report*. Available at https://www.legalsportsreport.com/11775/us-sports-betting-david-stern-federal-framework/.

Gouker, D. (2017, April 3). "Manfred: Wants MLB Owners To Be Ready For A Dialogue About Legal Sports Betting" *Legal Sports Report*. Available at https://www.legalsportsreport.com/13584/mlb-commissioner-dialogue-on-sports-betting/.

Green, W. (2015, September 12). "These Factors Can Shrink the Size of the Potential Legal US Sports Betting Market." *Legal Sports Report*. Available at www.legalsportsreport.com/11519/us-sports-betting-market.

Gruetze, M. (2016, April 10). "Expansion of Sports Betting Moves From 'What If' to 'When.'" Available at http://triblive.com/aande/gambling/10270770-74/sports-million-betting.

Katsilometes, J. (2016, February 1). "Monday by the Numbers: A Statistical Summary of Super Bowl 50." *Las Vegas Sun*. Available at http://lasvegassun.com/blogs/kats-report/2016/feb/01/monday-numbers-statistical-summary-super-bowl-50-/.

Levinson, M., and Soshnick, S. (2014, September 4). "NBA's Silver Says Legal Sports Gambling in U.S. Is Inevitable." Bloomberg.com. Available at www.bloomberg.com/news/articles/2014-09-04/nba-s-silver-says-legal-sports-gambling-in-u-s-is-inevitable.

Maese, R. (2016, May 30). "MLB is Keeping a Close Eye on Gambling to Protect the Sport's Integrity." *Washington Post*. Available at www.washingtonpost.com/sports/nationals/mlb-is-keeping-a-very-close-eye-on-gambling-to-protect-the-sports-integrity/2016/05/30/0581b24a-1ed5-11e6-b6e0-c53b7ef63b45_story.html.

McCann, M. (2014, November 14). "Judge's Injunction Deals Major Blow to New Jersey's Sports Betting Plan." *Sports Illustrated*. Available at www.si.com/more-sports/2014/11/21/new-jersey-sports-betting-judge-issues-injunction.

McCann, M. (2015, August 25). "Analyzing the Future of New Jersey Sports Betting After Denied Appeal." *Sports Illustrated*. Available at www.si.com/more-sports/2015/08/25/new-jersey-sports-betting-appeal-denied.

Mierswa, M. T. (2014). "Poor Man Wanna Be Rich, Rich Man Wanna Be King: The Battle to Legalize Sports Betting in the Garden State." *Seton Hall Law Legislative Journal* 38: 447.

Montero, D. (2016, October 28). "Once Unimaginable, Las Vegas Is Finally Ready to Bet Big on the NFL." *Los Angeles Times*. Available at www.latimes.com/nation/la-na-vegas-nfl-20161010-snap-story.html.

New Jersey Senate Bill No. 3375, 217th Legislature. (2017, June 26). Available at http://www.njleg.state.nj.us/2016/Bills/S3500/3375_I1.HTM.

Peltz, J. (2016, February 1). "Super Bowl 50 to Draw an Estimated $4.2 billion in Bets—Most of Them Illegal." *The Los Angeles Times*. Available at.latimes.com/business/la-fi-agenda-super-bowl-20160201-story.html.

Public Hearing Before Senate Economic Growth Committee on Senate Concurrent Resolution 49, 2010 Leg. (N.J. Apr. 5, 2010). Available at http://www.njleg.state.nj.us/legislativepub/pubhear/seg04052010.pdf.

Purdum, D. (2015, February 5). "MLB to Talk Betting With Owners." ESPN.com. Available at www.espn.com/chalk/story/_/id/12286521/mlb-commissioner-rob-manfred-says-legalized-sports-betting-needs-fresh-consideration.

Purdum, D. (2016a, September 30). "Former NBA Commissioner David Stern Hopes to See Legalized Sports Betting in U.S." ESPN.*com*. Available at www.espn.com/chalk/story/_/id/17678528/former-nba-commissioner-david-stern-hopes-see-legalized-betting-expand-us.

Purdum, D. (2016b, October 21). "Congress Reviewing 'Obsolete' Federal Gambling Laws, to Introduce New Legislation." *ESPN.com*. Available at www.espn.com/chalk/story/_/id/17848529/congressional-committee-reviews-federal-gambling-laws-plans-introduce-new-legislation.

Purdum, D. (2016c, October 26). "Congress to Review Sports Betting Prohibition." *ESPN.com.* Available at www.espn.com/chalk/story/_/id/17848529/congressional-committee-reviews-federal-gambling-laws-plans-introduce-new-legislation.

Purdum, D. (2017, May 25): "'GAME Act' Proposing Repeal of Federal Prohibition of Sports Betting Revealed" *ESPN.com.* Available at https://www.legalsportsreport.com/13584/mlb-commissioner-dialogue-on-sports-betting/.

Purdum, D., and Rodenberg, R. (2016a, October 26). "Future of Sports Betting: The Marketplace." ESPN.com. Available at http://abcnews.go.com/Sports/future-sports-betting-marketplace/story?id=43129610.

Purdum, D. and Rodenberg, R. (2016b, October 27). "Future of Sports Betting: The Bettors." *ESPN.com.* Available at www.espn.com/chalk/story/_/id/17900400/the-future-sports-betting-bettors-landscape-legalized-sports-betting-us.

Purdum, D., and Rodenberg, R. (2016c, October 28). "Future of Sports Betting: The Pitfalls." ESPN.com. Available at www.espn.com/chalk/story/_/id/17910253/the-future-sports-betting-go-wrong-sports-betting-was-legal-united-states.

Ranjo, J. (2010). "Game Over? The Potential Demise of the Professional and Amateur Sports Protection Act." *Rutgers Law Journal* 42: 213.

Rodenberg, R. (2015). "The Shield Stands Alone: Why Does the NFL Hate Sports Gambling." *Vice Sports.* Available at https://sports.vice.com/en_us/article/the-shield-stands-alone-why-does-the-nfl-hate-sports-gambling.

Rodenberg, Ryan M. (2016, November 4). Brief as *Amicus Curiae* in Support of Petitions for Writ of Certiorari, *Christie v. National Collegiate Athletic Ass'n, Inc.*, Case Nos. 16-476 & 16-477 (U.S. Nov. 4, 2016). Available at https://papers.ssrn.com/sol3/papers.cfm?abstract_id=2867011.

Rodenberg, R. & Holden, J. (2017, June): "Sports Betting Has An Equal Sovereignty Problem" *Duke Law Journal Online* 67: 1. Available at http://scholarship.law.duke.edu/cgi/viewcontent.cgi?article=1024&context=dlj_online.

Ruddock, S. (2016, September 12). "These Factors Can Shrink the Size of the Potential Legal US Sports Betting Market." *Legal Sports Report.* Available at www.legalsportsreport.com/11519/us-sports-betting-market.

Senate Report No. 102-248. 102nd Cong., 1st Sess. 4 (1991), *reprinted in* 1992 U.S.C.C.A.N. 3553.

Silver, A. (2014, November 13). "Legalize and Regulate Sports Betting." *The New York Times*, at A27. Available at www.nytimes.com/2014/11/14/opinion/nba-commissioner-adam-silver-legalize-sports-betting.html?_r=0.

Soshnick, S. (2016a, August 12). "NBA Said Close to $250 Million Data Deal with Sportradar." Bloomberg.com. Available at www.bloomberg.com/news/articles/2016-08-12/nba-said-close-to-250-million-data-deal-with-sportradar.

Soshnick, S. (2016b, August 23). "NHL Hires Gambling Watchdog Ahead of Vegas Move." Bloomberg.com. Available at www.bloomberg.com/news/articles/2016-08-23/nhl-hires-sportradar-as-gambling-watchdog-ahead-of-vegas-move.

Stutz, H. (2015, November 11). "Casino Group to Study Rational Alternative to Sports Betting Laws." *Las Vegas Review-Journal.* Available at www.reviewjournal.com/business/casinos-gaming/casino-group-to-study-rational-alternative-to-us-sports-betting-laws/.

Thompson, David C., and Wachtell, M. (2009). "An Empirical Analysis of Supreme Court Certiorari Petition Procedures: The Call for Response and the Call for the Views of the Solicitor General." *George Mason Law Review* 16(2): 237. Available at https://papers.ssrn.com/sol3/papers.cfm?abstract_id=1377522.

U.S. Department of Justice, Office of the Legal Counsel. "Whether Proposals by Illinois and New York to Use the Internet and Out-of-State Transaction Processors to Sell Lottery Tickets to In-State Adults Violate the Wire Act/" 35 Op. O.L.C. (2011). Available at www.justice.gov/olc/2011/state-lotteries-opinion.pdf.

Wallach, D. (2016, August 31). "How to Legalize Sports Betting." *Deadspin*. Available at http://deadspin.com/how-to-legalize-sports-betting-1786002079.

Wallach, D. (2017, June 23): "Seven Reasons Why The New Jersey Sports Betting Case May Get Its Day In The Supreme Court" *Legal Sports Report*. Available at https://www.legalsportsreport.com/14481/scotus-may-grant-nj-sports-betting-appeal/.

Wyshinski, G. (2016, September 9). "Gary Bettman's Sports Gambling Flip-Flop." *Yahoo Sports*. Available at http://sports.yahoo.com/news/gary-bettmans-sports-gambling-flip-flop-162345685.html.

Zwerling, J. (2015, May 4). "Betting on the Future: Imagining the NBA Fan Experience with Regulated Gambling." *Bleacher Report*. Available at http://bleacherreport.com/articles/2324874-betting-on-the-future-imagining-the-nba-fan-experience-with-regulated-gambling.

Cases

Conant v. Walters, 309 F.3d 629, 646 (9th Cir. 2002).

National Collegiate Athletic Ass'n v. Christie (*Christie I*), 926 F. Supp. 551 (D.N.J. 2013).

National Collegiate Athletic Ass'n, Inc. v. Christie (*Christie I*), 730 F.3d 208 (3d Cir. 2013).

National Collegiate Athletic Ass'n v. Christie (*Christie II*), 61 F. Supp. 2d 488 (D.N.J. 2014).

National Collegiate Athletic Ass'n v. Christie (*Christie II*), 832 F.3d 389 (3d Cir. 2016).

New York v. United States, 505 U.S. 144 (1992).

Printz v. United States, 521 U.S. 898 (1997).

Office of the Commissioner of Baseball v. Markell, 579 F.3d 293 (3d Cir. 2009).

United States v. Anderson, 542 F.2d 428 (7th Cir. 1976).

United States v. Baborian, 528 F. Supp. 324 (D.R.I. 1981).

United States v. Cohen, 260 F.3d 68 (2d Cir. 2001).

United States v. Lyons, 740 F.3d 702 (1st Cir. 2014).

United States v. McDonough, 835 F.2d 1103 (5th Cir. 1988).

United States v. Ross, 1999 WL 782749, at *5 (S.D.N.Y Sept. 16, 1999).

United States v. Rozenfeld, 2014 WL 917057, at *3 (S.D.N.Y. Mar. 10, 2014).

United States v. Scavo, 593 F. 2d 837 (8th Cir. 1979).

CHAPTER 17

THE ENDURING POWER OF THE SPORTS BROADCASTING ACT

NATHANIEL GROW

1. Introduction

National television agreements are one of the largest and most important sources of revenue for professional sports leagues today. Nowhere is this more evident than in the case of the National Football League (NFL), which currently generates more than $7 billion per year from its national broadcast contracts with various television networks and cable providers (NBC, CBS, Fox, ESPN, and DirecTV). Not only do these contracts provide sports leagues with considerable revenue, but they also play an important role in each league's competitive balance efforts as well. Because national television revenues are generally split evenly among a league's franchises, this money helps to level the playing field between teams situated in larger, more lucrative media markets and those residing in less populated areas.

While most sports fans are well aware of the importance of television revenue to the professional sports industry, far fewer appreciate the important ways in which the law has shaped sports leagues' broadcasting activities. But for a little-known statutory provision—the Sports Broadcasting Act of 1961 (SBA) (15 U.S.C. §§ 1291-1295)—any broadcast agreement between a sports league (on behalf of all of its individually owned and operated teams) and a television network would be vulnerable to legal challenge as an illicit restraint of trade in violation of Section One of the Sherman Antitrust Act (15 U.S.C. §§ 1-2). Indeed, in the only reported court decision to date—issued just months before the enactment of the SBA in 1961—a federal trial court judge prohibited the NFL from entering into a league-wide broadcasting contract with CBS, finding that the agreement would improperly eliminate the then-existing competition among the NFL's individual franchises for television contracts. In other words, rather than allowing its teams to compete with one another to each sign their own television agreements, the court believed that the NFL had effectively created a monopoly over its teams' broadcasting rights by negotiating with CBS exclusively on a league-wide basis. The SBA was enacted in order to overturn this decision, helping establish the sports broadcasting structure that fans have grown accustomed to today.

While some have questioned the continued significance of the SBA over the years in light of various technological advances in the broadcasting industry (cable television, pay-per-view broadcasting, and Internet streaming video, among others), the SBA remains vitally important to the professional sports industry. Not only does the SBA continue to provide legal protection—either explicitly or implicitly—to many of the leagues' most common broadcasting activities, but it has also given Congress political leverage over the industry, allowing the legislature to challenge various league activities over the years. Thus, the SBA continues to play an important role in helping to shape professional-sports-related public policy in the United States today.

2. The Origins of the Sports Broadcasting Act

The origins of the SBA date back to a pair of judicial decisions issued more than fifty years ago by a federal trial court judge in the first—and, to date, only—government antitrust prosecution of a U.S. professional sports league. In the early 1950s, the U.S. Department of Justice took an interest in sports leagues' burgeoning broadcasting activity, believing that some of these practices were inconsistent with the Sherman Act. Along these lines, the Justice Department filed suit in 1953 challenging a variety of the NFL's early television policies under federal antitrust law, a suit known as *United States v. National Football League* ((*NFL I*). Unlike today, where the NFL negotiates all of its regular and postseason television contracts on a league-wide basis, in the early 1950s the league allowed each of its teams to negotiate its own individual contracts with television networks. At the same time, however, the league imposed a series of rules to prevent its franchises from competing with one another within each team's metropolitan area. Thus, the league effectively granted each of its franchises a monopoly over its local television market.

Under Article X of the NFL bylaws, for instance, teams were forbidden from broadcasting their games via television or radio within seventy-five miles of a fellow league member's stadium on any day when the league rival was also playing a game—home or away—unless the rival team authorized the broadcast. Moreover, the league's rules gave the NFL commissioner the unlimited power to block the broadcast of any game in any market. The Justice Department alleged that these provisions violated Section One of the Sherman Act, constituting an illicit "contract, combination . . ., or conspiracy, in restraint of trade."

Judge Alan K. Grim issued a split decision, upholding one part of the NFL's television restrictions, while permanently enjoining the league from enforcing other portions of its broadcast policy. The court premised its decision on the observation that "[p]rofessional football is a unique type of business," one in which teams depended upon their rivals' continued existence for their own economic survival (323). In light of this economic reality, Judge Grim found that the NFL's rule prohibiting its teams from broadcasting their games into another's host city at a time when the other team was hosting a game of its own was arguably procompetitive, helping to protect a critical source of revenue for the league's teams: home ticket revenue. Because ticket sales were the predominant source of income for NFL teams at the time, and in light of the fact that the league had presented evidence showing that the existence of competing games on television could harm in-stadium attendance, the judge concluded that some restraints in this area were warranted in order to ensure the league's survival. Indeed, not only did such a restriction help increase weaker teams' ticket sales, but it also served to reduce the amount of television revenue that the stronger franchises were able to generate, thereby enhancing competitive balance across the league.

Judge Grim was less receptive to other aspects of the NFL's broadcasting policy, however. For instance, although the court was willing to uphold the league's restriction on television broadcasts into another franchise's market on days when the other team was hosting a game, it was unwilling to extend this same protection to days in which the fellow league member was playing on the road. Because competing broadcasts during a road game would not directly cut into a rival franchise's home ticket sales, the court concluded that the only plausible purpose for such a restriction would be to provide each team with a monopoly over its local television market, in contravention of the Sherman Act. Similarly, because the NFL had failed to present any evidence showing that radio broadcasting impacted attendance in the same way that television did, Judge Grim also struck down the league's prohibition of radio broadcasts into another team's home territory on game days, home or away.

Despite seeing significant portions of its broadcasting policy struck down in *NFL I*, the NFL ultimately opted not to appeal Judge Grim's ruling. The league feared that an appellate court might go one step further and prevent it from enforcing any of its television restrictions at all, including the prohibition on broadcasting into another franchise's territory while it was hosting a game (Banner, 2013). As a result, the NFL agreed to operate subject to the limitations imposed by Judge Grim's decision in *NFL I* for the rest of the decade.

By the start of the 1960s, however, the NFL faced competition from a new rival league—the American Football League (AFL)—which employed a very different television broadcasting model. Unlike the NFL—which at the time continued to allow its individual teams to sign their own television contracts—the AFL signed a single, league-wide television agreement with ABC, giving the network the exclusive rights to broadcast all of the AFL's games. Because the AFL then split the resulting television revenue evenly between its teams, this arrangement placed all of the league's franchises on equal financial footing from a television perspective. In the process, the arrangement also helped to enhance competitive balance among the league's teams, preventing franchises in larger media markets from exploiting any potential broadcast revenue disparities into eventual competitive dominance on the playing field.

Motivated by the AFL's new television contract, the NFL entered into its own exclusive, league-wide agreement with CBS for the 1961 season. Because the Justice Department believed that the NFL's new agreement violated Judge Grim's still-binding 1953 decision in *NFL I*, however, the league was forced to return to court to seek approval of its contract with CBS. In *United States v. National Football League* ((*NFL II*), the judge quickly decided that the league's new agreement with CBS did, in fact, contradict the terms of his 1953 ruling. As Judge Grim explained, with the exception of the limitation on broadcasts in another team's territory on days on which it was hosting a game, his prior ruling prohibited the NFL from restricting the areas within which its teams' games could be broadcast. Under the terms of the league's new contract with CBS, however, the NFL agreed to allow the network to decide which of the league's games would be broadcast in a particular market. As a result, the court determined that the NFL had improperly entered into an agreement authorizing the restriction of the areas within which its games may be broadcast, a violation of the still-binding decision in *NFL I*.

3. Congress's Enactment of the Sports Broadcasting Act

Rather than appeal the *NFL II* ruling to a higher court, the NFL pursued a different legal strategy. Shortly after Judge Grim issued his decision, the league reached out to members of Congress to request that the legislature enact a new law specifically exempting television contracts like the NFL's agreement with CBS from antitrust law.

Congress was ultimately quite receptive to the NFL's request. Even before Judge Grim's decision in *NFL II*, the legislature had recently held a number of hearings concerning the status of professional sports leagues under the Sherman Act, and therefore had already developed extensive expertise regarding the unique antitrust issues presented by the sports industry. Moreover, the NFL's legislative efforts were also aided by the fact that its request was supported by each of the nation's other major professional sports leagues. Indeed, even the rival AFL supported the NFL's legislation, for fear that its own league-wide television contract with ABC might one day face antitrust scrutiny under the *NFL II* precedent (*Telecasting of Professional Sports Contests*, House Committee on the Judiciary (1961)).

Although the NFL's proposed legislation was opposed by the Justice Department—due to the bill's failure to provide any safeguards to protect the public interest—it nevertheless quickly sailed through Congress and was enacted into law a mere seventy-two days after Judge Grim issued his decision in *NFL II*. In particular, Congress believed that legislation along the lines of that proposed by the NFL was necessary to ensure that smaller-market sports franchises were able to generate the television revenue and exposure necessary to remain competitive in their leagues. As Representative John Byrnes noted during the congressional debate over the bill, for instance, a team residing in a small city like Green Bay, Wisconsin, could never hope to secure the same sort of television revenue for itself that a team from a major metropolis like New York could command (*Congressional Record* (1961)). Thus, Congress feared that larger market teams would eventually use their inherent advantages in the television marketplace to invest in better players, ultimately allowing them to establish their competitive dominance on the playing field as well, to the detriment of the entire league. As a result, Congress agreed to pass the SBA in order to ensure that a sufficient share of each league's television revenue went to its financially weaker, but nevertheless essential, teams (*Telecasting of Professional Sports Contests*, S. Rep. No. 87-1087 (1961)).

As initially enacted, the SBA included three main sections. The most important of these provisions was Section 1, which effectively repealed the *NFL II* precedent by stating that the federal antitrust laws:

> Shall not apply to any joint agreement by or among persons engaging in or conducting the organized professional team sports of football, baseball, basketball, or hockey, by which any league of clubs . . . sells or otherwise transfers all or any part of the rights of such league's member clubs in the sponsored telecasting of the games of football, baseball, basketball, or hockey, as the case may be, engaged in or conducted by such clubs.
>
> (15 U.S.C. § 1291)

In other words, Section 1 of the SBA generally permits professional sports leagues to collectively sell their teams' broadcast rights to television networks without fear of antitrust liability. This provision thus gave legislative sanction to the NFL's television agreement with CBS, as well as similar contracts existing at the time between various television networks and the AFL and National Basketball Association (NBA).

Importantly, however, Section 1 of the SBA included several limitations. First, the provision only applied to leagues in the following sports: football, baseball, basketball, and hockey. While this list captured all of the relevant sports leagues in existence in 1961, it does impose a potentially more significant limitation today. Indeed, any professional league operating in a different sport—such as Major League Soccer (MLS)—would not appear to be eligible for protection under the SBA, even if it were to enter into the exact same type of contract sanctioned for the leagues in the four traditional "major" sports.

Perhaps more significant, Section 1 of the SBA also applies only to an agreement between a sports league and a television network for the "sponsored telecasting" of the league's games. In 1961, this particular term of art was understood to refer only to television broadcasts that were subsidized entirely by advertising revenue, rather than through subscription fees charged to viewers. This means that the protection afforded by the SBA was intended to only cover broadcast agreements between a sports league and an over-the-air broadcast network, such as NBC, ABC, CBS, or (today) Fox. Indeed, at the time the SBA was enacted, Congress emphasized the fact that the Act would not apply to television agreements covering other, emerging broadcast technologies such as pay-per-view or closed-circuit television, an interpretation confirmed by then-NFL Commissioner Pete Rozelle (107 Cong. Rec. Pt. 15 (1961); *Telecasting of Professional Sports Contests*, House Committee on the Judiciary (1961)). Thus, while sports leagues' television agreements with over-the-air networks are protected by the SBA, leagues' analogous contracts with subscription cable networks such as ESPN or TNT would not have been considered to be "sponsored telecasting," and therefore are not exempt under the Act.

Section 2 of the SBA (15 U.S.C. § 1292) then dealt with the issue of television blackouts, clarifying that the SBA does not apply to any broadcasting agreement that prohibits a network "from televising any games within any area, except within the home territory of a member club of the league on a day when such club is playing a game at home." Put differently, this provision codified the rule established by Judge Grim's decision in *NFL I*, only permitting a league to block the broadcasts of competing games from another franchise's home market on days in which the other team is hosting a game of its own. As with Judge Grim's original ruling, this provision was thus intended to protect a home team's ticket sales from competition from television broadcasts.

The blackout provision was included in the SBA at the behest of several congressmen who believed that the initial version of the legislation could potentially be interpreted as overturning not only Judge Grim's ruling in *NFL II* but also his decision in *NFL I*, thereby giving the NFL free reign to black out its games as it saw fit (*Telecasting of Professional Sports Contests*, House Committee on the Judiciary (1961)). Thus, Congress added Section 2 to the SBA to ensure that the NFL—or any other league—would not revert to the prior practice of blacking out other teams' games from a market on days in which the local team was not hosting a game of its own. Notably, however, Section 2 of the Act fails to define exactly what constitutes the "home territory of a member club" for blackout purposes. Instead, the provision appears to defer to each league to define the scope of its home broadcast territories (Roberts, 2001).

Third, Section 3 of the SBA imposed some restrictions on when the NFL or AFL could broadcast their games while still receiving protection under SBA Act. During Congress's consideration of the legislation, several congressmen expressed concern that the NFL might use its new antitrust immunity to begin televising games on new days of the week beyond its traditional Sunday afternoons. In particular, these legislators feared that the league could potentially begin competing directly with college football, which had always held its games on Saturdays (*Congressional Record* (1961)). These concerns ultimately resulted in the inclusion of an additional provision in the bill specifying that any professional football league would lose its exemption under the SBA if it permitted any of its teams' games to be broadcast:

> On any Friday after six o'clock postmeridian or on any Saturday during the period beginning on the second Friday in September and ending on the second Saturday in December in any year from any telecasting station located within seventy-five miles

of the game site of any intercollegiate or interscholastic football contest. (15 U.S.C. § 1293)

The provision goes on to define an "intercollegiate football contest" as one played between two four-year colleges, while an "interscholastic football contest" is defined as one played by high schools "offer[ing] courses continuing through the twelfth grade." Thus, the SBA sought to ensure that Friday nights and Saturday afternoons in the fall would continue to be reserved for high school and college football, respectively, while Sundays would be the domain of the professional game.

The SBA has subsequently been amended on two occasions. The first came in 1966, when Congress inserted an additional clause into Section 1 of the statute, stating that the antitrust laws "Shall not apply to a joint agreement by which the member clubs of two or more professional football leagues . . . combine their operations in expanded [*sic*] single league . . . if such agreement increases rather than decreases the number of professional football clubs so operating" (15 U.S.C. § 1291). This language was added to the SBA to legislatively sanction the proposed merger between the NFL and AFL, which by the mid-1960s believed that their continued competition had become unsustainable and would eventually lead to the financial ruin of one or both leagues. Because such a merger would have resulted in the monopolization of the professional football industry—arguably in violation of Section 2 of the Sherman Act—the leagues sought congressional preapproval of the proposed agreement. Before Congress would sign off, however, its members extracted a few concessions from the two leagues, requiring them to collectively add four new franchises (to be located in Cincinnati, New Orleans, Seattle, and Tampa Bay) (Surdam, 2015). This compromise explains the amendment's requirement that the merger increase the overall number of professional teams.

The SBA was amended a second time in the mid-1970s in order to address growing public outcry over the NFL's blackout policy. As permitted under Section 2 of the SBA, the NFL at the time continued to refuse to allow a team's home games to be televised in its local market, even on days on which tickets to the game were sold out. As a result, many local fans often found themselves completely unable to watch their favorite team play at home, as they could neither attend the game in person (due to the sellout) nor tune into the game on television (due to the blackout).

In order to rectify this state of affairs, Congress passed a provision in 1973 limiting permissible blackouts to home games that had not been sold out at least seventy-two hours in advance (Pub. L. No. 93-107, 87 Stat. 350). Congress hoped that this amendment would balance the NFL's concern that enhanced television-viewing options would decrease in-stadium attendance, while at the same time also ensuring that fans would be able to watch games that they were unable to attend in person. Importantly, however, the amendment included a sunset provision expressly stating that it would expire on December 31, 1975. Nevertheless, the NFL subsequently agreed to continue to abide by the seventy-two-hour sellout window even after the provision officially expired in 1975, in order to avoid Congress permanently writing the restriction into the SBA. The NFL continued to voluntarily abide by that policy until 2015, when it announced that it was indefinitely suspending its local blackout policy in its entirety.

Finally, it is worth noting that despite these amendments, one glaring omission that remains in the SBA is the lack of any provision actually requiring the beneficiary sports leagues to split the revenue they receive from their national television contracts evenly among their franchises. This shortcoming is particularly surprising given the fact that Congress justified the Act in no small part on competitive balance concerns. This omission, among others, has also led to criticism of the SBA on the grounds that it failed to include any consumer protections at all within the text of the statute (Fisch, 1995; Mitten and Hernandez, 2013).

4. Judicial Interpretations of the Sports Broadcasting Act

To date, courts have rarely been called upon to interpret the SBA, undoubtedly due to its limited scope and reasonably clear purpose. In the relatively few instances in which courts have needed to apply the SBA, judges have typically interpreted the statute narrowly, consistent with the Act's legislative history and intended scope.

The first court decision applying the SBA came in 1982. In *WTWV, Inc. v. National Football League* the court was asked to interpret Section 2 of the SBA, the statute's blackout provision. The suit arose after the NFL and the Miami Dolphins refused to authorize a Florida television station residing outside the Dolphins' broadcast territory to televise the team's un-sold-out home games. Even though the network's antenna was located ninety-six miles away from Miami—and thus was outside the seventy-five-mile radius constituting the club's home broadcast territory under the NFL Constitution—the team and league nevertheless opposed the broadcasts because the station's signal could reach homes located within forty miles of the Dolphins' stadium.

The court ultimately sided with the Dolphins and the league, ruling that the SBA's blackout provision applied to any television station whose signal could be received within a seventy-five-mile radius of a team's stadium, even if the station's antenna itself stood more than seventy-five miles away. In particular, the court reasoned that allowing a station to broadcast a team's games into its market simply because the antenna was physically located outside the team's protected radius would defeat the provision's intended purpose of protecting teams' home attendance from competition with television broadcasts.

While the SBA's blackout provision was the first to spawn litigation, the issue that has been most frequently litigated under the SBA involves the scope of the antitrust exemption established in Section 1. Specifically, several courts have been called upon to construe the language limiting the provision to agreements dealing with the "sponsored telecasting" of a league's games. For instance, in *Shaw v. Dallas Cowboys Football Club,*

Ltd., the legality of the NFL's Sunday Ticket service—a pay-per-view package allowing fans to watch all of the league's games each week, including those not broadcast on a fan's local television networks—was challenged under the Sherman Act. The NFL defended itself in the case in part by arguing that the SBA shielded the Sunday Ticket service from antitrust scrutiny. Specifically, although the Sunday Ticket service was offered only on a pay-per-view basis, the league contended that the service was nevertheless covered by Section 1 of the SBA because it constituted "residual rights" to games that were originally and primarily broadcast via over-the-air broadcast networks.

The Court of Appeals for the Third Circuit rejected this argument, concluding that the SBA's use of the phrase "sponsored telecasting" referred only to broadcasts that were "provided free to the general public." Because the Sunday Ticket service was provided to subscribers for a fee, it therefore did not constitute "sponsored telecasting" in the view of the court, and thus was not entitled to protection from antitrust liability by the SBA. Other courts have reached the same conclusion in lawsuits considering both other leagues' analogous pay-per-view services as well as their national television contracts signed with cable—as opposed to over-the-air broadcast—networks available only on a subscription basis (*Chicago Professional Sports Limited Partnership v. National Basketball Association*; *Kingray, Inc. v. National Basketball Association*; *Laumann v. National Hockey League*).

Finally, courts have also considered whether the SBA exempts only one contract between a sports league and a single broadcast network, or whether one league can permissibly enter into agreements with multiple networks while still receiving protection under the SBA. Specifically, in *United States Football League v. National Football League*, the upstart USFL (United States Football League) accused the NFL of illegally monopolizing the football industry. In particular, the rival league contended that the fact that the NFL had entered into television agreements with all three of the national over-the-air broadcast networks made it difficult for a competing league to obtain sufficient airtime and television revenues of its own. Along these lines, the USFL asserted that the SBA should be read to only shield a single contract between a sports league and television network from antitrust law.

The Second Circuit rejected the USFL's contention, noting that Congress had expressly considered the possibility that a league could enter into protected agreements with more than one television network under the SBA during its consideration of the Act. Nevertheless, the court noted that this did not necessarily mean that the SBA shielded the NFL from all antitrust liability arising out of those contracts, noting that the existence of multiple television contracts could be evidence of illegal monopolization if it were proven that a league entered into those agreements with the intent of preventing rivals from securing television deals of their own. In other words, the court concluded that while each of the NFL's three broadcast agreements were individually exempt from antitrust scrutiny under the SBA, the fact that the league had entered into agreements with all three broadcast networks could potentially serve as evidence of its intent to monopolize the professional football industry.

5. The Legacy and Continued Importance of the Sports Broadcasting Act

Despite the SBA's relatively modest scope and limited litigation history, the statute has nevertheless had an outsized impact on the professional sports industry. Indeed, because the SBA has effectively allowed the four major U.S. professional sports leagues to monopolize their national broadcasting activities—eliminating any potential competition among a particular sport's teams for the sale of their national broadcast rights—the leagues have been able to demand much higher broadcast fees than would be obtainable in a competitive marketplace in which teams individually competed against one another for television contracts (Quirk and Fort, 1999).

For example, in 1960, the year prior to the enactment of the SBA, NFL teams collectively generated approximately $3 million total for the sale of their individually negotiated broadcast rights. In contrast, by 1964—the first year in which the NFL negotiated a league-wide television contract in a competitive market[1]—the league was able to secure $16.2 million in television revenue. Thus, the ability to monopolize its teams' broadcast rights allowed the NFL to demand roughly an additional $13 million from television networks, an increase of more than 433%. Similarly, Major League Baseball (MLB) saw its national television revenues more than double following the enactment of the SBA, increasing from around $2.6 million per year in 1961 to just under $6 million per season in 1965 (ABA Section of Antitrust Law (2007)).

As sports fans are well aware, these dollar values have only increased exponentially in the decades following the SBA's enactment. Today, the NFL generates more than $7 billion per year from its league-wide, national television contracts, while the NBA is earning $2.7 billion per season under a new set of agreements that took effect in 2016. Meanwhile, MLB currently earns over $1.5 billion per year from its national television contracts, while the National Hockey League (NHL) gets around $615 million per season from its agreements. Absent the SBA, these contracts would be subject to challenge under federal antitrust law. Indeed, each agreement would arguably reflect an anticompetitive restraint of trade among the respective league's individually owned and operated teams, thereby eliminating competition among potential competitors for national broadcasting revenue.

Nevertheless, some scholars have questioned the continued significance of the SBA. Since the statute only shields a league's agreements with over-the-air broadcast networks from antitrust scrutiny, and because leagues are increasingly entering into non-exempt national television contracts with cable networks, some believe that the SBA has "been rendered largely obsolete" (ABA Section of Antitrust Law (2007)). As the argument goes, not only does the growing prevalence of these non-exempt cable agreements imply that the leagues are increasingly willing to disregard the protection afforded by the SBA, but the fact that these unprotected television contracts have rarely been challenged under antitrust law—and never successfully so—would appear to suggest that these agreements are now effectively considered lawful (despite Judge Grim's apparent 1961 ruling to the contrary in *NFL II*) (Boliek, 2014).

However, while the fact that sports leagues are increasingly willing to enter into league-wide broadcast agreements with non-over-the-air networks could be interpreted as suggesting that leagues are disregarding the protection afforded to them under the SBA, this interpretation is overly simplistic. As an initial matter, while it is true that the NBA, NHL, and MLB have each increasingly—but not entirely—shifted their national broadcasting activity to cable stations, the NFL continues to rely heavily on television contracts with over-the-air broadcast networks, and thus continues to benefit greatly from the protection afforded by the SBA. Indeed, of the more than $7 billion that the league generates in television revenues on an annual basis, over half of this money comes from its contracts with over-the-air broadcast networks NBC, CBS, and Fox. In this respect, then, the SBA arguably serves a legitimate policy objective, helping to ensure that at least a portion of professional sports broadcasts remain available on free television.

Moreover, although it is true that sports leagues' television contracts with cable networks are not covered by the SBA, and yet have never been seriously challenged under federal antitrust law, this does not mean that the SBA has not played a role in helping to shape the legal treatment of these agreements. Back in 1987, for instance, Congress held hearings to consider the applicability of the SBA to the NFL's recently announced television contract with the cable station ESPN, under which the league awarded the network the right to air Sunday evening games on a national basis. As part of these hearings the Federal Trade Commission (FTC) submitted a letter considering the legality of the contract (Moran, 1999).

Although the FTC concluded that the SBA did not appear to apply to the NFL's contract with ESPN, the agency nevertheless explained that it had elected not to challenge the agreement for fear that doing so could result in unintended consequences. In particular, the FTC expressed the concern that if broadcast agreements between a sports league and cable station were challenged under the antitrust laws, then the resulting threat of liability could disincentivize the leagues from negotiating with cable broadcasters. As a result, the FTC feared, the safe harbor provided by the SBA might actually result in the over-the-air broadcast networks acquiring an effective monopoly over professional sports telecasts on a national level, potentially decreasing the number of games available for fans to watch on television.

Somewhat perversely, then, even though Congress went to great lengths in 1961 to limit the SBA to only shield broadcasting agreements between a sports league and over-the-air broadcast network, the existence of this limited exemption has nevertheless indirectly benefited in sports leagues' contracts with cable stations as well. Indeed, as long as the SBA remains in force, it appears unlikely that the federal government will challenge a sports league's television contract with a non-exempt cable station. Thus, while the broadcasting industry may eventually evolve to the point that the SBA truly becomes irrelevant, the statute will likely continue to either directly or indirectly protect the leagues' national television contracts well into the foreseeable future. As a result, the SBA's alleged obsolescence appears to have been overstated.

Relatedly, the SBA has also had a profound effect in helping to establish and reinforce the by now well-entrenched sports broadcasting practices with which fans have grown accustom. Prior to the SBA's enactment in 1961, sports broadcasting was still in its relative infancy, with most television agreements traditionally negotiated between a station and an individual team. Had Congress not passed the SBA—leaving Judge Grim's ruling in *NFL II* intact—then this practice likely would have continued forward today, as any attempt to collectively negotiate a television contract on behalf of an entire league of teams would have been viewed as presumptively unlawful under Section One of the Sherman Act.

Instead, by ratifying the legality of league-wide broadcasting agreements in the SBA, Congress sanctioned the practice of sports leagues entering into collective national television contracts on behalf of their teams. Sports leagues' television broadcasting practices were thus allowed to evolve along a now familiar—but far from inevitable—path, with leagues uniformly negotiating any national broadcast agreements collectively on behalf of their franchises. As a result, individual teams in the NBA, NHL, and MLB currently retain only the authority to enter into local broadcasting agreements with regional networks in their own markets, while NFL clubs may only individually negotiate local pre-season television contracts (as all regular and post-season NFL broadcasts are subject to the league's national television contracts). Had Congress not enacted the SBA, the sports broadcasting industry likely would have developed in a very different manner, with teams actively competing against one another for television agreements in both the national and regional broadcast marketplaces.

Whether or not such an alternative structure would have been preferable to the existing norm is uncertain. Had individual teams continued to compete for national television contracts, then one would expect that this competition would not only have driven down the price that the leagues and their teams could demand for their broadcast rights but also increased the number of games broadcast on both a national and regional level. Had the sports industry's television practices evolved differently, then, fans today would likely be able to watch a greater number of games on their local cable packages, all the while paying a reduced price—in the form of lower cable subscription fees—for the privilege of doing so.

At the same time, however, this sort of competition among franchises may have further exacerbated competitive balance issues within each league, allowing teams residing in the largest markets to sign the most lucrative contracts with the most widely distributed television networks. And because these television revenues would have been generated exclusively by individual franchises, leagues would have undoubtedly found it more difficult to persuade their richest teams to share their television revenues equally with their smaller market counterparts. Consequently, the resulting television revenue disparities among franchises may have eventually caused significant competitive disparities to develop among teams on the playing field, ultimately resulting in a less compelling product for fans.

Thus, had the SBA not been enacted, the sports broadcasting industry would have undoubtedly developed quite differently, with both potential benefits and disadvantages for sports fans. For better or worse, then, sports fans can thank the SBA for helping to establish and reinforce the sports industry's now customary broadcast practices.

Along these same lines, another often underappreciated effect of the SBA is the extent to which the law helped reinforce the by now well-established cultural paradigm in which fall Saturdays are the exclusive domain of college football, with Sundays reserved for the NFL. While this structure had taken root prior to the SBA's enactment in 1961, the statute helped to legally reinforce this cultural tradition. As discussed earlier, Section 3 of the SBA expressly retracts the NFL's antitrust protection for any broadcast agreement that the league enters into in which the league allows its games to be televised on a Friday evening or Saturday between the second Friday in September and the second Saturday in December. Considering that the NFL has increasingly expanded its television footprint since 1961—first through the creation of Monday Night Football, and more recently Thursday Night Football—but for the SBA, the league may very well have launched its own slate of Saturday games by now, in direct competition with the college game. Thus, to the extent that fans enjoy having fall Saturdays reserved for college football, with NFL games on Sundays, they can thank the SBA for helping weave this tradition into our cultural fabric.

Last, but by no means least, one final impact of the SBA that often tends to be overlooked is the extent to which the statute has given Congress political leverage over the four major U.S. professional sports leagues, and the NFL in particular. Because the SBA could potentially be repealed at any time, Congress has routinely used the threat of rescinding a league's antitrust immunity to pressure the league to either take some sort of action or else refrain from engaging in a particular activity. In 2015, for example, a bill was introduced in Congress threatening to strip the NFL of its protection under the SBA as long as the league continued to allow its Washington franchise to use the racially insensitive nickname the "Redskins" (*Respect for Native Americans* (2015)). Similarly, years earlier, Congress threatened to retract the NFL's and MLB's protection under the SBA if the leagues moved the broadcasts of the Super Bowl or World Series, respectively, from free, over-the-air broadcast networks to subscription television (Cox, 1995).[2]

While one can, of course, question whether these matters warrant significant congressional attention given the plethora of other pressing issues facing the nation, these incidents do provide a level of governmental oversight that would otherwise be lacking in the professional sports industry. Indeed, considering that each of the four major U.S. leagues operates in many respects as an unregulated monopoly within its sport—facing no significant competition and relatively little direct governmental oversight—these sorts of congressional interventions provide one of the few chances for the government to try to ensure that the leagues are operating in a manner roughly consistent with the public interest. Given the extent to which sports leagues benefit from public largess—most significantly through the construction of state-of-the-art playing facilities built at taxpayer expense—the SBA thus provides an altogether rare opportunity for the public to attempt to influence the way in which the professional sports industry is run (Grow, 2012, 2015).

6. Conclusion

Although most sports fans are unaware of its existence, and despite the fact that some scholars have questioned its continued significance, the SBA nevertheless remains an important piece of legislation for the professional sports industry. In addition to shielding the four major U.S. professional sports leagues' national broadcast agreements with over-the-air television networks from antitrust scrutiny, the statute also indirectly protects the leagues' analogous contracts with cable stations by deterring the federal government from challenging these non-exempt agreements. Meanwhile, because the leagues value the protection afforded by the SBA, the threat of repealing the statute has also given Congress leverage over the industry, allowing the legislative branch to attempt to exert some level of oversight over the leagues' operations. Consequently, as long as professional sports are broadcast on television, the SBA is likely to continue to play an important role in shaping the way in which the sports industry operates.

Notes

1. Although the SBA granted the NFL permission to enter into league-wide television contracts beginning in 1961, the league was only able to negotiate an agreement with one network, CBS, for the 1961, 1962, and 1963 seasons, as the network already held the rights to nine of the league's ten teams' games for these years under preexisting contracts. Thus, the 1964 season marked the first in which the NFL was able to solicit competing bids from other networks U.S. Congress, House Committee on the Judiciary, *Telecasting of Professional Sports Contests* (1961).
2. For other examples of Congress using the threat of repealing the SBA to pressure the leagues, see Delrahim (2007); Phelps (2004); and Raut (2011).

References

ABA Section of Antitrust Law. (2007). *Federal Statutory Exemptions from Antitrust Law* (Chicago: American Bar Association).

Banner, S. (2013). *The Baseball Trust: A History of Baseball's Antitrust Exemption*(New York: Oxford University Press).

Boliek, B. (2014). "Antitrust, Regulation, and the 'New' Rules of Sports Telecasts." *Hastings Law Journal* 65: 545–549.

Cox, P. (1995). "Flag on the Play? The Siphoning Effect on Sports Television." *Federal Communications Law Journal* 47: 571–591.

Delrahim, M. (2007). "Oversight and Overwork: What the Change in Control of Congress Means for Antitrust Enforcement and Policy." *Antitrust* 21 (Spring): 17–20.
Fisch, A. (1995). "Compulsory Licensing of Blacked-Out Professional Team Sporting Event Telecasts (PTSETS): Using Copyright Law to Mitigate Monopolistic Behavior." *Harvard Journal on Legislation* 32: 403–429.
Grow, N. (2012). "In Defense of Baseball's Antitrust Exemption." *American Business Law Journal* 49: 211–273.
Grow, N. (2015). "Regulating Professional Sports Leagues." *Washington and Lee Law Review* 72: 573–652.
Mitten, M., and Hernandez, A. (2013). "The Sports Broadcasting Act of 1961: A Comparative Analysis of Its Effects on Competitive Balance in the NFL and NCAA Division I FBS Football." *Ohio Northern University Law Review* 39: 745–772.
Moran, D. (1999). "Illegal Procedure? The Antitrust Implications of NFL Sunday Ticket." *Journal of Law and Commerce* 18: 397–413.
Phelps, Z. (2004). "Stadium Construction for Professional Sports: Reversing the Inequities Through Tax Incentives." *Saint John's Journal of Legal Commentary* 18: 981–1029.
Raut, A. (2011). "Antitrust in the 112th Congress." *Antitrust Source* 10 (August): 1–10.
Respect for Native Americans in Professional Sports Act of 2015. HR 3487, 114th Cong., 1st Sess. (Sept. 10, 2015).
Roberts, G. (2001). "The Legality of the Exclusive Collective Sale of Intellectual Property Rights by Sports Leagues." *Virginia Journal of Sports and the Law* 3: 52–78.
Quirk, J., and Fort, R. (1999). *Hard Ball: The Abuse of Power in Pro Team Sports* (Princeton, N.J.: Princeton University Press).
Surdam, D. (2015). *The Big Leagues Go to Washington: Congress and Sports Antitrust, 1951-1989* (Urbana: University of Illinois Press).
107 Cong. Rec. Pt. 15, 87th Cong., 1st Sess. (1961).
Telecasting of Professional Sports Contests. House Committee on the Judiciary, 87th Cong., 1st Sess. (Aug. 28, 1961).
Telecasting of Professional Sports Contests. S. Rep. No. 87-1087, 87th Cong., 1st Sess. (1961).

Cases

Chicago Prof'l Sports Ltd. P'ship v. National Basketball Ass'n, 808 F. Supp. 646 (N.D. Ill. 1992).
Kingray, Inc. v. National Basketball Association, 188 F. Supp. 2d 1177 (S.D. Cal. 2002).
Laumann v. National Hockey League, 907 F. Supp. 2d 465 (S.D.N.Y. 2012).
Shaw v. Dallas Cowboys Football Club, Ltd., 172 F.3d 299 (3d Cir. 1999).
United States v. National Football League, 116 F. Supp. 319 (E.D. Pa. 1953).
United States v. National Football League, 196 F. Supp. 445 (E.D. Pa. 1961).
United States Football League v. National Football League, 842 F.2d 1335 (2d Cir. 1988).
WTWV, Inc. v. National Football League, 678 F.2d 142 (11th Cir. 1982).

CHAPTER 18

YOUTH AND HIGH SCHOOL SPORTS LAW ISSUES

BRIAN L. PORTO

1. Youth Sports

The American penchant for entrepreneurship is more evident in youth sports today than ever before, with mixed results. A record number of American children, some 41 million, according to one observer, now play organized sports (Hyman, 2012). But parental angst and aspiration drive much of this participation, according to Michael Messner, a sports sociologist at UCLA. He observes: "There's a thought that your kid has to have every advantage because the world is a competitive place. To give your kid that edge is considered a sign of love" (Hyman, 2012).

The prospect of financial gain for individuals and communities also fuels a push for more and better games and tournaments in bigger and better facilities. Since the early 1990s, youth sports have been an engine for tourism, as tournaments in baseball, softball, basketball, volleyball, and other sports became a means for communities to cash in on the youth sports craze. Among the early converts to youth sports tourism as a revenue source were Panama City, Florida; Rockford, Illinois; Kingsport, Tennessee; Frisco and Round Rock, Texas; and Virginia Beach, Virginia. But the temple of America's devotion to youth sports is the ESPN Wide World of Sports Complex at Disney World, a 200--acre campus near Orlando, Florida that features two field houses, a 9,500-seat ballpark, eight all-purpose outdoor fields, four baseball diamonds, six softball diamonds, a track-and-field complex, a cross-country course, and ten tennis courts accompanied by an 8,500-seat tennis stadium (Hyman, 2012). And the event that most epitomizes youth sports tourism may be the National Softball Tournament held each July in Round Rock, Texas, which, when author Mark Hyman visited in 2010, included 143 teams of fifteen girls each, accompanied by parents, grandparents, and siblings and hailing from as far away as California and Puerto Rico (Hyman, 2012).

The youth sports craze is about profits and economic development for merchants and their communities, but for at least some athletes and parents, it is about developing young athletic talent in the hope that, someday, John or Sally can earn a college athletic scholarship or perhaps even "turn pro." Tom Farrey, executive director of the Aspen Institute's "Project Play," says, "Youth sport[] is not just about orange slices and kids running free. It's about aggregating talent in as elite a setting as possible so that your kid can receive a reward at 17 or 18" (Jovenal, 2015, A1).

1.1. A Short History of Youth Sports

Youth sports were not always so commercialized and professionalized. They became organized at the end of the nineteenth century, led by the "Playground Movement" and a religious and social phenomenon known as "Muscular Christianity," which later gave way to national sports entities, such as Little League Baseball and the American Youth Soccer Association. The Playground Movement created playgrounds in many American cities and organized games for children. It was a first step in organizing youth sports, but ultimately it failed because it was unable to reach the children of immigrant and working-class families (Spies, 2006). Muscular Christianity preached that a strong, healthy body coincided with a strong, healthy soul. A perceived moral corruption in big cities during the Industrial Age spurred Christian groups to introduce organized sport to boys as a means of socialization and education. An outgrowth of Muscular Christianity was the Young Men's Christian Association (YMCA), founded in 1851 as a way to "nurture the healthy development of children . . . [and] strengthen[] families" through transmitting the important social values, such as "caring, honesty, respect and responsibility" found in sports (Spies, 2006, 276). By 1892, 348 YMCA's were open throughout the United States.

Little League Baseball, founded in 1939, had similar, although not expressly Christian, aims: to teach boys (and, starting in 1974, girls too) "the qualities of citizenship, discipline, teamwork and physical well-being" (Spies, 2006, 277). Growth was slow at first, with only twelve leagues nationwide in 1946, but the baby boom enabled Little League to expand to 1,500 leagues nationwide by 1952, and its annual World Series became a television staple by 1963. Today, the championship game draws up to 40,000 live spectators and is televised on ABC, with ESPN televising the earlier-round games.

If baseball was the baby boomers' game of choice, soccer has played the same role for Generation X and the Millennials. This is evidenced by the increasing prominence of the American Youth Soccer Organization (AYSO), which began in Torrance, California, in 1964 and by the mid-1990s, encompassed nearly 40,000 teams and half a million children in forty-six states. AYSO stressed two principles: "Everybody Plays" and "Balanced Teams." Under the former, every child who registers to play is guaranteed playing time for at least half the game. Under the latter, each team will be balanced according to the players' skills and will be reorganized each year to ensure that balance. These principles are admirable, but because AYSO is no longer the leading organizer of youth soccer in the United States, many soccer-playing children cannot benefit from them.

Indeed, the dominant trend in youth sports during the past generation has not been inclusion but, rather, the evolution of all-star and elite traveling teams. These teams are especially common in soccer and basketball. Based on a tryout, adults select the most talented children in a particular sport from a particular age group. The resulting teams are compilations of the best athletes in that sport from a certain town or community, who travel to other cities and states to play other elite teams.

These arrangements, which can begin as early as age seven or eight, have consequences. They encourage young athletes to specialize in one sport by playing it year round, and they foster what one commentator calls "a keep-up-with-the-Joneses mentality" of near-constant training and competition (Spies, 2006). That mentality can produce "overuse injuries," such as tendonitis, bursitis, and stress fractures, which are not the result of one big blow but, rather, of "an accumulation of repetitive microtraumas" (Spies, 2006). When children played sports only for enjoyment, they could stop when tired or injured. Now that they play on teams and in leagues, they may feel pressure to continue playing despite fatigue or injury for fear of disappointing coaches, parents, or teammates. One commentator has observed: "Gone are the days of pickup games of sandlot baseball; those days have been replaced with leagues that treat children as miniature professional athletes" (Spies, 2006, 285).

1.2. Legal Implications of Professionalism

When professionalization takes hold, lawsuits follow, even in youth sports. In 2015 Audrey Dimitrew won a place on a club volleyball team in Chantilly, Virginia. She was sixteen years old and hoped to impress the coach at her high school and perhaps college coaches too. But when the coach of the club team "benched" her and the league would not let her move to another team, she and her parents sued. She feared a lack of playing time during the spring 2015 season. For its part, the league feared that if it allowed Audrey to move to another team, other disappointed players would make the same request. In March 2015 the Dimitrews sought an injunction that would enable Audrey to play the rest of the season with a new team. But the trial court denied the request, stating that it could not intervene in the decision making of a private organization (Jovenal, 2015, A1).

Sadly, parental actions arising out of youth sports disputes have involved not only civil courts but criminal courts too. Parental intrusiveness has led to ugly altercations, such as when a father broke an umpire's jaw at his son's Little League game because the father objected to a particular call, when a "soccer mom" slapped a fourteen-year-old referee at a youth soccer game, and, most tragically, when a "hockey dad" beat another father to death after arguing at their sons' practice.

The latter incident occurred in 2000 between Thomas Junta and Michael Costin, while Costin was supervising a hockey practice for ten-year-old boys, including his three sons and Junta's son at an ice rink in Reading, Massachusetts. Junta objected to excessive body checking, and he left the stands and went onto the ice, where he shouted at Costin. In response, Costin attacked Junta. A rink employee separated the two men and asked Junta to leave. Junta left the rink with his son, but later returned to retrieve his son's two friends. When he saw Costin, a second argument ensued, followed by punches. Junta threw Costin to the floor and repeatedly beat him about the head and neck. After being transported to a hospital, Costin lapsed into a coma and was put on a ventilator. The following day, he was removed from the ventilator after being declared brain dead and died soon thereafter.

Thomas Junta was convicted of a lesser charge of involuntary manslaughter, an unintentional killing resulting from a battery that he knew or should have known would endanger Costin's life. Although he could have been sentenced to twenty years in prison under Massachusetts law, in 2002 he received a sentence of six to ten years instead (Fiore, 2003).

Misconduct by parents and youth coaches has prompted sports leagues to devise measures designed to protect their young athletes from abuse and themselves from liability for tortious or criminal behavior by adults. Some youth sports leagues require that coaches undergo criminal background checks to obtain coaching positions. The National Alliance of Youth Sports (NAYS), a nonprofit, offers certification programs for persons who wish to coach in a youth sports organization affiliated with NAYS. To become certified, coaches must undergo training and sign a code of ethics. If a coach violates the code, NAYS can revoke that coach's certification on the recommendation of a league's board of directors, which would bar the coach from participating in affiliated youth sports associations (Fiore, 2003).

The Jupiter-Tequesta Athletic Association, a youth-sports association in Florida, was the first such group to require its athletes' parents to enroll in classes that teach appropriate behavior at sporting events. Parents must take an oath to support the coaches and officials. If a parent fails to take the course, that parent's child will be ineligible to play. In Massachusetts, representatives from the Governor's Committee on Physical Fitness and Sports responded to the Junta case by implementing the Massachusetts Sport Parent Code of Conduct, a written contract that parents must sign before their children can play. Parents agree to follow a set of guidelines when attending a youth sporting event. Besides youth sports associations, the Massachusetts Department of Education and the Massachusetts Interscholastic Athletic Association have adopted the code, ensuring it applies to middle school and high school games too. For its part, Little League Baseball International has created a "Parent's Pledge" to be used within its organization. Parents promise to "teach all children to play fair . . . positively support all managers, coaches, and players . . . [and] respect all decisions of the umpires" (Spies, 2006, 289). Says President Fred Engh of NAYS: "No organization that runs sports for children should allow parents to register their child without the parent going through an orientation and training program on ethics and sportsmanship" (Fiore, 2003).

New Jersey has enacted legislation that holds parents and coaches accountable for their bad behavior at youth sporting events (N.J. Stat. Ann. § 5:17-1). The New Jersey law empowers school boards and youth sports associations (i.e., leagues organized by private nonprofits or county or municipal recreation departments) to establish athletic codes of conduct. The codes are to set guidelines for appropriate behavior at youth sports events and to enable school boards and youth sports associations to:

> ban the presence of any person at youth sports events (competitions, instructional events, and practices) who 1) engages in verbal or physical threats or abuse aimed at any student, coach, official, or parent, or 2) initiates a fight or scuffle with any student, coach, official, parent, or other person if the conduct occurs at or in connection with a school or community sponsored youth sports event.
>
> (N.J. Stat. Ann. § 5:17-1(a))

Typically, youth sports associations are private, so they are not "state actors" within the meaning of the Fourteenth Amendment to the U.S. Constitution. Therefore, their decisions are generally not subject to legal challenges based on constitutional claims of the denial of liberty or due process. School districts, however, are state actors; hence, they may be subject to constitutional challenges arising out of their operation of sports programs.

But in *Nichols v. Western Local Board of Education*, a state court in Ohio held that even though the education and upbringing of one's children is a recognized liberty interest under the Constitution, a parent does not have a constitutional right to attend school activities or be present on school property. In that case, school administrators had banned a parent from attending school activities at her child's school for three months because of a verbal altercation between the parent and her daughter's coach in the locker room after a volleyball game. The parent appealed, but the school superintendant upheld the ban, as did the school board at a meeting with the parent, who had counsel with her. The meeting was not a full-dress due process hearing, though. The parent then took her case to court, but the court rejected her constitutional claim, reasoning that Ohio school boards may govern school activities and school property without adopting formal rules on all aspects of such governance, subject to an "abuse of discretion" standard, which was satisfied in this case. The court then concluded that because no constitutional "liberty interest" exists for parents to attend school activities or be present on school property, school authorities may exclude them from school activities and property without a due process hearing.

Even without constitutional claims, private youth sports associations face an array of potential legal issues arising out of rule enforcement, the conduct of coaches and parents, and, increasingly, concerns about player safety, especially the prevention and treatment of concussions. The latter will figure prominently in the following section, which addresses high school sports. Other legal issues to be addressed in the next section are preventing hazing, creating opportunities for disabled and transgender athletes, improving opportunities for female athletes, and protecting athletes' freedom of expression.

2. High School Sports

As this section explains, neurological injuries associated with contact sports and hazing abuses are two of the most significant challenges facing high school sports.

2.1. The Concussion Scare

For many young athletes, playing high school sports can be a life-changing experience, but for some, it can be a life-damaging or even a life-ending experience because of a traumatic brain injury resulting from a concussion. These injuries can occur in youth sports, too, but they have figured most prominently in high school (and middle school) sports.

Perhaps the most publicized young victim of a sports-induced concussion was Zackery Lystedt of Washington State, who was initially injured during the first half of a middle school football game, when his head hit the turf hard while he was making a tackle. He left the game at that time, but returned in the second half. Although he finished the game, he collapsed afterward and had to be airlifted to a hospital. Zack and his parents settled a civil suit with his school district for $14.6 million, which reflects the gravity and extent of his injuries (Brandwein, 2013). In a 2012 interview with *Seattle Magazine*, Zack's father recounted those injuries: "He was on life support for seven days; he couldn't speak for nine months. After 13 months, he could move his left arm a little; it took two years to get rid of the feeding tube and four years before he could move his right leg purposefully" (Mickool, 2012).

Under these circumstances, Zack's ability to stand and walk a few steps, haltingly, as he did in 2011 at his classmates' high school graduation, was a major accomplishment. He will need a lifetime of assistance.

Zack and his parents were instrumental in the passage of the first state law establishing a protocol for the recognition and treatment of concussions in young athletes. The law, which Washington's state legislature enacted in 2009 and which is codified at Wash. Rev. Code § 28A.600.190, bears his name.

Contrary to popular belief, a concussion is not a bruise on the brain (Cook, King, and, Polikandriotis, 2014). Instead, it is a mild brain injury, caused by trauma to the head, which results in a temporary disruption of normal brain functions. More precisely, it is (a) an injury to the head arising from blunt trauma, an acceleration force, or a deceleration force; that (b) then disrupts the normal functioning of the brain; (c) causing the victim to exhibit one of many indicators, either observed or self-reported; and (d) which indicator is attributable to the injury (Harvey, 2014). Because evidence of a concussion will not appear on a CT scan or an MRI, a key line of defense in preventing long-term injury is attention by coaches, fellow athletes, and parents to typical symptoms, such as vomiting, confusion, or loss of consciousness. These symptoms usually occur within minutes after the injury, but they may also appear several hours, or even days, later.

Immediate removal from play of anyone who exhibits such symptoms is essential to preventing a mild brain injury from becoming a traumatic brain injury. For people ages fifteen to twenty-four, sports are the second leading cause of traumatic brain injuries, behind only automobile accidents. When an athlete has suffered one concussion, the risk of a second one increases by three to six times, putting the athlete in danger of "second-impact syndrome," which Zackery Lystedt experienced. Second-impact syndrome is most dangerous for young, developing brains and, although the most heavily publicized cases have involved male football players, research shows that girls exhibit more symptoms and experience a longer recovery period (Lowrey, 2015).

2.1.1. *The Legislative Response*

In response to the injuries that Zackery Lystedt and other children have suffered, the legislatures of all fifty states and the District of Columbia have enacted laws that establish protocols for identifying and treating young athletes suspected of having been concussed. Indeed, the rapidity with which the states responded to the concussion emergency, from Washington in 2009 to Mississippi in 2014, has been extraordinary (Lowrey, 2015). Washington's Zackery Lystedt Law set guidelines to help individuals who work with youngsters to recognize concussion symptoms and protect their players from immediate reinjury after an initial concussion. Unfortunately, the U.S. Congress has been unable to pass S. 307, "The Concussion Treatment and Care Tools Act," introduced in January 2015, which would "establish guidelines for states on the implementation of best practices for diagnosis, treatment, and management of [concussions] in school-aged children" and would offer states grants to pursue those goals.

Because the Washington law was the model for those enacted in other states, its definition of the problem to be solved as "reinjury" is crucial to understanding the customary policy response to sports-related concussions nationwide. The Washington law and its descendants are designed to prevent second-impact syndrome instead of initial concussions; hence, they feature secondary prevention measures, such as (a) educating athletes, coaches, and parents about how to recognize concussion symptoms; (b) removing from a practice or a game an athlete who is suspected of having suffered a concussion; and (c) prohibiting that athlete from returning to play without clearance from a licensed health care professional.

The National Football League (NFL) was the prime mover behind the concussion legislation in the states. Its commissioner, Roger Goodell, urged legislators to adopt the three components of the Washington law. According to one commentator, "By lobbying and providing resources and recommendations for state legislatures, the NFL was able to frame the issue (reducing negative outcomes of concussions) and shape the response accordingly (facilitating overwhelmingly uniform laws and not directly regulating the content, rules, or procedures of football itself)" (Harvey, 2014, 102). In following the NFL's lead, this commentator contends, states missed an opportunity to experiment and innovate by requiring changes in game rules, practice drills, or equipment that could prevent or mitigate initial concussions. Perhaps, he adds, because the NFL faced a large class action lawsuit by former players during most of the time period when states were considering concussion legislation, it wished to divert attention from the frequency of initial concussions and focus instead on remedies that would not affect its bottom line by changing the nature of football.

Whatever the NFL's motivation was for emphasizing secondary prevention measures, its lobbying has resulted in a remarkable uniformity among the state laws that address sports-related concussions. No state has banned any sport that has a high risk of concussions. Forty-one states and the District of Columbia require the distribution of information about traumatic brain injuries to parents and athletes, although only thirty-four jurisdictions require the annual distribution of that information. A parent or guardian must sign a release form acknowledging receipt of the information. Forty-six states and the District of Columbia mandate the removal from play of an athlete who may have suffered a concussion, and all but two of those states require that removal last for at least twenty-four hours. And forty-four states and the District of Columbia require written clearance before a return to play, although only eight states insist that a medical doctor provide that clearance. Thirty-two jurisdictions require that the clearance provider, whether a doctor, nurse, or athletic trainer, be specially trained in the recognition and management of concussion symptoms.

Unfortunately, most of these concussion laws do not extend to the sorts of youth sports associations featured in the previous section, that is, athletic clubs and leagues sponsored by nonprofits or municipalities. Only a handful of states include non-scholastic athletic leagues in their concussion laws, meaning that children participating in those leagues may receive a lower standard of care if they suffer concussions. Similarly, only a handful of states extend their concussion protocols to children participating in school-based physical education classes.

A possible remedy for this failure is for local governments to condition the use of public athletic facilities by such leagues on their agreement to adhere to the three requirements of the Lystedt Law: concussion education, immediate removal of anyone suspected of having sustained a concussion, and no return to play without medical clearance. Says Professor Douglas Abrams, who proposes this remedy:

> In the exercise of its broad police power to manage athletic fields and other public property, a local decision-maker such as a city council may condition grant of a permit or license on a private applicant's adherence to reasonable conditions that advance public health and safety without working forfeiture of a constitutional right.
>
> (Abrams, 2015, 6)

Another solution, of course, is to amend one's law to cover recreational leagues, as Arkansas has done. Similarly, California has extended its concussion law to charter and private schools, and Indiana and Virginia have extended their respective statutes (Ind. Code § 20-34-7-1.5; Va. Code Ann. § 22.1-271.5) to cover any sports association that uses school property.

2.1.2. *The Need for Primary Prevention Measures*

The principal shortcoming of the existing youth sports concussion laws, though, is that they address secondary prevention measures, not primary ones. Only Massachusetts, in the original version of its concussion law, prohibits coaches, athletic trainers, and others from encouraging or allowing an athlete to use sports equipment as a weapon or to employ unreasonably dangerous sports techniques, such as helmet-to-helmet hits (Mass. Gen. Laws Ann. ch. 111, § 222). The Massachusetts law also requires school superintendants to maintain records of statutory compliance and empowers the state's health department to set penalties for noncompliant school districts.

Still, other states also seem increasingly aware of the need for primary prevention measures. In 2014, for example, California amended its law to limit full-contact football practices to two per week and to stipulate that the full-contact portion of a practice cannot exceed ninety minutes per day (Cal. Educ. Code § 49475 (2014)). A full-contact practice is defined as one in which "[a] drill[] or live action is conducted that involves collisions at game speed, [and] players execute tackles and other activity that is typical of an actual football game" (Barwald, 2015, 353). California and Texas have established reconditioning standards for the helmets used in high school football; in California, high school athletes may only use helmets approved by a recognized certifying agency, and in Texas, helmets may not be used for more than sixteen years, and helmets that are ten years old or more must be reconditioned at least once every two years (Lowrey, 2015).

Technology may help to reduce the frequency and severity of concussions in the future. One commentator notes that "helmet impact sensors or accelerometer devices [which are being developed] would provide real-time monitoring of head impact exposure to identify high-risk impacts and potentially alert sideline personnel that a concussion assessment is warranted" (Lowrey, 2015, 69). A more immediate solution may be the one that Dartmouth College's head football coach, Buddy Teevens, adopted in 2010: the elimination of full-contact practices. Instead of hitting their teammates in practice, Dartmouth players hit pads and tackling dummies and a "mobile virtual player," a motorized tackling dummy that moves across the field the way a player would. The result, says Teevens, has been a reduction in concussions from about twenty per season to just a handful, along with a reduced number of neck, back, and shoulder injuries. And keeping players healthy has enabled Dartmouth to move up from third place to second place to a tie for first place in the Ivy League during the years without full-contact practices. Those outcomes have so impressed Teevens's fellow Ivy League football coaches that in February 2016, they voted unanimously to eliminate full-contact practices during the regular season. The mobile virtual player may become a fixture on high school and college football practice fields in the future. So may helmetless tackling drills, in which players learn to absorb the blow of a tackle with their bodies, not their heads (King, 2014).

No technological improvement or modified tackling drill, however, can compensate completely for the absence of enforcement mechanisms in state concussion statutes. Few states have followed the lead of Pennsylvania, which requires the governing body of a school to suspend for the remainder of the season a coach who fails to properly remove an athlete from play, or of Connecticut, where the State Board of Education may revoke the coaching permit of a coach who makes that same mistake or who fails to complete training and refresher courses on the recognition and treatment of concussions (Harvey, 2014).

Moreover, twenty-five jurisdictions have attempted—directly or by inference—to limit liability for school districts, volunteers, health care providers, and others who might face lawsuits filed by athletes and their families based on how these persons responded to concussions on the athletic field. These laws usually permit lawsuits, though, for gross negligence and willful or wanton misconduct. Willful or wanton misconduct, first defined by the Massachusetts Supreme Judicial Court in *Commonwealth v. Welansky*, is intentional conduct, either of commission or omission, in the face of a duty to act, which conduct involves a high degree of likelihood that substantial harm will result to another person. For example, Wisconsin's law removes civil liability for "[a]ny athletic coach, official involved in an athletic activity, or volunteer who fails to remove a person from a youth athletic activity [who is suspected of having a concussion]" (Wis. Stat. § 118.293(5)(a) (2012)). But coaches must provide adequate supervision, know if medical staff is available and, if not, determine where medical staff will be, aid an injured athlete before emergency help arrives, and send that athlete to receive medical assistance (Amberg, 2012).

Besides limiting liability, state concussion laws lack a provision for baseline neuropsychological testing and a requirement that medical personnel be present on the sidelines during games. Best practices in the identification of concussions include pre-competition baseline measurements of an athlete's overall brain function. Once the baseline information is recorded, a medical provider can compare it with an injured athlete's post-injury responses to determine whether the athlete exhibits cognitive symptoms that suggest a concussion. To achieve this capability would require (a) creating a baseline assessment for all athletes; (b) establishing a reporting regime that requires coaches, hospitals, and schools to publicly identify instances of concussions across sports and school districts; and (c) reporting baseline assessments of athletes over time to measure any decline in performance and determine whether the decline may be the result of a concussion.

A survey of individuals in thirty-five states who were responsible for implementing concussion laws found that access to medical personnel trained in the recognition and treatment of concussions, who could assess potential injuries and make informed return-to-play decisions, was quite limited (Lowrey and Morain, 2014). Accordingly, improving the future availability of both baseline neuropsychological testing and medical providers for high school athletes will likely require partnerships between school districts and medical schools or nursing schools to collect data and to provide sideline medical personnel during games. State legislators could jump-start such partnerships by providing funds to cover at least some of the associated costs.

Thus, the first generation of remedies for concussions in young athletes has raised awareness about concussions and about establishing a protocol for reducing the likelihood of second-impact syndrome. The next generation of remedies should, and likely will, include new legislation, new technology, and partnerships between educators and medical providers designed to prevent concussions from occurring in the first place.

2.2. Preventing and Punishing Hazing

In the spring of 2016 Chester County (Pennsylvania) District Attorney Thomas Hogan charged three seniors at Conestoga High School in Berwyn, a Philadelphia suburb, with crimes related to an assault that occurred inside their football team's locker room. This assault was the latest in a spate of such activities since December 2015. During that month, in Sevier County, Tennessee, three high school basketball players were charged with raping another player with a pool cue so violently that the victim needed surgery for internal injuries. Two months later, in Norman, Oklahoma, four high school wrestlers were charged with raping two other wrestlers, including a twelve-year-old boy, in a school bus on the way home from a tournament. In the Pennsylvania case, seniors held a freshman player and assaulted him with a broomstick (including penetration) while others watched (Macur, 2016, B9). Explaining the necessity for criminal charges, the district attorney observed:

> If you want to have a kid stand up and sing a silly fight song, then it's all right, or [to] let the freshmen carry the Gatorade onto the practice field, go ahead. But kids have to stop doing things that will [cause] lasting physical or psychological damage to other kids.
>
> (Macur, 2016, B9)

The National Federation of State High School Associations, the umbrella group for the organizations that run high school sports in the fifty states, defines hazing as "any humiliating or dangerous activity expected of a student to belong to a group, regardless of their willingness to participate" (McMullen, 2014, 184). In athletic hazing, veteran players typically will initiate newer players, often by means of humiliating or even dangerous practices. Depending on the age of the participants, the rituals can include physical and verbal abuse, coerced same-sex sexual activity, coerced binge consumption of alcohol, sleep deprivation, physical assaults, and being kidnapped, transported, and abandoned.

When asked to justify hazing, athletes have usually cited the development of bonds among players and of team cohesion as positive consequences of the rituals. But studies have shown that no correlation exists between hazing and such beneficial results. Indeed, a recent report notes that "[t]he victims end up feeling disenfranchised from their team and are sometimes less excited about participating in team activities, even when the incidence of hazing diminishes as competition ensues" (New York University Sports and Society Program, 2014, 11-12).

American society surely condemns hazing, as evidenced by its criminalization in forty-four states, thirty-four of which make it a misdemeanor. Most states limit criminal liability for hazing to students, while also construing hazing as part of an initiation into or continued membership in a particular organization (Bittner, 2016). One exception is Oregon, which extends potential criminal penalties to "volunteers, coaches and faculty advisors of a student organization" (Or. Rev. Stat. Ann. § 163.197 (2015)). Still, hazing persists, usually perpetrated by adolescents, whose physical maturity and emotional intensity far exceed their capacity for self-restraint. Pediatric psychiatrist Ronald E. Dahl notes: "The pubescent youth has several years with a sexually mature body and brain systems that are activated for sexual and romantic interest and passions, but a relatively immature set of neurobehavioral systems for self-control and affect regulation" (Dahl, 2004, 18).

Under these circumstances, the best antidote to hazing is supervision by mature adults. Litigation often reveals the lack of adult supervision. In *Bashus v. Plattsmouth Community School District*, the plaintiff, a freshman football player, sued the defendants under Title IX, the federal law that prohibits sex discrimination in education, claiming that they were deliberately indifferent to his sexually charged hazing by a fellow student. The defendants moved to dismiss. A varsity player had harassed the plaintiff by exposing his genitals to the plaintiff, touching him offensively, and generally humiliating and intimidating him. Contrary to the school's staff handbook, which required faculty supervision of student activities in the building after regular school hours, no coaches or other supervisory personnel were in the locker room when the harassment occurred.

The magistrate judge noted that because this case involved alleged student-on-student sexual harassment, the Supreme Court's decision in *Davis v. Monroe County Board of Education* controlled. Under *Davis*, damages are not available for simple acts of teasing and name-calling between children. To hold a school district liable under the *Davis* rule, a plaintiff must show that the district (a) had actual knowledge of, and (b) was deliberately indifferent to, (c) harassment that was so severe, pervasive, and objectively offensive, that it (d) deprived the victim of access to the educational benefits or opportunities the school offered. In *Bashus*, the magistrate judge denied the defendants' dismissal motion because the facts featured no "insuperable bar to relief" for the plaintiff.

Similarly, in *Roe ex rel. Callahan v. Gustine Unified School District*, a freshman football player who attended a two-school summer football camp alleged that he suffered several acts of hazing, including an assault. The defendant's four coaches were responsible for supervising the team's sixty players off the field. On the second day of the camp, four older players chased the plaintiff into the locker room, held him down, and inserted a battery-powered air pump into his rectum. Later, one older player, using an effeminate tone of voice, called the plaintiff a homosexual and grabbed the plaintiff's buttocks in the shower. And, during a subsequent pillow fight, the older players hit the plaintiff in the head and face with pillow cases filled with heavy objects, causing him injuries.

Citing *Davis*, the trial court noted that a school district may be liable for damages under Title IX for student-on-student harassment. The test of a school district's prior knowledge of the harassment is whether the appropriate official knew enough about it to have responded with remedial measures to address it. In this case, a coach had seen four players put an air hose up a younger player's shorts during the camp, which sufficiently apprised him of harassment that he could have responded to with remedial measures. Therefore, a jury should decide whether that observation constituted actual knowledge of harassment under Title IX, so the court denied the defendants' motion for summary judgment.

The *Bashus* and *Roe* cases underscore the experts' conclusion that adolescent athletes require adult supervision. One expert, psychologist Susan Lipkins, equates leaving high school athletes in control of their own locker room to leaving "the inmates in charge of the asylum" (Macur, 2016, B9). According to Lipkins, any coach who does so is asking for trouble because the boys are often aggressive and power hungry. Leaving them unsupervised is especially dangerous today, when the hazing is more violent and sexual than in the past, because the perpetrators keep upping the ante of pain and humiliation to put their unique stamp on the ritual. A legal commentator agrees, advising, "The only way to break the tradition of hazing is to make the adults in the building responsible for the behavior" (Short, 2013, 422).

Thus, although criminal prosecutions may be appropriate when serious physical or psychological injuries result from hazing, they are unlikely to deter hazing because teenage boys are often impulsive and short-sighted. The best deterrent is to educate coaches about hazing and to put them in locker rooms before and after practices and games. Perhaps then they can demonstrate that manhood is about taking responsibility, not taking advantage. Schools that fail to supervise their athletes could face civil liability under Title IX on a sexual harassment theory.

2.3. Creating Opportunities for Athletes with Disabilities

Two federal statutes, the Rehabilitation Act of 1973 (Rehab Act) and the Americans with Disabilities Act of 1990 (ADA), require public schools, as recipients of federal funds (Rehab Act) and as "public accommodations" (ADA), to make "reasonable accommodations" that enable disabled students to participate in activities from which they would otherwise be excluded. Section 504 of the Rehab Act seeks to eliminate discrimination based on disability in any program or activity receiving federal financial assistance. It states: "[N]o otherwise qualified individual with a disability . . . shall, solely by reason of his or her disability, be excluded from the participation in, be denied the benefits of, or be subjected to discrimination under any program or activity receiving Federal financial assistance." Under Section 504, as articulated in *Dennin v. Connecticut Interscholastic Athletic Conference, Inc.*, athletes with disabilities who challenge their exclusion from competition must show that (a) they have a disability as defined by the Act; (b) they are "otherwise qualified" to participate in high school athletics or may be "otherwise qualified" (i.e., able to meet the essential requirements of the program they seek access to) by means of "reasonable accommodations"; (c) they are being excluded solely on the basis of a disability; and (d) the defendant school district receives federal funds. Similarly, to succeed in discrimination actions under the ADA, students must show (a) a disability; (b) a denial of an opportunity to participate in or benefit from services or accommodations because of that disability; and (c) the ADA's applicability to the defendant (Looby, 2012).

Neither statute identifies the requirements of a "reasonable accommodation," but subsequent regulations and court decisions have helped to do so. In sports, an accommodation is not reasonable if it imposes undue financial and administrative burdens on a school or requires a fundamental alteration in the nature of the game or event. The controlling court decision is *PGA Tour, Inc. v. Martin*. The case concerned a professional golfer's request to use a cart in professional tournaments because a severe circulatory condition in his leg prevented him from walking the course without suffering extreme fatigue and risking further injury. The U.S. Supreme Court held that "an individualized inquiry must be made to determine whether a specific modification for a particular person's disability would be reasonable under the circumstances as well as necessary for that person, and yet at the same time not work a fundamental alteration" (1896). Therefore, state high school athletic associations must first determine whether the requested accommodation would remove an essential feature of the sport. If not, they must decide whether granting the accommodation would provide the disabled athlete with an unfair advantage when competing.

In *Martin*, the Court concluded that his use of a cart would not fundamentally alter tournament golf because it would not affect an essential aspect of the game, nor would it advantage Martin because his disability already subjected him to greater fatigue than his competitors experienced. The cart would merely give him a fair chance to qualify for and compete in professional tournaments.

The "individual inquiry" that *Martin* requires now governs cases in which high school athletes with disabilities seek accommodations that would enable them to compete. That inquiry has helped to determine, for example, whether a high school should let a nineteen-year-old who was two years behind his age-group peers in school because of a learning disability play football during his senior year. In *Cruz v. Pennsylvania Interscholastic Athletic Association*, the athlete stood 5 feet, 3 inches tall, weighed just 130 pounds, and was a marginal player; the court granted the request because his participation would not alter the games in which he played or give his team an unfair advantage. In *Baisden v. West Virginia Secondary Schools Activities Commission*, though, the athlete stood 6 feet, 4 inches, weighed 280 pounds, and exhibited excellent speed for his size. The court denied his request because his participation would threaten younger, smaller players' safety and unfairly advantage his team.

A thornier issue has been whether to allow direct competition in track and field between wheelchair athletes and able-bodied athletes. In *Badgett v. Alabama High School Athletic Association*, the plaintiff sought to compete on her high school track team as a wheelchair athlete. Alabama allowed wheelchair athletes to compete, but only in a separate wheelchair division, with their times recorded at each meet. The eight fastest wheelchair athletes in each event during the season would advance to the state championship meet, where the qualifiers in each event would compete in the wheelchair division.

But Mallerie Badgett wanted to compete directly against able-bodied athletes, because competing alone made her feel that she was an exhibition rather than part of a team. She also wanted to be eligible to earn points for her team. A federal district court rejected the first request on safety grounds, fearing collisions between wheelchair athletes and their able-bodied competitors, and reasoning that separate wheelchair divisions or staggered starting times are customary in marathons and similar races, so the Association's proposed accommodation was reasonable. The court also rejected the second request because awarding Mallerie points would be unfair to rival schools that lacked wheelchair athletes.

The point-scoring issue also arose in *McFadden v. Grasmick*, in which Tatyana McFadden, a world class Paralympic Games wheelchair racer, sought to compete and earn points for her high school team. A federal district court in Maryland held that allowing her to earn points would not be a reasonable accommodation because the few teams with wheelchair racers would be able to earn points that their rivals without wheelchair racers could not.

Both decisions were correct under the *Martin* rule, although undoubtedly disappointing to the respective plaintiffs. Direct competition in close quarters between wheelchair athletes and able-bodied athletes presents a safety hazard, necessitating at least that wheelchair athletes start first, as they often do in long-distance running races. Allowing a lone wheelchair athlete to score points would give her team a source of points that other teams lacked, hence an unfair advantage. Thus, granting Mallerie Badgett's request would have posed a safety risk to all the competitors, while giving her team an unfair advantage. Granting Tatyana McFadden's request would have had the latter result.

Besides, both plaintiffs could compete against themselves and the clock, which lies at the heart of track and field and is a "reasonable" accommodation after all, if not the accommodation they preferred (Looby, 2012). In the longer term, perhaps the prevalence of wheelchair athletes in adult long-distance running will spur a younger generation to compete for their high schools, enabling them to vie for team points with rival "wheelers." Even then, courts will continue to wrestle with defining a "reasonable accommodation" for high school athletes in various sports under the Rehab Act and the ADA, in light of the *Martin* rule.

2.4. Improving Opportunities for Female Athletes and Creating Them for Transgender Athletes

Title IX, codified at 20 U.S.C. §§ 1681-1688, has improved the quantity and the quality of athletic opportunities for high school girls dramatically since its enactment in 1972. In 1975, the regulations implementing the statute went into effect, including those pertaining to sports. The key regulation states: "No person shall, on the basis of sex, be treated differently from another person or otherwise be discriminated against in any interscholastic, intercollegiate, club or intramural athletics offered by a recipient . . ." (34 CFR § 106.41(a)). Numerous court decisions have interpreted Title IX and its regulations to improve, if not equalize, athletic life for high school girls, relative to high school boys, throughout the United States.

For example, in *McCormick v. School District of Mamaroneck*, the U.S. Court of Appeals for the Second Circuit held that the defendant school district's scheduling of girls' soccer in the spring and boys' soccer in the fall violated Title IX by depriving the girls of a chance to play for regional and state championships, which occurred in the fall. Of the 714 public schools in New York State that offered girls' soccer, 649 offered it in the fall. As a result, the plaintiffs, two high school girls who played soccer, would have to pass up participating in an Olympic Development Program that operated in the spring in order to play for their respective high schools, a choice no boy had to face. Citing the Title IX regulations, which define "equal opportunity" to include equity in the "[s]cheduling of games and practices," the plaintiffs argued that the defendants' spring soccer schedule for girls violated the statutory intent.

The appellate court agreed, rejecting the defendants' claim that moving soccer to the fall would result in fewer opportunities for girls to play spring sports. The court reasoned that "[t]he school districts have not offered persuasive evidence that the other sports the schools offer in the spring will not be able to accommodate the girls; nor have they claimed an inability to add another spring sport" (299). The court also rejected the defendants' claim that moving soccer to the fall would force girls to choose between it and other fall sports. That would be a temporary problem, the court observed, because younger girls would choose their sports based on a fall soccer season, thereby avoiding the disruption of a change. Therefore, the court ordered the defendants to move girls' soccer to the fall.

Similarly, in *Parker v. Franklin County Community School Corporation*, the Seventh Circuit considered whether the defendant's requirement that its girls' basketball team play half of its games on Monday through Thursday nights, enabling the boys' team to play almost all of its games on Friday and Saturday nights, violated Title IX. It considered evidence showing the negative effects of the arrangement on the girls, including disproportionate academic burdens caused by a larger number of weeknight games, reduced school and community support because of smaller crowds at the weeknight games, and a feeling of inferiority relative to the boys' team. Thus, the appellate court reversed a grant of summary judgment for the school district because the plaintiffs had presented sufficient evidence of a Title IX violation for a jury to consider.

McCormick, *Parker*, and other cases have enabled high school girls to successfully challenge entrenched practices that denied them opportunities to play interscholastic sports or limited those opportunities, subjected them to second-class treatment, and punished them for complaining about the inequities they faced. But one long-standing practice that Title IX has endorsed is sex-segregated sports teams; ordinarily, this arrangement goes unchallenged, except by the occasional high school boy who wants to play field hockey.

Sex-segregated sports pose a challenge, though, for transgender students in American high schools. Although physiological differences between boys and girls support segregating sport participation by gender, that segregation nevertheless forces the issue of whether transgender athletes will compete according to their gender at birth or their gender identity.

One possible source of guidance in providing opportunities for transgender athletes is the "Stockholm Consensus," an agreement reached in 2003 that has become a template for sports organizations worldwide on this subject. Under this agreement, transgender athletes can compete in their newly assigned gender after undergoing sex reassignment surgery. Unless the surgery occurred before puberty, the athlete must also undergo hormone therapy to minimize "gender-related advantages," observe a two-year waiting period after surgery, and obtain government recognition of the newly assigned gender (Buzuvis, 2011).

These requirements are impractical and unduly prohibitive for high school athletes, who have only a small window of time in which to compete. The surgical requirement would effectively operate as a ban because psychologists commonly recommend against surgical reassignment for children. And even for the teenager who has had surgical reassignment, the two-year waiting period after surgery would render the athlete ineligible for half of the high school years. Even a required hormonal transition is problematic because it would deny athletic eligibility to transgender students who lacked financial access to such treatment or who were not emotionally ready for it.

Therefore, the best approach regarding eligibility for transgender high school athletes seems to be that of the Washington Interscholastic Athletic Association (WIAA). In 2007, the WIAA became the first interscholastic athletic association to adopt a formal policy for transgender athletes, which permits students to participate in sports "in a manner that is consistent with their gender identity, irrespective of the gender listed on a student's records" (Buzuvis, 2011, 25). Since then, fourteen other states have joined Washington in not requiring a transgender high school athlete to undergo surgery or hormone treatment to be eligible to compete. In Washington, the process of becoming eligible to play according to one's gender identity includes a hearing before an eligibility committee to determine if the request is legitimate. Medical evidence is not required, but written statements from the student and a parent or guardian, or a health care provider, are necessary. The student can appeal an adverse decision to the executive director of the WIAA; a favorable decision will remain in effect throughout a student's high school years. This arrangement is fair because it seeks to include transgender athletes who have a genuine transsexual gender identity, while excluding anyone who claims a particular gender identity for athletic purposes only. It also maintains the sex-segregated model of athletic participation that has been associated with exponential expansion of athletic opportunities for women under Title IX.

Just as Title IX has benefited female athletes since its enactment, it could well benefit transgender athletes in the future, especially in those states that either have no policy regarding transgender high school athletes or that restrict students to competing according to their gender at birth rather than their gender identity. The Supreme Court is unlikely to create a new suspect classification based on gender identity, so a constitutional challenge to discrimination against transgender athletes, based on the Equal Protection Clause, is not foreseeable. But the Court has been willing to construe "discrimination based on sex," which Title IX prohibits, broadly, suggesting that it may be amenable to including discrimination resulting from gender nonconformity within the ambit of Title IX. That conclusion would enable transgender high school athletes to challenge schools' refusal to let them compete according to their gender identity. It would equalize life for such athletes nationwide.

2.5. Protecting Athletes' Free Speech

In *Tinker v. Des Moines Independent Community School District*, the Supreme Court observed that neither students nor teachers "shed their constitutional rights to freedom of speech or expression at the schoolhouse gate" (506). Under *Tinker*, schools may prescribe and control student conduct, but they may not practice viewpoint discrimination. To restrict student speech, they must show facts from which they could reasonably forecast "substantial disruption of or material interference with school activities" if the speech were allowed. Mere "undifferentiated fear or apprehension of disturbance" cannot justify restricting speech.

Subsequent Supreme Court decisions have limited *Tinker*, though, holding that students lack the same free-speech rights enjoyed by adults outside school because the needs of schools affect the expressive rights of students. For example, a school can discipline a student for using sexually explicit language during a speech at a school assembly. A school can refuse to allow certain articles to be published in its newspaper because they are inconsistent with its basic educational mission, even though government could not censor the same speech outside of school. And a school district can discipline a student who, during a school event, unfurls a large banner "reasonably viewed as promoting illegal drug use."

In two cases involving athletes, a coach conditioned team membership on apologizing to teammates and the athletes refused. The plaintiff in the 1996 case *Seamons v. Snow* was a hazing victim whose football teammates had assaulted him in the locker room. He reported the incident to the police; afterward, in a bizarre twist, the coach required him to apologize to his teammates for having done so. When the victim refused, the coach dismissed him from the team. Reversing a grant of summary judgment for the defendants, the Tenth Circuit held that "coaches may not penalize players for engaging in peaceful speech activit[ies], which [do] not create substantial disorder, materially disrupt class work, or invade the rights of others." The court did not rely on *Tinker* explicitly, but it appeared to hold that merely upsetting team unity did not create "material disruption" sufficient to restrict speech under *Tinker*.

In *Wildman v. Marshalltown School District*, a junior varsity basketball coach conditioned continued team membership on the plaintiff's apologizing to her teammates for writing a letter critical of the coach. The letter had complained about the coach's refusal to promote the plaintiff to the varsity, used some vulgar language, and invited her teammates to join her in defying the coach. The Eighth Circuit weighed the school's considerable interest in maintaining unified athletic teams against the plaintiff's interest in playing sports and concluded that the former should prevail. Accordingly, it affirmed a grant of summary judgment for the defendant.

In *Pinard v. Clatskanie School District 6J*, members of a boys' high school basketball team drafted a petition seeking their coach's removal and refused to board the bus to an away game. The trial court granted summary judgment for the defendant, but the Ninth Circuit reversed and remanded. Relying on *Tinker*, the court reasoned that the school could not punish the players for the petition, which aired their grievances privately and gave the school no reason to anticipate disruption. But the boycott was punishable because it had materially disrupted the school's basketball program; the school had invested time and money in its sports offerings, so *Tinker* did not entitle the players to disrupt it.

A related school interest—a coach's right to maintain order and discipline—conflicted with athletes' First Amendment rights in *Lowery v. Euverard*. In *Lowery*, high school football players drafted a petition seeking their coach's removal and obtained signatures before the coach learned of the petition and dismissed its leading supporters from the team. Here, unlike in *Pinard*, the petition alleged abusive conduct by the coach and a violation of state-association rules. And, unlike the Ninth Circuit in *Pinard*, the Sixth Circuit here sought to balance an athlete's expressive freedom and a coach's need to maintain order and discipline. Emphasizing a coach's authority to lead and to achieve team goals, the court held that a petition alone can cause the requisite disruption under *Tinker*; therefore, it reversed the trial court's denial of summary judgment for the defendants.

Because courts weigh high school athletes' First Amendment rights against coaches' interests in controlling their teams and schools' interests in preserving their athletic programs, athletes face constraints on expression that do not apply to non-athletes. *Tinker's* "material disruption" test governs, so when a petition is aired privately and is confined to the necessary audience, disruption is unlikely and a court will presumably protect the free-speech right. When, however, the speech causes or is likely to cause a team to refuse to practice or compete, a court will likely find a material disruption, allowing the speech to be restricted. Similarly, when the speech complains about a lack of playing time, thereby challenging a coach's authority, the coach's interest in maintaining that authority will likely prevail.

A disturbing situation occurs when a petition identifies abusive, unethical, or even illegal behavior by a coach, and the coach seeks to punish the players for causing a disruption, even though the true cause was the coach's behavior, not that of the players. This situation may have existed in *Lowery*, but the Sixth Circuit discounted it by bowing to the authority of coaches. It calls for the application of a modified *Tinker* rule, whereby a court would determine whether the speech could be considered "whistleblower" conduct that reveals inappropriate or unlawful behavior (Donnelly, 2009). If so, the court would then have to determine whether the defendant either ignored the claimed wrongdoing, and punished the athletes on "disruption" grounds, or retaliated against the athletes for blowing the whistle on misconduct. Under either conclusion, the First Amendment claim should prevail. This modification reflects the spirit of *Tinker*, which teaches that public schools should not be "enclaves of totalitarianism" where officials "possess absolute authority over their students."

3. Conclusion

Youth sports and high school sports generate many legal issues, as befits their high degrees of organization. In youth sports, civil actions have challenged decisions by coaches and league administrators, and criminal prosecutions have punished bad behavior by coaches and parents. Organizations and communities nationwide have responded to bad behavior by drafting conduct codes for coaches and parents and by requiring both to attend training sessions before participating (even as a parent-spectator) in youth sports. Some states have also responded to the concussion crisis by extending to youth sports associations their concussion protocols for middle and high school athletes.

Concussions have prompted the principal legislative action in high school sports in recent years: the enactment of recognition and treatment protocols in all fifty states. Another persistent challenge is hazing, which most states have criminalized, but only responsible adult supervision can prevent. High schools will likely face increasing demands for the "reasonable accommodation" of athletes with disabilities, and both female and transgender athletes will use Title IX to challenge "discrimination based on sex." The latter will argue that those words include discrimination based on gender non-conformity. Public schools, bound by the Fourteenth Amendment, can also anticipate constitutional challenges by athletes who allege violations of their free-speech rights.

References

Abrams, D. (2015). "Concussion Safety in Children's Sports: A Central Role for the 'Power of the Permit.'" *Journal of Business & Technology Law* 10: 1.

Amberg, P. A. (2012). "Protecting Kids' Melons: Potential Liability and Enforcement Issues With Youth Concussion Laws." *Marquette Sports Law Review* 23: 171.

Barwald, C. (2015). "Practicing Concussion Prevention: Enacting State Legislation Regulating Contact in High School Football Practices." *Thomas Jefferson Law Review* 37: 337.

Bigelow, B. (2001). *Just Let the Kids Play: How to Stop Other Adults from Ruining Your Child's Fun and Success in Youth Sports* (Deerfield Beach, Fla.: Health Communications, Inc.).

Bittner, N. (2016). "A Hazy Shade of Winter: The Chilling Issues Surrounding School Hazing and the Litigation that Follows." *Jeffrey S. Moorad Sports Law Journal* 23: 211.

Brandwein, K. (2013). "Goals and Obstacles in Legislating Concussion Management in Youth Sports." *Willamette Sports Law Journal* 10: 28.

Buzuvis, E. (2011). "Transgender Student-Athletes and Sex-Segregated Sport: Developing Policies of Inclusion for Intercollegiate and Interscholastic Athletics." *Seton Hall Journal of Sports and Entertainment Law* 21: 1.

Cook, A., King, Harold, and Polikandriotis, J. A. (2014). "Where Do We Go from Here? An Inside Look into the Development of Georgia's Youth Concussion Law." *Journal of Law, Medicine, & Ethics* 42): 284.

Dahl, R. (2004) "Adolescent Brain Development: A Period of Vulnerabilities and Opportunities." *Annals of the New York Academy of Science* 1021: 1.

Donnelly, E. (2009). "What Happens When Student-Athletes Are the Ones Who Blow the Whistle? How *Lowery v. Euverard* Exposes a Deficiency in the First Amendment Rights of Student-Athletes." *New England Law Review* 43: 943.

Fiore, D. (2003). "Parental Rage and Violence in Youth Sports: How Can We Prevent 'Soccer Moms' and 'Hockey Dads' from Interfering in Youth Sports and Causing Games to End in Fistfights Rather than Handshakes?" *Villanova Sports and Entertainment Law Journal* 10: 103.

Harvey, H. (2014). "Refereeing the Public Health." *Yale Journal of Public Health Policy, Law, & Ethics* 14: 66.

Hyman, M. (2012). *The Most Expensive Game in Town: The Rising Cost of Youth Sports and the Toll on Today's Families* (Boston: Beacon Press, 2012).

Jouvenal, J. (2015). "For benched Va. teen, it's not just a game." *Washington Post* Apr. 1: A1.

King, P. (2014). "Helmetless Football? It's the New Practice at New Hampshire," http://mmqb.si.com/2014/12/04/helmetless-football-practice-univserity-of-new-hampshire. Accessed November 4, 2016.

Looby, J. (2012). "Reasonable Accommodations for High School Athletes with Disabilities: Preserving Sports While Providing Access for All." *Sports Lawyers Journal* 19): 227.

Lowrey, K.M. (2015). "State Laws Addressing Youth Sports-Related Traumatic Brain Injury and the Future of Concussion Law and Policy." *Journal of Business & Technology Law* 10: 61.

Lowrey, K.M. and Morain, S. (2014). "State Experiences Implementing Youth Sports Concussion Laws: Challenges, Successes, and Lessons for Evaluating Impact." *Journal of Law, Medicine, & Ethics* 42: 290.

Macur, J. (2016). "Something is Missing in High School Hazing Stories: Adults." *New York Times* Mar. 14: B9.

McMullen, J. (2014). "Addressing Abusive Conduct in Youth Sports." *Marquette Sports Law Review* 25: 181.

Mickool, S. (2013, April 9). "The Story Behind the Zackery Lystedt Law." Seattle Magazine. Available at http://www.seattlemag.com/article/story-behind-zackery-lystedt-law.

New York University Sports and Society Program. (2014). *Changing the Culture of Youth Sports: An Initiative to Combat Abusive Behavior and All Forms of Intolerance In Order to Promote Civility and Respect Among Athletes* (New York: New York University Sports and Society Program).

Short, S. (2013). "Warriors, Machismo, and Jockstraps: Sexually Exploitative Athletic Hazing and Title IX in the Public School Locker Room." *Western New England Law Review* 35: 377.

Spies, J. (2006). "Only Orphans Should Be Allowed to Play Little League: How Parents Are Ruining Organized Youth Sports for Their Children and What Can Be Done About It." *Sports Lawyers Journal* 13: 276.

Cases

Badgett v. Alabama High Sch. Athletic Ass'n, 2007 U.S. Dist. LEXIS (N.D. Ala. May 5, 2007).
Baisden v. West Va. Secondary Sch. Activities Comm'n, 568 S.E.2d 32 (W. Va. 2002).
Bashus v. Plattsmouth Cmty. Sch. Dist., 2006 WL 2226338 (D. Neb).
Commonwealth v. Welansky, 55 N.E.2d 902 (Mass. 1944).
Cruz v. Pennsylvania Interscholastic Athletic Ass'n, 157 F. Supp. 2d 485 (E.D. Pa. 2001).
Davis v. Monroe County Bd. of Educ., 526 U.S. 629 (1999).
Dennin v. Conn. Interscholastic Athletic Conference, Inc., 913 F. Supp. 663 (D. Conn. 1996), vacated as moot and appeal dismissed, 94 F.3d 96 (2d Cir. 1996).
Lowery v. Euverard, 497 F.3d 584 (6th Cir. 2007).
McCormick v. School Dist. of Mamaroneck, 370 F.3d. 275 (2d Cir. 2004).
McFadden v. Grasmick, 485 F. Supp. 2d 642 (D. Md. 2007).
Nichols v. Western Local Bd. of Educ., 805 N.E.2d 206 (Ohio Com. Pl. 2003).
Parker v. Franklin County Cmty. Sch. Corp., 667 F.3d 910 (7th Cir. 2012).
PGA Tour, Inc. v. Martin, 532 U.S. 661 (2001).
Pinard v. Clatskanie Sch. Dist. 6J, 467 F.3d 755 (9th Cir. 2006).
Roe ex rel. Callahan v. Gustine Unified Sch. Dist., 678 F. Supp. 2d 1008 (E.D. Cal. 2009).
Seamons v. Snow, 84 F.3d 1226 (10th Cir. 1996).
Tinker v. Des Moines Indep. Cmty. Sch. Dist., 393 U.S. 503 (1969).
Wildman v. Marshalltown Sch. Dist., 249 F.2d 768 (8th Cir. 2001).

Statutes

Federal
Rehabilitation Act, Section 504, 29 U.S.C. § 794 (1973).
Americans with Disabilities Act, 42 U.S.C. §§ 12101 et seq. (1990).
Title IX, 20 U.S.C. §§ 1681-1688 (1972).

State
Cal. Educ. Code § 49475 (2015).
Ind. Code § 20-34-7-1.5 (2014).
Mass. Gen. Laws Ann. ch. 111, § 222 (2016).
N.J. Stat. Ann. § 5:17-1 (2002).
Or. Rev. Stat. Ann. § 163.197 (2015).
Va. Code Ann. § 22.1-271.5 (2016).
Wash. Rev. Code § 28A.600.190 (2009).
Wis. Stat. § 118.293(5)(a) (2012).

Regulations
34 CFR § 106.41(a).

CHAPTER 19

COLLEGE ATHLETICS

The Growing Tension Between Amateurism and Commercialism

WARREN K. ZOLA

1. Introduction

IN the twenty-first century, college athletics has evolved from quaint contests between colleges into a burgeoning business unto itself. As interest explodes, so too do media broadcast rights fees, creating a multi-billion-dollar-a-year industry. Not surprisingly, with greater revenue available, the stakes have skyrocketed for all constituents including institutions, students, conferences, and the governing body—the National Collegiate Athletic Association (NCAA).

Intercollegiate athletics is no longer solely viewed as merely an instrument that provides educational opportunities for students but as an essential revenue stream for higher education. The obvious consequence is that many institutions experience tremendous tension between their mission to educate and commercial opportunities with regard to college athletics. To combat this new paradigm, the NCAA crafts additional rules to govern and the bureaucracy grows, further engulfing college athletics.

The end result is inevitable: frequent disputes arise from the friction between academics and the increasing commercialism, triggering an abundance of legal challenges. This chapter discusses the development and mission of the NCAA, and how it shaped the growth of college athletics during the twentieth century. The chapter analyzes the creation, and subsequent protection, of the concept of amateurism. And, finally, we'll examine the various legal challenges to how the NCAA strives to protect its version of amateurism.

The intersection of law and college athletics is unique from other sports given the role of the NCAA as a private membership association, yet eerily similar to professional leagues in dealing with the collection and distribution of associated revenue. There are several related topics that other chapters cover, and thus for brevity I do not address them here, including general eligibility issues, gender equity (Title IX specifically), youth sports, agents, and player entry drafts.

Ultimately, by seeking to protect college athletics from the commercialism found in professional athletics, the NCAA often clashes with the law—and it is these conflicts this chapter examines.

2. History of the NCAA

> *Our purpose is to govern competition in a fair, safe, equitable and sportsmanlike manner, and to integrate intercollegiate athletics into higher education so that the educational experience of the student-athlete is paramount.*
>
> (NCAA Publications, 2014, p. 3)

2.1. Founding and Mission

In 1852, the crew teams of Harvard and Yale staged a boat race on Lake Winnipesaukee in what is likely the nation's first intercollegiate sporting event (Whitmer, 2015). Seventeen years later, on November 6, 1869, Princeton and Rutgers played a game of football in New Jersey, as teams of twenty-five men played under rugby-style rules (Crowley, 2002[1]). Like the modern game we know today, the contest was "replete with surprise, strategy, prodigies of determination, and physical prowess" (ScarletKnights.com, 2016).

From the seeds of those initial competitions, college athletics has evolved into a multi-billion-dollar-a-year industry, replete with virtually all of the same pressures and challenges of professional sports. Moreover, in order to manage the expanding complexities of this thriving enterprise, rules governing participation, eligibility, competitive balance, discipline, oversight, and fair competition have been created.

By the turn of the twentieth century, college football was both popular and profitable for many major institutions. Reports state that Yale University maintained a reserve account worth more than $100,000 (about $2 million today) and the 1905 Harvard University football game against its rival Yale attracted a crowd of about 45,000 spectators (Yeager, 1991). While colleges reaped financial rewards, safety concerns rose as participants in football games were injured at an alarming rate. There were an astounding eighteen fatalities during the fall 1905 season alone, and, coupled with an additional 149 players suffering serious injuries, public outcry sent a clear message: reform the game or outlaw the sport (Yeager 1991).

Among the many players injured during that season was President Theodore Roosevelt's son Ted, who broke his collarbone playing football for Harvard University (Miller, 2011). Using his son's injury as a catalyst for change, President Roosevelt conducted meetings at the White House during the 1905 season in which he urged the presidents of Ivy League schools Harvard, Princeton, and Yale to address the issue of athlete safety (Miller, 2011). As a result of those meetings, sixty-two colleges met in December 1905 and the Intercollegiate Athletic Association of the United States (IAAUS) was formed on March 31, 1906. The IAAUS became the rule-making body for college athletics (Yeager 1991). In 1910, the IAAUS was renamed the National Collegiate Athletic Association, and since that time, it has governed intercollegiate athletics ("The NCAA Century Series—Part I: 1900-39," 2016).

To distance themselves from professional sports during the 1920s, college presidents determined participants in college athletics ought to be amateurs; however, as a nascent organization, the NCAA lacked the ability to enforce this directive effectively (*O'Bannon v. NCAA*). As such, college athletics developed unfettered from any substantive national oversight for several decades. Competition among institutions became fierce for college athlete talent as on-campus stadiums were constructed, commercial air travel became more common, and growing paydays for postseason bowl games developed (Yeager 1991). To compete for their share of the blossoming revenue stream, schools expanded their player scouting and recruiting to a national scale.

These developments ultimately led to change. The NCAA passed the "Sanity Code" in 1948 in an effort to once again distinguish college athletics from the developing professional leagues. The Sanity Code strictly prohibited schools from providing financial aid based on a student's athletic abilities ("NCAA Answers Call to Reform," 2016). Thus, funding based on athletic talent was banned in an attempt to address perceived "cheating" by schools offering lucrative scholarships. In order to enforce this new regulation, the Sanity Code increased the NCAA's need to monitor member institutions to ensure compliance ("NCAA Answers Call to Reform," 2016). Then, just eight years later in 1956, for no obvious reason, the NCAA reversed course and eliminated the Sanity Code by changing its rules, permitting schools to offer college athletes scholarships based on their athletic ability (Lazaroff, 2007). While a complete reversal of philosophy, the growth, authority, and scope of the NCAA was firmly established in those eight years.

Today, the NCAA consists of member schools, each of which is categorized into one of three Divisions: I, II, and III. The three divisions were created in 1973 to "align like-minded campuses in the areas of philosophy, competition and opportunity" ("Our Three Divisions," 2016). Headquartered in Indianapolis, Indiana, the NCAA regulates virtually all aspects of competitive intercollegiate athletics including student eligibility requirements, recruiting standards, and guidelines for high school athletes. Of paramount concern to the NCAA is its intent to maintain a clear line of demarcation between professional and amateur athletics, and this task is undertaken by defining amateurism. This distinct mission necessitates that the NCAA play a significant role in navigating and regulating commercial opportunities available to college athletics and athletes.

The NCAA is a nonprofit, private organization with an entirely voluntary membership. As a private entity, it is not bound by the individual liberties guaranteed by the U.S. Constitution that are imposed on government agencies or officials. Thus, its ability to impose rules and restrictions on student-athletes is virtually absolute ("NCAA's Tax-Exempt Status," 2011). The *NCAA Division I Manual* (2016–2017) consists of exactly 296 pages of operating and administrative bylaws that define the manner in which all college players must (1) gain initial eligibility; (2) maintain their academic and athletic eligibility; (3) follow the constraints of the NCAA's self-defined "amateur" status; and (4) be allowed to represent their university and the NCAA in competition.[2]

Though a nonprofit organization itself, the NCAA generates over $1 billion a year in revenue by the latest reports (Berkowitz, 2016a). A whopping 81% of the NCAA's direct revenue derives from media broadcast rights and fees with another 11% from NCAA-sponsored championships in the form of ticket and apparel sales ("Revenue," 2016). The single largest contributor to the NCAA's coffers is its recent $8.8 billion, eight-year extension of its multimedia rights agreement with CBS Sports and Turner for the Division I Men's Basketball Championship executed in April 2016 ("Turner, CBS and the NCAA Reach Long-Term Multimedia Rights Extension . . .," 2016). The NCAA itself is but a small component of the money generated by intercollegiate athletics, and if you were to aggregate all income from each member institution, the annual revenue was projected to be just short of $12 billion in 2014, an amount more than the most lucrative professional sports leagues in America.[3]

2.2. Evolution

While there are over 1,200 active NCAA member institutions across three levels, it is abundantly evident that the concerns, and the legal challenges, within college athletics—conference realignment, the power of coaches, multi-billion-dollar contracts for broadcast rights, rights of publicity, and the growing issues of college student welfare—involve only a small number of them.

Breaking down intercollegiate athletics within the United States, there are 757 colleges competing at the Division II and III levels ("Our Three Divisions," 2016). These schools embrace athletics as an opportunity to enrich a student's education by allowing them the opportunity to compete in sports. These schools provide athletic opportunities as a way to teach transformative skills that are virtually impossible to replicate in a classroom. Decisions are made with the express purpose of enhancing a student's athletic and educational experience—with little focus on maximizing revenue or selling tickets.

Moving to the larger institutions within college athletics, there are 347 schools at the Division I level—further divided by the Football Championship Subdivision (FCS) and Football Bowl Subdivision (FBS). This bifurcation between the FCS and FBS, developed in 2006, speaks primarily to the financial investments schools make in their football programs. Football teams within the FBS are allowed a maximum of eighty-five players, each of whom may receive up to a full athletically based scholarship per year (*NCAA Division I Manual*, 2016–2017). FCS football teams may only provide an amount of aid equivalent to 63 full scholarships to their students (*NCAA Division I Manual*, 2016–2017).

Schools often further align themselves into conferences to create a sense of stability and alliance among, at least historically, similarly situated institutions of higher learning

While the landscape of conference memberships has changed over time, the NCAA defines a conference as a "group of colleges and/or universities that conducts competition among its members and determines a conference champion in one or more sports" (NCAA Membership). There are just three schools, competing at the FBS level, that are independent and unaffiliated with a football conference: Army, BYU, and Notre Dame ("FBS Independents Will Count . . .," 2015).

Today, viewers watch television primarily at a time most convenient to them. Sporting events are among the only broadcasts that are consistently watched during the initial, live airing—making them increasingly more valuable to sponsors. Since media broadcast rights for college football are primarily negotiated at the conference level, the importance of intercollegiate conference affiliation has become vital economically. Historically, schools would align themselves with conferences based on geographic proximity and institutional mission, but now membership is often tied to television market size and ability to generate interest, and therefore revenue, for the conference.

3. Commercialization

> *A college racing stable makes as much sense as college football. The jockey could carry the college colors; the students could cheer; the alumni could bet; and the horse wouldn't have to pass a history test.* (Sheehan, 1996, 261)
>
> – Robert Hutchins, former president at the University of Chicago

The development of commercialism within college athletics benefited from the convergence of two events in the 1980s: (1) the Supreme Court eliminating the NCAA's restrictions on television appearances in 1984 in *NCAA v. Board of Regents* and (2) the growth in cable television that followed government deregulation. Thus, televised college football games hit the open market at the same time cable television was exploding in popularity, along with newly created "all-sports" networks clambering for content to fill their airtime. The symbiotic relationship between television and football blossomed, driving ratings, advertising revenue, and broadcast rights.

As the financial value of conference media deals continued to escalate at the turn of the twenty-first century, increased attention was paid to the revenue captured by a smaller number of conferences. Thus, while college athletics enjoyed relative stability throughout the 1980s and early 1990s, the gap in revenue available to various athletic conferences expanded. For example, the Big East Conference was formed in 1979 when athletic directors at several private institutions located in the Northeast sought stability in basketball scheduling. With tremendous success in basketball, leaders of these schools recognized the growing value of football within the college landscape and invited several more institutions to join the conference—launching a football schedule in 1991 (Moran, 1994). This stability was shattered in 2005 when three Big East Conference teams, Boston College, the University of Miami, and Virginia Tech, migrated to the Atlantic Coast

Conference (ACC). The departure of these three schools triggered a domino effect, and twenty-three schools would change conference affiliations over the next decade.

When the dust settled, there were sixty-five schools in five conferences—the ACC, the Big Ten Conference, the Big 12 Conference, the Pac-12 Conference, and the Southeastern Conference—that now dominate the college athletic landscape. Dubbed "the Power 5" the members of these conferences command most of the revenue college athletics generates. When combining their three biggest revenue streams—(1) college football playoffs and bowl payouts; (2) NCAA basketball tournament prize money; and (3) television rights agreements—these five conferences generated just over $1.9 billion in the 2015–2016 academic year (Smith, 2016). And, based on recent legislation, these five conferences have greater autonomy to manage themselves under recently passed NCAA rules.

In August 2014, the NCAA Division I board restructured how schools and conferences within Division I could operate ("Board Adopts New Division I Structure," 2016). This new "autonomy structure" was formally passed by the Power 5 Conferences on January 17, 2015, giving these schools, predominantly the largest institutions in the country, more power, and flexibility by granting them the ability to develop their own rules (Bennett, 2014). This legislation thereby opened the door for these schools to treat their Division I student-athletes differently from those in other conferences. This maneuver by the NCAA was, largely, a response to the growing criticism of college athletics and concerns regarding the welfare of the athletes competing at the highest levels. Ultimately, this restructuring was a direct recognition of the growing tension between academics and commercialization within college sports and can be interpreted as an attempt to develop legislation that addressed this evolution.

4. Judicial Scrutiny of the NCAA

Just as it does with any private organization, including professional sports leagues, the court system has granted tremendous deference to the NCAA. The courts are reticent to intervene on questions surrounding the enforcement of a private organization's internal bylaws and rules. Thus, the ability of college athletes or coaches to successfully challenge NCAA decisions is severely limited, which is an important factor when considering the growing commercial nature that the NCAA enterprise now embraces.

Two U.S. Supreme Court cases from the 1980s have sharply defined the concept of due process within, and therefore the direction of college athletics: *NCAA v. Board of Regents* and *NCAA v. Tarkanian*. Together, these cases unquestionably developed the groundwork for the existing tension between academics and commerce within college athletics. Perhaps the single point in time when the NCAA's role in shaping college athletics irrevocably morphed was in 1984, when the Supreme Court rendered its decision in the *NCAA v. Board of Regents* case, a decision that continues to impact the industry thirty years later.

KDKA AM in Pittsburgh, Pennsylvania, became the first radio station to air a college football game when West Virginia University played the University of Pittsburgh in 1921 (Sciullo, Jr., 1991). Eighteen years later, in 1939, the first televised college football game was broadcast as Waynesburg College visited the campus of Fordham University (AmericanSportscastersOnline.com, 2016). Over the next several years, a small number of college football games were televised. Due to limited interest and availability during the first several decades of college football, the NCAA allowed member institutions to negotiate their own radio, and then television, broadcast rights contracts.

Throughout the 1940s and into the 1950s, debate ensued as to whether or not television broadcasts hurt game attendance. However, with this new potential stream of revenue available, the NCAA developed a test case in 1951, and entered into a national contract with Westinghouse Corporation to televise a limited number of games. The contract called for the broadcast of three national games during the course of the season and four regional games for each Saturday (Porto 2012).

The public responded favorably, and as a result of the growing television ratings, the next year NBC paid the NCAA $1.14 million for the rights to televise the 1952 football season. When the University of Pennsylvania, a football power at the time, decided it would be more lucrative for it to sign its own television deal and defy the national contract, the NCAA responded swiftly. Using its newly created legislative power, the NCAA declared Pennsylvania no longer to be in "good standing" and pressured their Ivy League opponents to cancel their games with the school unless Pennsylvania capitulated and joined the NCAA's Football Television Plan—a maneuver which ultimately succeeded.

The Football Television Plan, which allowed for the broadcast of merely one game nationally, and only a few games regionally each Saturday, remained in existence into the 1970s (Porto 2012). By this time the popularity of college football had increased, and so too had television broadcast viewership. As free markets are intended to do, an increase in television ratings brought greater revenue to the television deals. In 1976, in order to capitalize upon this opportunity, the nation's most powerful football schools formed the College Football Association (CFA). The CFA intended to wrest power away from the NCAA relative to television broadcast rights, allowing its members to collectively negotiate far more profitable television contracts.

At this time, the development of cable television began to play an influential role and new channels (including some devoted entirely to sports) sought content. Cable stations became a viable outlet to air college football games, and the CFA realized gains in negotiating substantial television deals for its members. The growing trend of the NCAA's member schools ignoring restrictions on television appearances prompted the organization to issue a threat: the imposition of sanctions on any school that participated in CFA-negotiated television deals. Unhappy with the impact this would have on their revenue stream, the University of Georgia and the University of Oklahoma sued the NCAA in 1982. The schools alleged that by controlling television rights for all of its member institutions, the NCAA was illegally and unreasonably restraining trade in violation of the protections provided by the Sherman and Clayton Antitrust Acts. Passed in 1890, Section 1 of the Sherman Act takes aim at restraint of trade and states:

> *Every contract, combination in the form of trust or otherwise, or conspiracy, in restraint of trade or commerce among the several States, or with foreign nations, is declared to be illegal. Every person who shall make any contract or engage in any combination or conspiracy hereby declared to be illegal shall be deemed guilty of a felony....*

Section 2 of the Sherman Act addresses monopolies in our country by declaring:

> *Every person who shall monopolize, or attempt to monopolize, or combine or conspire with any other person or persons, to monopolize any part of the trade or commerce among the several States, or with foreign nations, shall be deemed guilty of a felony....*

The Clayton Act, passed in 1914, addresses the vagueness of the Sherman Act and closed several loopholes that enabled large corporations to continue to engage in certain restrictive actions. The Clayton Act also provides unusual statutory deterrence against restraining trade by holding that any finding of a violation of the Sherman Act shall trigger a trebling of damages.

Known as *NCAA v. Board of Regents*, the case pitted competitive balance rights against consumer welfare, and it wound its way through the court system, ultimately arriving in front of the Supreme Court in 1984. The plaintiffs' central argument was that by restricting television appearances for their football programs, the NCAA was unreasonably restraining trade in a defined market—college football fans. Schools felt they could generate more revenue on football television contracts without the NCAA restriction. As with most antitrust cases, the outcome would necessitate a rule-of-reason analysis, predominantly decided by balancing the procompetitive effects against the anticompetitive effects of this restraint. As a legal doctrine to evaluate whether or not a restraint is unreasonable, the rule of reason is quite simply a balancing test, which asks: do the benefits of the restraint to the industry outweigh the harm created?

The NCAA offered three primary procompetitive benefits resulting from restricting television broadcasts on college athletics: (1) protecting game attendance, (2) promoting competitive balance within college football, and (3) the overarching principle of maintaining amateurism. The Supreme Court agreed with the third benefit, stating:

> *In order to preserve the character and quality of the "product," athletes must not be paid, must be required to attend class, and the like. And the integrity of the "product" cannot be preserved except by mutual agreement; if an institution adopted such restrictions unilaterally, its effectiveness as a competitor on the playing field might soon be destroyed. Thus, the NCAA plays a vital role in enabling college football to preserve its character, and as a result enables a product to be marketed which might otherwise be unavailable. In performing this role, its actions widen consumer choice—not only the choices available to sports fans but also those available to athletes—and hence can be viewed as procompetitive.*
>
> (*NCAA v. Board of Regents*, 468 U.S. at 102)

However, despite accepting this broad interpretation of the NCAA's role in protecting amateurism, the Court took exception to other procompetitive arguments made by the

NCAA. Specifically, the Court declared, "by seeking to insulate live ticket-sales from the full spectrum of competition because of its assumption that the product itself is insufficiently attractive to consumers, petitioner forwards a justification that is inconsistent with the basic policy of the Sherman Act" (*NCAA v. Board of Regents*, 468 U.S. at 117).

Ultimately, Justice John Paul Stevens delivered the opinion of the court in declaring that the NCAA television plan unreasonably restrained trade based on its rule-of-reason analysis, and thereby violated antitrust law. The Court opined: "there can be no doubt that the challenged practices of the NCAA constitute a 'restraint of trade' in the sense that they limit members' freedom to negotiate and enter into their own television contracts" (*NCAA v. Board of Regents*, 468 U.S. at 98). With this ruling, the NCAA's restrictions on television appearances on individual schools were struck down, allowing the CFA to move forward with its negotiations for national television contracts.

Though the NCAA lost this case, the Supreme Court's ruling still provided ammunition for the NCAA regarding amateurism. Justice Stephens wrote:

> *The NCAA plays a critical role in the maintenance of a revered tradition of amateurism in college sports. There can be no question but that it needs ample latitude to play that role, or that the preservation of the student-athlete in higher education adds richness and diversity to intercollegiate athletics and is entirely consistent with the goals of the Sherman Act. But consistent with the Sherman Act, the role of the NCAA must be to preserve a tradition that might otherwise die; rules that restrict output are hardly consistent with this role.*
>
> (*NCAA v. Board of Regents*, 468 U.S. at 120)

This specific passage declaring that the NCAA plays a "critical role in the maintenance of a revered tradition of amateurism in college sports" has been argued by the NCAA in every legal challenge to its governance or actions since 1984.

Of note in this case is also the dissent, written by Justice Byron "Whizzer" White, a former All-American and professional football player, whose stellar legal career took him to the Supreme Court. White writes that "non-commercial goals play a central role" in college athletic programs, and the Court errs "in treating intercollegiate athletics under the NCAA's control as a purely commercial venture in which colleges and universities participate solely, or even primarily, in the pursuit of profits" (*NCAA v. Board of Regents*, 468 U.S. at 121). In essence, White argues that the NCAA ought to be extended latitude in its operations as the mission of college athletics is a noble one, playing an important role in the education of students.

The decision rendered the NCAA's restriction on television appearances for its member institutions a violation of antitrust law, yet dicta in the decision and language in the dissent buttress the NCAA's claim it is granted rights to "retain a clear line of demarcation between college athletics and professional sports" (*NCAA v Board of Regents*, 468 U.S. at 122) While the NCAA was no longer able to limit a school's right to chase revenue, the Supreme Court accepted its version of amateurism. Despite this loss, the NCAA was still left with another weapon at its disposal to protect its manifest power—enforcement.

Having lost the ability to mitigate the impact that commercialism would have on the development of college football, the NCAA flexed its muscles in order to advance its version of a level playing field. A growing investigative and enforcement staff began policing and imposing new levels of oversight on intercollegiate athletics, ostensibly under the rubric of protecting amateurism. Not surprisingly, the unchecked authority of the NCAA was challenged four years later in 1988 in the high profile case *NCAA v. Tarkanian.*

5. Due Process

5.1 *NCAA v. Tarkanian*

Jerry Tarkanian spent the majority of his career as a NCAA Division I men's basketball coach—first at Long Beach State and then, most famously, at the University of Nevada, Las Vegas (UNLV). His tenure at UNLV stretched from 1973 to 1992, clearly highlighted by an NCAA National Championship in 1990 for the Running Rebels. His impact on college athletics is far more significant than his time chewing on a towel on the sidelines. Tarkanian challenged the NCAA's unfettered ability to enforce its own rules as violation of the U.S. Constitution.

Tarkanian first came to the attention of the NCAA in the early 1970s when he wrote two columns in local newspapers chiding the organization for ignoring violations of larger institutions while punishing smaller ones ("Jerry Tarkanian Dies at 84 . . . ," 2015). This perception led him to declare "the NCAA is so upset at UCLA they'll put Northridge on two years' probation". When legendary head coach John Wooden led the UCLA men's basketball team to eleven consecutive national championships, Tarkanian often quipped that a new recruit would "put them over the salary cap".

Thus, not surprisingly, while he was at Long Beach State, the NCAA began investigating Tarkanian and his program for recruiting violations. In 1973, Tarkanian left Long Beach State to assume the reigns of the UNLV men's basketball team, a program already under NCAA investigation. Shortly after Tarkanian's hire, the NCAA charged the men's basketball program at UNLV with seventy-eight rules violations. These alleged NCAA violations were subsequently pared to thirty-eight charges but included new additional violations against Tarkanian.

Acting swiftly, the NCAA decided that UNLV had violated its rules, and sent a letter to the university recommending penalties. As was its right under NCAA legislative rules, UNLV appealed to the NCAA Council, which promptly upheld all findings and recommended penalties, including the probation and suspension of Tarkanian. Despite UNLV's determination that many of the charges leveled against its program and Tarkanian were unfounded and unsubstantiated, in order to comply with the NCAA's mandate UNLV had no choice but to suspend Tarkanian.

In response, Jerry Tarkanian sued UNLV in Nevada Trial Court. He claimed the school, based on the NCAA's findings, had no legal right to suspend him without providing him due process, as guaranteed in the Fourteenth Amendment to the U.S. Constitution. The Fourteenth Amendment holds that no state, or state actor, shall "deprive any person of life, liberty, or property, without due process of law." The Nevada Trial Court agreed that due process was not provided to Tarkanian and struck down the suspension. UNLV, at the behest of the NCAA, then appealed to the Nevada Supreme Court. In an amicus brief, the NCAA asserted the Nevada Trial Court erred and the case against UNLV should be dismissed because any due process claims to be raised were against the NCAA and not UNLV—an argument the Nevada Supreme Court accepted. Tarkanian then brought his suit against the NCAA instead of UNLV.

The Fourteenth Amendment issue is whether or not the NCAA ought to be defined as a state actor, thereby triggering due process protections. Tarkanian argued that by suspending him with evidentiary standards well below the threshold required for due process, the NCAA clearly violated the U.S. Constitution. This argument began a decade's-long battle, winding its way to the U.S. Supreme Court.

In a 5-4 vote in 1988, the Supreme Court determined that the NCAA should not be defined as a state actor and is thus exempt from any requirement to provide due process to Tarkanian or anyone else it seeks to punish. The majority held that the NCAA is a private entity and accordingly is not obligated to provide the constitutional rights that attach to government actions (*NCAA v. Tarkanian*).

In a span of just four years, the Supreme Court decided two cases, *Board of Regents v. NCAA* and *Tarkanian v. NCAA*, that would significantly alter the landscape of college athletics. Brian Porto (2012) describes the tremendous impact these two cases continue to have on college sports. As a result of these cases, the Supreme Court has shaped college athletics by limiting the NCAA's ability to restrict commercialism while failing to curb the organization's ability to punish wrongdoing within the enterprise (Porto, 2012).

5.2. *Law v. NCAA*

During the 1980s, the NCAA and its member institutions became increasingly concerned with the escalating costs of college athletics. One of the primary areas of increasing expenses for athletic departments was coaching salaries. As schools sought to woo the best high school players, they recruited high-profile, and often expensive, head and assistant coaches to help build a program.

In men's basketball at this time, the *NCAA Division I Manual* rules permitted a school to have three full-time coaches—a head coach and two assistants. The rules also allowed for two part-time coaches, in the form of part-time assistants, graduate assistants, or volunteers. In 1992, after much debate from many within college athletics unhappy with escalating coaching salaries, the NCAA passed Bylaw 11.6.4, which limited the number of coaches for men's basketball to one head coach, two assistant coaches, and one "restricted earnings coach" (REC). The bylaw further held that compensation for the REC position would be capped at $12,000 for the academic year, with another $4,000 allowed in the summer, for a maximum annual salary of $16,000.

Stemming from the 1992–1993 basketball season, the coaches in REC positions filed *Law v. NCAA*, a class-action lawsuit. The plaintiffs challenged the restricted compensation as an unreasonable, and therefore unlawful, restraint of trade. The case started in district court, and on appeal, wound up in front of the U.S. Court of Appeals for the Tenth Circuit. Using a rule-of-reason analysis, the NCAA argued the REC positions provided significant procompetitive benefits: promoting balanced competition among all Division I institutions, retaining entry-level positions so access to the coaching industry was available to coaches starting their careers, and, finally, quite simply, limiting costs, which was good for college athletics.

The plaintiffs' argument was based on the assertion that the NCAA possessed and used market power to artificially deflate salaries, and that there was no legally justifiable procompetitive benefit. Neither the district court nor the appellate court found the NCAA's procompetitive arguments compelling, with both finding for the plaintiffs. As a result of the appellate court's decision, the NCAA was ordered to pay over $22 million in damages, which, thanks to the Clayton Act, was trebled to $67 million. Rather than face more delays and potentially another appeal, the plaintiffs settled the case for $54.5 million (Branch, 2011).

6. Amateurism

The NCAA's "Principle of Amateurism" states:

> *Student-athletes shall be amateurs in an intercollegiate sport, and their participation should be motivated primarily by education and by the physical, mental and social benefits to be derived. Student participation in intercollegiate athletics is an avocation, and student-athletes should be protected from exploitation by professional and commercial enterprises.*
>
> (*NCAA Division I Manual*, 2016–2017)

On paper, the distinguishing characteristic between amateurism and professionalism is simply "whether or not the athletes are paid." However, the concept of amateurism, particularly in regard to the NCAA, is far more pliable and illusory (Zola, 2013). In fact, despite trumpeting the notion of amateurism, the NCAA bylaws and rules do not contain a definition of the term.

6.1. Employee Status

Walter Byers was the first executive director of the NCAA, governing the organization from 1951 until 1987. Byers's ambition transformed the NCAA from an essentially powerless organization to one that dominated the college athletics landscape and generated millions of dollars of revenue for its members.

In the nascent years of college athletics, payments to players were common despite the NCAA's insistence that participants be "amateurs." As the NCAA's organizational strength increased and its rulebook grew, as discussed earlier, member institutions were finally granted the ability to give student-athletes scholarships based on athletic ability in 1956. The value of scholarships was capped at the amount of a full "grant-in-aid," which was defined as the total cost of "tuition and fees, room and board, and required course-related books" (*NCAA Division I Manual* l, 2016–2017).

With the payment of scholarships to students, college athletics, and therefore the NCAA, was faced with all sorts of new and complicated issues. Those issues included whether or not students ought to be defined as employees under the law. Byers coined the term "student-athlete" in the 1950s in a deliberate attempt to insulate colleges from workers' compensation claims. The term promoted the idea that athletes were students and not employees (Byers, 1995). This misdirection was strategic in its goal of attempting to insulate colleges from workers' compensation claims which includes having to provide long-term disability payments to players injured while playing their sport (Byers, 1995).

> *We crafted the term "student-athlete," and soon it was embedded in all NCAA rules and interpretations as a mandated substitute for such words as players and athletes. We told college publicists to speak of "college teams," not football or basketball "clubs," a word common to the pros.*
>
> (Byers, 1995, 69)

This strategy was successful and the term "student-athlete" stands today, over half a century later. However, Byers himself had a change of heart relative to college athletics, and in 1995 penned a book titled *Unsportsmanlike Conduct: Exploiting College Athletes*. In this memoir, Byers strongly critiques the NCAA, making several confessions and accepting blame for its evolution. Byers is so emphatic in his dislike toward the NCAA he calls it "a nationwide money-laundering scheme" (Byers 1995, 73). Once the principal architect of today's NCAA, Byers evolved into one of its fiercest critics.

6.1.1. *Waldrep v. Texas Employers Insurance Association*

The NCAA's position that a college athlete is not an employee was directly challenged in 1974 by Alvis Kent Waldrep Jr. in a lawsuit against Texas Christian University (TCU). (*Waldrep v. Texas Employers Insurance Association*) Heavily recruited to play football for TCU, Waldrep graduated from high school in 1972. In a regular-season game during his sophomore year against the University of Alabama, Waldrep sustained a severe spinal cord injury leaving him paralyzed below the neck. Finally, in 1991, under Texas law, Waldrep was awarded workers' compensation benefits by the Texas Workers' Compensation Division.

Shortly thereafter, the Texas Employers Insurance Association appealed the award, claiming that Waldrep was not an employee of TCU at the time of the injury and thus was ineligible for workers' compensation benefits. Workers' compensation is "no fault" insurance coverage providing employees medical treatment, wage replacement, and permanent disability insurance compensation for job-related injuries or illness. Thus, workers' compensation rules provide that an employer is strictly liable for any damages resulting from an injury to an employee incurred as a result of his or her employment.

The common law definition of employee is "a person who performs services for another under a contract of hire, subject to the other's control or right of control, and in return for payment" (Restatement of Agency, 1958). Yet, in order for the courts to determine whether an employer and employee relationship exists under the law, there are traditionally two tests used: (1) the "right of control" test and (2) the "relative nature of the work" test. Under the "right of control" test, the relationship between a business and an individual is reviewed to determine the extent to which an employer is able to control or manipulate the employee. A true employee/employer relationship exists if the employer retains the right to supervise the employee and control the work to be performed as well as how it should be done. Under the "relative nature of the work" test, there is an employment relationship if an individual relies on income from the business, and the work performed by the individual is an integral part of the activities of the business.

Waldrep claimed that as a scholarship football player for TCU he met the "right of control" definition. After considerable testimony supplied by TCU, the district court determined the school's control over Waldrep was not all encompassing. The court stated:

> *The record reflects that TCU exercised direction and control over all of the athletes in its football program, including on scholarship players, while they were participating in the football program . . .. (however) the evidence is clear that TCU did not have the right to direct or control all of Waldrep's activities during his tenure at the school.*
>
> (*Waldrep v. Texas Employers Insurance Association*, 21 S.W.3d at 703)

The appeals court declared that Waldrep was not an employee of TCU—making him ineligible for workers' compensation. The court noted in its final decision in 2000, decades after the injury and the filing of the case:

> *We are aware college athletics has changed dramatically over the years since Waldrep's injury. Our decision today is based on facts and circumstances as they existed almost twenty-six years ago. We express no opinion as to whether our decision would be the same in an analogous situation arising today; therefore, our opinion should not be read too broadly.*
>
> (*Waldrep v Texas Employers Insurance Association*, 21 S.W.3d at 707)

This case served as national precedence until a recent, and highly publicized, challenge.

6.1.2. *Northwestern University & College Athletes Players Association*

Ramogi Huma, a former UCLA football player, began his advocacy on behalf of college athletes when he launched the National College Players Association (NCPA) in 2006. (Nocera and Strauss, 2016). The NCPA's mission is "to provide the means for college athletes to voice their concerns and change NCAA rules" (Hawkings, 2010, 144). As a player, Huma witnessed a teammate endure an NCAA suspension for accepting a bag of groceries left on his doorstep when he had no food (Who We Are, 2016). Huma's opinion of the NCAA solidified when the NCAA notified him that its rules prohibited UCLA from paying his medical expenses for an injury he incurred during summer workouts. At that point, Huma dedicated himself to becoming a pioneer in the college athletes' rights movement (Who We Are, 2016).

Kain Colter, a quarterback on the Northwestern University football team, stood up for fellow college athletes prior to the 2013 season at the Big Ten media day when he announced his support for Ed O'Bannon's lawsuit against the NCAA. Seeking reform, Colter was connected to Huma, and on January 28, 2014, a group of Northwestern University football players announced their intentions to unionize. As a necessary first step, members of the football team signed union cards signifying their plan to file with the National Labor Relations Board (NLRB) as a union based on their employee status at Northwestern (Nadkarni and Putterham, 2014).

In their announcement, the players cited the need for athletes to have a voice in the college football industry. Indicated if allowed to unionize, the players had selected the College Athletes Players Association (CAPA) to serve as their union (Nadkarni and Putterham, 2014). CAPA, formed by Colter, Huma, and former college athlete Luke Bonner, declared themselves to be "a labor organization established to assert college athletes' status as employees with the right to collectively bargain for basic protections" (Who We Are, 2016).

Under the National Labor Relations Act (NLRA), it became Northwestern University's burden to justify denying its scholarship football players employee status (*Northwestern & CAPA*, 2014). The central issue in the case was, as in *Waldrep v. Texas Employers Insurance Association*, the definition of "employee." In general, the U.S. Supreme Court has determined that the concept of "employee" ought to enjoy a broad definition (*NLRB v. Town & Country Electric*). In doing so, the NLRB often relies upon the common law definition, provided earlier, of an employee being "a person who performs services for another under a contract of hire, subject to the other's control or right of control, and in return for payment" (Restatement of Agency, 1958).

The case was argued before the 13th Region of the United States NLRB, which reached a decision on March 26, 2014. NLRB Regional Director Peter Sung Ohr declared that scholarship football players at Northwestern met the legal standard as employees, and thereby had the right to unionize. In making his decision, Ohr accepted the considerable testimony of the players regarding the ultimate control Northwestern, through its football coaches, had on their daily lives.

The NLRB held that the threshold level of control required to define students as employees was met based on a variety of factors including practice time, length of season, mandatory workouts, ability to influence academic choices (including classes and majors), what the players could wear, media accessibility, and the fact that these players were recruited to the university to play football. Not inconsequential to Ohr's analysis was the fact that the Northwestern football team generated significant revenue for the university (*Northwestern & CAPA*).

In his decision, Ohr wrote "as the record demonstrates, players receiving scholarships to perform football-related services for the Employer under a contract for hire in return for compensation are subject to the Employer's control and are therefore employees within the meaning of the Act" (*Northwestern & CAPA*, 14). Now granted employee status, the players were permitted under the NLRA to vote on whether or not they wished to unionize. As a result, Ohr directed a vote be taken by the scholarship football players on unionization.

As required by law, both the students and university were granted time leading up to the students' vote to debate whether or not to unionize. After much discussion, and some significant lobbying efforts by both sides, the players held an election on April 25, 2014. The vote on whether or not to join CAPA and engage in collective bargaining was taken, but the ballots were sealed—as a formal request to review the regional director's decision was filed with the NLRB's national headquarters in Washington, D.C.

Hearings were held in front of the NLRB's national board nearly ten months later in February 2015. Finally, on August 17, 2015, the NLRB released its ruling. Noting the case involved "novel and unique circumstances," the NLRB declined to assert jurisdiction in this case, determining that doing so would not serve to promote stability in labor relations (*Northwestern & CAPA II*, 3). This decision immediately rendered the Regional Board's decision moot, stripping Northwestern players of their employee status and thereby prohibiting them from voting on unionization.

A significant part of the ruling, or lack thereof, centered on the fact that Northwestern University is a private institution, and of the 125 colleges and universities participating in FBS football, all but seventeen are public institutions (*Northwestern & CAPA II*). Accordingly, the NLRB did not wish to make a ruling (by asserting jurisdiction over Northwestern) when the decision would not impact the majority of its competitors—including the rest of the Northwestern's fellow members in the Big Ten Conference (*Northwestern & CAPA II*).

The NLRB reasoned:

> *After careful consideration of the record and arguments of the parties and amici, we have determined that, even if the scholarship players were statutory employees (which, again, is an issue we do not decide), it would not effectuate the policies of the Act to assert jurisdiction. Our decision is primarily premised on a finding that, because of the nature of sports leagues (namely the control exercised by the leagues over the individual teams) and the composition and structure of FBS football (in which the overwhelming majority of competitors are public colleges and universities over which the Board*

> *cannot assert jurisdiction), it would not promote stability in labor relations to assert jurisdiction in this case.*
>
> (*Northwestern & CAPA II*, 3)

Many legal scholars and noted labor law attorneys scoffed at the NLRB's continued repetition of the argument that "asserting jurisdiction would not promote stability in labor relations" in their decision (*Northwestern & CAPA II*, 3,). Given the very nature of collective bargaining, the role of unions and the resulting negotiations are, by their intent, disruptive. Yet, collective bargaining is one of the most important foundations of antitrust and labor law within the United States.

While this decision was strictly limited to the Northwestern football players and does not directly address other parties engaged in college football, the NLRB is clear that their decision did not officially decide whether college football players are employees. Nor does this ruling preclude a "reconsideration of this issue in the future" (*Northwestern & CAPA II*). In fact, the NLRB concludes by indicating that "recent changes" in the landscape of college athletics continue to have an impact on how they may interpret this issue in the future (*Northwestern & CAPA II*, 6).[4] However, as things stand today, college athletes have not been granted employee status by either the court system or the NLRB.

6.1.3. *Taylor Branch*

Tired of waiting for NCAA reform, one noted Pulitzer-Prize winning historian's efforts raised the public's consciousness to the cause of college athletes. In an insightful article entitled "The Shame of College Sports" in *The Atlantic*, Taylor Branch took direct aim at the NCAA's concept of amateurism (Branch, 2011). Frank Deford, a member of the National Association of Sportscasters and Sportswriters Hall of Fame and six-time Sportswriter of the Year, declared Branch's piece "may well be the single most important article ever written about college sports" (Taylorbranch.com, 2016).

Branch asserts that the NCAA's definition and implementation of amateurism regarding college athletics (at least in the sports of basketball and football) is an outright sham. He further argues that payment to the participants—the athletes themselves—is a moral and legal obligation (Branch, 2011). Taking his argument even further, Branch dropped a bomb on the NCAA when he declared the system "akin to the plantation mentality," pointing out the disproportionate impact the ruling class has on minority students (Branch, 2011).

Because of his credentials, Branch's argument could not be ignored as the rantings of the lunatic fringe. In eloquent and persuasive prose, Branch logically laid out a cogent argument declaring the NCAA's system of amateurism a product of a bygone era and the result akin to indentured servitude. His central argument was that commercialism has overtaken intercollegiate athletics, and it is time the revenue be shared with the labor that produces it.

6.1.4. *Bloom v. NCAA*

> *When I was a kid, I remember my parents telling me that going to college would broaden my horizons and give me all the opportunities in the world.*

> *What I've found out, though, is that the benefits of being a student become clouded when you add the word "athlete."* (*Bloom*, 2003)
>
> – *Jeremy Bloom*

At the age of 15, Jeremy Bloom became the youngest male freestyle skier to make the United States Ski Team. Bloom was a national champion by seventeen, and at the age of nineteen he was named to the first of two Olympic teams. Talent, paired with good looks, generated plenty of endorsement opportunities for him and he took advantage of them in order to cover the significant expenses of his skiing career. Endorsements with Under Armour and various ski equipment manufacturers, a modeling contract with Tommy Hilfiger, and entertainment opportunities with MTV and Nickelodeon all provided Bloom with money.

A phenomenal athlete growing up, Bloom excelled at both track and field and football in high school. His athleticism was so unique that despite his developing professional skiing career, the University of Colorado successfully recruited him to play wide receiver and punt returner for their football team. Before Bloom's freshman year, and on his behalf, the University of Colorado petitioned the NCAA seeking waivers from their eligibility and amateurism rules restricting student-athletes' endorsements and media opportunities.

The NCAA rejected Colorado's request, and in August 2002, Bloom moved into his dorm on campus after announcing he would give up his endorsement deals to play college football. Once on a college campus, he explained, "everyone is here because they had a big dream when they were young, and pursuing that dream is worth more than any amount of money" (SportsBusinessDaily, 2002). Bloom's success on the football field continued, and as a freshman he was selected to the first-team Freshman All-America list by collegefootballnews.com and the Football Writers Association of America (FWAA).

However, after his freshman year, Bloom's perspective changed and he brought a lawsuit against the NCAA and its rules relative to amateurism. Article 12 of the NCAA's Bylaws govern student-athlete eligibility as it pertains to amateurism, stating "only an amateur student-athlete is eligible for intercollegiate participation in a particular sport" (*NCAA Division I Manual*, 2016–2017, Art. 12.01.1). But there has always been an exception, as Article 12 further states "a professional athlete in one sport may represent a member institution in another sport" (*NCAA Division I Manual*, 2016–2017, Art. 12.1.3).

Thus, over the past several decades, it is common for a student to be a professional athlete in one sport while maintaining his or her amateur status in the eyes of the NCAA. For example, college football players John Elway, Ricky Williams, and Russell Wilson signed professional baseball contracts, playing minor league baseball during the summer months.

Given Bloom's success as a skier, the University of Colorado petitioned the NCAA on his behalf, seeking a waiver from its rules restricting student-athletes' endorsements and media opportunities. The NCAA swiftly rejected the University of Colorado's petition, and Bloom was forced to terminate his endorsement deals to maintain his place on the football team for the 2002 season.

Arguing his endorsement deals were necessary to support his professional skiing career and not based on his role as a college football player, Bloom sought declaratory and injunctive relief in court. He argued that since the NCAA rules allow a student-athlete to be a professional athlete in one sport yet maintain his or her amateur status in another, "a student-athlete is entitled to earn whatever income is customary for his or her professional sport, which in the case of professional skiers, primarily comes from endorsements and paid media opportunities" (*Bloom v. NCAA*, 93 P.3d at 625).

The trial court found for the NCAA and rejected Bloom's request for a preliminary injunction, determining that the NCAA's rules were applied neither arbitrarily nor unfairly, and as such, Bloom failed to demonstrate a reasonable probability of success on the merits. Bloom appealed. The appellate court found that "the NCAA bylaws express a clear and unambiguous intent to prohibit student-athletes from engaging in endorsements and paid media appearances" (*Bloom v NCAA*, 93 P.3d at 626). The court further determined that, under NCAA rules, it was irrelevant as to when the opportunity for endorsements arose or whether such income was customary for any particular sport (*Bloom v NCAA*, 93 P.3d at 626).

Bloom argued that his endorsements were specifically linked to his skiing career and wholly unrelated to his football exploits. Unfortunately for him, the NCAA resolved that it was unable to reach the same conclusion and, as such, needed to restrict all endorsement opportunities for Bloom as they would for any other college football player.

In determining whether the bylaws were fairly applied to Bloom under the law, the court of appeals gave tremendous deference to the Supreme Court's decision in the 1984 *Board of Regents* case, holding that the Supreme Court has recognized the NCAA as "the guardian of an important American tradition" (amateurism) in intercollegiate athletics (*NCAA v Board of Regents*, 468 U.S. at 101 & n.3). Furthermore, the court held the NCAA rules restricting Bloom's endorsement and media appearances were "rationally related" to preserving the legitimate purpose of maintaining the "clear line of demarcation between intercollegiate athletics and professional sports." (*NCAA v. Board of Regents*, 468 U.S. at 122)

Ultimately, the court determined that

> *Bloom has thus failed to demonstrate any inconsistency in application which would lead us to conclude that the NCAA was arbitrarily applying its rules. Finally, we are not convinced that the NCAA treated Bloom unfairly in this manner in which it denied the requests to waive or interpret its rules. . . . For these reasons, we agree with the trial court that Bloom failed to demonstrate a reasonable probability of success on the merits.*
>
> (*Bloom v. NCAA*, 93 P.3d at 628)

As a result of the court decision, Bloom departed the University of Colorado after two seasons. He immediately began to accept ski-related endorsement and sponsorship money, opting not to pursue his legal challenge against the NCAA but rather to enter the

NFL draft. In the 2006 NFL draft, Bloom was a fifth-round selection of the Philadelphia Eagles. After time with the Philadelphia Eagles and then Pittsburgh Steelers, Bloom left the NFL and returned to skiing in 2008—earning his way back onto the 2010 United States Ski Team.

6.2. Antitrust Law: *O'Bannon v. NCAA*

In 1995, UCLA won the national championship in men's basketball behind the stellar play of Ed O'Bannon. For his efforts that year, O'Bannon was named the NCAA Tournament Most Outstanding Player and a first-team All-American, and he also won the John R. Wooden Award as the nation's most outstanding player. He was drafted by the New Jersey Nets as the number 9 pick in the 1996 NBA draft but played just 128 games over parts of three seasons before heading overseas to play professional basketball for another seven years. After his professional basketball career, O'Bannon moved to Las Vegas and began working as a salesman at a car dealership (Nocera and Strauss, 2016).

The story has been told countless times: O'Bannon was playing a video game with one of his friend's sons. Created by EA Sports, the college men's basketball video game allowed the players to select not only teams from the most recent year but also several other championship teams including O'Bannon's 1995 UCLA Bruins team. After playing several games,

> *"Dude, you're on a video game!" the boy said. O'Bannon and the others gathered around to watch the game. "It was definitely me," says O'Bannon. "A left-handed black guy." His friend turned to him and said, "You know what is crazy? EA Sports is getting all that money, and you're not getting any of it."*
>
> (Nocera and Strauss, 2016, 162)

Their realization that O'Bannon had neither consented to the use of his name, image, or likeness (NIL) nor been compensated for their use, coupled with the efforts of several visionary people including Sonny Vaccaro, Michael Hausfield, Jon King, and Andy Schwarz, led to a seminal lawsuit by O'Bannon against the NCAA in 2009.

In a California district court, Ed O'Bannon sued the NCAA, the Collegiate Licensing Company (CLC), and Electronic Arts (EA) for using college athletes' names and likenesses in television broadcasts and video games without compensating the players. Specifically, O'Bannon alleged that the NCAA's amateurism rules were an illegal restraint of trade under Section 1 of the Sherman Act insofar as they prevent college athletes from being compensated for their NILs (*O'Bannon v. NCAA*).

> *. . . For more than a century, the National Collegiate Athletic Association (NCAA) has prescribed rules governing the eligibility of athletes at its more than 1,000 member colleges and universities. Those rules prohibit student-athletes from being paid for the use of their names, images, and likenesses (NILs). The question presented in this*

> *momentous case is whether the NCAA's rules are subject to the antitrust laws and, if so, whether they are an unlawful restraint of trade.*
>
> (*O'Bannon v. NCAA II*, 802 F.3d at 1052)

In the early years of college athletics, payments to players were common despite the NCAA's insistence that participants be "amateurs." However, over time, the NCAA's strength increased and its rulebook grew. In 1956, the Sanity Code was struck down and member institutions were finally granted the ability to give student-athletes scholarships based on athletic ability. The NCAA capped scholarships at the amount of a full "grant-in-aid," which was defined as the total cost of "tuition and fees, room and board, and required course-related books" (*NCAA Division I Manual* 2016–2017, Art. 15.02.5).

Any amount above the grant-in-aid would be deemed an extra benefit and immediately render the recipient permanently ineligible for intercollegiate competition under NCAA rules. There are also countless other rules that address a college athlete's "amateur" status that seeks to separate intercollegiate athletics from professional sports including signing contracts with professional teams, entry in professional entry drafts, or the use of agents.

Most important, NCAA rules strictly prohibit any college athlete from receiving any pay based on his or her athletic ability, including endorsements or licensors of the athlete's NIL (*NCAA Division I Manual*, 2016–2017, Art. 12.01.2). These rules confounded O'Bannon, who had accepted them while he was a college athlete at UCLA but now, more than a decade later, seemed preposterous. Thus, the "gravamen of O'Bannon's complaint was that the NCAA's amateurism rules, insofar as they prevent student-athletes from being compensated for the use of their NILs, were an illegal restraint of trade under Section 1 of the Sherman Act, 15 U.S.C. §1" (*O'Bannon v. NCAA II*, 1055).

At about the same time, Sam Keller, a former quarterback at both Arizona State and the University of Nebraska, was suing the same defendants for essentially the same restrictions. The *Keller* and *O'Bannon* cases were initially consolidated during pretrial proceedings. Citing the First Amendment and right-of-publicity grounds, the defendants sought to dismiss Keller's lawsuit. However, these efforts were swiftly dismissed as "EA's use of the likenesses of college athletes like Samuel Keller in its video games is not, as a matter of law, protected by the First Amendment" (*In re NCAA Student-Athlete Name & Likeness Licensing Litigation*, 724 F.3d at 284).

After a three-week bench trial, Senior Judge Claudia Wilken of the U.S. District Court for the Northern District of California concluded on August 8, 2014, that the NCAA's compensation rules were an unlawful restraint of trade (*O'Bannon v NCAA*). As a result, Judge Wilken enjoined the NCAA from prohibiting its member institutions from capping student-athlete scholarships below the full cost of attendance (*O'Bannon v. NCAA*). Judge Wilken also granted the ability for schools to provide up to $5,000 per year in deferred compensation, which would be held in trust for the students until after they leave college (*O'Bannon v. NCAA*).

In January 2015, seventy-nine of eighty members of the five largest athletic conferences in the country voted to allow member institutions to increase scholarships up to the full cost of attendance (Tracy, 2015).

The NCAA appealed Judge Wilken's decision and on September 30, 2015, the U.S. Court of Appeals for the Ninth Circuit rendered a decision that concurred in part and dissented in part (*O'Bannon v. NCAA II*). On appeal, the NCAA argued there were three primary reasons why the Sherman Act should not apply but the strongest was that the Supreme Court, in *Board of Regents*, determined that the NCAA's amateurism rules are "valid as a matter of law" (*O'Bannon v. NCAA II*, 1061). The appellate court did determine that "amateurism is integral to the NCAA's market" (*O'Bannon v. NCAA II*) and that the "preservation of amateurism is a legitimate pro-competitive purpose for the NCAA to pursue" but that they were not bound "to conclude that every NCAA rule that somehow relates to amateurism is automatically valid" (*O'Bannon v. NCAA II*, 1063). As such, the appellate court would engage in a rule-of-reason analysis on the NCAA amateurism rules.

Under a rule-of-reason analysis, the plaintiffs bear the initial burden of showing that the restraint produces significant anticompetitive effects within a relevant market (*Tanaka v. University of Southern California*). If the plaintiffs meet this burden, the defendants may then come forward with evidence of the restraint's pro-competitive effects (*Tanakav. University of Southern California*). Finally, if the defendants meet this hurdle, the plaintiffs can then prove that any legitimate objectives may be achieved in a substantially less restrictive manner (*Tanaka v. University of Southern California*).

The court determined that the college education market was the relevant market and that the plaintiffs met their burden in showing that the NCAA's amateurism rules did restrain trade (*O'Bannon v. NCAA II*). The NCAA proffered several procompetitive arguments but two were specifically recognized by both the district court and the court of appeals: "integrating academics with athletics, and 'preserving the popularity of the NCAA's product by promoting its current understanding of amateurism'" (*O'Bannon v. NCAA II*, 1073).

In deciding that there was a restraint of trade in a relevant market, but some level of procompetitive benefits, the court was left to determine if these legitimate objectives could be achieved in a less restrictive manner. This is where the court of appeals disagreed, in part, with the district court. Judge Wilken of the district court "identified two substantially less restrictive alternatives: 1) allowing NCAA member schools to give student-athletes grants-in-aid that cover the full cost of attendance; and 2) allowing member schools to pay student-athletes small amounts of deferred cash compensation for the use of their NILs" (*O'Bannon v. NCAA II*, 1074).

The court of appeals disagreed with the second part of the district court's judgment, primarily because they embraced the argument that they "must afford the NCAA 'ample latitude' to superintend college athletics" (*O'Bannon v. NCAA II*, 1079) As such, the decision declared:

> *The difference between offering student-athletes education-related compensation and offering them cash sums untethered to education expenses is not minor; it is a quantum*

> *leap. Once that line is crossed, we see no basis for returning to a rule of amateurism and no defined stopping point; we have little doubt that the plaintiffs will continue to challenge the arbitrary limit imposed by the district court until they have captured the full value of their NIL. At that point the NCAA will have surrendered its amateurism principles entirely and transitioned from its "particular brand of football" to minor league status . . .. we must afford the NCAA "ample latitude" to superintend college athletics.*
>
> (*O'Bannon v. NCAA II*, 1079)

The decision thus reaffirms that:

> *NCAA regulations are subject to antitrust scrutiny and must be tested in the crucible of the Rule of Reason . . .. The NCAA is not above antitrust laws, and courts cannot and must not shy away from requiring the NCAA to play by the Sherman Act's rules. In this case, the NCAA's rules have been more restrictive than necessary to maintain its tradition of amateurism in support of the college sports market. The Rule of Reason requires that the NCAA permit its schools to provide up to the cost of attendance to their student athletes. It does not require more.*
>
> (*O'Bannon v. NCAA II*, 1079)

Seeking clarity, both the NCAA and the plaintiffs appealed this case to the Supreme Court. However, on October 3, 2016, the Supreme Court declined to review the *O'Bannon* case, effectively leaving the Ninth Circuit's ruling intact. While the path of this case ended at the Supreme Court, Ed O'Bannon's legacy continues as important concerns surrounding college athletics, and in particular the system of amateurism, continue to be raised.

7. Pay-to-Play Cases

While the *Bloom* and *O'Bannon* cases challenge the NCAA's legal ability to restrict access to commercial opportunities as part of their efforts to protect amateurism, direct attacks on the NCAA's limitations to pay college athletes have arisen lately. Higher education touts the existing NCAA amateurism model as a necessary instrument to ensure competitive balance among member institutions. According to both NCAA rules and the legal system, as of today, compensation to college athletes is capped at the full cost of attendance, meaning no institution has the ability to "pay" its athletes more.

Former West Virginia football player Shawne Alston filed a class action lawsuit against the NCAA and the five major conferences in the U.S. District Court for the Northern District of California on March 5, 2014 (*Alston v. NCAA* et al.). Alston alleged that the NCAA and its conferences violated Section I of the Sherman Act's antitrust laws in their collusion of artificially depressed compensation available to college athletes—the grant-in-aid cap, set below a school's full cost of attendance, is an unreasonable restraint of trade (*Alston v NCAA* et al.). This case seeks to permit each athletic conference the ability to determine its own regulations, thereby allowing free markets and competition to determine college athlete compensation rather than NCAA rules.

Alston sought two specific remedies: first, that the NCAA and Power 5 Conferences be enjoined from limiting compensation to grant-in-aid amounts; and second, that damages be awarded for the difference between grant-in-aid and full cost of attendance for all members of the class (Seivert, 2015). The first remedy became moot when the Power 5 Conferences voted to allow institutions to provide compensation up to the level of full cost of attendance in their vote in January 2015 (Tracy, 2015). However, the second claim for damages based on the gap between grant-in-aid and full cost of attendance survives.

The *Alston* case merged with a similar antitrust case filed against the NCAA by Jeffrey Kessler on June 4, 2015 (*Jenkins et al. v. NCAA*). Kessler looms over this case as one of the most powerful antitrust lawyers in the country who uses his skill in sports litigation, having successfully represented the MLBPA, NBPA, NFLPA, and NHLPA over a career spanning forty years. Among his most notable cases were *McNeil v. NFL*, which led to the establishment of free agency in the NFL, and *Brady v. NFL*, which led to the end of the 2011 NFL lockout. Moreover, it is apparent that Kessler's skill and record of accomplishment strikes fear in the NCAA (Solomon, 2016).

In *Jenkins et al. v. NCAA*, Clemson University football player Martin Jenkins served as the lead plaintiff and was joined by other college athletes: Bill Tyndall of the University of California, Kevin Perry of the University of Texas-El Paso, and J. J. Moore of Rutgers University as plaintiffs. More aggressive, yet simple, *Jenkins* seeks to eliminate NCAA rules that restrain scholarships and other benefits provided to college athletes (*Jenkins et al. v. NCAA*). Thus, while the *O'Bannon* decision struck down the $5,000 stipend for deferred compensation for NILs, the *Jenkins* case seeks to strike down any NCAA restraints on compensation—opening up the doors to an entire free market system for college athletics.

If successful, the *Jenkins* case (or the *Kessler* case as it is often referred), will destroy the existing amateur model presently employed by the NCAA. While the *Alston* case seeks damages, *Jenkins* seeks to implode the current landscape of college athletics—at least for men's basketball and football players. In December 2015, Justice Claudia Wilken of the Court of Appeals for the Ninth Circuit and the presiding judge in the *O'Bannon* case, certified the injunctive relief cases, allowing them to proceed as class actions (Berkowitz, 2016b). Two additional Ninth Circuit justices upheld this decision without further comment in February 2016 (Berkowitz, 2016b).

In May 2016, the NCAA sought dismissal of these cases, arguing the decision in the *O'Bannon* case, also issued by the Ninth Circuit, ought to serve as binding (Berkowitz, 2016b). Specifically, the language stating that antitrust law "requires that the NCAA permit its schools to provide up to the cost of attendance to their student athletes. It does not require more" (*O'Bannon v NCAA II*, 1079).

8. Conclusion

Not surprisingly, college athletics has evolved dramatically since that first crew match in 1852. As the governing body for this industry, the NCAA has decided that amateurism is the defining characteristic of intercollegiate athletics. Accordingly, the NCAA has consistently and vigorously defended all attacks on its efforts to protect its concept of amateurism. Revenue, created primarily because of the popularity of sports, and the corresponding media rights fee deals have complicated college athletics.

Until the early 2010s, the NCAA's hold on the direction and future of college athletics was virtually absolute. However, the efforts of many activists including Jeremy Bloom, Ed O'Bannon, Taylor Branch, Ramogi Huma, Kain Colter, Malcolm Jenkins, and others, have generated enough national attention to force meaningful conversations on the future of college athletics and, specifically, the welfare of college athletes.

The result is that the concept of paying college athletes is no longer unfathomable, as writers from the *New York Times, Wall Street Journal, Time Magazine, U.S. News & World Report*, and *Chronicle of Higher Education* have all joined in the debate on the merits of compensating student athletes for the revenue they generate for their schools and their conferences.[5]

The issue squarely in front of the courts now is whether this concept of amateurism can coexist, legally, with the laws ensuring free economic competition. Wrapped up in this debate are questions of whether schools are acting as a cartel and engaging in collusion in order to restrain trade. Finally, even greater scrutiny arises when one recognizes the growing revenues generated from this system made possible as schools embrace their version and self-definition of amateurism.

It is this stark tension between ideology and commercialism that forms the basis of many of the recent, current, and imminent legal challenges to college sports—a tension that will undoubtedly continue into the future.

Notes

1. This is an electronic book, written by former University of Nevada President Joseph N. Crowley, for the celebration of the NCAA's 100th birthday in 2006. It is available for download at www.ncaapublications.com/p-4039-in-the-arena-the-ncaas-first-century.aspx. Last accessed July 11, 2016.
2. These specific principles are discussed in the *NCAA Division I Manual*, both Article 1.2 in (Purposes) and Article 2 (Principles for Conduct of Intercollegiate Athletics).
3. The NCAA's latest IRS filing made public was in 2013 and it is available online here: http://990s.foundationcenter.org/990_pdf_archive/440/440567264/440567264_201408_990.pdf. You may download data from the U.S. Department of Education's web site and aggregate all of revenue generated in college athletics here: http://ope.ed.gov/athletics/.

4. For a summary of the *Northwestern and CAPA* case, please refer to *The Daily Northwestern* for comprehensive coverage of the proceedings available online at http://dailynorthwestern.com/sports/northwestern-nlrb-union-effort/. Last accessed July 13, 2016.
5. There are a bounty of opinion pieces written advocating that the NCAA ought to begin compensating college athletes. Some of the best ones include Nocera (2011); Cohen, (2011); Gregory (2013); Debate Club (2013); Wolverton (2014).

References

Bennett, Brian. (2014, August 8). "NCAA Board Votes to Allow Autonomy." ESPN.com. Accessed May 2, 2016.

Berkowitz, Steve. (2016a, March 11). "NCAA Nearly Topped $1 Billion in Revenue in 2014." *USA Today*, March 11, 2016.

Berkowitz, Steve. (2016b, May 16). "NCAA Asks for Dismissal of '*Kessler*,' *Alston* Cases." *USA Today*. Accessed June 5, 2016, www.usatoday.com/story/sports/college/2016/05/16/ncaa-seeks-dismissal-kessler-alston-cases/84463368/.

Bloom, Jeremy. (2003, August 1). "Opinion: Show Us the Money." *New York Times*.

"Board Adopts New Division I Structure." Accessed May 22, 2016, www.ncaa.org/about/resources/media-center/news/board-adopts-new-division-i-structure.

Branch, Taylor. (2011, October). "The Shame of College Sports." *The Atlantic*.

"Buffaloed! Judge Denies Bloom's Injunction Against NCAA." (2002, August 16). *SportsBusinessDaily*.

Byers, Walter. (1995). *Unsportsmanlike Conduct: Exploiting College Athletes* (Ann Arbor: University of Michigan Press).

"CAPA: More Information." Accessed April 21, 2016, www.collegeathletespa.org/more.

Cohen, Ben. (2011, September 16). "The Case for Paying College Athletes." *Wall Street Journal*.

Crouthamel, Jake. (2000, December 2000). "A Big East History and Retrospective, Part 1." SUAthletics.com. Accessed October 26, 2011.

Crowley, Joseph N. (2002). *In the Arena: The NCAA's First Century*. Available at www.ncaapublications.com/p-4039-in-the-arena-the-ncaas-first-century.aspx. Accessed July 11, 2016.

Debate Club. "Should NCAA Athletes Be Paid?" (2013, April 2). *U.S. News & World Report*. Accessed June 6, 2016, www.usnews.com/debate-club/should-ncaa-athletes-be-paid.

"FBS Independents Will Count as Nonconference Power 5 for Big Ten." (2015, September 22). Accessed July 11, 2016, www.si.com/college-football/2015/09/22/big-ten-nonconference-power-five-notre-dame-byu-army.

Gregory, Sean. (2013, September 16). "It's Time to Pay College Athletes." *Time Magazine*.

Hawkings, B., (2010). *The New Plantation: Black Athletes, College Sports, and Predominantly White NCAA Institutions* (New York: Springer).

"Jerry Tarkanian Dies at 84, Basketball Coach Turned UNLV into a Force." (2015, February 11). *Los Angeles Times*. Available at www.latimes.com/local/obituaries/la-me-jerry-tarkanian-20150212-column.html.

Lazaroff, Daniel E. (2007). "The NCAA in Its Second Century: Defender of Amateurism or Antitrust Recidivist?" *Oregon Law Review* 86: 320, 333.

Miller, John D. (2011). *The Big Scrum: How Teddy Roosevelt Saved Football* (New York: HarperCollins).

Moran, Malcolm. (1994, March 10). "Rutgers and West Virginia Are Invited to Join Big East." *New York Times*.

Nadkarni, Rohan, and Putterham, Alex. (2014, February 7). "In Focus: From Locker Room to Courtroom: How the Union Movement Came to Northwestern." *The Daily Northwestern*.

NCAA Academic and Membership Affairs Staff. (2011–12). *NCAA Division I Manual*. Available at www.ncaapublications.com/productdownloads/D112.pdf.

"NCAA Answers Call to Reform." Accessed June 23, 2016, http://fs.ncaa.org/Docs/NCAANewsArchive/1999/19991122/active/3624n24.html.

"The NCAA Century Series—Part I: 1900-39." NCAA.org. Accessed July 15, 2016, http://fs.ncaa.org/Docs/NCAANewsArchive/1999/19991108/active/3623n27.html.

"NCAA Membership." Accessed July 1, 2017, www.ncaa.org/governance/membership.

"NCAA's Tax-Exempt Status." Accessed October 9, 2011, www.ncaa.org/wps/wcm/connect/public/NCAA/Issues/Commercialism/NCAA+tax+exempt+status.

NCAA Division I Manual. (2015–2016).

NCAA Division I Manual. (2016–2017).

NCAA Publications. (2014). "NCAA Strategic Plan, Core Purpose." Accessed April 9, 2016. Available for download at www.ncaapublications.com/p-4111-ncaa-strategic-plan.aspx.

"NCPA Mission." Accessed April 21, 2016, www.ncpanow.org/about/mission-goals.

Nocera, Joe. (2011, December 30). "Let's Start Paying College Athletes." *New York Times*.

Nocera, J., and Strauss, B. (2016). *Indentured: The Inside Story of the Rebellion Against the NCAA* (New York: Portfolio/Penguin).

"Our Three Divisions." Accessed June 6, 2016, www.ncaa.org/about/resources/media-center/ncaa-101/our-three-divisions.

Porto, Brian. (2012). *The Supreme Court and the NCAA: The Case for Less Commercialism and More Due Process in College Sports* (Ann Arbor: University of Michigan Press).

Restatement (Second) of Agency. (1958). Section 2(2).

"Revenue." Accessed June 28, 2016, www.ncaa.org/about/resources/finances/revenue.

"Rutgers 6, Princeton 4." Accessed April 18, 2016, www.scarletknights.com/sports/m-footbl/archive/first-game.html.

Sciullo, Sam, Jr. ed. (1991). *1991 Pitt Football: University of Pittsburgh Football Media Guide* (Pittsburgh, PA: University of Pittsburgh Sports Information Office).

Seivert, Justin. (2015, November 4). "The Forgotten Antitrust Case: How an NCAA Loss in *Alston* Could Impact College Athletics." *Sporting News*. Accessed on June 5, 2016, www.sportingnews.com/ncaa-football/news/ncaa-antitrust-case-shawne-alston-effects-college-athletics/1uro6chmw5naj106n150pblfmy.

Sheehan, Richard. (1996). *Keeping Score: The Economics of Big Time Sports* (South Bend, IN, Diamond Communications).

Smith, Chris. (2016, July 18). "The Most Valuable Conferences in College Sports: Can the SEC Be Caught?" *Forbes*. Accessed July 19, 2016, www.forbes.com/sites/chrissmith/2016/07/18/the-most-valuable-conferences-in-college-sports-can-the-sec-be-caught/#6b48026dff4d.

Solomon, Jon. (2016). "Meet Jeffrey Kessler, Lawyer Whose Suit Strikes Fear in NCAA's Heart." *CBS Sports*. Accessed June 5, 2016, www.cbssports.com/college-football/news/meet-jeffrey-kessler-lawyer-whose-suit-strikes-fear-in-ncaas-heart/.

"Television's Sports Heritage." Accessed May 22, 2016, www.americansportscastersonline.com/waynesbergarticle.html.

Tracy, Marc. (2015, January 1). "Top Conferences to Allow Aid for Athletes' Full Bills." *New York Times*.

"Turner, CBS and the NCAA Reach Long-Term Multimedia Rights Extension for NCAA Division I Men's Basketball Championship." Accessed June 28, 2016, www.ncaa.org/about/resources/media-center/news/turner-cbs-and-ncaa-reach-long-term-multimedia-rights-extension-ncaa-division-i-men-s-basketball?sf24203015=1.
Whitmer, *Michael.* (2015, June 6). "Harvard and Yale Crews Celebrate the 150th Boat Race." *Boston Globe.*
"Who We Are." Accessed April 21, 2016, www.collegeathletespa.org/about.
Wolverton, Brad. (2014, February 10). "How Should Big-Time College Sports Change?" *The Chronicle of Higher Education.*
Yeager, Don. (1991). *Undue Process: The NCAA's Injustice for All* (Champaign, IL: Sagamore.
Zola, Warren K. (2013, February 11). "The Illusion of Amateurism in College Athletics." *Huffington Post.* Accessed July 19, 2016, www.huffingtonpost.com/warren-k-zola/college-athletes-pay-to-play_b_2663003.html.

Cases

Alston v. NCAA et al., No. 14-cv-01011 (N.D. Cal. Mar. 5, 2014).
Bloom v. NCAA, 93 P.3d 621 (Colo. Ct. App. 2004).
Brady v. NFL, 640 F.3d 785 (8th Cir. 2011).
Jenkins et al. v. NCAA, No. 33-cv-0001 (D.N.J. Mar. 17, 2014).
Law v. NCAA, 134 F.3d 1010 (10th Cir. 1998).
McNeil v. NFL, 790 F.Supp. 871 (1992).
NCAA v. Board of Regents, 468 U.S. 85, 101, 104 S. Ct. 2948, 2960, 82 L. Ed. 2d 70 (1984).
NCAA v. Tarkanian, 488 U.S. 179 (1988).
NCAA Student-Athlete Name & Likeness Licensing Litig. ("Keller"), In re, 724 F.3d 268, (9th Cir. 2013).
NLRB v. Town & Country Elec., 516 U.S. 85 (1995).
Northwestern & Coll. Athlete Players Ass'n (CAPA), Case 13-RC-121359 (2014).
Northwestern & Coll. Athlete Players Ass'n (CAPA), 362 NLRB No. 167, Case 13-RC-121359 (2015).
O'Bannon v. NCAA, 7 F. Supp. 3d 955 (N.D. Cal. 2014).
O'Bannon v. NCAA II, 802 F.3d 1049 (9th Cir. 2015).
Tanaka v. University of Southern California, 252 F.3d 1059 (9th Cir. 2001).
Waldrep v. Texas Employers Ins. Ass'n, 21 S.W.3d 692 (Tex. App. 2000).

CHAPTER 20

TITLE IX AND U.S. COLLEGE SPORTS

Contemporary Challenges to Compliance

ERIN E. BUZUVIS

TITLE IX of the Education Amendments of 1972 (Title IX)[1] is a federal statute that prohibits federally funded educational institutions from discriminating on the basis of sex. Forty-five years have passed since Title IX became law, and many aspects of its application to college athletics programs are still controversial, misunderstood, and ignored. This chapter examines several aspects of gender inequality in college athletics, including inequitable allocation of resources and opportunities, inadequate institutional response to allegations of sexual violence against college athletes, and employment discrimination against female coaches and administrators. College and university athletic departments still struggle to comply with Title IX requirements in these areas even though the law provides for both private and public enforcement that subjects noncompliant institutions to an array of penalties. Those penalties include money damages, injunctive relief, and, potentially, the withdrawal of federal funding. This chapter suggests possible explanations for persistent gender inequality in college athletics and proposes potential solutions that promote Title IX compliance and broader issues of climate and culture as well.

1. Inequality of Opportunities and Resources

Title IX is widely and appropriately credited for expanding and improving opportunities for girls and women to play interscholastic and college sports. When Title IX became law in 1972, there were only about 300,000 girls playing high school sports—a number that has increased exponentially to over 3.2 million today. In college sports, the focus of this chapter, women's opportunities increased from 16,000 to over 200,000 in that same time frame (Carpenter & Acosta, 2014). Notably, however, female athletes are still outnumbered by their male counterparts and generally receive fewer athletic department resources and scholarship dollars (Bracken & Irick, 2012). These indicia of aggregate inequality raise questions about individual institutions' compliance with the requirements of Title IX.

1.1. Title IX's Requirements for Equitable Athletic Opportunity

When the law passed in 1972, educational institutions that receive federal funding—a category that includes nearly all private and public colleges and universities—were prohibited from discriminating on the basis of sex. Initially, the statute's application to athletics was unclear, as members of Congress engaged in very little discussion of the matter as the bill that would become Title IX worked its way through the House and Senate. In fact, the only mention of sports was Senator Bayh's reassurance to a colleague that the statute would not require schools to put women on their football teams (Brake, 2010). Congress's virtual silence on the issue of athletics created initial confusion for regulators as they began the task of promulgating the statute's implementing regulations. As a result, Congress soon amended the two-year-old statute to clarify that athletics should be included in the regulations' scope. This time, however, there was more congressional debate about what Title IX should mean for athletics. Several senators proposed exempting football and other revenue-generating sports, but all such measures failed (Festle, 1996).

Title IX's implementing regulations,[2] promulgated in 1975 and substantially unchanged since then, allow schools to retain sex-segregated athletic teams (34 C.F.R. Pt. 106). But schools must provide equitable athletic opportunities to both sexes, which the regulations define in three principal ways. First, schools must equitably distribute resources such as equipment, facilities, coaching staff, and publicity to its men's and women's programs. Second, schools must award scholarship dollars in proportion to the ratio of male and female athletes. Third, they must ensure that the number of athletic opportunities available to students is equitable to both sexes.

The third requirement has been the subject of additional regulatory as well as judicial interpretations. In 1979, the Office for Civil Rights issued a policy interpretation that defined in greater detail the distribution of athletic opportunities that would satisfy Title IX. Specifically, the policy interpretation set forth three alternative compliance standards. A school that satisfies any one of the three-part test satisfies the regulatory requirement for an equitable distribution of athletic opportunities.

In order to qualify for compliance under the first part, schools must offer athletic opportunities to men and women in a ratio that is substantially proportionate to the ratio of men and women in the student body. For example, a school with a student body that is 55% female must offer close to 55% of its athlete opportunities to female athletes to comply with this prong. If it does not, it must comply with either the second part—showing a history and continuing practice of expanding women's athletic opportunities—or the third part—"fully and effectively" accommodating women's interests and abilities in athletics.

1.2. Noncompliance with the Three-Part Test

When the three-part test was promulgated, there were few athletic opportunities available to women, but the college student population was predominantly male. As a result, the first prong was easy to attain relative to the other prongs. Today, however, women make up the majority of the college student population, a fact that makes proportionality compliance more difficult for many colleges to attain. According to a study that used data from the 2001–2002 academic year, between 82 and 89% of a 700-school sample failed to come within three to five percentage points of proportionality; schools with football teams are less likely to attain proportionality compliance than those without (Anderson, Cheslock, & Ehrenberg, 2006). The most recent study of proportionality compliance, which relied on data from 2004, found that a similar percentage of institutions do not have a proportionate distribution of athletic opportunities (Cheslock, 2007).

For schools that do not satisfy the proportionality prong, the two remaining options for compliance can complicate a school's decision to downsize its athletic offerings in response to economic pressure. This is because the federal appellate courts have uniformly held that cutting a viable women's team usually disqualifies a school from compliance under prong two (continuously expanding opportunities for women) as well as prong three (effectively accommodating women's interests and abilities). As the Court of Appeals for the First Circuit concluded in *Cohen v. Brown University*, a school that decides it must cut teams cannot subtract opportunities from the sex that is already underrepresented.

Yet college athletic departments continue to eliminate women's teams, even in the absence of proportionality compliance. Title IX litigation involving Quinnipiac University provides one such example. In 2009, the university announced the elimination of its women's volleyball team. When the team members sued, the university argued that even without volleyball, it complied with the proportionality prong and so its elimination was permissible under Title IX. This claim required the court to scrutinize Quinnipiac's numbers, which it found lacking in two primary respects: first, the university had counted opportunities in the nascent sport of competitive cheer, even though the team did not compete regularly against varsity-level opponents. Second, it also triple-counted members of the women's cross-country team who were also on the roster of the indoor- and outdoor-track team, even though they were injured or redshirted and did not actually compete in either sport. When Quinnipiac's participation figures were revised to exclude these opportunities, the percentage of women's athletic opportunities at Quinnipiac was not substantially close to the percentage of female undergraduates. This meant that the institution did not comply with prong one of the three-part test, and it therefore could not eliminate women's volleyball because that would violate prongs two and three.

As a result of this litigation, not only was Quinnipiac's volleyball team reinstated, but the public became increasingly aware of roster manipulation tactics that college athletic departments routinely utilize to maintain the appearance of proportionality. For example, the *New York Times* exposed universities that inflated women's team rosters with names of nonparticipants, some of whom did not even know they were listed as members of the team (Thomas, 2011). These and other acts of "subterfuge" allow universities to evade their obligations to protect or increase women's opportunities, which are triggered by the absence of proportionality compliance.

1.3. Title IX and men's sports

Notwithstanding declining opportunities in certain men's sports, the total number of college teams and participation opportunities for both men and women have increased in the Title IX era. According to the most recent NCAA participation data, men account for 56.6% of the 472,625 athletes who participate in NCAA-championship sports (Irick, 2014), even though women are the majority on most college campuses today. The increase in men's athletic opportunities is partially attributable to the growing rosters of football teams, where the average squad size across all three divisions has increased from 82 to 107 since 1981, as well as the increasing number of football teams (Irick, 2014). Newly added teams in sports like lacrosse and track have also contributed to the overall rise in men's athletic participation. In 2013–2014, for example, men received almost as many new teams (145) as women (181) despite being overrepresented among college athletes. At the same time, almost as many women's teams (56) as men's (61) were eliminated in that same year.

As Figure 20.1 shows, while the number of women participating in college sports has significantly increased since Title IX's passage, women's participation still lags behind men's, whose opportunities have also increased in that same time frame. Interestingly, the few years of negative growth for men's sports that occurred in the 1980s coincided with a period of Title IX's history when the statute was at its least powerful. Indeed, Title IX's application to athletics was temporarily neutralized by litigation culminating in the Supreme Court's 1984 decision *Grove City College v. Bell*. Eventually, Congress passed the Civil Rights Restoration Act of 1987[3] to ensure that Title IX reached athletics as well. Thus, not only has the passage of Title IX failed to adversely affect men's athletic opportunities in the long term, there is evidence that when men's sports do experience a short-term loss, it is for reasons other than Title IX.

Yet despite the evidence of the overall expansion of men's athletics, there is a widely held belief that Title IX harms men's sports. This misperception may be partially

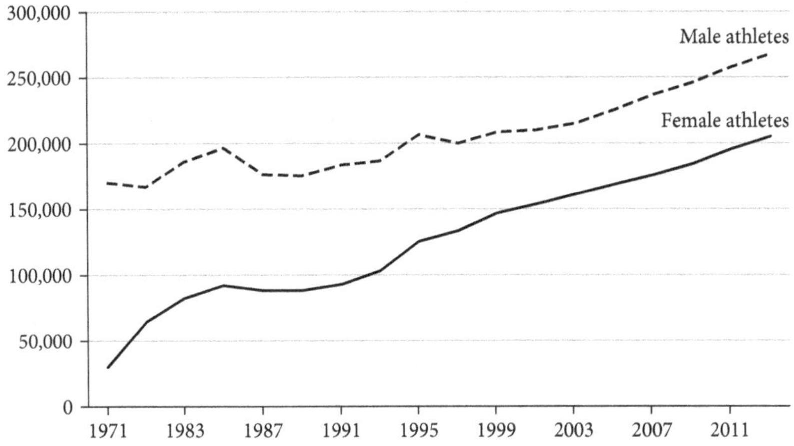

FIGURE 20.1. Men still outnumber women in college sports.

attributable to the fact that college athletic departments (and/or the media) may frame the decision to eliminate men's teams as a Title IX requirement, overinflating the role that Title IX plays in such a decision (Staurowsky, 2013). While it is true that Title IX prohibits the elimination of women's teams when athletic opportunities for women are disproportionately low, it is athletic departments themselves that are responsible for the decisions that lead to that imbalance in the first place. These departments could have pursued proportionality as a compliance strategy all along and yet did not. Moreover, the decision to achieve compliance by contracting men's opportunities, rather than expanding women's opportunities, reflects an institutional preference for large football rosters rather than a robust offering of men's and women's teams. Universities also tend to shirk responsibility for the financial conditions that predicated the decision to eliminate teams in the first place—such as the prioritization of football expenditures even though the majority of football programs run a deficit.[4] As a result, supporters of commonly downsized men's sports such as wrestling, swimming, and gymnastics, have become vocal critics of Title IX and have attempted to weaken the law through litigation and political pressure. This manner of advocacy on behalf of vulnerable men's sports is unfortunate not only because it seeks to weaken legal protection for other vulnerable sports, but also because it misses an opportunity to advocate against the commercialization that has distorted athletic department priorities to favor football over everything else.

1.4. Inequitable Allocation of Resources

Title IX requires educational institutions to ensure not only that the number of athletic opportunities is equitably distributed to both genders but that the quality of those opportunities is nondiscriminatory as well. The Department of Education takes into account facilities, equipment, coaching staff, publicity, and other factors to determine whether the men's and women's programs are comparable overall. While the regulations do not require equitable expenditures per se, the fact that men's athletic programs generally receive more resources than women's suggests widespread noncompliance with this requirement. Additionally, universities spend more on athletic financial aid for male athletes than for female athletes. For example, among Division I institutions in the Football Bowl Subdivision, the median difference is over $1 million (Bracken & Irick, 2012), a figure that still proportionately favors male athletes even when factoring in the degree to which female athletes are outnumbered.

Though the potential for revenue that athletic departments see in certain men's sports (football and basketball) may explain why they are willing to provide greater support to male athletes and men's programs, Title IX does not permit schools to provide inferior treatment to women's teams based on third-party (consumer) preferences for men's sports. Despite the increasing commercialization of college athletics, institutions claim to offer varsity athletic opportunities as an extension of their educational mission and benefit from the public money and tax benefits that educational affiliation provides. Fittingly, therefore, Congress has chosen to regulate college athletic departments like educational institutions, not like businesses. That includes imposing civil rights laws like Title IX that constrain market-based choices by prioritizing equal treatment over the pursuit of revenue.

2. Sexual Harassment and Sexual Violence

Despite its broad application to all aspects of education, Title IX used to be frequently mistaken for a statute that only addressed athletic opportunities. Today, however, Title IX's application to institutional responses to sexual harassment and sexual violence is equally well-known. Though this aspect of Title IX is not specific to athletics, sexual violence cases involving athletes have shaped the law and continue to be the most high-profile and controversial. For example, in 2007, the U.S. Court of Appeals for the Tenth Circuit held that a university could be liable for damages under Title IX to victims of sexual assault that resulted from the athletic department's failure to supervise football recruits. This decision helped to establish institutions' legal obligation to respond to threats of sexual violence even when that threat is not specific to the perpetrator, but to a particular program or activity (*Simpson v. University of Colorado*). In *Williams v. University of Georgia*, another appellate court held that a university could be liable for the gang-rape of a female student by three male athletes. In that 2007 decision, the court reasoned that university athletic department officials' decision to ignore notice that one of the athletes had a prior history of sexual misconduct would, if proven, constitute "deliberate indifference" required for institutional liability under Title IX. Additionally, the court faulted the university for postponing disciplinary action for eleven months, allowing the athletes involved to finish their respective seasons or careers.

Both decisions produced six-figure settlements. They were also among the several cases involving athletics that prompted the Department of Education to clarify, in its 2011 Dear Colleague Letter,[5] that charges of athlete misconduct are subject to the same Title IX requirements for prompt and equitable resolution as charges that arise outside the context of athletics. Since the Dear Colleague Letter, the Department has concluded, or is conducting, more than 200 investigations into claims that universities responded inadequately to reports of sexual assault. In one prominent example, the Department of Education (jointly with the Department of Justice), concluded that the University of Montana had delayed disciplinary proceedings for over a year in a matter that involved accusations of sexual assault against three football players.[6] Several of these pending investigations are believed to arise out of sexual misconduct claims involving football players, such as those against Florida State, Vanderbilt, and the University of Tennessee. Florida State, for example, has been accused of conducting a slow and inadequate investigation of charges that star quarterback Jameis Winston had sexually assaulted a female classmate. The complainant in that case also sued Florida State for damages, and her case settled for $950,000 (Cauterucci, 2016). The University of Tennessee also recently settled a lawsuit of a similar nature for reportedly $2.48 million (Slaby & Dopirak, 2016).

In another example, Baylor University admitted in May 2016 that the athletics department had actively concealed matters of sexual misconduct involving football players in order to immunize those players from disciplinary action that could have interfered with their ability to play. Baylor also admitted to having ignored the risk posed by accepting a transfer student who was dismissed from his prior team for misconduct issues that included domestic violence (Baylor University Board of Regents, 2016). That student, who went on to play football for Baylor, was later convicted of sexual assaulting another Baylor student. As part of its rare, public admission of responsibility for these and other Title IX problems, Baylor fired its head football coach and demoted the university president.

These high-profile cases raise questions about the extent to which other university athletic departments have made similar decisions to prioritize the success of its football program by shielding players from discipline for sexual assault.

3. Employment Discrimination and Retaliation

Today there is an enormous gender disparity among collegiate head coaches and athletic administrators, as women fill less than a quarter of head coach and athletic director positions in college athletics, and are even minorities among coaches of women's teams (Carpenter & Acosta, 2014). This glass ceiling is particular vexing because prior to Title IX, women dominated leadership positions in women's sport. The reasons for this trend are more complicated than simply discriminatory termination of existing female coaches (Buzuvis, 2015). Yet, Title IX cases challenging such adverse employment actions provide a partial explanation for this trend because they reveal working conditions for women in college athletics that explain why women leave or are forced out of leadership positions in college athletics. They may also illuminate why women are reluctant to pursue those positions in the first place.

Under Title IX, it is unlawful for educational institutions to discriminate on the basis of sex in their recruiting or selection of employees or in the terms and conditions of employment. In *Jackson v. Birmingham Board of Education*, the Supreme Court confirmed that retaliation is also covered by Title IX, including retaliation against a coach who complains about sex discrimination directed at him- or herself, coworkers, or students. In the wake of this decision, dozens of coaches and administrators have filed lawsuits against college athletic departments to challenge unlawful retaliation (Brown, 2016). An early example of this wave of retaliation cases involved the University of California at Fresno, which was sued by a female administrator and two female coaches, all of whom alleged they had lost their positions in the athletic department for complaining about inferior resources for women's teams, salary discrimination against female coaches, sexual harassment, and a hostile, homophobic environment. The university settled the administrator's claim for $3.5 million but took the coaches' cases to trial. Each of the coaches' juries ruled in her favor and assessed millions of dollars in damages. The cases then settled for $4.5 and $9 million, respectively (Buzuvis, 2010).

Notwithstanding these and other past cases in which coaches and athletic administrators have successfully challenged employment discrimination on the basis of sex, university athletic departments continue to take adverse employment action against female employees that is plausibly interpreted as discrimination in violation of Title IX. For example, in 2015, the University of Minnesota-Duluth (UMD) was sued by three former coaches, including Shannon Miller, who won four national championships during her sixteen years as the head coach of UMD's powerhouse women's hockey team. In December 2014, the athletic director informed her that her contract would not be renewed at the end of the season because the university was unable to afford her salary—notwithstanding the fact that other coaches in the department (all men) with higher salaries than hers were retained. At the same time, the university terminated Miller's entire staff, including the director of hockey operations, Jen Banford, who also doubled as the university's softball coach. Later, the women's basketball coach, Annette Wiles, resigned under alleged pressure after she complained to university officials about a hostile environment and sex discrimination within the department (Blount, 2015).

The University of Iowa is also defending a high-profile lawsuit filed by its former field hockey coach, Tracey Griesbaum. Griesbaum was fired after the athletic department received complaints that she had bullied and was verbally abusive toward players—even as internal investigators found no evidence to substantiate any violation of university policy. Griesbaum alleges that her termination is part of a pattern of adverse employment against female coaches, noting the current athletic director, Gary Barta, has forced out five female coaches in six years (Brown, 2016). Additionally, Griesbaum's partner, senior associate athletic director Jane Meyer, was reassigned outside the athletic department in the wake of Griesbaum's firing. Meyer has also filed a lawsuit against the university, challenging her transfer as reassignment and also claiming that she had been paid less than male counterparts during her tenure with the department (O'Leary, 2015).

The lawsuits pending against UMD and the University of Iowa reflect some common themes seen in Title IX employment discrimination cases. One such theme is the various double standards that apply differently to male and female coaches. The double standards are reflected in UMD's public statement that they could not afford Miller's salary while, by contrast, making no effort to control similar costs in men's sports. These double standards are also evidenced in Griesbaum's allegation that the university was quick to fire her for ostensible misconduct when worse behavior is commonly tolerated when committed by male coaches and in the allegations by all the UMD and Iowa coaches that their athletic departments provided their teams fewer resources than their male counterparts while expecting similar levels of success.

A second theme reflected in both the UMD and Iowa cases, and which is reminiscent of earlier employment discrimination cases like Fresno State, is the intersection of sex and sexual orientation discrimination, suggesting that despite increased social acceptance for homosexuality, college athletic departments are still places where it may be dangerous to be openly gay. The perception that lesbians do not comply with expected social roles for women and are thus destabilizing to male-dominated culture makes them vulnerable to discrimination (Griffin, 1998; Sartore & Cunningham, 2007). "In general, it is perceived that lesbians are bad for the 'image of women's sport.' Lack of sponsorship, fan support, and respect for women's sport is often blamed on the 'lesbian presence.'" (Krane & Barber, 2005, 68).

4. Understanding the Persistence of Sex Discrimination in Athletics

Considering the forty-five year history of Title IX, how can sex discrimination continue to persist in college athletics? Part of the answer to this question lies in the limitations of Title IX, and of law in general, to remedy and prevent discrimination. The persistence of sex discrimination in athletics is also understood by examining the particular role that sport plays in maintaining the deeply rooted gender order in our culture.

4.1. Title IX's Limited Ability to Remedy and Prevent Discrimination

Though Title IX is enforced by both government regulators and private litigants, neither enforcement mechanism has proven threatening enough to motivate universities to undertake the expensive and unpopular steps that compliance would require, such as adding women's teams, equalizing resources, and holding male athletes accountable for misconduct like sexual assault. The Department of Education's Office for Civil Rights (OCR) investigates educational institutions against whom Title IX complaints have been made. A university that does not comply with Title IX could potentially lose all federal funding administered by the Department, including the opportunity to participate in federal student loan programs. Typically, however, universities found to have violated Title IX agree to correct their mistakes so that OCR does not withdraw federal funds. As a result, OCR enforcement provides little incentive for institutions to comply with Title IX prospectively or on their own initiative, since there is little downside to waiting for an enforcement action to begin the process of coming into compliance.

In private lawsuits, plaintiffs may seek money damages against institutions that have violated their rights under Title IX. Yet despite the examples of successful plaintiffs noted previously, such as the coaches and students who prevailed in cases described earlier in this chapter, it still appears that that the threat of litigation has not drastically improved Title IX compliance. One reason may be that there are many aspects of Title IX compliance that Title IX lawsuits do not commonly address. Except when a university decides to drop a women's team, it is rare to see a lawsuit challenging inequitable participation opportunities or resources. This is because any plaintiffs who initiated such a process would likely graduate before having the opportunity to benefit from their efforts. And even when lawsuits do challenge a university's decision to eliminate a women's team, the relief at stake is a court order to undo or postpone the decision, not an expensive damages award.

As for employment discrimination cases, there is likely much gender-based inequality in the athletic department workplace that goes unchallenged, notwithstanding the examples of litigation discussed in this chapter. Plaintiffs who still have their jobs or who hope to secure another one in athletics may be reluctant to file suit. Additionally, they may be deterred by the notorious difficulty of satisfying the burden of proof on the issue of discriminatory motive or the publicity that accompanies such a lawsuit. For example, even if it is not true that Iowa coach Tracey Griesbaum verbally abused and bullied her players, her lawsuit necessarily draws attention to the fact that such allegations were made. Some coaches in her position may reasonably decide not to challenge a discriminatory termination because of the perceived threat of injury to their reputation and how they are seen not only by future employers but by future recruits on whom the coach's success relies. Plaintiffs seeking to challenge universities' handling of sexual misconduct charges against a prominent athlete must be particularly thick-skinned. For example, the female student who accused Florida State's star quarterback Jameis Winston of sexual assault endured such egregious retaliatory harassment that she was forced the leave the university. Her lawsuit against Florida State, alleging that the university did not satisfy its obligation under Title IX to promptly and adequately address her case eventually settled for $950,000, but not before she had endured frightening and humiliating vitriol from Florida State fans. This seemingly inevitable mistreatment combined with the uncertainty of justice likely suppresses many Title IX whistleblowers.

From an economic standpoint, therefore, institutions may not perceive a sufficiently high enough threat of enforcement, or consequences for having violated Title IX, to motivate proactive efforts to comply. These limitations may partially explain why Title IX compliance is still a challenge, even in the statute's forty-fifth year.

4.2. Sports, Power, and Gender

An examination of the interconnected nature of sport, power, and gender provides a related set of explanations for the recalcitrance of sex discrimination in college athletics. Sport has historically served to bolster masculinity and ascribe power to men (Hargreaves, 1994). For example, early youth sports organizers in the United States were motivated by the perception that the industrial revolution threatened masculinity by relocating the labor of fathers outside the home and leaving boys to the feminizing influence of their mothers. The rise of college sport in the years that followed was also a strategic effort to bolster masculinity against the feminizing effects of intellectualism and higher education (Messner, 1992). In this way, sport participation served to symbolically and visibly valorize athletic traits that are both positively viewed, and associated with, power—traits like strength, leadership, character—and simultaneously reinforcing of an association with masculinity through the exclusion of women[7] (Messner, 1988). While outright exclusion of women from sport is no longer permitted under Title IX, women's participation is minimized by structural and cultural barriers that operate to suppress their interests and ability. These barriers include having to contend with inferior levels of resources and support as well as encountering negative stereotypes about female athleticism. When women do play sports, they must often accept conditions that serve to differentiate women's sports from men's, such as a different set of rules, distinctly feminized team names, and obligations to convey (hetero)sexuality and femininity (Festle, 1996). When women's sports are minimized and differentiated, they can be dismissed as merely inferior copies of the real thing. As such, they pose no threat to the hegemonic masculinity sustained by the association between masculinity and power that is facilitated by sport.

This relationship between gender, sport, and power helps to explain the continued inequitable allocation of opportunities and resources, the imperviousness of college athletic departments to leadership of women, and failures to hold male athletes responsible for sexual misconduct. Additionally, it explains why efforts to secure equality are met with backlash, such as the commonly heard rhetoric, belied by statistics and history, that Title IX is responsible for the demise of men's sports, and the vitriol levied against women who call out college football stars for rape. Thus, given that the purpose of sport is to construct and sustain the association of masculinity and power, it is no wonder that sport organizers make minimal efforts to comply with Title IX, and only do so when the law requires it and the risk of enforcement is a sufficiently strong motivator.

5. Moving Forward

By first understanding *that* and *why* gender inequality persists in college athletics, we can better understand the diverse array of solutions that are needed to mitigate discrimination, inequality, and sexual violence. Some of these remedies require government intervention, including, as a starting point, aggressive enforcement by the Department of Education to ensure that institutions are held accountable for noncompliance even when victims of discrimination are deterred from filing lawsuits by the associated financial, emotional, social, and professional costs. For its part, Congress could pressure college athletic departments to address the rampant commercialization that puts economic pressure on athletics departments to engage in discriminatory practices that favor football in the allocation of opportunities and resources and that immunize football players from discipline. One possibility along these lines is to exempt the National Collegiate Athletic Association (NCAA) from antitrust laws, which are being used as the basis for challenging the associations' restrictions on athlete compensation. In exchange for the exemption, Congress could require the NCAA to impose limits on athletic department spending. Without high costs, institutions will be under less pressure to generate revenue by winning at any cost.

Even without Congress's involvement, colleges and universities could do a better job policing themselves, such as by agreeing to condition NCAA membership status on Title IX compliance. Recently, however, the NCAA has taken a step in the opposite direction, by abandoning its past practice of conditioning membership of Division I members on the results of the institution's evaluation of its commitment to gender equity across a variety of measures. By restoring and strengthening that program, the NCAA would create stronger incentives for institutions to strive for Title IX compliance and beyond. The NCAA could revoke membership or impose other penalties on institutions found to have sheltered athletes from discipline for sexual assault or who have turned blind eyes to risks posed by student-athletes with records of sexual misconduct.

Whether individually or collectively, colleges and universities have an obvious role to play. Strong presidents must resist economic pressure to give football and other revenue sports priority over other values of an academic community, including equality, well-being, and accountability. They should establish Title IX and gender equity as a clear priority and support that priority by educating and training athletic department staff on how to attain and sustain equitable participation opportunities, combat the implicit bias that serves as a barrier to women's athletic leadership, and effectively carry out their duties to report and address accusations of sexual violence. They must also be willing to hold that staff accountable when these objectives are not met.

To be successful, however, institutional leaders must have the support of alumni, fans, faculty and staff, and students and parents. These stakeholders must refrain from conditioning their institutional support on the football team's success and, instead, withdraw support from institutions that fail to do right by other measures. By choosing carefully which college athletics programs to attend and support, the public can increase the pressure on universities to denounce and desist inequitable allocations of resources, biased hiring practices, and tolerance for sexual violence. By withholding support from athletics programs that engage in these practices, stakeholders can ensure that institutions lack both the resources and the motivation to support discrimination, while also weakening the role that sport plays in sustaining the gender order.

Notes

1. 20 U.S.C. §§ 1681–1688.
2. 34 C.F.R. Part 106.
3. Pub. L. No. 100-259, 102 Stat. 28 (1988).
4. While 55% of Division I football programs in the Bowl Subdivision reportedly generated greater revenue than expenditures, only 2% of the Division I football programs in the Championship subdivision reported the same (Fulks, 2015a, tbl. 3.6, 4.6). No Division II or III football programs generated net revenue.
5. Letter from Russlynn Ali, Assistant Secretary for Civil Rights, Department of Education (Apr. 4, 2011).
6. Department of Justice & Department of Education Letter to University of Montana President Royce Engstrom (May 9, 2013).
7. Women's athletic opportunities existed before Title IX, but these opportunities generally existed in an entirely different paradigm—participatory, not competitive; companionate, not adversarial; and minimized to avoid conflict with gender stereotypes and expectations (Festle, 1996). These differences permitted mainstream (men's) sport to create and sustain associations between masculinity and power.

References

Anderson, D. J., Cheslock, J. J., & Ehrenberg, R. G. (2006). "Gender Equity in Intercollegiate Athletics: Determinants of Title IX Compliance." *Journal of Higher Education* 77(2): 225–250.

Baylor University Board of Regents. (2016). *Findings of Fact*. Retrieved from https://assets.documentcloud.org/documents/2843361/Baylor.pdf.

Blount, R. (2015, September 28). "Three Former Duluth Coaches File Discrimination Lawsuit. *Star Tribune*. Retrieved from www.startribune.com/3-former-duluth-coaches-file-discrimination-lawsuit/329788221/.

Bracken, N. M., & Irick, E. (2012). *Gender Equity Report 2004-2010* (Indianapolis, IN: National Collegiate Athletic Association).

Brake, D. L. (2010). *Getting in the Game: Title IX and the Women's Sports Revolution* (New York: New York University Press).

Brown, A. (2016, May 5). "A Man's Game: Inside the Inequality That Plagues Women's College Sports." *Reveal News*. Retrieved from www.revealnews.org/article/a-mans-game-inside-the-inequality-that-plagues-womens-college-sports/.

Buzuvis, E. E. (2010). "Sidelined: Title IX Retaliation Cases and Women's Leadership in College Athletics." *Duke Journal of Gender, Law & Policy* 17: 1–45.

Buzuvis, E. (2015). "Barriers to Leadership for Women in College Athletics." In *Introduction to Intercollegiate Athletics*, edited by E. Comeaux (Baltimore: John Hopkins University Press), 272–284.

Carpenter, L. J., & Acosta, V. (2014). *Women in Intercollegiate Sport: A Longitudinal, National Study, Thirty-Seven Year Update*. Unpublished manuscript. Retrieved from www.acostacarpenter.org.

Cauterucci, C. (2016, January 25). Florida State Pays Landmark Title IX Settlement over Alleged Jameis Winston Rape. *Slate*. Retrieved from www.slate.com/blogs/xx_factor/2016/01/25/florida_state_pays_landmark_title_ix_settlement_over_alleged_jameis_winston.html.

Cheslock, J. (2007). *Who's Playing College Sports? Trends in Participation* (East Meadow, NY: Women's Sports Foundation).

Department of Health, Education and Welfare, Office for Civil Rights. (1979, December 11). "A Policy Interpretation: Title IX and Intercollegiate Athletics." *Federal Register* 44: 71,413.

Festle, M. J. (1996). *Playing Nice: Politics and Apologies in Women's Sports* (New York: Columbia University Press).

Fulks, D. (2015a). *Revenues and Expenses: NCAA Division I Intercollegiate Athletics Report 2004-2014* (Indianapolis, IN: National Collegiate Athletic Association).

Fulks, D. (2015b). *Revenues and Expenses: NCAA Division II Intercollegiate Athletics Report* (Indianapolis, IN: National Collegiate Athletic Association).

Griffin, P. (1998). *Strong Women, Deep Closets: Lesbians and Homophobia in Sport* (Champaign, IL: Human Kinetics).

Hargreaves, J. (1994). *Sporting Females: Critical Issues in the History and Sociology of Women's Sport* (London: Routledge).

Irick, E. (2014). *Student-Athlete Participation 1981-82–2013-14* (Indianapolis, IN: National Collegiate Athletic Association).

Kane, M. (2001). "Leadership, Sport, and Gender." In *Women on Power: Leadership Redefined*, edited by S. J. Freeman, S. C. Bourque, & C. M. Shelton (Boston: Northeastern University Press), 114–146.

Krane, V., & Barber, H. (2005). "Identity Tensions in Lesbian Intercollegiate Coaches." *Research Quarterly for Exercise and Sport* 76(1): 67–81.

Messner, M. (1988). "Sport and Male Domination: The Female Athlete as Contested Ideological Terrain." *Sociology of Sport Journal* 5: 197–211.

Messner, M. A. (1992). *Power at Play: Sports and the Problem of Masculinity* (Boston: Beacon Press).

O'Leary, J. (2015, November 6). "'Strong Women Are Not Welcome' in Iowa Athletics Department, Ex-Official Says." *Iowa City Press-Citizen*. Retrieved from www.press-citizen.com/story/news/local/2015/11/06/ui-athletics-department-gender-sexual-orientation-discrimination/75293780/.

Sartore, M. L., & Cunningham, G. B. (2007). "Explaining the Under-Representation of Women in Leadership Positions of Sport Organizations: A Symbolic Interactionist Perspective." *Quest* 7: 244–265.

Schultz, J. (2014). *Qualifying Times: Points of Change in U.S. Women's Sports* (Urbana: University of Illinois Press).

Slaby, M. J., & Dopirak, D. (2016, July 5). "University of Tennessee Settles Title IX Lawsuit for $2.48 Million." *Knoxville News Sentinel*. Retrieved from http://archive.knoxnews.com/news/local/ut-settles-title-ix-lawsuit-for-248-million-36cfb409-2921-4d9c-e053-0100007f0d02-385623781.html

Staurowsky, E. J. (2013). "Revisiting James Madison University: A Case Analysis of Program Restructuring Following So-Called 'Title IX Cuts.'" *Journal of Intercollegiate Athletics* 6: 96–119.

Thomas, K. (2011, April 26). "College Teams, Relying on Deception, Undermine Gender Equity." *New York Times*, p. A1.

Cases

Biediger v. Quinnipiac Univ., 728 F. Supp. 2d 62 (D. Conn. 2010).

Cohen v. Brown Univ., 101 F.3d 155 (1st Cir. 1996).

Grove City College v. Bell, 465 U.S. 555 (1984).

Jackson v. Birmingham Bd. of Educ., 544 U.S. 167 (2005).

Simpson v. University of Colo., 500 F.3d 1170 (10th Cir. 2007).

Williams v. University of Georgia, 477 F.3d 1282 (11th Cir. 2007).

CHAPTER 21

RECREATIONAL SPORTS LAW

THOMAS A. BAKER III

1. Introduction

This chapter will introduce the reader to critical and significant legal issues in recreational sports law. The term "recreational sports law' is a generic one used to describe the application of law to recreational sport activities. This description is important because the reader needs to understand that recreational sports law is not an area of law distinct from sport law. So many of the same legal issues inherent in professional, intercollegiate, and interscholastic sports are also found within subjects considered to be recreational sports. Thus, the aim of this chapter is not necessarily to identify specific legal applications that are unique to recreational sports. In most cases, there is substantial overlap in terms of the way the law applies to sport, as recreation or not. The key to understanding this chapter is to identify aspects unique to recreational sport activities and how the law adapts, or does not adapt, to those distinctions. In this task, the reader needs to understand that the concept of recreational sports is too broad in reach to be covered comprehensively in this chapter. Instead, specific attention is placed on trends within recreational sports law that have generated interest from legal scholars and practitioners charged with managing sport recreation activities.

So what are recreational sport activities? A conventional definition of the term "recreational sports" is all sport activities engaged in purely for pleasure. The problem with this definition is that people engage in activities for multiple reasons. For example, someone may engage in a recreational sport for educational or health-related purposes as well as for the joy of participation. Perhaps the practical application of the term provides the best parameters for understanding it. In practice, recreational sports is an umbrella term used to cover all sporting activities other than professional, intercollegiate, or interscholastic sports. To control for breadth of application, this chapter refers to "recreational sport activities" in the general sense as involving adult participants, but also includes the following subcategories that cover more specific types of activities: (1) recreational youth sports, (2) intramural sport competitions on college or university campuses (rec sports), and (3) adventure sport activities.

Recreational youth sports are considered in this chapter to broadly include all non-scholastic youth sport activities. These activities can involve participation in organized youth sport leagues like Little League (baseball) or Pop Warner (football). They can also include sport involvement in activities that can transition into college, professional, or even Olympic development. Most elite-level athletes began participating in their sport as a child. The overwhelming majority of young athletes do not advance to the point that they earn athletic scholarships or have professional opportunities. For some, however, their talents allow them, at early ages, to progress from recreational sport involvement to something closer resembling career training or professional development. For example, while gymnasts start training with coaches at young ages, that training can become more advanced and more elite over time—even to the point where the line between participation in recreation and professional training becomes blurred.

Intramural sports are those offered on college campuses as a means for providing recreational opportunities for students. Intramural sports are commonly structured offerings that take the form of competitions for individual or team sports. However, intramural sports should be distinguished from collegiate or club sports. Participants in intramural sports, unlike those in collegiate and club sports, typically do not compete against students from other institutions. Intramural sports exist on college campuses purely for recreational purposes and the number and type of intramural sport offerings vary from institution to institution. Some common and popular intramural sports include activities like flag football, bowling, soccer, tennis, and slow-pitch softball.

Finally, this chapter also considers a group of activities labeled "adventure sports." The term "adventure sports" is given to nontraditional sport activities like skateboarding, wakeboarding, snowboarding, hiking, mountaineering, and adventure racing. These types of activities have not always been considered sports, but participants and adventure sport organizations have worked together to have them recognized as new disciplines within sport (Greer, 2012). Some use the terms "extreme sports" and "action sports" as interchangeable with adventure sports. One common similarity among the types of adventure sport activities is the inclusion of dangers that are more extreme than those that are normally expected in traditional types of recreational sport activities.

The categories designated for recreational sports in this chapter are broad and the subjects covered are not exclusive. "Recreational sports" is a term that includes an incredibly wide range of indoor and outdoor activities, and the range of legal applications to those activities is just as wide and diverse. For this reason, entire books are written exclusively on the subject of recreational sports law. Thus, one chapter cannot cover all the interesting and important facets of recreational sports law. Still, from reviewing the relevant research, two themes (legal threats and prevention strategies and legal defenses) emerged that provide the foundation for this chapter. Within these two themes there are topical subsections that cover some of the more relevant issues influencing recreational sport law.

The legal threats and prevention section of this chapter is thematically designed to cover legal responsibilities for recreational sport service providers (i.e., duty of care and duty to warn) as well as measures for preventing legal liability and the harms that give rise to litigation. The threat of litigation is a constant in recreational sports. After all, recreational sport activities inherently pose risk and mismanagement can mollify or intensify those risks. Furthermore, people who engage in recreational aspects may not appreciate or accept the fact that they are subjecting themselves, or perhaps their children, to dangerous activities. Adult participants, or the parents of child participants, may have a false sense of security based on the fact that the dangerous activities are recreational. Consequently, when those activities result in harms to adult participants or children, the victims and their families may feel wronged and hold the service provider responsible.

The very real possibility of litigation involving recreational sport service providers necessitates legal defenses for mitigating or eliminating the threat of liability. This section of the chapter provides a recreational sport context for topics like immunity, defenses to tort liability (i.e., assumption of risk), and the use of participation agreements and negligence release agreements (waivers). Still, even if recreational sport service providers were to have no legal duty or have contractually removed the threat of legal liability, activity providers must still take reasonable steps to protect participants. Society imposes responsibilities on recreational sport providers, particularly when children are involved. Accordingly, service providers should always be concerned with the court of public opinion—its verdict can sometimes have more of an impact than those rendered by a court of law.

2. Legal Threats and Prevention Strategies

The title of this section was carefully crafted to cover various types of problems and preventative measures for those problems. This chapter is, by no means, inclusive of all legal concerns for recreational sport providers. Instead, it addresses those concerns that generate significant interest from legal scholarship and that provide a frequent source of controversy in the courts. To put the problems discussed in this section in the proper perspective, we first need to discuss the general legal responsibilities and injury preventions required from recreational sport providers. In law, this responsibility is referred to as the duty of care and whether such a duty exists is a question of law for the judge to determine based on interpretation of common law, or through application of legislation requiring care for specific parties in specific instances.

2.1. The Duty of Care in Recreational Sports

Legal obligations for one person engaged in recreational sport to protect another stem from special relationships between two persons that result in a need for one to protect another from unreasonable risks of harm. Some relationships giving rise to legal duties are established by statutes, but most legal duties in recreational sports are judicially recognized as inherent and necessary for comporting with the kinds of mutually dependent relationships commonly found in recreational sports. For example, the relationship between the coach of a recreational sport and an athlete is the type of mutually dependent relationship that necessitates care from the coach to not expose the athlete to certain risks. A coach's duty of care to an athlete may be found to include duties to provide proper supervision, safe instruction, warning of risks inherent to the activity, safe equipment, matching of participants with similar skill level and size, means for handling emergencies (an emergency action plan), and timely and appropriate medical care. To this end, the relationships and resulting duties of care in recreational sports are not very different, if at all, from those also found within sport activities that are not for recreation. And like those other types of sport activities, there exists a hesitance in the majority of jurisdictions to impose an obligation on recreational sport participants and service providers to safeguard sport participation from the types of harm that are inherent to the activity. Along those lines, there are certain risks that cannot be removed without altering the nature of the activity significantly. If anything, the reluctance to find a duty of care for recreational sport participants and providers may be more pronounced than that which also exists for nonrecreational sports. The reluctance in requiring legal care can be found in the judicial and legislative desire to preserve recreational sport opportunities from being sued into nonexistence. More specifically, the majority of jurisdictions seem to be of a common mind-set that subjecting recreational sport participants and providers to an exacting legal scrutiny would (1) substantially reduce participation and (2) dramatically decrease recreational sport opportunities. Participants would be afraid to engage in risky recreational activities that could cost them in civil court. Insurers, for their part, would refuse to cover recreational sport providers based on the costs of defending them against legal claims.

Legislative acts that shield recreational sport providers, coaches, and officials tend to provide immunity for risks and harms resulting from behavior that is neither intentional nor reckless. Further discussion of the types of statutory immunity available for recreational sports is found in section "3. Legal Defenses" in this chapter. When courts refuse to find a duty of care in recreational sports cases, they typically focus on the voluntary nature of the activities. In doing so, courts often merge the duty-of-care analysis with a legal defense called "assumption of risk," a term which is also discussed in section "3. Legal Defenses" in this chapter. Determining the existence of a special relationship that creates a duty of care on the part of the defendant is the first step for courts in negligence cases. Accordingly, it may seem confusing that some courts would include within that initial step an examination of a defense to negligence. Courts consider the assumption-of-risk defense at this stage to assess whether the plaintiff voluntarily assumed the risks of harm, thus relieving the defendant of any duty to prevent that harm. The result is an approach in which courts have generally refused to find a duty of care on the part of those engaging in recreational sport (either by participating, officiating, coaching, or organizing) to protect voluntary participants in recreational from reasonable risks that are inherent to the activities.

Even in the case of recreational youth sports, the role of the law in preventing injury in youth sports should not be exaggerated (Abrams, 2011). Those who expect the law to safeguard recreational youth sports will likely be disappointed by the limited safety protections available to courts. For adventure sports, the judicial reluctance to impose liability extends to include types of risks that are often more extreme than those reasonably expected in more traditional sport settings. The duty owed by colleges and universities to intramural sport participants is very similar to that owed by other recreational sport providers. However, the recognition of a limited duty of care in intramural sports is a relatively recent development. At one time colleges and universities stood *in loco parentis*, in the place of the parents, in regard to stewarding moral welfare, physical well-being, and mental training for students under their charge (White, 2005). However, the responsibilities imposed by *loco parentis* on colleges and universities have eroded over time. Where before there may have existed a duty of care on the part of higher education to safeguard most aspects of student life, now responsibility tends to rest with the students to protect themselves. The Third Circuit put it best with its statement in *Bradshaw v. Rawlings* that "the modern American college is not an insurer of the safety of its students" (612 F.2d at 138). This modern view matches student demand for increased autonomy and decreased regulation from colleges in terms of student life, both on and off campus (Spaziano, 1994). And the modern view has extended to include what is required from colleges in protecting students engaged in intramural sports.

The limited duty that schools owe to intramural sport participants needs to be distinguished from the duty of care owed to varsity or junior varsity collegiate athletes. Courts have consistently found the existence of a special relationship that gives rise to an obligation by schools to protect collegiate athletes from injuries, even in the case of nonfeasance. To discern whether a special relationship exists between a college and an athlete, courts place emphasis on whether the college actively recruited the athlete to play a particular sport as well as the degree of control the school exerts over the collegiate athlete. Unlike collegiate athletes, intramural participants are not recruited by colleges to play intramurals. And while schools control the operation of intramural sport activities, they do not exercise the same degree of control over the lives of intramural participants as they do college athletes. For these reasons, courts have distinguished college sports from intramural sports by finding that the latter are private recreational pursuits that do not impose a duty of care on the part of colleges to protect participants from inherent risks of harm (*see Kyriazis v. University of West Virginia; Ochoa v. California State University*).

For all types of recreational sports, however, courts have found a duty of care to protect harms that are not inherent to the activities but within the control of defendant.

First, the limitations on the duty of care do not extend to include risk exposure that falls well outside that expected for the activity. Specifically, a duty of care exists that covers reckless conduct that harms participants in recreational sport activities. Reckless conduct (or recklessness) is a heightened form of negligence that is found when the defendant did not intend to cause the harm but intended to do the act with a strong probability that harm would result. When an act rises to the level that it is deemed to be reckless, that conduct is no longer connected to the competitive scope of the sport and is no longer voluntarily assumed by the participant.

Second, those who provide recreational sport opportunities owe a duty to their participants to provide a reasonably safe event and abide by industry standards and practices. For this reason, all recreational sport providers must stay up to date on industry trends in risk prevention. Recreational sport organizations often provide standards, guidelines, and/or best practices suggestions that courts will look to in setting the standard of care required under the duty of care to protect participants. Examples of organizations that provide safety standards in youth sports include, but are not limited to, the National Alliance of Youth Sports (NAYS), the National Council for Youth Sports (NCYS), the Little League Baseball, Pop Warner (football), USA Hockey, and US Youth Soccer. In addition to those, the National Athletic Trainers' Association (NATA) and the Youth Sport Safety Alliance (YSSA) are actively engaged in advocating for safety standards and influencing policy on recreational youth sport safety. Similarly, recreational sport providers for adult or adventure sports need to look to regulatory policies established for the specific activities that they operate. For example, a recreational softball operator should, at minimum, comply with the safety equipment required by the World Baseball Softball Confederation (WBSC) before sanctioning a match. An example for adventure sports is found in the regulatory policies developed for adventure racing by the United States Adventure Racing Association (USARA).

Third, proper supervision is required from those who operate recreational sport activities so that they can respond in a careful and immediate manner when participants incur injuries. When a service provider negligently supervises recreational sport activities the risks inherent to those activities may be increased to such a degree that they are no longer voluntarily assumed by the participants. In supervising recreational sport activities, service providers should also have proper risk management strategies in place that include emergency action plans. Advanced discussion of risk management and emergency action plans, in general, is beyond the scope of this chapter. However, some mention of emergency action preparation is needed when discussing the supervision of recreational sports. Also, all personnel must be well-versed on emergency action plans and those plans must be rehearsed in order to be effective. With these general understandings of the duty of care in recreational sports in mind, the focus in this chapter will now shift to discussing certain specific threats that are very relevant in recreational sport settings.

2.2. Violence in Recreational Youth Sports

Violence in recreational youth sports is a growing concern, so much so that the term "epidemic" has been used to describe the problem with some degree of regularity in both the press and in research articles that have examined the topic. It is important to differentiate the violence that is considered problematic from violence that is common and natural to the recreational sport activity. Many types of recreational youth sports involve contact that is, to some degree, violent. For example, sports like football, basketball, lacrosse, soccer, and softball are types of ballistic activities in which players propel their bodies in ways that result in collisions with other players. Even still, the dangerous nature of sport does not excuse all types of violent contact. When players engage in dangerous acts that fall well outside the constitutive rules of the game their conduct rises to the level of recklessness and results in risks of harm that are not assumed by other participants.

Reckless conduct is a serious problem for recreational youth sports. Findings from injury prevention studies have revealed a connection between reckless conduct (illegal under the constitutive rules of the game) and injuries sustained by participants. A study conducted in 2008 by the Center for Injury Research and Policy at Nationwide Children's Hospital found that more than 98,000 injuries in youth sports occurring between 2005 and 2007 were directly connected to conduct that was not allowed by the constitutive rules of the games surveyed in the study (Abrams, 2013). Citing that study, NATA identified effective and consistent enforcement of rules that punish illegal conduct as a control measure for reducing injury rates in youth sports. The general consensus from those who investigate violence in youth sports is that rules tend to be violated by participants based on the desire to win at all costs. Accordingly, the NATA and youth sport organizations like National American Boosters Club and Little League Baseball have called for an increased emphasis on sportsmanship (the nongendered version of the concept is sportspersonship) and respect for fellow competitors during youth sport competitions.

Unfortunately, the desire to win at all costs is not just prevalent to participants. Too often, parents and coaches promote illegal conduct from the children under their charge. Recreational youth sports provide many teachable life lessons (e.g., learning how to win, lose, and work as a team); yet, those moments are lost when a coach or parent's desire to win dwarfs their desire to teach children valuable life lessons through sport. In fact, Plato opined that "[t]he moral values of exercises of sport far outweigh the physical value" (Plato, 1920, 46). Research supports the position that participation in youth sports facilitates the development of necessary life skills in children (Gould & Carson, 2008). Most experts recommend that youth sport organizations focus on educating both the adults (parents, coaches, and officials) and the child participants on the importance of following the rules. This policy is often regarded as the best step toward preserving the valuable aspects of youth sports while also best protecting participants. In addition to education, most experts suggest that local youth sport organizations have measures in place for removing coaches and parents from competition when they overemphasize winning at the expense of safety. Every instance of unnecessary violence in youth sports cuts into the constructive values that children should learn from their participation (Fiore, 2003).

Another pressing problem in recreational youth sports involves violence from parents directed at other parents, coaches, officials, and even participants. This type of violence is referred to as "parental sports rage." Like in-game violence from child participants, parental sports rage is linked to the win-at-all-costs mind-set now permeating recreational youth sports (Schutte, 2001). The problem is so pervasive that fourteen states have passed or proposed legislation aimed at increasing penalties for persons who assault coaches or officials (Fiore, 2003). While legislation may be needed to help prevent parental sports rage, perhaps the best protections remain those that come from recreational youth sports organizations. Similar to efforts at curbing participant violence during games, education and training by youth sport organizations are considered by experts as the necessary means for preventing parental sport rage. Sport administrators and coaches should communicate with parents as to what is acceptable and unacceptable behavior. One interesting measure was taken by the Jupiter-Tequestra Athletic Association in Florida, which required parents to enroll in classes on appropriate behavior at sporting events and swear an oath to support coaches and officials (Fiore, 2003). The measures appear to have an impact. Youth sport officials in Jupiter have noticed improvements as a result of the required sportspersonship classes, and there have been no further reported incidents of parental sports rage.

Coaches, officials, and other types of league administrators are likewise prone to acts of violence in recreational youth sports. Sometimes these acts manifest in violence committed against other adults, while other times the violence is directed at the child participants. When violence directed at child participants is traced to the desire to win, then the same educational methods for managing parents should apply to coaches and other support staff. In particular, coaches need to be educated on the types of behaviors that are forbidden. However, coach and staff education in youth sports should be coupled with adequate screening procedures and supervision to best protect participants from coaches and staff who have a propensity for violence. Before those protective measures are discussed in more detail, specific attention must be provided for the threat of sexual violence in recreational youth sports.

Recreational youth sports have been described as a means for providing pedophiles with a ready-made pool of potential victims (Peterson, 2004). Through recreational youth sports, a minority of coaches and other officials have used the power their positions provide them to access child athletes and coerce acts that constitute sexual abuse (Brackenridge & Kirby, 1997; Brackenridge, 2001). Compounding the problem is how predatory coaches hide in plain sight—so few expect that the men and women engaged in coaching or officiating sports would be capable of sexual violence (Baker & Byon, 2014). Take the case of Norman Watson, a successful and popular coach and umpire for the East Base Line Little League. Watson pled guilty to thirty-nine counts of lewd acts with children, all of whom were his players during the six years he worked in the league (Nack & Yaeger, 1999). Watson is just one of many high-profile cases involving sexual violence and recreational youth sports. Just as disturbing, experts believe that most cases go unreported as victims are afraid or ashamed to speak up.

Violent coaches and staff can create legal problems for recreational sports leagues. Following Watson's conviction, his victims were able to sustain legal claims against the local Little League affiliate based on theories of negligent hiring, negligent supervision, and the doctrine of respondeat superior. These three legal theories are commonly asserted by plaintiffs in legal actions brought against recreational youth sport leagues for violence committed by coaches or staff. By understanding these theories, recreational sport organizations can adopt strategies to both reduce legal liability and best protect child participants.

The tort of negligent hiring is used to establish liability on the part of employers for harms caused by persons who were hired despite a record for violent conduct. To prevail on a negligent hiring claim, the plaintiff must show that (1) the employer knew or should have known at the time of hiring of the employee's unfitness for the position, and (2) the employee's dangerous characteristics proximately caused the plaintiff's injuries. The "knew or should have known" aspect is particularly problematic for youth sport organizations because it means that they could be found negligent by failing to properly screen applicants for paid or volunteer positions within their organizations (Baker, Connaughton, and Zhang, 2010). If reasonable hiring practices would have revealed a history of violence for a coach or staff member, then the youth sport organization is potentially responsible for harms caused by that violent coach or staff member.

Typically, courts define reasonable hiring practices as including an application, an interview, and reference checks. If the interview and reference check alerts the employer of the applicant's potential for violence, a more exacting investigation by the employer into the applicant's work history may be warranted. Few jurisdictions require criminal records checks as part of a reasonable background search (Baker, Connaughton, and Zhang, 2011). Some states have exceptions to the general rule and now require criminal records checks when employees are provided with access to the public, particularly when they would have access to children (Gibbons & Campbell, 2003). It's important to note that criminal records checks are much more affordable than they once were, and youth sport organizations like Little League Baseball and Pop Warner now require criminal records checks for all personnel at their affiliates. The growing industry trend of youth sport organizations requiring criminal records checks has led some to suggest that the use of criminal records checks has become part of the standard of care that is expected from all youth sport organizations (Baker & Byon, 2014). In Oregon, the state legislature proposed that bill that would have required youth sport coaches to be certified by the Youth Sports Commission within Oregon's Department of Human Services (Fiore, 2003). The bill would have also encouraged background checks for all coaches. Texas, however, passed legislation that protects employers from liability for negligent hiring merely based on the evidence that the employee had been convicted of a crime. Legislation like this exists to shield employers in situations in which they are giving someone who has committed a crime a second chance. However, legislative protection typically does not extend to include either offenses committed while performing job duties similar to the position for which the person was hired or certain violent or sexual offenses such as murder, aggravated robbery, or sexual assault.

Still, even the most exacting of screening practices will not expose all violent coaches and staff. Many are never accused of violent acts, let alone caught in the act. This is why youth sport organizations need to rely on supervision to supplement their screening practices. Supervision, in this use, means more than a mere physical presence at practices and games. After all, managerial staff for recreational youth sport organizations are unable to be in all places at all times. Instead, managers need to implement effective—and reasonable—supervision strategies for monitoring practices and games. Failure to do so could result in a claim for negligent supervision if victims are harmed at times and locations that should have been supervised. For this reason, managers of recreational youth sport organizations need to look to the industry practices developed by national organizations for the sports they manage (e.g., US Youth Soccer or Pop Warner) for guidance in keeping with industry trends on supervision and education. Like most safety protocols, supervision strategies should not be stagnant. Managers must evolve their approach based on need and industry-wide changes.

Youth sport administrators must also be responsive and sensitive to allegations of violence and terminate all involvement with personnel who have shown a propensity for violence. Failure to terminate involvement with an unfit coach or staff member could result in a negligent retention claim against the youth sport organization. Because most incidents of violence go unreported, youth sport organizations should consider educating parents and participants on what is allowed and disallowed and the need to report problems. Adopting such an approach may help the organization in fostering an environment in which parents and participants feel comfortable reporting suspect behavior.

In addition to being found liable for their own negligence in hiring, supervision, and retention of unfit coaches and staff, the possibility also exists that the organization could be found liable for violence committed by its employees and volunteers through the doctrine of respondeat superior (Baker, Connaughton, & Zhang, 2011). Respondeat superior is a legal doctrine that holds employers responsible for wrongful acts committed by their employees during the scope of employment. The traditional view of respondeat superior did not apply the doctrine to cover intentional, often criminal, acts of violence on the basis that intentional acts were not performed in furtherance of the employer's enterprise and therefore fell outside the scope of employment. However, the modern application, adopted by many jurisdictions, now extends the doctrine to include intentional violence that is closely related to the person's position. Courts have found a close relationship in situations in which the employee used opportunity provided by their employment to commit the violent act. Most of those cases have also focused on the role of the aggressor as having some degree of authority over the victim that is provided through the employment (e.g., authority a coach enjoys over athletes).

The plaintiffs in the case involving Norman Watson were able to sustain a respondeat superior claim against East Baseline Little League claim by showing that Watson used the authority afforded by his coaching position to harm players on his team (*Hickman v. Little League Baseball, Inc.*). It is important to note that Little League Baseball, Inc. was able to dismiss the claims against it on the grounds that it was a franchisor, but the claims against the affiliate were allowed to continue. Similar to that case was another involving a little league affiliate in *Southport Little League v. Vaughan*. In *Vaughan*, the doctrine of respondeat superior was found to include sexual violence committed by an equipment manager. The affiliate's attempt to dismiss the claims based on the traditional application of resopndeat superior were rejected because the affiliate cloaked the manager with authority and provided him with authorization and opportunity to molest child participants in an equipment room under the pretense that he was fitting the children for uniforms. Cases like *Vaughan* and *Hickman* are not typical in that plaintiffs are unlikely to prevail in court against youth sport organizations for intentional acts of violence committed by coaches and officials. Rarely do intentional acts of violence fall within the scope of authority for the purpose of respondeat superior. Similarly, prevailing against youth sport organizations for negligent hiring, retention, and supervision in these types of cases is also difficult because the plaintiffs must establish that the organization's hiring, retention, and supervision practices were a proximate cause for the plaintiff's injuries. In other words, the plaintiffs must demonstrate with evidence that the youth sport organization could have prevented the violence through more reasonable practices. However, the threat of liability, even if slight, exists and the threats posed to child participants by violent coaches and staff are very real.

2.3. Concussions in Recreational Sports

A concussion is an injury to the brain that may be caused either by direct impact to the head, face, neck or by impact to somewhere else on the person's body that results in an "impulsive" force transmitted to the head (McCrory et al., 2013). Concussions most often cause an immediate but short-lived impairment of neurological function; however, symptoms of concussion may evolve over time and may manifest neuropathological changes. The types of symptoms for concussions are graded and typically resolve in a sequential order. It is important to note that concussions may or may not involve loss of consciousness. Concussions are a threat to any recreational sport that includes the possibility of collisions with other participants or hard surfaces. Recent concussion-related litigations involving professional sports leagues like the NFL and NHL have placed a spotlight on the risks posed by concussions and made necessary risk management strategies for preventing and managing concussions in sports, including recreational sports.

The NFL's concussion litigation and the major motion picture *Concussion* both addressed the threat of chronic traumatic encephalopathy (CTE) as a long-term effect of concussions in sport. While CTE is a product of long-term exposure to concussions throughout a life, some studies have found symptoms in sport participants as young as twenty-five (e.g., see, McKee et al., 2009). The symptoms of CTE are progressive and start with memory loss and develop into dementia that could include Alzheimer's disease or Parkinsonism. CTE has long since been traced to boxing and has most recently been linked to football and basketball. The disease, however, is linked to any recreational activity in which participants suffer repeated head traumas for a prolonged period of time. While it is possible to suspect the disease in athletes based on symptoms, the disease can only be confirmed postmortem evaluation of the brain.

CTE is also a serious risk for participants in non-contact sports in which frequent and hard impact falls over years of participation are common (e.g., gymnastics and high-risk adventure sports like skateboarding). The disease was diagnosed by neuropathologists in BMX legend Dave Mirra following his death from suicide at the age of 41 in 2016. For some adventure sports like BMX and skateboarding the threats from concussions and CTE are compounded by the trend for athletes to elect not to wear protective equipment, especially helmets. Another concussion-related problem pertaining to those adventure sports is that they are often performed without any organizational supervision, meaning that athletes may be solely responsible for their own concussion recognition and management.

Second-impact syndrome is a second type of injury that results from multiple concussions and can sometimes be fatal for sport participants. This type of injury occurs when someone sustains a second concussion while still symptomatic from a first concussion. The athlete with second-impact syndrome may become unresponsive for up to 15 seconds following the second concussion as a result of a massive edema (brain swelling) or elevated intracranial pressure. When these phenomena occur, the mortality rate is near 50% while the morbidity rate (chance of sustaining a disabling impairment) is 100% (Wilson, 2010). Concussion identification and postconcussion management procedures are the best defense for preventing second-impact syndrome. Problems exist in the lack of uniform concussion managements for sports and the difficulties in identifying concussions in situations in which athletes are not rendered unconscious. Further complicating identification difficulties is the fact that participants may hide concussion symptoms in order to continue sport participation. For this reason, coaches, administrators, officials, and staff who manage recreational sport activities need to look for situations in which participants are demonstrating symptoms that suggest that they are concussed.

Recreational youth sport participants are particularly prone to suffering from concussions and second-impact syndrome because their brains are still developing. In fact, children between ages of six and fourteen are at the highest risk of any age group for sustaining head traumas, which is the leading cause of death among children and adolescents (Danov, 2006). Children also may hide symptoms so that they can continue playing, or may not even appreciate that they are experiencing symptoms of a concussion. Those who supervise youth sport activities need to be particularly mindful in identifying concussions and managing for them through return-to-play (RTP) protocols. Second-impact syndrome for child athletes is so serious that some medical and sport experts have urged for rule changes that would fundamentally alter high-risk youth sports as a means for reducing the risk of injury from concussion. There exists a long-standing debate in hockey about the appropriate age for allowing young athletes to body check (Wilson, 2010). Also, the US Soccer Federation released safety initiatives in 2015 that prohibit anyone age ten and under from heading the ball, and that ban headers in practice (not games) for eleven- to thirteen-year-olds. The US Soccer Federation's initiatives were made to resolve a proposed class action lawsuit. Participation in flag football has increased given parental concerns over concussions in youth football. The NFL and USA Football started Heads Up Football, a program designed with the goal of improving concussion safety in youth football. The program required for all teams a player safety coach who has been trained in teaching proper approaches to blocking and tackling. There have been conflicting studies concerning the effectiveness of the Heads Up program.

In terms of legal liability for concussion-related injuries, little guidance can be found in the literature or in the case law on what is expected from those who provide recreational sport services. Also, the concussion litigations involving professional sports leagues are of limited applicability to recreational sport organizations or leagues. However, a related line of cases exists that involves interscholastic sport leagues and schools. It may shed a light on the possibility that recreational sport providers could be found liable for concussion-related injuries sustained by participants. What can be learned from those cases is that there is a reluctance from courts to hold governing bodies and associations that regulate recreational sports responsible for claims related to concussions and failures to provide RTP rules and protocols (see *Serrell v. Connetquot Central High School District* and *Mohr v. St. Paul Fire & Marine Insurance Co*). Yet, those decisions may not protect schools, coaches, doctors, and athletic trainers who fail to take proper steps to protect participants from concussions and second-impact syndrome.

Furthermore, what is expected from sport providers may evolve based on what is learned from improved research on concussions. Increased knowledge on the subject has already led to the development of legislations in several states that require safety training for staffs in recognizing the signs of concussion. Some of these laws even include RTP procedures. From 2009 to 2013, forty-nine states had passed concussion laws, most of which were based on Washington's Lynstedt Law, a concussion act named for Zachery Lystedt, a middle school football player who suffered a brain injury in 2006 because he returned to play while concussed. The Lystedt Law and those like it have provided means for managing concussions in interscholastic sports. Federal legislation has also been proposed that would provide states with money to develop concussion management strategies. However, none of the extant legislative acts extend to include requirements, or even resources, for managing concussions in recreational youth sports or any other form of recreational sport activity.

Complicating the matter is the fact that disagreement exists among various medical and political factions in terms of the best RTP measures and how to administer those measures. The Zurich Consensus Statement on Concussion in Sport is one of the latest efforts from scientists to develop an effective concussion protocol for sport. The Consensus Statement discourages same-day RTP for any athlete who suffers a head injury and requires that no athlete be allowed to continue participation in the activity until he or she is asymptomatic. The Consensus Statement also suggests that RTP standards be stricter for younger athletes and states that these athletes should only be allowed to RTP following permission by a physician following an examination (McCrory et al., 2013). It's important to keep in mind that concussions are an inherent risk for various recreational sport activities. Along those lines, sport activity providers are rarely held responsible for injuries resulting from inherent risks unless their actions have made the risks more dangerous or likely. Second-impact syndrome is the type of inherent risk that sport activity leaders can make more likely or dangerous by failing to administer proper RTP protocols. This is why recreational sport providers need to follow the science on the subject. They must also stay well-informed on how governing bodies and fellow providers manage concussions so that the concussion protocols for the sport activities they provide do not fall below the standard of care that may be established through changes in guidelines and industry norms.

3. Legal Defenses

This section of the chapter concerns the legal defenses to tort liability that are most commonly asserted in cases involving recreational sports. The defenses are broken down into three primary types: (1) assumption of risk, (2) waivers, and (3) statutory protections. The first two defenses involve participant consent to take responsibility for their own safety. For this reason, the first two defenses involve agreements, whether explicit or implied. Yet, key distinctions exist in the types of risks assumed through assumption of risk in comparison to waivers. The third defense type discussed in this section involves protections stemming from state statutory law. State legislation exists in a number of jurisdictions that insulates those who conduct recreational sport activities and those who allow their properties to be used by participants in recreational sport activities. While the types of legislations discussed may vary in degree and in application, they have a common purpose in encouraging recreational sport participation. This section provides a general overview of these defense types, which vary considerably in application from state to state.

3.1. Assumption of Risk

Assumption of risk is an often misunderstood defense to liability that remains very relevant in recreational sport cases involving harms resulting from dangers associated with activities. Assumption of risk emerged in the nineteenth century as a tool for shielding defendants in situations in which the plaintiff has voluntarily assumed the risk of harm. Yet, over time, the doctrine has been confused by the fact that courts in many jurisdictions used assumption of risk as an umbrella term that covered two very different defenses to liability: (1) primary assumption of risk, and (2) secondary assumption of risk. Primary assumption of risk acts as a complete defense to liability because it removes the existence of a legal duty on the part of the defendant in situations in which the plaintiff knowingly consented to risk exposure. Primary assumption of risk is assumption of risk in the truest sense because the defense exists even in the absence of negligence on the part of the defendant. For this reason, when judges and scholars use the term "assumption of risk" in a recreational sport context, they are discussing, more often than not, primary assumption of risk.

The key to primary assumption of risk is that the plaintiff's injuries must result from known, understood, and appreciated risks inherent to activities in which the plaintiff voluntarily participated. Throughout this chapter, there has been mention of how recreational sport providers are generally not liable for harms resulting from inherent risks—that is, those risks that cannot be removed from the activity without fundamentally altering its nature. Accordingly, the contexts for each sport must be examined to discern whether the injuries for which the plaintiff is suing result from risks that are natural to the activity. For some risks, their inherent natures are very straightforward to assess. An ankle sprain suffered while grabbing a rebound in an intramural basketball game would be an example of an easily identified and commonly understood risk inherent to that particular activity. However, there are other risks that are less clear and require case-by-case determinations. For example, think about the risk of a batter being hit by an intentionally thrown pitch during a game administered as part of an adult recreational baseball league. The constitutive rules of baseball do not allow pitchers to intentionally throw at batters, but the customs of the game may lead the trier of fact to determine that the batter should have appreciated that risk. The point of this exercise is to highlight how some risks of injury may be natural to activities, even though they result from conduct prohibited by the official rules of the game. There is no bright-line test that can be applied to all recreational activities and in all cases. Thus, the trier of fact is left to evaluate the contexts of each case to decide whether the plaintiff's harm should have been anticipated as part of the activity. To further illustrate, the risks associated with certain adventure sports (e.g., rock climbing, white-water-rafting, and base jumping) may greatly exceed the risks that would be anticipated in other types of recreational activities (e.g., golf, tennis, and badminton) and could even include the risk of death.

Another core aspect of assumption of risk involves the fact that the participant must know, understand, and appreciate the inherent risks for the activity in which he was injured. The trier of fact must determine whether, based on an objective view of the facts for each case, the plaintiff's familiarity, or lack thereof, with the activity provided the requisite knowledge, understanding, and appreciation needed for the plaintiff to assume the risk that caused the injury at issue. Accordingly, recreational sport activity providers need to warn their participants of inherent risks. If the participants are minors, then the warnings must also be provided to the participant's parents or legal guardian.

Plaintiffs can assume risks inherent to recreational sport activities by either express or implied assumption. Express assumption of risk occurs when the participant communicates his voluntary assumption of the risk. Typically, this occurs through the use of words or language that is either spoken or written. While any form of expression will work, recreational sport activity providers often use participation agreements as a means for evidencing the plaintiff's express assumption of risk. Participation agreements are the sport version of informed consent agreements that are commonly used to inform of risks prior to participation in a medical procedure or experimental study. The key to an effective participation agreement is in the use of language that effectively communicates the risks, including a list of possible injuries, which are to be assumed by the participant for that particular activity. Accordingly, recreational sport activity providers should use a participation agreement that was drafted for their specific activity and for their specific types of participants. No single participation agreement will effectively apply in all recreational sport settings. Participation agreements need to also confirm the participant's ability to take part in the activity and provide consent for treatment in the case of injury. Participation agreements are contracts and should be drafted by attorneys in order to maximize the effectiveness of their application and best ensure their enforceability in courts of law. Because participation agreements are contracts, participation agreements should be signed by the participant's parents or legal guardian in order to be enforced against a minor in a court of law. Remember, minors lack the legal ability to consent to risk exposure.

Implied assumption of risk involves the plaintiff's assumption of the risks through participation in the risky activity rather than communication. Since this type of assumption of risk does not involve evidence of the plaintiff communicating his willingness to risk exposure, the defendant must convince the court that the plaintiff understood and appreciated the risks for that activity and participated willingly with that information in mind. The plaintiff's pre-existing familiarity with the activity and its risks is central to implied assumption of risk. Not all recreational sport activities are organized in ways that facilitate or necessitate the use of lawyers who write up participation agreements. For example, a group of former high school basketball players decide to meet up at a college campus rec facility and play a pickup game of basketball. The participants in this game should not be forced by the law to require contractual protections in the case that one inadvertently injures another during a defended play or as part of a rebound. After all, the participants in this match should have the requisite knowledge, understanding, and appreciation of all the risks inherent to basketball based on their experiences playing the game. By engaging in the pickup game, the participants in this hypothetical likely assumed the risks of injury from dangers inherent to basketball.

3.2. Waivers and Recreational Sports

Similar to participation agreements, waivers are contractual tools that, if enforced by courts of law, can safeguard recreational sport providers from legal liability. The well-drafted waiver for a recreational sport activity will include warnings of the inherent risks in the same way that an effective participation agreement does; however, waivers also include language that contractually releases the activity provider from liability resulting from negligent acts or omissions that harm participants. Waivers are controversial and not all states enforce them the same way, or at all. The controversial nature of waivers is found in the fact that they permit service providers to be negligent with participant safety by contractually shifting risk avoidance from the provider to the participant. Keep in mind that recreational sport providers are in the best position to bear the burden of safeguarding their activities from injuries that are caused by the providers' own negligence. After all, they should know the activities and the services they provide better than their participants. Yet, the waiver contractually shifts the burden of injury prevention from the provider to the participant. Their controversial nature is why states like Louisiana, Montana, and Virginia still do not legally enforce waivers in courts of law as a matter of public policy. However, those three states are in the minority because waivers that are well-drafted, properly administered, and voluntarily signed by an adult will be enforced in forty-three states, D.C., Puerto Rico, and the Virgin Islands (Cotten, 2013).

States that enforce waivers also tend to cite public policy as the main justification. These states, however, focus on the policy behind protecting the public's interests in maintaining the services that are covered by the waiver. The accompanying fear is that without the enforcement of waivers, the costs of litigation would drive service providers out of business. This pro-waiver policy is thought to be particularly true for recreational sport activities because they often involve services that expose participants to high degrees of risk. Sport event operators for high-risk activities like triathlons (e.g., Ironman), adventure racing (e.g., USARA), and obstacle racing (e.g., Tough Mudder and Spartan) should consider the enforceability of waivers when assessing host locations as a means for mitigating the risk of legal liability for their events.

For fourteen states, the pro-waiver policy has also provided the basis for enforcing, to varying degrees, parental waivers. The parental waiver is a contractual release provided by the parent or legal guardian for the minor. As with participation agreements, minors lack the contractual capacity to consent to waivers. But unlike participation agreements, waivers authorized by parents or legal guardians are legally unenforceable in seventeen states,[1] and enforcement remains unclear in twenty-one other states.[2] To date, only twelve states enforce parental waivers, but that number continues to increase at a rate that suggests the existence of a trend favoring enforceability. The pro-parental waiver states focus on the fact that participation in extracurricular and recreational activities is never essential and always voluntary (*Sharon v. City of Newton*). Those states also respect the fundamental rights of parents and legal guardians in making decisions concerning the child's care, custody, and upbringing (*Woodman v. Kera, LLC*). The anti-parental waiver states, instead, have expressed reluctance, as a matter of public policy, to permit service providers to behave negligently with minors. For these jurisdictions, those who provide services to children must exercise reasonable care. Importantly, this requirement cannot be contractually removed by children, parents, or legal guardians (*Scott v. Pacific West Mountain Resort*).

In addition to public policy violations, courts have refused to enforce recreational sport waivers that (1) attempt to release liability for heightened degrees of negligence, or (2) use inconspicuous language. First, waivers in general only cover acts or omissions that involve ordinary negligence. Behavior that is considered by the trier of fact to include gross negligence, reckless conduct, or willful or wanton conduct may not be waived in the overwhelming majority of legal jurisdictions (Cotten, 2013).[3] Waivers must also be conspicuous in the sense that they must provide the reader with a clear notice that they release the activity provider for its negligent conduct. Some states require use of the word "negligence" in the release. Courts tend to scrutinize waivers carefully before enforcing them. If enforced, a waiver holds harmless someone who negligently harmed another, meaning that the victim of negligence leaves the court empty handed. Waivers are always enforced on a "case-by-case" basis. Put another way, the contexts of each contractual relationship are considered carefully by courts in determining whether the waiver applies to a given set of facts. Accordingly, recreational sport activity providers must appreciate the significance of waivers and the need for legal expertise in waiver drafting. Waivers must be written in a way that complies with the laws for the state in which the activity is provided. Hiring an attorney to draft a waiver is not without cost, but that cost could pale in comparison to the compensatory damages that a recreational sport activity provider could have to pay for its own negligence or the negligence of its employees.

3.3. Statutory Defenses for Recreational Sports

State legislators in a number of states have enacted laws that shield some recreational sport activity providers from legal liability for inherent risks and negligence. First, intramural sport activity providers may qualify for the governmental (sovereign) immunity protections that cover public colleges and universities and their employees. Sovereign immunity is qualified by the courts to protect government employees only for their discretionary decisions and functions. For example, an intramural director would be protected for a decision as to which teams play on which fields or how many officials are needed to staff a match. No sovereign immunity exists for ministerial acts, which are defined as any act performed (1) based on orders provided by a superior; (2) or as a result of duties that are "absolute, certain, and imperative" (*Yanero v. Davis*, 522). In an intramural setting, a ministerial act could include any task that must regularly be performed prior to a game (e.g., inspecting equipment).

States like Rhode Island, Georgia, and Mississippi have enacted legislation that extends immunity (similar to that provided for government employees) to persons who provide athletic services (coaches, officials, volunteers). Rhode Island's athletic services immunity, however, does not extend to willful, wanton, or reckless disregard for the safety of participants (R.I. Gen. Laws 1956 § 9-1-48(b)). Georgia's statute provides immunity for nonprofit sport associations or those sponsoring sports programs (Ga. Code Ann § 51-1-20). Mississippi provides immunity from negligence for volunteers and sports officials (Miss. Code Ann. § 95-9-3). California has a statute (Cal. Gov't Code § 831.7) that immunizes public entities and employees from liability for injuries to persons engaged in hazardous recreational activities. In *Ochoa v. California State University,*

Sacramento, a California court interpreted California's hazardous recreational activity statute to immunize a university from negligence that resulted in a student being injured during an intramural soccer match. However, the *Ochoa* case is a bit of an anomaly as other California courts have refused to extend the hazardous recreational activity statute to school sport settings because the law was intended protect public entities for allowing use of public land for hazardous activities like hang gliding, rock climbing, or for building a skate park that is open to the public (*see Acosta v. Los Angeles Unified School District*,).

More common, however, is a specific type of legislative immunity that exists to encourage public and private land owners to make available their property to those who would use it for recreational purposes, collectively called recreational user statutes. Some states require the land to be undeveloped, while others do not. Some statutes limit liability only for private landowners; others extend to include state or federal properties. Many statutes list examples of the types of recreational activities that are covered, even if those lists are not exclusive. However, courts tend not to extend protections to activities that are not purely recreational. Thus, protected activities are typically outdoor, more physical than not, and are not spectator sports (Easter, Hardin, and Stenger, 2002).

Notes

1. Alabama, Hawaii, Louisiana, Michigan, Pennsylvania, Utah, West Virginia, Arkansas, Iowa, Montana, Tennessee, Virginia, Illinois, Maine, New Jersey, Texas, and Washington.
2. Georgia, Kentucky, North Carolina, New Hampshire, Oklahoma, South Carolina, Wyoming, Idaho, Missouri, Nebraska, New Mexico, Oregon, South Dakota, Kansas, Nevada, New York, Rhode Island, and Vermont.
3. Florida, Illinois, Kentucky, and North Carolina have allowed waivers to include releases of liability for gross negligence.

References

Abrams, D. E. (2011). "Player Safety in Youth Sports: Sportsmanship and Respect as an Injury-Prevention Strategy." *Seton Hall Journal of Sports and Entertainment Law* 22(1): 1.

Abrams, D. E. (2013). "Confronting the Youth Sports Concussion Crisis: A Central Role for Responsible Local Enforcement of Playing Rules." *Mississippi Sports Law Review* 2: 75.

Baker, T. A., III, & Byon, K. K. (2014). "Developing a scale of perception of sexual abuse in youth sports (SPSAYS)." *Measurement in Physical Education and Exercise Science*, 18(1): 31–52.

Baker, T. A., III, Connaughton, D. P, and Zhang, J. J. (2010). "An Examination of Immunity Statutes Regarding the Liability of Recreational Youth Sport Organizations for the Pedophilic Actions of Coaches, Administrators, and Officials." *The ICHPER-SD Journal of Research in Health, Physical Education, Recreation, Sport & Dance* 5(1): 54–59.

Baker, T. A., Connaughton, D. P., and Zhang, J. J. (2011). An Examination of Case Law Regarding the Liability of Recreational Youth Sport Organizations for the Pedophilic

Actions of Coaches, Administrators, and Officials Based on the Theory of Respondeat Superior." *Applied Research in Coaching and Athletics Annual* 26: 1–30.

Brackenridge, C. H. (2001). *Spoilsports: Understanding and preventing sexual exploitation in sport.* (London: Routledge).

Brackenridge, C. H., & Kirby, S. (1997). "Playing safe: Assessing the risk of sexual abuse to elite child athletes." *International Review for the Sociology of Sport* 32: 407–418.

Cotten, D. J. (2013). Negligence theory. In D. J. Cotten & J. T. Wolohan, (Eds., 6th ed.), *Law for recreation and sport managers,* (pp. 42–53). Dubuque, IA: Kendall-Hunt.

Danov, R. (2006). "Pediatric Traumatic Head Injuries." In *Foundations of Sport-Related Brain Injuries,* edited by S. Slobounov and W. J. Sebastianelli(New York: Springer Science), 298–299.

Davis, T., National Sports Law Institute (US). Board of Advisors, and Marquette University. Law School. (2006). *Symposium, National Sports Law Institute Board of Advisors.* National Sports Law Institute, Marquette University Law School.

Easter, B. A., Hardin, S. E., and Stenger, T. L. (2002). "Legal Issues Related to Adventure Racing." *Journal of Legal Aspects Sport* 13: 253.

Epstein, A. (2009). "Incorporating the Criminal Law in Sport Studies." *The Sport Journal* 12(3).

Fiore, D. K. (2003). "Parental Rage and Violence in Youth Sports: How Can We Prevent 'Soccer Moms' And 'Hockey Dads' From Interfering in Youth Sports and Causing Games to End in Fistfighting Rather Than Handshakes?" *Villanova Sports & Entertainment Law Journal* 10: 103.

Gibbons, M., & Campbell, D. (2003). "Liability of recreation and competitive sport organizations for sexual assaults on children by administrators, coaches, and volunteers." *Journal of Legal Aspects of Sport* 13: 185–229.

Gould, D., & Carson, S. (2008). "Life skills development through sport: Current status and future directions." *International Review of Sport and Exercise Psychology* 1: 58–78.

Greer, A. (2012). "Extreme Sports and Extreme Liability: The Effect of Waivers of Liability In Extreme Sports." *DePaul Journal of Sports Law & Contemporary Problems* 9: 81.

Kounang, N. (2016, May 25). "Late BMX Biker Dave Mirra had CTE." CNN.com. Retrieved on July 15, 2016 from: www.cnn.com/2016/05/24/health/dave-mirra-cte-bmx-biker/.

McCrory, P., Meeuwisse, W. H., Aubry, M., Cantu, B., Dvořák, J., Echemendia, R. J., and Sills, A. (2013). "Consensus Statement on Concussion in Sport: The 4th International Conference on Concussion in Sport Held in Zurich, November 2012." *British Journal of Sports Medicine* 47(5): 250–258.

McKee, A. C., Cantu, R. C., Nowinski, C. J., Hedley-Whyte, E. T., Gavett, B. E., Budson, A. E., and Stern, R. A. (2009). "Chronic Traumatic Encephalopathy in Athletes: Progressive Tauopathy After Repetitive Head Injury." *Journal of Neuropathology & Experimental Neurology* 68(7): 709–735.

Nack, W., & Yaeger, D. (1999, September 13). "Every parent's nightmare: The child molester has found a home in the world of youth sports, where as a coach he can gain the trust and loyalty of our kids-and then prey on them." *Sports Illustrated* 91: 40–53.

National Athletic Trainers Association and National American Boosters Club Association. (n.d.). "Sports and Safety Checklist to Help Prevent Common Athletic Injuries." www.shapeamerica.org.

Peterson, J. (2004). "Don't trust me with your child: Non-legal precautions when the law cannot prevent sexual exploitation in youth sports." *Texas Review of Entertainment & Sports Law,* 5, 297–323.

Plato. (1920). Protagoras. In: A. Cubberly (Ed.), *Readings in the history of education* (p. 46). New York, NY: HoughtonMifflin.

Pound, R. (1908). "Mechanical Jurisprudence." *Columbia Law Review* 8: 605.

Schutte, J. R. (2001). "When Prosecutors Play Referee, Making Criminals out of Child Athletes, But Are They the Real Culprits?" *Northern Illinois Law Review* 21: 515.

Schwarz, A. (2016, July 27). "N.F.L.-Backed Youth Program Says It Reduced Concussions. The Data Disagrees." *The New York Times*. Retrieved August 1, 2016, from: www.nytimes.com/2016/07/28/sports/football/nfl-concussions-youth-program-heads-up-football.html?_r=0.

Spaziano, J. L. (1994). "It's All Fun and Games Until Someone Loses an Eye: An Analysis of University Liability for Actions of Student Organizations." *Pepperdine Law Review* 22: 213.

Stier, W. F., Jr., Schneider, R. C., Kamp, S., Haines, S., and Gaskins, B. (2008). "Selected Risk Management Policies, Practices, and Procedures for Intramural Activities at NIRSA Institutions." *Recreational Sports Journal* 32: 28–44.

Strauss, B. (2015, November 9). "US Soccer, Resolving Lawsuit, Will Limit Headers for Youth Players." *The New York Times*. Retrieved on July 16, 2016, from www.nytimes.com/2015/11/10/sports/soccer/us-soccer-resolving-lawsuit-will-limit-headers-for-youth-players.html?_r=0.

White, N. (2005). "Taking One for the Team: Should Colleges Be Liable for Injuries Occurring During Student Participation in Club Sports?" *Vanderbilt Journal of Entertainment Law and Practice* 7: 193.

Wilson, M. F. (2010). "Young Athletes at Risk: Preventing and Managing Consequences of Sports Concussions in Young Athletes and the Related Legal Issues." *Marquette Sports Law Review* 21: 241.

Cases

Acosta v. Los Angeles Unified School Dist., 37 Cal. Rptr. 2d 171 (1995).
Bradshaw v. Rawlings, 612 F.2d 135 (3d Cir. 1979).
Commonwealth v. Junta, 815 N.E.2d 254 (Mass. App. 2004).
Hickman v. Little League Baseball, Inc. (2006).
Mohr v. St. Paul Fire & Marine Ins. Co., 674 N.W.2d 576 (Wis. Ct. App. 2003).
Scott v. Pacific West Mountain Resort, 834 P.2d 6 (Wash. 1992).
Serrell v. Connetquot Cent. High Sch. Dist., 721 N.Y.S.2d. 107 (N.Y. App. Div. 2001).
Sharon v. City of Newton, 437 Mass. 99, 769 N.E.2d 738 (2002).
Southport Little League v. Vaughan (2000).
State v. Forbes, No. 63280 (Hennepin Co. Minn. Dist Ct., dismissed Aug. 12, 1975).
Woodman v. KERA LLC, 785 N.W.2d 1, 486 Mich. 228 (2010).
Yanero v. Davis, 65 S.W. 3d 510 (Ky. 2002).

CHAPTER 22

ARBITRATION AND THE OLYMPIC ATHLETE

SEAN F. NOLON

1. Introduction

The organization of the Olympics—also known as the Olympic Movement—traces its roots to the first Olympic games. The Olympic Movement consists of three primary constituents: The International Olympic Committee (IOC), international sports federations, and national Olympic committees. Of these three groups, the IOC "is the supreme authority of the Olympic Movement," and is responsible for organizing these governing bodies as well as collaborating with other parties, such as the Organizing Committees for the Olympic Games (OCOGs), athletes and coaches, broadcasting partners, and United Nations agencies (IOC, Olympic Charter, 2015). All affiliated organizations must comply with the Olympic Charter, which sets forth the Fundamental Principles of Olympism, rules, and bylaws adopted by the IOC.

The IOC carries out the goals of the Olympic Movement, as dictated in the Olympic Charter. The Olympic Charter is the Movement's constitution. The Charter begins with General Principles, which serve as the ideological declarations of the Charter. The remaining sections set forth sixty-one legislative rules and thirty-five bylaws. The Movement's main goal is laid out in the Olympic Charter, and states: "The goal of the Olympic Movement is to contribute to building a peaceful and better world by educating youth through sport practised in accordance with Olympism and its values."

The Charter outlines judicial powers in Rule 23. This judicial rule grants IOC bodies and disciplinary commissions the authority "to punish violations of the Olympic Charter, the World Anti-Doping Code or of any other regulation, as the case may be." According to the Olympic Charter, the IOC can impose sanctions against an individual IOC member, international federations (IFs), national organizing committees (NOCs), host cities and OCOGs, applicant cities, and recognized associations and organizations.

As another important part of the Olympic Movement, NOCs serve as country representatives, and work to "develop, promote and protect the Olympic Movement in their respective countries." Currently, there are over 200 NOCs throughout the world, each promoting sport within their country and eventually sending athletes to compete in the Olympic games. The NOCs must adhere strictly to the Olympic Charter and remain neutral in the face of "political, legal, religious or economic pressures." As such, government officials of any NOC country may not specifically pick NOC members, but they may be elected as a member through the appropriate election process as outlined in the Olympic Charter. For a country to have its NOC officially recognized, it must show that it has sports programs that align with those conducted in the Olympic games and that those in charge of these sports programs have a "voting majority" in all NOC meetings. In their annual meetings, the NOC's obligations are to its athletes: conducting an appropriate selection process for athletes and further providing for adequate training, travel, and overall well-being of the selected athletes.

The United States Olympic Committee (USOC) joined as an early member of the IOC forming twenty-seven years after the IOC started in the late 1800s. Under U.S. federal law the USOC is a nonprofit sports organization designated to coordinate all Olympic-related athletic activity in the United States.

Specifically, the USOC is governed by the Ted Stevens Olympic and Amateur Sports Act. This Act identifies the purpose and authority of the USOC. Among its many objectives, the USOC's stated goals are to "establish national goals for amateur athletic activities, promote . . . amateur athletic activities . . . physical fitness and public participation . . . [and] exercise exclusive jurisdiction . . . over all matters pertaining to United States participation in the Olympic Games, the Paralympic Games, and the Pan-American Games" (Ted Stevens Act).

The wide and contrasting array of decision-making bodies—NOCs, IFs, and doping agencies determining the fate of Olympic athletes—means that disputes are inevitable. As financial benefits for athletes increase, so too do the stakes of athlete-related decisions. Eligibility decisions, the imposition of sanctions, and the review of those determinations all present important dispute resolution questions. To best serve the interests of the athletes and the sporting association community, an efficient and fair mechanism for reviewing official decisions must be available. Other nations have created different structures to administer their Olympic activities.

2. Olympic Disputes and the Court of Arbitration for Sport

Experiences with Olympic disputes over the last several decades have guided athletes and associations to rely on arbitration mechanisms as the principal way to streamline decision making while still delivering fair results. The experience of U.S. sprinter Harry

"Butch" Reynolds in the 1990s demonstrates the need for a consistent and efficient mechanism for resolving sporting disputes.

In August 1990, Reynolds tested positive for banned substances. The International Association of Athletic Federations (IAAF) imposed a two-year ban from international competitions which barred him from participating in the 1992 Barcelona Olympics. Reynolds filed suit in the U.S. District Court for the Southern District of Ohio challenging the suspension. The court issued an injunction that prevented the national federation—then called The Athletic Congress (TAC)—and the IAAF from banning Reynolds from the Olympic trials (McArdle, 2003). On appeal, the U.S. Court of Appeals for the Sixth Circuit ruled against Reynolds and set aside the injunction. Then, on appeal to the U.S. Supreme Court, Justice Stevens lifted the Sixth Circuit's stay and cleared the way for Reynolds to compete in the U.S. qualifying Olympic trials. Complying with the court order, the national association—TAC—allowed Reynolds to compete and he eventually qualified for the U.S. Olympic Team as an alternate. At the same time, the IAAF refused to accept the jurisdiction of the U.S. courts and forced TAC to remove him from the team and refused to let him compete in Barcelona.

After Reynolds defied the IAAF by participating in the U.S. Olympic Trials, the IAAF imposed an additional year on his suspension (Epstein, 2002). Reynolds supplemented his complaint in the Ohio lawsuit and the trial court awarded him $27.4 million in damages. The Sixth Circuit eventually dismissed this judgment, finding that the U.S. district court lacked personal jurisdiction over IAAF. This long saga ended—with Reynolds as the loser—when the U.S. Supreme Court refused to hear an appeal of the Sixth Circuit's dismissal. Partly in response to this convoluted experience with legal challenges, the IOC began requiring all participants in the Olympics to sign an agreement to resolve disputes through the Court of Arbitration for Sport (CAS).

3. Making the Court of Arbitration for Sport Operational

According to the Olympic Charter, "[a]ny dispute arising on the occasion of, or in connection with, the Olympic Games shall be submitted *exclusively* to the Court of Arbitration for Sport, in accordance with the Code of Sports-Related Arbitration." In addition, most NOCs require their athletes to sign an agreement stating that athletes may not "commence proceedings in any court or tribunal other than [the] CAS[.]" (New Zealand Olympic Committee, 2016). The IOC created the CAS in 1983. The CAS then became operational in 1984, operating its headquarters in Lausanne, Switzerland. As originally enacted, the CAS Statutes established the sixty-member pool of arbitrators and one form of dispute resolution, regardless of the nature of the dispute. Today the number of arbitrators has grown and mediation has been added as another form of dispute resolution.

Olympic participants must sign an arbitration agreement committing them to submit all disputes to the CAS. In addition to constituent organizations, any person "play[ing] any part whatsoever in the Olympic Movement, shall accept the supreme authority of the IOC and shall be bound by its Rules and submit to its jurisdiction" (Simma, 2006). Therefore, any corporate body, legal person as determined by public law, or natural person involved in the Olympics can submit a case to the CAS. In addition to claims by athletes, television broadcasters and radio sponsors may also initiate proceedings before the CAS.

The International Equestrian Federation (FEI) was the first Olympic Movement constituent to adopt a CAS arbitration clause. In 1992, an FEI member, Elmar Gundel, utilized the arbitration clause to review sanctions imposed by the FEI. The CAS upheld the sanctions but reduced his suspension to one month. Still unhappy, Gundel appealed to Switzerland's highest court—the Swiss Federal Tribunal—arguing that the CAS arbitration award was invalid due to the CAS's partiality and connections with FEI. The Swiss Federal Tribunal rejected Gundel's argument and determined that the CAS was sufficiently independent from the FEI and certified the CAS "as a true court of arbitration."

At the same time, however, the Swiss Federal Tribunal noted that the CAS's financial dependence on the IOC might undermine the court's neutrality if the IOC appeared as a party before the CAS. The opinion strongly suggested that the CAS needed to be organizationally and financially independent from the IOC. The Swiss Tribunal was concerned with the CAS's funding since the IOC almost exclusively financed the CAS. The Tribunal also expressed concern that the IOC had authority to modify the CAS Statues and that the IOC and its president appointed the CAS members.

Following the Swiss Tribunal's decision in *Gundel*, the CAS adopted two major reforms. The first reform established the International Council of Arbitration for Sport (ICAS) to separate the CAS from the IOC. The ICAS was set up to supervise and finance the CAS. The second major reform created the Code of Sports-Related Arbitration (CAS Code). This Code "defines the structure and procedures of the CAS," and developed two arbitration divisions: the Ordinary Arbitration Division and the Appeals Arbitration Division. By establishing greater autonomy for the CAS, the reforms arguably offered greater protections for parties appearing before the CAS. In addition, the CAS clarified that it could alter its own statutes without IOC approval, and was not subject to an IOC decree ordering noncompliance with a CAS decision.

Subsequently, the CAS's decisions have established a body of authoritative rules for international sports law. For example, CAS rulings have established the general principle for "fairness of rules and procedures." Under this philosophy, the CAS has consistently upheld the athlete's right to be heard in a fair proceeding (Mestre, 2009). Similarly, the CAS can invalidate rules that appear unreasonable or arbitrary. The CAS has issued rules that address jurisdictional conflicts. Specifically, the CAS rulings have consistently established the priority of international federations over national governing bodies in jurisdictional disputes. For example, if an international federation and national federation issue different sanctions for a doping offense, the international federation's sanctions triumph.

While CAS arbitrators are not bound by earlier decisions, in practice they typically follow the principles of *stare decisis*. CAS awards thus contribute to a *lex sportiva*, or the body of sports law. Establishing a level of consistency among decisions enhances the confidence and integrity in the system (McLaren, 2001-2002).

3.1. The Jurisdiction of the Court of Arbitration for Sport

The CAS's jurisprudence has developed rules regarding the extent of their power to review decisions and the types of decisions it can review. For instance, the CAS does not review "on-field-of-play" sporting disputes. Notably, the Olympic Charter leaves the jurisdiction of technical decisions, such as referee calls on the field, to International Federations with one exception: a CAS panel will hear a field-of-play dispute "when there is an element of arbitrariness or maliciousness or when an error of law has been made" (McLaren, 2001, 58).

Aside from field-of-play disputes, the Olympic Charter and the arbitration provisions of athlete agreement state that all disputes in connection with the games must be submitted to the CAS exclusively (Locklear, 2003). This broad authority is consistent with purposes enumerated in the Court of Arbitration for Sport's CAS Code. The CAS Code specifies that the CAS arbitrates private disputes "arising out of the practice or development of sport . . . [and] all activities pertaining to sport." Article 4 of the CAS Statute further articulates the CAS jurisdiction: the CAS will hear disputes concerning doctrinal problems of sport as well as associated "pecuniary, commercial issues." The practical effect of these provisions is that the CAS hears a variety of disputes related to Olympic activity. As a result, the Court of Arbitration for Sport handles conflicts related to eligibility challenges, disciplinary sanctions, qualifying on and participating in national teams, contractual relationships, organizing sporting events, and selling and purchasing sports equipment.

Depending on the nature of the case, the CAS Court Office assigns arbitration proceedings to either the Ordinary Arbitration Division or the Appeals Arbitration Division. Generally, the Office assigns commercial disputes to the Ordinary Arbitration Division and disciplinary matters to the Appeals Arbitration Division. According to the CAS Code, the Appeals Division has jurisdiction over challenges to decisions regarding disciplinary matters and challenges of decisions addressing athlete qualification and official recognition of events.

3.2. Ordinary Arbitration Division

The Ordinary Arbitration Division hears cases of "first instance," namely, problems arising out of contracts as well as advisory opinions. The Ordinary Arbitration Division resolves disputes pertaining to corporate sponsorship, merchandizing, and the sale of television rights, as well as employment and agency contracts. Further, the division hears civil liability claims, which may arise when an athlete experiences an accident during a sports competition. Ordinary Arbitration proceedings on these commercial matters generally last from six to twelve months.

When adjudicating these disputes, the Ordinary Arbitration Division applies Swiss law if the parties have not specified which law will apply. Additionally, the parties may allow the panel to decide a case *ex aequo et bono*, meaning that the arbitrators are not bound by legal rules and can consider what is just and fair under the circumstances. The parties to the dispute can determine how the arbitrators are appointed and how many arbitrators will hear the case. The president of the Division will determine the number of arbitrators if the parties' arbitration agreement does not specify.

To commence an ordinary arbitration with the CAS, a party must file a written request along with the corresponding filing fee. The request must include the name and address of respondent(s), a brief statement of the facts and legal argument, claimant's request for relief, a copy of the contract or document containing the jurisdictional arbitration clause, and any information regarding the number and selection of arbitrators.

After filing a complete arbitration request, parties can go through either a written or an oral proceeding. After consulting with the parties, the panel can decline to hold a hearing if it deems itself sufficiently informed. The CAS arbitrators decide written proceedings based on submitted documents. Alternatively, the parties could participate in an oral proceeding. Since the CAS Code grants discretion to the panel to award the prevailing attorneys' fees and costs of witnesses and interpreters, parties should consider the potential cost of an oral proceeding.

Proceedings before the Ordinary Arbitration Division are confidential. The CAS Code specifies that the parties, the arbitrators, and the CAS cannot disclose information about a dispute or proceeding to any third party. Moreover, arbitrators have a strict duty of confidentiality that continues even after the arbitration proceedings end. Further, under Swiss law, arbitrators are subject to civil liability and damages for violating this duty. The Code also states that the award will not be made public unless the award itself provides for it or the parties agree to public disclosure. Many awards have been made public and can be found on the "Jurisprudence Database" at the website for the Court of Arbitration for Sport (www.tas-cas.org).

3.3. Illustrative Case: *United States Olympic Committee v. International Olympic Committee*

United States Olympic Committee (USOC) v. International Olympic Committee (IOC) demonstrates how the Ordinary Arbitration Division functions. In 2008, the IOC adopted a regulation limiting the eligibility of athletes suspended for doping-related violations. The regulation provided that any athlete banned in excess of six months for doping-related violations could not participate in the next Olympic games. In 2011, this regulation was tested when it was imposed on LaShawn Merritt, a U.S. sprinter.

Merritt had tested positive for DHEA, a banned substance, in a series of out-of-competition tests in violation of the World Anti-Doping Agency (WADA) regulations (Gandert, 2012). He appealed the positive test results to the North American Court of Arbitration for Sport (NACAS). The NACAS panel determined that the USOC could not use the IOC regulation to prevent Merritt from competing in the Olympic Trials or from entering into the Olympic games.

This placed the USOC on a potential collision course with the IOC. If Merritt qualified and won a place on the U.S. team, the IOC would not accept his nomination. Recognizing the uncertainty, the USOC and IOC agreed to submit the case to the CAS for an advisory opinion—referred to as a "consultation proceeding." The arbitration agreement entered into by the USOC and IOC granted CAS authority to hear the case following the rules applicable to the Ordinary Procedure of the CAS Code.

The CAS panel first addressed whether the IOC Regulation was a sanction or an eligibility requirement. From the athlete's perspective, this distinction was very important. If the IOC Regulation operated as a sanction, athletes would be subject to double jeopardy for one infraction. To make this determination, the panel relied on both the regulations and previous CAS case law to analyze the express language of the WADA Code. Article 10.1 of the WADA Code, entitled "Sanctions on Individuals," provides that athletes may be ineligible for a fixed period of two years for the first violation of Article 2.1, 2.2, or 2.6. Further, Appendix One of the WADA Code defines ineligibility as "barred for a specified period of time from participating in any Competition." In addition, according to CAS case law, eligibility requirements serve to facilitate the organization of an event rather than "sanction undesirable behavior by athletes." Unlike sanctions, eligibility requirements are not used to punish athletes for a specific behavior. The panel held that the 2008 IOC regulation was not an eligibility requirement because it sanctioned athletes based on undesirable behavior.

Next, the panel addressed whether this regulation—as a sanction—was consistent with the WADA Code. Article 23.2.2 of the WADA Code requires signatories to accept, without substantive changes, the mandatory provision of the WADA Code. As a signatory, the IOC must comply with the terms. Since the adoption of the 2008 IOC regulation imposed additional disciplinary action that is not provided within Article 10 of the WADA Code, the panel found this imposition of additional consequences to be a "substantive change" in violation of Article 23.2.2 of the WADA Code. The panel concluded that the IOC Regulation was not in compliance with the WADA Code and thus invalid and unenforceable. The panel directed the IOC to take the necessary measures to ensure the IOC Regulation is not enforced against any athlete pending its abrogation.

3.4. Appeals Arbitration Division

The Appeals Arbitration Division hears appeals of decisions made by a sports-related body. The CAS will only hear disputes concerning a sports organization's internal decisions when the appellant has exhausted all avenues available under the implicated sports association. Although rare, the Appeals Division can also hear appeals of CAS arbitral awards when the CAS was the initial decision-making body rather than decisions made by a sports federation (Krahe, 2006). If the parties have not specified which law the panel shall apply, the panel will adjudicate the dispute according to the law of the domicile country of the federation, association, or sports body, or the law the panel deems appropriate (McLaren, 2011).

In regard to timing, unless the relevant federation's or association's arbitration clause explicitly states a period of limitations, the appellant must raise the appeal within twenty-one days from when the sports body rendered a decision (CAS Code R57). A party commencing an action through the Appeal Division, must comply with the same statement filing and court fee process as those required by the Ordinary Arbitration Division. Where applicable, the appellant's Statement of Appeal must include a request to stay the sports organization's decision that the appellant is challenging, along with reasons for that request.

The Appeals Arbitration Division reviews cases de novo. Accordingly, the panel is not constrained to the challenged decision but rather can reexamine the facts and legal consequences of the decision being contested. This allows the panel discretion to exclude evidence that was available or reasonably discoverable to the parties before the challenged decision was rendered. The panel "may issue a new decision which replaces the decision challenged or annul the decision and refer the case back" to the initiating organization (CAS Code R57). The panel must render a decision within three months after receiving the case.

3.5. Illustrative Case: *Pistorius v. International Association of Athletics Federations*

Oscar Pistorius, a disabled South African track athlete, relied on the Appeals Arbitration Division to review a decision of an international sporting federation that barred him from competing against able-bodied athletes. Pistorius, a double amputee, utilized two J-shaped carbon fiber prostheses attached below his knees to compete in track and field events. Pistorius experienced unprecedented success in Paralympic sprinting events while also competing against able-bodied runners. In 2004, Pistorius began to compete in IAAF events against able-bodied athletes, with the eventual goal of sprinting against able-bodied athletes at the 2008 Beijing Summer Olympics. In March 2007, the IAAF Council introduced an amendment to IAAF Rule 144.2 that regulated the use of technical devices. Rule 144.2(e) prohibits "use of any technical device that incorporates springs, wheels or any other element that provides the user with an advantage over another athlete not using such a device."

Initially, Pistorius was still eligible to compete after the rule was instituted. However, Pistorius agreed to participate in a series of tests conducted by IAAF-selected scientists in Germany to determine if his prostheses were prohibited under the new rule. In January 2008, based on the scientists' conclusions, the IAAF stated that Pistorius's limbs used 25% less energy than runners with complete natural legs to run at the same speed, and that they led to less vertical motion combined with 30% less mechanical work for lifting the body.

Based on these findings, the IAAF ruled that the prostheses were to be considered a technical device and therefore violated Rule 144.2(e). Accordingly, Pistorius was declared ineligible to compete in IAAF-sanctioned events against able-bodied athletes, including the 2008 Beijing Summer Olympics. IAAF Competition Rules permit an appeal of the Council's decision to the Court of Arbitration for Sport in Lausanne, Switzerland. Pistorius delivered his Statement of Appeal to the CAS in February 2008. In preparation for his appeal, Pistorius retained his own experts and scientists and ran tests to contradict the findings of the German report. The CAS determined that the IAAF's burden of proof is to prove "on the balance of probability" that Rule 144.2(e) is contravened by Pistorius' use of the prostheses (*Pistorius v. IAAF*). This burden equates to the "preponderance of the evidence" standard within American jurisprudence.

In May 2008, a panel of the Appeals Arbitration Division upheld Pistorius's appeal and revoked the decision of the IAAF with immediate effect. The CAS Panel unanimously determined that the IAAF did not meet its burden of proof for multiple reasons. First, the German scientist only tested Pistorius's biomechanics at full speed when he was running in a straight line, unlike a real 400-meter race. Second, the CAS Panel determined that the IAAF report did not consider the *disadvantages* that Pistorius suffers at the start and acceleration phases of the race, and that overall there was no evidence that Pistorius had any *net* advantage over able-bodied athletes. The IAAF only asked the German experts to determine if Pistorius had an advantage; the scientists did not look for disadvantages that would have balanced against any advantages.

The CAS later found that the correct determination, based upon the correct interpretation of the rule, should have been whether Pistorius had an overall *net* advantage. The CAS Panel interpreted Rule 144.2(e) as a "masterpiece of ambiguity" and said that the actual question was whether Oscar gained an overall *net* advantage (*Pistorius v. IAAF*). Furthermore, the CAS Panel found that the new rule was drafted to prevent Pistorius from competing against able-bodied athletes and that the IAAF Council members behaved improperly prior to the IAAF Council's vote, as several IAAF officials had commented to the press that Pistorius would be deemed ineligible (Crincoli, 2011; Charlish and Riley, 2008). The CAS ruling cleared the way for Pistorius to participate in qualifying events for the 2008 Beijing Olympics. When the CAS Panel delivered its ruling, months after he thought the IAAF had crushed his dream to compete in the Olympics, Pistorius wept.

3.6. Ad Hoc Division/Olympic Division

In 1995, the ICAS established a new division to hear cases more quickly. The Ad Hoc Division (AHD) or Olympic Division to the Court of Arbitration for Sport operates during the games to address disputes that arise between the opening and closing ceremonies. The Division may also have jurisdiction over "first instance" disputes, such as an athlete bringing a tort action against the Games' organizing committee or the IOC. The

Ad Hoc Division presides over all disputes connected to the operation of the Games. The CAS created the Ad Hoc Division to resolve disputes within twenty-four hours, without any cost to the athlete. (CAS Arbitration Rules for the Olympic Games, Art. 18, 2012). The AHD was created, in part, as a reaction to the legal challenges brought by U.S. sprinter Harry Reynolds in the early 1990s.

As with the Ordinary and Appeals Divisions, the Ad Hoc Division "holds a seat" in Lausanne, Switzerland. The practical effect of this decision is that although arbitration proceedings take place at the venue of Games, Chapter 12 of the Swiss Federal Act on Private International Law of 18 December 1987 ("PIL Act") governs the panelists. As is expected, the CAS Code distinguishes the Ad Hoc Division's rules from those applicable to the Ordinary and Appeals Divisions. The arbitration rules for the Olympic games require panelists to resolve disputes "pursuant to the Olympic Charter, the applicable regulations, general principles of law and the rules of law, the application of which it deems appropriate." The "applicable regulations" include the IOC Medical Code pertaining to doping and IF regulations concerning each sport's practice and event organization (Kaufmann-Kohler and Bärtsch, 2006). The "general principles of law" refers to public and criminal law principles such as the proportionality of sanctions and canons of statutory interpretation.

The athlete's Olympic entry form contains an arbitration clause as an eligibility condition. For example, the entry form for the 2004 Athens Summer Olympic Games stated the following:

> I agree that any dispute, controversy or claim arising out of, in connection with, or on the occasion of, the Olympic Games, not resolved after exhaustion of the legal remedies established by my NOC, the International Federation governing my sport, [Athens Organizing Committee for the Olympic Games] and the IOC, shall be submitted exclusively to the Court of Arbitration for Sport (CAS) for final and binding arbitration in accordance with the "Arbitration Rules for the XXVIII Olympiad in Athens," which form part of the Code of Sports-related Arbitration.
>
> (Blackshaw, 2013)

To commence an arbitration with the Ad Hoc Division, the challenging party must file an application specifically with the Division. This application triggers the president of the Division to select a three-member arbitration panel from the ICAS's approved list and appoint the panel's president. Despite broad discretion to formulate procedure, the Arbitration Rules for the Olympic Games require that the panel initiate at least one hearing where each party presents its case and all of its evidence. The panel must render its decision within twenty-four hours.

3.7. Illustrative Case: *U.S. Swimming v. Fédération Internationale de Natation Amateur*

The Fédération Internationale de Natation Amateur (FINA) is considered an "umbrella organization" that oversees all national sports federations for swimming (CAS Ad Hoc

(O.G. Atlanta) 96/001 US Swimming v. FINA). The IOC has tasked FINA with overseeing the admissibility and entry of swimming athletes at the Olympic Games. In 1996, a swimmer representing Ireland identified as "S," was properly entered into the Olympic games before the July 5, 1996, deadline for five events not including the 400-meter freestyle. However, "S" was later permitted to replace another Irish swimmer competing in the 400-meter freestyle. On July 20, FINA concluded that "S" could substitute for the other Irish swimmer. Such a determination falls within FINA's authority. However, Germany, the Netherlands, and the United States sought reversal of FINA's determination from the Ad Hoc Division. The request for arbitration was sent to CAS by fax at 6:10 p.m. on July 21, 1996. The panel of arbitrators convened for a hearing at 11:00 p.m., which concluded at 12:30 a.m. on July 22, 1996.

Because Article 17 of the Ad Hoc Rules specifies that the panel must rely on the Olympic Charter, applicable regulations, and general principles of law when deciding a case, this panel focused on the applicable regulations—specifically, FINA's bylaws and the IOC's Guide to Entries for Sports Competitions and Accreditation, both of which provide requirements for entries to the Olympic games.

FINA's bylaws provided that entries for the Olympic games must be determined "on or before the date determined" by the IOC. The entry deadline was determined to be July 5, 1996, by the IOC. The dispute centers around whether "S" was entered into the Olympic games before the July 5 deadline or, as *U.S. Swimming* contends, on July 20. In determining the date of entry, the panel had to determine the scope of the term "entry."

First, the panel looked to Article 6.3.2 of FINA's bylaws for clarification. However, Article 6.3.2 does not state whether "entry" refers only to the identification of an athlete and his or her sport, or if it encompasses each specific event. Thus, Article 6.3.2 failed to provide any guidance for the panel to interpret the term "entry."

The Panel then reviewed the IOC's Guide to Entries and examined the common practices of the IOC and FINA. The IOC's Guide to Entries provides, in part, that deadlines are firm unless otherwise approved. In fact, the IOC and FINA, respectively, followed a consistent practice of leniency in allowing entry of athletes past the determined deadline. The IOC sports director stated that roughly 1,000 athletes were permitted to enter the 1996 Atlanta Olympic Games past the determined July 5 deadline. Additionally, the IOC sports director testified that correspondence between the IOC and FINA supported the finding that the IOC and FINA together made an exception allowing "S" to participate in the 400-meter freestyle.

The panel noted that the IOC and FINA have displayed, over the years, flexibility in the entry of certain athletes. The panel explicitly stated that change to this common practice "must be the result of calm policy deliberations, and not an abrupt exclusion which penalizes an unsuspecting and blameless athlete" (CAS Ad Hoc (O.G. Atlanta) 96/001 US Swimming v. FINA at para. 15). In doing so, the Panel acknowledged that such a decision must be left to the experience within the IOC because it would negatively affect countless athletes. The Ad Hoc Division of CAS concluded that *U.S. Swimming* failed to demonstrate that the participation of "S" would violate a clear requirement of applicable rules. The ambiguity contained in FINA's bylaws, in addition to IOC and FINA common practice and policy rationale, compelled the panel the defer to the experience of the IOC. As a result, "S" was allowed to compete in the event.

3.8. Enforcing a CAS Arbitration Award

A CAS award governs the parties that were in front of the panel. The parties are expected to comply with the CAS's award. If the parties are uncertain about their rights or obligations stemming from the award, either or both parties can request an interpretation from the panel that rendered the decision within one month of when the award was made.

Applicable municipal legislation and international conventions can execute a CAS award if parties do not voluntarily comply. Also, the Swiss Federal Act on Private International Law says that a panel arbitrator can request assistance from a local judge if a party is not complying with an award voluntarily. Specifically, CAS awards are enforceable in countries that are signatories to the New York Convention on the Recognition and Enforcement of Foreign Arbitral Awards. However, a signatory to the New York Convention can refuse to enforce the award if the country denying enforcement determines that sports-related disputes are ineligible for settlement under that country's laws.

3.9. Remedies: Provisional or Conservatory Measures

Procedural rules allow parties to apply to the CAS for protective measures known as "provisional or conservatory measures" that essentially serve as stays of execution. According to Article R37 of the CAS Code, parties may apply for these protective measures only after filing a request for arbitration or statement of appeal. These documents affirm that the petitioner has exhausted all internal remedies available to it by the applicable federation or sports body. The CAS offers these measures when the parties have exhausted the rules outlined in their respective federation or sports organization. If a complainant requests a protective order, the respondent has ten days to reply with its position. By submitting disputes to the CAS, the petitioner expressly waives his or her rights to request provisional or conservatory relief from other courts. Under the CAS Code, "in cases of utmost urgency," the CAS can issue provisional or conservatory measures upon a "mere presentation of the application, provided that the opponent is heard subsequently."

The CAS may authorize provisional and conservatory measures for three reasons. First, the CAS may issue a protective measure "to facilitate the proceedings, such as orders to safeguard vital evidence." Also, the CAS may order a provisional measure to preserve the *status quo* during the proceedings. Finally, the CAS may authorize conservatory measures in order to protect the decision's future enforceability, such as disputes relating to property.

Given the nature of sporting events and deadlines, the CAS Code allows the CAS to conduct expedited proceedings with the parties' consent. Such expeditious proceedings are particularly pertinent in eligibility disputes where an athlete or team has been denied eligibility to participate in an event that is scheduled to take place soon. The CAS often applies expedited proceedings in cases where a party is appealing a doping suspension. Under urgent circumstances, the CAS may grant a stay of execution of a challenged decision. The CAS can only issue a stay if the complainant requested this relief when they filed the statement of appeal.

Another provisional and conservatory measure the CAS can order is a "stay of execution" on the decision being appealed. As with other protective orders, the party must request this relief at the time of filing the statement of appeal with the CAS. When granting such a stay, the panel considers whether the applicant needs this relief to prevent irreparable harm, "the likelihood of success on the merits of the claim, and whether the interests of the Applicant outweigh those of the Respondent(s)" (CAS Code R37). As with expedited proceedings, a stay of execution is particularly suited for appeals of a doping suspension.

4. Reviews of and Challenges to CAS Awards

As explained below, parties can invoke available procedures to challenge to unfavorable CAS panel awards.

4.1. Internal Review of a CAS Award

A party can request a review of a CAS panel award if the arbitration agreement or clause, which granted the CAS jurisdiction over the dispute, permits such review (Simma, 2006). The CAS will only review a panel's award if a request establishes two prerequisites. First, the party must present a new fact which would have had a decisive influence on the CAS award had the panel been aware of the fact. Second, the applicant was unaware of this fact before the oral proceedings ended. If these two conditions are satisfied, the CAS Executive President can order a new panel to hear the dispute.

4.2. Judicial Review

Because the CAS is headquartered in Lausanne, Switzerland, the Swiss Federal Tribunal has jurisdiction to hear challenges to CAS awards. According to Swiss law, parties to an arbitration have limited grounds to contest an arbitral award. First, the Swiss Federal

Tribunal may terminate an arbitration award if the panel did not have proper authority to hear the case. Thus, an award can be vacated if the CAS "ruled on matters beyond the submitted claims, or failed to rule on a claim" (Mitten and Davis, 2011, 232). Second, a decision may be vacated if the panel violated the principles of good faith and equal treatment. This concern arises when a CAS panel did not treat parties equally or did not respect a party's right to be heard. Third, the Swiss Federal Tribunal can vacate an arbitral award if it contradicts Swiss public policy.

While CAS awards can be challenged in the Swiss Tribunal, success is very rare. One of those exceptions arose in 2007 when the Swiss Tribunal vacated a CAS Ordinary Arbitration Division award. The Tribunal found that the panel had violated the athlete's right to a fair hearing by rejecting substantive arguments without response. In *Cañas v. Association of Tennis Professionals (ATP)*, an Argentinean tennis player, Guillermo Cañas, appealed the CAS's decision concerning his use of a banned substance during the Mexican Open in 2005. The Tribunal found that the CAS panel did not sufficiently consider the player's right to be heard. Further, the Swiss Federal Court concluded that the ATP's standard waiver of the right to file an appeal with the Tribunal was unenforceable. As a result, the Tribunal ordered the CAS to reconsider Cañas's case.

In *Marc Boilley v. Association Turkish FA*, the Swiss Tribunal upheld a panel's award despite the athlete's challenge that the arbitrator was biased (*Marc Boilley v. Association Y. & TAS*). Boilley's case involved an appeal of a CAS Ordinary Arbitration Division award. Boilley alleged that one of the arbitrators on the CAS Panel was associated with the opposing party and the relationship was not disclosed. The Swiss Tribunal required proof that the arbitrator systematically found for the party whose counsel was affiliated with a party or other objective evidence of impartiality. Thus, mere association alone was not enough to prove impartiality.

Finally, a well-publicized case in Germany upheld the arbitration regime described in this chapter. In 2009, the anti-doping governing bodies barred Claudia Pechstein, a German speed skater, from competition for two years after blood tests displayed evidence of illegal substances. Pechstein proclaimed her innocence and claimed the condition was the result of a congenital blood disorder. After Pechstein's appeals to the CAS and the Swiss Federal Tribunal were unsuccessful, she challenged the sanctions, as well as the authority of the CAS to uphold those sanctions in German courts.

In January 2015, Pechstein's efforts made headlines when the Munich Higher Regional Court of Germany ordered the International Skating Union to pay 4.4 million Euros for lost income. The court's sweeping decision held that the CAS decision upholding the ban and the arbitration clause were invalid. The court found that Pechstein did not voluntarily agree to the arbitration clause with the International Skating Union because she had no choice. If she wanted to compete in the World Speed Skating Championship she had to sign the agreement. In addition, the German court found that the procedures to select the CAS arbitration panel violated the governing standards by running afoul of German cartel law. First, the court was concerned that the list of arbitrators available to the parties was compiled by the sport federations and did not include input from athletes. Second, the fact that the chair of the panel was selected by the CAS staff, again without involvement from the athlete, concerned the court. The case was appealed within the German system to the German Federal Court of Justice. In June 2016, the appeals court overturned the lower court ruling and upheld the sanctions against Pechstein. This decision kept intact the Olympic dispute resolution mechanism involving the Court of Arbitration for Sport.

The initial ruling raised significant concerns in the sporting community. Allowing the decision to stand would have undermined the system of arbitration set up in response to legal challenges like these. At the same time, the decision addressed tensions inherent in any arbitration regime. In exchange for decision-making efficiency, athletes forego the possibility of a review on the merits. Many athletes feel that the arbitration regime is unfairly imposed on them and does not offer adequate opportunity for appeals. If an athlete does not sign the arbitration agreement, he or she will not be able to compete. The mandatory nature of these arbitration clauses raises significant due process concerns that remain unaddressed. Despite successes like that experienced by Oscar Pistorius, many athletes feel frustrated by the mandatory nature of the arbitration agreement and the limited grounds for appeal available through the CAS and the Swiss Tribunal.

5. Conclusion

Disputes involving Olympic athletes raise serious concerns for individuals, sporting associations, and the community. Sporting association decisions can have a severe impact on reputations and financial opportunities, as well as the outcomes of athletic competitions. Athletes accused of doping can be barred from competition, cut from marketing contracts, and alienated from their community. Ensuring that disciplinary and eligibility decisions are based on reliable facts presented in a fair hearing is essential to ensure an effective and credible decision-making process. Providing athletes with an effective mechanism to challenge unfavorable decisions has been a goal of the Court of Arbitration for Sport since its inception in 1993. While this arbitration system has limitations that frustrate some athletes, the system offers benefits that are not available through any existing alternatives.

References

Blackshaw, I. (2013). "ADR and Sport: Settling Disputes Through the Court of Arbitration for Sport, the FIFRA Dispute Resolution Chamber, and the WIPO Arbitration & Mediation Center." *Marquette Sports Law Review* 24: 1.

Charlish, P., and Riley, S. (2008). "Should Oscar Run?" *Fordham Intellectual Property, Media & Entertainment Law Journal* 18: 929.

Crincoli, S. (2011). "You Can Only Race If You Can't Win? The Curious Cases of Oscar Pistorius & Caster Semenya." *Texas Review of Entertainment & Sports Law* 12: 133.

Epstein, A. (2002). *Sports Law* (Mason, Ohio: Cengage Learning).

Gandert, D. (2012). "The Battle Before the Games: The British Olympic Association Attempts to Keep Its Lifetime Ban for Athletes with Doping Offenses." *Northwestern Journal of International Law and Business* 32(4): 53A.

Kaufmann-Kohler, G. (1997). "Arbitration and the Games or the First Experience of the Olympic Division of the Court of Arbitration for Sport." *Mealey's International Arbitration Report* 12: 20.

Kaufmann-Kohler, G. (2001). *Arbitration at the Olympics: Issues of Fast-Track Dispute Resolution and Sports Law* (The Hague, Netherlands: Kluwer International). 107.

Kaufmann-Kohler, G., and Bärtsch, P. (2006). "The Ordinary Arbitration Procedure of the Court of Arbitration for Sport." In *The Court of Arbitration for Sport 1984-2004*, edited by I. S. Blackshaw, Janwillem Soek, and Robert C. R. Siekmann (The Hague, Netherlands: Asser Press).

Krahe, C. (2006). "The Appeals Procedure of the Court of Arbitration for Sport." In *The Court of Arbitration for Sport 1984-2004*, edited by I. S. Blackshaw, Janwillem Soek, and Robert C. R. Siekmann (The Hague, Netherlands: Asser Press).

Locklear, J. (2003). "Arbitration in Olympic Disputes: Should Arbitrators Review the Field of Play Decisions of Officials?," *Texas Review of Entertainment & Sports Law* 4: 199.

McArdle, D. (2003). "Reflections on the Harry Reynolds Litigation." *The Entertainment and Sports Law Journal*, 2(2): 6. DOI: http://doi.org/10.16997/eslj.141.

McLaren, R. (2001-2002). "Introducing the Court of Arbitration for Sport: The Ad Hoc Division at the Olympic Games." *Marquette Sports Law Review* 12: 515.

McLaren, R. (2011). "The Court of Arbitration for Sport." In *Handbook on International Sports Law*, edited by J. Nafziger and S. Ross (Cheltenham, UK: Edward Elgar), 32.

Mestre, M. (2009). *The Law of the Olympic Games* 11–12 (Robert C. R. Siekmann & Janwillem Soek, eds.) (The Hague, Netherlands: Asser Press).

Mitten, M., and Davis, T. (2011). "Athlete Eligibility Requirements and Legal Issues." In *Handbook on International Sports Law*, edited by J. Nafziger and S. Ross (Cheltenham, UK: Edward Elgar), 223.

New Zealand Olympic Committee Incorporated, Rio 2016 Athlete Agreement. www.olympic.org.nz/assets/Uploads/Rio-Athlete-Agreement-Printed-v2.pdf.

International Olympic Committee, Olympic Charter, 17, *entered into force* Aug. 2, 2015.

Simma, B. (2006). "The Court of Arbitration for Sport." In *The Court of Arbitration for Sport 1984-2004*, edited by I. S. Blackshaw, Janwillem Soek, and Robert C. R. Siekmann (The Hague, Netherlands: Asser Press), 21, 22.

The Federal Act on Private International Law of 18 December 1987.

Ted Stevens Act, 36 U.S.C.A. § 2205, et al.

World Anti-Doping Agency (2015) World Anti-Doping Code.

Cases

Cañas v. Association of Tennis Professionals (ATP), 4P.172/2006 (1st Civ. Law Ct., March 22, 2007)

Marc Boilley v. Association Y. & TAS, 4A_506/2007 (2008) (Switz.), *translated* 2 Swiss Int'l Arb. L. Rep. 191 (2008).

Pistorius v. IAAF, Arbitration CAS 2008/A/1480, p. 2 (Ct. of Arb. for Sports, May 2008).

US Swimming v. FINA, 96/001 (Ct. of Arb. for Sports, Ad Hoc, O.G. Atlanta).

CHAPTER 23

COMPETITION LAW, FREE MOVEMENT OF PLAYERS, AND NATIONALITY RESTRICTIONS

RYAN GAUTHIER

1. Introduction

Professional sports leagues restrict how and when players are able to move between teams or clubs (from here on, I will use the North American term "teams" to refer to teams and clubs). Although restrictions may be placed on employees from moving between employers in other industries—such as notice provisions, or noncompete clauses—these restrictions are required to be narrowly-tailored. Further, employees generally retain the right to leave their current employer and seek out new employment in their particular field with a high degree of freedom (Ball, 2014: 710; Lembrich, 2002). In professional team sports, players are rarely able to move freely from one team to another team on their own initiative—often only a maximum of two or three times over a twenty-year career (for the few who play that long). Instead, players are more likely to be moved at the whims of teams, or subjected to complex negotiations over the sale of their rights from one team to another.

This chapter outlines the basic restrictions on player movement among teams in the North American and European professional leagues. Certainly, the "North American" and "European" models of sport are not monolithic (Nafziger, 2011: 88). However, enough similarities between the leagues of each system remain so that a comparison is useful. As is often the case with a North American/European comparison, the North American system consists of the "Big Four" North American leagues (National Basketball Association (NBA), National Football League (NFL), National Hockey League (NHL), and Major League Baseball (MLB)), while the "European" system is the one implemented by the Fédération Internationale de Football Association (FIFA), and down through the "pyramid" of regional soccer regulators (namely, the Union of European Football Associations (UEFA)) and national leagues (e.g., the Premier League, Bundesliga). Notably, Major League Soccer (MLS) is a hybrid of both systems in regard to player movement, but it will be discussed more thoroughly in section 4, "Player Movement and Nationality Restrictions."

Section 2 of this chapter outlines the general private and public law regulatory regimes that apply to player movement. Section 3 discusses the general methods of player movement that are used in the North American and European systems. Section 4 outlines restrictions placed on players through nationality restrictions in two North American leagues and in European soccer. Section 5 undertakes an examination of how these restrictions comport with antitrust/competition law, and whether they may be seen as valid under these laws. Section 6 offers some concluding thoughts as to the way forward.

2. General Regulation of the Player Market—Private and Public Law

This section outlines the regulatory approaches taken by sporting organizations through their private legal regimes. I highlight the differences between the negotiated regime that exists within the North American "Big 4" leagues, and soccer's top-down approach. This section also discusses the public law regimes that act as a backdrop to these private legal regimes, revealing their similarities and key differences.

2.1. Private Law Regulations

The North American players' market is currently constructed through negotiations between the leagues and the players' unions. It has not always been this way. In the late nineteenth and early twentieth century, leagues imposed restrictions on player movement in a top-down fashion. An example of this is the imposition of the "reserve clause," first formally imposed by baseball's National League in 1879. The reserve clause allowed teams to "reserve" the rights to players after their contracts expired, preventing players from signing contracts with other teams (Kahn, 2000: 76). There was debate over whether these clauses were perpetual, or were limited in duration (*Philadelphia World Hockey Club, Inc. v. Philadelphia Hockey Club*; *Robertson v. NBA*). Ultimately, it was a 1975 baseball arbitration decision by Peter Seitz in regard to Andy Messersmith and Dave McNally that decreed that the reserve clause only created a one-year option on players (unsuccessfully appealed by MLB in *Kansas City Royals Baseball Corp. v. Major League Baseball Players Association*. This decision, which clarified that renewal rights in player contracts are not perpetual, essentially spelled the end of the reserve clause

(Irwin, 1991: 296–297). In the background of these attacks on the reserve clauses, players' associations began their rise. Forming in the mid-1950s, their first collective bargaining agreements were completed in the 1960s and 1970s (Kahn, 2009: 862).

Today, restrictions on player movement in North America are partially negotiated, and partially set out unilaterally by the leagues. Generally, negotiated restrictions are those that involve players who are out-of-contract (e.g., free agents). Restrictions on in-contract players are often set forth in league bylaws, which are unilaterally established by leagues, and are incorporated by reference into the collective bargaining agreement (CBA) or the standard players' contract (which itself is incorporated into the CBA). These latter two documents often prevail over the league bylaws in the event of conflict (NHL and NHLPA, 2013, art. 30.1; NFL and NFLPA, 2011, art. 2, s. 1), demonstrating an emphasis on negotiation over imposition.

In contrast to North America, the European players' market remains regulated in a top-down manner. Using the example of soccer, FIFA, the global governing body for soccer (and a not-for-profit association based in Switzerland (FIFA, 2015, art. 1.1)), has enacted the *Regulations on the Status and Transfer of Players* (Transfer Regulations). The Transfer Regulations set forth general principles that are then implemented by the national football associations (FAs) and the relevant national leagues. The Transfer Regulations apply to transfers between teams in different national associations, while national associations establish their own rules for intra-association transfers (arts. 1.1, 1.2). These rules were enacted in their modern form after the landmark decision of *Union Royale Belge des Sociétés de Football Association ASBL v. Jean-Marc Bosman*, known simply as the *Bosman* case, which removed restrictions on out-of-contract players. The Transfer Regulations were established following consultation between FIFA, UEFA, and the European Union Commissioners in charge of competition, sport, and social affairs. Notably, it appears that the players' association, the Fédération Internationale des Associations de Footballeurs Professionnels (FIFPro) was part of the original consultations but was marginalized in the final stages (García and Meier, 2012).

2.2. Public Law Regulatory Background

The most significant public law consideration for sports law as a whole is antitrust/competition law. Sports leagues often operate as monopolies within a particular state, while a sports regulatory body such as FIFA oversees a global monopoly on the regulation of that sport more broadly. As the leagues and governing bodies use their monopolistic power to restrict the free operation of the labor market, questions of abuse of monopoly position, prohibited in both North America and Europe, arise. In North America, these questions are considered under the American Sherman Antitrust Act (15 U.S.C. §§1-7), or, to a lesser extent, under Canada's Competition Act (R.S.C., 1985, c. C-34). In the European Union, the articles 101 and 102 (2008 O.J. C 115/47) of the Treaty on the Functioning of the European Union (TFEU) are the touchstones when applying competition law to sport, although the competition laws in the individual EU (European Union) member states may also play a role.

Labor law, as alluded to previously, plays a larger role in the North American system than in the European system. The North American leagues are subject to the rules of the National Labor Relations Act (29 U.S.C. §§151-169) (Aubut, 2003: 191). A complication in the matter is that the Canadian teams are subject to Canadian provincial labor laws. However, when it comes to collective bargaining between the owners of the teams/league with the players associations, Canadian provincial labor boards have been loath to exercise their jurisdiction, preferring to leave issues of collective bargaining to the parties and to perhaps the American National Labor Relations Board (*National Hockey League Players' Association v. Edmonton Oilers Hockey Corp.*; *Orca Bay Hockey Limited Partnership and the NHL v. B.C. Chapter of the NHLPA*). In the European context, collective bargaining is less common at both the national level, and Europe-wide (Frodl, 2016: 5). Instead of collective bargaining, negotiations have taken place between the European Professional Football Leagues, and the European Club Association on the league/team side, and FIFPro on the players' side. These negotiations have been conducted under a process known as "social dialogue," where industry and workers take part in a dialogue at the European level, and may be supported by the bodies of the EU itself (TFEU arts. 153-155). These negotiations encourage the parties to work together on policies, and may lead to informal or formal agreements (Pierre and Buisine, 2013: 581; McArdle, 2015: 164–179). However, it is unlikely that social dialogue will lead to a CBA similar to the one seen in North American sports (Parrish, 2016). As of November 2016, the only agreement reached under the social dialogue has been one that sets out the minimum requirements for contracts between teams and players (i.e., what elements of the employment relationship must be addressed by the contract) (UEFA, EPFL, ECA, and FIFPro, 2012). As of this writing, it appears that the transfer system is not part of the social dialogue process, and that its inclusion is likely to be a long-term prospect.

In the EU, restrictions on player movement have also been shaped by other articles of the TFEU—free movement of workers and the specificity of sport. First, TFEU Article 45 guarantees freedom of movement for workers within the EU. Regulations that restrict this movement between member states are subjected to an extra element of scrutiny that North American leagues do not face. Second, TFEU Article 165 states: "The Union shall contribute to the promotion of European sporting issues, while taking account of the specific nature of sports, its structures based on voluntary activity and its social and educational function." Sport organizations (leagues and international federations in particular) in Europe have regularly argued that the "specificity of sport" requires the imposition of restrictions that would otherwise violate EU law, although its value as an actual legal principle is not yet settled.

3. General Methods of Player Movement

In principle, when a player signs a contract with a team, both sides initially expect that the player will play out the entire term of the contract with that team. However, teams and players may wish to make a change for various reasons. For instance, teams may wish to move a player to improve the competitiveness of the team. Alternatively, a team may be guided by financial/salary cap reasons, or for reasons particular to the player (e.g., behavior or role on the team). For his or her part, a player may wish to move to another team for similar reasons—to have a better chance of winning a championship, to play a different role on the other team, or for personal reasons (e.g., to be closer to family). Movement of players while they are "in-contract" is governed by a series of private law regulations that largely leave players at the whims of the teams. Once the contract has expired, regulations on player movement loosen significantly, often providing players a choice as to what team they could play on next.

3.1. In-Contract Player Movement

In the North American system, players are moved among teams within a league via "trades." Technically, a "trade" is the assignment of a player's contract to another team, which players are bound to honor. For example, the NHL's Standard Players' Contract, which is part of the CBA, reads:

> It is mutually agreed that the Club shall have the right to Assign or to Loan this SPC, and the Player agrees to accept and be bound by such Assignment or Loan, and will faithfully perform and carry out this SPC with the same purpose and effect as if it had been entered into by the Player and such other club.
>
> (art. 11).

The NBA has substantially similar language (NBA and NBPA, 2011, Uniform Player Contract, art. 11), while MLB and the NFL have similar rules (MLB and MLBPA, 2011, Uniform Player Contract, art. 6; NFL and NFLPA, 2011, NFL Player Contract, art. 17). In more practical terms, a trade involves a player being sent from his current team to a new team in exchange for some form of consideration. The most common forms of consideration from the new team are: a player on the roster, a player in the minor leagues that the new team holds the rights to (a "prospect"), or the rights to a team's future draft pick. In the NBA and MLB, cash can be exchanged for a player (NBA and NBPA, 2011, art. VII, s. 8(a); MLB and MLBPA, 2011, art. XXIII, C(2)(b)(iii)), although this practice is uncommon.

The establishment of salary caps in the NFL, NBA, and NHL require teams to consider not only sporting factors when engaging in trades but also financial factors. In particular, the salary numbers that matter for the salary cap are often required to "balance" (e.g., if a team trades a player whose salary cap figure is $3 million for that season, the team is likely seeking to receive consideration (player, prospect, or pick) whose salary cap figure is as much or less than $3 million). In the NHL, for example, teams are now allowed to retain up to 50% of the departing player's salary, both in actual dollars and "salary cap dollars," allowing teams with more salary cap room greater leverage in making trades (NHL and NHLPA, 2013, art. 50.5(e)(iii)(A)).

In regard to player input on his destination, the default rule is that players have no say in their destination. For example, NHL player Sam Gagner was traded twice in one day, June 30, 2014, first from Edmonton to Tampa Bay, and then ninety minutes later from Tampa Bay to Phoenix (Whyno, 2014). However, in some leagues, player contracts may allow players to negotiate restrictions on who they may be moved to, if they can be moved at all. These are known as "no-trade" (player cannot be traded to another team, without his consent), "no-movement" (player cannot be traded to another team, or "sent down" to the minor leagues), or "limited trade" (player can provide a list of x number of teams he would consent to being traded to) clauses. The NHL has these clauses (NHL and NHLPA, 2013, art. 11.8(a)), as does the NFL (whose CBA refers to the clauses but does not explicitly set them out). The MLB Basic Agreement sets out that players with more than ten years of services, the last five of which have been with the same club, may withhold their consent to trades (MLB and MLBPA, 2011, art. XIX A(1)). Only the NBA specifically bars no-trade clauses (NBA and NBPA, 2011, art. XXIV s. 1). Players can also request trades to another team, but it is ultimately up to their current team to accommodate the request. Trade demands often see a player seeking to be traded to a "contender" after years on a low-performing team, for personal reasons (*see* Compton, 2015), or for financial reasons (e.g., players requesting trades to New York or Los Angeles in part for increased media exposure and financial opportunities outside the sport (Ziller, 2015)).

If a player does not have control over where he is traded due to one of the clauses mentioned previously, and disagreed with the trade, he can refuse to report to a team. However, this would lead to fines and other discipline (e.g., NHL and NHLPA, 2013, art. 11). As such, players tend to report, even if they are disappointed in a trade. For instance, Jeff Carter was traded from the Philadelphia Flyers, a team he had just signed an eleven-year deal with the year before, to the struggling Columbus Blue Jackets. Carter was publicly unhappy with the trade, and after only playing thirty-nine games with Columbus, was traded again, this time to Los Angeles (NHL.com, 2012; Wyshynski, 2012).

The league's commissioner's office is required to approve trades. Generally, trades are approved as a matter of course. However, some trades have been nullified by the commissioner, such as the trade that was the subject of *Finley v. Kuhn*. Finley, the owner of the Oakland Athletics, saw that the new free agency regime would greatly raise the salary of his players, and instead of having to pay the higher salary or lose the players to free agency, he "traded" three players to the Boston Red Sox and New York Yankees for cash. The Commissioner vetoed the trade in "the best interests of baseball," a move that was later upheld by the courts. Over thirty years later, the NBA Commissioner refused to approve a trade of Chris Paul from the New Orleans Hornets to the Los Angeles Lakers in 2011. However, complicating the situation was that the NBA was the owner of the Hornets at the time. The NBA officially nixed the trade due to "basketball reasons," but was apparently under pressure from other owners to cancel the trade as it would be too unfair to the Los Angeles Lakers. Paul was traded to the Los Angeles Clippers soon thereafter (Wyman, 2013: 171–172).

Trades are allowed to take place year-round, with one significant exception. Trades cannot take place following the "trade deadline." Leagues set a deadline for trades that begins a few months before the commencement of the playoffs. The practice of trades following the trade deadline differs by league. The NBA prohibits any trades whatsoever until the end of the regular season (NBA, 2001); the MLB requires teams to place the player on waivers first, allowing any team to claim the player for free for one month, and following that deadline, players who are traded are not eligible for the playoffs (MLB, 2007); while the NHL allows trades but stipulates that the player cannot be on that team's roster for the playoffs (NHL, n.d., Bylaws, s. 28.1).

Under the European system, in-contract player movement is accomplished through a "transfer." A transfer refers to the transfer of a player's registration from one club to another. A player (amateur or professional) must be registered with the relevant national association to play for a particular club (FIFA, 2016, art. 5.1; The Football Association Premier League, 2016, Rules U.1, U.25). When a player changes teams, he must also register with the new team. However, while the player is under contract with a club, a player cannot change his registration to another club unless his current club provides its consent to terminate the current registration. To terminate/transfer the registration, the current club will often request a payment from the future club. This payment is known as the "transfer fee."

Less commonly, players may be "loaned" from one club to another (FIFA, 2016, art. 10). A "loan" is a temporary assignment of the player to another club, although the original club maintains the player's registration. Teams may loan players, instead of transferring them, for a variety of reasons. A strong club may loan a young player to a weaker club, where the younger player is able to obtain more playing time and develop his skills (similar to the North American "farm team" concept—although some countries, such as Spain and the Netherlands, have the concept of "B" teams, which are somewhat equivalent to "farm teams"), while the weaker club benefits from having a highly skilled young player on its roster that it may not be able to afford otherwise. Teams may also have a surplus of players at a particular position, and could not find a suitable transfer partner for the player, making a loan a preferable alternative.

Players appear to have at least some say in transfers. When a transfer is made, the playing contract of the player is usually mutually terminated by the player and the selling team. The player then signs a new playing contract with the buying team. Therefore, a player could refuse to sign a new playing contract with the buying team, scuttling the transfer. However, the buying team has generally done its due diligence by reaching out to the player to gauge his interest in playing for the buying team, so as not to take any risks. In addition, a player who scuttles a transfer may find himself out of favor with the selling team, seeing reduced playing time, and so forth. An example of a player refusing a transfer is Kaka. Manchester City offered AC Milan more than £100 million, more than double the world-record transfer fee at the time, for Kaka. However, he refused to consent to the transfer, and the transfer simply failed (BBC, 2009). Players may also request transfers, although there may be some risk in doing so. Many players have a "loyalty bonus" worth about 20% of their contract, and a transfer request would cause the player to forfeit this bonus.

A tool available to the players in the European system that is unavailable to those in the North American system is the possibility of breaching their own contracts to render themselves "free agents." Penalties for such breach of contracts may be negotiated between the players and the teams. However, if the contract does not explicitly allow for breach, players may breach their contracts under the FIFA Transfer Regulations Article 17, pay damages, and begin play with a new club (although a player may be suspended for four to six months for breaching his contract within two to three seasons or years of signing the contract (FIFA, 2016, art. 17.3). As of this time, however, breaches under the FIFA Transfer Regulations are risky adventures for the players, as the kind and quantum of damages awarded, at least at the Court of Arbitration for Sport, have been inconsistent (*Wigan Athletic & Andrew Webster v. Heart of Midlothian*; *FC Shakhtar Donetsk v. Matuzalem & Real Zaragoza*; *Sevilla & Morgan de Sanctis v. Udinese Calicio*; Czarnota, 2013).

Transfers are approved by the national football associations. These football associations appear to rarely deny transfers. However, they will impose "transfer bans" on teams as a punishment for violating transfer rules (FIFA, 2016, art. 9.4). For example, Barcelona was issued a fourteen-month transfer ban for violating rules that regulate the transfer of players who are under the age of eighteen (*Fútbol Club Barcelona v. Fédération Internationale de Football Association (FIFA)*).

Football transfers take place twice per season, during "transfer windows." These windows are mandated by FIFA, although the particular dates are left to the national associations. These windows are generally divided into a "pre-season" transfer window that lasts up to twelve weeks, while the second window is a "mid-season" transfer window that lasts up to four weeks. Other sports, notably basketball, use a "transfer deadline," similar to the North American system. This system was examined and upheld by the European Court of Justice in *Lehtonen v. Fédération royale belge des sociétés de basket-ball ASBL*.

3.2. Out-of-Contract Player Movement

North American players whose contract with a team has ended become "free agents." Not all "free agents" are alike. Players with only a few years' experience whose contracts have expired are "restricted free agents" (RFAs), and exist in the NBA, NFL, and NHL. RFAs are free to sign with other teams, but the team that holds the rights of the RFA has the right to match the offer made by the other team, to retain the rights to the RFA. In the event that RFAs are signed by another team, the original team has the right to compensation, generally, in the form of draft picks, from the signing team (NHL and NHLPA, 2013, art. 10.4; NFL and NFLPA, 2011, art. 9, s. 2). Some categories of RFAs in the NHL and MLB may have the right to have their salary determined by an arbitrator, if they are unable to reach agreement with their team (NHL and NHLPA, 2013, art. 12.3; MLB and MLBPA, 2011, art. VI(E); Aubut, 2003; Buckstein, 2011).

After several years of service, players who reach the end of their contract become "unrestricted free agents" (UFAs). These players are able to negotiate with, and sign with, any team in the league. To stem the tide of free agents leaving their initial teams, leagues have negotiated mechanisms that enable the team that most recently employed the UFA to offer more money and longer-term contracts than other teams are able—such as the "Larry Bird Rule" (NBA and NBPA, 2011, art. VII, s. 6). This gives the initial team more leverage in negotiations with their UFAs on this front.

In the European system, out-of-contract players are also able to exercise free agency, moving between teams on what is known as a "free transfer." Prior to 1995, players whose contracts had expired were still registered with their teams, meaning that teams were still able to demand transfer fees for players, and prevent them from playing elsewhere, reminiscent of the "reserve clause" in North America. This system was struck down in the *Bosman* case, allowing players to complete a "free transfer" once their contract has expired, without the future club paying a transfer fee to the current club.

4. Player Movement and Nationality Restrictions

In addition to restricting the movement of players by contract, some leagues have attempted to restrict the movement of players by nationality. These rules are often implemented as a counter to the internationalization of sport. In a perfectly liberalized market, top teams will seek to have the best players on their team, regardless of nationality, and will draft, trade, or transfer as needed to achieve this goal. However, some sport regulators argue that this approach is detrimental to the development of local (i.e., national) players. As top teams seek to obtain the best players, they will ignore the development of local players—which may be longer-term and higher-risk than obtaining a "known commodity" from another team (Chaplin, 2005; Downward et al., 2014; 494;). Some regulators also argue that a lack of local players may alienate local fans (Chaplin, 2005).

The "Big 4" North American leagues do not have nationality rules. This may be due to North American leagues viewing their oversight of the sport from the perspective of a business, where nationality takes a back seat to on-field (and financial) performance. Additionally, development of local players is often left to either high school/colleges or junior leagues, rather than to the teams themselves. This is in contrast to the European system, where national federations have more influence, and teams are responsible for development of players from the youth teams to the top-flight professional teams. As such, national federations attempt to influence the teams to develop their national players.

This does not mean that no league in North America has nationality restrictions. Both the Canadian Football League (CFL) and MLS have such restrictions. The CFL, based in Canada, divides players into "national" and "international" players (CFL, 2016). The CFL considers players to be "Nationals" if they are (a) Canadian citizens at the signing of the player's first contract, or (b) a player who is resident in Canada for five years prior to turning eighteen. Of the forty-four-man CFL team roster, there must be a minimum of twenty-one "nationals." Of the twenty-four "starters," seven must be nationals. Quarterbacks are not designated as "nationals" or "internationals."

Nationality restrictions are slightly more complex in the MLS, given its Canadian and American team base. MLS divides players into "domestic" and "international" (MLS, 2016). The terms are defined differently for American and Canadian teams. For American teams "domestic" players are those who are U.S. citizens, permanent residents, or holder of a special status (e.g., refugee or asylum seeker). "Domestic" players for Canadian teams are those who are Canadian citizens, who are seeking refugee or asylum status in Canada, or are considered American "domestic" players (although a Canadian permanent resident is not listed on the publicly available document, it is likely that he would also be considered in this category). In numerical terms, MLS teams have rosters of eighteen to twenty players. MLS established 160 "international" spots, which are then divided across the twenty teams. While teams initially began play with eight international spots, these spots can be traded among the teams in a manner similar to players—meaning that some teams will have more or less than the initial eight. The remaining spots on the club must be filled by "domestic" players. In addition, Canadian teams are required to have a minimum of three Canadian domestic players on their rosters at all times. MLS also provides incentives for teams to develop talent through their youth academies by making them unavailable to be drafted by other teams.

MLS has likely taken its cue from international soccer, where both FIFA and UEFA have proposed or implemented nationality restrictions. Some leagues implemented severe nationality restrictions in the past, such as Italian restrictions limiting participation in professional or semi-professional competitions only to Italian nationals, a practice that was deemed incompatible with EU law in *Donà v. Mario Mantero*. Prior to the *Bosman* ruling, UEFA maintained the "3+2 Rule," which allowed teams to field three players who were not nationals, in addition to two players who were "assimilated" (having played for five years in the country, including three years for junior teams) (García, 2007: 207). This rule was struck down in the *Bosman* case. Following *Bosman*, in 2008 FIFA proposed a rule known as the "6+5" rule. At the beginning of the match, the club would be required to field at least six players who would be eligible to play for the national team of the country that the club was located in (however, this limit did not apply to either the overall roster, or to substitutions made during the match) (Freeburn, 2009: 182–183). This rule was met with strong opposition by the European Parliament, and was likely to be found contrary to EU competition law by the European Commission (Freeburn, 2009: 184–187). The rule was quietly shelved by FIFA in 2010.

More relevant is UEFA's current "Home-Grown Player Rule" (UEFA 2016a, ss. 43.02-43.06; UEFA 2016b, ss. 43.02-43.06—both of which use the term "locally trained players"). UEFA's rule applies only to teams playing in European club competitions (i.e., the Champions League and Europe League). The rule requires that the club name eight "home-grown players" as part of their twenty-five-man roster. Four of these players must be "club-trained"; that is, they must have been registered with that club for three years between the ages of fifteen and twenty-one. The other four players must be "association-trained," meaning that they have been registered with a club within the club's national association for three years between the ages of fifteen and twenty-one. If the club does not have the minimum eight players, then the squad size is reduced by one sport for every home-grown player that the club is short.

The restrictions in the North American leagues have not been challenged. MLS has taken the position that its system is legal under American law, as long as Canadians are not treated as "domestic" (Devos, 2013). The European systems have faced a more difficult road, as they are subject to EU law—namely, Article 45 TFEU, which establishes the free movement of workers throughout the EU. The courts have established a test in examining restrictions on freedom of movement and their legality under the TFEU. The restriction must be (1) applied in a nondiscriminatory manner; (2) justified by imperative requirements in the general interest; (3) suitable to attain the objectives; and (4) proportional to the objective (*Gebhard v. Consiglio dell'Ordine degli Avvocati e Procuatori di Milano*). In regard to step (1), scholars appear to agree that the rules do not engage in direct discrimination but do engage in "indirect discrimination" (Freeburn, 2009: 209). A non-national can be classified as a "home-grown player" if he were trained by the club or within the national association at issue. However, this status is likely to be difficult for a non-national to achieve, for practical reasons. For step (2), UEFA could attempt to justify the rule by arguing that the rule preserves competitive balance, and encourages the training of young players (these rationales are discussed more later). For step (3), some commentators suggest that a court would defer to the expertise of UEFA in regard to attaining these sporting objectives, similar to the approaches of the court in *Deliège v. Ligues fancophone de judo* and *Meca-Medina and Majcen v. Commission* (Downward et al., 2014). The trouble for UEFA defending the Home-Grown Player Rule would appear to arise in the final step, proportionality. A review conducted in 2014 found that the gains in regard to competitive balance were "very limited," and that there was little evidence to suggest that improvements in youth soccer had been made (Downward et al., 2014: 507, 510). The study suggested that alternative measures could potentially achieve similar effects on competitive balance and youth training, suggesting that other measures might be just as successful. The study also intimated that alternatives such as club licensing that required teams to have high-quality youth development programs, cost-control mechanisms (similar to "Financial Fair Play"—which may itself be challenged under EU competition law (Peeters and Szymanski, 2014)), financial incentives to develop young players, revenue sharing, and so forth, might achieve the same aims, without restricting freedom of movement (Downward et al., 2014: 509).

5. Player Movement and Relationship with Competition/Antitrust Law

It is uncontroversial to state that sports leagues have market power in regard to the labor market (Kahn, 2000: 76; Ross, 2004: 51–52). At the national level, sports leagues do not have rivals with which to compete for players, and attempts to set up rival leagues are met with significant practical barriers (Che and Humphreys, 2015: 127; Pijetlovic, 2015: 53–73;). In regard to North American professional leagues, some alternative leagues exist at the international level for hockey (Kontinental Hockey League), basketball (Chinese Basketball Association), and baseball (Nippon Professional Baseball Organization), but these are usually seen as second-class alternatives. Soccer is somewhat different in that there are multiple credible national leagues to compete in, although the regulatory body itself is pan-European or global. Thus, antitrust/competition laws are central in both the North American and European sports models.

5.1 Competition Law in USA and EU

Both American and European competition law prohibits abusive conduct by entities that have market power (Fox, 1997: 340). While there are differences in specifics, the overall goals are the same. A significant point of difference is the enforcement of competition law. Antitrust law in the United States is enforced through a collection of government agencies, but also through cases brought to the courts. In contrast, European enforcement of competition law is more "regulatory and bureaucratic," with the European Commission taking a leading role (Fox, 1997: 341).

Without getting into the particular tests of each regime, it has been noted that in short, following a finding of an abuse of a dominant position (to use the European parlance), "courts tend to uphold restraints when reasonably tailored to achieve a legitimate goal, but find them illegal when no legitimate justification is accepted or where the challenged restraint is found to be overly restrictive" (Ross, 2011: 312). Sports leagues in North America and Europe exercise market power in regard to labor. Restrictions on player movement have the potential to depress the wages of players, and otherwise distort the efficiency of the labor market (Ross, 2004: 51). As such, examinations of restrictions on player movement generally turn to the justifications advanced by the leagues/regulators and their proportionality.

5.2. Justifications for Restrictions on Player Movement

Restrictions on player movement are generally justified using three rationales: (1) contractual stability, (2) competitive balance, and (3) incentivizing training and development. The latter two have been accepted by courts in North America and Europe as *prima facie* justifications.

Contractual stability has been cited by FIFA as the primary reason for maintaining the current transfer system. For instance the Transfer Regulations require national associations to "include in its regulations appropriate means to protect contractual stability" (art. 1.3(b)). FIFA states that contractual stability is of "paramount importance in football," requiring "a regulatory system which responds to the specific needs of football and which strikes the right balance between the respective interests of players and teams and preserves the regularity and proper functioning of sporting competition" (FIFA, 2001). The justification of contractual stability has not been used to a significant degree by the North American leagues.

Competitive balance is the second oft-used justification for restrictions on player movement. The term itself is broad, but it is often reduced to the idea of uncertainty of outcome for a particular game or season (McKeown, 2011: 521–526 (citing Fort, 2005); Rottenberg, 1956: 246). The premise is that unless outcomes are uncertain, fan interest in the sport will dwindle. Competitive balance can be undermined by a small group of teams obtaining the majority of top players, a concern raised in the case of *Finley v. Kuhn*, where the cash-strapped Oakland owner attempted to sell his players to the teams in New York and Boston. At the extreme end, wealthy teams could "hoard" the best players, paying them high salaries to simply be on the team (not necessarily to play) in a bid to keep these players away from other teams (Downward et al., 2014: 494). The European Court of Justice recognized the need to maintain "a balance between teams by preserving a degree of equality of and uncertainty as to results" as a legitimate objective for sport regulators in *Bosman* (para. 106), and seemingly in *Lehtonen* (para. 53). Similarly, organizers of athletic competitions in the United States have raised this argument (*O'Bannon v. NCAA*; *Philadelphia World Hockey Club*). While the U.S. Supreme Court has recognized "the interest in maintaining a competitive balance" among teams in athletic competitions, it has not addressed or endorsed this justification as thoroughly as its European counterparts (*NCAA v. Board of Regents* (cited in *American Needle Inc. v. National Football League*).

Incentivizing training and development is a third common justification for various player restrictions. The basic argument behind this justification is that investments in the training of players are uncertain, and the results may not appear for years. If teams could simply obtain already-developed talent from other teams, then the incentives to train players would be reduced. Namely, the wealthiest teams would rather obtain the top players, while the less-wealthy teams would not have an incentive to train players, as they would lose them to the wealthier teams. A system, such as the transfer system, compensates a club for the training of a player, thereby increasing the incentives for less-wealthy teams, while also increasing the costs for wealthier teams. Additionally, the benefits for a team in engaging in the training would be more certain, and on a shorter timeline (*Olympique Lyonnais v. Bernard*, para. 42). This argument has been accepted by the courts in Europe (*Bernard*, paras. 41-50; *Bosman*, para. 106), and has been made by leagues United States courts (*Flood*, 316 F. Supp. at 275).

5.3. Analyzing the Justifications and Proportionality of Restrictions on Player Movement

If player restrictions are justified, they must also be proportional to achieving their aims—that is, they are both necessary and not overly burdensome. This is known as the "rule of reason" test in the United States (*Chicago Board of Trade v. United States*), and the "proportionality" test in the European Union (*Wouters v. Algemene Raad van de Nederlandse Orde van Advocaten*, para. 97). This test is often conducted by examining the existence of less-restrictive alternatives.

The first justification, stability of contract, is not per se achieved by a transfer system, or restrictions on free agency. It is possible to characterize the justification as "basically nothing else than to reinforce contractual stability, i.e. to strengthen the principle of *pacta sunt servanda* in the world of international football, by acting as deterrent against unilateral contractual breaches and terminations" (*Matuzalem*, para. 80). Perhaps then, contractual stability can be ensured by other, less restrictive alternatives, such as liquidated damages, or other sorts of damages as contemplated in the FIFA Transfer Regulations. Proponents of restrictions on player movement may argue that the services that players provide cannot be offset by damages. This was the argument raised in the century-old case involving baseball player Hal Chase (*American League Baseball Club v. Chase* ()). Chase was under contract to the Chicago White Sox of the American League but had signed a contract to play for the Buffalo Blues of the Federal League. In considering whether to enjoin Chase from playing for Buffalo, the court famously found that Chase was "reputed to possess special, unique and extraordinary characteristics as a baseball player" (*Chase*, 86 Misc. at 444), which militated in favor of an injunction. Ultimately, the court ultimately refused to grant the injunction, as the contract between Chase and his former employer lacked mutuality of obligation and remedy (*Chase*, 86 Misc. at 455-457).

Second, restrictions on player movement have not been shown conclusively to address the competitive balance concerns of the leagues. The Court in *Bosman* was critical of claims that the transfer system enabled competitive balance, as the wealthier teams were still able to acquire top players more easily than less wealthy teams (para. 107). It is also difficult to separate one element of competitive balance (e.g., player restrictions) from the myriad other mechanisms imposed in the name of competitive balance, such as the entry draft, salary caps, or financial fair play. Additionally, leagues have chosen not to exhaust every avenue of competitive balance. For instance, leagues have not imposed restrictions on salaries for coaching or management staff, which may have competitive balance implications. Less restrictive alternatives to achieving competitive balance could include elements such as a salary cap or a mechanism such as financial fair play—although these may be themselves attacked as anticompetitive. Revenue sharing would also be a less restrictive alternative that could achieve the goal of maintaining competitive balance, and may not be seen by a court as anticompetitive as it is redistributive rather than restrictive. Additionally, scholars have questioned whether competitive balance is a vital element in maintaining fan interest in a sport at all (Scelles et al., 2013; Pawlowski and Budzinski, 2013).

Third, in regard to youth development, little evidence has appeared to suggest that player restrictions promote youth development. In the context of North American leagues, professional teams often do not develop players. Rather, this task is carried out by development leagues (amateur or professional), or by colleges. Additionally, it has recently been suggested by Kevin Clark that, as an effect of the NFL's recent caps on the salaries of young players, NFL teams are using more young players. However, the teams are unable to develop them properly, creating a decline in the quality of play (Clark. 2016), although fans admittedly may not be too worried this turn of events (Clark, 2015). In Europe, it has been reported that the current transfer system does not promote youth development (KEA—CDES, 2013: 256). Even if youth development is promoted, which is debatable, the question remains as to whether less restrictive alternatives exist. For soccer, an alternative does exist. UEFA requires that teams entering into UEFA competitions have an approved youth development program that has appropriate financial and training resources, amongt other elements, including youth teams (UEFA, 2015: arts. 17, 18). Such a scheme may be scrutinized under the TFEU but may be justified as inherent to the organization of football (Parrish and Miettinen, 2007).

5.4. Imposed vs. Negotiated Systems

Ultimately, for the North American leagues, the aforementioned antitrust concerns are somewhat moot. This is because the player restrictions in North America are collectively bargained, which is not the case for the European system. This distinction is important, as restrictions that are collectively bargained for are protected from antitrust/competition law scrutiny. In the United States, this is largely governed by the "nonstatutory" labor exemption to antitrust law (Schwochau, 2000). In Canada, the Canadian Competition Act (R.S.C., 1985, C-34) excludes labor agreements (s. 4(1)(a), 4(1)(c)), and a number of professional sporting activities (s. 48(3)). The European Union also protects collectively bargained agreements from competition law scrutiny (*Albany International BV v. Stichting Bedrijfspensionenfonds Textielindustrie*). The basic rationale behind such protections is that collective agreements are inherently collusive. Along those lines, to subject such collectively bargained restrictions to antitrust/competition law scrutiny would undermine collective agreements, which is against the interests of fostering stable labor relations in which employees have a voice (*United States v. Hutcheson*). Given that the professional leagues in the United States/Canada have CBAs, they have protected various practices from antitrust scrutiny, such as the entry draft (*Clarett v. NFL*).

The European system, on the other hand, is one that is largely imposed by the governing bodies onto players. While there may be CBAs at the domestic level, this is not the case at the European-level, given the differences between the needs of the twenty-eight EU member states (and non-EU member states) (McArdle, 2015: 164–165). As such, European-wide rules, such as the transfer rules, are subject to competition law scrutiny. Although the European Commission worked with the leagues to establish the transfer rules following the *Bosman* case, these rules were "not the result of negotiations between management and labour . . . nor do they have the effect of improving players' working conditions, which is what matters according to the case law" (Egger and Stix-Hackl, 2002: 83; Weatherill, 2003: 69). In addition, the EU has not addressed the interests of players more generally (McArdle, 2015: 113–114). Concerns about the effectiveness of social dialogue remain, although it may be the best option available outside legal challenges by the players (McArdle 2015: 169–171; Pearson, 2015: 238).

Nevertheless, systems that have been imposed by leagues or regulators have been found to run afoul of competition law, both in America (*Mackey v. NFL*), and in Europe (*Bosman*). As such, leagues and regulators have an incentive to negotiate player restrictions with those who are affected the most—players. One scholar has even suggested that MLB might have prevented the demise of the reserve clause, had it simply negotiated it into the CBA (Edmonds, 2010: 567). Reminiscent of the demise of the reserve clause, in 2015, FIFPro filed a complaint with the European Commission in regard to the transfer system, calling for its dismantling (FIFPro, 2015). If the regulators of soccer do not do something to obtain the consent of the players to the transfer system—whether through social dialogue or some other means—it is possible that the transfer system may meet a similar demise.

6. Conclusion: Toward a Collectively Bargained Transfer System?

The North American and European systems have evolved since the 1970s into their current form. The North American system is likely to be relatively stable. Although issues such as when players may become free agents are likely to surface with each round of collective bargaining, there is no wholesale attack on the system. The European system, in contrast, is under a much more full-frontal attack from FIFPro and is under scrutiny by the European Commission and the courts. The question then, is whether, and how, the systems continue to evolve.

I suggest that it is likely some convergence between the two systems will occur. Already, North American leagues are seeing some elements that resemble the European transfer system. These elements can be seen in the transfer agreements that the NHL has with the Kontinental Hockey League and that MLB has with the Japanese and Korean baseball leagues. Additionally, the "stability of contracts" is the subject of collective bargaining in North America, as there is discussion about the elimination of "guaranteed" contracts in the NHL, NBA, and MLB, while the NHL already allows teams to "buy out" contracts (NHL and NHLPA, 2013, art. 50.9(i)). Might a system where players are allowed to "breach" their contracts through the payment of liquidated damages, similar to the system permitted under the FIFA Transfer Regulations, be the flip-side of that coin? Europe, meanwhile, appears set to move to a system that relies on consultation with the players. If FIFPro is successful in having the transfer system ruled incompatible with the TFEU, what system might take its place? Perhaps MLS and its hybrid of the European and North American system might take its place?

The way forward for regulators, leagues, and players is uncertain. Although some authors have called for government regulation of sport in a broad sense as of late (Grow,

2015; Koller, 2016), it is unlikely that this will occur, as the harm to the public interest is not sufficiently clear (Edelman, 2015; Ross, 2004: 53–54).

Restrictions on player movement are likely to remain a source of litigation in Europe and contentious collective bargaining in North America. Regardless of the direction taken in the future, leagues and regulators must continue to take into account the interests of the players if they seek to shield the decisions from the courts or other regulatory bodies.

References

Aubut, M. (2003). "When Negotiations Fail: An Analysis of Salary Arbitration and Salary Cap Systems." *Sports Lawyers Journal* 10: 187–239.

Ball, S. R. (2014). *Canadian Employment Law* (student ed.) (Toronto: Canada Law Book).

BBC. (2009, January 20). "Man City Move for Kaka Collapses." *BBC.com*. Viewed December 5, 2016, http://news.bbc.co.uk/sport2/hi/football/teams/m/man_city/7838966.stm.

Buckstein, S. (2011). "A New Solution for Salary Disputes: Implementing Salary Arbitration in the National Basketball Association." *Marquette Sports Law Review* 25: 25–60.

CFL. (2016). "Game Rule Ratio." *CFL.com*. Visited oDecember 5, 2016, www.cfl.ca/game-rule-ratio/.

Chaplin, M. (2005, February 3). "Homegrown Player Plans Revealed." *UEFA.com*. Viewed December 3, 2016, www.uefa.org/protecting-the-game/protection-young-players/news/newsid=276829.html.

Che, X., and Humphreys, B. R. (2015). "Competition Between Sports Leagues: Theory and Evidence on Rival League Formation in North America." *Review of Industrial Organization* 46: 127–143.

Clark, K. (2015). "NFL's Quality of Play Hits Rock Bottom, No One Cares." *Wall Street Journal*, October 27, www.wsj.com/articles/nfls-quality-of-play-hits-rock-bottom-no-one-cares-1445988922.

Clark, K. (2016, September 14). "The NFL Has an Age Problem." *The Ringer*, https://theringer.com/the-nfl-has-an-age-problem-7068825845e4#.9jomyziwr.

Compton, B. (2015, November 19). "Islanders' Hamonic Cites Family Matter for Trade Ask." *NHL.com*. Viewed December 3, 2016, www.nhl.com/news/islanders-hamonic-cites-family-matter-for-trade-ask/c-788701.

Corcoran, K. M. (1994). "When Does the Buzzer Sound? The Nonstatutory Labor Exemption in Professional Sports." *Columbia Law Review* 94: 1045–1075.

Czarnota, P. A. (2013). "FIFA Transfer Rules and Unilateral Termination Without 'Just Cause.'" *Berkeley Journal of Entertainment and Sports Law* 2: 1–47.

Devos, J. (2013, March 5). "Will Canadian Players Ever Be Treated Equally in MLS?," *TSN.ca*, Viewed December 3, 2016, www2.tsn.ca/blogs/jason_de_vos/?id=417461.

Downward, P., Parrish, R., Pearson, G., and Semens, A. (2014). "An Assessment of the Compatibility of UEFA's Home-Grown Player Rule with Article 45 TFEU." *European Law Review* 39: 493–510.

Edelman, M. (2015). "In Defense of Sports Antitrust Law: A Response to Law Review Articles Calling for the Administrative Regulation of Commercial Sports." *Washington and Lee Law Review* 72: 210–226.

Edmonds, E. (2010). "At the Brink of Free Agency: Creating the Foundation for the Messersmith-McNally Decision—1968-1975." *Southern Illinois University Law Journal* 34: 565–619.

Egger, A., and Stix-Hackl, C. (2002). "Sports and Competition Law: A Never-Ending Story?" *European Competition Law Review* 23: 81–91.

FIFA. (2001, August 24). "FIFA Circular No. 769: Revised FIFA Regulations for the Status and Transfer of Players," www.fifa.com/mm/document/affederation/administration/ps_769_en_68.pdf

FIFA. (2015). *FIFA Statutes*. Fédération Internationale de Football Association, Zurich.

FIFA. (2016). *Regulations on the Status and Transfer of Players*. Fédération Internationale de Football Association, Zurich.

FIFPro. (2015, September 18). "FIFPro's EU Competition Law Complaint—Executive Summary," www.fifpro.org/attachments/article/6156/FIFPro%20Complaint%20Executive%20Summary.pdf.

Football Association Premier League. (2016). *Handbook Season 2016/17: Premier League Rules*, http://pulse-static-files.s3.amazonaws.com/premierleague/document/2016/08/09/b81992f4-cf2a-4c5e-a9c1-155169074163/2016-17_Premier_League_Handbook.pdf.

Fort, R. (2005). "The Golden Anniversary of 'The Baseball Players' Labor Market." *Journal of Sports Economics* 6: 347–358.

Fox, E. M. (1997). "US and EU Competition Law: A Comparison." In *Global Competition Policy*, edited by J. D. Richardson and E. M. Graham (Washington, D.C.: Institute for International Economics).

Freeburn, L. (2009). "European Football's Home-Grown Players Rules and Nationality Discrimination Under the European Community Treaty." *Marquette Sports Law Review* 20: 177–220.

Frodl, C. (2016). "Neuer, Hummels, Müller, Götze & Co: The Legal Framework Governing Industrial Relations in German Professional Football." *International Sports Law Journal* 16: 3–21.

García, B. (2007). "UEFA and the European Union: From Confrontation to Co-Operation?" *Journal of Contemporary European Research* 3: 202–223.

García, B.. and Erik Meier, H. (2012). "Limits of Interest Empowerment in the European Union: The Case of Football." *Journal of Economic Integration* 34: 359–378.

Grow, N. (2015). "Regulating Professional Sports Leagues." *Washington and Lee Law Review* 72: 573–652.

Irwin, R. L. (1991). "A Historical Review of Litigation in Baseball." *Marquette Sports Law Review* 1: 283–300.

Kahn, L. M. (2000). "The Sports Business as a Labor Market Laboratory." *The Journal of Economic Perspectives* 14: 75–94.

Kahn, L. M. (2009). "Sports, Antitrust Enforcement and Collective Bargaining." *The Antitrust Bulletin* 54: 857–881.

KEA—CDES (2013). *The Economic and Legal Aspects of Transfers of Players*. Viewed November 11, 2016, http://ec.europa.eu/sport/library/documents/cons-study-transfers-final-rpt.pdf.

Koller, D. L. (2016). "Putting Public Law into 'Private' Sport." *Pepperdine Law Review* 43: 681–741.

Lembrich, G. T. (2002). "Garden Leave: A Possible Solution to the Uncertain Enforceability of Restrictive Employment Covenants." *Columbia Law Review* 102: 2291–2323.

McArdle, D. (2015). *Dispute Resolution in Sport: Athletes, Law and Arbitration* (London: Routledge).

McKeown, J. T. (2011). "The Economics of Competitive Balance: Sports Antitrust Claims After *American Needle*." *Marquette Sports Law Review* 21: 517–550.

MLB. (2007, July 31). "Trade Deadline FAQ." *MLB.com*. Visited December 5, 2016, http://m.mlb.com/news/article/2119863/.

MLB and MLBPA. (2011). *2012-2016 Basic Agreement*, http://mlb.mlb.com/pa/pdf/cba_english.pdf.

MLS. (2016). "Roster Rules and Regulations." *MLS.com*. Visited December 5, 2016, http://pressbox.mlssoccer.com/content/roster-rules-and-regulations.

Nafziger, J. A. R. (2011). "European and North American Models of Sports Organization." In *Handbook on International Sports Law*, edited by J. A. R. Nafziger and S. F. Ross (Cheltenham, UK: Edward Elgar).

NBA. (2001). "Roster Regulations," *NBA.com*, 22 October, viewed 10 May 2016, https://web.archive.org/web/20160510033338/http://www.nba.com/analysis/00421026.html.

NBA and NBPA. (2011, December). *NBA Collective Bargaining Agreement*, www.scribd.com/doc/172760974/NBA-NBPA-CBA-2011.

NFL and NFLPA (2011). *Collective Bargaining Agreement*, https://nfllabor.files.wordpress.com/2010/01/collective-bargaining-agreement-2011-2020.pdf.

NHL. (2012, February 23). "Blue Jackets Trade Jeff Carter to LA Kings for Jack Johnson, 1st-Round Pick." *NHL.com*. Viewed December 5, 2016, www.nhl.com/news/blue-jackets-trade-jeff-carter-to-la-kings-for-jack-johnson-1st-round-pick/c-618601.

NHL. (n.d.). *Constitution of the National Hockey League*.

NHL and NHLPA. (2013). Collective Bargaining Agreement Between National Hockey League and National Hockey League Players' Association, September 16, 2012—September 15, 2022, http://cdn.agilitycms.com/nhlpacom/PDF/NHL_NHLPA_2013_CBA.pdf.

Parrish, R. (2016). "The European Social Dialogue: A New Mode of Governance for European Football?," In *The Legacy of Bosman: Revisiting the Relationship Between EU Law and Sport*, edited by A. Duval and B. van Rompuy (The Hague, The Netherlands: TMC Asser Press).

Parrish, R., and Miettinen, S. (2007). "National Discrimination in Community Law: An Assessment of UEFA Regulations Governing Player Eligibility for European Club Competitions (the Home-Grown Player Rule)." *Entertainment and Sports Law Journal* 5: xiv–xxvi.

Pawlowski, T., and Budzinski, O. (2013). "The Monetary Value of Competitive Balance for Sport Consumers: A Stated Preference Approach to European Professional Football." *International Journal of Sport Finance* 8: 112–123.

Pearson, G. (2015). "Sporting Justifications Under EU Free Movement and Competition Law: The Case of the Football 'Transfer System.'" *European Law Journal* 21: 220–238.

Peeters, T., and Szymanski, S. (2014). "Financial Fair Play in European Football." *Economic Policy* 29: 343–390.

Pierre, J., and Buisine, S. (2013). "Social Dialogue in the Sports Sector at EU Level." *Transfer: European Review of Labour and Research* 19: 581–595.

Pijetlovic, K. (2015). *EU Sports Law and Breakaway Leagues in Football* (The Hague, The Netherlands: Springer).

Ross, S. F. (2011). "Competition Law and Labor Markets." In *Handbook on International Sports Law*, edited by J. A. R. Nafziger and S. F. Ross (Cheltenham, UK: Edward Elgar).

Ross, S. F. (2004). "Player Restraints and Competition Law." *Marquette Sports Law Review* 15: 49–61.
Rottenberg, S. (1956). "The Baseball Players' Labor Market." *Journal of Political Economy* 64: 242–258.
Scelles, N., Durand, C., Bonnal, L., Goywau, D., and Andreff, W. (2013). "Competitive Balance Versus Competitive Intensity Before a Match: Is One of These Two Concepts More Relevant in Explaining Attendance? The Case of the French Football Ligue 1 over the Period 2008–2011." *Applied Economics* 45: 4184–4192.
Schwochau, S. (2000). "The Labor Exemptions to Antitrust Law: An Overview." *Journal of Labor Research* 21: 535–555.
UEFA. (2015). *UEFA Club Licensing and Financial Fair Play Regulations, Edition 2015* (Union of European Football Associations, Nyon).
UEFA. (2016a). Regulations of the UEFA Champions League 2015-18 Cycle: 2016/17 Season, www.uefa.org/MultimediaFiles/Download/Regulations/uefaorg/Regulations/02/35/87/89/2358789_DOWNLOAD.pdf.
UEFA. (2016b). Regulations of the UEFA Europe League 2105-18 Cycle: 2016/17 Season, www.uefa.org/MultimediaFiles/Download/Regulations/uefaorg/Regulations/02/35/92/45/2359245_DOWNLOAD.pdf.
UEFA, EPFL, ECA, and FIFPro. (2012, April 19). *Agreement Regarding the Minimum Requirements for Standard Player Contracts in the Professional Football Sector in the European Union and in the Rest of the UEFA Territory*, http://ec.europa.eu/social/BlobServlet?docId=7678&langId=en.
Weatherill, S. (2003). "'Fair Play Please!': Recent Developments in the Application of EC Law to Sport." *Common Market Law Review* 40: 51–93.
Whyno, S. (2014, June 29). "Sam Gagner Traded Twice in Under Two Hours, Ends up with Coyotes." *Thestar.com*. Viewed December 8, 2016, www.thestar.com/sports/hockey/2014/06/29/sam_gagner_traded_twice_in_under_two_hours_ends_up_with_coyotes.html.
Wyman, A. C. K. (2013). "Collective Bargaining and the Best Interests of Basketball." *Virginia Sports and Entertainment Law Journal* 12: 171–197.
Wyshynski, G. (2012, January 31). "Is Jeff Carter's Unhappiness in Columbus Scaring off Trade Partners?" *PuckDaddy*. Viewed December 3, 2016, https://ca.sports.yahoo.com/blogs/nhl-puck-daddy/jeff-carter-unhappiness-columbus-scaring-off-trade-partners-173947886.html.
Ziller, T. (2015, February 19). "Goran Dragic Has the Most Stereotypical Trade Request Ever." *SBNation*. Viewed December 3, 2016, www.sbnation.com/nba/2015/2/19/8068793/goran-dragic-trade-diva-suns-stereotype.

Cases

Albany Int'l BV v. Stichting Bedrijfspensionenfonds Textielindustrie, (1999) C-67/96, [1999] ECR I-5751).
American Needle Inc. v. National Football League, 560 U.S. 183, 204 (2010).
American League Baseball Club v. Chase, 86 Misc. 441 (N.Y. 1914).
Chicago Bd. of Trade v. United States, 246 U.S. 231 (1918.
Clarett v. NFL, 306 F.Supp. 2d (2d Cir. 2004)
Deliège v. Ligues fancophone de judo, Case C-51/96, ECR [2000] I-02549.
Donà v. Mario Mantero, Case C-13/76, ECR [1976] 1333.

FC Shakhtar Donetsk v. Matuzalem & Real Zaragoza, CAS 2008/A/1519-1520.
Finley v. Kuhn, 596 F.2d 527 (7th Cir. 1978).
Flood v. Kuhn, 316 F. Supp. 271, 275 (S.D.N.Y. 1970).
Fútbol Club Barcelona v. FIFA, CAS 2014/A/3793.
Gebhard v. Consiglio dell'Ordine degli Avvocati e Procuatori di Milano, Case C-55/94, ECR [1995] I-04165.
Kansas City Royals Baseball Corp. v. Major League Baseball Players Ass'n, 409 F. Supp. 233 (W.D. Mo. 1976).
Lehtonen v. Fédération royale belge des sociétés de basket-ball ASBL, Case C-176/96, ECR [2000] I-02681.
Mackey v. NFL, 543 F.2d 606 (8th Cir. 1976).
Meca-Medina & Majcen v. Comm'n, Case C-519/04, ECR [2006] I-06991.
National Hockey League Players' Ass'n v. Edmonton Oilers Hockey Corp., 2012 CANLII 58944 (AB LRB)
NCAA v. Board of Regents, 468 U.S. 85, 117 (1984).
O'Bannon v. NCAA, 7 F. Supp. 3d 955 (N.D. Cal. 2014), aff'd 802 F.3d 1049 (9th Cir. 2015).
Olympique Lyonnais v. Bernard, Case C-325/08, para. 42.
Orca Bay Hockey Ltd. P'ship and the NHL v. B.C. Chapter of the NHLPA, [2007] B.C.L.R.B.D. No. 172
Philadelphia World Hockey Club, Inc. v. Philadelphia Hockey Club, Inc., 351 F. Supp. 462 (E.D. Pa. 1972).
Robertson v. NBA, 389 F. Supp. 867, 891 (S.D.N.Y. 1975).
Sevilla & Morgan de Sanctis v. Udinese Calicio, CAS 2010/A/2145-2147.
Union Royale Belge des Sociétés de Football Ass'n ASBL v. Jean-Marc Bosman, [1995] ECR I-4921.
United States v. Hutcheson, 312 U.S. 219 (1941).
Wigan Athletic & Andrew Webster v. Heart of Midlothian, CAS 2007/A/1298-1300.
Wouters v. Algemene Raad van de Nederlandse Orde van Advocaten, Case C-309/99, ECR [2002] I-01577, para. 97.

CHAPTER 24

ATHLETE TRADEMARKS

Names, Nicknames, and Catchphrases

ALEXANDRA J. ROBERTS

THE mixed martial artist and Olympic judo gold medalist Ronda Rousey is the proud owner of the registered trademark RONDA ROUSEY for clothing and entertainment services, along with nine additional pending applications for ROWDY RONDA ROUSEY. But when NBA player Jeremy Lin applied to register LINSANITY as a trademark just a few days after fans coined the term, he learned that several other applicants had beat him down the court. NFL running back Marshawn Lynch, meanwhile, has applied for marks such as BEAST MODE, POWER PELLETS, BOUT THAT ACTION, and I'M JUST HERE SO I WON'T GET FINED; some speculate that his assertiveness at the U.S. Patent & Trademark Office helped him secure lucrative endorsement deals with sponsors including Nike, Skittles, Progressive, and Activision.

Athletes at all stages of their careers are increasingly attempting to register their names, nicknames, catchphrases, and fan slogans as federal trademarks (Hilbert, 2013).[1] But their goals in filing those applications are often notably distinct from the traditional goals of trademark law, and the types of use that athletes make of those marks differ somewhat from the types of use theoretically required for protection. Athletes' recent attempts to rely on trademark laws to monetize their fame and cultural capital reveal a mismatch between this trend and the legal doctrines on which it relies. Those who work at the intersection of sports law and business are therefore poised to help shape this area of law while advocating for their clients' interests.

A trademark is any word, name, symbol, or device that identifies the source of goods or services and distinguishes them from competitors' goods and services. Their worth can be staggering—the Nike brand name has been valued at $26 billion dollars, for example; ESPN, $17 billion; the New York Yankees, $361 million. Trademarks associated with individual athletes can also be worth quite a lot: Forbes has valued marks associated with Tiger Woods's name and likeness at $38 million; David Beckham's, $26 million; and Kobe Bryant's, $18 million. The estimated worth of marks associated with Jeremy Lin at the peak of the "Linsanity" craze was $14 million. Yet the fee that an applicant must pay to register a trademark with the federal government starts at only $225 per class.

It should come as no surprise, then, that so many athletes are applying to register their names and associated phrases as trademarks. They figure they might as well.

But names, brands, and trademarks are not synonymous. Words and symbols are only protectable under federal trademark law if they meet certain requirements. To qualify as trademarks, matter must be distinctive, either inherently or as a result of use over time. It must be used to indicate the source of goods or services or distinguish its owner's products from those of competitors. To obtain federal registration for a trademark, owners must specify the goods or services for which the matter serves as a mark and must actually sell those goods or services. And trademarks must not deceive consumers by creating a false association or likelihood of confusion with another person, group, or mark. The word NIKE and the company's ubiquitous "swoosh" symbol are trademarks for sneakers and athletic apparel; ESPN is a source-indicator for entertainment and broadcasting services; NEW YORK YANKEES distinguishes one baseball team from others. For what goods or services (if any) is DAVID BECKHAM a trademark? Is WORK HARD STAY HUMBLE a distinctive mark, or just a descriptive slogan? And are marks like THORPEDO and REVIS ISLAND being used in commerce as trademarks or merely as references to well-known athletes?

This chapter begins with an overview on trademark use and registration. Next, it discusses limitations for trademark protection, including those based on distinctiveness, false association, and confusion, and explores how those doctrines affect athletes' ability to protect certain words or phrases as trademarks. Finally, it considers how the general goals of trademark law comport with an athlete's desire to protect words and phrases associated with him or her and prevent others from appropriating them.

1. Trademark Use and Trademark Registration

Trademark rights in the United States stem from use: the person or entity that has the right to register or enforce a mark is not the one who first came up with a phrase or said it out loud but the one who first used it in commerce in connection with the sale of goods or services. While many other countries and jurisdictions have primarily registration-based systems, U.S. trademark users' rights derive from use.

And while trademark owners can enjoy many of the benefits of ownership under common law based solely on using a mark in commerce, whether or not they register it, registration provides some additional bells and whistles that many find worth obtaining. Those include the right to use the ® symbol, block infringing imports at customs, obtain foreign registrations, and sue in federal court for statutory damages, treble damages, and attorneys' fees. Registration also helps discourage others from using the same or similar marks, puts competitors on notice of the owner's use of a mark, grants nationwide rights, and provides additional protection after five years of registration, when many marks may become eligible for "incontestable" status. Registration is helpful in enforcing a mark against cybersquatters or parties whose use dilutes a famous mark by tarnishing or blurring it. Finally, registration creates a presumption of validity in litigation.

After NFL linebacker Terrell Suggs referred to his alma mater Arizona State University as "Ball So Hard University" on national television, a quick-thinking fan named Brian Bussells began using the phrase as a trademark in connection with apparel and immediately applied to register it as a trademark. When Suggs's company filed several applications to register the phrase just a week after Bussells had applied, Suggs lost out. The fact that he had uttered the phrase first publicly did not endow him with trademark rights superior to those of Bussells, even if fans thought it should, because it didn't qualify as the type of use that trademark law protects.

When athletes seek trademark protection for their given names or famous nicknames, they're far less likely to lose out to another party like Suggs did, because their names are already associated with them and the use of those names by someone else could potentially deceive fans. That's why the U.S. Trademark Office ultimately refused to grant a registration for LINSANITY to anyone other than Jeremy Lin.

But if athletes want to register their names as trademarks, they are still bound to use them in commerce *as* trademarks, not just as personal names, and they must specify in their applications the particular goods or services with which they're using their marks. Goods and services are grouped into forty-five different international categories, known as the "Nice Classes" for the French city in which the list was first created. The word mark ESPN, for example, is registered in International Class 41 for entertainment services; IC 16 for paper goods; IC 28 for electronic games; and IC 9 for cell phones and mobile apps. NIKE, meanwhile, is registered in class 25 for shoes and apparel; 18 for bags; 42 for retail store services; 16 for school supplies; 28 for sports equipment; 9 for ear plugs and eyeglasses; 14 for stopwatches; 9 for software and electronic devices; and—somewhat inexplicably—class 30 for sandwiches.

While trademarks can run the gamut of goods and services, athlete trademark registrations are most prevalent in two categories: apparel and entertainment services. Quarterback Donovan McNabb successfully registered his name, DONOVAN MCNABB, for clothing and entertainment services, including personal appearances and television shows in the field of sports. Quarterback Joe Flacco registered JOE FLACCO for clothing and entertainment services, including football games, personal appearances, and "promoting the brands, goods, and services of others." RONDA ROUSEY is registered for clothing and entertainment services, including martial arts competitions and live appearances. Yet another quarterback, Colin Kaepernick, applied to register his name for clothing. Tennis champions and sisters Venus and Serena Williams each applied to register their names for "promoting the goods and services of others" via product endorsements, though they later abandoned their applications. Golfer Phil Mickelson once owned a registration for PHIL MICKELSON for golf-related entertainment services—services that included providing a website detailing his own professional accomplishments. The MICHAEL PHELPS registration covers advertising, promotional, and publicity services for the most decorated U.S. Olympian of all time. Basketball player Amar'e Stoudemire's name is registered for personal appearances, endorsement services, and online entertainment.

Clothing and entertainment services also predominate in athletes' applications to register their nicknames as trademarks. Baseball players Manny Ramirez and Randy Johnson applied to register MANNY BEING MANNY and THE BIG UNIT for clothing, respectively, and hockey player Johnny Gaudreau applied to register JOHNNY HOCKEY for similar goods. Basketball player Shaquille O'Neal's numerous registrations include SHAQ ATTAQ for clothing and footwear. And a slew of football players have applied to register their catchphrases for apparel, including Robert Griffin III's RGIII; Darrelle Revis' REVIS ISLAND; and Vincent Wilfork's WILFORK U UP. Colin Kaepernick applied to register six different trademarks that feature his last name or a portion of it, including KAP7, KAEPERNICK7, KAEPERNICK CK7, a CK7 logo, and most famously KAEPERNICKING, all for clothing.

Are you beginning to see a pattern? Athletes' trademarks for their names, nicknames, and catchphrases consistently cover the same few classes of goods and services. Generally, when a company develops a product and registers a trademark for it, like DRAFTKINGS for a daily fantasy sports website or GU for energy gels, it presumes that consumers will be interested in the goods or services themselves and will use the trademark to find them, such as by searching Google to locate the DraftKings website or requesting the energy gels by name in a supermarket.

But when an athlete registers her name for apparel, she does so to capitalize on her fame, reputation, and athletic prowess. Consumers who buy RONDA ROUSEY sweatshirts and COLIN KAEPERNICK hats likely do so in most cases because they are fans of those athletes, rather than because the sweatshirts and hats are themselves particularly fashionable, functional, or otherwise desirable. In other words, the trademark serves less as a way to find something and distinguish it from other products and more as a way to express allegiance and fandom. In almost all cases, the athlete is not actually the source of the apparel in the traditional sense, anyway—the athlete doesn't manufacture it but merely sells it under his imprimatur. And when an athlete registers his name for entertainment services like endorsements or personal appearances, the use of the trademark is even less like a traditional trademark use. The name essentially functions as a trademark for the athlete himself, without even a semblance of separate services.

Of course, not all athlete name and nickname trademarks are limited to these two categories of use. Runner Usain Bolt's name is registered for sports equipment in addition to clothing and bags. Registrations for MICHAEL JORDAN cover a variety of goods and services from counseling, restaurants, and product endorsement to perfume and skin cream. Figure skater Nancy Kerrigan's application to register her name as a trademark listed ice skates as well as clothing, entertainment services, and product endorsements. Hockey player Gordie Howe's registrations for GORDIE HOWE include sporting goods, memorabilia, and entertainment services. Soccer player DAVID BECKHAM is a registered trademark for clothing, toys, paper goods, toiletries, and entertainment services, as well as CDs, DVDs, and video games on a broad variety of topics. Tiger Woods's name has been registered for apparel, golf equipment, art, video games, personal appearances, golf course design, flavored water, and more. Earvin "Magic" Johnson, likewise, capitalized on his celebrity with registrations covering restaurant services, clothing, blood testing services, career counseling books, live comedy shows, amateur golf tournaments, charitable services, and credit cards, among other goods and services. Tennis player Anna Kournikova's six trademark applications for her name listed goods including eyewear, electronic devices, sporting goods, clothing, accessories, and cosmetics, as well as marketing services.

Nickname registrations for goods and services other than clothing include baseball player Reggie Jackson's MR. OCTOBER for paper goods; football player Chad Johnson's MAD CHAD for videogames; hockey legend Wayne Gretzky's THE GREAT ONE 99 for skates; football player Marshawn Lynch's BEAST MODE for headphones and candy; basketball player Pete Maravich's PISTOL PETE for athletic coaching; and Shaquille O'Neal's SHAQTACULAR for charitable fundraising.

As part of the registration process, an applicant must establish that he has made and continues to make use in commerce of his trademark in connection with the goods and services listed. He does so by submitting one or more specimens showing how the mark is used, along with a signed affidavit. USPTO (United States Patent and Trademark Office) trademark examining attorneys, who review applications and issue refusals or clear marks for registration, may reject a specimen for any number of reasons, some of which are more relevant to athletes than others. One of those bases for refusal is "ornamentality": a mark cannot be registered if its use is merely decorative. Ornamentality is a particular challenge for applicants seeking to show trademark use on apparel when the mark is featured in large font on the front of clothing. Trademark law presumes that consumers will perceive as a trademark matter that appears as a logo or insignia on the breast pocket or sleeve of a shirt, or inside apparel on a permanent or temporary tag, but will perceive words displayed across the front of the apparel as mere decoration.

A single company may produce t-shirts with twenty different slogans on them, and not all of those slogans will be regarded as trademarks. Put another way, fans will expect that they can only get a shirt with the Under Armour logo on the front pocket from a single company—Under Armour—but that they can get a shirt that says "Go Big or Go Home" from more than one source or brand. A number of the applications discussed in this chapter received initial refusals for reflecting only ornamental use, prompting their owners to revise their use or send a new specimen to demonstrate it. Athlete applicants and their lawyers, then, should pay careful attention to this rule to avoid an ornamentality refusal or address one when they receive it. That might mean using the mark in a trademark way on the apparel, or it might mean choosing not to seek registration if the athlete doesn't actually intend to use the matter as an indication of source.

As demonstrated by the foregoing examples, trademarks for athletes' names, nicknames, and slogans tend to be heavily concentrated in two classes of goods and services. Athletes' tendency to use their marks in connection with apparel or with services that only they can perform—endorsements, appearances, or athletic demonstrations—suggests a different use for trademark law than that made by other categories of applicants, like chain restaurants or dry cleaners or producers of useful tangible items. But these uses are allowed by trademark law and are not necessarily problematic. Athletes and the lawyers and agents who advise them are simply taking advantage of an existing legal regime and adapting it for their own purposes. And, of course, athletes are not the only celebrities to see the opportunities that trademark registration offers; applications from actors, musicians, reality television stars, and even the architects of social media memes like Grumpy Cat are on the rise. It's important for owners to ensure legitimate use in commerce in case a mark is challenged, since courts will delve more deeply into use, distinctiveness, and validity in enforcing a mark than the USPTO typically does in granting one. But it's also worth noting that athlete name marks are categorically less prone to litigation, because an athlete will almost always have a greater claim to his own name than will an unaffiliated entity. This concern, then, is more relevant when it comes to a nickname or catchphrase that's also in use by another.

2. Trademark Distinctiveness

In addition to requiring use in connection with goods or services, trademark law mandates that marks be distinctive in order to earn protection. Distinctiveness refers to a trademark's ability to distinguish the goods or services in question from those of competitors—in other words, to be perceived by consumers as a source indicator, not just a descriptive phrase. Courts and USPTO examining attorneys evaluate whether a word mark is inherently distinctive, and thus automatically capable of functioning as a trademark; merely descriptive, and thus only capable of acquiring trademark meaning through use over time; or generic, and incapable of ever becoming a trademark. To aid them in that determination, they typically place marks in one of five categories, deeming them fanciful, arbitrary, suggestive, descriptive, or generic. But athlete trademarks often defy these categorizations, leading to different results than the traditional framework would predict.

Registration of a trademark, as we learned earlier, provides for certain presumptions, one of which is the distinctiveness of the mark. For example, plaintiffs who owned a registration for CROSSOVER KING found that presumption helpful when they sued Nike for using the phrase; a federal court denied Nike's motion for summary judgment, finding the shoe company's argument that the mark was merely descriptive of Tim Hardaway unpersuasive because its status as a registered mark created a presumption of distinctiveness, whether inherent or acquired (*S.B. Designs v. Nike, Inc.*).

While this chapter focuses primarily on word marks, remember that a trademark is any word, symbol, or device that functions as a source indicator—logos (Nike's swoosh), images (Usain Bolt's "lightning" pose), colors (Boise State University's blue football field), patterns (Alabama football coach Bear Bryant's houndstooth hat), shapes, product packaging, and even sounds and smells can all be protected as trademarks if they satisfy the requirements.

A fanciful mark is a made-up term, like UMBRO or ASICS, which is not found in any dictionary. An arbitrary mark is an existing term used in connection with goods or services to which it has no logical relationship, such as COBRA for golf clubs. And suggestive marks are those that connote or hint subtly at characteristics of the goods or services without describing them explicitly, like AQUARIUS for hydrating sports drinks or SPEEDO for bathing suits. The majority of professional team names would likely be classified as suggestive, because they indirectly convey aspirational qualities about the team or its players—the PHILADELPHIA FLYERS are quick; the DETROIT TIGERS, fierce; the SAN DIEGO CHARGERS, aggressive.

Trademarks characterized as fanciful, arbitrary, or suggestive are deemed inherently distinctive and granted protection from their earliest use in interstate commerce. Trademark law assumes that consumers will perceive them as trademarks right away. Generic terms and phrases, on the other hand—think THE SKATEBOARD STORE for a company that sells skateboards or MITT for baseball gloves—are not protectable as trademarks, because they are incapable of becoming distinctive and must remain in the public domain for competitors to use. In some cases, protectable marks can become generic over time, and their owners can lose protection: a once-distinctive mark like ZAMBONI could fall victim to genericide if the relevant consumers understand the term to refer to any ice-resurfacing machine, rather than a specific brand of ice-resurfacing machine.

Between inherently distinctive trademarks and generic terms lie descriptive marks. Descriptive marks are those that directly describe some aspect of the goods or services on which they're used, such as their purpose, appearance, materials, taste, quality, intended audience, or place of origin. Many sports-related publications, from SPORTS ILLUSTRATED to THE JEWISH SPORTS REVIEW, have descriptive names that tell readers what content they cover. A number of sports networks also use descriptive trademarks, including NESN (New England Sports Network) and ESPN (Entertainment and Sports Programming Network). Other examples include 5-HOUR ENERGY for a drink that purports to provide five hours of energy and NEW YORK CITY FOOTBALL CLUB for a soccer team. Laudatory terms that tout the quality of the goods and services, like "best," "supreme," "premier," or "#1," are also treated as descriptive. A federal court held the trademark STAR CLASS for yachts and a yacht association merely descriptive for that reason.

Likewise, under the federal trademark statute, a mark that consists of a person's last name is deemed "primarily merely a surname" and treated like a descriptive mark unless consumers would be unlikely to perceive it as a surname, either because it is rare or because it doubles as a common word like "king" or "golden." Sports-related goods and services include plenty of surname brands named for their founders, from WILSON tennis rackets to RAWLINGS baseball gloves. When Daniel Philbrick, the owner of two stores known as "Philbrick's Sports," sued a competitor for trademark infringement and cybersquatting in 2009, a federal court granted summary judgment for the defendant, finding the PHILBRICK'S SPORTS mark was not inherently distinctive and its owner failed to establish secondary meaning despite its twenty-five years of use and extensive advertising (*Philbrick v. eNom, Inc.*). Full names like DAVID BECKHAM or RONDA ROUSEY are treated as merely descriptive under common law and by some courts, but they are more often categorized as inherently distinctive, including by the USPTO.

Unlike those classified as fanciful, arbitrary, or suggestive, trademarks deemed descriptive are only granted protection under federal law after they have been in use for such a time and in such a way that consumers have come to recognize them as trademarks, rather than as mere descriptors of the goods or services. The quality that renders a descriptive trademark protectable is known as "acquired distinctiveness" or "secondary meaning," because the words acquire an additional, "second" meaning as a trademark in addition to their primary, descriptive meaning. A trademark owner can establish secondary meaning by providing evidence of proxies for consumer recognition such as advertising expenditures, sales success, unsolicited media coverage, attempts by others to copy the mark, consumer surveys, and consumer testimony. In many cases owners claim acquired distinctiveness based on five years or more of continuous, exclusive use of the mark in commerce. Of course, even if a descriptive mark acquires trademark protection, competitors can still use its component terms to describe their own products. CHAMPION is a well-known sportswear brand with extensive secondary meaning, but other apparel companies would be free to call their shorts "the best for champions at play" or describe them as "the official shorts of the 2016 World Cup champions" without confusing consumers or infringing the CHAMPION trademark. This is known as "descriptive fair use."

Like the laudatory and surname marks noted above, slogans are often grouped with descriptive marks and are even, in some cases, flatly unregistrable as trademarks.[2] The Trademark Trial and Appeal Board (TTAB) hears applicants' appeals of initial registrability decisions as well as *inter partes* disputes like oppositions and cancellations. It has held that informational slogans like "Drive Safely," "Proudly Made in the USA," and "Once a Marine, Always a Marine" could not be granted trademark registration because they were incapable of functioning as marks, even when used in commerce in connection with specific products. And the Court of Appeals for the Federal Circuit deemed the mark THE BEST BEER IN AMERICA "so highly laudatory and descriptive of the qualities of its product that the slogan does not and could not function as a trademark to distinguish Boston Beer's goods." According to black-letter trademark law, then, it should be difficult to obtain registration for a catchphrase or slogan-type mark without at a minimum demonstrating secondary meaning.

And yet players, coaches, and sportscasters have successfully registered a number of catchphrases and fan slogans for goods and services similar to those used in connection with personal name trademarks. Those applications are rarely, if ever, refused on the basis that they are informational slogans or lack distinctiveness. Examples include football's Terrell Owens' GETCHA POPCORN READY and I LOVE ME SOME ME and Jared Allen's GOT STRANGE?, basketball coach John Calipari's REFUSE TO LOSE, and basketball player Anthony Davis' FEAR THE BROW and RAISE THE BROW, all for clothing. Baseball player Ernie Banks's LET'S PLAY TWO registration covers clothing, trading cards, and baseball bats. MMA (mixed martial arts) ring announcer Bret Freeman's IT'S GO TIME is registered for announcing and voice services. Bart Scott registered CAN'T WAIT for clothing, retail stores, and educational and entertainment services. Boxing announcer Michael Buffer owns LET'S GET READY TO RUMBLE! for clothing and coffee cups as well as entertainment, advertising, and promotional services. And the late boxing legend Muhammad Ali owned a registration for THRILLA IN MANILA for books, clothing, and toys.[3]

Perhaps those registrations have been allowed because they're substantively different from "Proudly Made in the USA" and "Once a Marine, Always a Marine"—many are less broadly informational and thus less useful to competitors. Slogans like REFUSE TO LOSE, CAN'T WAIT, and IT'S GO TIME, though, seem analogous to those examples and are equally unlikely to be source-indicating from their first use or perhaps ever. It's also worth considering that athlete slogans and catchphrases are often already strongly associated with the athletes who apply to protect them. While the U.S. system is based on the principle that the first to use a mark in commerce is entitled to protect and register that mark, and prior use equates to superior rights, there are exceptions to that rule. If consumers are likely to associate a name, term, or phrase with an athlete or celebrity, even if that person never used it as a mark in commerce, then registration will not be granted to that first user.

If a trademark is a name—whether full name, first name, surname, or nickname—an applicant will encounter several other hurdles to federal registration besides distinctiveness. 15 U.S.C. § 1052(c) bars registration of any mark that comprises a name, portrait, or signature that identifies a living individual without that individual's written consent to the registration. § 1052(a), meanwhile, bars registration of a mark that "consists of or comprises . . . matter which may disparage or falsely suggest a connection with persons, living or dead . . . or institutions . . . or bring them into contempt, or disrepute." The disparagement portion of the prohibition, which recently led a federal court to cancel several registrations for REDSKINS trademarks and logos, is currently being challenged as unconstitutional under the First Amendment, with implications for a number of team names and logos that reference Native Americans. But the portions of the Lanham Act prohibiting registration of marks that create a false association or connection aren't going anywhere, as they serve the fundamental purpose of preventing consumer confusion as to source, sponsorship, or endorsement.

Those two prohibitions explain why an entrepreneur was unable to register the mark BO BALL for a football-baseball hybrid ball without the express permission of Bo Jackson—the USPTO presumed consumers would expect that the ball was being sold with Jackson's permission or endorsement. They are also two of the reasons that opportunistic applications by people other than the named or referenced athletes have been refused for trademarks including TEBOWING, TIGER WOODS, JUSTIN BLACKMON, MICHAEL PHELPS, NEYMAR, THE BIG HANDSOME, MANNY BEING MANNY, KOBE BRYANT FLIGHT 24, LEBRON 3:16, CR7 CRISTIANO RONALDO, THE HOUSE THAT JOHNNY BUILT, FAMOUS JAMEIS, LEO

MESSI—GOAL!, and MONEY MANZIEL. The USPTO refused to register those marks because it concluded that they identified living individuals and created false associations with them.

Jeremy Lin applied to register LINSANITY just a few weeks after it was coined, only to find three others had already filed applications for the LINSANITY mark. Even if Lin wasn't using LINSANITY as a trademark when those others applied, the USPTO recognized that consumers would be likely to associate goods or services bearing that mark with him—especially basketball-related goods or services—and assume he either produced or endorsed the products or licensed his name to their seller. Granting the mark LINSANITY to someone unconnected with Lin without his permission would risk deceiving a substantial portion of the public. And the consumers most likely to be deceived were the same consumers who would be interesting in buying something bearing that mark in the first place.

Likewise, the applicant who sought to register FEAR THE BROW received a refusal based on false association: according to the examining attorney, "the term at issue need not be the actual, legal name of the party [to create a false association, but] must . . . be so uniquely and unmistakably associated with [him] as to constitute [his] name or identity." The examining attorney attached evidence "showing that the phrase . . . is associated so uniquely with the physical appearance of Anthony Davis that it constitutes his identity" (Second Office Action, 2011, 2-3). To the USPTO, FEAR THE BROW was already so closely associated with Anthony Davis that granting the registration to someone else had the potential to confuse or deceive members of the public, even though Davis had not begun using the phrase as a trademark at the time the applicant filed.

This issue also applies to well-known coaches. USC's Steve Sarkisian applied to register SARK for clothing and sports websites, along with COACH SARK and BARK FOR SARK (both later abandoned) for the same goods and services, only to discover others had already applied to register SARK TANK and BARK FOR SARK without his permission. The USPTO refused to grant the trolls' applications, noting that "Sark" was a known nickname for Coach Sarkisian and one that he himself had embraced. The examining attorney even appended Sark's Twitter page as evidence that consumers would perceive an association between the marks and the coach. The rule has also been applied to athletic institutions, although inconsistently: the TTAB held that SYDNEY 2000 created a false association with the Olympics Games taking place that year in Sydney, Australia, but it allowed an apparel company to register MARATHON MONDAY, finding that the public didn't closely associate that phrase with the entity that runs the Boston Marathon. Decisions by the USPTO can also be inconsistent. When Skechers applied to register #GOMEB for footwear, the trademark examining attorney allowed the application without requiring written proof that Olympic athlete and marathon winner Mebrahtom "Meb" Keflezighi had granted the shoe company permission to use his nickname. In another case, an individual applied to register a design mark "meant to resemble Kobe Bryant's tattoo on his arm" and featuring the initials KB. The USPTO did not issue a false association or false identification refusal. Such refusals will only be triggered when the USPTO recognizes a mark as a reference to an individual and presumes that consumers will too, but dictionaries and online searches can supply cultural or subcultural knowledge that individual examining attorneys might lack.

In addition to the false association and identification prohibitions discussed previously, 15 U.S.C. § 1052(d) prohibits the registration of any mark that will cause a likelihood of confusion with another registered mark. An applicant who hoped to use LET'S GET READY TO RUMBLE as a clever trademark for earthquake emergency survival kits, for example, was unable to register it because the USPTO predicted consumers might think the product associated with or endorsed by Buffer, the boxing announcer with whom it originated. An applicant who hoped to obtain a registration for I LOVE ME SOME ME for apparel saw his application refused based on a likelihood of confusion with Terrell Owen's registration of the same mark for the same goods. The applicant who sought to register LEBRONASTY as a trademark for hats, jackets, and shirts was met with a refusal based on the likelihood consumers would be confused that the LEBRONASTY apparel was related to apparel sold under the trademark LEBRON.

This registration principle mirrors the federal cause of action for infringement: when a party uses in commerce matter that is identical or confusingly similar to a mark owner's trademark, whether or not the owner has registered that mark, the mark owner can sue that party to enjoin its use as long as he can establish a likelihood of consumer confusion. For example, an equipment company that had an endorsement deal with Mark Messier sued a competitor that was printing "Messier" on its hockey sticks, ostensibly to suggest that those particular sticks were the same shape as the one Messier played with. The court sided with Messier and his sponsor, prohibiting the defendant from producing or selling sticks bearing the word "Messier" in the future.

Often, a trademark examining attorney will cite all three prohibitions—false association, false identification, and likelihood of confusion—as bases for refusing a registration, as applicants discovered when they tried to register WATCH WHAT LEBRON.COM for athletic apparel and LEBRON LAMES for hats and shirts. And while many marks refused registration on these bases are fan marks that celebrate the player's fame and accomplishments, some—LEBRON LAMES; JUDAS & BRUTUS & BENEDICT & LEBRON.; possibly also LEBRONASTY—come from haters who want to reserve the exclusive right to use those negative slogans on apparel. While the *use* of such phrases is often a permissible expressive use allowed under fair use doctrine, in part because consumers are not likely to believe that LeBron is affiliated with clothing that bashes him, trademark registration is typically still barred. This is an important distinction: even when trademark registration is not permitted, a mark or phrase can still be used; a refusal to register is not the same as an injunction against selling products bearing that phrase. The TTAB recently affirmed that principle in siding with the Yankees when the team challenged the USPTO's decision granting registration for THE HOUSE THAT JUICE BUILT, a play on the Yankees slogan THE HOUSE THAT RUTH BUILT. While the use of that slogan is likely a permissible parody that won't confuse consumers, the Yankees successfully argued that it diluted their mark and tarnished their reputation given its reference to players' reported steroid use, and its registration was thus barred.

To be sure, not all similar or even identical trademarks will be disallowed as confusing consumers or creating a false association. PISTOL PETE has been registered to Peter Maravich since 1975 for athletic instructional services, but that didn't keep other applicants from successfully registering PISTOL PETE for clothing, fishing flies, and gaming devices. CHAMPION is a registered trademark for target launchers, dental floss, nutritional supplements, motor oil, and windshield wiper fluid, among other things; consumers are not expected to confuse those products with the sportswear sold by Champion USA. And despite the rejections of SARK TANK and BARK FOR SARK mentioned earlier, certainly not all trademarks containing the letters "sark" will create an association with Steve Sarkisian—applications for SARK for coffee, toys, and food have been allowed, and CUTTY SARK is a famous, decades-old mark for alcohol. Applications to register "sark"-marks for goods or services related to sports, or those which use the colors of a school where Sarkisian coaches, are most likely to confuse consumers and thus garner a false association refusal. But the more famous and well-known an athlete, and the more closely the applied-for mark references his name, the more likely the USPTO is to refuse it or require the athlete's written permission, no matter how far afield the goods or services are from the sport he plays. Trademark examining attorneys and courts have explained their reasoning by asserting that even though the athlete or coach is not connected with the goods or services for which the applicant seeks to register the trademark, he "is so famous that consumers would presume a connection." In other words, Michael Jordan and Shaquille O'Neill—like Apple and Nike—have such broad and far-reaching fame that consumers would expect any goods or services bearing their names or nicknames to be endorsed by them, even if the goods are not basketballs or sneakers but musical instruments or lawn-mowing services.

3. Trademark Goals

The primary goals of trademark law are protecting consumers from confusion or deception, rewarding producer investment in quality products by building their brand equity, and minimizing consumer search costs to promote marketplace efficiency. Granting federal trademark registration protection for the Nike swoosh serves all three goals: it protects consumers by preventing them from being misled by a manufacturer producing lower-quality sneakers and using a confusingly similar logo on them. It rewards Nike for investing in the swoosh mark and generating substantial goodwill in it by prohibiting the registration of confusingly similar marks and granting Nike the ability to enforce its mark against anyone using a similar symbol to free-ride on Nike's fame. And it minimizes search costs by enabling Nike fans to find what they're looking for quickly—they can scan a rack of shoes for that iconic symbol and try on only those sneakers made by their preferred producer.

Athletes no doubt share many of the same goals as other producers when they use, register, and enforce trademarks. But media coverage suggests that athletes may prize other goals even more highly. Some athletes and coaches who have applied to register name or catchphrase marks report doing so not because they want to create a new business venture or capitalize on their celebrity by selling particular products but because—like Sarkisian—they feel pressure to "protect their names" (Solomon, 2014). They use trademark registration defensively to prevent others from capitalizing on their reputations, rather than affirmatively to protect trademarks they use or plan to use in connection with goods or services. Tim Tebow told reporters he filed to register multiple trademarks including TEBOWING, less for financial gain and more "to just control how it's used, make sure it's used in the right way" (ESPN, 2012). How does an athlete use the registration system to protect a mark that she does not use in commerce? The Intent to Use (ITU) registration system helps here.

Athletes' use of trademark law may diverge from the mainstream particularly when it comes to ITU-based applications. U.S. trademark rights are based on use, as discussed previously. Traditionally, owners acquire rights they can protect and enforce based simply on using a mark in commerce, and they can—but are not obligated to—then register the mark. Since 1989, though, an alternative approach is available. An applicant can submit an application based on her bona fide intent to use a mark with specified goods or services in the future. The application will be examined and published, and the owner can perfect the application by using the mark in commerce within a limited period of time after that. The ITU application requires use in commerce within six months, but a user can obtain up to five extensions, giving her a total of three years to use the mark and submit a specimen of use to the USPTO. While the registration does not actually issue without use, the ITU application provides constructive notice to competitors and other potential users that an owner plans to employ a particular mark in the near future. As long as the mark is not merely descriptive or barred by any other trademark doctrines and the applicant truly intends to use it in the future, she can reserve it for future use. If the applicant changes her mind later and abandons the ITU application or lets it lapse without ever making technical use in commerce, she will be out a few hundred dollars but suffer no other adverse consequences.

Entrepreneurs have used the ITU process in a variety of ways. Some want to begin the registration process before their business or product is ready to launch so they can perfect the registration from the first day of use in commerce. Others believe they've struck marketing gold with a clever trademark and want to ensure priority over any other users. Applicants might reserve several different potential marks while they conduct market research on them. In some cases, companies would like to begin producing and selling goods and services but are waiting for something, such as regulatory approval, an appropriate manufacturer for a component, completion of construction, or adequate capital. The ITU application enables them to explore a mark's protectability in advance—if the examining attorney finds it deceptive, or descriptive, or too similar to another mark, or if a competitor objects to the application as likely to cause confusion with one of its own marks, the applicant has time to modify the mark or select a different one before introducing the goods or services to consumers.

Athletes have made use of ITU applications in creative ways that aren't always consistent with the stated goals of trademark law. They have discovered that an ITU application can scare off other applicants from trying to "poach" the mark or catchphrase, since the athlete has already staked his territory. If those applicants do apply, it can ensure that the trademark examining attorney will issue refusals based on likelihood of confusion, as well as false identification and false association. It also saves athletes the resources required to contest those other applications and the time involved in waiting them out. On top of those more common justifications, the ITU application can serve additional functions for amateur athletes. It can reserve a source of future income for college athletes who are barred by the National Collegiate Athletic Association (NCAA) from monetizing their names, identities, and catchphrases at the time the application is filed, assuming those trademarks are still valuable once the athlete is no longer bound by rules governing amateurs. And once perfected, the registration provides nationwide rights from the date of filing; that is, the trademark's priority date can predate the athlete's status as a professional. One sports lawyer has gone so far as to assert that the NCAA and universities ought to inform student-athletes of their "right to protect their trademarks for future commercial use" by filing ITU applications, and coaches' and universities' failure to do so "has caused undue burdens for many of these athletes once they hit the professional ranks" (Heitner, 2013). The characterization of an ITU application as a "right" is questionable, given it assumes specific plans to commercialize the athlete's name, nickname, or slogan as a trademark. But the comment reflects a growing appreciation of the importance of trademark registration and the potential for amateur athletes to use ITU applications to maximize future opportunities.

Johnny Manziel discovered the benefits of ITU applications for amateurs somewhat accidentally when he was the first freshman to win the Heisman Trophy in 2012 and his nickname, JOHNNY FOOTBALL, became nationally known. With unauthorized "Johnny Football" merchandise surfacing across the country, Texas A&M University encouraged Manziel and his family to apply to register the nickname in order to bolster his efforts to keep others from using it and thus maintain his eligibility as an amateur (Cho, 2015). The NCAA bylaws not only prohibit an athlete from using his name to promote the sale of commercial products, they also require him to take affirmative steps to prevent unauthorized commercial use of it by others (NCAA Academic and Membership Affairs Staff, 2013). By filing an ITU application, the amateur athlete can protect trademarks associated with him, but has three years to actually use the mark in commerce before it is considered "abandoned." Thus, if a college player avails himself of the opportunity to apply to register trademarks at the end of his freshman year based on an intent to use them in future, he can protect his trademark from unauthorized use and begin using the mark in commerce after he graduates without jeopardizing his NCAA eligibility.

By the time the Manziels applied to register JOHNNY FOOTBALL, another application for the mark was already pending, although the USPTO ultimately refused it because it clearly referenced Manziel. The family also sued two other entities that were using Manziel's nicknames in connection with merchandise, ultimately settling with both. The NCAA surprised many when it ruled that Manziel was entitled to keep any "financial earnings" that resulted from the legal actions without jeopardizing his amateur status (Cho, 2015). More recently, Manziel applied to register JOHNNY CLEVELAND and THE HOUSE THAT JOHNNY BUILT after unrelated entities attempted to beat him to the punch. Enterprising fans have also applied to register other phrases that reference Manziel, including JOHNNY BROWNS and MONEY MANZIEL (unsuccessfully) and JOHNNY BE GOOD and JUANITO FÚTBOL (successfully).

Manziel's goals in applying to register his nickname while playing college football were not the same as the ostensible goals of typical trademark registrants—capitalizing on a near-term plan to sell goods and services. Rather, Manziel, whose football career is now in limbo due to unrelated legal issues, was motivated to preserve his eligibility to play college football, prevent others from profiting from his famous nickname, and reserve his own ability to trade on that nickname once he went pro, including perhaps clearing the path for agreements with major sponsors. Other college athletes have had the same idea, filing ITU applications to protect trademark rights without jeopardizing amateur status. Ohio State University football player Ezekiel Elliott applied to register nicknames ZEKE and EZE for merchandise, as well as HERO IN A HALF SHIRT and IN CROP TOP WE TRUST for apparel and ZEKE'S CROP TOP BAR AND GRILL for restaurant services. Mississippi State University quarterback Dak Prescott applied to register his name as a trademark, along with DAK ATTACK and WHO DAK. Like Johnny Manziel, football players Jameis Winston and Kenny Hill also took advantage of the ITU process to apply to register name or nickname trademarks while still playing college ball.

In addition to preserving rights and running defense, applying to register a trademark can improve an athlete's bargaining position when it comes to future sponsors or endorsement opportunities, because the sponsor will likely need to license the trademarks back from the player in order to use them. As one of Jeremy Lin's lawyers noted in connection with his successful registration of LINSANITY, "having a clean plate with rights in place makes it a lot easier to negotiate licenses and endorsements deals" (Soshnick, 2012). It also demonstrates the athlete's marketability and business savvy and shows potential partners that the path to exploiting the athlete's already-well-known names, nicknames, logos, or catchphrases is unobstructed. On top of that, given fans' hunger for sports news and fascination with players as celebrities, the mere fact of a player applying to register a name, nickname, or catchphrase mark can increase publicity for that player. Applications and registrations often generate headlines about the player's athletic prowess and popularity, underscoring that he or she is "having a moment" and in turn making the player even more marketable to sponsors.

At least some sports insiders have acknowledged that in choosing between two athletes close in talent, savvy managers are likely to choose the one who has a bigger social media and fan following. Trademark applications and merchandising efforts amplify both (Mooney, 2014). An early ITU application might have helped Vince Young who, as a student athlete at the University of Texas, led his team to a national championship in 2005 and gained some traction with fans using his initials, VY, and the word

INVINCEABLE, both of which appeared on merchandise. Shortly after he declared for the draft, it occurred to Young to apply to register both nicknames as trademarks. To his chagrin, he discovered others had already filed applications for both trademarks. Young sued. According to press reports, the litigation and pending applications prevented Young from securing several potential marketing deals, including one that was allegedly in the works with Reebok (Wyatt, 2008).

If an applicant does not eventually make use in commerce of his applied-for mark and convert the ITU-based application into a use-based one, the mark will be deemed abandoned.[4] It's unsurprising, then, that the Principal Register lists a large number of abandoned marks. But it seems noteworthy that so many athlete trademarks are abandoned. The late football coach Dennis Green's THEY ARE WHO WE THOUGHT THEY WERE, swimmer Ryan Lochte's JEAH, football player and media personality Michael Strahan's STOMP YOU OUT, Robert Griffin III's UNBELIEVABLY BELIEVABLE and WORK HARD STAY HUMBLE, basketball player and commentator Jalen Rose's FAB FIVE, Kenny Hill's KENNY TRILL, baseball player Bryce Harper's THAT'S A CLOWN QUESTION, BRO, and baseball's Brian Wilson's FEAR THE BEARD, all for goods including apparel, are just a few examples in which athletes or coaches filed ITU applications for trademarks but never saw them through. The surplus of abandoned applications seems to support the proposition that athletes who apply to register persona trademarks don't particularly want to sell things, so much as they want to increase their fame, assert control over what they understand to be their property, and stake their territory defensively to avoid exploitation by others. The law requires ITU applicants to submit a sworn affidavit attesting to their bona fide intent to use the mark in the future, though, and the TTAB has required that an applicant be able to demonstrate that intent with documentary evidence. So filing an application for a phrase with no intent to use it in commerce could constitute fraud on the USPTO.

Athletes' goals may also differ from those of other applicants or of trademark law itself when it comes to mark ownership. Typically, the person or company that applies to register a trademark is the same person or company that is using it or plans to use it in commerce. The applicant may have devised the mark herself or hired an external marketing firm to assist in naming the goods or services; trademark law is agnostic as to who actually selected the mark. In some cases, applicants register a mark with plans to license it, but those stories are the exception rather than the rule.

When it comes to athlete trademarks, the stories differ somewhat. Athlete nicknames and slogans are often devised by loyal fans and spread quickly via social media, press coverage, and live audiences. The athletes themselves may be the applicants, or their sponsors may register and own the marks as part of an endorsement contract that negotiated those rights in exchange for a large payday. LeBron James, for example, registered LEBRON for clothing, bags, and sporting goods through LBJ Trademarks, LLC, and then assigned all three registrations to Nike, for which he is a spokesperson. He registered LEBRON JAMES HOME COURT for furniture and retail services and THE LEBRON JAMES FAMILY FOUNDATION for apparel and charitable services using the same LLC and then assigned those registrations to a furniture store and a nonprofit, respectively. Meanwhile, Nike itself applied to register a number of marks that referenced James with James's written permission, including five applications for KING JAMES, seven for LEBRON, three for LBJ, and one for LEBRON JAMES, covering a variety of apparel and accessories. James reportedly sold Nike the rights to many of those marks as part of a $90 million endorsement deal in 2003.

In the case of coaches at both the professional and the university level, the employer may be the listed registrant based on provisions folded into the coach's employment contract, or the coach may apply to register trademarks under his own name. A number of European teams and leagues own U.S. registrations for their coaches' or players' names, nicknames, or catchphrases. The Liverpool Football Club has registered THE NORMAL ONE, a nickname for manager Jurgen Klopp, in the United States for seven classes of goods including hardware, software, games, apparel, kitchen utensils, and leather accessories. Auburn football coach Gus Malzahn applied to register his catchphrase HURRY UP NO HUDDLE for glassware and clothing, but it was his employer who applied for GUS BUS for t-shirts. Coaching contracts have become more explicit regarding how a school can or cannot use a coach's name, image or likeness, with some coaches agreeing to assign those rights to their employers in exchange for substantial remuneration—in some cases, tens of millions of dollars (Solomon, 2014). The Ohio State University owns the registrations for URBAN MEYER and URBAN MEYER KNOWS for clothing and reportedly has contracted for the right to use Meyer's name and likeness in connection with various other goods and accessories, while Meyer retains the right to use his name for charitable endeavors and other opportunities that don't conflict with his employer's rights. Clemson coach Dabo Swinney, on the other hand, has registered DABO and DABO SWINNEY for clothing and DABO'S ALL IN for clothing and charitable services; his agreement with Clemson enables the university to take advantage of merchandising rights while Swinney remains the owner of the marks.

4. Conclusion

This chapter has focused on the protectability and registration of athletes' names, nicknames, and catchphrases as trademarks under federal law, and attempted to highlight some of the unique features of those marks as well as athletes' particular goals in applying to register them. The Trademark Act also includes a cause of action for false endorsement that comes into play when someone makes commercial use of a famous person's name, image, or likeness in a way that misleads consumers to believe the celebrity has sponsored or endorsed the products. But trademark and false endorsement causes of action overlap and intertwine with rights of publicity, which are primarily a product of state law. Rights of publicity are based on the premise that every individual has the right to control the commercial value of his or her identity and prevent others from exploiting it without his or her permission. "Identity" can include a person's name, image, likeness, signature, voice, or anything else that the public associates with that person—in one case, a racecar driver prevailed on a right-of-publicity claim against RJ Reynolds Tobacco when an ad using a car that resembled his led members of the public to believe the driver was sponsored by the cigarette company (*Motschenbacher v. R.J. Reynolds Tobacco Co.*).

Where trademark rights and rights of publicity overlap, athletes are encouraged to avail themselves of relief under both sets of doctrines. Lawyers encourage this "belt-and-suspenders" approach whenever multiple forms of protection are available to their clients. But trademark law offers some advantages over right of publicity law that make it particularly appealing to athletes.

First, the right of publicity comprises a patchwork of laws that vary state by state, encompassing different definitions of "identity," different rules regarding descendability and transferability, and different requirements for relief. Federal trademark law is more uniform across jurisdictions, so results are more consistent and predictable. Second, an athlete may call upon right of publicity laws only once he has been wronged; he can assert trademark protection affirmatively and publicly, on the other hand, as discussed earlier. Finally, college athletes are currently barred from taking advantage of their rights of publicity while they are amateurs. Those rights are instead assigned to the university for which the athletes play (although legal challenges to that principle are ongoing).

Trademark law, then, seems to be an increasingly appealing avenue for amateur and professional athletes looking to put others on notice of their claims to words or phrases and protect themselves proactively from unscrupulous companies that would trade on their names and reputations, if not their likenesses. Arguably, the marks discussed in this chapter represent a trend in which athletes increasingly rely on trademark law as a back-door way to protect their publicity rights.

While trademark law is traditionally understood to reward and protect producer investment in trademark goodwill and prevent consumer confusion or deception, athletes are increasingly using it creatively to promote themselves as celebrities. For athletes, the registration process doubles as a tool to expand their fan base, generate publicity, and increase desirability to potential sponsors. And while trademark doctrines are designed to accommodate the use of marks as source indicators for tangible goods or identifiable services of value to consumers, athlete trademarks are predominantly used on apparel or for entertainment services in which the athlete's trademark serves primarily as a trademark for the athlete himself, rather than a source-indicator for separate goods and services. The ability of these marks to reference a specific athlete from their earliest use may defy the trademark principle that some categories of marks are only protectable once they acquire secondary meaning. Finally, athletes often use trademark applications, and in particular ITU applications, defensively to prevent others from exploiting marks connected with their identity, rather than to capitalize on those marks themselves. This principle has particularly interesting implications for amateur athletes, who are barred from fully exploiting their publicity rights but have availed themselves of ITU applications to reserve marks for professional use and enjoin infringers even without making actual use in commerce.

For better or worse, those who work in sports law and business should be aware of the variety of goals that athletes use federal trademark law to serve, and should keep clients informed of their opportunities for protection.

Acknowledgments

For helpful conversations and comments, the author thanks Roger Ford, Yvette Liebesman, Michael McCann, Daniel Roberts, and participants in the Junior IP Scholars Association's summer 2016 meeting.

Notes

1. Hilbert notes "today's athletes seem to be filing trademark applications earlier and earlier and likely will continue to do so."
2. Trademark Manual of Examining Procedure (TMEP) § 1202.04
3. Note that while short phrases may function as trademarks, they are almost always ineligible for copyright protection, which typically covers more substantial written works like novels, plays, poems, and films, rather than mere slogans. Book titles are never copyrightable.
4. Marks may also be abandoned before registration when an applicant doesn't respond (satisfactorily or at all) to a USTPO Office Action listing bases for refusal or when the applicant notifies the USPTO of his intent to abandon the mark. Registered marks can also be abandoned explicitly or deemed abandoned when a registrant fails to file paperwork renewing registration at certain junctures in the mark's life.

References

Cho. C. (2015). "Protecting Johnny Football®: Trademark Registration for Collegiate Athletes." *Northwestern Journal of Technology and Intellectual Property Law* 13: 65, 66–67.

ESPN. (2012, October 20). "Tim Tebow Trademarking 'Tebowing.'" *ESPN.com*. Available at http://espn.go.com/new-york/nfl/story/_/id/8525097/tim-tebow-new-york-jets-trademarking-tebowing.

Heitner, D. (2013, December 9). "Should Current NCAA Student-Athletes File for Federal Trademark Protection?" *Forbes.com*.

Hilbert, R. (2013). "Maintaining the Balance: Whether a Collegiate Athlete's Filing of a Federal Trademark Application Violates NCAA Bylaws." *Berkely Journal of Entertainment and Sports Law* 2.

Mooney, L. (2014, April 28). "Five Key Trends That Are Driving the Business of Sports." *Stanford GSB Insights*. Available at www.gsb.stanford.edu/insights/five-key-trends-are-driving-business-sports.

NCAA Academic and Membership Affairs Staff. (2013). *NCAA Division I Manual* (Indianapolis, Ind.: NCAA).

Solomon, J. (2014, August 21). "Which College Football Coaches Have Tried To Trademark Their Name?," *CBSsports.com*. Available at www.cbssports.com/collegefootball/eye-on-college-football/24671319/which-college-football-coaches-have-tried-to-trademark-their-name.

Soshnick, S. (2012, May 12). "Linsanity Belongs to Jeremy Lin After Point Guard Wins Trademark." *Bloomberg.* Available at www.bloomberg.com/news/articles/2012-05-25/linsanity-belongs-to-jeremy-lin-after-point-guard-wins-trademark.

Wyatt, J. (2008, December 18). "Vince Young Sues Friends for Use of 'VY' Trademark." *USA Today*. Available at http://usatoday30.usatoday.com/sports/football/nfl/titans/2008-12-18-young-trademark_N.htm.

Cases and Administrative Office Actions

Motschenbacher v. R.J. Reynolds Tobacco Co., 498 F.2d 921 (9th Cir. 1974).

Philbrick v. eNom, Inc., 593 F. Supp. 2d 352 (D.N.H. 2009).

S.B. Designs v. Nike, Inc., 2002 U.S. Dist. LEXIS 24637, *7 (N.D. Ill. Dec. 20, 2002).

Second Office Action, FEAR THE BROW, U.S. Trademark Application Serial No. 85477805 (filed Nov.21, 2011) (abandoned) at 2-3.

CHAPTER 25

TRADE SECRETS AND INFORMATION SECURITY IN THE AGE OF SPORTS ANALYTICS

ROGER ALLAN FORD

1. Introduction

PROBABLY the most important recent advance in professional sports has been the rise of sports analytics. In the last few decades, teams and outside observers have used increasingly sophisticated statistical methods and data to assess and improve their odds of winning, relying on data to evaluate and make decisions about everything from player signings and trades to game strategy to allocating practice time. And these tools have been valuable: teams that embrace statistical methods, like baseball's Oakland Athletics and Boston Red Sox and basketball's Houston Rockets and San Antonio Spurs, have been successful, winning more than their fair share of games and titles.

As analytics has become increasingly important to team success, the latest methods have become increasingly sophisticated and increasingly secretive. Most of the work is done in-house: teams have built large analytics staffs and have kept the results of those efforts secret. They have also invested substantial amounts of money to gather increasingly granular data to use in their analysis. And while some outsiders continue to do important analytic work, often they do so in the hopes of getting hired by teams. In this trend toward secrecy, professional sports increasingly resembles other industries, like Wall Street, in which proprietary data and algorithms are critical to firm success. And it resembles other industries in a way that is more troubling: security breaches and industrial espionage have come to sports.

The increasing amount of valuable information in professional sports has highlighted the need for teams to protect their secrets. This chapter discusses the rise of sports analytics and surveys the five basic means teams have to protect the value of secret information: league rules and norms, nondisclosure and noncompete agreements, trade-secrecy law, criminal law, and information-security efforts. It then discusses likely future trends as secret information becomes increasingly valuable. Teams should expect to see more efforts to obtain this secret information and should expect to invest more in legal and technical countermeasures.

2. The Rise of Sports Analytics

Professional sports is one of the many industries that have been revolutionized by technology. Besides better tools of the game—faster balls, lighter and stronger rackets, better padding and helmets, and so forth—information technology has allowed coaches and teams to analyze information that did not exist or could not easily be analyzed a few decades ago. It is no exaggeration to say that data has changed how games are played, revealing inefficiencies and tendencies that teams can exploit. In baseball, analytics led teams to recognize the value of walks, on-base percentage, and pitch counts; in basketball, it underscored the value of three-point shooting and spacing the floor and the inefficiency of long two-pointers. Teams like the 2015 Golden State Warriors, which won the NBA title after a historically dominant season built on small ball and threes, simply would not exist in the same form without modern analytics. (The notable exception is football, where teams still kick field goals and punt far more often than statistics show is optimal. But even there, teams have started assembling analytics staffs; likewise, the explosion of fantasy football has fueled a boom in analytics work, much of it highly sophisticated and done by outsiders.)

Sports analytics has two distinct uses. One is to simplify the process of using the kinds of information teams have used for decades to prepare for games and opponents. Rather than spend hours reviewing game film, for instance, a coach with access to good analytic tools can quickly learn things like which plays an opponent prefers in different circumstances, or which pitches a hitter is least likely to hit, or which shots a team is particularly bad at defending. In this form, analytics lends efficiency and analytical precision to inferences that teams have long made. The other use—and the more transformative use—of analytics is to generate new insights. By analyzing data from previous games or other players, teams can uncover new correlations that help them do everything from evaluating draft prospects to optimizing players' rest.

Sports analytics came of age in baseball in the 1960s, 1970s, and 1980s. Early steps came with the publications of books like Earnshaw Cook's *Percentage Baseball* (1964) and Bill James's first *Baseball Abstract* (1977), and with the founding of the Society for American Baseball Research (1971). Baseball had two key features that made it ideal for an early analytics revolution. First, there was a need: teams and players had long made decisions based on apocryphal wisdom handed down over the generations and dubious measures like whether someone looked like a baseball player. This left a lot of room for improvement. Second, that need could readily be filled: baseball has long been one of the most statistically documented sports, though that data had mostly been used poorly, and the development of inexpensive computers in the second half of the twentieth century made processing the data much easier. So when James and his contemporaries mined that data for new truths about how teams could optimize their rosters and strategies, there was a built-in audience that could make productive use of those truths.

The problem was that the teams weren't receptive, at least at first. The prototypical baseball manager or general manager at the time was an ex-player who grew up in the old system and had a vested interest in perpetuating it. It took outsiders without preconceptions to bring some of the new ideas into practice, and even then it happened only when those outsiders had little choice. One of the first was Sandy Alderson, general manager of the Oakland Athletics from 1983 to 1997 (and now of the Mets), who was a Marine Corps officer and law firm partner before he became the team's general counsel and then general manager (GM). This unusual background positioned him well to question preconceived notions, but even so it took new team owners demanding that he slash the team's payroll. Having less money to work with than most competitors, the A's had to find ways to get better value out of its payroll, and the easiest way to do so was to have more players on cheap rookie contracts. But the traditional scouting tools had a terrible track record of predicting which players would pan out, so Alderson and his successor Billy Beane—himself one of those failed predictions—relied more heavily on statistics than on scouting to predict which players would pan out. They also looked for undervalued traits, like a high rate of walks, which correlated with run production and wins. This led to a remarkable run of success, with the A's making four consecutive playoff runs in the early 2000s despite having one of the lowest payrolls in Major League Baseball (MLB). And this success was noticed by other teams, which quickly hired Athletics front-office alumni or set up analytics operations of their own. (It didn't hurt when, in 2003, Michael Lewis published the bestseller *Moneyball: The Art of Winning an Unfair Game.*)

Baseball took quickly to analytics because the data existed and because the nature of the game facilitates statistical thinking. Baseball is less a team game than a series of individual pitcher-hitter encounters, which made it easy to develop statistics that predict, rather reliably, the number of runs a team will score and the number of games it will win per year. (The failure of the game to take to analytics earlier was probably a historical accident, since many of the classic statistics turn out to be of dubious value. Some—RBIs (runs batted in), wins and losses, saves, errors—are unreliable because they depend as much on what other players do as on what the player in question does. Others—batting average, hits—ignore walks, which can often be just as valuable as hits.) To a surprisingly good approximation, a hitter who makes it on base *X*% of the time more than another hitter will produce *Y* marginal runs and *Z* marginal wins a year. Comparing players is fairly easy, then, and as a result most of the low-hanging fruit has been solved, at least in baseball, with most of the teams exploiting the same techniques and eliminating many of the previous inefficiencies.

(Besides providing these sorts of insights, there's another key advantage of analytics. In the salary-cap era, analytics staffs are one of the most cost-effective ways to increase team quality. Entry-level analytics salaries are rounding errors compared to those of most professional athletes.)

Things become more complicated in sports like basketball and football in which the data is more complex and player interactions matter more. The data is more complex because geography becomes important: in baseball, a pitcher and catcher are always located in the same places, while in most other sports it matters greatly exactly where each player is located. This is why a basketball player's field-goal percentage has only limited value: three-pointers are more valuable than two-pointers, as are shots that are well-positioned for offensive rebounds or that are likely to lead to foul calls. Data of the kind kept for more than a century in baseball—*X* pitcher threw to *Y* batter, who struck out or hit a home run—would be mostly worthless in basketball. And player interactions add to this complication. When a batter in baseball hits a home run or strikes out, two players affect the play: the batter and the pitcher. When a basketball player scores, it's usually the result of a complex sequence of movement and passes and screens by several different players. So individual statistics like field-goal percentage or points per game have limited predictive value.

The second, post-*Moneyball* generation of sports analytics has worked to fill this gap by generating the kinds of detailed spatial data that can permit better analysis. Basketball has been at the forefront of this trend, with the National Basketball Association (NBA) installing SportVU tracking systems in each arena. The systems use cameras and image-processing software to generate second-by-second data about where each player and the ball are during a game. (SportVU began in soccer, a sport with its own monetary inequalities that reward efforts to find and exploit inefficiencies.) This provides a set of data so large that teams and others can use it to do complex analyses that wouldn't be possible with simpler data. For instance, SportVU data can be used to examine how a player shoots from each spot on the court, how much a player runs during a game, how a player's game changes over time, whether a player is a good passer, and how effective different players are on the defensive end of the court. Most notably, SportVU data is especially valuable for evaluating defensive play, which is otherwise notoriously hard to quantify. SportVU data lets analysts identify and explore effects from the interaction of multiple players, since there's enough data to infer matchups and isolate those effects.

Basketball is not alone in this analysis; similar spatial-tracking systems are in use or development in baseball, football, soccer, and hockey. In the 2015–2016 National Football League (NFL) season, for instance, players wore real-time tracking beacons that let the league and teams measure how quickly players run and accelerate, when a player becomes fatigued or injured, and what sorts of routes are most effective. The potential uses of this spatial information are limited only by analysts' statistical creativity; some of the work is so new that it's being published in peer-reviewed academic journals, at least when it's not developed by teams that consider it proprietary. (Kirk Goldsberry, for instance, is a geographer who famously published numerous pieces on spatial analytics in sports before leaving the academy to join the San Antonio Spurs.)

Drawing novel insights from data sources like spatial-tracking systems are not the only cutting-edge analytics tools used by leagues and teams; teams are increasingly investigating ways to analyze other aspects of the game. Two notable areas of focus are health and team chemistry. Better understandings of health have long been a holy grail of professional sports: injuries are unpredictable events, yet a team that can avoid them has a substantial competitive advantage. Teams have tackled the problem in two ways. One is to use standard analytics tools to look for patterns that predict when a player is more likely to be injured—investigations that have largely pointed to fatigue. The other is to look for ways to avoid fatigue. Several NBA teams, for instance, use biometric tracking devices during practice, and even outside practice and games, to measure exertion, movement, and sleep. Until recently, teams and leagues had mostly ignored the implications of these tools for medical privacy and contract negotiations; that is starting to change, with the next collective bargaining agreement between the NBA and players' union establishing an advisory committee that will study players' privacy concerns.

Measuring team chemistry may be the most unexpected use of analytics, since the importance of chemistry is often cited as a limitation on the effect analytics can have. But with the right tools, chemistry can be measured and engineered as much as anything else. One key line of research, for instance, looks to teams as social communities with cliques and fault lines dividing different subcommunities—say, pitchers and infielders and outfielders, or Spanish and English and Japanese speakers, or veterans and rookies. This research finds that when players span these subcommunities—when the three Venezuelans play different positions, or when a player speaks multiple languages—the team is more likely to perform well. Baseball teams with extensive overlap win about three extra games compared to teams with not much overlap. That might sound like not much, but to a team it has about the same value as $15 million in free agent signings.

The next analytics frontier may be finding better ways to integrate analytics methods and data throughout a team's management and decision-making structure. Analytic insights are only useful if anyone listens, but many coaches, general managers, and other decision makers have long been resistant to the idea that analytics has anything valuable to offer. Integrating analytic analysis into an organization, then, is an important challenge for teams. This requires several distinct steps. First, data sources need to be combined, checked for errors, and cross-referenced. If a database of college stats contains information for someone named Chris Jones, for instance, while another database of pro stats calls him Christopher Jones, then data analysis is less likely to give useful insights. Second, coaches and general managers need to understand and appreciate the kinds of questions to which analytics can provide answers. This essentially requires a translation step between analytics staffs and the rest of a team's management. And third, coaches and players need to implement the strategies that analytics suggest are most likely to be successful, which requires its own translation process.

Analytics has become a critical part of most professional sports, and there is no reason to think that that trend will reverse itself. This means teams will have to maintain more and more secret information. Professional sports teams have always possessed information that they took pains to keep from competing teams, like playbooks, signal calls, preparations for opposing teams, and so forth. But new information will be increasingly important and increasingly sophisticated, as many of the easiest analytics insights are adopted throughout sports and the marginal benefits come from subtler analyses. This proprietary information will come in several forms. New data sources are an obvious example: if a team invests in tracking players' movements or pitches' arcs or any other new source of data, that provides a valuable leg up over other teams. Insights based on these data sources may be more valuable, since the data itself is becoming increasingly common and commoditized; teams that develop novel strategies to combat a certain kind of play, or learn the kinds of plays an opponent is least likely to be able to stop, have another advantage. And player information, including health information and data-backed assessments, will become more detailed and more granular as they are based on more information and more advanced analytic tools. Teams, then, will have to look for ways to ensure their secret information remains secret.

3. League Rules and Norms

Historically, professional sports teams have mostly relied on a mixed bag of league rules, informal social norms, and unilateral security measures to protect their secret information. In the pre-analytics age, much of this information concerned game strategy: playbooks, signal calls, preparations for opposing teams, and so forth. Playbooks have long been considered sensitive, for instance, and are generally collected by teams when players leave; in recent years many teams have moved to electronic playbooks that can be remote-wiped when a player leaves the team. At the same time, though, these security measures can only do so much, since the information in playbooks becomes publicly known when plays are executed during games and seen by opposing teams and the public. Similarly, play-calling signals can be observed in public, but teams often change them between games—an effective security measure, but one that imposes costs—and leagues have also enacted rules to prevent their interception. And informal conduct norms in some sports frown on collecting certain information about opposing teams. In baseball, for example, there is an unwritten rule against a batter trying to see the catcher's signs and location while batting. But it is a rule with no clear enforcement; and many similar practices are not taboo, like the long-standing practice in football of teams signing players from division rivals for their intel as much as for their play.

Sports analytics is new enough that there is no obvious way to apply this assortment of rules, norms, and security measures. Partly this is because enough time hasn't passed; mixed systems of rules, norms, and unilateral protections develop in path-dependent ways that play out over many years. But mostly this is because many of the kinds of information that are valuable in the analytics age are new, with little parallel in the pre-analytics era. And even when the same kinds of information are at issue, the scope of that information has expanded. Analytics is game-changing (no pun intended) because it allows for better inferences, but that means that information becomes substantially more valuable. The implications of these increased values are unpredictable: teams should have a greater incentive to obtain other teams' information, but the higher stakes may lead leagues to impose anti-spying rules, or may lead teams into a game of high-stakes data chicken backed up by steps to protect the security of proprietary information.

There are at least some reasons to expect teams to try to obtain and exploit this information, seeking new ways to cheat. Teams in both MLB and the NFL have, in recent years, landed in trouble for spying on other teams. In football, the New England Patriots were disciplined by the NFL for videotaping the New York Jets' defensive signal calls during a game; in baseball, the former scouting director of the St. Louis Cardinals was sentenced to forty-six months in federal prison for accessing a database used by the Houston Astros to track trade offers and other internal information. And it is doubtful that these are the only significant instances of spying in the last decade. The Patriots and Cardinals were caught because they were sloppy: the Patriots chose a form of spying that required an employee with a camera to act in view of opposing teams, and the Cardinals (apparently) leaked the Astros' secrets to the press instead of using them. But although there have been rumors of other instances of spying, there would be little way to know if teams were taking similar steps if they did do so without getting caught.

Leagues undoubtedly have the power to ban and punish spying. Such rules, though, are fundamentally harder to enforce than most league rules because the proscribed conduct is much harder to detect. When teams break on-field rules, referees or television cameras can see it; when players break substance-abuse rules, testing can detect it. But when a team hacks into another team's server to see its player evaluations or learn what trades a competitor has offered, there is no inherent means of detection. Even when misconduct is detectable, leagues may be unable to deter or punish it, for any number of reasons. Leagues may not have rules in place banning a category of conduct, or they may have inadequate remedies. Collective action and principal agent problems can also block adequate enforcement, since a league and a team may value secret information differently or a league may have incentives to sweep misconduct under the rug. Social norms between teams could also help deter and punish attempts to obtain another team's information, but they are unlikely to be a sufficient answer. Social norms can be an effective means of regulation in contexts in which property rights, contracts, and other types of legal rules are too cumbersome, inflexible, or otherwise costly. But they depend on a degree of transparency that is unlikely to apply between sports teams. Social norms are enforced through social sanctions, but teams and individuals cannot enforce norms if they are unaware of violations. And social sanctions may be ineffective in professional sports because teams have limited power to affect rival teams off the playing field; for instance, widespread suspicions in the NFL that the New England Patriots routinely bend or break rules do not appear to have hurt the team. General managers are sometimes unwilling to trade with certain teams—like the Houston Rockets or Oakland Athletics—but that may be due less to social sanctions and more to a fear of coming out worse in the trade.

4. Nondisclosure and Noncompete Agreements

When league rules and norms aren't enough to protect a team's secrets, the team may choose to rely on various unilateral measures to do so. The simplest unilateral measure a team can take is to require employees with access to proprietary information to sign nondisclosure or noncompete agreements. These two types of contracts use different mechanisms to protect secrets: nondisclosure agreements prohibit signers from disclosing covered information to third parties, while noncompete agreements prohibit a team's employees from working for a competitor for a fixed period after leaving the team. Both types of contracts, though, have the effect of making it less likely that secrets wind up in a competitor's hands, whether by prohibiting disclosure outright or by prohibiting the most likely mechanism of disclosure.

Nondisclosure agreements are the simpler option but may prove less effective at protecting team information. Nondisclosure agreements are relatively straightforward in structure: they just need to define the scope of the protected information and the employees who are prohibited from disclosing that information. An agreement could prohibit members of a team's analytics staff from disclosing any of the raw data it uses to analyze player performance, or the details of an innovative method of analysis, or any of the conclusions drawn from that analysis. But it can be difficult to detect or prevent some disclosures. If a team concludes, for instance, that a mediocre pitcher would become excellent with minor mechanical tweaks (as the Houston Astros did with Collin McHugh, based on the unusually high spin rate on his curveball), it may be impossible to tell whether another team obtained that information or came to the same assessment based on different data. Even the simple act of attempting to acquire a player from another team can elevate the player's perceived value, on the assumption that the prospective acquirer must see something that other teams are missing.

Noncompete agreements try to solve this detection problem by targeting the most common mechanism by which secrets are disclosed to outsiders: when an employee leaves a job for a new job with a competitor. Because the act of going to work for a competitor is more observable than the act of disclosing information, noncompete agreements can be more resistant to cheating and cheaper to enforce than nondisclosure agreements. Their disadvantages, though, are substantial. Preventing an employee from going to work for a competitor is far more disruptive than prohibiting her from disclosing secrets, since it can affect her basic livelihood. Assuming reasonable bargaining power on both sides of the transaction, then, it should be costlier for an employer to obtain a noncompete agreement, since it would have to compensate the employee for the potential lost income. And in many cases, obtaining a noncompete agreement may be impossible, since some states ban them outright or significantly limit their scope. There may also be nonlegal constraints that make it impossible to obtain a noncompete agreement, since in a relatively small and close-knit industry like professional sports, moves from one team to another can be a common means of learning new skills and advancing in one's career. This can make it politically difficult to demand that new hires sign noncompete agreements.

Neither nondisclosure nor noncompete agreements, then, are likely to completely solve a team's or league's secrecy problems. They can nevertheless be an important part of a comprehensive data strategy. Nondisclosure agreements can be hard to enforce, but when copying is clear, having them in place is necessary for a team to recover from either an employee or a competing team. And having nondisclosure agreements in place also helps demonstrate that a team's secrets are valuable enough to protect legally as trade secrets, as discussed in the next section.

Noncompete agreements also have their proper role. A team might, for instance, insist that an employee with access to especially valuable information sign a noncompete agreement with a "garden leave" provision, which would impose a mandatory paid waiting period before the employee leaves for a competitor. These agreements are more likely to be upheld because many of the legal and policy arguments against noncompete agreements go away if an employee is compensated for the time between jobs; it is hard to argue that someone is deprived of the chance to earn a basic livelihood if he or she earns her normal salary for the time between jobs. And the risk that an employer will require too many employees to sign agreements that are too heavily slanted in its favor goes away if an employer must internalize the cost of preventing employees from working for competitors. Such an employer is more likely to limit noncompete provisions to the most valuable employees and employees with access to the most valuable information.

5. Trade Secrecy

Once a company's secrets have been disclosed to a competitor, trade secrecy may provide an after-the-fact remedy for that disclosure. Like league rules and norms and noncompete and nondisclosure agreements, though, trade secrecy can be an imperfect tool for professional sports teams. For trade secrecy to be an effective tool, teams must think ahead and take steps to protect their investment, since, if they haven't done so before secrets are disclosed, they can wind up without any real remedy.

The economics of trade secrecy are simple. For literally thousands of years, people have relied on secrecy as a form of self-help to protect valuable information, using everything from buried boxes of treasure to passwords and encryption to keep others from taking valuable information or property. Doing so is costly, though, since protecting secrets requires investments in those security measures. Trade secrecy provides a set of legal protections that backs up these self-help efforts with legal force, making it easier to protect valuable secrets without overinvesting in wasteful security measures. Trade secrecy does this by granting a limited form of intellectual property (IP) that protects valuable secrets from misappropriation, a form of IP distinct from the patents, trademarks, and copyrights with which most people are familiar.

A trade secret is any piece of information that is economically valuable due to (1) not being generally known to others who could obtain value from it, and, in most states, (2) not being readily ascertainable by proper means by those who could obtain value from it. (In this chapter, I use "secret" to refer generally to any piece of valuable information that a team wants to keep confidential, and "trade secret" to refer more specifically to a secret that is legally protectable as a trade secret.) A trade secret is legally protected as long as its owner takes reasonable efforts, under the circumstances, to protect the secret. As long as a trade secret is protected, trade-secrecy law provides a remedy against a third party who misappropriates that secret, such as by hacking into a server or hiring a competitor's employee to learn the secret. Unlike with other forms of IP, legal protections for trade secrets are largely tools of state law, not federal, with almost all states having enacted versions of the Uniform Trade Secrets Act. In 2016, though, Congress enacted the federal Defend Trade Secrets Act, which provides a uniform set of federal protections that supplements those provided by state laws.

Unlike other forms of IP, trade secrets can consist of almost any kind of information, as long as that information derives economic value from its secrecy. The scope of trade secrecy, then, can be much broader than patent law (which covers useful inventions), copyright law (which covers creative works like books, music, and art, along with some additional categories like computer software), or trademark law (which covers brands and logos). Classic examples of trade secrets include manufacturing methods, algorithms, marketing plans, customer lists, pricing information—anything a company would want to keep its competitors from getting.

Notably, essentially every kind of secret information a sports team relies on likely qualifies for trade-secret protection. Raw tracking data from games and practices, analytic insights based on that data, algorithms generating those insights, player health information, trade talks with other teams, plans to increase attendance or concession revenue—all this information could be used by a competitor to gain a competitive advantage, and so derives economic value from its secrecy. And although some of it could be generated by other teams—more than one team can generate spatial game data by analyzing game video, for instance—the cost of doing so suggests it is unlikely to be considered "readily ascertainable" by teams. Indeed, in a zero-sum game like professional sports in which success (at least on the field or court) comes at the expense of competitors, keeping secrets becomes especially critical.

Much of the information a team relies on, then, could be legally protected as long as the team takes reasonable steps to maintain its secrecy. And this reasonable-steps requirement is relatively easy for a diligent team to satisfy. The requirement does two things: (1) it helps ensure that information a company seeks to protect actually merits trade-secret protection (because if a firm does nothing to protect a category of information, that suggests the information isn't that valuable), and (2) it helps ensure that the law responds only when information has been wrongfully misappropriated (because if the firm doesn't protect certain information, then it is just as plausible that a competitor obtained that information through no wrongdoing than that the competitor misappropriated it). The amount of protection required depends on the circumstances, but basic security best practices are likely sufficient: teams should use strong encryption, limit information access to employees with legitimate needs, use strong passwords and two-factor authentication, log accesses, even keep especially sensitive information under physical lock and key. Having employee policies that prohibit disclosure and requiring employees to sign nondisclosure agreements likewise help show that a team takes reasonable steps to maintain secrecy.

Though trade secrecy protects a wider variety of information than do other forms of IP, the other side of the coin is that the scope of that protection is far narrower. Other forms of IP give broad exclusive rights: patent law gives an inventor a legal monopoly over an invention that applies even when someone else independently invents the same thing; copyright law governs any copying, regardless of how the copier obtained access; and trademark law provides nationwide notice of exclusive rights, at least for federally registered marks. But trade secrecy protects only against wrongful misappropriation by another. If someone obtains the exact same information through legitimate means, then there's no problem. And there are several legitimate means of obtaining information: independent development (such as by processing game video or scouting opposing teams), reverse engineering (such as by inferring a team's opinions or processes from its actions), or even innocently obtaining information from a third party (such as by reading press reports—even those reporting leaks).

The law of what constitutes a misappropriation is complex, with both states and the federal government supplying governing rules. The Uniform Trade Secrets Act defines several specific actions as misappropriation, including acquiring a trade secret by "improper means," disclosing a trade secret when one is subject to a duty to maintain its secrecy, and knowingly obtaining a trade secret from someone who had such a duty. (Uniform Trade Secrets Act § I(2).) (Federal law uses a functionally identical definition. (18 U.S.C. § 1839(5).) The upshot of all of these forms of misappropriation, though, is fairly simple: efforts by one company to obtain the trade secrets of another company are likely to constitute misappropriation as long as they involve some improper means, like inducing an employee to breach a confidentiality provision, hacking an email server, or committing some sort of fraud. Indeed, nearly all trade-secret cases finding a misappropriation involve some sort of independent legal wrong like a tort, breach of contract, or criminal act; such actions are clearly "improper means." (E.g., *Rockwell Graphic Systems, Inc. v. Dev Industries, Inc.*.)

A team that obtains another team's information through wrongful means, then, would likely be subject to liability for misappropriation of a trade secret. This would include, at a bare minimum, cases like the Cardinals accessing the Astros' private computer server. It could also include more common actions, like a team hiring the employee of another team to learn that team's secrets, when the employee is bound by a nondisclosure agreement. And it's conceivable that it could include actions like the Patriots videotaping other teams' signals, if a court considered a breach of league rules serious enough to constitute misappropriation and if there weren't other ways to acquire the same information.

Trade secrecy, then, might provide a useful tool for teams to protect their secrets—albeit one they may be reluctant to use. That even the Astros, a team that would seem to have a strong misappropriation claim against the Cardinals, hasn't sued suggests that other constraints may keep teams from taking advantage of trade secrecy. These constraints likely arise from league rules and norms. Leagues have reasons to keep disputes in house, since publicly airing dirty laundry might cast doubt on the integrity of the game; this could hurt fan interest and reduce revenues and franchise values. And leagues can readily do so, since they have their own internal sanctions available in the form of lost draft picks, monetary penalties, and so forth. So teams may have little need to use legal remedies like misappropriation lawsuits.

6. Criminal Law

For especially egregious misappropriations, criminal law may provide some relief. Such cases are rare, though. And the benefit to the victim of criminal prosecution is limited, since the main effect of a criminal conviction is prison time for the defendant. But criminal law may provide one substantial benefit: it provides a strong disincentive to take another team's secrets in the first place. There are several different criminal laws, at both the federal and state levels, that could apply to different means of acquiring another team's secrets.

The most clearly relevant criminal statute is the federal Economic Espionage Act of 1996. The Act prohibits various methods of misappropriating trade secrets, including by stealing, fraudulently obtaining, and purchasing secret information. (18 U.S.C. § 1832(a).) The Act would straightforwardly apply to most intentional trade-secret misappropriations: it covers any trade secret that relates to a product or service used in interstate or foreign commerce, which would include secrets kept by professional sports teams and leagues, and it prohibits knowing misappropriations carried out in any of a large variety of specified means. It also contains an intent element: the perpetrator must intend to convert the trade secret to the benefit of someone other than its owner, and intend or know that the owner will be harmed. An effort by one team to take another team's secrets would predictably harm the victim team while benefiting the perpetrator team, so the Act would likely apply to intentional efforts by one team to take another team's secrets. The Act is not often used by prosecutors, though, because of the uncertainty created by the intent element; other, simpler criminal laws are available in most cases.

Of more generally applicable criminal laws, the federal Computer Fraud and Abuse Act is the most important one that teams might rely on to protect their secrets. The Act prohibits unauthorized access of computers in a variety of circumstances, including unauthorized access of a computer used in interstate or foreign commerce. (18 U.S.C. §§ 1030(a)(2)(C), 1030(e)(2)(B).) Accessing a rival team's server by guessing a password, using stolen credentials, or using a software exploit to bypass security measures would almost certainly qualify. And there is a history of using the statute when a team takes another team's secrets: Christopher Correa, the Cardinals' former Director of Baseball Development, pled guilty to five counts of violating the Act for his role in breaking into the Astros' server by guessing a password. The Act is useful only when a team's method of obtaining secrets involves unauthorized access of a computer, but like most businesses, modern professional teams are highly dependent on networked computers and data to operate. So the Act is likely to be useful in many cases in which one team gains illicit access to another team's secrets.

For the Computer Fraud and Abuse Act to apply, a defendant must access a computer "without authorization," a requirement the meaning of which has been hotly debated. It may or may not qualify, for instance, as unauthorized access if someone accesses a computer in violation of an employment policy or website terms of service. This debate could matter in borderline cases. If a team employee violated team policies to download data to a personal flash drive, and only later provided that data to a rival team, it might or might not count as unauthorized access since physical access to the computer was authorized but the scope of the access was not. Similarly, a team that used a third-party vendor to provide data or analytics services and obtained illicit access to a rival team's information through that vendor's computer server has been authorized to access the server, but not to use it to access the rival team's information. (For a good discussion of the many issues raised by this debate, see Kerr (2016).) But any ambiguity is unlikely to matter in the mine-run case, since an employee of one team will almost never have the authority to access another team's systems.

Various other criminal laws could apply when a team takes a rival team's secrets, depending on the means employed:

- Mail- and wire-fraud statutes ban the use of the mail or most telecommunications services to commit fraud or obtain another's property or money. 18 U.S.C. §§ 1341, 1343. These statutes could apply to efforts to obtain another team's trade secrets, for instance by gaining access to a team's secrets stored on computer servers run by a cloud service provider. The mail- and wire-fraud statutes could also apply to efforts to bribe another team's employee to reveal secrets or work as a double agent, as a scheme to deprive an employer of an employee's "honest services." (18 U.S.C. § 1346)
- A team that made it a practice of seeking other teams' trade secrets could conceivably even run afoul of the Racketeer Influenced and Corrupt Organizations (RICO) Act, which provides enhanced penalties when someone commits more than one of a specified list of crimes in connection with a corrupt "enterprise." (18 U.S.C. §§ 1961 et seq.) Notably, mail and wire fraud are included in the list of predicate offenses. RICO prosecutions are uncommon, and the law is unlikely to be the first concern of a team accused of stealing trade secrets. But it could come into play if a team, or a part of a team's organization, repeatedly obtained another team's trade secrets. Most notably, since 2015 numerous officials of FIFA (Fédération Internationale de

Football Association) have been prosecuted for RICO violations, albeit for taking bribes rather than anything involving trade secrets.

- Though federal law enforcement agencies are likely to be involved in economic crimes committed between teams located in different states, state criminal laws can also apply to acts to misappropriate trade secrets. Many states have analog laws to the federal laws discussed previously. Additionally, traditional state crimes like larceny could apply to trade-secret misappropriation. Under the common law of larceny, the stolen property must be tangible personal property, which would not cover theft of a trade secret (though would cover theft of, say, a laptop computer containing trade secrets). In many (but not all) states, though, larceny statutes are broad enough to cover theft of intangible property like trade secrets. In those states, such laws could be used to prosecute a team or employee who took another team's trade secrets.

Criminal law can be a powerful tool after a secret has been taken and, because criminal penalties are a strong deterrent, before as well. It is only useful, though, if the victim knows about the crime; had the Cardinals never leaked the Astros' secrets to the press, the fact that they obtained those secrets may never have been detected. And when criminal law can be used, it comes at some cost. Because criminal investigation and prosecution are in the hands of law enforcement agents and prosecutors instead of private lawyers, teams must give up a lot of control. This means meeting and cooperating with investigators and prosecutors; handing secrets over to them and, potentially, the public; and ignoring a large distraction, both inside and outside the team. In many cases, then, a team may conclude that the benefits of prosecution do not outweigh the costs, weakening the deterrent effect of criminal prosecution in the first place.

7. Information Security

Most of the time, the legal remedies discussed previously are not perfect solutions; indeed, in many cases they may be effectively worthless. That leaves, then, the option of preventing secrets from being taken in the first place. To do this, teams should implement effective information-security measures to protect their secrets. There are two components of an effective security system: technical measures and human factors.

On the technical side, teams should implement robust security systems to prevent intruders from gaining access to secrets. The details of effective security technologies are well beyond the scope of this chapter, since best practices evolve quickly and the details depend greatly on the specifics of a team's situation and needs. But there are several basic components of such a system. Teams should maintain information using up-to-date encryption and give access only to those who need it. When possible (though it may not be possible in many circumstances), teams should use systems that aren't connected to the Internet. Teams should use individual authentication instead of common passwords so that access can be revoked and should maintain access logs and periodically examine those logs so they can detect intrusions. Teams should use two-factor authentication or hardware token authentication instead of relying solely on passwords. And teams should use modern software systems and regularly and promptly update those systems with security updates and bug fixes. Most important, teams should hire specialists to keep their systems maintained and updated as best practices evolve. This is a partial list, but even this much is more than many businesses do to protect their secrets.

Human factors are as important as technical measures and require each team to instill a culture of security throughout the organization. Sometimes a security breach happens because an intruder gains access by using some technical exploit, but just as often the weak link is a human. This can happen when a user clicks on a malicious URL in a phishing email, opens a booby-trapped email attachment, visits a website that installs a piece of malware, or inadvertently reveals information to a caller or social network user exploiting social engineering techniques. Some of these attack vectors can be blocked using effective security software, but not all of them or all the time. Training, then, is critical. Employees throughout an organization need to know how to use and maintain security systems, how to avoid becoming victim to a phishing attack, and how not to inadvertently reveal secret information to an intruder, among other things. This sort of training is still relatively rare, but it is becoming more common as companies in numerous industries discover the importance of human factors in information security.

Information security is far from a team's core competency; for as culturally important as they are, professional sports teams are, in the grand scheme of things, fairly small businesses with limited expertise in information technologies. Nevertheless, teams should be able to get sufficiently up to speed on security to protect their trade secrets, for a couple of reasons. One is that businesses are starting to tackle the problem of building off-the-shelf, scalable security apparatuses that can be installed throughout an organization. Security is difficult today, but like a lot of other information technologies, it should become more user-friendly over time as standard tools become widespread. And the other is that the threat models are relatively limited. Most big companies need to guard against a lot of different threats: industrial espionage; thieves seizing customer data to sell on the black market; hackers installing ransomware to extract ransom payments; even nation-state actors like North Korea's hack of Sony Pictures. But with teams, there are just two big threat models. One is other teams conducting espionage, but just as teams aren't that sophisticated about their own security, they probably aren't that sophisticated about how to spy on their competitors. So basic security measures may be enough to foreclose that threat model. The other is professional gamblers seeking an inside edge before placing bets; this may be a more likely threat to come to pass. But the consequences of such a security breach are less immediate for teams, since the costs are borne by casinos and other outsiders, so the threat of criminal prosecution may be enough to protect teams' interests.

8. Conclusion: The Future of Information and Sports Analytics

Sports is an old-fashioned, tradition-bound industry full of close-knit relationships between repeat players, but it is also a zero-sum game. Every time two teams play, one wins and one loses (setting aside the rare tie). Every season, one team wins the title and the rest come up short. And so for a team to do better, it needs to get better players than other teams (by making more-efficient draft picks and free-agent signings) and get more out of those players (by keeping them healthy, improving their skills, and playing them in the right spots). All these things are made easier by analytics. In an industry in which the Boston Red Sox and Chicago Cubs broke 86- and 108-year-old curses by hiring the same analytics-minded leadership, the debate over the value of statistics is over; the quantitative side won, and the only question is how far they can go.

In such a zero-sum game, there is a constant pressure to get better at the expense of others. Without reasons for a team to respect other teams' secrets, we should expect that pressure to lead teams, at least some of the time, to try to discover other teams' secrets. If this prediction comes to pass, then the Cardinals' hack of the Astros' database and the Patriots' videotaping of opponents may just be the tip of the iceberg, with teams that are better at keeping secrets (or just luckier) getting away with it when they spy on rival teams. And in response, we should expect teams and leagues to make greater efforts to protect their secrets, with teams spending more time and money on security and leagues coming down hard on teams that get caught. This sort of arms race is far from unique to sports; firms in nearly every industry have dealt with outside intruders by beefing up their security measures, though in other industries those intrusions come as often in the form of malicious hacks as in the form of industrial espionage.

The tools discussed in this chapter, then, are key pieces of a system of incentives for teams to respect others' secrets. League rule and norms, nondisclosure and noncompete agreements, trade secrecy, criminal law, and security efforts all make it harder, costlier, or both to take another team's secrets. League rules and norms, trade secrecy, and criminal law all impose sanctions, whether legal or social, for security breaches. And nondisclosure and noncompete agreements, along with information security, try to prevent breaches from happening in the first place. None of these tools are perfect; there is room for each of them to play a role. But with data and secrets becoming increasingly important to sports, like most industries, we should expect that the competitive pressure to use that data will only increase.

Acknowledgments

Roger Allan Ford thanks Alexandra Roberts, Jennifer Berk, Mike McCann, and Nicholson Price; the panelists at a University of New Hampshire Sports & Entertainment Law Society forum on Protecting Secrets in Sports & Entertainment, Bob Ryan, Mandy Petrillo, Mark Szpak, and Sean Smith; and participants at the tenth MIT Sloan Sports Analytics Conference and the Franklin Pierce Center for Intellectual Property's fifth IP Roundtable. Nicholas Danforth provided outstanding research assistance.

References

Alamar, B. C. (2013). *Sports Analytics: A Guide for Coaches, Managers, and Other Decision Makers* (New York: Columbia University Press).

Anderson, C. (2013). *The Numbers Game: Why Everything You Know About Soccer Is Wrong* (New York: Penguin).

Berger, K. (2015, June 3). *Warriors 'wearable'" weapon? Devices to monitor players while on the court.* CBS Sports, www.cbssports.com/nba/writer/ken-berger/25203846/warriors-wearable-weapon-devices-to-monitor-players-while-on-the-court.

Bryant, H. (2010, January 15). *The Revolutionary.* ESPN, http://sports.espn.go.com/espn/otl/columns/story?columnist=bryant_howard&id=4357166.

Cook, E. (1964). *Percentage Baseball* (Baltimore: Waverly Press).

Davenport, T. H. (2014). *Analytics in Sports: The New Science of Winning*, SAS/International Institute for Analytics Whitepaper, www.sas.com/content/dam/SAS/en_us/doc/whitepaper2/iia-analytics-in-sports-106993.pdf.

Franks, A., Miller, A., Bornn, L. & Goldsberry, K. (2015a). "Characterizing the Spatial Structure of Defensive Skill in Professional Basketball." *Annals of Applied Statistics* 9: 94.

Franks, A., Miller, A., Bornn, L. & Goldsberry, K. (2015b, February 27–28). *Counterpoints: Advanced Defensive Metrics for NBA Basketball*, MIT Sloan Sports Analytics Conference, www.sloansportsconference.com/?p=15794.

Goldsberry, K. (2013, March 29). *The Evolution of King James*, Grantland, http://grantland.com/features/how-lebron-james-transformed-game-become-highly-efficient-scoring-machine/.

Goldsberry, K. (2015, February 24). *Department of Defense*, Grantland, http://grantland.com/features/department-of-defense/.

James, B. (1977). *Baseball Abstract: Featuring 18 Categories of Statistical Information that you Just Can't Find Anywhere Else* (Lawrence, Kansas: Self-Published).

Jazayerli, R. (2016, November 3). *The Curious Have Won*, The Ringer, https://theringer.com/2016-world-series-chicago-cubs-theo-epstein-analytics-war-9f1248c44eb7.

Kerr, O. S. (2013). *Computer Crime Law* (3rd ed.) (Eagan, Minn.: West).

Kerr, O. S. (2016). "Norms of Computer Trespass." *Columbia Law Review* 116: 1143.

Leitch, W. (2015). "The Cardinals' Hacking Scandal Has Brought Sports into the Surveillance Era." *New York Magazine*, July 13, http://nymag.com/daily/intelligencer/2015/07/cardinals-hacking-scandal.html.

Lewis, M. (2003). *Moneyball: The Art of Winning an Unfair Game* (New York: W.W. Norton).

Lewis, M. (2009). "The No-Stats All-Star.", *New York Times Magazine*, February 13.

Lowe, Z. (2013, March 19). "Lights, Cameras, Revolution." *Grantland*, http://grantland.com/features/the-toronto-raptors-sportvu-cameras-nba-analytical-revolution/.

Lowe, Z. (2015, September 17). "From BMI to TMI: The NBA Is Leaning Toward Wearable Tech." *Grantland*, http://grantland.com/the-triangle/from-bmi-to-tmi-the-nba-is-leaning-toward-wearable-tech/.

Maxcy, J. G., & Drayer, J. (2014). "Sports Analytics: Advancing Decision Making Through Technology and Data." *IBIT Report*, http://ibit.temple.edu/blog/2014/04/13/sports-analytics-advancing-decision-making-through-technology-and-data/.

Miller, S. (2013, October 26). "The Happiness Project." *ESPN Magazine*, http://espn.go.com/mlb/story/_/id/9749026/oakland-athletics-success-due-player-chemistry-not-metrics-espn-magazine.

Paine, N. (2014, June 12). "What Analytics Can Teach Us About the Beautiful Game." *FiveThirtyEight*, http://fivethirtyeight.com/features/what-analytics-can-teach-us-about-the-beautiful-game/.

Petchesky, B. (2014, June 30). "Leaked: 10 Months of the Houston Astros' Internal Trade Talks," *Deadspin*, http://deadspin.com/leaked-10-months-of-the-houston-astros-internal-trade-1597951970.

Rowe, E. A., and Sandeen, S. K. (2017). *Trade Secret Law: Cases and Materials* (2nd ed.) (Eagan, Minn: West).

Torre, P. S., & Haberstroh, T. (2014, October 27). "New Biometric Tests Invade the NBA." *ESPN Magazine*, available at http://espn.go.com/nba/story/_/id/11629773/new-nba-biological-testing-less-michael-lewis-more-george-orwell.

Twilley, N. (2015, September 10). "How Will Real-Time Tracking Change the N.F.L.?," *New Yorker*, www.newyorker.com/news/sporting-scene/how-will-real-time-tracking-change-the-n-f-l.

Wagner, K. (2014, March 7). "Two Days At Sloan: How Sports Analytics Got Lost in the Fog," *Deadspin*, http://regressing.deadspin.com/two-days-at-sloan-how-sports-analytics-got-lost-in-the-1535046292.

Wagner, K. (2015, February 27). "'Sports Analytics' Is Bullshit Now." *Deadspin*, http://regressing.deadspin.com/sports-analytics-is-bullshit-now-1688293396.

Winston, W. L. (2009). *Mathletics: How Gamblers, Managers, and Sports Enthusiasts Use Mathematics in Baseball, Basketball, and Football* (Princeton, N.J.: Princeton University Press).

Cases

Rockwell Graphic Sys., Inc. v. Dev Indus., Inc., 925 F.2d 174 (7th Cir. 1991) (Posner, J.).

Skilling v. United States, 561 U.S. 358 (2010).

Statutes

18 U.S.C. §§ 1341, 1343, 1346 (prohibiting mail and wire fraud).

Computer Fraud and Abuse Act of 1986, codified as amended at 18 U.S.C. § 1030.

Defend Trade Secrets Act of 2016, codified at 18 U.S.C. § 1836.

Economic Espionage Act of 1996, codified as amended at 18 U.S.C. § 1831 *et seq*.

National Conference of Commissioners on Uniform State Laws, Uniform Trade Secrets Act with 1985 Amendments.

CHAPTER 26

THE ROLE OF BIOETHICS IN SPORTS LAW

ALAN MILSTEIN

1. Introduction

Bioethics, as the name suggests, is the application of ethical principles to life's critical biological choices, with particular focus on how advances in the biological sciences may impact those choices. It is not so much an area of law as it is a discipline that crosses a variety of fields. Bioethicists can be not only lawyers and law professors but philosophers, physicians, and clergy. Bioethicists ask questions that do not always have answers; indeed, they often question whether the answers themselves are relative to time and place and context. What is right in the world of sports may or may not be right outside the arena. But the sports world is often a good laboratory for issues that perplex society as a whole.

As with most of life's controversies, when disputes arise as to the questions bioethicists ask, judges may provide the answers to those questions based on the value both the law and the community place on concepts such as individual autonomy, the sanctity of life, the greater good, and human dignity. Because sports is by its nature an exploration into the limits of human physical potential, bioethics has played and will continue to play an ever-increasing role in sports law.

2. The Role of the Team Doctor

In virtually every organized sport, a physician is required to be present during the practices as well as the contests. For example, Article 39 of the National Football League's collective bargaining agreement (CBA) expressly obligates each club to carry a board-certified orthopedist and either a board-certified internist or a physician specializing in one other relevant field. In addition, while the CBA requires hiring the physician to be "the responsibility of the club," it states that the physician's duty with respect to care, confidentiality, and disclosure shall be to the player.

Such language, however, may not solve all potential conflicts of interest. Consider a soccer match in England between Chelsea and Swansea. After being tripped, Belgian Chelsea player Eden Hazard lay on the grass writhing in pain. Team doctor Eva Carneiro felt ethically bound to run out to attend to what looked like a serious injury, which meant Hazard could not return to the field. Consequently, Chelsea was left one player short for the rest of the contest, which ended in a 2-2 tie. After the game, Chelsea's manager, Jose Mourinho, was not happy, commenting that the physician was "impulsive and naïve" and "did not understand the game." He then announced Dr. Carneiro would not be on the sidelines in the upcoming match against Manchester (BBC, 2016).

As this incident makes clear, the role of the team physician is rife with conflicts of interests. Who is his or her master? The doctor is hired by the team but theoretically has a doctor-patient fiduciary relationship with each player he or she treats. Coaches may believe, as Vince Lombardi famously said, that "winning is the only thing." Owners, however, may want to protect their investment and not risk a valuable asset. This is particularly true at a time when a trade is imminent. Further, the player may want to avoid risk at a given moment to keep his own salary value high for the next contract or he may want to conceal an injury from his coach and teammates. To whom or to what can the physician turn in such circumstances?

One choice might be the Code of Medical Ethics, propounded by the American Medical Association. Opinion 10.03 provides that the physician employed by a company, which would include a professional sports team, must "(1) Evaluate objectively the patient's health or disability" and not be "influenced by the preferences of the patient-employee, (or) employer," and has a responsibility to "inform the patient about important health information or abnormalities that he or she discovers during the course of the examination" (AMA Code, 2001).

At bottom, the team physician must conform to the standard of care of any doctor treating a patient with a similar injury, regardless of the urgency of the competition. The physician's duty is primarily to the player, with one caveat. This duty includes the following ethical obligations:

1. Assess properly the athlete's condition;
2. Provide the player with full disclosure as to the nature and extent of his injuries and the risks of continuing to play;
3. Aim to protect athletes from injury, reinjury, or permanent disability; and, generally,
4. Practice good medicine consistent with the standard of care.

The caveat is this: While physician-patient confidentiality still exists with respect to treatment that has no impact on the player's ability to perform, if it would have such impact either presently or in the future, the team physician may also have a duty to disclose the nature of the player's injury to the team so that all parties can make a decision as to whether the player should play, rest, or be put on the disabled list. In addition, league rules may require disclosure of a player's injury to the public and other teams.

Courts have had varying responses to the issue of what duties teams and their physicians owe with regard to a player's health. Most courts agree that a special duty exists between the team and the athlete. With respect to professional sports, that duty is specifically defined by the athlete's individual player contract as well as the CBA. But colleges and high schools also have a special duty to their athletes over and above the duties owed to the student population as a whole.

In *Kleinknecht v. Gettysburgh College*, a lacrosse player suffered cardiac arrest during practice. No trainer or physician was present, nor did anyone present have CPR training. In the days before cell phones were omnipresent, the coach did not even have a radio and the nearest phone was two fields away over an eight-foot fence. Kleinknecht died before the ambulance even arrived. In denying the motion to dismiss, the Court of Appeals for the Third Circuit concluded that colleges owed an athlete "a duty of care in his capacity as an intercollegiate athlete engaged in school sponsored intercollegiate athletic activity for which he had been recruited" (3d Cir op: p1369).

With respect to the specific duties owed by team physicians, the case of *Krueger v. San Francisco Forty Niners*, is quite instructive. After he retired, Charlie Krueger sued his former team, alleging that its physicians had concealed the true nature of his knee injuries and the potential adverse effects of the steroid injections he was given to keep him in the game. Krueger insisted that this substandard care resulted in his suffering traumatic arthritis and a crippling degenerative knee condition. The court observed:

> In its desire to keep (Krueger) on the playing field, (the 49ers) consciously failed to make full, meaningful disclosure to him respecting the magnitude of the risk he took in continuing to play a violent contact sport with a profoundly damaged left knee (p584).

The team argued that its physicians did not misrepresent the risks of continuing to play; they simply did not tell him what those risks were. This, the court said, was not sufficient given the ethical duties of a physician to his patient. The court stated:

> A physician cannot avoid responsibility for failure to make full disclosure by simply claiming that information was not withheld (p583).

With respect to the defense that Krueger was making his own choices, the court cogently responded:

> (Krueger) demonstrated throughout his football career a courageous—some might say foolhardy—willingness to endure pain and injuries for the sake of his team and employer, but no credible evidence suggests that he ever assessed and accepted the prospect of permanent disability (p584–585).

Other players did not fare so well in the courts, though the cases were a harbinger of things to come. In *Zimbauer v. Milwaukee Orthopaedic Group*, the court dismissed the claim of a Milwaukee Brewers pitcher that the team physician failed to properly diagnose and treat his shoulder injury, holding that "plaintiff's occupation as a pitcher invoked particular concerns that fall within the specialized realm of sports medicine: the appropriate level of pain the plaintiff could expect to experience and physical therapy tailored to his profession as a major league pitcher" p965. In *Stringer v National Football League* (2007), the court dismissed the complaint of the Estate of Korey Stringer, who died of heat stroke during Minnesota Vikings training camp. The court concluded that the claim that the team and its physicians had a duty "to use ordinary care in overseeing, controlling and regulating practices . . . to minimize the risk of heat-related injuries" (p687) was preempted by Section 301 of the Labor Management Relations Act of 1947, also known as the Taft-Hartley Act. Chicago Bear linebacker Richard Dent's suit was also dismissed on preemption grounds. In what some called the "drug pushing class action," Dent had claimed team doctors and trainers had given him and other players thousands of injections and pills to keep them playing while they concealed dangers of repeated drug use. The court stated,

> No decision in any state (including California) has ever held that a professional sports league owed such a duty to intervene and stop mistreatment by the league's independent clubs and that it was only through the CBAs (that) players' medical rights have steadily expanded.
>
> (*Dent v. National Football League*, 2014 U.S. Dist. LEXIS 174448).

Such a view was soon to change as a result of the various class actions brought by retired National Football League (NFL) players suffering from long-term brain injury, called chronic traumatic encephalopathy (CTE) as a result of concussive and subconcussive head injuries experienced both in games and practice. The players claimed the league as well as team physicians and trainers understood what the long-term impact was of such injuries and fraudulently concealed it from the players. Perhaps even more egregiously, the players contended that the NFL contributed to false and errantly researched scientific literature, which had the effect of misleading the public as to the risk of anyone playing or allowing their children to play sports where the chance of concussive injuries is significant (*Brody* (2014)).

The players argued that, as the medical community grew concerned about the long-term effects of head injuries in contact sports, the NFL created the Mild Traumatic Brain Injury Committee (MTBI) to obfuscate the connection between head injuries and CTE, a connection the scientific community as well as the league knew then and now accepts as fact. The MTBI was purportedly composed of independent researchers and physicians but arranged for the publication of ghost-written and at times demonstrably false articles in medical journals. The NFL ultimately settled the cases for approximately $1 billion to cover the care of 20,000 retired players over the next sixty-five years (*Brody*

(2014)). Concussion litigation involving other sports and sports organizations will likely have similar results.

What is clear from these cases and the billion-dollar NFL settlement is that teams and their physicians and trainers have not just an ethical but a legal obligation to disclose to the players under their care the full nature of any injury they suffer, to provide treatment consistent with the standard of care irrespective of the exigencies of competition, and to disclose the risks of any such treatment as well as of returning to the field of play.

3. Performance-Enhancing Therapies

New technologies have always played a role in the advancement of athletic achievement. Everything from the playing surface to a player's clothing and shoes to the equipment used to strike the balls to the makeup of the balls themselves to advances in training equipment have allowed athletes to run faster, jump higher, hit further, and endure greater. Advances in medical therapies have had no less an impact, though not without considerable if not uneven controversy.

Near the end of the 1974 baseball season, Dodger left-hander Tommy John heard his arm snap after throwing a pitch and knew he had torn a ligament in his elbow, an injury that ended most pitching careers. Fortunately for John, the Dodgers employed orthopedic surgeon Frank Jobe as a special consultant. With John's consent, Jobe snipped a six-inch tendon from the pitcher's right arm and wove it through holes he made in John's elbow to replace the ligament destroyed by a career of overuse. It worked so well for John that Pete Rose remarked: "I know they had to give Tommy John a new arm. But did they have to give him Koufax's?" (LA Times, 1989). Since then, fully a third of major league pitchers have undergone ulnar collateral ligament (UCL) reconstruction, what is now known as "Tommy John surgery." Absent a patient's need to be able to pitch a baseball at the major league level, however, one cannot imagine any physician performing such a procedure.

Another surgical innovation impacting performance in sports, though one the general public also enjoys, is Laser-Assisted in Situ Keratomileusis, or Lasik for short. In a procedure that takes about an hour, the surgeon creates a thin flap in the cornea using a laser, folds it back, removes corneal tissue, and lays the flap back in place.

The first and most prominent athlete to take advantage of the procedure was Tiger Woods in the fall of 1999. Prior to the surgery, Woods had not finished first in sixteen straight events; afterward, he won seven of the next ten including the Masters. Dr. Mark Whitten, Woods's eye surgeon, has said of the surgery "Golfers get a different three-dimensional view of the green after Lasik (and) can see the grain . . . small indentations. It's different. Lasik actually produces, instead of a spherical cornea, an aspherical cornea. It may be better than normal vision" (Slate, 2005).

Not to be outdone, a number of golfers soon underwent the procedure, as did numerous players in virtually every sport where better than 20/20 vision is an advantage, even some who did not have impaired vision and for whom Lasik surgery was not medically indicated (Slate, 2005).

Without question surgeries such as that performed on Tommy John and Tiger Woods are performance enhancing, as are new training techniques to improve cardiovascular conditioning and muscle tone, specialized diets, and dietary supplements. So why the obsession with performance-enhancing drugs (PEDs)?

The use of elixirs thought to be performance enhancing is not confined to the current era. As far back as the Ancient Greek Olympic Games, athletes brewed a tea to improve their strength and endurance made of crushed animal testicles—in other words, testosterone tea, though nutritionists today consider ingesting crushed testicles an inefficient means of boosting testosterone levels (Yesalis and Barke, 2002).

What the Ninth Circuit, in reviewing the conviction of Barry Bonds, called "the Steroid Era" (*United States v. Bonds*) really began in 1889 with French American physician Charles Brown-Sequard, known as the Father of Endocrinology. This branch of medicine deals with the body's system of endocrine glands, its diseases, and its production of hormones. That year Brown-Sequard developed an animal testosterone mixture, which he tested first on himself and later on James "Pud" Galvin, baseball's first 300-game winner for the Pittsburgh Alleghenys (now the Pirates) and the St. Louis Browns (now the Baltimore Orioles). In his first game after becoming a human research subject, Gavin pitched a complete game shutout and excelled at the plate to the cheers of the crowd and the local media. Shortly after the public learned of Brown-Sequard's potion, the *New Haven Register* announced: "The discovery of a true elixir of youth by which the aged can restore their vitality and renew their bodily vigor would be a great thing for baseball nines. We hope the discovery . . . is of such a nature that it can be applied to rejuvenate provincial clubs" (Pud Galvin, 1889).

Compare that sentiment to an editorial appearing in the same newspaper more than 100 years later during the 2016 Rio games. In a piece titled "Shaming could be the best fix for Olympic Doping," the legal scholar Cass Sunstein asks:

> Will it work? The challenge is that here, as elsewhere, people's behavior is a product of numerous incentives, not just one. A spot in the Olympics, or a shot at gold, can be hard to resist; if a drug really would make the difference, some athletes will always be tempted. In these circumstances, it's not entirely pleasant to see Olympic gold medalists acting as village elders or self-appointed drug police—but if we want a level playing field in the future, it's probably a good idea.
>
> (Rio, 2016)

Gavin, the first baseball player to experiment with what today are called PEDs, was easily voted into the Hall of Fame. The same, of course, cannot be said of more recent PED users who include the game's all-time home run leader, arguably its best right-handed pitcher and numerous other stars whose career numbers would otherwise have ensured enshrinement in the Hall.

The most common PEDs fall into three main categories. The first and perhaps most notorious are anabolic steroids or, more accurately, anabolic-androgenic steroids (AAS). These are laboratory-produced derivatives of the hormone testosterone, far more effective at building muscle, called an anabolic effect, than crushed testicle tea. Such steroids are different than corticosteroids, those steroids typically prescribed to the general public to treat inflammatory, immunological and allergic conditions (Fahey, 1998).

Whether ingested or injected, AAS attach to androgen receptors of muscle cells promoting muscle growth, regeneration, and repair. AAS may also reduce muscle soreness associated with strenuous physical exercise, enabling the athlete to work harder to achieve his or her goals. Under the Controlled Substances Act (21 U.S.C. §§ 801 et seq.), they are a Class III drug, meaning they can only be obtained with a physician's prescription, and have a currently acceptable medical use and a potential for abuse. Like many drugs, AAS pose a risk of side effects, some quite serious, including liver and heart damage, as well as psychiatric and sexual dysfunction.

A related substance favored by some athletes is human growth hormone (HGH). Growth hormones, made up of 190 amino acids, occur naturally in the body and are produced by the pituitary gland. They spur the liver production of the hormone called "insulin-like growth factor-1" (IGF-1). Together, these hormones regulate the growth of muscles, bones, and other organs through cell multiplication. Physicians prescribe synthetically produced HGH to treat mostly growth-related disorders in children and adolescents. Advertised by proponents as "the Fountain of Youth," the drugs have been used by athletes who believe they help them not just repair their injured bones but keep them young (Saugy et al., 2006).

Like steroids, the use of HGH carries risk because too much HGH is as bad as too little and can increase the risk of disease and lead to conditions such as bone deformities, arthritis, vision problems, and heart failure.

The third most common PED is blood doping or the artificially induced means of increasing the blood's ability to bring oxygen to muscles. This is accomplished in one of three ways. Before a competition or practice, an athlete can get an autologous transfusion of his or her own blood removed and stored for later use, or a homologous transfusion of the blood of someone else with the same blood type. The third type of blood doping, and the easiest to detect, is the injection of synthetically produced erythropoietin or EPO, a hormone naturally produced by the kidney that regulates the production of red blood cells (FIFA, 2004).

Each of these methods increases the amount of the body's hemoglobin, the protein that transports oxygen in the blood to the muscles. When athletes are engaged in long-distance events such as bicycling or marathons, they tire as the heart struggles to continue to deliver blood-carrying oxygen to the muscles. Boosting the concentration of hemoglobin and blood mass slows muscle fatigue and improves stamina.

Blood doping, too, is not without its risks. Artificially increasing the number of red blood cells when no increase is warranted may end up damaging the heart, thickening the blood, and increasing the chance of a heart attack, stroke, phlebitis, or pulmonary embolism.

In the 1980 Moscow Olympics, before blood doping was banned, trainers transfused Finnish long-distance runner Kaarlo Maanika with two pints of blood and he went on to win two medals in the five and ten-kilometer races. After the 1984 Los Angeles games where the U.S. cycling team won nine medals—the first medals won since 1912—the team revealed that a full third of its athletes had received autologous transfusions before their races. It seemed clear blood doping helped athletes endure the grind of long-distance competition and improved performance.

The next year, the International Olympic Committee banned blood doping, though no test was available at the time, and other sports organizations soon followed suit. In 1999, the United States Olympic Committee (USOC) formed the United States Anti-Doping Agency (USADA) to test and police the use of blood doping in sports. Its most famous action was to strip Lance Armstrong, the world's most well-known cyclist, of his seven consecutive Tour de France titles. Armstrong sued the USADA, alleging it had no jurisdiction over him because he had retired and that its actions violated his right to due process; the court dismissed the suit, holding most of Armstrong's claims were pre-empted by "The Sports Act" establishing the USOC (*Armstrong v. Tygart*).

All of the major professional leagues and athletic organizations now employ policies restricting the use of these PEDs and numerous other drugs which found their way on an ever-growing list of banned pharmaceuticals. The names of world-class athletes sanctioned for their use is legion. As the 2007 Mitchell Report to the Commissioner of Baseball explained, it is wrong to assert that baseball had not outlawed these substances until 2002, when the league and the players agreed on a testing protocol. To the contrary, the league had since 1971 "prohibited the use of any prescription medication without a valid prescription" (Mitchell Report, 2007). One bioethical inquiry is whether such substances should be banned with a prescription and under a doctor's supervision, since they undoubtedly have a therapeutic use and might be administered safely under a physician's supervision. After all, is this not a matter of personal choice and decision making?

Policymakers have asserted several arguments to support aggressive testing and policing of the use of PEDs with or without prescriptions: (1) these substances are detrimental to the health of athlete; (2) the use of these substances by some coerce others to use them as well; (3) the use by athletes who are role models will encourage aspiring young athletes to use them; and (4) such performance enhancers cheapen the achievements and records of the past and make it impossible to make a fair comparison of athletes of different eras. Some of these reasons are more convincing than others, but all are undercut by too broad of a brush in their implementation or by their failure to achieve the stated goals.

The most persuasive justification is the concern for player health and the health of youngsters who believe they must use these substances if they are to achieve their goals. Athletes and their admirers certainly should be discouraged from using prescription drugs without a prescription and thus not under a doctor's supervision. Evidence suggests that when players use AAS, HGH, or other PEDs, they use them in doses far beyond what has been suggested by their manufacturer and beyond what has been clinically proven as safe. In addition, athletes have been known to "stack" these substances in an attempt to find the perfect combination to enhance their performance.

But what if a physician prescribes a safe dose of a PED and closely observes the player for any adverse effects? That would eliminate any concern for the player's health. What if a player has been diagnosed ADHD and prescribed Ritalin or Adderall, both of which are on the banned substance list?

Consider the case of Robert Mathis of the Indianapolis Colts and one of the top linebackers in the NFL. He and his wife already had three children but they wanted a fourth grandchild for Mathis's mother after she was diagnosed with stage four cancer. The couple sought the assistance of Atlanta fertility doctor Steven Morgenstern, who prescribed the drug Clomiphene, better known by its trade name Clomid, a selective estrogen receptor modulator (SERM). The drug is on the NFL's banned substance list because it increases testosterone. Clomid is by far the most widely prescribed fertility drug for women and is also prescribed off-label for men. The theory is that if you lower the body's production of estrogen you increase the production of testosterone and sperm counts rise. As soon as Ms. Mathis became pregnant, her husband went off the drug. But a random NFL drug test detected the presence of Clomiphene, which stays in the body for some time after discontinuation, resulting in a four-game suspension for the expectant father.

Is any drug that increases testosterone levels a performance-enhancing drug? Does it matter if the purpose for taking the drug is not performance on the field but at that most critical of human physical endeavors: making babies?

In a written statement, the NFL explained:

> A cornerstone of the program is that a player is responsible for what is in his body. Consistent application of the policy's procedures is critical to the integrity of the program.
>
> (NFL, 2014)

The league says players should check with it before taking any substance prescribed by a physician. Indeed, the NFL rules provide for a therapeutic use exception (TUE), but a player must first apply with his physician for the right to take a banned substance for therapeutic reasons. Mathis says he never thought whether a fertility drug could be on the banned list and the doctor says he, too, never made the connection. In what job, however, does anyone have to share such personal and private matters with his employers? Should not the decision to have a child under difficult circumstances remain a personal matter even for NFL linebackers?

Another drug that raises interesting bioethical questions is propranolol. This FDA-approved drug is a beta-adrenergic blocking agent that works by inhibiting the effects of the hormone epinephrine, otherwise known as adrenaline. As a beta-blocker, it is safe and effective and has long been proscribed to treat high blood pressure. Because it keeps the heart from racing without any sedative effect, even in the most stressful of circumstances, it soon became known as the "stage fright" drug, prescribed off-label by physicians for patients who were public speakers, actors, musical performers, even surgeons.

Before 2008, when the drug was banned by the IOC (International Olympic Committee), the PGA (Professional Golf Association), and the LPGA (Ladies Professional Golf Association), it was also a favorite of professional golfers wanting to cure what putters called the "yips" as well as of archers and sharpshooters for similar reasons. No one complains if a surgeon has steady hands as a result of a prescription drug, or if an actor or musician can perform beautifully without feeling her heart is about to pop out of her chest. Why restrict the athlete from performing at his or her best in the absence of any health concern?

The argument is that the public, as well as other competitors, want what they call "a level playing field." As the Mitchell Report stated:

> Clean athletes face three choices: (1) compete without performance-enhancing substances, knowing they may lose to competitors with fewer scruples; (2) abandon their quest because they are unwilling to use performance-enhancing substances to achieve decisive competitive advantage; or (3) use performance-enhancing substances to level the playing field.
>
> (Mitchell Report, 2007)

The problem with this argument is that the field is not and has never been level. A variety of economic, social, political, and cultural factors, including race, create competitive advantages for some and disadvantages for others. One need only look at the athletic careers of Jesse Owens, Jackie Robinson, Curt Flood, Joe Louis, and Muhammad Ali to understand how much remarkable athletes have achieved despite a field that is anything but level.

Perhaps the most hypocritical aspect of this obsession with ridding sports of PEDs is the list of drugs that are not included as banned substances. Cortisone, Torodol, Percoset: these and other pain-killers are routinely given to athletes before and during games to keep them on the field playing through pain. As former NFL Coach Tony Dungy has said: "Practically everybody in the NFL is using Toradol." As a result, numerous players have retired from professional sports, not only addicted to pain killers but with crippling permanent injuries as a result of playing their sport when team doctors should have insisted they rest and recover. Yet the league—and the public—seem to pay no mind to this sanctioned if not outright encouraged form of dangerous drug abuse, while condemning the use of other often less harmful drugs characterized as performance enhancers.

And then there is DNA, which makes some of us bigger or stronger or faster than the rest of us. Scientists have already isolated a few genes associated with elite endurance and athletic performance. The angiotensin converting enzyme (ACE) is active in muscle tissue and regulates blood flow. We all carry either an insertion or an absence of a gene sequence called "allele," giving us either high or low ACE levels. The lower the ACE level, the higher the maximum oxygen uptake, the greater the stamina, while a lower ACE level is associated with greater strength. Scientists have isolated two other "performance genes," known as ACTN 2 and ACTN 3, which influence the contraction of skeletal muscles.

What is interesting about these discoveries is not just the idea that genetic makeup plays a part in athletic performance. We probably did not need these discoveries to reach that conclusion. It is clear that an athlete like Usain Bolt is the fastest man alive not just because of technique and training; he is naturally engineered to run fast. But what if some form of gene therapy or gene splicing could alter our DNA to make us better athletes? Such an as-yet purely theoretical future already has a name: "gene doping." In one animal study, researchers experimented with the delivery of gene-encoded EPO (erythropoietin) as a potential cure for anemia. Could the next Lance Armstrong benefit from such a procedure and thus bypass the rules prohibiting artificial blood doping? Would such a procedure be akin to taking steroids or having Lasik surgery? Some say that future is not too far distant. The IOC is concerned enough to have issued the following statement:

> Gene therapy holds great promise for all people including athletes competing in Olympic sports. We endorse the development and application of gene therapy for the prevention and treatment of human disease. However, we are aware that there is the potential for abuse of gene therapy medicines and we shall begin to establish procedures and state-of-the-art testing methods for identifying athletes who might misuse such technology. This will require investment in modern detection methods including antigen detection, gene chip and proteomic analysis which are now becoming available. Wc are confident that we shall be able to adequately monitor abuses and establish the procedures for doing so using ethically acceptable methods. We call upon other sports, medical and scientific organizations to endorse our position.
>
> (IOC, 2001)

Such theoretical procedures involve what is called "somatic cell modification," meaning they involve the altering of an individual's existing nonhereditary genetic makeup. Even more ethically problematic: what if, when the technology allows, parents desirous of having a superior athlete undergo performance-enhancing in vitro fertilization so their physicians can produce a designer baby possessing all those genes that are markers for physical ability? Such a possibility, experts agree, is not just the stuff of science fiction.

4. Performance-Tracking Technologies

To return to the present day, if we could agree that sporting competition is better if the performance of athletes is not artificially enhanced, it follows that the leagues must be able to enforce the rules aimed at keeping the games "pure." But assuming the tests for detecting any of these artificial enhancements are effective, is it ethical to require athletes to take them? Do such tests violate our notions of privacy, of constitutional rights against self-incrimination, of essential human dignity? Should there at least be some reasonable suspicion of the use of PEDs before subjecting an athlete to such a test?

In *Vernonia School District 47J v. Acton*, the U.S. Supreme Court held that random drug testing of high school students as a condition of participating in sports was a reasonable search under the Fourth Amendment. These tests, of course, were not for PEDs but for drugs then illegal in Oregon like marijuana. Nonetheless, the opinion certainly could be read as endorsing randomized drug testing for PEDs as well. The Court's acceptance of the school district's reason for drug testing, however, was rather startling. The stated purpose by the school district for implementing the regimen was not to protect the health of student athletes and ensure they stayed away from harmful drugs; it was the idea that student athletes were perceived as role models by the general student population who would then take the athlete's guide and refrain from drug use. Quite a naive assumption. The Court must not have heard Charles Barkley remark: "I am not a role model. Just because I dunk a basketball doesn't mean I should raise your kids."

Not all advances in medical or pharmaceutical research attractive to the sports world necessarily enhance a player's performance. In 2005, Eddy Curry was in the last year of his contract with the Chicago Bulls when he collapsed during a team practice. Team doctors expressed concern that the 6'11" center had an enlarged heart, a genetic defect called hypertrophic cardiomyopathy (HCM). Boston Celtic Reggie Lewis and college star Hank Gathers had previously collapsed and died during games of this condition, traumatizing fellow players as well as shocked fans. This condition may be confirmed by a DNA test, though not all individuals with HCM test positive for the gene marker.

The Bulls insisted that before Curry could play again he had to submit to DNA testing. Curry refused. The issue was an important one. Could an employer insist on a DNA test as a condition of employment? After all, teams would love the opportunity down the road to know whether their potential players had the performance genes or perhaps genes that suggested a predisposition to gambling, alcoholism, or cancer. Congress answered that question by a near unanimous vote when approving funds for the Human Genome Project. The Genetic Information Nondiscrimination Act of 2008 (42 U.S.C. Chapter 21F) makes it illegal "for an employer to request, require or purchase genetic information." Ultimately, the Bulls decided to trade Curry to the New York Knicks, with whom Curry signed a multimillion-dollar contract.

Another new technology with ethical implications is already being utilized by some sports organizations. Teams are experimenting with the use of devices to monitor biometric data about their personnel 24/7. The Seattle Mariners, for instance, issued to players who agreed to participate a device called a Readiband. It is manufactured by Fatigue Science, a name seemingly plucked from a futuristic Cyberpunk novel. The company claims these monitors are "the only scientifically validated tool for measuring the impact of sleep on human performance."

One can envision a near future where athletes feel like those astronauts in the movie *Apollo 11*, except the overseers are monitoring not only their heart rate, blood pressure, and temperature but also their caloric intake, muscle growth, and mental acuity. While, of course, still being paid like kings, players may feel more like possessions, objects to be tinkered with, in such a Brave New World.

5. The Use of Animals in Sports

Animals find their way in sports in one of three ways. The first is where they are pitted against each other as in dogfighting or cockfighting or in dog racing, primarily so humans can bet on who will be the victor. The second is where the very purpose of the sport is for the human to kill the animal as in bullfighting or hunting. And the third is where the human and animal work together to compete against other human-animal teams as in horse racing or polo.

To assess the ethics of any of these sports, one need not necessarily engage in the philosophical argument of whether animals themselves have rights. Humans have used animals for a variety of non-sports-related purposes probably since the two first shared the planet together. The issue is really whether the treatment of animals in sport is "humane," that is, whether it comports to what we as humans consider morally acceptable.

Most of us would agree bullfighting and dogfighting or cockfighting are unethical and indeed such sports run counter to the laws and regulations of every state. Michael Vick was celebrated for years as a quarterback, but his participation in the sport of dogfighting quickly landed him in a federal prison. But is there an ethical difference between bullfighting and hunting, if indeed hunting is a sport? Is it the fact that bullfighting is a spectator sport while hunting is a relatively solitary activity that makes one illegal in most of the nations of the world and the other an accepted recreational activity? Or is it that the bulls seem to have to undergo a slow, torturous if not ritualistic death?

The question of whether horseracing, euphemistically called "The Sport of Kings," is ethical is more complicated. Certainly, the animals do not participate in the competition by choice. Most are bred for the very purpose of one day earning money for their owners by outrunning other horses, sometimes urged on by a whip. Yet the champions do seem to revel in the competition, at least that's what their trainers and jockeys tell us. The ethical issues with horse racing stem mostly from the overuse of drugs such as Lasix, which control bleeding in the lungs, and other anti-inflammatory substances which keep the horses racing when they should not. While proponents describe the easy life of past champions put out to stud, many more end up in slaughterhouses after their racing careers end.

6. The Ethics of Being a Fan

It is not just teams, team doctors, and players who should strive to behave ethically. What about the fans? Anyone who has seen the movies *Gladiator* or *Ben Hur* must have wondered how human beings could enjoy watching as sport the suffering of others. Can the same be asked about fans watching NASCAR for the crashes or the National Hockey League (NHL) for the fights? If we know a good percentage of boxers and football players will almost certainly be subjecting themselves to a life after sports of pain and disability, is it ethical to sit and cheer the big hit? What should be the ethical response to such violence: not buy a ticket or merchandise or even, perish the thought, not watch the games?

In his song "Who Killed Davey Moore," Bob Dylan asked the ethical question who was responsible for the death of a twenty-nine-year-old boxer who died as a result of injuries he sustained in a championship fight against Sugar Ramos in 1963. Was it the other fighter, the promoter, the gambler, or the sports writer, or was it the fans who sustained a sport where the outcome depended on how badly one athlete injured another?

We know that professional athletes are paid handsomely for the risks they take. We also know that, for the most part, they willingly consent to participate in the dangerous activity, just like policemen, firefighters, soldiers, and astronauts. Indeed, for many, their lifelong dream is to make it in professional sports. Many of us would trade places with them in a heartbeat if only we had the talent.

Each of us will have to answer these ethical questions for ourselves. Suffice it to say, either answer may be right ethically as long as the players are true volunteers and not coerced into participating or exploited, as long as they are not being deceived or misled about the risks, and as long as care is being taken to protect their health and safety as much as practical without sacrificing the integrity of the game.

7. Conclusion

As science and medicine continue to advance, creating new and safer drugs, as well as developing surgical techniques that can vastly improve one's physical condition, bioethics is sure to play an ever-increasing role in deciding which of these advances comports with the values we hold integral to fair competition. In addition, it seems certain athletes will become increasingly involved in understanding and controlling their critical health decisions. But the question remains open as to whether the future will be devoid of those sports which destroy rather than showcase the magnificent athletes who choose to participate.

References

AMA Code of Medical Ethics (2001).

BBC. (2016). www.bbc.com/sport/football/33931547.

Fahey, T. D. (1998, March 7). "Anabolic-Androgenic Steroids: Mechanism of Action and Effects on Performance." In *Encyclopedia of Sports Medicine and Science*, edited by T. D. Fahey (Internet Society for Sport Science), www.sportsci.org/encyc/anabster/anabster.html.

FIFA. (2004). EPO and Blood Doping-Oxygen Above All?, www.fifa.com/mm/document/afdeveloping/medical/6.10.4.%20epo%20and%20blood%20doping%20-%20oxygen%20above%20all,%20kgr_1511.pdf.

Galvin, Pud. (1889). www.findingdulcinea.com/news/sports/2009/june/Remembering-Pud-Galvin.html.

IOC. (2001). www.olympic.org/news/ioc-gene-therapy-working-group-conclusions.

LA Times. (1989). articles.latimes.com/2014/mar/07/local/la-me-frank-jobe-20140307.

Mitchell Report. (2007). http://mlb.mlb.com/mlb/news/mitchell/.

NFL. (2014). http://profootballtalk.nbcsports.com/2014/05/17/nfl-responds-to-agents-statement-regarding-robert-mathis/.

NFL Collective Bargaining Agreement, https://nfllabor.files.wordpress.com/2010/01/collective-bargaining-agreement-2011-2020.pdf.

Rio. (2016). www.bloomberg.com/view/articles/2016-08-11/shaming-could-be-the-best-fix-for-olympic-doping.

Saugy, M., N. Robinson, C. Saudan, N. Baume, L. Avois, and P. Mangin. (2006). Human Growth Hormone in Sport, www.ncbi.nlm.nih.gov/pmc/articles/PMC2657499/.

Slate. (2005). www.slate.com/articles/health_and_science/human_nature/2005/04/the_beam_in_your_eye.html.

Yesalis, C., and M. S. Barke. (2002). History of Doping in Sport. *International Sports Studies* 24(1): 42–76, library.la84.org/SportsLibrary/ISS/ISS2401/ISS2401e.pdf.

Cases

Armstrong v. Tygart, 886 F. Supp. 572 (W.D. Tex. 2012).

Brody: In re National Football League Player's Concussion Litig., 775 F.3d 570 (3d Cir. 2014).

Dent v. National Football League, No. 14-2324 (N.D. Cal. Dec. 17, 2014).

Kleinknecht v. Gettysburgh College, 989 F.2d 1360 (3d Cir. 1993).

Krueger v. San Francisco Forty Niners, 234 Cal. Rptr. 579 (Ct. App. 1997)

Stringer v. National Football League, 474 F. Supp. 2d 894 (S.D. Ohio 2007)

United States v. Bonds, 730 F.3d 890 (9th Cir. 2013).

Vernonia Sch. Dist. 47J v. Acton, 515 U.S. 646 (1995).

Zimbauer v. Milwaukee Orthopaedic Group, 920 F. Supp. 959 (E.D. Wis. 1996)

CHAPTER 27

THE ROONEY RULE'S REACH

How the NFL's Equal Opportunity Initiative for Coaches Inspired Local Government Reform

N. JEREMI DURU

1. Introduction

On January 6, 2016, the Portland, Oregon, city council passed a resolution requiring that any interview process for a bureau directorship in the city government include an interview of at least one minority candidate, one women candidate, and one candidate with a disability. The extent to which this groundbreaking resolution, named the Charles Jordan Standard, will help in diversifying the largely white and male city government, and the time that it will take to make a discernable impact, are as of now untold. Any impact it does have, however, is owed, in no small part, to sport, and specifically, to football. At first blush, this would seem an odd and incongruous connection. Indeed, no sports organizations sponsored the bill, no celebrity athletes endorsed or campaigned for it, and it houses no provisions relating to sport. Still, if not for developments in the National Football League (NFL) over a decade earlier, the Charles Jordan Standard would likely never have come to pass.

In 2003, the NFL enacted the Rooney Rule, which requires that before hiring a head coach a club must interview at least one person of color for the position. That rule, at times maligned and at times celebrated, is, by most accounts, the principal driver of increased diversity on the NFL's sidelines and has undoubtedly prompted a culture shift in the league. It has since bled out of the NFL, and out of the sports industry altogether, and has emerged in the personnel policies of a variety of entities seeking to diversify. The City of Portland is one such entity and is the first major city to adopt a form of the Rooney Rule. As such, the development of the Charles Jordan Standard is a sports story, or rather a story about sport's unique ability to impact society and push the law. It is by no means the first or most notable such story. Sport has long had a direct influence on

American society and the creation of law. Such influence is perhaps best exemplified by the impact that the desegregation of the NFL, Major League Baseball (MLB), and the National Basketball Association (NBA), in 1946, 1947, and 1950, respectively, had on the broader movement to desegregate American institutions. But the passage of the Charles Jordan Standard provides a contemporary example of the manner in which sport can impact society at large. It also reveals the import of individual activism to the creation of law, as neither the NFL's Rooney Rule nor the City of Portland's Charles Jordan Standard would have come to be without direct action by concerned citizens.

This chapter first details the origin of the Rooney Rule in the NFL and the impact it has had on the league. It then explores efforts to expand the Rooney Rule to collegiate football, the frustration of those efforts, and the State of Oregon's groundbreaking passage of a Rooney Rule analog, House Bill 3118. Next, the chapter examines the manner in which the Rooney Rule and House Bill 3118 influenced the creation of the Charles Jordan Standard. Finally, the chapter assesses key differences between the Rooney Rule on the one hand and the state and city provisions on the other. As part of that assessment, this chapter examines the extent to which those differences might impact the state and city provisions' ultimate efficacy.

2. Coaching Inequity in the NFL

Although at the turn of the twenty-first century the NFL had been in existence for eighty years, only five African Americans had served as head coaches in the league. However, three of them—the Minnesota Vikings' Dennis Green, the Tampa Bay Buccaneers' Tony Dungy, and the New York Jets' Herm Edwards—were in those positions as the 2001 season began, and with many promising assistant coaches of color sprinkled among the league's clubs, it seemed coaching diversity in the NFL was trending upward. All that would change by season's end.

At the start of the 2001 season, Green was the winningest African American head football coach in NFL history, and the second winningest head coach in Vikings history, behind only Bud Grant, who was a legend in the state and had led the club to four Super Bowls in eight years. Green, for his part, had won 63% of his games with the Vikings and in one season led the Vikings to a 15-1 record. In addition, he had taken the Vikings to the playoffs eight times and to the NFC (National Football Conference) championship game twice. The 2001 season, however, began in tragedy. On a sweltering day during training camp that summer, Vikings offensive lineman Korey Stringer collapsed and died from heatstroke, an uncontrollable rise in body temperature that shuts down vital organs. Stringer had not only been a Pro Bowler and one of the Vikings' best linemen, he had also been one of the most beloved players on the team and a steadying force in the locker room. His death devastated his teammates and the team as a whole.

Never able to get on track, the Vikings limped to a 5-10 record through fifteen games, and Green was fired three days before the season finale. It was Green's first and only losing season during his decade with the Vikings. Many in the NFL community viewed it as an unjust firing and believed that after an anomalous losing season scarred by Stringer's death Green should have been given more time at the helm. The NFL, however, can be cruel to head coaches, and although some in the community were disgruntled, termination after a disappointing season is always a possibility.

Two weeks later, the Tampa Bay Buccaneers fired their head coach, Tony Dungy. Dungy's tenure with the Buccaneers, although shorter, may have been even more impressive than Green's tenure with the Vikings. Whereas the Vikings were a respected franchise with a proud history of success when Green became head coach, when Dungy took the Buccaneers job the team was a joke—a lightly regarded perennial doormat that had not had a winning season in fourteen years. Dungy, however, resurrected the Buccaneers. Two years after Dungy took over, the Buccaneers were in the playoffs. Two years later, they played for the NFC championship and narrowly missed a trip to the Super Bowl. But two years after that, and on the heels of back-to-back playoff seasons, Dungy was surprisingly fired.

Those who were displeased with Green's firing grew even more displeased when the news of Dungy's firing broke. And although two firings of prominent and successful head coaches under circumstances that might have suggested a reprieve was noteworthy, that alone did not cause the concern. The concern was squarely about race. Roughly two-thirds of the NFL's players were African American, but after the Green and Dungy terminations only one of its thirty-two head coaches, Herm Edwards, was African American. This billion-dollar business, sustained by the toil of African American players, seemed reticent to allow an African American to lead them.

3. An NFL Civil Rights Movement

Critics within the NFL community, in the press, and elsewhere had noticed and complained in the wake of the Green and Dungy terminations, but the firings galvanized a new group of disgruntled NFL observers—civil rights lawyers. Cyrus Mehri, an NFL fan and employment discrimination lawyer based in Washington, D.C., took particular note. Having followed the NFL for years, he'd observed, as had others attuned to racial dynamics in the league, that positions on the field deemed thinking positions—such as center, middle linebacker, and most famously quarterback—disproportionately featured Caucasians. But this disproportionality, he noticed, paled in comparison to the disproportionality among NFL coaches. Viewing the Green and Dungy terminations through the employment discrimination lens that Mehri had previously reserved for his job rather than his sports interests, Mehri believed redress was necessary.

If isolated and taken out of context, each firing could easily be attributed to a club owner's hasty reaction to a season that failed to meet expectations. Taken together and viewed in the context of the league's racial dynamics, however, they could not so easily be dismissed. Mehri believed that discrimination in the league was systemic, and he set out to prove it with statistics, a tool he turned to regularly in his legal practice. Together with famed criminal defense and civil rights lawyer Johnnie Cochran, with whom Mehri was litigating an employment discrimination class action lawsuit against Johnson & Johnson and who shared Mehri's concern about both the NFL's racial dynamics and the Green and Dungy terminations, Mehri commissioned a labor economist at the University of Pennsylvania, Dr. Janice Madden, to study the matter.

3.1. Empirical Evidence of Discrimination

The lawyers asked Dr. Madden to compare the win-loss records of African American head coaches with those of white head coaches over the course of the previous fifteen years, from 1986 through 2001. Mehri and Cochran believed from anecdotal evidence that African American head coaches were typically the last hired and first fired and that they had to do more to obtain and maintain their jobs than did their Caucasian counterparts. As lawyers having previously litigated employment discrimination cases, however, they knew that anecdotes could only take them so far. To create the foundation for any sort of compelling argument, they needed statistical support.

Dr. Madden's study definitively revealed that African American head coaches did in fact win more games than their Caucasian counterparts. Over the NFL's sixteen-game season, African American head coaches averaged 9.1 wins while Caucasian head coaches averaged 8 wins. And that ninth game, which African -American head coaches on average won, often meant the difference between a successful season and an unsuccessful one. Indeed, during the fifteen years studied, 60% of teams with nine wins made the playoffs and fewer than 10% of those with eight wins made the playoffs. Moreover, in their years of termination, African American head coaches won 1.3 more games than Caucasian head coaches (Mehri and Cochran, 2002).

Dr. Madden's work, which was statistically significant and peer reviewed, confirmed Mehri and Cochran's hypothesis: African American head coaches were winning more games than Caucasian head coaches but were being given fewer opportunities. Using Dr. Madden's study as a foundation, Mehri and Cochran crafted a report detailing the inequity in the NFL's coaching ranks, titled it *Black Coaches in the NFL: Superior Performance, Inferior Opportunities*, and submitted it to the league shortly after a press conference during which they threatened litigation if the NFL did not take action.

3.2. Charting a Path Forward

Exactly what form any such litigation would take was unclear, as the NFL itself terminated neither Green nor Dungy. The Buccaneers and Vikings, respectively, terminated the coaches, and because courts had consistently held that the NFL was an umbrella organization of thirty-two autonomous football clubs rather than a single thirty-two club entity, holding the league accountable for the terminations seemed unlikely. Holding the clubs directly responsible, however, seemed similarly unlikely. Dr. Madden's study reflected league-wide averages, which would be compelling in a class or group action against the league but essentially meaningless in a suit against a particular club. Moreover, in individual cases, courts are deferential when defendants provide a legitimate, nondiscriminatory reason for a personnel decision. Since coaching relies so heavily upon hard-to-measure characteristics such as judgment, leadership ability, and temperament, any number of justifications for the termination would likely pass muster. On top of these challenges, there was no indication that Green, Dungy, or any other coach was interested in suing, so it was by no means certain Mehri and Cochran would even have a client to represent.

Notwithstanding these relatively obvious impediments to suit, the NFL did not dismiss the report or the lawyers who sent it to them. The league recognized the racial disproportionality between coaches and players, and race-conscious journalists had occasionally raised the issue over the years. Although the NBA and MLB, like the NFL and like American institutions generally, had historically struggled with race, both were well ahead of the NFL with respect to coaching diversity. The NFL had tried to address the issue, instituting various initiatives and bringing in consulting companies to advise club owners on best practices, but it had failed to make notable progress. Mehri and Cochran's report starkly highlighted that failure. Moreover, with Cochran involved, media attention was a certainty and something the NFL preferred to do without. So in October 2002, not long after the NFL's top officials received the report, they invited Mehri and Cochran to their offices to discuss the report and the lawyers' concerns.

3.3. Birth of the Rooney Rule

The October meeting began a sometimes congenial, sometimes contentious three-month-long process during which NFL Commissioner Paul Tagliabue, General Counsel Jeff Pash, and others at the league office as well as club owners and executives—with consistent input from Mehri, Cochran, and some retired African American players, coaches, and front office executives who had been inspired by their efforts—struggled to find solutions to the lack of diversity in the league's coaching ranks. In the end, support coalesced around an initiative that Mehri had used in settling employment discrimination cases in his legal practice. He called it "diverse candidate slate interviewing" and, to promote systematic change in companies that had long been racially homogenous, it required the company to interview at least one person of color for all open positions in identified job categories. The initiative was generally successful in diversifying those companies, and Mehri believed the same concept could have a similar impact on the NFL's coaching ranks.

Among the league insiders who shared Mehri's enthusiasm for the idea was Pittsburgh Steelers Owner Dan Rooney. As chairman of the league's new Committee on Workplace Diversity, which Commissioner Tagliabue created in response to Mehri/Cochran report, Rooney was charged with charting a path forward for the league on diversity. He believed diverse candidate slates could be helpful in doing so.

Along with several other like-minded club owners and with support from the Commissioner's Office as well as Mehri and Cochran, Rooney set out to convince the remaining club owners that they should collectively agree to adopt diverse candidate slate interviewing practices. While some owners were interested in the idea others were skeptical. The latter group complained that such a regulation would strip them of their autonomy in deciding who ought to run their football club. They also opined that it would be a waste time. Some owners believed that, even worse, clubs would be incentivized to conduct a quick sham interview of a person of color with no intention of considering him in order to get the regulation out of the way and get their coach selected in preparation for the new season. This outcome, they argued, would make a mockery of the rule and reflect poorly on the clubs and the league. Moreover, it would stigmatize and insult the coaches of color who would be subject to the sham interviews.

The debate culminated in a meeting of owners and executives, during which Commissioner Tagliabue asked the league's outside counsel, Tom Williamson, to discuss the merits and detriments of the proposal and to answer questions. The same skepticism that existed during the previous several weeks of quiet conversations emerged during the meeting. Williamson had had several conversations with Mehri by this point and was convinced that, notwithstanding its drawbacks, the diverse candidate slate concept had merit, and he grew frustrated that many in the room seemed unwilling to seriously consider it.

Finally, with the meeting at a standstill, Williamson recounted the league's poor record of diversity in coaching, the failed attempts over the years to address it, and the damage the league's image was suffering because of the lack of progress. He then asked those in the room whether they had any better ideas to address the problem. When none were offered, his point was made. The diverse candidate slate idea was the best idea the league office had at the time, and unless someone in the room had a viable alternative, Williamson urged, they should support the effort to adopt diverse candidate slate interviewing.

Ultimately, in late December 2002, all thirty-two NFL club owners reached a handshake agreement to interview at least one candidate of color for all head coaching positions. It was a breakthrough for the league's diversity efforts. When sportswriter Len Shapiro called Mehri with the good news and asked whether, when writing about the new NFL initiative, he should call it the Mehri-Cochran Rule or the Cochran-Mehri Rule, Mehri suggested he call it the Rooney Rule. The suggestion was made out of respect for Dan Rooney's efforts. But there was also strategy involved. Mehri knew that for the Rule to succeed the NFL community had to buy into it and that doing so would be easier if it carried the name of one of the league's most respected owners rather than two outside lawyers who introduced themselves to the community with a threat.

Shapiro took the suggestion and the Rooney Rule was born. Within a few months, several clubs implemented head coaching searches with different levels of dedication to the rule. The Dallas Cowboys ownership followed the letter of the rule but flouted its spirit, interviewing Dennis Green, who had been out of the league since the Vikings terminated him a year earlier, for a mere twenty minutes on the telephone before hiring Bill Parcells, whom they had interviewed for over eleven hours during two separate meetings. The Cincinnati Bengals ownership abided by the rule in text and spirit, interviewing two African American head coaching candidates, including Marvin Lewis, whom they ultimately hired. The Detroit Lions ownership disregarded the rule altogether, stating publicly, as soon as they terminated their then head coach, that they planned to hire Steve Mariucci, who is Caucasian, to replace him. The Lions thereafter invited African American coaches to interview, but of course none accepted, as the club's decision had clearly been made.

The Lions' violation of the Rooney Rule forced Commissioner Tagliabue to determine what consequences, if any, should follow. While the owners had agreed to the rule, no agreement existed as to the scope of punishment. As a result, Tagliabue was essentially left to determine whether the Rooney Rule would be a guideline clubs were simply encouraged to follow or a mandate. The loose coalition of former players, coaches, and front-office executives who had helped Mehri and Cochran lobby the league for equal opportunity initiatives in the wake of the report's release had by now formed an organization. They took the name Fritz Pollard Alliance—in honor of the NFL's first African American head coach, Fritz Pollard—and urged the Commissioner to signal the import of the rule by disciplining the Lions.

After hearing from the Fritz Pollard Alliance, Lions executives, and other interested parties, the commissioner concluded that a penalty was necessary and fined the Lions' general manager, Matt Millen, $200,000. The commissioner also warned that any future Rooney Rule violations would trigger a $500,000 fine and announced that to satisfy the rule, interviews of candidates of color had to be of the same quality as those of others. This meant that interviews should be of roughly the same length, conducted by the same decision makers, and conducted in the same manner, whether in person or by phone. In doing so, the commissioner established that an approach such as the Cowboys' would in the future be deemed a Rooney Rule violation.

3.4. The Rooney Rule's Impact in the NFL

In the years that followed, diversity among the NFL's head coaches tracked upward. With an enforcement mechanism in place, head coaching candidates of color began to get interviews and those interviews began to turn into employment offers. The year after Marvin Lewis was hired, two of the seven NFL clubs searching for new head coaches hired people of color, bringing the total number of head coaches of color to a historical high of five. By 2011, there were eight head coaches of color in the NFL, an 800% increase over the eight years since the Rooney Rule took effect. The NFL was so pleased with the Rooney Rule's impact on head coaching diversity that two years later it extended the rule to the front office. Accordingly, any club looking for a new general manager was required to interview a candidate of color. In short order, the league's general manager ranks diversified as well.

Different studies conducted during the Rooney Rule's existence have taken different positions on the extent of the rule's responsibility for changing the NFL's racial complexion, but none can reasonably question that it has dramatically changed. The numbers of head coaches and general managers of color have certainly increased: during the twelve years before the Rooney Rule's enactment, the NFL featured four head coaches of color and one general manager of color; during the twelve years after enactment, the NFL featured sixteen head coaches of color (two of whom have held multiple head coaching positions) and eight general managers of color. Just as notable, those head coaches and general managers of color have, on the whole, experienced success. During the twelve years before the Rooney Rule's enactment, the only head coach or general manager of color to lead a club to the Super Bowl was Baltimore Ravens' general manager Ozzie Newsome. In comparison, during the twelve years after enactment, ten head coaches and general managers of color led their club to the Super Bowl, two of whom did so twice.

4. The Collegiate Landscape

By 2007, only four years after the Rooney Rule's enactment and before it had been expanded to include searches for general managers, the rule's impact in the NFL was evident. Super Bowl XLI featured two African American head coaches, whereas the previous forty Super Bowls had featured none. This groundbreaking matchup, together with the increased diversity among NFL head coaches in just the first few years following the Rooney Rule's implementation, highlighted the lack of diversity among collegiate head football coaches. In 2007, only six of the 120 Division IA (now known as Football Bowl Subdivision) football programs had an African American head coach. Those who were concerned about these numbers wondered whether the Rooney Rule could do for the college game what it had appeared to do for the professional game.

The Fritz Pollard Alliance, which had by then become a well-respected voice for equal opportunity in sports, took particular interest in the matter and arranged a meeting in 2007 with then NCAA (National Collegiate Athletics Association) President Myles Brand and other NCAA officials to discuss the possibility of the NCAA adopting some sort of Rooney Rule analog to promote equal coaching opportunity in the NCAA. While cordial, the meeting was unproductive. Brand and his lieutenants stated flatly that the NCAA could issue no such mandate to its member institutions. They argued that the NCAA had no "authority to mandate campus-hiring requirements" and that member schools would be unwilling to "surrender" to the NCAA their autonomy in selecting a head coach. (Pike, 2011, 42-43).

The Fritz Pollard Alliance (FPA) was not alone in pressing for a collegiate version of the Rooney Rule. Other organizations advocated for an NCAA Rooney Rule as well.

Most notably, Richard Lapchick, the director of the Institute for Diversity and Ethics in Sport and a nationally renowned thought leader, pressed the issue. He called on the NCAA and its member institutions to adopt the basic principle of the Rooney Rule and to call it the Eddie Robinson Rule, to honor Eddie Robinson, the African American coaching legend at Grambling State University. Notwithstanding the pressure to act, the NCAA would not budge.

The NCAA did, however, suggest that the Division IA Athletic Directors' Association (the Association)—which, although composed of collegiate athletic directors is independent of the NCAA—might be willing to consider the concept. After several conversations between the FPA leadership and the Association's executive director, Dutch Baughman, the Association agreed to implement a best practice modeled after the Rooney Rule. The Association recommended that each member athletic director commit to interviewing one minority candidate when seeking to fill a head coaching position.

The Association's best practice was a step forward in a college football context essentially devoid of meaningful equal opportunity initiatives, and between its establishment in 2007 and the end of the 2009 head coach hiring cycle, the number of minority head coaches at Football Bowl Subdivision schools had increased from six of a possible 120 to 13 of a possible 120. Still, it was a guideline rather than a rule. Each athletic director was free to follow the guideline or not, meaning that a new executive director could easily abandon the recommendation, and even if not, adherence to the best practice would fluctuate from school to school.

5. The Oregon Approach

Critics of the disproportionately white NCAA coaching ranks were largely dissatisfied with the NCAA's inaction and the Association's non-binding recommendation to its members. They believed that more had to be done to level the playing field for coaches of color in collegiate football, but none of the scholars, activists, or organizations involved in the national conversation on the issue seemed to have any solutions. A senior student at Portland State University, Sam Sachs, however, did. Sachs knew nothing of the FPA's meeting with the NCAA or the NCAA's arguments against the feasibility of a collegiate Rooney Rule analog, but he knew of the Rooney Rule in the NFL. He supported the rule because it seemed a creative and effective means of breaking down barriers in what he had come to view, through his life experiences, as a fragmented and bigoted American society.

Sachs grew up in a small Oregon town with little racial, ethnic, or religious diversity, and being Jewish, he was keenly aware of the town's homogeneity. He knew of no other Jewish families in town, and his high school—at which the sports teams were named the Rebels and were represented by a confederate flag—had no more than a few dozen students of color among roughly 1,200 total students. Upon graduating from high school,

Sachs joined the Army and, while serving, was disquieted with the separation and at times distrust among soldiers of different races. After leaving the Army to attend college at Western Oregon University, he grew disturbed with the frequency with which he heard disparaging comments about Jewish people, particularly from his teammates on the school's football team. By the time Sachs found his way to Portland State—after leaving Western Oregon in his junior year to work as a corrections deputy and seeing racial inequity in the criminal justice system firsthand—he knew racial and social justice were important to him. He decided to major in black studies and committed to working for equal opportunity whenever he could.

When Portland State's longtime head football coach Tim Walsh resigned following the 2006 season to take a job as head football coach at Army, Sachs approached the administration to suggest that they follow a Rooney Rule-like interviewing process when selecting Walsh's replacement. When the administration declined his suggestion and went on to hire former NFL coach Jerry Glanville without interviewing any candidate of color, Sachs showed up at Glanville's February 28, 2007, introductory press conference and stationed himself in the back of the room. When Glanville invited questions from the crowd, Sachs raised his hand, and matter-of-factly asked, "Coach Glanville, what do you think about the fact that today is the last day of Black History Month and they're introducing you for this job even though they didn't interview one minority candidate in this whole process?" (Sam Sachs, telephone interview by N. Jeremi Duru, April 8, 2016). Glanville, who was stunned, haltingly responded that he wasn't part of the interview process and moved on to the next question, but Sachs's point was made: a template existed for a more inclusive hiring process and Portland State University had eschewed it.

The press conference question marked the beginning and end of Sachs's activism at Portland State, but his fascination with the Rooney Rule and its possibilities at the collegiate level would endure. He followed national trends in college football head coach hiring during the remainder of his time at Portland State and continued to follow them after he graduated in 2007 and took a job as a loss prevention officer at a Nordstrom's department store in Portland. He found himself pleased when it appeared that a school conducted a comprehensive and broad-based search that included minorities and was disgruntled when schools proceeded as Portland State had with Glanville. He also began to follow the careers of promising African American coaches and rooted for their success.

During the 2008 college football season, Sachs paid particular attention to two coaches—Turner Gill, the head coach at the University of Buffalo, and Charlie Strong, the defensive coordinator at the University of Florida—who were both widely respected and deemed by most pundits to be among the top candidates of any race for head coaching jobs in 2009. Neither, however, landed such a job, and race was widely perceived to be a factor for both. Not only were both men African American, but they were both married to white women. According to multiple commentators, as well as Strong himself who spoke publicly on the matter, such a combination damaged their opportunities to land interviews and secure head coaching positions with elite collegiate football programs.

Sachs shared the view that race played a part in Strong and Gill being left out during the hiring cycle, and although they had received some interviews, he felt that a collegiate Rooney Rule might have expanded their opportunities, and maybe more importantly, would likely open opportunities to the many aspiring collegiate head coaches of color who until then had never been considered for a head coaching position. Sachs felt the need to do something, but he had no connection to the NCAA and no influence in the collegiate football community. Moreover, he had experienced flat rejection when he had taken the idea directly to Portland State.

So, with no other recourse he could think of and largely out of frustration, Sachs cold-called his state representative, Mitch Greenlick, expecting to leave a message in voice-mail or with a staffer and to never have the call returned. Greenlick, however, answered the phone himself, leaving Sachs so surprised that he asked Greenlick if he could gather his thoughts and call back later. When they reconvened on the phone, Sachs expressed his frustration with the short shrift African American coaches seemed to be getting in collegiate football as well as his view that the Rooney Rule concept could, to some extent, level the playing field for those coaches. Sachs also mentioned his failed attempt to convince his alma mater to interview a candidate of color before hiring Glanville. Sachs recognized that Greenlick, as an Oregon state representative, had no responsibility for the rest of the country, but he suggested to Greenlick that he could have an impact in their home state by sponsoring a bill to require Oregon's public universities to implement a Rooney Rule-like interviewing requirement.

It was a bold suggestion. No state in the union had ever implemented such a law, and Oregon seemed an unlikely candidate to be the first to do so. Although nearly as geographically distant as possible from the heart of America's chattel slavery system in the South, Oregon has had an ugly racial history from its inception. When Oregon was granted statehood in 1859, it was the only state in the Union with a constitution prohibiting non-enslaved African Americans from moving to the state, or working or owning property there. Pursuant to the Oregon State Constitution, enacted in 1857:

> No free negro, or mulatto, not residing in this State at the time of the adoption of this Constitution, shall come, reside, or be within this State, or hold any real estate, or make any contracts, or maintain any suit therein; and the Legislative Assembly shall provide by penal laws, for the removal, by public officers, of all such negroes, and mulattoes, and for their effectual exclusion from the State, and for the punishment of persons who shall bring them into the state, or employ, or harbor them.
>
> (Art. 1, § 35)

While those prohibitions, of course, eventually dissolved, it remained illegal for African Americans to move to Oregon through the first quarter of the 20th century. By the time African American immigration to Oregon became lawful in 1926, the exclusionary constitutional provisions had served their purposes: scarcely any African Americans lived in the state, and that remained the case when Sachs began discussions with Greenlick.

Of the nearly four million people living in Oregon at the time, only 2% were African American.

Nevertheless, Sachs's suggestion intrigued Greenlick, and Greenlick invited Sachs to his office for the two to talk further. Greenlick wanted to be helpful but, politically, felt he needed support. He told Sachs that he would likely sponsor the bill if Sachs were able to also convince his state senator, Suzanne Bonamici, to co-sponsor. Sachs reached out to Bonamici and she agreed. Securing support for a Rooney Rule analog from his two representatives in the legislature was a tremendous accomplishment, but bill sponsorship meant nothing without eventual passage, and passage would require much more than the support of two legislators. It would need broad-based support in the House and in the Senate and then, ultimately, from the governor.

So, despite working full time at Nordstrom's, Sachs made it his business to garner that support. He used virtually all of his scheduled off days as well as his vacation days to drive the 100 miles roundtrip between Portland and the state capitol in Salem to lobby for the bill. Between February and June 2009, Sachs made at least fifty trips to Salem, during which he personally met with every Oregon state legislator. The lawmakers expressed the same concerns NFL owners had about tokenism and the potential for sham interviews, but the rule's success in the NFL proved persuasive at the state House. On July 22, 2009, having received the bill from the house and senate with overwhelming support in both chambers, Governor Ted Kulongoski signed Oregon's Rooney Rule, House Bill 3118, into law.

Notably, House Bill 3118 goes well beyond the scope that either the FPA or Lapchick had envisioned in terms of a collegiate mandate proposal. Both had restricted their advocacy to ensuring diverse candidate slate interviewing with respect to collegiate football head coaching positions, and so had Sachs when he approached Greenlick. However, during one of Sachs' many trips to Salem—when the bill was still being debated in the House Education Committee—Sachs met with state representative Betty Komp, who reasoned that if the Rule made sense for football it could make no less sense for other head coaching positions. By the time the Committee sent the bill to the floor, it required each of the state's seven public universities to utilize diverse candidate slate interviewing when seeking to fill all head coaching positions as well as athletic director positions, and that is the version of the bill that became law.

6. The Charles Jordan Standard

With the Rooney Rule in place on the state level, it was only a matter of time before it found its way to the state's most populous city, Portland, which, despite being substantially more diverse than the state of Oregon as a whole, had long struggled with diversity in the upper levels of city government. The city has 26 governmental bureaus, each of which is headed by a bureau director, such as the Police Chief, Fire Chief, and Parks Director, and as of 2015 those positions had been disproportionately held by white males. Indeed, by August of that year, white males had been selected for seven consecutive bureau directorships. It was an embarrassing state of affairs in need of remedy, and Sachs, by then one of Portland's Human Rights Commissioners, proposed a form of the Rooney Rule.

Were the Rooney Rule still restricted to the NFL, a multi-billion dollar private sports enterprise, it may have been hard for Portland's mayor and city council to view it as a potential solution to the city's lack of diversity among bureau directors. But the Oregon legislature brought the Rule into the public realm, and since then, non-sports related private entities such as Xerox, Intel, Facebook, and Pinterest had adopted forms of the Rule. It was a well-established best practice, and an intuitive step for the City of Portland to take. Dante James, the director of Portland's Office of Equity and Human Rights, supported the idea, as did Mayor Charlie Hales and the city council. Thus, on January 6, 2016, the Charles Jordan Standard—named after the first African American ever elected to the Portland city council—went into effect. Just as Oregon adjusted the NFL's Rooney Rule concept to suit its needs in applying it to all public-sector collegiate coaching and athletic director searches, Portland adjusted the Oregon Rooney Rule to suit *its* needs in drafting the Charles Jordan Standard to require city commissioners to interview not only a person of color but also a woman and a person with a disability when conducting interviews for bureau directorships.

7. The Potential Impact of House Bill 3118 and the Charles Jordan Standard

Oregon's Rooney Rule and the Charles Jordan Standard both take the NFL's Rooney Rule to another level. Oregon's legislation extends the NFL's Rooney Rule beyond football and Portland's resolution extends it beyond sport entirely, applying it to not only race but also gender and disability. While these extensions would suggest that these initiatives may have a broader equal opportunity impact than the NFL's Rooney Rule, other differences between the NFL's Rooney Rule and the Oregon and Portland initiatives may suggest otherwise.

7.1. Enforcement Mechanism

While far narrower in scope, the NFL's Rooney Rule contains something the Oregon and Portland initiatives do not: an enforcement mechanism. As Commissioner Tagliabue established in 2003, a Rooney Rule violation will result in a $500,000 fine. By contrast, neither House Bill 3118 nor the Charles Jordan Standard set forth a punishment mechanism.

In the state context, the consequence of this shortcoming played itself out in 2013 when Oregon State University failed to interview a diverse candidate slate when hiring a softball coach and suffered no consequence. Moreover, because House Bill 3118 was passed with no reporting or monitoring requirements, barring a self-report (which is how Oregon State's failure came to light) there was no way to determine whether other state universities were abiding by the law. In 2015, to rectify the monitoring problem, the Oregon legislature passed a provision requiring the state's Higher Education Coordinating Commission to work with the public universities in structuring a means of monitoring compliance with House Bill 3118. When the City of Portland passed the Charles Jordan Standard, perhaps learning from the state's initial oversight with respect to monitoring, it included a provision requiring that commissioners report on the interviewing processes for bureau directorships. Still, with no mechanism for punishment on the city or state level, the extent to which decision makers will adhere to the interview requirements, and therefore the extent to which the interviewing requirements will be effective, is unclear.

7.2. Public vs. Private Enterprise

The Rooney Rule applies in private industry whereas House Bill 3118 and the Charles Jordan Standard apply in government. While it would be beyond the scope of this chapter to fully explore the respects in which legal analysis of a private-sector policy considering race would differ from such analysis of a public-sector policy considering race, a brief discussion of the potential differences is in order.

Although critics have argued that the Rooney Rule is an affirmative action program that unfairly and unlawfully requires NFL clubs to consider race in making employment determinations, in thirteen years the rule has never been challenged in court, and if it were challenged, the challenge would likely fail. The Rooney Rule neither advantages candidates of color nor disadvantages white candidates for head coaching and general manager positions. It does not bear on hiring at all. Once a candidate of color is interviewed, decision makers can hire whomever they want irrespective of race. Moreover, the rule does not cap the number of interviews, so providing a candidate of color an interview does not mean denying an interview to a Caucasian candidate.

Even if the Rooney Rule were considered an affirmative action program triggering analysis under Title VII of the Civil Rights Act of 1964—which applies to both private and public employers—a line of U.S. Supreme Court Title VII cases, beginning with *United Steelworkers v. Weber* and *Johnson v. Transportation Agency*, suggests it would pass muster. Those cases permit affirmative action programs that are designed to "eliminate manifest racial imbalance in traditionally segregated job categories," that do not "unduly trammel the interests of majority group members," and that are temporary rather than permanent (Sullivan, 2004, 1052). Unless the Rooney Rule were determined to be a permanent program—an unlikely outcome in that the NFL has expressed that it looks forward to the day when the rule is no longer necessary—the Rooney Rule would likely survive Title VII scrutiny.

If House Bill 3118 and the Charles Jordan Standard were deemed affirmative action programs, they would, as public enactments, face scrutiny under not only Title VII but also the Equal Protection Clause of the U.S. Constitution's Fourteenth Amendment. A different line of U.S. Supreme Court cases, including *Richmond v. J.A. Croson Co.* and *Adarand Constructors, Inc. v. Pena*, set out a different, arguably more searching analysis of public employment affirmative action programs that is inapplicable to private employment affirmative action programs. Both *Adarand* and *Croson* hold that the Equal Protection Clause requires "strict scrutiny of *all* race-based action by state and local governments" (*Adarand*, 515 U.S. at 226 meaning that even though the interviewing protocols in House Bill 3118 and the Charles Jordan Standard have a nonexclusionary impact on the interviewing process and no impact at all on the actual hiring decision, they may well trigger strict scrutiny review.

However, under strict scrutiny review, which requires that governmental race-based actions serve a compelling interest and be narrowly tailored, neither House Bill 3118 nor the Charles Jordan Standard would likely be invalidated. They are both factually distinct from race-based actions such as those involved in *Adarand* and *Croson*, in that they do not involve quotas or set-asides. They are also distinct from more mild Supreme Court-approved, narrowly tailored race-based actions such as the University of Michigan's admission practice—which was unsuccessfully challenged in *Grutter v. Bollinger*—of giving a "plus factor" to applicants based on a wide range of identified characteristics, including race (*Grutter*, 539 U.S. at 392). Indeed, it is hard to imagine a more narrowly tailored race-based action than granting one interview among an uncapped total number of interviews to a person of color.

Moreover, the *Grutter* court established the pursuit of diversity as a compelling interest that would justify narrowly tailored race-based actions, and both House Bill 3118 and the Charles Jordan Standard were inarguably instituted in the pursuit of diversity. It bears noting, though, that *Grutter* was a university admissions case rather than an employment case, and while the *Grutter* Court's opinion detailed the import of diversity not only in the classroom but in the workplace and relied on amicus briefs from public employers supporting the diversity rationale, the Supreme Court has never held in an employment case that diversity is a compelling interest under strict scrutiny analysis. As such, a court reviewing a challenge to House Bill 3118 or the Charles Jordan Standard could conceivably decline to accept diversity as a compelling governmental interest in employment. It would instead require a showing of past discrimination requiring remedy, which would complicate the analysis and put a greater burden on Oregon or the city of Portland.

Unless and until their diverse candidate slate interviewing protocols are legally challenged, however, neither the state of Oregon nor the city of Portland will have to defend or justify its policy. Whether those policies will have the impact in Oregon and Portland that the Rooney Rule has had in the NFL, however, remains to be seen.

8. Conclusion

What began as a provision that civil rights lawyer Cyrus Mehri used to settle employment discrimination cases became a linchpin in the NFL's effort to diversify its coaching ranks. The NFL's version of diverse candidate slate interviewing, the Rooney Rule, has since found traction in a variety of contexts, including in one of America's least diverse states, Oregon. Oregon's House Bill 3118 requires that all public universities apply the practice when searching for a head coach or athletic director, and Oregon's largest city, Portland, has incorporated the concept into its protocols for interviewing aspiring bureau directors. Whether diverse candidate slate interviewing will impact the state of Oregon and city of Portland as profoundly as it has impacted the NFL has yet to be determined, but Oregon's and Portland's implementation of the concept illustrates the Rooney Rule's reach and provides a template for public entities seeking to diversify in any number of ways.

References

Mehri, C., and Cochran, J. (2002). "Black Coaches in the National Football League: Superior Performance, Inferior Opportunities" (Washington D.C.: Mehri & Skalet).
Pike, J. (2011). "From the Rooney Rule to the Robinson Rule: NCAA Football and the Quest for Equal Opportunity in Head Coaching." *Widener Journal of Law, Economics & Race* 3: 42–43.
Sullivan, C. (2004). "Circling Back to the Obvious: The Convergence of Traditional and Reverse Discrimination in Title VII Proof." *William and Mary Law Review* 46: 1049–1051.

Cases

Adarand Constructors, Inc. v. Pena, 515 U.S. 200 (1995).
Grutter v. Bollinger 39 U.S. 306 (2003).
Johnson v. Transportation Agency, 480 U.S. 616 (1987).
Richmond v. J.A. Croson Co. 488 U.S. 469 (1989).
United Steelworkers v. Weber, 443 U.S. 193, 99 S. Ct. 2721, 61 L. Ed. 2d 480 (1979).

CHAPTER 28

SPORTS IN THE CONTEXT OF SOCIAL MEDIA LAW

JON M. GARON

1. Social Media in the Sports Law Context

To assess whether social media matters in the context of sports law, one need look no further than the 2016 U.S. National Football League (NFL) draft. Laremy Tunsil, a contender for the top draft pick in the 2016 season, dropped to the thirteenth pick after a video surfaced on social media depicting the former collegiate athlete smoking marijuana from a bong attached to a gas mask (Bishara and Martin, 2016). The video was placed on Tunsil's Twitter account by hackers who accessed the account without authorization. The video may be responsible for Tunsil's being taken later in the round than had been expected, a delay that reduced his initial contract by millions of dollars.

Shortly after Tunsil's selection, his Instagram account was also hacked and a text message conversation was revealed, allegedly showing Tunsil in an apparent exchange with his college coaches about a payment to the player. Although the funds were for help in paying his mother's utility bill, such compensation would violate U.S. collegiate rules.

Rather than making allegations about the player's conduct, his critics put the damaging information into the player's own social media accounts. The medium greatly enhanced the immediacy of the allegations and highlighted one of the many challenges to social media for athletes seeking to manage their media image. This chapter explains the nature of social media and highlights areas where the legal consequences of social media may vary or expand from those of traditional mass media.

1.1. Understanding Social Media

One of the greatest changes to the economics of global sports has been the growth of revenue available to teams and leagues from broadcast industries. Deloite projects recent increases in global premium sports broadcast rights at $28 billion as of 2015. This represents roughly 20% of total revenue. "Global sports revenues were valued at US $121.4 billion in 2010" (PriceWaterhouseCoopers, 2011). This number will likely exceed $150 billion in 2018.

The continued growth is expected to continue well into the future. Similarly, PriceWaterhouseCoopers (PWC) predicts continued expansion of sports revenue along with continued integration between traditional entertainment and sport broadcasting (PWC, 2011). The powerful economic role of traditional mass media (discussed more fully in Section 6) provides the context needed to assess the role of social media on sports revenues and business structures. This is because sports broadcasting drives many of the legal rules and league structures.

Because social media varies, it is difficult to define. Some jurisdictions have attempted to provide legal definitions. California law defines the term as follows: " 'social media' means an electronic service or account, or electronic content, including, but not limited to, videos, still photographs, blogs, video blogs, podcasts, instant and text messages, email, online services or accounts, or Internet Web site profiles or locations" (Cal. Lab. Code § 980 (2016)). This definition focuses on the tools and media that may be used to create and distribute content rather than the nature of the producer and the engagement of the audience. The legal definition casts a very wide net that likely includes professional mass media as well as social media.

Social media serves as both a complement and competitor to mass media in terms of market share, but it differs from mass media in significant ways. In traditional mass media, the content producer creates all the content for distribution, and then it disseminates that content to the public. Typically, television broadcasters would create a single broadcast to be distributed across an entire country or region. Radio and newspapers typically do the same, although the smaller market for those media allow them to make modest changes from market to market. A newspaper, for example, might have a city edition, a national edition, and a few separate editions with unique local sections for each community within the newspaper's subscriber base. The newspaper editions remain very similar in all but a few pages in each daily edition. In mass media, the vast bulk of the content and mechanisms for distribution would be standardized for all customers.

In contrast, social media distributors may combine content from any number of traditional content producers and from any number of individual members of the public. Social media is sometimes created exclusively from content that is wholly "user generated," meaning the content is created solely by individuals who are nonprofessional content producers (Mandiberg, 2012). Each individual contributes a small portion to the collective project. Wikipedia, the world's largest encyclopedia, is such a user-generated collaborative project.

At the other extreme of social media, the content is produced by the same mass media companies that produce traditional broadcast and print content. Using social media channels, these mass media companies use Internet and mobile-device platforms to distribute their content, and, at the same time, they enable audience members to interact with the content by liking, sharing, or promoting the content. Websites and apps with such professionally produced content are enabling a participatory media experience for the users. Consequently, such engagement falls within the scope of social media (Mandiberg, 2012).

Social media platforms typically combine some aspects of the user-generated content and the professional, mass media content. The mix varies from platform to platform and may vary from day to day, depending on the interest of the public and perceived value to the mass media producers.

Finally, social media technology enables the content platforms to predict which content is most likely to be of interest to each user and thus narrow the range of content highlighted for that individual. In the same way, the user can choose to promote or limit sources of content. The combined effect of this content selection process is that the experience for each audience member is somewhat unique, and the scope of content presented to each audience member is much more selective and self-reinforcing than from mass media. This "echo chamber" effect means that audience members are not exposed to content with which they are likely to disagree. At its simplest, for example, a sports fan might be offered only versions of a broadcast match which features commentators who are supporters of that audience member's team. Traditional mass media broadcasts do not give the viewer such a choice.

Social media networks include such well-known companies as YouTube, Facebook, LinkedIn, Twitter, Pinterest, Tumblr, Instagram, VK (ВКонтакте), flickr, Vine, Meetup, Kik, and many others. In Europe, the more popular sites include Partyflock, iWiW, Badoo, Netlog, and Nasza-klasa, among others. Some emphasize sharing music, videos, or still photographs; others emphasize sharing published commentary; and others focus on group chats or sharing short comments. A number of social media sites for sports have been launched but these have had limited success.

For purposes of this chapter, then, social media is any non-mass media content. Social media may be distributed by any party and the content is generally distributed in a platform that allows the audience members to engage with the content through each audience member's ability to evaluate/like, alter, and/or redistribute that content. If a television broadcaster simultaneously broadcasts a sports event on network television and through a mobile app, the network television broadcast is mass media. The content on the mobile app, which includes the user's ability to like, share, repost, or otherwise engage that content, will be social media. On the other hand, if the mobile app provides the convenience of watching the televised content in substantially the same broadcast mode as a television, then the use of a mobile device will not transform the broadcast into social media.

1.2. Importance

Social media is increasingly moving to supplant mass media in market share. The revenue from advertising, ticket sales, and product sales continues to grow in size and importance. As PriceWaterhouseCoopers noted "[i]n an era of 24-hour news and player tweets, fans want to know everything and be as close to the action as possible, or even inside it" (PWC, 2011). Even a modest shift of audience to social media networks is worth billions of dollars in revenue. And over time, this shift will likely be far more than modest as broadcast television, satellite, and cable risk losing their dominant role.

Clarifying the scope and structure of social media will have increasing importance to the distribution of sports content, sources of sporting revenue, and interpretations of contracts and regulations involving media licenses and player management. For example, as sports leagues develop new techniques to engage their fans, the leagues will seek to extend their own content into online Internet sites and mobile apps. Their ability to do so will be limited by the exclusive broadcast contracts they have previously entered with television, cable, radio, and satellite networks.

Social media poses other puzzles. For example, which party has the right to upload a clip of a game-ending goal to social media website—the player who scored, the team for whom he plays, the league which regulates team play, or the broadcaster who recorded the footage and copyrighted the broadcast? The answer will likely be found in the contracts between the league and the broadcaster as well as the collective bargaining agreement regulating the player. At the same time, the clip may have been uploaded dozens or hundreds of times by fans who celebrated the event and shared the clip without authorization. The player and the team may wish for unlicensed clips to remain available online while the league and broadcaster requires the copyright in the clip to be aggressively enforced.

In drafting regulations and agreements to create a common understanding among players, teams, leagues, mass media broadcasters, and social media networks, a common understanding of these expectations will need to be developed. These understandings also need to take the fan expectations into account so the reputations of the players, teams, and leagues are not harmed by the unintended consequences of excessive policing of social media or a failure to police when necessary.

1.3. Fantasy Leagues and Specialized Sports Social Media

In addition to the importance sports content plays on general social media sites like Twitter, Facebook, and YouTube, there are also sites devoted exclusively to sports content and lifestyle. SportsFanLive, which is available at www.sportsfanlive.com/, provides newsfeeds, team coverage, meet-ups, and other fan support. A number of similar platforms have launched but few have remained viable. In contrast, fantasy sports leagues such as DraftKings and FanDuel have become the new platform for fans interested in engaging in their fan interest through a highly interactive platform. The National Basketball Association (NBA) became an equity investor in FanDuel. The NHL became an equity investor in rival DraftKings, as did two NFL teams (Schrotenboer, 2015).

For social media platforms such as Yahoo and CBS, the fantasy sports league opportunity complements the active engagement of the audience. The fantasy betting sites transform the interaction between fan and sport, gamifying the experience. DraftKings and FanDuel—both of which are discussed in greater detail in the accompanying chapter on daily fantasy sports law—are less social media and closer to sports wagering websites, using the structure of the user-generated team structure to skirt sports gambling laws.

It is likely the convergence will continue between mass media, social media, and fan gamification. This convergence will likely move to social media platforms that incorporate both sporting and non-sporting aspects of the individual's life. Eventually a dominant social media host, whether Facebook or a next-generation successor to its open architecture, will serve to integrate live broadcast, fan participation, merchandise consumption, and gaming in a single interface. All participants in sports' economic model are jockeying to be at the center of this new medium. Still, it is likely that the dominant host will not emerge for a number of years to come. The winner of the power struggle will likely be determined both by the economics of the marketplace and by the legal regulations that emerge in the next few years.

2. Social Media as Sports Broadcasting

Sports broadcasting did not always include the comprehensive television coverage that makes the home experience better than the experience watching the game live from the stadium or arena. When sports were covered only by newspapers and radio, much of the information was necessarily left to the imagination of the fan.

2.1. The Origins of Social Media Sports Broadcasting

Television coverage of broadcast shows provides both play-by-play coverage of each game and replays of all significant action.

Still, for many fans, live television coverage has unacceptable restrictions. The rules on out-of-market broadcasts sometimes limit the geographic region in which a game is broadcast. At other times, fans find themselves unable to watch TV and must rely on intermittent updates of the game without access to the television broadcast.

In 1996, Motorola, Inc. created a product named SportsTrax, which was designed to fill the content gap for fans who could not attend games and could not stay home to watch those games on television. SportsTrax offered the ability to stay current with (NBA) games. "SportsTrax displays the following information on NBA games in progress: (i) the teams playing; (ii) score changes; (iii) the team in possession of the ball; (iv) whether the team is in the free-throw bonus; (v) the quarter of the game; and (vi) time remaining in the quarter" (*National Basketball Association v. Motorola*, 105 F.3d at

843–844). This information is a far cry from the full game experience, but it did allow the Motorola customers to stay current with the scoring and the flow of the game. As the litigation progressed, similar information was available to America Online (AOL) customers through Motorola's STATs service.

The NBA sued to enjoin Motorola and AOL under a U.S. federal common law doctrine known as "hot news misappropriation." The Second Circuit held that hot news misappropriation continued to be a viable legal claim, but then determined that neither Motorola nor AOL had violated the very narrow right to prevent third-partying copying of information.

Under the test for hot news misappropriation, five elements must be established for the plaintiff to prevail:

> (i) a plaintiff generates or gathers information at a cost; (ii) the information is time-sensitive; (iii) a defendant's use of the information constitutes free riding on the plaintiff's efforts; (iv) the defendant is in direct competition with a product or service offered by the plaintiffs; and (v) the ability of other parties to free-ride on the efforts of the plaintiff or others would so reduce the incentive to produce the product or service that its existence or quality would be substantially threatened.
>
> (*NBA*, 105 F.3d at 845)

As viewed by the court, the NBA is in the business of producing basketball games and in the business of producing and selling copyrighted broadcasts of basketball games. U.S. copyright protection does not extend to the facts, scores, or statistics of the game and the NBA cannot logically be in the business of manufacturing those facts. Motorola did not free-ride on either the games themselves or the broadcasts, since SportsTrax merely reported the factual information that resulted from the games. As the court explained, "there is no evidence that anyone regards SportsTrax or the AOL site as a substitute for attending NBA games . . .. In fact, Motorola markets SportsTrax as being designed 'for those times when you cannot be at the arena, watch the game on TV, or listen to the radio . . .' " (*NBA*, 105 F.3d at 853–854).

Neither Motorola nor AOL was stopped from offering its service. The court speculated whether a product owned by the NBA could become a direct competitor of Motorola. Writing in 1997, the court found such an occurrence unlikely. The situation, however, has evolved. Today both the leagues and the competitors are actively distributing this content.

2.2. Tweeting Scores and Posting Play-by-Play

Unlike the 1996 experience of SportTrax, a sports fan unable to watch the game on TV or at the stadium can turn to Twitter, Instagram, mobile apps, or social media sites for a comprehensive production of photos, videos, statistics, and commentary regarding the ongoing, real-time status of a game. In fact, the potential is so great that the U.S.

National Football League has entered into an agreement with Twitter to authorize live game tweets and provide official Twitter feeds to augment or replace fan content during the live broadcast of American football games.

Partnerships between leagues and the social media sites Facebook and Twitter provide links to purchase Internet-based broadcasts of those league games. This phenomenon increasingly shifts the point-of-purchase for broadcast to an on-demand model. This will ultimately reduce the value of the mass media broadcast license and shift revenue structure toward direct payment for broadcast to the leagues.

At the same time, there is a significant interest in dual-screen interactivity, by which fans are engaged both in watching a mass media broadcast and in accessing the content through their Internet connection or mobile device. For the leagues, the dual-screen fan becomes the ultimate at-home customer. The fan can receive commentary from self-selected feeds based on the fan's own team and player favorites. The fan can be offered goods and merchandise tailored to that fan's profile and history of engagement with the league. And the fan can be part of a social network, which engages the fan and rewards him for remaining part of the fanbase. Such fans are likely to generate far higher loyalty and revenue than any others, and they are likely to be less expensive to retain on a weekly and seasonal basis. For social media content curated by the league, dual-screen interactivity is the next step in fan support and marketing.

2.3. Exclusive Broadcast Licenses and the Threat of User-Generated Coverage

Much of the social media content, however, remains user generated. As noted in *NBA v. Motorola*, the scores and statistics are not covered by copyright law. Broadcasts of the games, in contrast, are protected by copyright laws. Because copyright protection begins at the moment of fixation, the recording of a live game is sufficient to vest copyright protection in the author of the broadcast, which is typically the league under U.S. contracts.

The NFL is among the most aggressive in policing its intellectual property interests among the various sports leagues. Using the takedown provisions first promulgated under the WIPO Copyright Treaty and the WIPO Performances and Phonograms Treaty (17 U.S.C. §512 (2016)), the NFL regularly sends notifications of copyright infringement to social media sites to remove links to the images. Generally, this results in only the links to the copyrighted video clips being removed.

The NFL is now a contractual partner with Twitter. So when two Twitter accounts were deactivated after the NFL filed a takedown regarding video clips, concerns were raised that the companies were seeking to punish the account holders rather than the individual posts (Bieler, 2015). The two sites were restored by Twitter and the NFL disclaimed any request for the removal of the sites. But the incident raised additional concerns that the terms of service on the social media sites could give rights to even greater restrictions on what content can be posted by the system users.

The NFL owns the copyright in the American football broadcasts. As copyright holder, this may give the league the right to remove short clips, though such short clips may also fall within the definition of copyright fair use, since the short clips when used in the context of the commentary may constitute a form of comment or criticism.

At the same time, the league cannot own fan photographs taken during the sporting events. These photos (as well as videos taken by the fans themselves) are not copied from the copyrighted work owned by the league. The league does not own a copyright in the game but rather in its depiction of the game. As a result, original photographs filling social media sites should be immune from copyright complaints.

For the leagues and broadcasters there are still strong economic incentives to control the distribution of this content. They may attempt to assert additional control by negotiating for restrictive terms of service for the social media site end user license agreements. Although these policies are rarely read by social media users, they determine whether content is permitted or prohibited on the social media site. A restrictive terms-of-service agreement could threaten the user-generated fan content and return control of social media from the fans to the leagues. As leagues enter into licensing agreements with the social media platforms or begin to acquire equity ownership of these platforms, it is likely that this interest will lead to some restrictions in the end user license agreements.

3. Athlete and Coach as Social Media Broadcaster

In addition to the social media content generated by the fans and by the leagues, another source of significant social media may be generated by the individual athletes.

3.1. Role of the Athlete in Social Media

As the Professional Football Association (of England and Wales) (PFA) explains on its player's website (http://www.thepfa.com/) regarding social media, "[p]ositive use of social media allows you to communicate and interact directly with fans thereby instilling a sense of loyalty and connection between supporters, players and clubs." The PFA highlights other incentives, explaining that social media "can also enhance your own and your club's commercial activities and revenue generation by allowing you to globally and publicly promote any commercial ventures you may have."

At the same time, the instructions of the PFA highlight the concerns that many teams and leagues have regarding the social media activities of their athletes:

> Recent cases have established that anything posted on a social networking site, regardless of the intended recipient, may be considered public information.

> As blogging is therefore considered to be information in the public domain, anything which is written should be treated in exactly the same way as you would approach any comment given to the press, for example by way of an interview or a press conference.
>
> Furthermore, messages which are intended to be private and for a particular person can be forwarded on or published without your consent. Take great care therefore with what you write and to whom and always be confident that if a message were to be published this could in no way leave you open to criticism or punishment.
>
> In addition, posting false or defamatory material might not only leave you open to punishment from your club and/or from The FA and legal action, it may also have the effect of seriously damaging your public image.
>
> Finally, discussing team mates or fellow professionals in a negative light may not only impact on team morale but in extreme circumstances could lead to criticism of you, for instance if a controversial incident then occurs on the pitch or if there is any problems between rival supporters.

These concerns represent a modest set of the potential controversies that can erupt if team members post derogatory information about family, friends, or other players and their teams. Misinformation and disinformation can affect trade deals among teams and harm relationships between a player and the team or league.

As a result of the unintended consequences of ill-conceived posts and tweets, social media has become a significant concern for amateur and professional athletes alike.

3.2. Privacy and Defamation in the Social Media Context

At the most extreme, the harmful publication on social media of a statement that is defamatory or an invasion of privacy can lead to financial liability for the harm caused by the statements. Both tort law and privacy law vary significantly from jurisdiction to jurisdiction, both within the United States and throughout the world. "Under typical state defamation law, the defamed private citizen had to prove only a false publication that would subject him to hatred, contempt, or ridicule. Given such publication, general damage to reputation was presumed, while punitive damages required proof of additional facts" (Gertz v. Robert Welch, Inc., 418 U.S. at 370 (1974)).

With the advent of the Internet and recognition of press freedoms in various countries, some governments have substantially revised the harm required to prove defamation. In the United Kingdom, for example, the Defamation Act of 2013 transformed UK law, requiring that serious harm resulted from the false publication as a condition of a defamation action. The UK also adopted a rule first established in the United States that immunized Internet Service Providers from the defamatory statements posted by their users.

In other countries, however, it may be easier to succeed in a claim of defamation. The outcomes will vary greatly. In Australia, for example, the rugby league player Andrew Ettinghausen brought a successful defamation lawsuit against *HQ Magazine* for publication of a nude photograph published without permission. "The court found that the photograph led him to be ridiculed because it showed his genitals to readers of a magazine with widespread readership. The court accepted that the publication lowered the public's estimation of Etttinghausen by implying he had authorised the taking and publication of the photograph" (*Unauthorised Use of Your Image*, 2016).

Because the laws of defamation vary so greatly and athletic competitions are often international in nature, athletes must pay very careful attention to posts and comments that hold others up to harm or ridicule. If a UK footballer were to comment on a competitor from another country, that footballer risks having the case heard in that other country and being subject to that country's legal system. The global nature of the Internet adds an additional risk for those accused of defamation, because the party bringing suit can try to find countries with sympathetic laws willing to hear the case.

Like defamation, the law regarding invasion of privacy varies significantly from jurisdiction to jurisdiction. Invasions of privacy may involve the unwanted disclosure of private facts or it may be so broad as to include the unauthorized publication of a person's image. In some situations, those photographs might result in liability even if taken in public.

Under Article 8 of the European Convention on Human Rights, there is at least theoretical protection against unauthorized publications of photographs taken in public.

> [A] person's image constitutes one of the chief attributes of his or her personality, as it reveals the person's unique characteristics and distinguishes the person from his or her peers. The right to the protection of one's image is thus one of the essential components of personal development. It mainly presupposes the individual's right to control the use of that image, including the right to refuse publication thereof...
>
> (*Von Hannover v. Germany (no. 2), § 96; see also* European Court of Human Rights, 2016)

Despite the rather broad language of the European Court of Human Rights, this right to control publication of one's image is balanced by Article 10, covering freedom of expression and access to public information. As a result, cases brought in various European courts under Article 8 have rather inconsistent outcomes, often depending on factors such as the public interest in the publication of the information and the public exposure of the individual at the time the photograph was taken. The public setting of the photograph is not sufficient, however, to make the photograph automatically publishable without restriction.

This snapshot of defamation and privacy is not in any way exhaustive. Instead, it provides a context in which to understand the risks athletes undertake when they choose to enhance their public presence through social media.

3.3. Potential for Obligations to Stop Harassing Speech Under Title IX

In the context of U.S. student athletics, an additional category of potential liability exists for the student athlete, the coach, and the athlete's institution as a result of Title IX of the

Education Amendments of 1972 (Title IX). Title IX provides that "no individual may be discriminated against on the basis of sex in any education program or activity receiving Federal financial assistance" (U.S. Department of Education, 1997). This very broad-ranging regulatory regime extends to student athletes, coaches, schools, and fans.

A school, for example, would be liable for any actions taken by its employee that constituted sexual harassment. If a coach were to coerce a player into providing nude photographs which the coach then distributed using social media, both the coach and the school would be liable under Title IX for the violation of the player's civil rights. Unfortunately, a number of coaches have been fired or arrested for sending their own nude photographs to student players.

More typical of some social media is the highly charged language that can sometimes be used by players and fans. "Sexually harassing conduct of third parties, who are not themselves employees or students at the school (e.g., a visiting speaker or members of a visiting athletic club) can also cause a sexually hostile environment in school programs or activities" (U.S. Department of Education, 1997). A concerted social media campaign aimed at a student can result in actionable sexual harassment, obligating the home institution of those involved to take action, even if the harasser and the victim are at different schools. Social media posts and comments sometimes become quite hurtful and vindictive. When such attacks include language or images, the school has the obligation to protect the students and stop the abuse.

3.4. Potential for Unintended Interference with Contractual Rights of Other Teams

Coaches and team management personnel face another risk from ill-conceived tweets, posts, or comments. Many leagues have very specific rules regarding the right of a team to engage players and coaches regarding their rights to change teams. Posts discussing player movement of one's own teammates or the prospects of landing new players and coaches could violate these rules.

Many leagues have anti-tampering rules which apply to owners, teams, coaches, and players. These rules generally include public statements and press statements, which often extend to the public statements made in social media. Tweets by players calling on other players to join their teams, comments by coaches or owners of ongoing interest in other teams' players, and commentary on contract disputes in other teams may all violate the league rules.

These rules apply with equal force to press conferences and other media interaction, but unlike those venues, the ability to send a quick tweet, make a Facebook post, or comment on a posted photograph can occur before the author considers the legal implication of the action. Social media is the same as all other media in its power, but it differs because of the access. For players and coaches, in particular, this difference often results in unintended consequences and difficult situations.

A similar set of rules applies to collegiate athletics. In the United States, the National Collegiate Athletic Association (NCAA) maintains strict rules regarding the interaction between prospective players and future recruitment. These strict rules are conceptually at odds with the casual nature of social media. Teams, players, coaches, and agents must be very careful not to reach out to potential recruits in violation of these regulations. Public comments are prohibited in these situations just as private communications are prohibited. So even a seemingly innocuous tweet or post has jeopardized the ability to sign a recruit because the post violated NCAA communications restrictions.

4. Regulating Social Media for the Athlete by Law

In the United States, the market power of social media has long been recognized as unique among media. This may be a result of the intimacy of social media for the user or the ability to intersperse more explicitly commercial advertisement amongst the editorial nature of content provided by friends and neighbors. As a result, the U.S. Federal Trade Commission (FCC) has established regulations that specify minimum disclosures which must occur as part of any commercial social media marketing campaign.

4.1. In the United States—Endorsement Guidelines

For athletes and others involved in the lucrative endorsement business, these guidelines establish how they can be compensated for their commercial social media endeavors. The FCC guidelines do not prohibit commercial advertisements or endorsements by paid spokespersons. Instead, the guidelines establish regulatory expectations requiring that the information provided to the public is accurate and honest, and that any payments or incentives provided to the endorsing individual be disclosed.

Under the Guides Concerning Use of Endorsements and Testimonials in Advertising, the first guideline requires that any endorsements "reflect the honest opinions, findings, beliefs, or experience of the endorser" (FTC Guides, 2010). This requires an athlete to actually use a product if he claims to use it on social media or to believe in the benefits of a product if an athlete posts positive comments about the benefits. The belief in the benefits is further limited. "[A]n endorsement may not convey any express or implied representation that would be deceptive if made directly by the advertiser." So an athlete may only make health claims or efficacy claims if she both believes those claims and the statements would be permitted as verified if the same statements were claims made by the manufacturer. Whether conducted on mass media or social media, these commercial activities will be treated as endorsements by the FTC.

The honest opinion requirement includes a temporal limitation that protects the athlete. Not only must the endorsement honestly reflect the opinion of the athlete, it must be accurate when used. So if a young athlete spoke glowingly of a product but then switched products a few years later, the manufacturer could not continue to promote the out-of-date promotional material.

A second category of guideline expectations focuses on the public disclosure of the relationship between the advertiser and the endorser. "When there exists a connection between the endorser and the seller of the advertised product that might materially affect the weight or credibility of the endorsement (i.e., the connection is not reasonably expected by the audience), such connection must be fully disclosed." As a result, most endorsements over social media must include some form of disclosure that the person providing the endorsement has been compensated.

This is an area where mass media and social media diverge. Because the television audience understands that celebrities and athletes appearing in television ads are paid for their services, there is no need to disclose the relationship. In contrast, a celebrity athlete discussing a product during a television talk show would be required to disclose the relationship with the advertiser because the context of the talk show would fail to inform the audience the product was being endorsed.

Social media generally falls into this second category. Tweets, Facebook posts, Snapchat photographs, and similar content should all require that an athlete receiving compensation for promoting those products must disclose the financial nature of the relationship. At the same time, an advertisement that scrolls before a YouTube video clip has the characteristics of the television ad and the public would generally understand that an appearance in that clip was a paid performance.

The guidelines also recognize the practical nature of athletic endorsements. It is common practice for athletes to enter into product endorsements which require the athlete to wear clothing that features the insignia or trademarks of the manufacturer. Images of the athlete wearing the logos appear in paid advertisements, sporting events, news coverage, and media engagement. As long as the athlete is not making any representations about the clothing, the appearance of the insignia in the media does not trigger a requirement to disclose the endorsement.

Many advertisers raised concerns about the challenge to provide conspicuous disclosures in the limited space available through social media platforms. The FTC has published a guide entitled "How to Make Effective Disclosures in Digital Advertising" specifically to explain the techniques to make the disclosures clear and conspicuous. Although the guide has lengthy explanations, the simple requirement is that the endorser must make the disclosure appear reasonably close to the claims in a readable and visible font.

Endorsers are responsible for avoiding false or undisclosed endorsements. Advertisers are responsible for adherence to the guidelines both for the advertiser and for all its endorsers.

4.2. In the EU and Other Jurisdictions

Like the regulatory regime in the United States, most other jurisdictions provide for similar rules that require some form of notice regarding a relationship between an athlete or endorser and the advertiser, and all typically have some combination of antifraud provisions and truthful advertising provisions that result in obligations to be truthful, accurate, and sufficiently informative to avoid misleading the public. In Europe, for example, EC Directive 2005/29/EC provides foundational regulation on misleading advertising. The British CAP Code provides a self-regulatory supplement to the EC Directives and other laws. As the CAP Code explains, however, "trading privileges may be revoked . . . and . . . noncomplying parties can be referred to Trading Standards for action, where appropriate, under the Consumer Protection from Unfair Trading Regulations 2008 or the Business Protection from Misleading Marketing Regulations 2008." So these advertising self-regulations take on the force of regulatory law.

The CAP Code does not use social media in its remit. Instead, it covers such activities as advertorials, advertisements in non-broadcast electronic media, emails, text transmissions, and, most generally, sales promotions in non-broadcast media. These illustrations of advertising all reflect particular aspects of social media advertising and illuminate how the scope of regulations is very broad and complete. Nonetheless, the specificity of the methods to advertise helps put the athlete and team on notice regarding the promotional activities they might undertake.

The CAP Code promotes truthful advertising. "The central principle for all marketing communications is that they should be legal, decent, honest and truthful. All marketing communications should be prepared with a sense of responsibility to consumers and society and should reflect the spirit, not merely the letter, of the Code."

At the same time, the CAP Code does not provide the level of specificity as the FTC Guidelines regarding endorsements. Under the CAP Code, "[c]laims that are likely to be interpreted as factual and appear in a testimonial must not mislead or be likely to mislead the consumer." A marketer can utilize an accurate statement produced in published sources for advertising purposes without the express permission of the endorsing person. So under this provision, an advertiser can repurpose an athlete's statement if it is correct and beneficial to the advertiser.

The CAP Code does limit other forms of athlete endorsements. Athletes cannot endorse medicines. Nor can athletes be used to suggest that alcohol improves athletic performance.

In Canada, the Competition Act is supplemented by the Deceptive Marketing Practices Act, which provides a brief introduction to the challenges of digital advertising. Volume I of the Deceptive Marketing Practice Act focused, in part, on the practice of "astroturfing," in which a marketing firm utilizes what appears to be broad-case social media support for a product or service, but which in fact is comprised of either falsely created posts or posts provided by employees and other paid individuals. These fake versions of grass-roots public support can readily deceive readers of the reviews and constitute an unfair trade practice in Canada as well as the United States and UK.

5. Social Media's Risk of Harm to the Athlete

Although the various national guidelines provide the most detailed and comprehensive regulatory discussion of social media endorsements, they do not stand alone. Myriad laws in each state and jurisdiction bar untrue, deceptive, or misleading advertising. Every state has a law barring fraudulent advertising. These state laws often include the right to contract damages, injunctive relief, financial penalties, and even criminal actions for intentionally fraudulent advertising. There are very few instances in which the athlete, coach, team, or league will be found violating such provisions.

5.1. Fraud with the Athlete as Victim

On the other hand, online bulletin boards, chat rooms, and similar social media gathering places provide natural opportunities to take advantage of naïve athletes hoping to find opportunities to launch their careers. These online venues create an excellent platform for predators to take advantage of vulnerable athletes seeking jobs or endorsement opportunities. False business fronts can create interesting and dynamic opportunities that are too-good-to-be-true investment opportunities for athletes looking to break into business or endorsement deals. False sports agencies or management firms can offer the illusion of services and yet steal from the players with impunity. European football players often extend their careers in Asia or Central America. Reports continue to surface that when looking for these opportunities, many players who thought they had obtained lucrative employment contracts and skilled representation find themselves the victims of Internet fraud.

On Twitter, many of the accounts purporting to be owned by athletes are actually owned by unrelated third parties. A good many of these accounts are obvious parodies, but others are subtler and allow the unauthorized controller of the account to speak on behalf of the athlete. These false accounts or similar false social media identities may allow identity thieves to pose as the athletes and seek out payments for legitimate—or improper—opportunities that enable the impersonator to exploit the athlete's public career.

Since the enforcement tools of the FTC do not generally reach to individual complaints among private individuals, the state law antifraud and false advertising statutes become much more important for the athlete. The first step in such a situation is typically to reach out to the social media platform to free the unauthorized account. Because such fraud is so common, the social media companies are quite efficient at this process. If the fraudulent account has created financial harm in addition to emotional embarrassment, then the athlete must rely on state criminal authorities or else attempt a private lawsuit in state or federal court. This process is complicated, of course, because the offending party may not be in the same state as the athlete. As a result, the challenges for recourse against such fraud are great and the likelihood of success only modest.

5.2. Blackmail, Revenge, and Other Abuses of Social Media

As outlined at the beginning of the chapter, American football player Laremy Tunsil paid a tremendous price for his college indiscretions when his misconduct was promoted on the eve of his professional draft. Tunsil, however, is not alone. American hockey player Jaromir Jagr (at age 43), was shown in bed in a photo with an eighteen-year-old Czech Republic model (Bleier, 2015). Jagr was allegedly asked to pay $2,000 to stop the release of the photo, but he refused, resulting in both the blackmail story and the photo going viral.

Television celebrity and professional wrestler Hulk Hogan received a jury verdict of $140 million against social media platform Gawker.com for intentionally posting an edited version of a surreptitiously recorded videotape of the wrestler in an adulterous relationship with a friend's wife. Unlike many of the other examples, Hogan chose to fight the unauthorized posting, and he had good information about the company posting the content.

These examples highlight the difficult and increasingly common experience for athletes being targeted for negative media in their personal lives as well as their professional lives. In such situations, the athlete likely did participate in the behavior in question. But unlike traditional mass media—which tends to limit such coverage to newsworthy event—social media platforms have few, if any, editorial policies. Everything gets posted and every moment of an athlete's personal life may be caught on camera. The effect has certainly impacted the private lives of the athletes. It may be that the athletes are becoming increasingly unavailable to the public. There may be greater need for confidentiality agreements and media release in prenuptial agreements. Conceivably, some athletes may seek confidentiality agreements as a condition of dating relationships and as part of any staff or management hired by the athlete. These contracts may provide limited protection, but they offer some degree of control for the athlete who otherwise risks giving up a personal life as a condition of participation in the sport.

5.3. Sexism and Hate Speech Directed at Female Athletes and Journalists

Social media makes the personal life of female athletes and journalists even harder than for their male counterparts. For both men and women, the barroom culture of some social media platforms leads to intolerant, violent, racist, and shameful comments. But the threats to women often take on a predatory tone and the situations can escalate to the point where women athletes and journalists are put at risk by the abusive culture acceptable to some sports fans.

The Online News Association, the largest association of digital journalists, began to lead an effort to respond to this culture with a 2015 national program on the topic. In 2016, sports journalist Erin Andrews won a $55 million jury verdict against a Nashville Marriott hotel and the man who stalked her before posting a nude video of her. The stalker easily tricked the hotel into providing Andrew's hotel room information. He mounted a video camera to the peephole in her hotel room door to capture the surreptitiously filmed content. The stalker was separately convicted for his criminal behavior.

Rare wins in the courts and panels by news organizations are doing little to address the broader culture of sexism in social media, which occurs in every field but is particularly rampant in sports commentary. As discussed in Section 3, there is a duty for schools to protect students from such sexual abuse and there is a more general duty for employers to protect their employees from such a work environment.

The employers in the sports industry and in journalism have generally shrugged off the issue as endemic to the public rather than addressing it directly. But just as any bar has an obligation to police its patrons, and any amusement park must work to ensure that customers do not get out of hand, these employers have the same obligations. Increasingly, athletes and journalists seek greater responsibility from these employers. Change, however, is slow. In all likelihood then, it will require a number of high-profile claims against the larger mass media companies and social media platforms before mechanisms are put in place to safeguard the female employees.

6. Regulating the Athlete's Social Media by Contract

Almost every amateur and professional sport has some regulatory body which establishes the professional conduct expected of the athletes. In the United States, this power is vested in the universities, which, in turn, are held accountable by the NCAA. The professional sports leagues place this authority in the league commissioner or president. For example, in the NBA, this obligation is embodied in the "good moral character" clause. Similarly, in the NFL, the policy requires players to avoid "conduct detrimental to the integrity and public confidence" of the league.

6.1. Behavior Policies

As discussed earlier, one of the challenges raised by social media is the extent to which a player's personal life is made accessible to the public through social media posts by those surrounding the athlete. Such disclosure of an athlete's misconduct by third parties is not materially different if it is reported through social media rather than through other means. Of course, when misconduct is shown on video, it generally carries more weight than when merely described. And when misconduct is distributed to the public for millions of viewers, it requires a stronger response from the governing body than when the situation is known only to the clubs, leagues, and players. But the public nature of social media does not materially alter the standards or process of discipline.

In contrast, social media has become a common source of discipline for athletes because of the content they share themselves. Players, coaches, owners, and others have regularly posted, tweeted, and shared offensive content that can trigger discipline for violation of league policies. Professional athletes may be criticized for their online activities, but there has been only a modest number of consequences to player's continuing employment. NFL running back Larry Johnson was suspended in 2009 for an anti-gay comment. NBA athlete Amare Stoudemire was fined $50,000 for an anti-gay slur in 2012. Greek Olympic athlete Voula Papachristou was expelled from her Olympic team after posting a racist tweet. Rio Ferdinand was suspended by the Premiere League Football Association for three matches and fined £25,000 for a sexist tweet. While not epidemic, these situations continue to occur with regularity.

More than the professionals, it is primarily the collegiate athletes who are punished for inappropriate social media activities. School policies sometimes ban players from using Twitter or other certain social media platforms to create a prophylactic protection against short-sighted comments and posts. Where not banned from use of social media, some student athletes post inappropriate comments about opponents, opposing schools, or other issues that result in school discipline.

Technically, public universities are bound to respect the free speech rights of their students, but in practice this has not posed a significant limitation on social media bans. Team discipline and cohesion may be a sufficient rationale to uphold these bans. More likely, the players cannot risk losing playing time or other support from their coaches, so they would not be likely to challenge these rules. So despite the questionable legal basis for these bans at public universities they are likely to continue to become popular with more and more schools.

6.2. Concerted Action and Player's Right to Collective Bargaining

For most industries in the United States, drafting social media policies continues to prove exceptionally difficult. This is because any ban on social media usage by an employee directly interferes with that employee's right to collectively bargain and right to take concerted activity regarding wages or working conditions. When disciplining an employee for violating a social media policy, the employer must be able to rely on a lawful policy. Creating a policy which allows for the employee's right to discuss working conditions, wages, and similar aspects of employment while prohibiting harmful or disparaging speech regarding others has proven to be quite a challenge. If the policy itself is unlawful, then the discipline exacted under the policy violates the labor rules.

Athletic teams and leagues are not exempt from these general labor regulations. As social media continues to expand as a predominant platform for player communication with the public, there will be an increasing number of high-stakes disciplinary cases which challenge the basis of these disciplinary policies. The failure to adhere to the strict U.S. National Labor Relations Board protocols on these policies would likely undermine the enforceability of these provisions.

In fact, the sanctions discussed earlier have all been focused on racist, sexist, anti-gay, or similar forms of intolerant speech. Such speech is far outside the categories of speech afforded protection under employment laws, so it may be that this is the reason that the disciplinary proceedings have had this common focus. Punishment regarding this category of speech is one of the most likely to be upheld by courts and regulators. Over time, the policies will continue to be refined and the scope of the enforceable provisions clarified. As such language becomes more common in industry, the sports leagues will also embrace these additional constraints on player posts.

6.3. Exclusive Endorsement Agreements

Another significant limitation on what a player can post will come from the agreements already entered by that player. Many athletes enter exclusive endorsement agreements as a significant source of revenue. These agreements typically include explicit obligations about mass media content and public appearances. With the rise of social media as a major marketing platform, these endorsement agreements now typically include language that limits what the endorser can say on social media about both the endorsed products and the competing products.

Sports teams' colors, names, and insignias are a valuable asset for the endorsing athlete. These tools, however, may be limited by team or league rule. The endorsement agreement likely requires the athlete use "best efforts" to use the team colors, names, and insignias in the social media activities of the player rather than making such use an express requirement of the contract. A player will likely post or repost photos of games. How closely the endorsement content can be associated with these posts will be covered by league rules rather than the endorsement agreement.

Endorsement agreements generally specify appearance and commercial filming activities. As the value of social media revenue increases, these agreements will begin to utilize more specific language regarding the number and type of social media posts that include the endorsed products, in photos or discussion. Potentially, these posts could be separately monitored and the value of the contract could incorporate the popularity of those posts. Since online and mobile content is much more trackable than traditional television, it is inevitable that such tracking tools will move into the calculation of pricing for the endorsements.

A well-drafted endorsement agreement will clarify how the endorsement activity will occur for the athlete. As discussed earlier, at a minimum, the athlete will need to comply with the full-disclosure requirements of the jurisdictions' media endorsement regulations. Negative comments are also a form of endorsement activity which the athlete should avoid. A tweet complaining about a brand of golf club to disparage that brand could run afoul of the contract and the jurisdiction's marketing guidelines. If the tweet was not the true opinion of the athlete, it could trigger a claim of fraud or unfair competition. The athlete should also seek a contract that carefully specifies which products and services are covered by the agreement. Such contractual language would help the athlete avoid discussing conflicting products and services on social media.

The terms of the agreement will also require morals clauses. The endorsement agreement may be significantly broader in scope than those required by the leagues. In such a "conduct unbecoming" clause, the advertiser will generally reserve the right to cancel the contract if the athletes engage in any form of conduct that places the advertiser or the athlete in a negative or disparaging light. The provision may be reciprocal, allowing the athlete to also drop the endorsement if the advertiser acts in a negative or disparaging light that would embarrass the athlete.

6.4. Social Media Athlete Provisions in the End User License Agreement

The final source of management and regulation of content on the social media platforms can come from the various platforms themselves. There is tremendous competition between the existing platforms to gain traffic, boost advertising revenue, and generate other forms of market value. Over time, more and more sports leagues will be entering into contractual relations with particular platforms.

As with the agreement between the NFL and Twitter, these agreements will often specify that the league will provide some exclusive content in exchange for payment and revenue sharing. The agreement may require the social media platform to limit content from other sources. In addition, these league-based agreements may extend obligations through the collective bargaining agreement or individual agreements to require some or all of the athletes to participate in that "official" social media platform as part of the player's obligations to support the league.

Just as athletes today must participate in some broadcast journalistic exercises, the new wave of social media arrangements will make online participation a part of the player's future obligations. If an endorsement agreement can require an endorsing athlete to make a minimum number of positive posts regarding the product, a league could similarly require that each player (or each team) make a required minimum of posts, photos, and comments to support the league and promote the sport.

Contractual agreements in the End User License Agreement may also change the way some social media platforms handle sports coverage. These platforms often have no-disparagement language. To protect themselves and their players, leagues may begin to filter the accounts of their athletes to look for content that could give rise to such problems. Leagues may begin to introduce this authority through the collective bargaining process or through contracts with individual athletes.

Like the required five-second delay on many live broadcasts, these filters could serve to enforce both league policies and End User License Agreement terms to stop athletes, coaches, and owners from distributing harmful pictures and posts. The introduction of these tools may require an increase in the revenue from these platforms, but the trend continues to show an increase in advertising and traffic onto social media and away from mass media. As that trend continues, the value of these prophylactic measures increases. The ability to update the End User License Agreement to require these additional tools and the potential to attract exclusive league agreements by provision of these additional services makes it highly likely that this next generation of filtering tools will be made available in the near future.

7. Conclusion: Sports in the Context of Social Media Law

Social media continues to challenge traditional mass media in its appeal to both the athlete and sports fan as the home of sports coverage. The immediacy of the interactions, the ability to focus very specifically on the athletes, games, teams, and leagues of particular interest, the mobility, and the global nature of the medium all give social media an edge over traditional mass media. Since players continue to use the medium themselves, the platforms will continue to thrive.

Social media is a source of great economic opportunity for the leagues and the players. Agreements between leagues and social media platforms are aligning the interests of both. Yet the vast diversity of social media platforms will continue to make this a difficult terrain to manage, regulate, and navigate for years to come. Individual players, in particular, remain the most vulnerable to making mistakes. These mistakes will come from posting inappropriate content such as content that is disparaging speech, content that violates endorsement guidelines, or content that violates tampering or recruiting rules. Athletes will also be vulnerable to the victimization that can come from the deluge of hate speech and sexually harassing speech which remains all too common in social media.

Nonetheless, despite the challenges to athletes, the opportunity to connect with fans, to promote themselves, and to promote their endorsed products makes social media highly attractive. Ultimately, athletes will remain on social media because the sports fans will remain on social media. Social media's role will only continue to grow in years to come. Social media is the new home for sports.

References

Bieler, Das. (2015). "Twitter Suspends Deadspin and SBNationGIF Accounts, Allegedly at NFL's Behest.'" *Washington Post*, October 13, www.washingtonpost.com/news/early-lead/wp/2015/10/12/twitter-suspends-deadspin-and-sbnationgif-accounts-allegedly-at-nfls-behest.

Bishara, Motez, and Martin, Jill. (2016, April 29). *Laremy Tunsil: Twitter Hack Could Cost Him Millions After Pot Video Goes Viral*, CNN, http://www.edition.cnn.com/2016/04/29/sport/laremy-tunsil-ole-miss-nfl-draft-twitter-hack.

Bleier, Evan. (2015). "Blackmail Selfie? Be My Guest." *Daily Mail*, September 15, www.dailymail.co.uk/news/article-3245282/Jaromir-Jagr-selfie-Catherine-Moravia-popular-Instagram-meme.html.

Deloitte. (2014). *Television's Business Model: Fit for a Digital World*, p. 11, www2.deloitte.com/content/dam/Deloitte/global/Documents/Technology-Media-Telecommunications/gx-tmt-ibc-report-2014.pdf.

European Court of Human Rights. (2016). *Factsheet—Right to the Protection of One's Image*, p. 1, www.echr.coe.int/Documents/FS_Own_image_ENG.pdf.

FTC Guides Concerning Use of Endorsements and Testimonials in Advertising. (2010). 16 C.F.R. § 255.1.

Kim, Janine Young, and Parlow, Matthew J. (2009). "Off-Court Misbehavior: Sports Leagues and Private Punishment." *Journal of Criminal Law & Criminology* 99: 573, 577–578.

Mandiberg, Michael. (2012). *The Social Media Reader* (New York: NYU Press), 1–2.

ONA15. (2015, June 16). "Keynote Takes Aim at Online Harassment of Women in Media." *Reuters*, www.reuters.com/article/idUSnMKWLCQrha+1f8+MKW20150616.

Patten, Dominic. (2016, March 7). "Erin Andrews Wins $55M in Hotel Peephole Lawsuit; Jury Blames Hotel & Stalker." *Deadline*, www.deadline.com/2016/03/erin-andrews-wins-55-million-peephole-lawsuit-espn-dancing-with-the-stars-1201715915.

PriceWatershouseCoopers. (2011). *Changing the Game: Outlook for the Global Sports Market to 2015*, p. 11, www.pwc.com/gx/en/hospitality-leisure/pdf/changing-the-game-outlook-for-the-global-sports-market-to-2015.pdf.

Schrotenboer, Brent. (2015, January). "Leagues See Real Benefits in Daily Fantasy Sports." *USA Today*, www.usatoday.com/story/sports/2015/01/01/daily-fantasy-sports-gambling-fanduel-draftkings-nba-nfl-mlb-nhl/21165279.

Social Media, The Positives . . . (2014, May 3). PFA, www.thepfa.com/players/socialmedia/positives.

Unauthorised Use of Your Image. (2011). (Woolloomooloo: Arts Law Centre of Australia), www.artslaw.com.au/info-sheets/info-sheet/unauthorised-use-of-your-image (last visited May 6, 2016).

U.S. Department of Education. (1997). *Sexual Harassment Guidance*, www2.ed.gov/about/offices/list/ocr/docs/sexhar01.html (citing 20 U.S.C. § 1681 et seq., as amended; 34 C.F.R. 106.1, 106.31(a)(b)).

Cases

Gertz v. Robert Welch, Inc., 418 U.S. 323 (1974) (White, J., dissenting).

National Basketball Ass'n v. Motorola, 105 F.3d 841 (2d Cir. 1997).

Von Hannover v. Germany (no. 2), [GC], nos. 40660/08 and 60641/08, § 96, ECHR 2012.

CHAPTER 29

PUBLIC DEVELOPMENT FOR PROFESSIONAL SPORTS STADIUMS

IRWIN P. RAIJ AND ALEXANDER CHESTER

1. Introduction

This chapter discusses the process of development and financing for stadiums used by the teams in the largest American professional sports leagues, including Major League Baseball (MLB), the National Football League (NFL), the National Basketball Association (NBA), the National Hockey League (NHL), and Major League Soccer (MLS), and the role of government in that process. With the exception of antitrust issues, there may be no aspect of American sports in which the government is as involved as the construction and financing of the stadiums in which the games are played. Stadium development, which was initially a private matter, entered the public interest because of the dramatic growth in construction costs coupled with the appearance of economic and societal benefits to a region that hosts a major league team. It will come as no surprise that venue projects are challenging and often controversial. This chapter analyzes how teams, leagues, and government entities negotiate for venue development projects. The analysis touches on the legal, practical, and political challenges that have emerged over the years. Can the site be acquired? Can it be entitled on zoned property? Is financing available? Are public funds available? Is the project in compliance with league rules? Are there environmental challenges? What kind of opposition, if any, will arise if public funds are invested? These are the questions and challenges that force parties to become more creative and forward thinking to avoid failure. Stadium financing is also unique because negotiations are open to public approval and scrutiny. Teams and governments cannot simply negotiate a good deal; they must be able to sell it to voters. Given the fluctuations in the economy as well as the public and political reception to public development, teams and their counsel must always be ready for unique and novel approaches to complete a successful stadium project.

2. History of Stadium Development

The rise in stadium development has mirrored the rise in professional sports in American life. Professional baseball emerged in the 1860s, but it wasn't until the late 1880s that the National League (NL) and the American Association began drawing a critical mass of spectators.

2.1. Emergence of Major League Baseball Ballparks

The rise of baseball as a spectator sport required the games to be played in specially designed ballparks that could seat thousands of fans rather than public parks. The first such ballpark was the Philadelphia Base Ball Grounds (later called the Baker Bowl), which opened in 1887 as the home to the NL's Philadelphia Phillies with a capacity of 12,500. The ballpark was constructed by the team's owners at a cost of $80,000 ($2.1 million in 2017 dollars; the exponential increase in construction costs is discussed in section2.3 in this volume) and was quickly followed by similar ballparks, including the Polo Grounds in New York (1890, which was actually initially built not for baseball but for polo), League Park in Cleveland (1891), and Robison Field in St. Louis (1893) (Jordan, 2010).

In the first fifteen years of the new century, a booming economy coupled with the emergence of the American League (AL) and the World Series to explode baseball's popularity, and teams built themselves ballparks across the country, including Shibe Park in Philadelphia (1909, $301,000 ($8 million in 2017 dollars) (Kuklick, 1991)), Sportsman's Park in St. Louis (1909, $300,000 ($8 million in 2017 dollars)), Forbes Field in Pittsburgh (1909, $1–2 million ($26–$53 million in 2017 dollars) (Leventhal and MacMurray, 2000)), Comiskey Park in Chicago (1910, $750,000 ($19 million in 2017 dollars)), Griffith Stadium in Washington (1911, $100,000 ($2.6 million in 2017 dollars) (Snyder, 2004)), Fenway Park in Boston (1912, $600,000 ($14.9 million in 2017 dollars) (Stout, 2011)), Crosley Field in Cincinnati (1912, $225,000 ($5.6 million in 2017 dollars) (Rhodes and Erardi, 1995)), Tiger Stadium (then known as Navin Field, 1912, $300,000 ($7.5 million in 2017 dollars)), Ebbets Field in Brooklyn (1913, $750,000 ($18 million in 2017 dollars) (Hollander, 2012)), Wrigley Field in Chicago (1914, $250,000 ($6 million in 2017 dollars)), and Braves Field in Boston (1915, $600,000 ($14.3 million in 2017 dollars)). Each of these venues was privately developed by team owners who maintained complete control over their facilities and all revenues they generated. Baseball was still the only team sport in America attracting mass crowds in the early decades of the twentieth century, but as other sports and leagues developed, they would play in the existing baseball stadiums.

2.2. The Rise of Public Investment

The first stadium built with public funds was City Stadium in San Diego, built in 1914 as part of the 1915 Panama-California Exposition, and primarily used for track and field events (Amero, 2013). City Stadium was followed by the Los Angeles Coliseum, which cost less than $1 million ($13.4 million in 2017 dollars) (Benson, 1989). It was constructed in 1922–1923, in part to help Los Angeles compete for the Olympic Games, which the Coliseum would eventually host in 1932 (and again in 1984). The Coliseum immediately became the home of the University of Southern California Trojans football team, and other tenants arrived in succeeding years, including the University of California-Los Angeles Bruins football team, the Los Angeles Rams, the Los Angeles Raiders, and other professional football, baseball, and soccer teams.

During the Great Depression venue construction was seen as a public works project. The Works Progress Administration oversaw the construction of 2,302 stadiums, grandstands, and bleachers, including War Memorial Stadium (originally Roesch Memorial Stadium) in Buffalo (1937), Roosevelt Stadium in Jersey City, New Jersey (1937), and the Rubber Bowl in Akron, Ohio (1940) (Leighninger, 1996). With the belief that stadiums and the teams they attracted as tenants generated revenue and created jobs, cities began to invest further in stadiums, especially as the economy boomed in the aftermath of World War II. As Americans moved from industrial centers to suburbs or younger cities to the south and west, cities and states discovered that professional sports teams were an avenue of competition and a point of civic pride. In many instances, these teams gave midsize cities national media coverage they would otherwise not receive.

By the 1950s public investment in stadiums was the norm, usually via tax-exempt bonds issued by municipalities. From the 1950s through 1986, major league stadiums were almost exclusively built with financing from the public sector (e.g., twenty-seven of the thirty MLB/NFL stadiums built between 1953 and 1970) (Kishner, 2011). This shift was precipitated by four interrelated factors: economic prosperity, expansion of the major leagues (in the 1960s the NFL expanded from twelve to twenty-six teams and MLB expanded from sixteen to twenty-four teams; the NBA expanded from ten teams in 1967 to twenty-two teams in 1976), the threat of losing a team to a new city offering a newer and more favorable stadium (between 1953 and 1963 six of the sixteen MLB teams and seven of the nine NBA teams relocated), and skyrocketing construction costs. Even as the economy slowed in the 1970s, public investment of major venues was seen as important development for the broader community, including employing idle workers.

The primary benefit of public investment to teams and leagues was the minimal level of risk: teams took on no debt and paid low rent. But teams also lacked complete control over venues and their revenue streams. With the public developing and owning venues, the public cut costs where possible, and venues tended to be multiuse, shared by MLB and NFL (and college football and soccer) teams, with arenas shared by NBA and NHL teams. This trend would continue until the 1990s, when teams began to demand new facilities that granted the teams more control over facility operations to control costs and the design process to improve the fan experience, and broader rights to revenue streams generated by the venue (partly as a result of free agency and the attendant escalation of player salaries).

2.3. Skyrocketing Construction Costs

The dramatic increase in construction costs can best be understood by looking at the relative costs for construction of a given city's MLB and NFL stadiums over the past century (*all of the figures in this section, 2.3 and all its subsections, are adjusted for inflation in 2017 dollars*).

2.3.1. *New York City*

Yankee Stadium was built with private funds in 1923 for $43.9 million (Durso, 1972). New York City official Robert Moses offered Dodgers owner Walter O'Malley a publicly owned stadium in Queens in the late 1950s, which the city would rent to the team, with the city retaining ancillary revenue to pay off the construction bonds. But despite the growing trend for public development, O'Malley preferred to fund his own construction costs so that he could own the ensuing stadium outright and control all of its revenue. When Los Angeles offered O'Malley complete ownership of a stadium, he moved the team. The Dodgers' biggest rival was the New York Giants, and O'Malley thought it would be a wise business move to have a second team in California, so he convinced Giants owner Horace Stoneham to move his team to California as well. With the departure of the Dodgers and Giants, New York was left without NL baseball in 1958, and the city built Shea Stadium for the expansion Mets in 1964 for $187 million.

New York's NFL Giants and Jets shared space with MLB's Yankees and Mets, respectively, until Giants Stadium was opened in 1976 in East Rutherford, New Jersey for $328 million (Bagli, 2013). The stadium was built by the New Jersey Sports and Exposition Authority (NJSEA), an independent authority established by the state. (For further discussion as to why governments form such authorities, see section 3.2, in this chapter) After decades of discussions related to different sites around New York City (including the Meadowlands in New Jersey and Manhattan's West Side for the Yankees and Nassau County, Long Island, Sunnyside Yard in Queens, and the West Side in Manhattan for the Mets), the Yankees and Mets each received new stadiums next to their existing ones in 2009 (each stadium is owned by the team). The stadiums were built simultaneously for a total cost of $3.5 billion ($2.5 billion for Yankee Stadium and $1 billion for Citi Field), including $2 billion in public subsidies, which included the sale of New York City municipal bonds, to be repaid by the teams with interest, with the payments offsetting property taxes for the stadiums' lifetimes. (For further discussion of such payments, see section 3.2.)

The Giants and Jets moved into a new stadium in East Rutherford when MetLife Stadium opened in 2010. A plan for public financing for a Jets stadium on Manhattan's Upper West Side collapsed in 2005 after New York state representatives rejected the proposed state funding, resulting in the Jets joining the Giants to co-own MetLife Stadium. The stadium itself was privately financed by the teams (at a total cost of $1.76 billion), but the land was owned by the NJSEA (New Jersey Sports and Exposition Authority). The state also gave the teams twenty acres each for training facilities, the right to seventy-five acres for further development, and hundreds of acres of parking surrounding the structure. The teams no longer share revenue from suites and club seats, parking, naming rights, and other events with the state, but they pay a total of approximately $6.3 million in annual rent and other expenses. The state also contributed $265 million toward infrastructure, roadways and public transportation (Bagli, 2013).

2.3.2. *Baltimore*

The Baltimore Colts joined the NFL in 1953 and the Baltimore Orioles moved from St. Louis (where they were the Browns) in 1954 and they shared Memorial Stadium, built in 1950 during the public development era for $65 million. Camden Yards opened for the Orioles in 1992 and was considered the first of the baseball-specific ballparks that MLB teams have moved into over the past twenty-five years. Camden Yards was built for $361 million, 96% of which was publicly funded through lease revenue bonds and revenue notes and lottery funds (Kilar, 2011). Although the Colts moved to Indianapolis in 1984, the Cleveland Browns moved to Baltimore in 1996 and became the Ravens, largely because 90% of the $323 million construction cost for the now-named M&T Bank Stadium came from the public sector.

2.3.3. *Washington*

As mentioned in section 2.1 in this chapter, Griffith Stadium was built by the Washington Senators in 1911 for $2.6 million and also became home to the Washington Redskins when the NFL team moved from Boston (where they were the Braves) in 1937. Robert F. Kennedy Memorial Stadium (RFK Stadium) was built for the two teams to share in 1961 for $192 million. With teams demanding single sport facilities, which they could design themselves to improve the fan experience and maximize revenue, the Redskins paid for 72% of FedEx Field, which opened in Landover, Maryland, in 1997 and cost $374 million. The Senators moved to Minnesota in 1961 where they became the Twins, and the replacement Senators moved to Arlington, Texas in 1972 where they became the Rangers. Washington finally got its own baseball team again in 2005, when the Montreal Expos moved to RFK Stadium and became the Nationals. Nationals Park opened in 2008 as a baseball-specific stadium at a cost of $918 million. It was publicly financed through general obligation bonds and a special higher sales tax for concessions, beverages and tickets on the nineteen-acre stadium and parking site, though the team also pays rent.

2.3.4. *Minneapolis*

With an interest in attracting either an MLB team from the East Coast or an expansion team, Metropolitan Stadium was publicly financed in Bloomington, Minnesota (which was near the airport and considered equidistant between the downtowns of the rival Twin Cities of Minneapolis and St. Paul) in 1956 for $75 million. In 1961 it became the home of the Twins and the NFL's expansion Minnesota Vikings. The Hubert H. Humphrey Metrodome was publicly financed in downtown Minneapolis in 1982 for $181 million. It hosted the Twins, Vikings, and the University of Minnesota Gophers football team. Each team has since moved into its own facility. The Gophers moved into TCF Bank Stadium, an on-campus football stadium that cost $339 million. A public university, Minnesota's stadium was primarily financed by the state (plus certain student fees) (Muret, 2009). The Twins moved into Target Field in 2010, which cost $598 million, of which 64% was born by Hennepin County, with the remainder paid for by the team (Mannix, 2009). The Vikings moved into U.S. Bank Stadium in 2016, which cost over $1 billion, split between the team (53%), state (33%), and city (14%) (Associated Press, 2015).

2.4. Government Reaction: The Tax Reform Act of 1986

Government concern over corporate use of public financing led Congress to pass the Revenue and Expenditure Control Act of 1968.[1] The statute intended to curb the proceeds from tax-exempt bonds from flowing to private activities. In order to avoid classification as a private activity bond, a project needed to meet either of two tests: (1) "Private Business Use Test": 25% or less of the bond proceeds were to be used by a private business; or (2) "Private Security Test": 25% or less of the debt service was secured by the property used directly or indirectly in the private business. However, sports facilities were exempt from the Revenue and Expenditure Control Act under subsection 103(c)(4)(B), so the statute had no effect on stadium development. The fact that sports venues were excluded from a statute initially intended to target them is an example of the political challenge surrounding this issue. While public and political dissent to public investment in sports stadiums exists, the popularity of sports teams also results in political pull in the opposite direction. To many elected officials, the only thing worse than investing public funds in a stadium is being seen as responsible for a team moving to another city.

The next legislative shot across the bow of stadium development came from the Deficit Reduction Act of 1984,[2] which denied tax exemption for bonds issued to finance "sky boxes" in sports venues. However, the real challenge arose as a result of the Tax Reform Act of 1986,[3] which lowered the threshold for the Private Business Use and Private Security Tests from 25% to 10% and removed the exemption for sports facilities. Though venues already in a planning stage would be grandfathered in, the clear legislative intent was to put an end to public financing of stadiums under the traditional model. No stadium project could realistically meet the Private Business Use Test, since the purpose of the bonds would be for the stadium. However, stadium projects could creatively pass the Private Security Test as long as at least 90% of the debt was serviced using non-stadium revenues. In other words, rent payments from the team to the public jurisdiction would have to be capped at 10% of the bond revenue. Thus, despite the intent of the Tax Reform Act to limit public financing for stadiums through tax-exempt bonds and end a certain form of public subsidy, the result was an *increase* in public funding by limiting the amount of stadium revenue that could be used to repay debt on the tax-exempt bonds. A record pace of stadium development ensued, with MLB, NFL, NBA, and NHL teams receiving more than $5.2 billion in tax-exempt bond issues in the 1990s (Kishner, 2011). That figure grew to $12 billion between 2000 and 2010 (Long, 2013) and $16.9 billion between 2006 and March 2016, according to Thomson Reuters (Fallor, 2016).

3. Variety of Sources: The Emergence of Complex Development Transactions

The confluence of the new legislation, rising construction costs, and the growing desire of teams to build top-of-the-market predominantly single-use stadiums that allow them to generate more revenue, control costs to compete in the industry, and allow for more team control have forced teams and local government to work more closely together to develop stadiums.

3.1. Sources of Team Contribution

Teams have a number of sources of private financing: contributions from the team and the league (e.g., the NFL has established a "G-4" stadium fund under which the league can loan a team up to $200 million, based on project and team qualifications) and loans and debt. Land and debt are secured by contractually obligated income, such as broadcast and cable rights, advertising and naming rights agreements, club seats and luxury suites, pouring rights and concession arrangements, and personal seat licenses (PSLs). If these private sources are sufficient to fund an entire venue, there is no tax increase or bond cost on taxpayers, there is less controversy and public opposition, and the team maintains complete control of all programming and revenue. The Atlanta Braves built Turner Field in 1997 with private funding and the San Francisco Giants built the now-named AT&T Park in 2000 with 96% private funding.

A PSL grants a fan an exclusive license to purchase season tickets for a given seat in a stadium. PSLs are particularly a helpful funding source for NFL stadiums, given the relative scarcity and high demand for NFL tickets compared to tickets for other major league sports. A majority of NFL stadium deals have included PSLs in the last twenty years. The Dallas Cowboys sold 56,314 PSLs for AT&T Stadium, which opened in 2009, generating total revenue of $650 million (Nelson, 2012). PSLs are advantageous to teams because their term is short—generally five years—and the team can reclaim the seats thereafter and sell new licenses. The shorter term and relatively smaller fee are more accessible to some fans. However, PSLs are inefficient for tax purposes, and the shorter term and smaller fee mean less revenue for the team. The shorter term also means that PSLs can only secure short-term debt. In addition, teams can suffer declining revenues if the PSL renewal rate decreases, and because PSL revenue declines over time, it does not help as a stadium ages and requires funding for renovations or repurposing. PSLs also alienate fans, especially because the cost of the tickets themselves is not built in.

An alternative to PSLs are equity seat rights (ESRs), a unique financing method that enables fans to obtain mortgages for purchases of a seat, rather than an outright purchase. They are more fan-friendly than PSLs because they are easier to transfer, there are no annual price increases, and the price of the ticket is built in. However, they present operational challenges to teams, including an uncertain interest rate structure for the mortgages and potential defaults on the mortgage payments. Because they are transferable teams cannot recapture revenue from the secondary market, as they can for PSLs.

Another emerging financing model has been to use the EB-5 program, created by Congress as part of the Immigration Act of 1990 to stimulate the economy through job creation and capital investment by foreign investors. Administered by the U.S. Citizenship and Immigration Services, EB-5 incentivizes foreign nationals to invest in American construction projects in exchange for an accelerated immigration process. A foreign national who commits $1 million ($500,000 in high-unemployment areas) to a development that creates ten American jobs gets a green card, which becomes permanent if the jobs exist for two years. Despite some concerns that the program is susceptible to corruption, it is politically popular (having been reauthorized nearly unanimously by Congress in 2012,[4] and again in 2016) because it comes at no cost to American taxpayers. And because the foreign nationals trade the added incentive of American immigration for very low interest rates and even lower return rates, EB-5 is an attractive financing source for developers. The program was used to finance part of the Atlantic Yards project in Brooklyn, which included the Barclays Center, home arena for the New York Islanders and Brooklyn Nets, and now is being used for stand-alone stadium projects, such as for the MLS franchises Orlando City, D.C. United, and Los Angeles FC. But the timing of EB-5 funds can be a challenge, causing several stadium project committees that planned on using EB-5 financing to decide against doing so. In addition, there is always the threat that Congress could abolish the program. On January 24, 2017, Senators Chuck Grassley (R-Ia.) and Diane Feinstein (D-Cal.) introduced a bill to abolish the program (S.232), though it seems unlikely that this legislation will become law in the near future.

These sources are far more costly to teams and their owners and may inhibit their ability to compete in their league and market. There are additional costs to the aforementioned funding sources. Most leagues have rules limiting teams from taking on debt, and teams are reticent to do so even when it is permitted. Though sports are generally insulated from economic downturns because of the passion of fans and the limited supply of major league teams, revenue opportunities such as advertising and naming rights can dip alongside the market as a whole, so teams open up their risk to the fluctuations of the economy when they depend on contractually obligated income as a source for project funding.

3.2. Sources of Public Investment

Public financing for stadiums can come in the form of nonreimbursable community contributions, such as public grants of funds, land, or both; taxable or tax-exempt bonds; or other sources described below. The loss of the federal tax exemptions can add up to 34% of the total bond costs (Phelps, 2004), and higher interest rates may be required to compensate investors for the taxes due. But given the limited payment of debt service on municipal tax-exempt bonds under the Internal Revenue Code described in section 2.4 in this chapter, occasionally teams and municipalities have agreed to publicly issued taxable bonds. For example, $191 million of taxable bonds was issued toward the construction of Globe Life Park in Arlington, Texas. The Rangers contributed approximately $30 million in cash up front and subsequently have paid approximately $3.5 million annually in rent and other expenses. The debt services payments on the bonds have been paid for with about $18 million collected annually, primarily from a one-half-cent sales tax approved by 65% of voters in a 1991 referendum (Noll and Zimbalist, 1997).

But as discussed previously, tax-exempt bonds serve as the most common form of public-sector financing for stadium projects. Tax-exempt bonds allow the government to pay below-market interest rates, which bondholders are willing to accept because the interest is exempt from federal taxes. Essentially, local governments subsidize the venue through the proceeds of the bonds they issue, while the federal government subsidizes the venue indirectly through the forfeited tax revenue. The argument in favor of the federal subsidy is that the benefits of public capital facilities extend beyond the jurisdiction that provides them (though it is hard to argue that voters in Topeka benefit from the new Yankee Stadium in the Bronx), and without public subsidy, the facilities would be provided at less than optimal levels.

As discussed in section 2.4, in order for bonds to be tax-exempt under the Private Security Test of the Tax Reform Act, team rent payments on the stadium must be capped under the lease arrangement to no more than 10% of the bond revenue. Debt service on bonds may be financed by other revenue sources: tourist taxes (i.e., hotels and car rentals in Indianapolis for Lucas Oil Stadium and in Chicago for U.S. Cellular Field, bed taxes in Miami-Dade County for Marlins Park), "sin taxes" (i.e., tobacco and alcohol taxes in Cuyahoga County, Ohio for Progressive Field and Quicken Loans Arena, state charitable gambling in Minnesota with the revenue dedicated to the bonds used for U.S. Bank Stadium), increase in sales tax (i.e., in Arlington for Globe Life Park and AT&T Stadium and in Washington for the Nationals Park use tax mentioned in section 2.3.3, in this chapter), and income surcharges on the salaries of team players and employees (though teams generally try to negotiate for protection from such future "targeted taxes" in project documents).

Despite the limitations on tax-exempt bonds, they are still the best financial option for teams pursuing stadium projects, less expensive and more efficient than the alternatives. However, there are costs: receiving any public money leads to public scrutiny, and it may require expensive public initiative campaigns. Depending on the local statutory and political climate, public approval may be necessary via referendum. Even if it is not, there are votes by city, county, or state officials. Construction may even trigger a land use review, which can require public hearings held by affected community boards, city planning commissions, and the like. In order to motivate elected officials and voters to support public funding, teams often need to cry poverty or issue veiled or explicit threats of moving the team. These actions can cost political capital and cause harm to the public perception of the team and its ownership.

There are additional sources of public-sector financing or public-private partnership that may be more palatable politically in a given jurisdiction. In addition to the taxes described two paragraphs earlier, these include capital investments to improve infrastructure and transportation upgrades, public reimbursable debts (revenue bonds) supported by stadium revenues, public rent credits or funding of stadium operation reserves, exemptions from property taxes, sales taxes, mortgage recording taxes, and mixed-use development and entitled land and ancillary development (discussed in section 3.3). Special business improvement districts can be created to increase a sales tax zone for stadium project funds. Special districts have the power to impose taxes on residents to be dedicated for one particular purpose, often infrastructure-related. They are seen as a way of fairly spreading the burden across a region that benefits from a particular project, rather than imposing the entire burden on the residents of the municipality where the project is built. Another way for governmental jurisdictions to avoid private activity bond status is to create a "stadium authority," such as the NJSEA. A tax is not considered to be stadium-related if it is "generally applicable." By establishing a stadium authority as a separate unit of the state government that manages several stadiums, the taxes on event tickets are generally applicable as long as they are applied to all events equally.

Until a recent Internal Revenue Service (IRS) regulation limited their availability as a source of public funding for stadium projects (Internal Revenue Bulletin, 2008), payments in lieu of taxes (PILOTs) were used when the stadium property was owned by the public and not subject to local property taxes, especially in New York City. PILOTs are defined as contracted payments made to an agency equal to the amount, or a portion of, the real property taxes that would have been levied if the project was not tax-exempt by reason of agency involvement. Under a PILOT agreement, the team would make payments using stadium revenues to pay off debt service from the public bond issue in amount equal to what it would be required to pay in property taxes were the stadium property privately owned.

New York Mayor Michael Bloomberg proposed a PILOT agreement for the stadium proposal for the New York Jets on Manhattan's Upper West Side in 2005, and PILOTs were used in New York for Barclays Center, Citi Field, and Yankee Stadium after the IRS issued private letter rulings in 2006 which permitted tax-exempt bonds to be paid off with PILOTs rather than tax revenues collected by New York City and the State of New York.[5] The letter rulings argued that the stadiums would serve the public interest by generating significant positive economic impact on the community. But the IRS later reversed course, introducing a new regulation that dramatically curtailed the ability to use PILOTs (Internal Revenue Bulletin, 2008). Because the regulation only applied to bonds sold after October 24, 2008, however, it did not affect Barclays Center, Citi Field, or Yankee Stadium, projects whose bonds had already been sold.

Under tax-increment financing (TIF), municipalities divert future increases in property tax revenues from a defined area toward a project in the community. These types of funds are often used for roads and infrastructure. Property taxes are locked at their current rate, and as they increase, the additional amount is used to fund such projects. The idea is that school districts and other programs that depend on property tax revenues will maintain their current rate of funding, while allowing project bonds against the incremental increase. But as costs of education and other property-tax-dependent services have risen beyond the standard cost-of-living adjustments, a shortfall has developed when property taxes have been tied up by TIFs. As a result, California, the first state in the county to embrace tax-increment financing (known as CRA in California), has also become the first state to abolish it.[6] Nevertheless, it is still being used elsewhere, such as Detroit, where the Downtown Development Authority announced TIF financing for a new Red Wings hockey arena in 2014. Some $250 million of the project cost would be financed using TIF financing to repay thirty-year tax-exempt bonds purchased by the Michigan Strategic Fund, the state's economic development agency (Shea, 2014).

3.3. Ancillary Development

Regardless of where one falls on the debate discussed in section 4.1 (in this chapter) over the local job creation, business development, and economic stimulation that a stadium development brings to a city, it is self-evident that the potential for the same increases significantly when the venue is part of a larger developmental plan. One survey of economic studies concluded that a municipality will benefit from public financing for a new stadium if it is part of a larger, more comprehensive development plan, pointing to the Verizon Center in Washington, D.C. as an example (Johnson, 2011). The Verizon Center opened in the Chinatown section of Washington in 1997. Prior to the arena's construction, the blighted neighborhood had virtually no tourist or entertainment activity. Currently the Verizon Center hosts between 200 and 250 major events per year, including home games for the NBA's Wizards, the WNBA's Mystics, the NHL's Capitals, the Georgetown University men's basketball team, and the Arena Football League's Valor. The area around the arena has been redeveloped and converted into a tourist destination with a dramatic increase in employment opportunities and tax revenue.

"Ancillary development" is a general term for taking the land surrounding or adjacent to a stadium and creating a project on that land that includes commercial, residential, or mixed-use development. When professional teams partner with the public sector to develop or redevelop a stadium, it is increasingly common for the development plans to address ancillary development as well. For the team, this can enhance the fan experience and generate additional revenue. For the public, the benefits extend beyond traditional stadium-related job creation and increased tax revenue, but actually result in dramatic urban revitalization, such as L.A. Live in Los Angeles, the San Francisco China Basin, the Baltimore Inner Harbor, Denver's LoDo District, and Downtown Detroit. Whereas many publicly funded stadiums of the 1960s and 1970s followed fans out to the suburbs, these new developments are drawing fans and their wallets back into the heart of America's cities.

Historically, ancillary development was controlled by the public sector (e.g., Baltimore and Denver). The municipality controlled the type and pace of development, and used the ancillary development to offset its stadium development risk (for which it was also responsible). The city was responsible for acquiring the land, refashioning it to make it attractive for development, entitling it (granting certain tax status), and "upzoning" for greater density or commercial uses. The team's risk exposure was limited to securing land-use restrictions to protect the fan experience and team revenue.

For the reasons stated in section 4.1, the public appetite for stadium projects is lower today than it was in the past. Accordingly, the availability of public funds for stadium development projects has shrunk, and the city-first paradigm for ancillary development has changed. Today the public sector offers ancillary development opportunities to the team, which takes additional risk but also benefits from additional upside to offset its increased investment in the stadium relevant to the previous generation (when the stadium investment came from the public). Although the recent dissolution of the California Redevelopment Agency (California Department of Finance, 2017) has created new challenges, team-funded ancillary development projects have continued in California, such as Downtown Commons (also called DoCo) in Sacramento, which includes the NBA Kings' new arena, Golden 1 Center.

Granting the team investment in ancillary development provides both benefits and costs to the public sector. The public gets an additional tool with which to finance stadium development, a reduction in its operational and financial risk in ancillary development, and a reduction in political exposure, and the city benefits from the team being incentivized to maximize development opportunities to create a new tax base and new jobs. But there are still risks for the public: this is still an additional expenditure that requires public funds, and taxpayers need to be convinced that shifting responsibility to the team is mitigating public exposure for a beneficial cost, not just giving the team additional free corporate incentives.

For teams, greater control over ancillary development means greater control over the fan experience and revenue generation. But professional sports teams are in the sports industry; they may not be comfortable with construction, management, and fiscal responsibilities for broader development projects. If a development is unsuccessful, the team has a long-term expense that could be difficult to unload, and it could create an underwater stadium deal that defeats the very purpose of a team pursuing a new stadium. To mitigate some of this risk, teams may request more land entitlements than a typical real estate developer would expect to receive in a typical development deal. These land entitlements help to make up for the team's additional capital outlay. Another option is for the team to partner with a third-party developer, as the St. Louis Cardinals did with the Cordish Companies in creating the St. Louis Ballpark Village, and the

Sacramento Kings did with The Hahn Company in DoCo. The developer provides experience in constructing and operating a commercial/residential development and may serve as an additional source of funds—though the team may have to give up some of the control it has received from the public sector in the first place.

4. Challenges to Public Investment

Section 3 of this chapter discussed a variety of sources for private and public investment for stadium projects. The complexities of these projects generally result in a mixture of private sources, public sources, and ancillary development. No one system works everywhere. Rather, teams, leagues, and government entities must work together to mix and match, finding the right combination of resources that work in a given community for a given project. However, there are many challenges to dedicating any public investment toward stadium projects.

4.1. The Public Debate For and Against Public Development

The benefits a team accrues from public financing for a new venue are obvious. In addition to new revenues, new stadiums generally result in a better fan experience and increased attendance, which in turn is tied to improved on-field performance (though some studies have challenged this assertion (Quinn et al., 2003)). But even if on-field performance improves, public-sector investment in professional sports stadiums still generates political opposition. The primary political argument against public investment is that it serves as a form of "corporate welfare." Along those lines, critics of public investments in sports stadiums sometimes charge that such allocation of public money enriches the billionaires who own professional teams and the millionaires who play for them. Of course, this claim implies that public funds are a zero-sum game, as if but for the stadium such funds would be going toward public education, health care, or some other purpose.

Stadium advocates also point to potential public economic benefits of a new stadium: job creation (including construction, operation, and tourist expenditures), increased tax revenue, and economic stimulation. Indeed, the Keynesian multiplier, an economic principal introduced by Richard Kahn in the 1930s, demonstrates that any government spending brings cycles of spending that increase additional employment and prosperity. This phenomenon can be evidenced with new stadiums: the economic impact of a new stadium is multiplied by fans spending at local businesses (as discussed vis-à-vis ancillary development in section 3.3). One study points to Nashville, Tennessee, as a success story. Tennessee had no major league sports teams until the late

1990s, when the state provided a $55 million construction bond and spent $12 million for road improvements, and the city financed an additional $144 million to construct a football stadium and hockey arena. The football stadium attracted the Houston Oilers to relocate to Nashville in 1997, and the arena helped result in the NHL awarding Nashville with the expansion Predators in 1998. The Nashville Convention and Visitors Bureau published a study which indicated that visitors traveled to Nashville specifically to attend events at the football stadium and hockey arena, and eighty-five major events at the two facilities between 1997 and 2005 generated over $300 million, making the public investment in the projects successful (Johnson, 2011).

Critics respond by citing economic research which indicates that new venues may not have much impact on the local economy because they tend to redistribute existing entertainment dollars rather than create new wealth. "The large and growing peer-reviewed economics literature on the economic impacts of stadiums . . . has consistently found no substantial evidence of increased jobs, incomes, or tax revenues for a community associated with" public subsidies for new venues, conclude two economists (Coates and Humphreys, 2008, 310). In addition, bond payments for stadiums can often balloon past initial projections. Legacy costs not only continue to rise, they can continue long past a stadium's life expectancy. Indeed, it is not unusual for the public to continue paying for stadiums even after they have been demolished (such as old Giants Stadium in New Jersey, the Kingdome in Seattle's King County, the RCA Dome in Indianapolis, and Veterans Stadium in Philadelphia) or after the team for whom it was built has moved away (such as in Houston, Kansas City, Memphis, and Pittsburgh).[7]

However, even some critics acknowledge that the public can benefit economically from new stadiums to the extent they steer purchases toward activities with higher tax rates or to the extent they recruit and tax out-of-town visitors (such as the claims made in Nashville). Hotels and rental cars are two examples that fall under both categories, as they are often taxed at high rates and new stadiums increase consumption of both. Furthermore, leagues often reward cities that build new stadiums by awarding them national events, such as the Super Bowl, all-star games, college basketball tournaments, and football bowl games. These events can draw additional revenue from out-of-town visitors and provide advertising and increased visibility to the area.

Perhaps most important, notwithstanding the unresolved debate over how much economic benefit a region gets from funding a stadium, absent infrequent expansion, the number of professional teams in the major leagues is a zero-sum game. The benefits a region gets from a team (and, conversely, the harm accruing to a city as a result of the threat of a team leaving) go beyond merely economic concerns. Major league teams and major league stadiums provide a region with civic pride. They serve as a unifying factor across demographics of race, socioeconomic status, and political affiliation. When the Cleveland Cavaliers won the NBA title in 2016, Cleveland's first major championship since 1964, more than 1.3 million people attended the championship parade in downtown Cleveland, more than three times as many people as the city's population (Hoppert, 2016). It is no wonder that cities have invested in publicly built stadiums even before teams commit to them in hopes of attracting them, such as Metropolitan Stadium in Minnesota in 1956, the Edward Jones Dome in St. Louis in 1993, and a variety of proposed football stadiums in Los Angeles before the Rams and Chargers moved there in 2016 and 2017, respectively.

4.2. Taxpayer Lawsuits

The doctrine of public purpose is a standard by which courts determine the legitimacy of state taxation legislation. The doctrine prevents taxpayers from funding private interests, but the definition of "public purpose" has been broadened by advocates such as Robert Moses. In four key cases taxpayers have filed suit against governmental jurisdictions seeking to prevent public money from paying for a professional team's stadium. All four times the court has sided with the team over the taxpayer plaintiffs.

4.2.1. *Meyer v. City of Cleveland*

After Cleveland voters approved a city council proposal to issue $2.5 million in bonds to construct a stadium for the local professional teams by a vote of 112,000 to 77,000, a taxpayer sued the city for financing a stadium intended for "primarily private use." The court rejected the taxpayer's argument, stating that cities are "not limited to policing the city [and] paving streets" and that "the power of cities to maintain institutions which educate and instruct as well as entertain and amuse their inhabitants is unquestioned" (35 Ohio App. at 22–23). The resulting Cleveland Stadium was built for $3 million ($47 million in 2017 dollars) (Cormack, 1997) and after opening in 1931 it served as the home for Cleveland's MLB and NFL teams for a combined 116 seasons, in addition to other teams.

4.2.2. *Martin v. City of Philadelphia*

Philadelphia's AL team, the Athletics, moved to Kansas City in 1954 after teetering on the edge of bankruptcy in its old stadium, Shibe Park. Philadelphia also lost the NBA's Warriors in 1962 when the team moved to San Francisco. Philadelphia's remaining MLB team, the NL's Phillies, was unhappy with Connie Mack Stadium, which had been built in 1909, and was considering moving to New Jersey after Pennsylvania banned alcohol sales at sporting events in 1959. In response, city voters authorized a loan of $25 million to build a stadium. A Philadelphia taxpayer sued to enjoin the city from enforcing Ordinance No. 546 of 1964. The Supreme Court of Pennslyvania ruled in favor of the city. As aptly described by the Court of Appeals of New York in a subsequent opinion, *Murphy v. Erie County*, the Supreme Court Pennsylvania held that "it is established that a city may lease its public improvements to private concerns so long as the benefit accrues to the public and the municipality retains ownership of the improvement" (28 N.Y.2d at 88). Ultimately, cost overruns required the voters to authorize an additional $13 million bond issue. The total cost of Veterans Stadium upon completion in 1969 was $63 million ($373 million in 2017 dollars), making it one of the most expensive stadiums to date (Westcott, 2005). It was home to the Phillies and Eagles for thirty-three and thirty-two years, respectively, in addition to the Temple Owls (for twenty-five years) and other teams.

4.2.3. *Murphy v. Erie County*

In May 1968 the New York state legislature enacted a law empowering the Erie County legislature to enter into contracts and incur indebtedness in connection with the building of a stadium for the Buffalo Bills. The county legislature adopted a resolution authorizing the issuance of bonds for $50 million to construct a domed stadium. The county negotiated a contract with the Kenford Company under which Kenford would operate the stadium as the tenant and would pay the county $63.75 million over forty years, to be reduced by tax revenues generated by the stadium. Taxpayer plaintiffs filed suit, alleging that certain terms of the contract violated provisions of the state constitution and effected a waste of county funds. The New York Court of Appeals held that a publicly funded stadium utilized for the benefit of a private corporation fulfilled a public purpose and did not necessarily represent a gift of public property to a private entity. "The private benefit is incidental to the conceded public purpose of the stadium" (28 N.Y.2d at 88).

Ultimately the domed stadium plan was cancelled after the project dissolved into unrelated litigation between the county and the developer, with the developer receiving a financial settlement. But when Bills owner Ralph Wilson publicly explored the option of moving the team to Seattle, Memphis, or Tampa, the county legislature approved new stadium bonds in September 1971. The ensuing stadium (now named after Wilson) was built for $22 million ($119 million in 2017 dollars) (Warner, 2013). It opened in 1973 and has been home to the Bills since.

4.2.4. *Poe v. Hillsborough County*

The Tampa Bay Buccaneers were bought by Malcolm Glazer in 1995 for $192 million. Though he announced his intention to stay in Tampa, he advised local public officials that without additional stadium-related revenue sources unavailable in the team's existing home (Tampa Stadium), such as luxury suites and club suites, the team could not remain financially competitive with other NFL teams and might have to move. The City of Tampa, Hillsborough County, the Tampa Sports Authority, and the team reached an agreement for a new stadium on August 28, 1996. Related to that agreement, the Hillsborough County Board of County Commissioners passed an ordinance on July 10, 1996, levying a one-half-cent local government infrastructure surtax for a period of thirty years to "acquire infrastructure for general government purposes, public educating, and public safety." As required by law, the surtax was approved by a public referendum, with 53% of voters supporting the tax, whose purpose as presented to the voters included "to finance infrastructure for . . . a community stadium" (695 So. 2d at 674) The interlocal agreement for distribution of the tax revenue dedicated $318 million of the proceeds for the new Tampa stadium. A taxpayer challenged the application of the funds for the stadium. The court ruled that public purposes provided by a stadium include the anticipated economic benefits as well as "national media exposure" and the "civic pride and camaraderie" associated with having a professional football team play in the city.

Raymond James Stadium opened in 1998 at a construction cost of $169 million ($248 million in 2017 dollars) (Testerman, 2001). It has been home to the Buccaneers, University of South Florida Bulls football team, and the Outback Bowl since. The Buccaneers were the worst team in the NFL from their inception through 1996, with a combined regular season record of 100–223 and no playoff appearances from 1983 to 1996. Within the team's first five years of play in the new stadium they made the playoffs four times, twice setting a team record for wins in a season, and culminating in a Super Bowl championship after the 2002 season. During those five seasons the Buccaneers averaged 99.4% capacity at their regular season home games at Raymond James Stadium, compared to 70.5% capacity during the previous five seasons at Tampa Stadium.

4.3. CEQA and Environmental Lawsuits

Environmental litigation can also slow down the process of developing a new stadium. This is especially true in California, thanks to the California Environmental Quality Act (CEQA).[8] Under CEQA, state and local agencies must give serious consideration to environmental protection when regulating public and private activities, and projects cannot be approved until they can prove that there are no feasible environmentally superior alternatives. The "heart of CEQA,"[9] according to the California appellate court, is the environmental impact report (EIR), a comprehensive report which informs the public and governmental agencies of a given project's environmental impact.

Because of the deliberateness of the process, as well as the fact that it is a "plaintiffs' bar," CEQA poses a challenge to development in California. This is especially true for sports projects, which are large and attract much more public attention than other types of development. Petco Park, the San Diego Padres' home field, was originally scheduled to open in 2002, but thanks in part to CEQA-related litigation, its opening was delayed until 2004. Because the process has been so burdensome for stadium development, the California state legislature has abrogated CEQA to expedite the appellate process, allowing stadiums to proceed without an EIR. The proposed construction of Los Angeles Stadium was exempted from CEQA in 2009, rendering moot an ongoing lawsuit brought by eight residents who were challenging the validity of the developer's EIR. The Sacramento Kings and Golden State Warriors have also benefited from targeted legislation reforming the CEQA process in the development of their arenas, and although the legislative abrogation did not stem environmental lawsuits against the teams, each prevailed in court.[10]

4.4. Further Attempted Legislative Reform

For the reasons stated in section 4.1, in addition to other political motivations (on the left, an opposition to corporate welfare; on the right, an opposition to any government spending), Congress has repeatedly considered further legislation aimed at curbing tax-exempt bond issuance to fund professional stadiums. Senator Daniel Patrick Moynihan (D-N.Y.) introduced the Stop Tax-Exempt Arena Debt Issuance Act in 1996, 1997, and 2000, though it never passed committee. Senator Arlen Specter (R-Pa.) introduced the Stadium Financing and Franchise Relocation Act in 1999. Specter's bill would have required the NFL and MLB to set aside 10% of their national television contract revenue each year to create a stadium construction fund. This fund would then provide up to 50% of the construction costs on new facilities. If the leagues did not comply, they would be penalized by the removal of their antitrust exemptions. Among other flaws, Specter's bill was unworkable because the MLB's network contract at the time of the proposal was nowhere near the size necessary to fund it, and this bill died like Moynihan's bills did.

Senator Tom Coburn (R-Okla.) called for a ban on federal tax-exempt financing for sports stadiums in 2014. President Barack Obama agreed, proposing the elimination of the Private Security Test in his 2016 and 2017 budgets (Fallor, 2016). On March 22, 2016, Representative Steve Russell (R-Okla.) introduced the No Tax Subsidies for Stadiums Act (H.R. 4838), which would prohibit tax-exempt financing for any location that serves as a venue for professional sports and seats more than 100 people for at least five days of the year. Like the previous legislation, Russell's bill has yet to generate widespread political support and has not passed committee.

5. Due Diligence in Preparation for Stadium Proposal

Before a team goes public with a stadium proposal, the team and its counsel and advisors need to conduct both legal diligence and research related to public affairs. Legal diligence includes identifying potential sources and funding vehicles and potential legal speed bumps related thereto, such as league rules, local laws forbidding certain kinds of funding, municipal noncompetes related to existing venues, and tax issues related to property taxes, sales taxes, ticket taxes, and income taxes. The team should study relevant examples of previous public/private partnerships in the region, and it should review recent local and national stadium development deals. The team needs to determine how much financial responsibility and management/operational control it wishes to assume over both the stadium and ancillary development, as well as its timing requirements in terms of construction. Related to site ownership, the team needs to understand whether land acquisition is necessary (including the potential of eminent domain issues) and determine who will own the stadium, the ancillary development, and the underlying land. Whether the team chooses to be an owner or not will affect its control, property taxes, and impact on financing.

Because the public sector is a partner in the project, the team needs to identify potential allies and opponents in local, state, and federal government. It should review the previous public stands and voting histories of public officials, as well as their private views, as well as how to position itself with elected leaders to maximize their support for the project. The team should also understand how local hot button political issues will affect its project, and it must present a good "story" or narrative for why it needs a new home and why it needs the public's support in creating it.

As a condition for providing public financing, the public entity often requires the team to make a contractual commitment not to move the franchise, either via a nonrelocation covenant within the operating agreement or a freestanding nonrelocation agreement. Nonrelocation language was first introduced into stadium leases in the late 1980s. A nonrelocation provision will typically grant the municipality exclusive rights to the team's name and history and provide injunctive relief to prevent an attempted move. But given the challenges in successfully seeking an injunction, there is no guarantee that an injunction would be successful were a team bound by nonrelocation language to seek to move anyway. Specifically, it is possible that a franchise could make a claim under the Bankruptcy Code to enable it to reject its lease and relocate. According to one study, in an executory contract the debtor can attempt to reject the nonrelocation clause, and may be permitted to do so if it is in the best interests of the estate under 11 U.S.C. § 365. The study notes the uncertainty of how a court may rule but suggests that a separate nonrelocation agreement is more likely to be enforceable than a nonrelocation clause in a lease, which is why stand-alone nonrelocation agreements are now standard (Williams, O'Quin, and Stein, 2012).

This chapter focused on the relationship between the team and the public sector in developing a venue, not the operation of the venue itself. But completing construction and then operating a stadium development project requires a variety of legal documents to be negotiated among the team, the government, and various third parties. These include, but are not limited to, the initial agreement between the team and the governmental jurisdiction (city, county, district, state, etc.), financing documents, documents related to the acquisition of the land, zoning, and land use; to operation of the venue itself (including concession agreements, naming rights, and marketing agreements); and to First Amendment Rights policies (pertaining to permitted signage at a venue that is owned by the public).

6. Conclusion

Unlike traditional corporate development transactions, stadium projects are always subject to public review at every stage of the development. Legal drafting that may be standard for more private developments must be able to withstand public scrutiny in order to succeed in the context of a stadium deal. Sports are generally insulated from economic fluctuations due to the passion of the fans and the civic importance that a team represents to a region. Thanks to a changing legal and political landscape, a team that wishes to create a successful development needs to be willing to think creatively. Doing so will allow a team to overcome the challenges and build a market-leading stadium that will allow the team and its host city to succeed for decades to come.

Notes

1. Public Law 90-364, 82 Stat. 266, I.R.C. § 103(c)(6).
2. Public Law No. 98-369, § 171(a).
3. Public Law 99-514, 100 Stat. 2085.
4. Public Law 112-176, 126 Stat. 1325.
5. Private Letter Ruling (PLR) 2006400001 (July 11, 2006); PLR 200641002 (July 19, 2006).
6. See, e.g., *California Redevelopment Association v. Matosantos* (2013).
7. Regarding this last concern, see the discussion of nonrelocation agreements in section 5 of this chapter.
8. California Pub. Res. Code §§ 21000 et seq.) (CEQA).
9. *County of Inyo v. Yorty* (1973).
10. See Saltonstall v. City of Sacramento, 234 Cal.App.4th 549 (3d Dist. 2015); Mission Bay Alliance v. Office of Cmty. Inv. & Infrastructure, 6 Cal. App. 5th 160 (Cal. Ct. App. Nov. 29, 2016).

References

Amero, Richard W. (2013). *Balboa Park and the 1915 Exposition*. 1st ed. (Charleston, S.C.: The History Press).

Associated Press. (2015, March 26). "Wilfs Pledge $19.5M More to Stadium." *ESPN*. Available at www.espn.com/nfl/story/_/id/12566029/wilf-family-pledges-195-million-more-minnesota-vikings-stadium?ex_cid=espnapi_public.

Bagli, Charles V. (2013, November). "Giants and Jets, Super Bowl Hosts, Have Already Been Richly Rewarded." *New York Times*. A30. Available at www.nytimes.com/2013/11/29/nyregion/giants-and-jets-super-bowl-hosts-have-already-been-richly-rewarded.html.

Benson, Michael. (1989). *Ballparks of North America: A Comprehensive Historical Reference to Baseball Grounds, Yards, and Stadiums, 1845 to Present* (Jefferson, N.C.: McFarland).

Brighton Allston Historical Society. *Braves Field*. Available atwww.bahistory.org/BravesField.html.

California Department of Finance. (2017). *Redevelopment Agency Dissolution*. Available at www.dof.ca.gov/Programs/Redevelopment/.

Coates, Dennis, and Humphreys, Brad R. (2008, September). "Do Economists Reach a Conclusion on Subsidies for Sports Franchises, Stadiums, and Mega-Events?" *Economic Journal Watch* 5(3): 294–315.

Cormack, George. (1997). *Municipal Stadium: Memories on the Lakefront, Vol. 1* (Cleveland, Ohio: Instant Concepts, Inc.).

Durso, Joseph. 1972. *Yankee Stadium: Fifty Years of Drama* (New York: Houghton Mifflin).

Fallor, Evan. (2016, March 28). "Bill Would Prohibit Tax-Exempt Bonds for Sports Stadiums." *The Bond Buyer*. Available at www.bondbuyer.com/news/washington-taxation/bill-would-prohibit-tax-exempt-bonds-for-sports-stadiums-1099959-1.html.

Goodman, Andrew H. (2002, Spring). "The Public Financing of Professional Sports Stadiums: Policy and Practice." *Sports Law Journal* 9.

Hollander, Sophia. (2012, April 19). "Soon on Display in Brooklyn: 'Holy Grails' of Baseball." *Wall Street Journal*. Available at www.wsj.com/articles/SB10001424052702304299304577345920613196782.

Hoppert, Melissa. "Cavaliers Parade Caps Off Cleveland Victory Party." *New York Times*. Available at www.nytimes.com/2016/06/23/sports/basketball/cleveland-cavaliers-parade-nba-champions.html.

Internal Revenue Bulletin. (2008, November 24). "Treatment of Payments in Lieu of Taxes Under Section 141," 2008-47, T.D. 9429. Available at www.irs.gov/irb/2008-47_IRB/ar07.html.

Johnson, Garrett. (2011). "The Economic Impact of New Stadiums and Arenas on Cities." *University of Denver Sports and Entertainment Law Journal* 10.

Jordan, David. *Closing 'Em Down: Final Games at Thirteen Classic Ballparks* (Jefferson, N.C: McFarland).

Kilar, Steve. (2011). "The Economics of Oriole Park." *Baltimore Urban Affairs Report* (Philip Merrill College of Journalism). Available at http://bmore.jschool.umd.edu/summer11/?p=65.

Kishner, Irwin A. (2011, October 3). "If You Build It, They Will Come: Financing Stadium Construction." *University of Maryland School of Law Journal of Business & Technology Law Fall Symposium*, Baltimore.

Kuklick, Bruce. (1991). *To Every Thing a Season: Shibe Park and Urban Philadelphia*. (Princeton, N.J.: Princeton University Press).

Leighninger, Robert D. (1996). "Cultural Infrastructure: The Legacy of New Deal Public Space." *Journal of Architectural Education* (1984-) 49(4): 226–236. Available at www.jstor.org/stable/1425295.

Leventhal, Josh, and MacMurray, Jessica. (2000). *Take Me Out to the Ballpark* (New York: Workman).

Long, Judith Grant. (2013). *Public-Private Partnerships for Major League Sports Facilities* (New York, Routledge Research in Sport Business and Management).

Mannix, Andy. (2009, March 2). "Twins: Target Field." *MinnPost*. Available at www.minnpost.com/infodoc/2009/03/twins-target-field.

Metropolitan Sports Facilities Commission. (2013). *Metrodome History*. Available at www.leg.state.mn.us/webcontent/lrl/issues/FootballStadium/MSFC_metrodome_history.pdf.

Muret, Don. (2009, September 21). "Gophers' Golden Moment." *SportsBusiness Journal*. Available at www.sportsbusinessdaily.com/Journal/Issues/2009/09/20090921/This-Weeks-News/Gophers-Golden-Moment.aspx.

Nelson, Tim. (2012, November 15). "NFL Stadium Personal Seat Licenses Compared." *MPR News*. Available at www.mprnews.org/story/2012/11/15/sports/nfl-personal-seat-licenses-compared.

Noll, Roger G., and Zimbalist, Andrew, eds. (1997). *Sports, Jobs, and Taxes: The Economic Impact of Sports Teams and Stadiums* (Washington, D.C.: Brookings).

Phelps, Zachary A. (2004, June). "Stadium Construction for Professional Sports: Reversing the Inequities Through Tax Incentives." *Journal of Civil Rights and Economic Development* 18(3): 981–1029. Available at http://scholarship.law.stjohns.edu/cgi/viewcontent.cgi?article=1178&context=jcred.

Quinn, Kevin G., Bursik, Paul B., Borick, Christopher B., and Raethz, Lisa. (2003, August). "Do New Digs Mean More Wins? The Relationship Between a New Venue and a Professional Sports Team's Competitive Success." *Journal of Sports Economics* 4(3): 167–182. Available at http://citeseerx.ist.psu.edu/viewdoc/download?doi=10.1.1.936.8950&rep=rep1&type=pdf.

Rhodes, Greg, and Erardi, John. (1995). *Cincinnati's Crosley Field: The Illustrated History of a Classic Ballpark* (Cincinnati, Ohio: Road West).

Shea, Bill. (2014, September 21). "On Cost, Financing of Wings Arena: Here Are Answers." *Crain's Detroit Business*. Available at www.crainsdetroit.com/article/20140921/NEWS/309219990/on-cost-financing-of-wings-arena-here-are-answers.

Smith, Curt. (2001). *Storied Stadiums* (New York City, Carroll & Graf).

Snyder, Brad. (2004). *Beyond the Shadow of the Senators*. (New York, McGraw-Hill Professional).

Stout, Glenn. (2011). *Fenway 1912: The Birth of a Ballpark, a Championship Season, and Fenway's Remarkable First Year* (New York, Houghton Mifflin Harcourt).

Testerman, Jeff. (2001, January 25). "Super Bowl 2001: We Paid for It; It Paid Off." *St. Petersburg Times*.

Warner, Gene. (2013, October 6). "The $130 Million Renovation Project at Ralph Wilson Stadium Will Make the Facility More Fan-Friendly." *Buffalo News*. Available at http://buffalonews.com/2013/10/06/the-130-million-renovation-project-at-ralph-wilson-stadium-will-make-the-facility-more-fan-friendly/.

Westcott, Rich. (2005). *Veterans Stadium: Field of Memories* (Philadelphia, Temple University Press).

Williams, Jack F., O'Quin, Jessica, and Stein, Joshua. (2012). "Public Financing of Green Cathedrals." *Albany Government Law Review* 5(1): 123–155. Available at www.albanygovernmentlawreview.org/Articles/Vol05_1/5.1.123-Williams.pdf.

Wrigley Field >> Ballpark Information >> History. Major League Baseball Advanced Media, http://chicago.cubs.mlb.com/chc/ballpark/information/index.jsp?content=history.

Cases

California Redev. Ass'n v. Matosantos, 212 Cal. App. 4th 1457, Cal. Ct. App. (2013).

County of Inyo v. Yorty, 32 Cal. App. 3d 795 (3d Dist. 1973).

Martin v. City of Philadelphia, 420 Pa. 14, 215 A.2d 894 (1966).

Meyer v. City of Cleveland, 35 Ohio App. 20 (1930).

Mission Bay Alliance v. Office of Cmty. Inv. & Infrastructure, 6 Cal. App. 5th 160 (2016).

Murphy v. Erie County, 34 A.D.2d 295 (N.Y. 1970).

Poe v. Hillsborough County, 695 So. 2d 672 (Fla. 1997).

Saltonstall v. City of Sacramento, 234 Cal. App. 4th 549 (3d Dist. 2015).

CHAPTER 30

DAILY FANTASY SPORTS AND PASPA

How to Assess Whether the State Regulation of Daily Fantasy Sports Contests Violates Federal Law

DANIEL L. WALLACH

1. Introduction

The recent well-chronicled controversies surrounding daily fantasy sports (DFS) have highlighted the need both to regulate the industry and also to clarify its legal status. State legislatures are now attempting to shore up the legal status of DFS while proposing regulations aimed at protecting consumers. Since the beginning of 2015, approximately thirty states have weighed in with some form of proposed DFS legislation. These bills run the gamut: several of the bills "authorize" DFS as legal; some propose a "licensing" regime (whereby operators are required to pay substantial annual sums for the privilege of doing business in that state); others simply "regulate" DFS without explicitly authorizing or licensing the activity, whereas, at the other end of the spectrum, a few states "exempt" fantasy contests from the ambit of those states' gambling codes.

These legislative proposals are laudable, and, perhaps, even necessary to protect consumers. However, they may be in violation of the Professional and Amateur Sports Protection Act (PASPA), a 1992 federal law that prohibits state-sponsored sports gambling.[1] While PASPA is commonly understood to prohibit state-sanctioned sports betting on the "outcomes" of professional and amateur sporting events, it also contains language that is arguably (and perhaps inarguably) directed at fantasy sports contests. Section 3702 of PASPA provides that a "governmental entity" (defined to include a state) may not "*sponsor, operate, advertise, promote, license, or authorize by law or compact*... a lottery, sweepstakes, or other betting, gambling, or wagering scheme based, directly or indirectly ... on one or more competitive games in which amateur or professional athletes participate, or are intended to participate, *or on one or more performances of such athletes in such games*."[2] The italicized language strongly suggests that state-sanctioned gambling or wagering schemes tied to athlete "performance" (e.g., a player's individual game statistics) would fall within the scope of PASPA's prohibitions.

Indeed, PASPA's legislative history makes clear that the statute is intended to have a "broad" reach covering a wide spectrum of schemes, regardless of the amount of "skill" or "chance" involved (Senate Report 248, at 3560). For these reasons, many commentators (and litigants) believe that PASPA's reach may extend beyond traditional, single-game sports betting and could also apply to bar state legislative measures to legalize or regulate daily fantasy sports contests, which are based on the individual "performances" of athletes in the real-world games (Moore, 2015; Rodenberg, 2016; Wallach, 2016).

Although PASPA has not yet surfaced as an obstacle to state legalization of DFS, it may emerge as an important issue as additional state legislative measures are introduced. To this point, the Massachusetts Gaming Commission (2016) cautioned that PASPA "potentially presents the greatest constraint to state action to address DFS," adding that "at first glance, PASPA may constrain [state legislatures] from any legislation that directly or indirectly permits or regulates DFS." Any analysis of a state DFS law under PASPA would likely center on three key issues: (1) whether the state has done any of the six things—"sponsor," "operate," "advertise," "promote," "license," or "authorize by law or compact"—that are expressly forbidden by PASPA; (2) whether state-sanctioned DFS contests are a "lottery, sweepstakes, or other betting, gambling or wagering scheme" for purposes of PASPA; and (3) whether DFS contests are "based on" the "performances" of professional or amateur athletes in one or more competitive sporting events. If all three elements are present, the State DFS law would violate PASPA, thereby leaving the state vulnerable to a civil enforcement action under the federal law.

2. Is the State Engaging in any of the Six Forbidden Activities?

Under the first inquiry, the state legislative measures that would be at the greatest risk are those that expressly "authorize" or "license" daily fantasy sports contests. Examples of states that have affirmatively authorized or provided for the licensure of DFS contests are Indiana, Colorado, Missouri, New York, and Tennessee.[3]

The state DFS laws that *expressly* "license" or "authorize by law" present a relatively straightforward and clear case for a PASPA violation. But several states—perhaps cognizant of the prohibitions imposed by federal law—avoid the use of any of the six forbidden PASPA verbs in their DFS legislative enactments. Instead, these states purport to set forth a scheme of "regulation" (ostensibly to protect consumers from fraud) without necessarily licensing, authorizing, approving or endorsing DFS contests. But, in my view, even those legislative enactments are tantamount to an "authorization by law" where: (1) the DFS law expressly grants permission to operate (either upon its effectiveness or through the later issuance of licenses and registrations by a state agency); or (2) the effect of the new state DFS law is to regulate activity that had previously been *unlawful* based on an interpretation of state law prior to the enactment of the new statute.

Each of these analyses would turn on the plain and ordinary meaning of the word "authorize," which is not defined by PASPA (*Hinds Investments, L.P. v. Angioli*).[4] According to *Black's Law Dictionary* (Garner, 2009), the word "authorize" means "to give legal authority; to empower; or to formally approve; to sanction." Similarly, the *American Heritage Dictionary* defines "authorize" as "to grant authority or power to. To give permission for (something); sanction." The *American Heritage Dictionary* supplements the foregoing definition of "authorize" with the following example of its usage: "the city agency that authorizes construction projects." These definitions suggest that the term "authorize" does not merely mean "to permit" or "to allow."[5] Rather, according to the plain and ordinary meaning of the word "authorize," there must be an affirmative granting of formal approval or permission to allow the conduct in question (*Norberto*, 373 F. Supp. at 156).

2.1. "Authorization by Law": State Grant of Permission to Operate

Several of the state DFS laws can be said to "authorize" DFS contests under this rubric through the granting of "permission to operate" in the form of state-approved and state-issued licenses, permits and/or registrations. For example, Colorado, Indiana, Missouri, and Tennessee require operators to obtain state-issued "licenses" before offering fantasy sports contests to in-state consumers.[6] That is the most clear-cut instance of "state permission," and, hence, an "authorization," although those situations are probably more appropriately addressed by PASPA's licensing prohibition. But even a "registration" requirement (the nomenclature used in New York and Virginia) is tantamount to an "authorization by law" since the state must still approve an operator's application and formally "issue" a registration certificate, based on certain enumerated criteria. For example, the New York DFS law requires operators to "register" with the New York State Gaming Commission as a condition of offering contests to New York consumers.[7] This registration requirement is not merely ministerial; the New York DFS law sets forth a number of detailed requirements for registration, and vests the state gaming commission with the authority to determine whether to approve or deny an application for registration.[8] Similarly, the Virginia DFS law requires operators to "register" with the Department of Agriculture and Consumer Services, and pay a $50,000 registration fee.[9] Just like the New York example, "registration" in Virginia is not a matter of right nor is it a ministerial act; the Virginia DFS Law empowers the state agency to determine whether a DFS operator has satisfied the criteria for registration, and, if so, formally issues a registration certificate.[10] The issuance of a registration certificate constitutes the formal state permission to operate, and, hence, is an "authorization" under the plain and ordinary definition of the word.

A similar outcome would likely be reached in Massachusetts. While not requiring DFS operators to apply for "permission to operate" (as in New York and Virginia), the Massachusetts DFS law is nonetheless an affirmative "enabling" statute—and therefore an "authorization by law"—since it places the state's imprimatur on fantasy sports wagering. In this vein, the Massachusetts DFS law provides, in pertinent part, that "a person or entity that offers fantasy contests for a cash prize to members of the public *may* offer a fantasy contest to residents of the commonwealth pursuant to and in accordance with regulations promulgated by the Attorney General."[11] By providing that fantasy sports operators "may" offer DFS contests, the Massachusetts DFS law is expressly permitting—and, hence, "authorizing"—DFS wagering.[12] For the same reasons, the Mississippi DFS law would likely be considered an "authorization by law" as well. Although there is no formal approval process in Mississippi requiring operators to apply for permission to operate (as in New York and Virginia), the Mississippi DFS law broadly permits operators to offer DFS contests for cash prizes, provided that they are "lawfully conducting business" within the state and submit certain "registration information."[13] By contrast, the DFS laws in Kansas and Maryland do not provide for "state-issued" licenses or registrations, or even a blanket permission to operate within the State. The DFS laws in Kansas and Maryland simply exclude fantasy sports contests from the ambit of the state gambling laws without providing for any regulatory oversight or approval mechanism. As such, they would likely not be considered an "authorization by law" under this analytical framework.

2.2. "Authorization by Law": Regulating Previously Unlawful Conduct

An unresolved question is whether state "regulation" of fantasy sports contests violates PASPA. Since the word "regulate" does not appear among PASPA's proscriptions, an argument could be made that a pure regulatory scheme would not violate the federal law. One federal judge has already advanced such a theory. During oral argument in *National Collegiate Athletic Association v. Christie*, which addressed New Jersey's efforts to legalize sports betting through a partial repeal of a state-law ban against the activity, Third Circuit Judge Marjorie Rendell suggested that it might be possible to read PASPA as *not* prohibiting the states from "regulating" sports betting. She observed that PASPA is so "specific" and that there are six verbs contained within PASPA identifying the activities that states may not engage in (e.g., "sponsor, operate, advertise, promote, license, or authorize by law or compact"), and noting that "regulate" is not one of them. She then posited that "some modicum" of state regulation could be "appropriate." Echoing that same point, the Massachusetts Gaming Commission opined in its white paper on fantasy sports that "regulation" is "arguably permitted" on the face of PASPA, "particularly where the regulations themselves do not establish a licensing or other heavy state oversight scheme" (Massachusetts Gaming Commission, 2016, at 15). While such an interpretation has some semantic appeal, it is difficult to envision a state regulatory scheme that does not—at least on some level—provide the state's imprimatur (and, hence, *authorization*) of fantasy sports contests.

A more useful tool in assessing whether a state regulatory scheme runs afoul of PASPA would be to ascertain the legal status of fantasy sports in the state in question *prior* to the enactment of the new regulatory scheme. This would entail evaluating whether DFS wagering was legal—based on then-existing state guidelines—prior to the enactment of the new law. Under this approach, if fantasy sports contests were already legal based on an interpretation of existing state law (prior to the effective date of any new legislation), then a new regulatory scheme would be much more likely pass muster under PASPA because a state would be regulating "previously lawful" conduct. In that situation, it cannot be said that the state is "authorizing" conduct that is already lawful.

By contrast, if fantasy sports contests were determined to be illegal based on an examination of state law prior to the enactment of the new regulatory scheme, then "regulating" such activity on a going-forward basis would be tantamount to "authorizing" conduct that would otherwise be impermissible or unlawful, and, as such, is a more likely violation of PASPA. Support for this type of analytical approach can be found in judicial decisions assessing whether a state regulatory scheme rises to the level of "state action" for purposes of 42 U.S.C. § 1983.[14]

Under this suggested approach, the DFS regulatory schemes that are the most vulnerable to a legal challenge under PASPA would be those states that define "gambling" broadly, or, put another way, employ a low threshold for determining what constitutes "gambling." Tennessee is right at the top of that list. In Tennessee, "gambling" is broadly defined as "risking anything of value for a profit whose return is *to any degree* contingent on chance," subject to various exceptions that are not relevant here.[15] Under Tennessee's "any chance" test, DFS contests fall within the broad definition of "gambling" because: (1) "participants pay an entry fee in order to win a prize"; (2) "a portion of the fees comprise the pot of funds that are paid out to the winning participants—by proffering these entry fees, participants agree to risk something of value for a profit and (3) winning a fantasy sports contest is contingent to some degree on chance."[16] As Tennessee's attorney general explained, fantasy sports participants "do not control how selected athletes perform in actuality on a given day. Athletes' performances are affected by many fortuitous factors—weather, facilities, referees, injuries, etc."[17] "Thus," Tennessee's attorney general concluded in his opinion, "fantasy sports contests constitute illegal gambling under Tennessee law."[18] Given the broad definition of "gambling" under Tennessee law and the Tennessee Attorney General's advisory opinion concluding that DFS contests constituted illegal gambling, the state's regulatory regime—enacted less than one month later—would likely be characterized as an "authorization" of DFS wagering since it would be regulating activity that was previously considered impermissible or unlawful.

A similar conclusion would likely be reached with respect to other DFS states that follow the "any chance" test, such as Colorado and Indiana. However, unlike the situation in Tennessee, the attorney generals of Colorado and Indiana have not addressed the legality of fantasy sports contests. Nonetheless, I believe that, given the low definitional threshold for "gambling" in those states, a court would likely find that the Indiana and Colorado DFS regulatory regimes legalized conduct that was previously *unlawful*, and, hence, constitutes a prohibited "authorization by law" under PASPA.[19]

Other DFS states that employ relatively low thresholds for gambling—and are also at risk of having their regulatory regimes viewed as a PASPA-forbidden "authorization"—are Missouri and New York. Both states follow the so-called material element/future contingent event definitional test for gambling. Under this formulation, "gambling" is said to exist when "a person stakes or risks something of value upon the outcome of a contest of chance or a future contingent event not under his control or influence, upon an agreement or understanding that he will receive something of value in the event of a certain outcome."[20] Applying this standard, New York's attorney general, Eric Schneiderman, asserted in a recent highly publicized court case that DFS contests are illegal "gambling" because: (1) contestants are placing bets on events "outside their control or influence," specifically on the real-game performance of professional athletes; and (2) numerous elements of chance, such as an athlete's injury, a hot streak, a slump, and even weather conditions, could directly and "materially affect" whether a particular DFS wager wins or loses. Crediting this argument—at least preliminarily—a New York State trial judge granted the attorney general's request for a preliminary injunction against DraftKings and FanDuel temporarily barring them from offering real-money DFS contests to New York consumers.[21] Although DraftKings and FanDuel secured a temporary stay of that injunction pending the outcome of a later-abandoned appeal, they voluntarily agreed to cease offering paid DFS contests in New York until New York expressly legalized such contests. Less than eight months after the preliminary injunction was issued, New York expressly legalized daily fantasy sports contests. Thus, the effect of New York's later-enacted DFS regulatory regime (and Missouri's too, since it employs the same definition of "gambling") was to regulate conduct that was previously *unlawful*. As such, a strong argument can be made that both the New York DFS law and the Missouri DFS law "authorized" fantasy sports wagering in violation of PASPA.

The Mississippi DFS law also regulates conduct that was previously unlawful, and, hence, arguably constitutes an "authorization" under PASPA. In Mississippi, there are two principal anti-gambling prohibitions, depending on whether the activity occurs "on a licensed gaming floor" or "off of a licensed gaming floor." As to the former, the Mississippi Gaming Control Act provides that "[n]o wagering shall be allowed on the outcome of any athletic event, nor on any matter to be determined during an athletic event, nor on the outcome of any event, which does not take place on the premises."[22] (The Mississippi DFS law eviscerates this prohibition by allowing "licensees" under the Gaming Control Act—namely, Mississippi's twenty-eight commercial casinos—to offer "on premises" fantasy sports contests in the licensee's licensed gaming establishment.[23] Prior to the May 12, 2016, effective date of the Mississippi DFS law, such on-site contests were clearly illegal in Mississippi. In an advisory opinion dated January 29, 2016, the Mississippi Attorney General concluded that "[f]antasy sports wagering is illegal in the state of Mississippi . . . on a licensed gaming floor" because such wagering "is controlled by matters that are determined during an athletic event, and by an event that does not take place on the premises. Specifically, the statistical performance of players is determined during an athletic event or events."[24] The Mississippi Attorney General reached a similar conclusion with respect to "off-site gaming"—under which wagering is prohibited upon "the result of any . . . event *or contingency* whatever"—because "the fantasy sports model involves a wager 'upon the result of any . . . event or contingency whatsoever,' namely, upon how the selected players perform."[25] The analysis of these two statutory provisions does not depend in any way on the mix between "skill and chance." As stressed by the Attorney General, "the possible existence of the element of skill in picking players in a fantasy sports game is *irrelevant* to any charge of gambling . . . under Section 97-33-1 of the Mississippi Code."[26] Thus, the Mississippi DFS law—which declares that "[f]antasy sports contests with an entry fee are *legal* in this state"—now permits activities that were previously determined to be *unlawful* by Mississippi's highest-ranking law enforcement officer. As such, it should be considered an "authorization by law" as well.

I am much less confident about the outcome of this particular analysis in Virginia because of the uncertainty over which gambling definitional test applies. While gambling is broadly defined in Virginia, with one commentator labeling Virginia as an "any chance" state (Tsai, 2016, 415), there is relevant authority—namely, a late-1980's attorney general opinion—suggesting that the "predominant factor" test governs the analysis of whether a particular contest is illegal gambling.[27] Moreover, the Virginia statutory definition of gambling does not include modifiers such as "*contingent in whole or in part upon . . . chance*" (like in Colorado and Indiana) or "*to any degree contingent on chance*" (as in Tennessee) that are indicative of a traditional "any chance" formulation. Additionally, the Virginia statute has an exception from the definition of "gambling" for "contest[s] of speed or skill between men, animals, fowl or vehicles, where participants may receive prizes or different percentages of a purse, stake or premium dependent upon whether they win or lose or dependent upon their position or score at the end of such contest."[28] Accordingly, there is a good possibility that a Virginia federal court would conclude that DFS contests were always legal as "skill contests" in Virginia (under Virginia Code Ann. § 18.2-333) and that the new DFS law did not effectively legalize conduct that was previously unlawful. Therefore, the outcome in Virginia—at least using this analytical framework—cannot be predicted with anywhere near the same level of confidence as with the indisputable "any chance" states of Tennessee, Colorado, and Indiana.

It is even less likely that the state DFS laws in Kansas, Maryland, and Massachusetts would be viewed as a PASPA-forbidden "authorization" under this analytical approach. Both Kansas and Massachusetts employ the less rigorous "dominant factor" definitional test for "gambling," under which contests must simply contain "more skill than chance" in order to be legal. Under such an analysis, DFS wagering would probably not be considered illegal gambling. Along those lines, it is worth noting that the attorney generals of four "dominant factor" states—Kansas, Massachusetts, Rhode Island, and West Virginia—have taken the position that DFS contests are legal under each state's "dominant factor" analysis. Since DFS wagering may have already been legal in these states—at least in the opinion of four separate state attorney generals (with no dissenting views from other "any chance" states)—it would be challenging to successfully argue that the DFS schemes in those states permit conduct that was previously unlawful.

2.3. Avoiding the PASPA Problem Through a Straight Repeal Law

States wishing to take a more conservative approach under PASPA—and thereby minimize (or eliminate) the risk of a legal challenge—could just simply exclude fantasy sports contests from the definition of "bet," "wager," or "gambling" under state law, without affirmatively authorizing, licensing or regulating such contests. In my opinion, such a measure would likely pass muster under PASPA since a state would not be doing any of the six things—"sponsor, operate, advertise, promote, license, or authorize by law or compact"—expressly forbidden by the statute. Such an interpretation also finds support in *NCAA, Inc. v. Christie*, which recognizes that a complete repeal of state law prohibitions on sports gambling would not violate PASPA. To date, only one state has utilized this narrow approach in legalizing fantasy sports contests. In 2015, Kansas amended its gambling statute to exclude "fantasy sports leagues" from the definition of "bet" under state law.[29] Notably, the Kansas legislation imposes no regulatory or licensing scheme. By contrast, every other state that has legalized fantasy sports contests requires operators to register with the state and/or apply for licenses or permits, and also subjects operators to varying degrees of state regulation. Such regimes—which have some level of state involvement in the conduct and operation of fantasy sports contests—face a heightened risk under PASPA.

3. DFS Contests Are a "Betting, Gambling or Wagering Scheme"

The second showing that must be made under PASPA is establishing that the state-sanctioned DFS contests qualify as a "lottery, sweepstakes or other betting, gambling or wagering scheme." PASPA does not expressly define these terms. However, many states—either by statute or through decisional law—define a "lottery" as consisting of three essential elements: (1) the furnishing of consideration, (2) for the chance to win a prize, and (3) the distribution of a prize by "chance." The definition of "sweepstakes" also varies from state to state but is generally defined as a legal contest or game where anything of value is distributed by lot, by chance, or based on the random selection of entries. The principal difference between a "lottery" and a "sweepstakes" is the element of consideration: most lotteries require the payment of an entry fee to enter the contest, whereas the hallmark of a traditional sweepstakes contest is the absence of any purchase requirement.[30]

Under this definitional approach, it would be difficult to categorize any of the existing state DFS regimes as being in the nature of a "lottery" or "sweepstakes." This is because, unlike a lottery or sweepstakes which typically award prizes by lot, chance, or random selection of entries, most traditional DFS contests award prizes based on the "skill" of the contestant in successfully constructing a winning lineup, even though some chance or luck is necessarily involved. The predominance of skill over luck in DFS will likely insulate it from any future PASPA challenge predicated on the activity being deemed a "lottery" or "sweepstakes."

It is a different story, however, when it comes to the other salient language in Section 3702 of PASPA: "*other betting, gambling or wagering scheme*." While the definitions of these terms also vary from state to state, generally, a "bet" or "wager" occurs whenever a person stakes or risks something of value on the outcome of a contest or a contingent event, in the hope of winning more money than was risked. This would seem to encompass most real-money DFS contests, since contestants are risking something of value (in the form of an entry fee) on the outcome of either a contest (the DFS contest) or a future contingent event (the performances of a group of real-world athletes who the DFS participant drafts for his or her fantasy team) in the hope that those performances will accumulate more points than the mythical teams put together by a participant's competitors and thereby enable him or her to win a prize.[31]

But one federal court decision may cast doubt on this assumption. In *Humphrey v. Viacom, Inc.*, a New Jersey federal district court concluded that the payment of an entry fee to participate in a season-long fantasy sports league did not constitute a "bet" or "wager" under New Jersey's qui tam statute. The court held that "entry fees do not constitute bets or wagers where they are paid unconditionally for the privilege of participating in a contest, and the prize is for an amount certain that is guaranteed to be won by one of the contestants (but not the entity offering the prize)" (2007 WL at *9).

Additionally, some might argue that DFS is not a "betting, gambling, or wagering scheme" within the meaning of PASPA because DFS is a "contest of skill" (with skill predominating over chance), whereas traditional sports betting (the main focus of PASPA) entails more "chance" than "skill" (although this distinction is debatable). Along those lines, the *Humphreys* decision recognizes that "the success of a fantasy sports team depends on the participants' skill in selecting players for his or her team, trading players over the course of the season, adding and dropping players during the course of the season and deciding who among his or her players will start and which players will be placed on the bench" (*Humphrey*, 2007 WL at *2).

While several of the state DFS laws explicitly state that fantasy sports contests do not constitute "gambling" or are exempt from prohibitions against betting, wagering, or gambling—how a state chooses to label its state-sanctioned fantasy sports contests should not control how a *federal law* (PASPA) is interpreted. This could lead to inconsistent—and potentially absurd—results, such as where a state characterizes DFS as "not gambling," yet provides for regulatory oversight by a state *gambling* commission (as is the case in Indiana, New York, Missouri, and Tennessee). One can easily envision a scenario whereby a state revises its definitions of "betting," "wagering," or "gambling" in order to insulate a fantasy sports law from a potential legal challenge under PASPA, thereby frustrating the statute's purpose. For example, New York's fantasy sports law expressly declares that such contests are not "games of chance," or "wagers on future contingent events," or even "gambling" under New York State law, even though New York's attorney general concluded otherwise just several months earlier.

This is why PASPA's legislative history is so instructive, and likely controlling of any determination as to whether a state DFS "scheme" is encompassed by PASPA. The Senate Report accompanying PASPA should dispel any notion that the scope and meaning of "betting, gambling or wagering scheme" is dependent on how a *state* chooses to define such terms. To the contrary, the Senate Report provides as follows:

> The prohibition of section 3701 applies *regardless of whether the scheme is based on chance or skill, or a combination thereof.* Moreover, the prohibition is intended to be *broad enough to include all schemes* involving an actual game or games, *or actual performance therein*, including schemes utilizing geographic references rather than formal team names (e.g., Washington vs. Philadelphia), or nicknames rather than formal names of players.
>
> (Senate Report 248, at 3553) (italics added)

This language could not be any clearer. It states that PASPA is "broad enough" to include "all schemes" involving "an actual game or games" or "actual performance therein," regardless of the amount of "skill" involved. As such, "skill-chance considerations should seemingly play no role in PASPA regulatory efforts" (Rodenberg, 2016). The Massachusetts Gaming Commission similarly observed that PASPA's legislative history "clearly demonstrates that the statute was designed to have a broad scope applying to a wide swath of 'schemes' regardless of the balance between chance and skill." (Massachusetts Gaming Commission, 2016, at 48). This legislative intent is further evidenced by the inclusion of the five words "*lottery, sweepstakes, betting, gambling* or other *wagering* schemes"—suggesting a broad rather than a narrow sweep. Based on the "broad scope" of PASPA, as evidenced by its plain language and legislative history, I believe that a court would likely find that most state-sanctioned DFS contests constitute a "betting, gambling or other wagering scheme" within the meaning of PASPA.

In an attempt to discount the seriousness of the PASPA risk, several DFS industry proponents have suggested that PASPA was "superseded" by the Unlawful Internet Gambling Enforcement Act (UIGEA),[32] which was enacted some fifteen years later. In fact, one well-known payment processor specifically requires a legal opinion from DFS operators on this point before it will agree to process DFS transactions. Presumably, lawyers drafting legal opinions for the use and benefit of DFS payment processors have opined that UIGEA "implicitly supersedes" PASPA. But any such opinion would strain credulity in my view. UIGEA, which generally outlaws Internet gambling, contains an exemption for fantasy sports contests that meet certain criteria. PASPA, on the other hand, prohibits states from authorizing or licensing sports gambling schemes based directly or indirectly on the "performance" of athletes in amateur or professional sporting events.

Under the interpretive principle known as *lex posterior derogat legi priori*, "a later statute takes away the effect of the prior one" (Garner, 2009, 995–996). To take effect, however, the later-enacted statute must either "expressly repeal" or be "manifestly repugnant" to the earlier one (Garner, 2009). This rule of interpretation militates heavily against any notion that the UIGEA supersedes PASPA. There are several reasons for this. First, the UIGEA does not expressly repeal PASPA. Neither the UIGEA statute nor the legislative history preceding its enactment makes so much as even a passing reference to PASPA. Second, the UIGEA is not "manifestly repugnant" to PASPA. The two federal statutes have entirely different aims: UIGEA targets the "recipients" of payments associated with unlawful Internet transactions, whereas PASPA simply forbids "governmental entities" (including states and federally recognized Indian tribes) from "authorizing" new sports gambling schemes. They are simply not in conflict with, much less manifestly repugnant to, one another.

Further, UIGEA's "Rule of Construction" makes clear that the UIGEA does not supersede other federal or state laws:

> No provision of this subchapter shall be construed as altering, limiting, or extending *any* Federal or State law or Tribal-State compact *prohibiting*, permitting, or regulating gambling within the United States.[33]

This clear and unambiguous statutory language should put to rest any contention that the UIGEA superseded, altered, or supplanted PASPA.

4. DFS Contests Are "Based on" the "Performances" of Athletes

The third and final prong of PASPA looks to whether the state-sanctioned DFS contests are directly or indirectly "based on" the "performances" of athletes in one or more competitive games.[34] This standard is easily satisfied since virtually all of the state DFS laws at issue explicitly recognize—as part of their statutory definition of "fantasy sports contests"—that the winning outcome of a fantasy sports contest is "**predominantly determined**" by the accumulated statistical results of athletes competing in the real-world sporting events.[35]

This is self-evident. Without the underlying performance statistics of the real-world athletes, there would be no "winners" or "losers" in a DFS contest. Until the athletes play and a complete tally is made, the identities of the winners and losers of any DFS contest are unknown and unknowable. As the Massachusetts Gaming Commission aptly put it, "the success of the individual athletes that make up a participant's team, when filtered through the scoring rubric set up by the DFS operator, will result in the win or loss of the participant." (Massachusetts Gaming Commission, 2016, at 14). While a DFS participant is not "betting" that a specific player will achieve a specific statistical milestone, such as scoring a certain number of touchdowns in a single game, the DFS participant is nonetheless betting that "the aggregate performance of the individual athletes on his team will exceed the aggregate performance of the individual athletes on his opponents' teams" (Massachusetts Gaming Commission, 2016, at 14). "Simply stated," as the Massachusetts Gaming Commission reasoned, "if there were no underlying athletic performances, there would be no DFS" (at 14). Based on this unassailable rationale and the plain language of the relevant state DFS laws, I believe that a court would likely find that most DFS contests are directly or indirectly "based on" one or more "performances" of amateur or professional athletes participating in real-world sporting events.

5. Assessing the State DFS Laws Enacted Through 2016

Through December 31, 2016, ten states had enacted laws expressly legalizing (and, in almost every case, regulating) real-money fantasy sports contests: Colorado, Indiana, Kansas, Maryland, Massachusetts, Mississippi, Missouri, New York, Tennessee, and Virginia. As many of eight of these laws could be seen as violating PASPA, in my estimation. The state DFS laws having the greatest vulnerability under PASPA are those enacted by Colorado, Indiana, Massachusetts, Mississippi, Missouri, New York, Tennessee, and Virginia. There are several reasons for such a conclusion. First, four of the states—Indiana, Colorado, Missouri, and Tennessee—have adopted an express "licensing" mechanism in their state DFS laws, requiring operators to become licensed by the state. Additionally, Colorado and New York expressly "authorize" fantasy sports contests. Both types of state sanctioning are prohibited by PASPA. Second, even those states that do not *expressly* license or authorize DFS wagering can still be found to have *de facto* "authorized" such activity by virtue of (1) granting permission to offer DFS contests (either immediately upon the statute's effectiveness or by requiring DFS operators to apply for permission) and (2) regulating activity that had previously been unlawful.

In my opinion, Tennessee is—far and away—the DFS state that is the most vulnerable to a successful legal challenge under PASPA. Tennessee checks all of the right boxes: it expressly "licenses" DFS wagering (which PASPA forbids), it requires operators to apply for state permission, and it regulates conduct that was previously considered unlawful (as determined by that state's attorney general). Additionally, the U.S. Attorney's Office for the Eastern District of Tennessee recently prosecuted a criminal theft case against a senior bank employee who embezzled nearly $1 million in customer monies to fund his DFS gambling addiction. The plea agreement—signed by a federal prosecutor—characterizes DFS contests as "online gambling," a potentially troubling development in the event a PASPA lawsuit is brought in the same judicial district (*United States v. Miller*).

After Tennessee, the state DFS laws that—in my view—are the most vulnerable under PASPA are those enacted by Colorado, Missouri, and New York. Both Colorado and Missouri have a PASPA-forbidden "licensing" scheme for DFS operators, and Colorado and New York expressly "authorize" DFS contests (also a PASPA violation). Moreover, all three states require DFS operators to apply for state permission, and also purport to regulate conduct that was previously unlawful based on each state's definition of "gambling" (e.g., the "any chance" test in Colorado and the "material element/future contingent test" in Missouri and New York). New York also has the added bonus of numerous court documents filed by the New York Attorney General—prior to the enactment of the New York DFS Law—asserting that DFS contests constitute illegal gambling under state law. Further, a good argument can be made that New York's "registration" and "permit" procedure functions just like a "license" requirement (a violation of PASPA) given the extensive amount of state oversight and state discretion in determining whether to grant permission to operate within the state.[36] It is also worth noting that a separate New York state court lawsuit has raised the specter of PASPA as part of a broader challenge to the constitutionality of the New York DFS law. That lawsuit—filed in the Albany County Supreme Court—asserts that the New York DFS law impermissibly expands gambling in New York in violation of the New York State Constitution, and also violates PASPA, although the lawsuit does not seek relief on that basis.

My third tier of "PASPA-vulnerable" state DFS laws is comprised of Indiana, Mississippi, Virginia, and Massachusetts (in that order), but each for different reasons. Indiana's express "licensing" regime for DFS puts it in direct violation of PASPA's prohibition against "state-licensed" sports gambling. Additionally, Indiana is one of the "any chance" states, meaning that its DFS Law regulates conduct that was previously considered unlawful, and, therefore, constitutes a *de facto* "authorization" in violation of PASPA. Mississippi is included in this category because its DFS Law explicitly recognizes that "[f]antasy sports contests with an entry fee are *legal* in this state,"[37] coming right on the heels of an earlier attorney general opinion stating that "[f]antasy sports wagering is *illegal* in the state of Mississippi." That opinion—coupled with the state's low definitional threshold for what constitutes "gambling" (and the exclusion of "skill" from that dynamic)—provides a compelling argument that the Mississippi DFS law "authorizes" DFS wagering in violation of PASPA by regulating activity that indisputably had been unlawful prior to the enactment of the new law. Finally, I include the Massachusetts DFS law in this category because it is an "enabling" law—stating that operators "may" offer fantasy sports contests to in-state residents—but do not rank it higher because unlike many of the other DFS states listed previously, Massachusetts does not expressly license or authorize DFS, or even require operators to apply for permission to operate.

Finally, Virginia is included in this third group because it requires DFS companies to obtain permission to operate via a state-issued "registration" (in other words, an "authorization"), and arguably employs the "any chance" definitional test for "gambling."

However, there is some authority in Virginia—in particular, a late-1980's attorney general opinion—suggesting that the more lenient "predominant factor" test would apply to any assessment of whether a particular scheme constitutes illegal gambling. Under that test, it would be more difficult to establish that DFS wagering was illegal gambling under Virginia law prior to the effective date of the new legislation. If the "predominant factor" test were to apply (or, alternatively, if a court were to determine that the Virginia statutory exception for "skill contests" removes DFS from the ambit of "gambling" under Virginia law), a plaintiff would be hard-pressed to argue that Virginia's DFS law "authorized" conduct that was already legal. That prospect—coupled with the absence of an explicit licensing scheme—makes Virginia a very risky proposition for a PASPA challenge. However, the statutory requirement that DFS operators obtain "permission to operate" (through a registration protocol, with the state "issuing" a registration) likely renders the Virginia DFS regime an "authorization by law" for purposes of PASPA.

6. The Scorecard: Ranking the States

In terms of their "PASPA vulnerability", here is how I would rank the state DFS laws from the most vulnerable to a successful legal challenge to the least vulnerable:

a) Tennessee:
- Expressly "licenses" DFS contests (forbidden by PASPA)
- Requires state permission to operate (an "authorization")
- Legalizes conduct that was previously unlawful
  - Follows "any chance" test
- Attorney General opinion says DFS = "illegal gambling"
- US Attorney's Office says DFS = "online gambling"

b) Colorado:
- Expressly "licenses" DFS contests (forbidden by PASPA)
- Expressly "authorizes" DFS contests (forbidden by PASPA)
- Requires state permission to operate (an "authorization")
- Legalizes conduct that was previously unlawful
  - A de facto "authorization" under PASPA
  - Follows "any chance" test

c) New York:
- Expressly "authorizes" DFS contests
- Requires state permission to operate (also an "authorization")
- Legalizes conduct that was previously unlawful
  - A de facto "authorization" under PASPA
  - Follows "material degree/future contingent event" test
- Attorney General court filings say DFS = "illegal gambling"
- Court decision (on TRO) sides with Attorney General

- Regulatory scheme that is akin to gambling-type "licensing"
  - Regulation by a state gambling commission
  - Extensive oversight—approval of all DFS platforms/contests
  - $50,000 annual fee + 15% of in-state gross revenues
  - Considerable discretion in approving/denying registration
  - Annual reporting requirement
  - Broad investigative powers
  - Right to initiate enforcement proceedings

d) Missouri:
- Expressly "licenses" DFS contests (forbidden by PASPA)
- Requires state permission to operate (an "authorization")
- Legalizes conduct that was previously unlawful
  - A de facto "authorization" under PASPA
  - Follows "material degree/future contingent event" test
- No Attorney General opinion, but has same definitional test as New York, which does have an Attorney General opinion + court decision

e) Mississippi:
- Provides for broad permission to operate (an "authorization")
- Legalizes conduct that was previously unlawful
  - A de facto "authorization" under PASPA
  - "Skill" is irrelevant under Mississippi test
- Attorney General opinion says DFS = "illegal gambling"
- No ban on college sports (potential for "cease-and-desist" letter)
- Con: No licensing requirement/only bare-minimum registration
- Con: No state permission to operate (thus not an authorization)

f) Indiana:
- Expressly "licenses" DFS contests (forbidden by PASPA)
- Requires state permission to operate (an "authorization")
- Legalizes conduct that was previously unlawful
  - A de facto "authorization" under PASPA
  - Follows "any chance" test
- No Attorney General opinion, but employs same definitional test for gambling as Tennessee, which does have an Attorney General opinion
- But has "bona fide contest of skill" statutory exception

g) Virginia:
- Requires state permission to operate (an "authorization")
- Lack of clarity over which definitional test applies
- Could be either "predominant factor" or "any chance" test
  - AG opinion days former
  - Other secondary sources suggest latter
- Has "skill contest" statutory exception
- Regulatory scheme that is akin to "licensing"
  - $50,000 registration fee

  - o Considerable discretion in approving/denying registration
  - o Annual audit requirement
  - o Disclosure requirements
  - o Right to conduct investigations on "reasonable cause"
  - o Subpoena power—witnesses and documents
  - o Broad revocation and suspension powers

h) Massachusetts:

- Provides broad state permission to operate (an "authorization")
- Contra: no license or registration requirement.
- Contra: no formal application process (like in other states)
- Contra: applies "dominant factor" test for gambling
- Contra: AG previously said DFS = "perfectly legal"

i) Kansas:

- No PASPA violation (just exempts DFS from definition of "bet")
- No state permission to operate (thus not an authorization)
- No regulation or licensing scheme either.
- Applies "dominant factor" test for gambling
- Attorney General opinion says DFS = "perfectly legal"

j) Maryland:

- No PASPA violation (functions as a "repeal" law)
- No state permission to operate (thus not an authorization)
- No license or registration requirement.
- Law is over 4 years old (SOL issues?)
- Recent AGO expresses doubt that it even applies to DFS
- Says Legislature needs to clarify whether law applies to DFS
- AGO also suggests a voter referendum may be required.

7. Navigating PASPA's "Standing" Restrictions

Despite the apparent applicability of PASPA to state-legalized fantasy sports contests, none of the recent state DFS laws have been challenged under PASPA. This is likely because of the "standing" limitations imposed by PASPA. Standing to sue under PASPA is limited to just three categories of potential plaintiffs: (1) the U.S. Attorney General; (2) "professional sports organizations"; and (3) "amateur sports organizations."[38] The standing of the latter two categories is further narrowed by the statutory requirement that a professional or amateur sports organization's own "competitive games" must be the basis of the alleged violation.

But the more plausible explanation for the absence of any PASPA challenge in the fantasy sports context is that the four major U.S. professional sports leagues have a strong financial disincentive against bringing such a lawsuit. The National Basketball Association (NBA) is an equity investor in FanDuel, one of the largest daily fantasy sports operators, and two other major professional sports leagues—Major League Baseball and the National Hockey League—have taken minority stakes in DraftKings, the major competitor to FanDuel. Additionally, many U.S. sports franchises (including twenty-eight of thirty-two National Football League teams) have entered into lucrative advertising sponsorships with either FanDuel or DraftKings. As investors or supporters of fantasy sports, the four major U.S. sports leagues are not considered likely candidates to bring PASPA challenges against state fantasy sports laws. That leaves just the U.S. Attorney General and the National Collegiate Athletic Association (NCAA) as the only realistic PASPA challengers. But the U.S. Attorney General has shown no inclination to wade into these waters, and the NCAA seems even less likely to file a PASPA lawsuit after securing an agreement from DraftKings and FanDuel to cease offering DFS contests involving collegiate, high school and youth sporting events.

There may be several workable solutions to this statutory impediment. One possibility might be for a private plaintiff—such as an anti-gambling or compulsive gambling group (or even a problem gambler who has suffered losses wagering on DFS)—to bring a PASPA lawsuit against a state under an "implied private right of action." While this novel approach has not yet been pursued in the more than twenty-five-year history of PASPA (and is unlikely to succeed given the Supreme Court's recent clamping down on implied private rights of action), an argument could be made that one of the goals of PASPA—other than to protect the integrity of sports—is to target problem gambling. The Report of the Senate Judiciary Committee—the primary source of PASPA's legislative history—identified a number of "harms" caused by sports gambling, including "the potential effect of legalized sports gambling on America's youth," noting that technological advances have made gambling more accessible to minors, who at the time comprised some one million of the nation's approximately eight million compulsive gamblers (Senate Report 102–248, at 3556). The Committee thus declared that "[g]overnments should not be in the business of encouraging people, *especially young people*, to gamble" (Senate Report 102–248, at 3556). One of the factors that a court would consider in determining whether a federal statute contemplates an implied private of action is whether the private plaintiff "is one of the class for whose especial benefit the statute was enacted." An anti-gambling group—or perhaps a compulsive gambler who has suffered losses wagering on DFS—might be able to persuade a court that he is part of the class that PASPA was designed to protect. But such a plaintiff "bears a relatively heavy burden" (as articulated by a number of recent federal decisions) of demonstrating that Congress affirmatively contemplated private enforcement when it passed PASPA. Such an option, therefore, would be highly unlikely to succeed, but may be worth considering.

Notes

1. Professional and Amateur Sports Protection Act, 28 U.S.C. §§ 3701 et seq.
2. 28 U.S.C. § 3702.

3. *See* Colo Rev. Code § 12-15.5-108 ([o]n or after July 1, 2017, an entity shall not operate as a fantasy sports operator unless the entity is *licensed* by the director."); *see also* Colo. Rev. Code § 12-15.5-108 ("Fantasy contests are *authorized* and may be conducted by a fantasy sports operator at a licensed gaming establishment[.] . . . [or] . . . at a licensed facility at which pari-mutuel wagering . . . may occur."); Ind. Code § 4-31-2-20.6 ("The division and the commission shall allow game operators who are operating in Indiana on March 31, 2016 to continue operating until they have received or have been denied a *license*."); Mo. Rev. Stat. § 313.910(2) ("A fantasy sports contest operator shall apply for and receive a *license* from the commission prior to offering fantasy sports contests for play in Missouri."); N.Y. Rac., Pari-Mut. Wag. & Breed. Law § 1411 ("Interactive fantasy Sports contests registered and conducted pursuant to the provisions of this chapter are hereby *authorized*."); Tenn. Code Ann. § 47-18-603 ("It shall be a violation of § 39-17-503 for any person to offer fantasy sports contests through an online digital platform that enables Tennessee consumers to participate in such contests without that person being *licensed* as a fantasy sports operator by the secretary of state.").
4. *Hinds Investments*, 654 F.3d at 850 ("Where terms are not defined within a statute, they are accorded their plain and ordinary meaning," which "can be deduced through reference sources, including . . . general usage dictionaries.").
5. *Gunther*, 452 U.S. at 169, 101 S. Ct. at 2247–2248 ("Although the word 'authorize' sometimes means simply 'to permit,' it ordinarily denotes affirmative enabling action." (citing *Black's Law* definition)).
6. Colo. Rev. Code § 12-15.5-108; Ind. Code § 4-31-2-20.6; Mo. Rev. Stat. § 313.910(2); Tenn. Code Ann. § 47-18-603).
7. N.Y. Rac., Pari-Mut. Wag. & Breed. Law § 1402 ("No operator shall administer, manage, or otherwise make available an interactive fantasy sports platform to persons located in New York unless registered with the Commission . . .").
8. N.Y. Rac., Pari-Mut. Wag. & Breed. Law § 1403.
9. Va. Code. Ann. § 59.1-557 ("No fantasy contest operator shall offer any contest in the Commonwealth without first being registered with the Department.").
10. Va. Code. Ann. § 59.1-557.
11. Mass. Legis. Serv. Ch. 219, § 135 [H.B. 4569]) (italics added).
12. *See* 7A C.J.S. *Authorize* 914 (defining "authorize" in part as "to permit"); *Gunther*, 452 U.S. at 199, 101 S. Ct. at 2263 (noting that "Black's Law Dictionary . . . defines 'authorized' to mean 'to permit a thing to be done in the future.' ").
13. Miss. Code Ann. § 97-33-3-7(1) ("A fantasy contest operator offering fantasy contests to be played by persons in this state must register with the office to conduct fantasy contests within this state.").
14. *See Sharrock*, 45 N.Y.2d at 161 ("For state action purposes, there is a fundamental distinction between a statute which, in regulating previously lawful conduct, does nothing more than merely acknowledge its lawfulness, and one which authorizes otherwise impermissible or unconstitutional conduct."); *Doe v. Harrison*, 2006 WL at *6 ("This is not to say that state regulation can never give rise to state action. Where the State 'authorizes otherwise impermissible or unconstitutional conduct,' State action may be found . . .. On the other hand, regulations that merely affix statutory imprimatur to lawful private conduct cannot constitute State action.").
15. Tenn. Code Ann. § 39-17-501(1).
16. Tenn. Atty. Gen. Op. 16-13, *Legality of Fantasy Sports Contests in Tennessee* (Apr. 5, 2016), at 2.

17. Tenn. Atty. Gen. Op. 16-13, *Legality of Fantasy Sports Contests in Tennessee* (Apr. 5, 2016), at 2.
18. Tenn. Atty. Gen. Op. 16-13, *Legality of Fantasy Sports Contests in Tennessee* (Apr. 5, 2016), at 3.
19. *Cf.* Texas Atty. Gen. Op. KP-0057, at 4–5 (Jan. 19, 2016) (opining that DFS contests constitute illegal gambling under the Texas iteration of the "any chance" formulation).
20. *See* N.Y. Penal Law § 225.00(2); Mo. Ann. Stat. § 572.010(4).
21. *DraftKings*, at 9 (holding that the New York Attorney General "established a greater likelihood of success on the merits under . . . the definitions of gambling and 'contest of chance' as currently stated in Penal Law § 225.00[1][2]."); *FanDuel*, at 9 (same).
22. Miss. Code § 75-76-33(3)(a).
23. Miss. Code § 97-33-307(5).
24. Miss. Atty. Gen. Op. *Fantasy Sports Wagering in the State of Mississippi* (Jan. 29, 2016), at 2.
25. Miss. Atty. Gen. Op. *Fantasy Sports Wagering in the State of Mississippi* (Jan. 29, 2016), at 3.
26. Miss. Atty. Gen. Op. *Fantasy Sports Wagering in the State of Mississippi* (Jan. 29, 2016), at 3 & 5 (italics added).
27. Va. Atty. Gen. Op. No. 287 (July 20, 1988) ("If chance is not the predominant factor in winning a prize, the machine is not a 'gambling device,' as defined in § 18.2–325(2)(b)").
28. Va. Code Ann. § 18.2-333; *see also Daniels v. Mobley*, 737 at 901 (stating that "even if the definition of illegal gambling . . . is 'read' as not having an exception for games of skill, . . . § 18.2–333 provides that skill be considered in determining whether [Virginia law] has been violated.").
29. Kan. Stat. Ann. § 21-6403.
30. *People v. Nasser*, 2014 WL at *7 n. 16 ("The difference between a lawful sweepstakes and an unlawful lottery is that a sweepstakes does not require that consideration be paid to enter."); *California Gasoline Retailers v. Regal Petroleum Corp.*, 50 Cal. 2d at 861–862 (promotional sweepstakes was not an unlawful lottery since consideration element was absent where no purchase was necessary to enter).
31. Massachusetts Gaming Commission, 2016 (opining that [t]he common law definitions of a "bet" as well as the Massachusetts definition strongly suggest that DFS would qualify as a "betting, gambling or wagering scheme" under PASPA where a sum is pledged on the outcome of a future unknown event.).
32. Unlawful Internet Gambling Enforcement Act (UIGEA), 31 U.S.C. §§ 5361 et seq.
33. UIGEA, 31 U.S.C. § 5361(b) (italics added).
34. PASPA, 28 U.S.C. § 3702.
35. Colo. Rev. Stat. § 12-15.5-102; Ind. Code § 4-33-24; Kan. Code § 21-6403; Miss. Code. § 93-33-303; Mo. Rev. Stat. § 313.905; Tenn. Code Ann. § 47-18-602; Va. Code Ann. § 59.1-556; *see also* 31 U.S.C. § 5362 (UIGEA) (emphasis added).
36. *See North Valley Baptist Church v. McMahon*, 696 F. Supp. at 528, *aff'd*, 893 F.2d at 1139.
37. Miss. Code. § 97-33305(1).
38. PASPA, 28 U.S.C. § 3703.

References

Garner, Bryan, ed. (2009). *Black's Law Dictionary* (9th ed.) (New York: Thomson West).

Massachusetts Gaming Commission. (2016, January 11). "White Paper on Fantasy Sports." Available at http://massgaming.com/wp-content/uploads/MGC-White-Paper-on-Daily-Fantasy-Sports-1-11-16.pdf.

Pennsylvania Gaming Control Board (2016): "Fantasy Sports Report," 20 May, available at http://gamingcontrolboard.pa.gov/files/communications/PGCB_Fantasy_Sports_Report_2016.pdf

Rhode Island Attorney General (2016): "Daily Fantasy Sports," 4 Feb., available at http://www.legalsportsreport.com/wp-content/uploads/2016/02/Rhode-Island-DFS-Opinion.pdf

Moore, A. (2015, December 8). "Does State Regulation of Fantasy Sports Violate PASPA." Law360.com. Available at www.law360.com/articles/734823/does-state-regulation-of-fantasy-sports-violate-paspa.

Rodenberg, Ryan M. (2016, November 4). Brief as *Amicus Curiae* in Support of Petitions for Writ of Certiorari, *Christie v. National Collegiate Athletic Ass'n, Inc.*, Case Nos. 16-476 & 16-477 (U.S. Nov. 4, 2016). Available at https://papers.ssrn.com/sol3/papers.cfm?abstract_id=2867011.

Senate Report 248. 102nd Cong., 1st Sess. 4, *reprinted in* 1992 U.S.C.C.A.N. 3553.

Tsai, M. (2016, Spring). "Fantasy (E)Sports: The Future Prospect of Fantasy Sports Betting Amongst Organized Multiplayer Video Game Competitions" *UNLV Gaming L.J.* 6: 93

Wallach, D. (2015, March 14). "Fantasy Sports Legislation by States May Run Afoul of PASPA." Sports Law Blog. Available at http://sports-law.blogspot.com/2015/03/fantasy-sports-legislation-by-states.html.

Wallach, D. (2016, January 11). "No Question, PASPA Applies to Daily Fantasy Sports." Sports Law Blog. Available at http://sports-law.blogspot.com/2016/01/no-question-paspa-applies-to-daily.html.

Cases

Daniels v. Mobley, 737 S.E.2d 895 (Va. 2013)

Doe v. Harrison, 2006 WL 2109433 (S.D.N.Y. July 28, 2006).

Hinds Inv., L.P. v. Angioli, 654 F.3d 846 (9th Cir. 2011).

Humphrey v. Viacom, Inc., 2007 WL 1797648 (D.N.J. June 20, 2007),

National Collegiate Athletic Ass'n v. Christie, 832 F.3d 389 (3d Cir. 2016).

North Valley Baptist Church v. McMahon, 696 F. Supp. 518 (E.D. Cal. 1988), *aff'd*, 893 F.2d 1139 (9th Cir. 1990).

People v. DraftKings, Case No. 453054/2015, Order, (N.Y. Sup. Ct. Dec. 11, 2015) (Mendez, J.).

Sharrock v. Dell Buick-Cadillac, Inc., 45 N.Y.2d 152 (1978).

People v. FanDuel, Case No. 161691/2015, Order (N.Y. Sup. Ct. Dec. 11, 2015).

People v. Nasser, 2014 WL 906798 (Cal. Ct. App. Mar. 10, 2014).

California Gasoline Retailers v. Regal Petroleum Corp., 50 Cal. 2d 844 (1958).

United States v. Miller, Case No. 2:16-cr-120 (E.D. Tenn. Oct. 19, 2016).

United States v. Norberto, 373 F. Supp. 2d 150 (E.D.N.Y. 2005).

County of Wash. v. Gunther, 452 U.S. 169, 101 S. Ct. 2242 (1981).

Index

Figures and tables are indicated by "f" and "t" following the page numbers.

www.ingramcontent.com/pod-product-compliance
Lightning Source LLC
Chambersburg PA
CBHW081708290526
45890CB00005B/170
9780190465957